NEW TESTAMENT

New Testament Theology

G. B. CAIRD

Completed and Edited by
L. D. HURST

CLARENDON PRESS · OXFORD

Oxford University Press, Walton Street, Oxford OX2 6DP
Oxford New York
Athens Auckland Bangkok Bombay
Calcutta Cape Town Dar es Salaam Delhi
Florence Hong Kong Istanbul Karachi
Kuala Lumpur Madras Madrid Melbourne
Mexico City Nairobi Paris Singapore
Taipei Tokyo Toronto
and associated companies in
Berlin Ibadan

Oxford is a trade mark of Oxford University Press

Published in the United States
by Oxford University Press Inc., New York

British Library Cataloguing in Publication Data
Data available

Library of Congress Cataloging in Publication Data
New Testament theology / G. B. Caird;
Completed and edited by L. D. Hurst.
Includes bibliographical references and index.
1. Bible. N.T.—Theology. I. Hurst, L. D. II. Title.
BS2397.C35 1994 230—dc20 93-36971
ISBN 0-19-826388-0

3 5 7 9 10 8 6 4 2

Printed in Great Britain
on acid-free paper by
Bookcraft (Bath) Ltd., Midsomer Norton

FOREWORD

The whole world is the memorial of famous men

Pericles

The pillar perished is whereto I leant

Sir Thomas Wyatt

He, being dead, yet speaks

Epistle to the Hebrews

It is an ever-present but sad fact of life that great figures are taken from us at the peak of their energies, with their work often left conspicuously unfinished.[1] So it was with George Bradford Caird, who died suddenly just at the point at which he seemed to be entering upon a most happy and productive period of his life. While to his family and friends the dimensions of such a loss could never be measured, its most obvious consequence to the professional field in which he laboured was the fact that at the time of his death he had not yet completed his eagerly awaited *New Testament Theology*. And at least one who heard this disturbing news at his funeral in Oxford had cause to reflect that George Caird, like so many of his greatest British predecessors such as Westcott and Hoskyns, had died without being allowed to give expression to the ultimate scholarly undertaking of his life.

Some months later, while visiting Caird's wife at Letcombe Regis, I had occasion to see the incomplete manuscript of the book. I remember at first feeling private reservations as to its possibilities; but I can also recall the building sense of excitement as I stayed up the entire night reading what he had left and wondering at its potential. After some discussion it was agreed that the work should go forward, if only one who knew Caird's heart and mind (for Caird was a scholar as much of the heart as of the mind) would be willing to undertake the task. I was then granted access to all of his writings, published and

---

[1] But see Caird's 1982 eulogy in Westminster Abbey to Eric Routley, which portended his own death two years later. There he observed that in the case of certain people it is misguided to think that their work could ever be 'finished'.

unpublished, appointed his literary executor, and commissioned with the task of seeing the work through to publication. Several weeks later the Delegates of Oxford University Press took the additional step of going ahead with the book if I could provide the necessary edition of the manuscript and somehow construct the missing second half.

Anyone who saw the manuscript would have been struck by its two most obvious features. First, it was intended to be the culmination of all that Caird had thought, written, and taught during his scholarly career. Second, the task of finishing it would take considerable time and effort, in so far as the manuscript was less than half-finished (65,000 words out of a contracted 150,000), with the three most crucial chapters missing. But in the end it turned out to be a labour of love and gratitude to a mentor who had given me much, with the compensations outweighing the tribulations.

Some description of what Caird left may be given. Of the five and a half first-draft chapters he had written, three (1, 2, and 4) were virtually complete, two (3 and 5) were mostly complete (pp. 166–173, for instance, were added later), and another (6) had been started. Caird's original manuscript ends at p. 203 of the present volume with the poignant words, 'Whatever the immediate consequences may appear to be, the outcome can be safely left in God's hands'. Some footnotes he had supplied in complete form, others were suggested, often by only one or two words, and still others were clearly needed but lacking. From the state of chapters 2 to 6 it was also obvious that he had intended some matters to be left for later (often indicated by scribbles in the margin, followed by a question mark). I have tried, as much as within reason, to follow up these items.

For the task of providing what constitutes more or less the second half of the work I was left largely to my own devices. Originally there was a flurry of hope that tape recordings of lectures given by Caird on the subject of New Testament theology in 1981–2 would be of considerable help. But as is often the case with Oxford dons, the lecturer pursued the topic only as far as he had written, and then promptly stopped.[2] These chapters I was therefore forced to construct out of the only sources which were to hand: unpublished papers, whether whole or (more commonly) in part; articles (in an atomized

---

[2] His last lecture on the subject, delivered in the University Schools, 11 March 1982, dealt with various aspects of the experience of salvation, covered in the first half of Ch. 6.

form) which Caird had published, but which in their current setting (usually *Festschriften* and obscure theological journals) were not likely to reach a large reading public; some lectures delivered in the mid-1970s; private conversations with Caird; contributions of my own (almost always to fill gaps); and, rarely, small sections from Caird's published books in an abbreviated and recast form.

It is inevitable that the final chapters are not in the form in which Caird would have passed them on to the Press. It is also certain that in a work such as this some deficiency of detail, logic, and subtle nuance has crept in which otherwise would have been noted and purged by the original author. It would be difficult for one born in the year in which George Caird became a professor of Old Testament to bring to such an enterprise the depth of erudition and subtle penetration he would have provided. But it is also becoming increasingly common that those who are taken from us suddenly have their unfinished work delegated to another, usually a friend or pupil—as George Caird was himself to discover[3]— and those like Caird who have trodden this path before me will testify that finishing a book begun by another is not an easy experience. The reader's forbearance is therefore requested in the event of any shortcomings the work may exhibit.

Caird's overall plan of attack was unique in at least two respects: his 'apostolic conference' model and his extraordinary decision to place the teaching of Jesus *last*. The latter idea, while presenting unforeseeable obstacles for the completion of the work, is far-reaching in its implications (see below). What he intended in Chapters 1–8 was a series of crisp, illuminating epitomes of New Testament thought which would interpret one another with the precision of pins on a war strategist's map. In attempting to follow his plan throughout I have at times had to make difficult decisions. Where might a potentially recurrent theme best be treated? Many of the same concepts could be treated in Chapters 5, 8, or 9. Should aspects of Jesus' death be inserted under Atonement (5) or deployed to Jesus' self-understanding (9)? Would the corporate aspects of kingship be properly dealt with in 5, 8, or 9? Should the 'Son of Man' be treated under the hope of salvation (7), the bringer of salvation (8), or Jesus' theology (9)? These, and countless other decisions, were always difficult, at times harrowing.

I have also provided the work with documentation where I felt it

---

[3] See W. H. Cadman, *The Open Heaven*, ed. G. B. Caird (Oxford: Basil Blackwell, 1969).

was needed, including works published since Caird's death. Those who knew him will scarcely be surprised to find that there are frequent references to Rudolf Bultmann, whom Caird personally admired but whom he also felt to be responsible (along with Albert Schweitzer and Johannes Weiss) for much that is wrong today with New Testament theology. But one would be mistaken to think that the book is therefore dated or narrow in its scope. Bultmann or Schweitzer are used to introduce lasting points. His admiration for, and indebtedness to, C. H. Dodd is likewise clearly and frequently expressed. Yet his esteem of Dodd never reached the point of uncritical acceptance. He did not think Dodd's work to be the last word on the subject, any more than his own ('merely an interim report', he liked to say).

While the outlines of Caird's career are known to many, a brief resumé may help to orient the reader to the larger scope of his life and work. As a young man he exhibited rare scholastic brilliance, which in his case made a career in the academy almost inevitable. After Peterhouse, Cambridge (BA first-class honours in both parts of the Classical Tripos, with distinction in Latin and Greek verse), Caird moved on to study theology at Mansfield College, Oxford, gaining an MA in 1943. A year later he produced a definitive study of the term *doxa* ('glory') in the New Testament, one of the earliest D.Phils. to be granted in theology. Then in 1946, following a three-year pastorate in London, Caird and his young bride moved to Canada, where he was to spend the next thirteen years, first as an Old Testament Professor at St Stephen's College, Edmonton, Alberta, and later as a New Testament Professor at McGill University and Principal of the United Theological College of Montreal. These were happy years, but Caird's heart had in some ways never left Oxford, and in 1959 he returned to Mansfield College, the place associated with such New Testament giants as Dodd, Peake, Moffatt, Manson, and Marsh. Serving as Senior Tutor and later as Principal, Caird now saw the steady growth of his international reputation as a biblical scholar of judiciousness and insight. Combining a penetrative knowledge of both Testaments with a rare fastidiousness with words, Caird analysed his texts in a way which for many set a new standard for the field. These traits, coupled with a fertility of imagination and an almost poetic approach to complex theological issues, produced a potent brew which any who took even a small draught were not likely to forget.

Such qualities brought him great honours and recognition, including the DD from Oxford, appointment to the Dean Ireland Chair of

Exegesis of Holy Scripture in the University of Oxford (1977–84), election to the British Academy (and the awarding of its famed Burkitt Medal for Biblical Studies), and the Collins Religious Book Award (for *The Language and Imagery of the Bible*, 1980). But honours, however prestigious, will hardly convey to the reader the impact of Caird's life and work on those who knew him. Some measure of his legacy, on the other hand, may be appreciated by consulting the six major works published in his lifetime.[4] His first book, *The Apostolic Age* (1955), is a brilliant and succinct historical study of the life, institutions, and thought of the early Church to the end of the first century. *Principalities and Powers* (1956), while ostensibly a discussion of one aspect of St Paul's theology, is in fact a compendium of that theology on a very wide range of topics. His three commentaries, *The Gospel of St Luke* (1963), *The Revelation of St John the Divine* (1966), and *Paul's Letters from Prison* (1976), bring to the text Caird's genius for beauty of expression combined with incisive historical-critical analysis. Lastly, his celebrated *The Language and Imagery of the Bible* is a treasure trove of linguistic and literary insights into the methods and meanings of the biblical authors.

This, his seventh and final work, in a number of ways adds a new dimension to a well-worked subject. Previous New Testament theologies have all stumbled over the critical question of how the historical Jesus is to be fitted into the overall subject. Bultmann made it the 'presupposition' of a New Testament theology, while Jeremias devoted his entire first volume (of a projected but unfinished multi-volume work) to *The Proclamation of Jesus*. Other attempts have simply worked in the 'historical Jesus' material throughout, assuming a priori that it has the same theological status as the New Testament writings. This of course is the method adopted by more conservative writers such as G. E. Ladd, D. Guthrie, and L. L. Morris.

Caird foresaw the problem, and, as we have seen, postponed his treatment of Jesus to the end. For him an apostolic conference *by definition* will end with Chapter 8. But it is also true that the dislocation of Jesus from critical New Testament theology results from faulty

---

[4] For a full bibliography of Caird's published works, see p. 427 below. An illuminating and full memoir of Caird's life is that of Henry Chadwick, in L. D. Hurst and N. T. Wright (eds.), *The Glory of Christ in the New Testament: Studies in Christology in Memory of George Bradford Caird* (Oxford, Clarendon Press, 1987), pp. xvii–xxii; cf. also James Barr, 'George Bradford Caird', *Proceedings of the British Academy*, 71 (1985), Oxford University Press, 493–521.

historical methods and a destructively narrow definition of the term
'theology'. For Caird Jesus' 'theology' and his 'politics' were inextricably intertwined; and it is the merit of studies of Jesus' message
published since Caird's death that the distinction between holiness
and politics is now finally being eroded.

How did Caird intend to solve the problem of Jesus and the apostolic
conference? The answer surely lies in distinguishing between an 'apostolic conference' and a 'theology of the New Testament'. The former is
one scholar's way of organizing the thought of the New Testament
writers; the latter is a certain amount of information included between
the covers of a book. The mistake would be to attempt to force Chapter
9 into the format of the rest of the book. What links Chapters 1–8 with
Chapter 9 is not the conference model, in other words, but the subject
matter: theology. Caird's decision to include Chapter 9 is an attempt to
show that the historical Jesus is a deeply theological figure in the same
sense as Paul, John, and the others. Jesus' teaching is recoverable and
identifiable as the starting point of much of the New Testament writers'
discussion of the issues surrounding salvation.

Chapter 9 none the less provided the greatest problems. While
outlines of what Caird had intended for chapters 6, 7, and 8 were
found among his papers, none was found for 9 (his wife and I searched
the files twice with no success). The only clues I therefore had to
work from were the title and the few hints he had laid in the earlier
chapters. While the plan is my own, it follows generally the order of
topics treated by Caird in lectures he gave in 1975 on 'The Teaching
of Jesus', and I am hopeful that it is compatible with what he would
have provided had he lived, although it is now impossible to be sure.

The observant reader will note that George Caird was by many
canons a relatively conservative scholar. He had little time for schools
of thought or 'the methodology of the month'. The latest scholarly fad
was for him as truth-bearing as a fortune cookie. While this might
appear to place him on the side of conservatives such as Ladd, Guthrie,
and Morris, what comes across most vividly from his work is a rebellion
against any kind of dogmatic regimentation of New Testament
thought. Caird was too fine a scholar to see a perfect harmony or
agreement as the criterion of an apostolic conference. Dialogue was
its essential characteristic. If the New Testament writers preserve lasting and harmonious truth, it is because their melodies allow for
occasionally dissonant tones. In this sense, although there are major
differences in method, scope, and literary orientation, Caird's last work

approximates at certain points J. D. G. Dunn's more historical study, *Unity and Diversity in the New Testament* (1977).

This volume is offered in the belief that George Caird would have wanted his last book to be published, and that, despite the lapse of time since his death, what he says about New Testament theology continues to be important. To those who knew him, personally or through his writings, he will be remembered as one who combined knowledge and wisdom with a disarming sense of humour, and who brought the Alexandrian sword of his intellect to the many tangled knots posed by modern biblical interpretation. For him the meaning of the language and imagery of the New Testament was what its writers intended it to mean; and the only way to understand that meaning was to read and reread the New Testament. His finest gift to his friends, pupils and readers will always be his enthusiasm for the central meaning and authority of the New Testament, offered in humility yet over-powering conviction, together with his contagious belief that God is never very far from those who are truly listening for His voice. Thus for Caird Paul's letters from prison will always be as relevant as anything to be found in this morning's edition of *The Times*.

The completion of this volume has required at certain points an adaptation of information in some of Caird's above-mentioned works.[5] These are as follows.

Chapter 6: *The Apostolic Age*, pp. 48–50, on sacraments and baptism; pp. 57–67, on the Holy Spirit; and several scattered paragraphs from *Paul's Letters from Prison* on baptism.

Chapter 7: *The Language and Imagery of the Bible*, pp. 243–71, on eschatology; *The Gospel of St Luke*, pp. 198–200, 228–34, on the Parousia; pp. 255 f. on Jesus' resurrection; and several paragraphs from *Paul's Letters from Prison* on resurrection.

Chapter 8: *The Gospel of St Luke*, pp. 30–1, on the Virgin Birth; pp. 76–7, on Jesus' baptism; and pp. 79–81 on Jesus' temptation.

Chapter 9: *The Language and Imagery of the Bible*, p. 215, on eyewitness testimony to historical events.

Of additional assistance has been material from the following published articles and lectures; I have indicated with brackets the chapters of this book in which they are used: Alexander Nairne, 'The Epistle

---

[5] The dependency upon this material amounts to approximately 3–4% of the present volume.

of Priesthood', *Exp.T.* 72 (1960–1), 204–6 [Ch. 8]; 'Paul's Theology', in James Hastings (ed.), *Dictionary of the Bible*, revised edition by F. C. Grant and H. H. Rowley (New York, 1963) [Ch. 8]; *Jesus and the Jewish Nation* (Ethel M. Wood Lecture) (London, 1965) [Ch. 9]; 'The Development of the Doctrine of Christ in the New Testament', in N. Pittenger (ed.), *Christ for Us Today* (London, 1968), 66–80 [Ch. 8]; 'Les Eschatologies du Nouveau Testament', *Revue d'histoire et de philosophie religieuses* (1969), 217–27 [Ch. 7]; 'The Christological Basis of Christian Hope', in G. B. Caird (ed.), *The Christian Hope* (London, 1970), 9–24 [Ch. 7]; 'Paul and Women's Liberty', *BJRL* 54 (1972), 268–81 [Ch. 6]; 'New Wine in Old Wine-Skins: I. Wisdom', *Exp.T.* 84 (1973), 164–8 [Ch. 8]; 'Eschatology and Politics: Some Misconceptions', in Johnston R. McKay and James F. Miller (eds.), *Biblical Studies: Essays in Honour of William Barclay* (London, 1976), 72–86 [Ch. 7]; 'Just Men Made Perfect', *London Quarterly and Holborn Review* (1966), 89–98, reprinted in Charles S. Duthie (ed.), *Resurrection and Immortality: Aspects of Twentieth-Century Christian Belief* (London, 1979), 89–103 [Ch. 7]; 'Jesus and Israel: The Starting Point for New Testament Christology', in Robert F. Berkey and Sarah Edwards (eds.), *Christological Perspectives: Essays in Honor of Harvey K. McArthur* (New York, 1982) 58–68 [Ch. 9]; 'The One and the Many in Mark and John', in Horton Davies (ed.), *Studies of the Church in History: Essays Honoring Robert S. Paul on his Sixty-Fifth Birthday* (Allison Park, Pa., 1983), 39–54 [Ch. 5]; 'Son by Appointment', in William C. Weinrich (ed.), *The New Testament Age: Essays in Honor of Bo Reicke*, i (Macon, Ga., 1984), 73–81 [Ch. 8]; 'Perfection and Grace', in C. R. Young, R. A. Leaver, and J. H. Litton (eds.), *Duty and Delight: Routley Remembered* (Carol Stream, Ill., 1985), 21–33 [Chs. 7 and 8]; and 'The Ethics of Jesus', in J. Green and S. McKnight, *Dictionary of Jesus and the Gospels* (Downers Grove, Ill., 1992), 210 ff.

The following publishers are to be thanked for their permission to use, in an adapted form, information from these copyright works: Gerald Duckworth & Co. Ltd.; Adam and Charles Black Ltd.; The Canadian Corporation for Studies in Religion (*The Canadian Journal of Theology: Studies in Religion/Sciences religieuses*); T. & T. Clark; The Ethel M. Wood Trust of the University of London; SCM Press; Basil Blackwell; The Inter-Varsity Press; *Bulletin of the John Rylands Library*; HarperCollins Publishers Ltd.; the Pilgrim Press; Pickwick Publications; Mercer University Press; Hope Publishing Company; SPCK; Oxford University Press; and Penguin Books.

Unless otherwise noted, translations from the Bible are those of the authors. All other quotations are from the Revised English Bible, used with the kind permission of the Syndics of Oxford University Press and the Cambridge University Press.

I would also like to record my thanks to the following for their help in this project: to the Hall-Houghton foundation, for a subsidy which greatly alleviated my numerous travelling expenses between Davis and Oxford; to the University of California, Davis, for a grant which helped offset the inevitable secretarial costs; to the Delegates of Oxford University Press, who accepted the proposal that the book should be completed.

Special gratitude is also due to the editors and staff of the Press: to John Cordy and Ann Ashby, who dealt with the book in its earliest stages; to Hilary O'Shea and Lucy Gasson, whose wise judgements helped in bringing the book to completion; to Robert Ritter, master of the crucial stages of desk-editing; and to Sylvia Jaffrey, whose sharp eye and equally sharp wit saved me from a number of blunders.

Finally, I would like to express my gratitude to a number of individuals who willingly gave of their time and wisdom in ways which greatly facilitated the completion of the work. Professor Robert Banks of Pasadena, California, carefully read through each chapter, making many helpful suggestions as well as providing much personal encouragement. Professor David Nystrom of Chicago, Illinois, my close colleague and friend during the years 1988–92, read every chapter, giving at many points the benefit of his shrewd judgement. My old friend Dr John I. Snyder of Fresno, California, read through several editions of the work and posed many helpful questions in the midst of much personal support. Dr A. A. Howsepian of South Bend, Indiana, read through parts of the work and through his friendship supplied more help than he knows. Two old Oxford friends deserve special mention. Catherine Wilson of Pembroke College, Oxford, provided useful assistance in the task of sorting through Caird's papers in the difficult days immediately following his death. Dr Jeffrey Gibson of Chicago, Illinois, generously lent me his tape recordings of Caird's lectures from 1979–1982, and showed great patience in awaiting their return. Thanks are due also to all those friends and relatives who by their presence in my life provided whatever else was needed to see the job to completion. My mother in particular stood by me during many difficult situations in the past eight years, while my friend Shannon Brandt helped enormously during the early stages of the project. Paul

Castelfranco of Davis was, as always, a pillar of strength and wisdom. Mary Doty conscientiously and faithfully typed through enough versions of the book to fill a small warehouse, and never ceased to be a source of cheerful encouragement. Much credit for the completion of the book goes to her.

Lastly, mention must be made of those who were closest to George Caird. Mollie Caird opened to me her husband's files, provided many helpful suggestions as to infelicities of style in the typescript, afforded much personal encouragement, and waited patiently, with enthusiasm, for the outcome. George's sons and daughter provided challenge and inspiration: James, the first to offer me the soundings of friendship during a removal from Mansfield College to Wantage in the 1970s; John and George, who through their thespian and musical efforts, respectively, have done much to further the George Bradford Caird Memorial Trust; and wonderful Meg, whose unceasing and cheerful support was first given under the giant sequoias of Yosemite. George Caird's family, as is well known, was one of the great strengths of his life. If what follows is not the same book he would have provided, I none the less dedicate it, with love and admiration, to them.

February, 1994

FOREWORD TO THE PAPERBACK EDITION

I would like to thank those friends and reviewers who kindly pointed out a number of errors and misprints in the hardback edition, which have now been corrected. I would also like to acknowledge two works to which I was indebted in the previous edition, but of which I did not make adequate mention in the wording required by the publishers:

Excerpts from 'Paul the Apostle' and 'Paul's Theology' by G. B. Caird are used by permission of Charles Scribner's Sons, an imprint of Macmillan Publishing Company, from DICTIONARY OF THE BIBLE, edited by James Hastings. Revised by Frederick A. Grant and H. H. Rowley. Copyright © 1963 by T. & T. Clark Ltd. and Charles Scribner's Sons.

Exerpts from 'The Bible and the Word of God', *Christian Confidence*, Theological Collections 14, pp. 105–20, are used by permission of the Society for Promoting Christian Knowledge, Copyright © 1970.

Davis, California   L.D.H.
March, 1995

CONTENTS

ABBREVIATIONS

Modern Sources

AJT	*American Journal of Theology*
AV	Authorized Version
BJRL	*Bulletin of the John Rylands Library*
BZ	*Biblische Zeitschrift*
BZNW	*Beiheft, Zeitschrift für die neuetestamentliche Wissenschaft*
CBQ	*Catholic Biblical Quarterly*
CJT	*Canadian Journal of Theology*
ERE	J. Hastings (ed.) *Encyclopedia of Religion and Ethics*, 12 vols. (Edinburgh, 1908–22)
EQ	*Evangelical Quarterly*
ET	English translation
Exp.T.	*Expository Times*
HDB	J. Hastings *et al.* (eds.), *Dictionary of the Bible*, 4 vols. (Edinburgh, 1899–1904)
HUCA	*Hebrew Union College Annual*
Int.	*Interpretation*
IDB	G. A. Buttrick (ed.), *The Interpreter's Dictionary of the Bible*, 4 vols. (Nashville, 1962)
JAC	*Jahrbuch für Antike und Christentum*
JBL	*Journal of Biblical Literature*
JETS	Journal of the Evangelical Theological Society
JSNT	*Journal for the Study of the New Testament*
JTS	Journal of Theological Studies
LXX	Septuagint Version
Midr.	Midrash
MT	Masoretic Text
NEB	New English Bible
NIDNTT	Colin Brown (ed.), *New International Dictionary of New Testament Theology*, 3 vols. (Grand Rapids, 1975–78)
NT	*Novum Testamentum*

NTS	*New Testament Studies*
RB	*Revue biblique*
REB	Revised English Bible
RGG	*Religion in Geschichte und Gegenwart*
RQ	*Revue de Qumran*
RSR	*Recherches de science religieuse*
RSV	Revised Standard Version
SJT	*Scottish Journal of Theology*
TB	*Tyndale Bulletin*
TDNT	G. Kittel and G. Friedrich (eds.), *Theological Dictionary of the New Testament*, trans. G. W. Bromiley, 10 vols. (Grand Rapids, 1964–76)
TDOT	G. J. Botterweck, H. Ringgren, and H. J. Fabry (eds.), *Theological Dictionary of the Old Testament*, trans. J. T. Willis, G. W. Bromiley, and D. E. Green (Grand Rapids, 1974–)
Th.Z.	*Theologische Zeitschrift*
VT	*Vetus Testamentum*
ZNW	*Zeitschrift für die neutestamentliche Wissenschaft*
ZTK	*Zeitschrift für Theologie und Kirche*

Ancient Sources

Aen.	Virgil, *Aeneid*
AJ	Josephus, *Antiquities of the Jews*
Asc. Isa.	Ascensio Isaiae
B	Codex Vaticanus, 4th c.
b	Codex Veronensis, Old Latin, 5th c.
Bereshith R.	*Bereshith Rabbah*
boh	Bohairic version of the Syriac
b.T.	Babylonian Talmud
Berak.	b.T. *Berakoth*
b.T.RH	b.T. *Rosh Hashanah*
C	Codex Ephraemi, 5th c.
Clem. Alex.	Clement of Alexandria
D	Codex Bezae, 5–6th c.
de Agric.	Philo, *de Agricultura*
de Cher.	Philo, *de Cherubim*
de Conf. Ling.	Philo, *de Confusione Linguarum*
de Plant.	Philo, *de Plantatione*
de Op. Mundi	Philo, *de Opificio Mundi*

de Somn.	Philo, *de Somniis*
de Spec. Leg.	Philo, *de Specialibus Legibus*
Dio Chrys. *Orat.*	Dio Chrysostomus, *Orationae*
1 En.	1 Enoch
2 Esd.	2 Esdras
Hippolytus, *Haer.*	Hippolytus, *Refutatio Omnium Haeresium*
Iren. *Haer.*	Irenaeus, *Adversus Haereses*
Jub.	Jubilees
L	Luke's Special Material
Leg. All.	Philo, *Legum Allegoriae*
M	Matthew's Special Material
Mem.	Xenophon, *Memorabilia*
Metaph.	Aristotle, *Metaphysica*
Ned.	b. T. *Nedarim*
Od.	Homer, *Odyssey*
Or. Sib.	Sibylline Oracles
Pes.	b. T. *Pesaḥim*
pesh	Peshitta version of the Syriac
Phdr.	Plato, *Phaedrus*
Q	The Q Source
Quaest. Exod.	Philo, *Quaestiones et Solutiones in Exodum*
4QFl	4Q p 317 l 19 Florilegium
1QH	Qumran Hymns
1QpHab	*Pesher on Habakkuk* from Qumran Cave I
RH	b.T. Rosh Hashanah
Shabbath	Mishnah, *Shabbath*
Sm.	Ignatius, *Letter to the Smyrnaeans*
Suet. *Nero*	Suetonius, *Nero*
Syr Sin	Sinaitic Syriac, 4–7th c.
Tac. *Hist.*	Tacitus, *Historiae*
Targ. Jer.	Targum Jeremias
Targ. Jon.	Targum Jonathan
Targ. Onk.	Targum Onkelos
Test. Jud.	Testament of Judah
Xenophon, *Mem.*	Xenophon, *Memorabilia*
33	MS 33, 9–10th c.

I.

Introduction: The Apostolic Conference

I.I. WHAT IS NEW TESTAMENT THEOLOGY?[1]

New Testament theology is a historical discipline. It is not to be confused with either dogmatics or apologetics: for its purpose is neither to provide scriptural authority for modern doctrinal beliefs nor to make those beliefs appear reasonable and defensible to the unconvinced inquirer. Its purpose is descriptive.[2] We may indeed believe that in the New Testament we have a divine revelation valid for all ages. But that revelation was made in historical events, and those who first

---

[1] The literature on the subject is enormous. In addition to the works cited below, cf. H. Boers, *What is New Testament Theology?* (Philadelphia, 1979); O. Merk, *Biblische Theologie des Neuen Testaments in ihrer Anfangszeit* (Marburg, 1972); R. Morgan, *The Nature of New Testament Theology* (London, 1973), 'Theology (New Testament)', in R. J. Coggins and J. L. Houlden (eds.), *A Dictionary of Biblical Interpretation* (London, 1990), 689 ff.; and 'Theology (NT)', in D. N. Freedman (ed.), *The Anchor Bible Dictionary* (New York, 1992), vi. 473 ff.; K. Stendahl, 'Biblical Theology, Contemporary', in G. A. Buttrick (ed.), *The Interpreter's Dictionary of the Bible* (Nashville, 1962), i. 418 ff; J. D. G. Dunn, 'The Task of New Testament Theology', in J. D. G. Dunn and J. P. Mackey (eds.), *New Testament Theology in Dialogue: Christology and Ministry* (Philadelphia, 1987), 1 ff.; G. Hasel, *New Testament Theology: Basic Issues in the Current Debate* (Grand Rapids, 1978); H. G. Reventlow, 'Theology (Biblical), History of', in D. N. Freedman (ed.), *The Anchor Bible Dictionary*, 6 (New York, 1992), 483 ff.; J. D. Smart, *The Past, Present and Future of Biblical Theology* (Philadelphia, 1979); G. Strecker (ed.), *Das Problem der Theologie des Neuen Testaments* (Darmstadt, 1975); B. S. Childs, *Biblical Theology in Crisis* (Philadelphia, 1970); and H. Räisänen, *Beyond New Testament Theology*. Introductions to the various New Testament theologies should also be consulted, including those of H. Conzelmann (London, 1969), L. Goppelt (Grand Rapids 1981–2), D. Guthrie (Downers Grove, 1981), W. G. Kümmel (London, 1974), G. E. Ladd (Grand Rapids, 1974), and L. L. Morris (Grand Rapids, 1986). The insights of Bishop Stephen Neill in *Jesus Through Many Eyes* (Philadelphia, 1976) characteristically cut through much of the nonsense of modern debate and present the reader with a coherent and unified vision of New Testament theology.

[2] See G. Ebeling, 'The Meaning of "Biblical Theology"', *JTS* NS 6 (1955), 210–25. For a contrary view see A. Richardson, *An Introduction to the Theology of the New Testament* (1968), 9–15.

thought out the significance of those events did so in relation to the circumstances of their time and with a pastoral concern for particular congregations; even their general statements were made with reference to the particular. They never dreamt that what they wrote would, centuries later, be subjected to the microscopic scrutiny of modern biblical scholarship, providing in every unusual phrase and every unexpressed assumption matter for a doctoral dissertation. Nor did they imagine that it might be used as a rule of faith and practice in a world changed beyond their imagining. Yet for us that scrutiny is necessary, since we cannot be confident in discerning the relevance of their teaching to our day until by all the resources of historical research we have learnt its relevance to their own. Karl Barth once properly warned us to be suspicious of a biblical research which loses itself in details of antiquarian reconstruction and forgets that the Bible is a book about God; but the Barthian revolt against *Historismus* all too easily becomes an indifference to history totally incompatible with the belief that God revealed himself in events which happened *sub Pontius Pilato*.[3]

The distinction between New Testament theology and other related disciplines is one which has all too often been ignored. Systematic theologians naturally wish their work to be regarded as biblical theology, in the sense that it is in harmony with what they find written in Scripture. But to confound dogmatics with New Testament theology is to assume that the New Testament writers had minds which worked exactly like ours and were interested in the same questions as we are. If, for example, we take it for granted that Christians in the first century attached much importance to the questions of church order which occupy the attention of modern ecumenical conferences, we shall certainly distort what little the New Testament has to say on this subject; for the Pastoral Epistles are more interested in the bishop's morals than in his authority. Romans 9–11 will certainly be misrepresented if we treat it as Paul's philosophy of history or as a treatise on predestination and free will, and not as a very practical wrestling with a problem of missionary policy. Paul, in Romans 13 was not

---

[3] Cf. e.g. *The Doctrine of the Word of God: Church Dogmatics I* (Edinburgh, 1975), 188, where the historical circumstances of the life of Jesus are represented not as the revelation but as the veiling of the word of God, and the historical Jesus, in so far as we can know him at all, is described as 'a little commonplace' in comparison with the founders of other religions. For the correct balance, see C. F. D. Moule, *Essays in New Testament Interpretation* (Cambridge, 1982), viii.

merely airing his views on the state but communicating something to a particular group of readers, so that we need to determine not only what he could have meant by the words but also what the readers could have been expected to understand by them. If we not only ask what a New Testament writer said, but also what he was communicating when he said it, we shall be chary of giving the New Testament doctrine about a question which the New Testament writers themselves never raised.

It is equally important to keep New Testament theology distinct from apologetics. It is one thing to ask what the New Testament teaches, and quite another to ask whether that teaching is credible to ourselves or to others. The nineteenth-century writers of lives of Jesus assumed that if they could strip from the gospel story the accretions of ecclesiastical dogma they would find a Jesus in whom it would be possible for a rational person to believe. Form Criticism—the quest of the historical *kērygma*—started from similar assumptions about the nature of the earliest Christian preaching. More recently Bultmann, believing that even the earliest Gospel was couched in thought forms and language which make it unacceptable to 'the modern mind', has demanded the demythologizing of the New Testament. But to make the New Testament intelligible is not the same thing as making it credible. The 'modern mind' can do what it likes with the teaching of Jesus and the apostles. But it can only have the freedom to do so if the New Testament theologian has first described the material honestly. We are thus involved with the reconstruction of the past, a past accessible to us not by direct scrutiny but only through the interrogation of witnesses. The possibility of conversation depends on the historian's skill in 'speaking the same language' as his or her source. Sources are sources only in virtue of the questions which the historian addresses to them, and, if one approaches them without a sufficient degree of sympathetic rapport, they will either remain silent or yield fantastic answers. To some extent the historian creates his or her own past by the choice of questions; and, since the responsible historian speaks both for the past and the present, it may be said in a quite literal sense that history is what we make of our own past. Furthermore, what we make of the past helps to determine what we make of the future. When Macaulay wrote that 'the history of England is emphatically the history of progress', he was, in effect, saying to the English people, 'Here is the way which your tradition has marked out for you to follow.' There is therefore an element of judgement in all history,

not merely in the sense that the historian must exercise critical discrimination, but in the sense that we are judged by what we make of
our past. This does not mean, however, that historians are hopelessly
imprisoned within the walls of their own subjectivity or of the subjectivity of their time. The work of creation is never *ex nihilo*. It must be
admitted that Winston Smith in George Orwell's *1984*, whose task it
was to 'correct' back issues of *The Times* in order to make them conform with party propaganda, has his counterparts in real life; and that
even those who adhere to the principle 'Comment is free, but facts
are sacred' are liable by inadvertence to impose on facts an interpretation they are incapable of bearing. But the moral of this long tale is
simply that historical accuracy is the product of free discussion, honest
criticism, and constant revision.

1.2. APPROACHES TO WRITING A
NEW TESTAMENT THEOLOGY

From what we have said above it follows that there is no such thing
as New Testament theology. It is not an entity waiting to be discovered
by industrious and perspicacious scholars. No perfect pattern of it is
laid up in heaven, to be contemplated by the learned, and then brought
down to earth for the release of the captives in this world's cave of
illusion. New Testament theology is nothing more than a book which
some scholar chooses to write, an attempt to describe in some sort of
orderly fashion what the writers of the New Testament believed, in
the hope that the book may be of benefit to readers of the New
Testament, to preachers of its gospel, to all who desire to put their
lives and the corporate life of the community to which they belong,
under its authority, and particularly to those who have responsibility
for the constant restatement of Christian doctrine. To ask 'What is
New Testament theology?' is to ask how an author may most effectively
write such a book. There are, hybrids apart, five types of answer.

1.2.1. *The Dogmatic Approach*

Until J. P. Gabler[4] published his essay on the distinction between biblical and dogmatic theology, nobody thought of writing 'biblical' theology. They wrote theology: and the shape of theology was dictated by the traditional doctrines of the creeds. The theologian turned to the Bible either as a source of proof texts or as *prolegomena* to the systematic formulation of doctrine. The earliest attempts at biblical theology were inevitably in the same mould.[5] It long continued to be common practice that any treatment of Christian doctrine should begin with one chapter on the Old Testament and one on the New, before proceeding to the Fathers and later church history, and so to a definitive statement of modern belief. And there have never been lacking books on such subjects as the biblical foundations of the doctrine of the Trinity.

This method has one obvious advantage. If New Testament theology is to be of value, it must be of value to the ongoing life of the Church; and one of its functions is to supply 'raw material' for systematic theology. Theologians have with justice complained that the findings of biblical scholarship have too often not been presented in a form which they could readily use;[6] and the dogmatic method is, superficially at least, exempt from that complaint. But the objections to it are overwhelming, for it raises at least four types of problem.

1. There is the problem of category, i.e. the confusion of doctrine with revelation. 'For the love of Christ leaves us no choice, when once we have reached the conclusion that one man died for all and therefore all have died' (2 Cor. 5: 14). Paul undoubtedly believed in the objectivity of God's saving and revealing act in Christ; but the impact of that event on his own life depended on his having reached a conclusion about it. Doctrines, ancient and modern, are the product of human

[4] J. P. Gabler, *De justo discrimine theologiae biblicae et dogmaticae regundisque recte utriusque finibus* (Altdorf, 1787). For a more modern treatment, cf. Morgan, *The Nature of New Testament Theology*.

[5] See W. M. L. de Wette, *Biblische Dogmatik Alten und Neuen Testaments* (Berlin, 1813); and for a modern counterpart, D. Guthrie, *New Testament Theology* (Downers Grove, Ill., 1981).

[6] This was what prompted Barth to write his commentary on Romans (1919, 1921[2]; ET 1933), which has been more significant as protest than as a guide to the mind of Paul (K. Barth, *The Epistle to the Romans*, trans. from 6th edn. by E. C. Hoskyns (London, 1933)).

thought about the revelation of God; they are not revealed truth.[7] We are saved by believing in God, not by believing doctrines, not even the doctrine of justification by faith.

2. There is the problem of interest. The dogmatist assumes that the New Testament writers dealt with matters of perennial significance, and concludes that what seems important to him or her must equally have been important to them. But the New Testament shows, for example, little interest in those questions of church order which have engrossed the attention of modern ecumenists. Paul, like Jesus, is impatient of protocol;[8] it did not matter to him who administered baptism, and there is not a shred of evidence that it mattered to him or to anybody else who presided at the eucharist. James Barr[9] has effectively shown that, while the biblical writers frequently use words for time in talking about other subjects, they never, with the one exception of Qoheleth, make statements about time itself: and he has reasonably questioned whether there is any value in speaking of 'a biblical concept of time'. When the Second Vatican Council decreed that there are not two sources of revelation (scripture and tradition) but only one (scripture as interpreted in tradition), there was an immediate danger that conservative scholars would start ransacking scripture to provide authority for those dogmas which had previously been believed on the basis of tradition alone.[10] E. P. Sanders has convincingly argued that the traditional Lutheran interpretation of Pauline theology, together with the picture of Judaism which it assumes, is the projection on to the first century of a sixteenth century controversy.[11] Personal interest is thus a common intruder into the study of the New Testament academic.

3. There is the problem of reference, i.e. the assumption that in

---

[7] 'I am not denying that the great Christian doctrines point to the truth, but propositions such as theological statements are not revealed from heaven, and if they were, they would of necessity be distorted in any possible human language. They arise out of man's intellectual travail. In revelation it is God who reveals and it is God who is revealed. Revelation is not doctrine' (N. Micklem, *Ultimate Questions* (Nashville, 1955), 20).

[8] Gal. 2: 6; 1 Cor. 1: 12 ff; cf. Mark 9: 35–9; 10: 35–45; Matt. 23: 8, 12.

[9] J. Barr, *Biblical Words for Time* (London, 1969).

[10] See G. B. Caird, *Our Dialogue with Rome* (Oxford, 1967), 28 ff.

[11] E. P. Sanders, *Paul and Palestinian Judaism: A Comparison of Patterns of Religion* (Philadelphia, 1977), 57: 'We have here the retrojection of the Protestant–Catholic debate into ancient history, with Judaism taking the role of Catholicism and Christianity the role of Lutheranism.'

the New Testament 'the speaker is referring to what we should be referring to were we speaking the words ourselves'.[12] When, for example, we read of a contrast between gospel and Law, we tend (if we are thinking dogmatically rather than historically) to suppose that the one refers to the Christian and the other to the Jewish religion. But Torah covers much more than what we mean by religion; it is also the code of civil and criminal law of the Jewish nation and the national ethos of the Jewish people, the Jewish way of life.

4. There is the problem of authority. Modern Christians naturally wish their teaching to be regarded as biblical, in the sense that it is in harmony with what they find in Scripture. This is an aim which any honest biblical scholar will hardly wish to criticize. But if that harmony is guaranteed from the outset by doctrinal authority, whether by the explicit statement that the doctrines of the Church are *ex sese irreformabiles* or by the unacknowledged infallibilities which are more characteristic of the churches of the Reformation,[13] it becomes nothing more than a tautology. Human beings hardly put themselves under the authority of the word of God in the Bible—under its criticism and judgement, its illumination and renewing powers—unless they allow the Bible to speak, above all the voices of ecclesiastical dogma, with its own original, authentic voice. Moreover, the dogmatic approach to the New Testament is inevitably selective. Theologians of various traditions have all appealed to the New Testament to provide warrant for their conflicting views, and so have made themselves vulnerable to the cynical epigram of Werenfels: 'This is the book in which every one searches for his own opinions, and every one with equal success finds his own opinions.'[14]

It should perhaps be added that dogmatism is not necessarily ecclesiastical. Critical scholarship creates its own dogma whenever one of its theories ceases to be regarded as a reasonable working hypothesis and becomes sacrosanct. As an example, C. F. D. Moule[15] has pointed out that W. Wrede, in his determination to eliminate theological dogma

[12] C. K. Ogden and I. A. Richards, *The Meaning of Meaning* (London, 1960), 15. In G. B. Caird, *The Language and Imagery of the Bible* (London, 1980), 80 ff., this point has been illustrated with regard to baptism and the words denoting ministry.

[13] e.g. E. Käsemann, *Perspectives on Paul* (London, 1971), 63.

[14] 'Hic liber est in quo quaerit sua dogmata quisque, invenit et pariter dogmata quisque sua.'

[15] In a review of J. D. Smart's *The Past, Present, and Future of Biblical Theology* (*JTS* NS 33 (1982), 195–7).

from historical and literary criticism, 'was applying a dogma—the dogma of the competence of the human reason to interpret scripture without invoking the transcendent'.

The whole tenor of the New Testament is opposed to dogmatism and authoritarianism. Jesus is represented in the Gospels as regularly teaching by questions and seeking to elicit a critical judgement from his hearers.[16] Paul spent so much of his career trying to prevent those who would turn the gospel into a new legalism that we may be sure he would have been shocked at the conversion of his own teaching into dogma. If ever he appears dictatorial, it is at the expense of the dogmatists, whether at Galatia, Corinth, or Colossae, i.e. those who are making extravagant demands of their fellow Christians or imposing unnecessary conditions upon them. His own, more relaxed attitude to the ordinary believer, the brother or sister for whom Christ died, arises out of his confidence in God; for he was convinced that, provided his friends adhered to the primacy of God's grace, no matter what hetero-dox ideas they might hold about other matters, God would in due course reveal the truth to them (Phil. 3: 15). Similarly, the author of 1 John writes to strengthen those whose faith has been shaken by an aggressive clique who have been priding themselves on the superiority of their religious experience and credentials; and he insists that the only *necessary* knowledge is the common possession of all Christians (2: 20). And John records two warnings against the idolatry of giving to the angel of Revelation the absolute status which belongs only to God (Rev. 19: 10; 22: 9).

1.2.2. *The Chronological Approach*

Those scholars who led the revolt against the dogmatic method, deeply impressed as they were by the variety of New Testament experience and thought, denied also that there could be a theology common to a collection of books which were the product neither of a single setting nor of a single generation, and undertook to substitute for the theology of the New Testament 'a history of New Testament thought'. The aim here is simple: we must trace the growth of Christian ideas from the seed-beds of Jewish or Graeco-Oriental thought, through the various stages represented in the New Testament, to the catholic

---

[16] e.g. Matt. 17: 25; Mark 4: 13, 8: 29; Luke 12: 54–7 (cf. also below, p. 417).

Christianity of the second century, in which some saw their full flor-
escence, others their incipient fossilization. There were some who
believed that by comparing early Christianity with contemporary
religions they could arrive at its distinctive and unique kernel of truth,
and others who, frankly humanist in their attitude to Christian origins,
were prepared to find truth only in universals. But all agreed that the
main object of New Testament research was to discover the place
taken by Christianity in the general history of religions; and that the
only unity to be looked for in the New Testament was that of continuous and organic development.

This approach to the New Testament enjoyed for a while a certain
popularity, partly because of its indisputable success in building up
vast stores of information about the background to primitive Christianity; this remains its positive and abiding achievement. Yet even this
success has proved to be an embarrassment. No one New Testament
scholar can be equally expert in the Old Testament, Greek philosophy,
Graeco-Oriental religions, Palestinian and Hellenistic Judaism, classical and biblical archaeology, and in the writings of the apocalyptists,
the Rabbis, Philo, Josephus, and the Qumran covenanters. Those who
have contributed to the history of early Christianity have come to it
from a particular field of research and with a predominant interest
which has coloured their view of the whole period. Thus Professor
Bultmann discovered in the New Testament evidence of Gnosticism,
where the Old Testament scholar sees only the natural and proper
development of Hebrew ways of thought; and the provocative writer
Stauffer, criticizing Deissmann and Dalman for attempting to illuminate the first century by the use of Hellenistic or Jewish documents
from later periods, represented early Christianity as merely one branch
of apocalyptic. Just as the nineteenth-century quest for the historical
Jesus, with its host of mutually contradictory lives of Jesus, ended in
a horrifying form of scepticism, so the mutually incompatible histories
of early Christianity have raised doubts about the validity of their
method and the very possibility of their objective.

Nobody will dispute that it would be desirable to possess an account
of the development of early Christianity which would command general agreement. But do we have the evidence to make this possible?
The chronology of the New Testament is notoriously problematic,
even for the life of Paul, where the evidence is strongest.[17] The attempt

[17] Cf. Robert Jewett, *A Chronology of Paul's Life* (Philadelphia, 1979).

of J. A. T. Robinson[18] to give an early date to the books of the New
Testament has not won many converts, but it has demonstrated the
precarious nature of the arguments by which dates have been assigned.
And if it is hard to date whole books, how much more speculative
must be the dating of their constitutive elements, the hypothetical
sources and redactional strands of the Gospels and such items as the
hymns which it has been fashionable to detect within the Epistles?
Scholarly terminology has frequently disguised the difficulties rather
than solving them. What, for example, does the term 'pre-Pauline'
signify? Is it that which antedates the conversion of Paul, or the writing
of his first letter, or the writing of the letter which happens to be under
discussion? And can we be sure that what is pre-Pauline in the second
and third senses is independent of the influence of Paul?

But is our ignorance confined to chronology? Paul apart, we know
nothing about the authors of the New Testament except the little that
we can infer from their books. Even in the case of Paul, there is
still a hot debate concerning the reliability of Acts[19] and the relative
importance of his Jewish and Greek backgrounds.[20] One reason for

---

[18] J. A. T. Robinson, *Redating the New Testament* (Philadelphia, 1975). Robinson argues
that all the books of the New Testament were written prior to AD 70.

[19] Those who take a negative view of its value for understanding Paul include P.
Vielhauer, 'On the "Paulinism" of Acts', in L. E. Keck and J. Martyn (eds.), *Studies in
Luke–Acts* (Nashville, 1966), 33 ff.; and E. Haenchen, *The Acts of the Apostles: A Commentary* (Philadelphia, 1971). Positive estimates include M. Enslin, 'Once Again, Luke
and Paul', *ZNW* 61 (1970), 253 ff.; W. W. Gasque, *A History of the Criticism of the Acts
of the Apostles* (Grand Rapids, 1975); and M. Hengel, *Acts and the History of Earliest
Christianity* (Philadelphia, 1979).

[20] As with the question above, the nature of Paul's religious background remains
extremely controversial. The dominance of his Jewish background has been vigorously
asserted by W. D. Davies, *Paul and Rabbinic Judaism* (London, 1980⁴), and by E. P.
Sanders, *Paul and Palestinian Judaism* and *Paul, the Law and the Jewish People* (Philadelphia, 1983). Other studies, with varying types of focus, include F. Watson, *Paul, Judaism
and the Gentiles: A Sociological Approach* (Cambridge, 1986); H. Räisänen, *Paul and the
Law* (Tübingen, 1987²), and *The Torah and Christ* (Helsinki, 1986); J. D. G. Dunn,
Jesus, Paul and the Law (Philadelphia, 1990); J. C. Beker, *Paul the Apostle* (Philadelphia,
1980); S. Kim, *The Origin of Paul's Gospel* (Grand Rapids, 1981); N. T. Wright, *The
Climax of the Covenant: Christ and the Law in Pauline Theology* (Minneapolis, 1992); and
J. A. Ziesler, *Pauline Christianity* (New York, 1983). The question of his upbringing is
well canvassed by W. C. van Unnik, 'Tarsus or Jerusalem: The City of Paul's Youth',
in van Unnik, *Sparsa Collecta* (Leiden, 1973), 259 ff., and J. Collins, *Between Athens
and Jerusalem* (New York, 1983). While not denying the importance of Paul's Jewish
background, Professor E. A. Judge of McQuarrie University has provided valuable
information on the social aspects of Paul's Hellenistic background in 'St Paul and
Classical Society', *JAC* 15 (1972), 19 ff.

this is that we know far less about first-century Judaism than has commonly been supposed; our sources for Palestinian Judaism are late, and our sources for Hellenistic Judaism derive almost wholly from Egypt, which was certainly not typical of the Diaspora.[21]

Even more serious difficulties attach to the concept of development. Similarities between systems of thought and religion are not necessarily evidence of causal links. Even where a connection can be demonstrated, we have to beware of the genetic fallacy, the besetting temptation of all historians of thought. To trace an idea to its origins is not to explain it, let alone to explain it away.[22] Words and symbols may at different times to the same people, and at the same time to different people, convey radically divergent meanings. Ideas and practices with a long history can be reborn into a new existence when taken up into a new and living system. We may illuminate the synoptic phrase 'the Kingdom of God' by referring to the Old Testament, intertestamental, and rabbinic usage, but we do not thus explain it: Jesus would not have devoted so much of his teaching to explaining what *he* meant by the Kingdom if this had been the meaning which the phrase bore in current parlance, or even in the teaching of any existing group. Much of the discussion of the title 'Son of Man' has been vitiated by the curious assumption that Jesus cannot have used the term in any way that is not totally explained from Jewish sources. Bousset's monumental work[23] on the use of *kurios* in Hellenistic religions helped to account for the attraction which Christianity held for devotees of these cults and suggests a reason why early Christian missionaries emphasized this title of Christ above others; but it does not determine the theological content of the word in its Christian setting. Christianity was not the mathematical product of existing factors, an amalgam of contemporary beliefs and practices; it was a new way of thought and life with the power to draw into itself elements of Jewish and pagan religion and to give them a new meaning and existence that can be understood only from within the New Testament.[24]

---

[21] Cf. the helpful discussion of R. H. Pfeiffer, *History of New Testament Times* (New York, 1949), 166 ff.

[22] The origin of the phrase 'genetic fallacy' is often traced to the ethical philosopher G. E. Moore, *Principia Ethica* (Cambridge, 1954).

[23] W. Bousset, *Kyrios Christos* (Göttingen, 1913; ET, Nashville, 1970).

[24] Cf. C. H. Dodd, *The Interpretation of the Fourth Gospel* (Cambridge, 1953), 212: 'The current conceptions of the higher religion of Hellenism have been taken up but entirely transformed.'

There are similar problems when we turn to consider the relationships between the New Testament books themselves. It was once almost axiomatic that parallels between books were due to dependence of the kind so decisively established by synoptic criticism. Today it is no longer obvious that 1 Peter copied from Romans and Ephesians, that John's Gospel is a meditation on drastically altered selections from the written record of the synoptics, or that the other John modelled his letters to seven churches on the collected letters of Paul. We have come to recognize that in the apostolic age the pen was less influential than the spoken word. But we have also come to recognize a much more important point, that, even where one author can be proved to be familiar with the work of another, this is no guarantee of theological continuity. Polycarp had read Paul without understanding him, and the author of the Pastoral Epistles was a person of similar limitations— Paul's disciple but not his heir. Luke had certainly read Mark, but his theology is his own, less sophisticated (some would say 'more primitive') than Mark's. If then it is unjustifiable to trace a development of thought where literary convictions are certain, must it not be even more questionable to do so when connections are dubious? Many critics once held, almost as a dogma, that Ephesians, the Pastorals, Peter, and Hebrews were 'deutero-Pauline'. But the relationship of these writings to Paul is too diverse to be usefully covered by a single portmanteau term. If Ephesians is not by Paul, it is by a disciple who picked up the threads of Pauline theology where Paul himself laid them down.[25] With such a one the author of the Pastorals had nothing in common except his admiration of the master. Hebrews and 1 Peter, even if they are post-Pauline (which is far from being generally agreed), and even if their authors had some acquaintance with Pauline teaching, are theologically so remote from Paul that they are best regarded as representatives of a Hellenistic Christianity largely independent of the Pauline circle.

Thus literary history provides an inadequate foundation for a history of early Christian thought. Nor can we make good the deficiency by appealing to some proven standard of logical development by which to distinguish the primitive from the mature. That Christians modified

---

[25] For a sympathetic discussion of the Pauline authorship of Ephesians, cf. G. B. Caird, *Paul's Letters from Prison* (London, 1976), 11–17, 20–2, and J. C. Kirby, *Ephesians, Baptism and Pentecost* (London, 1968), 3–56. A thoroughgoing defence of Pauline authorship is provided by D. Guthrie, *New Testament Introduction* (Downers Grove, Ill., 1990⁴), 496 ff.

their ideas with the passing years in response to exigencies of thought and conduct goes without saying. But this hardly means that the modifications followed any logical pattern or always constituted an advance towards greater maturity. The qualitatively primitive and the temporally primitive do not necessarily coincide. It was once generally accepted that in its doctrine of the person of Christ the New Testament displayed a steady development from the 'low' Christology of Jewish-Christian Messianism to the 'high' Christology of the cosmic Christ and the *logos* doctrine; but Dom Gregory Dix[26] has warned us against too facile an assumption that a Christology expressed in Greek terms of status is necessarily higher than one expressed in Jewish terms of function, and in any case there is no Christology in the New Testament higher than that of Phil. 2: 6 ff., which is earlier than any of the non-Pauline writings. B. Lindars has argued that the use of Old Testament quotations in the New Testament underwent a logical development dictated by the changing apologetic and pastoral needs of the Church; but he is careful to point out that this 'logical sequence . . . can be linked to historical development at some points, but not always';[27] and that, in one case at least, 'John preserves the oldest application, Acts the second, and Mark the latest'.[28] Whatever hypothesis we adopt about the 'primitive' beliefs of Christology or any other subject, we are liable to find that in some respects Matthew, Luke, and John are more 'primitive' than their predecessors.[29] In any religious community different degrees of development and different levels of profundity coexist; movements of thought rarely proceed in a single, straight line. Moreover, developments do not necessarily take place at the time when they are first recorded, nor are the processes by which new ideas are reached necessarily identical with the arguments by which they are subsequently defended.

The task of writing a history of early Christian thought is thus beset by at least as many pitfalls as the task of writing a life of Jesus, and

[26] G. Dix, *Jew and Greek: A Study in the Primitive Church* (Westminster, 1953), 79 f. (see also below, p. 284).

[27] B. Lindars, *New Testament Apologetic* (Philadelphia, 1961), 29.

[28] Ibid. 18. Cf. two essays by C. F. D. Moule, in which he attributes variations in Christology and eschatology to changing circumstance and purpose rather than to development (*Essays in New Testament Interpretation*, 165–99).

[29] On primitive elements in the Fourth Gospel, see W. C. van Unnik, 'The Purpose of St John's Gospel', in *The Gospels Reconsidered* (International Congress on 'The Four Gospels in 1957', Oxford (1960), 167 ff.), and C. H. Dodd, *Historical Tradition in the Fourth Gospel* (Cambridge, 1963).

scholars who attempt it are likely to find that their work commends itself only to their most ardent disciples. But even if such a work could be successfully completed it would in one respect differ from New Testament theology in that it would deliberately ignore the canon. If the apostolic age is to be treated simply as an important chapter in the continuously unfolding story of religious thought, or even of divine revelation, the books of the New Testament are not in principle different from any other book. According to this view, these books are normative for the life and teaching of the Church, not because of any intrinsic quality, but because the Church, after much wavering, has so decided.

It was perfectly natural, therefore, that the Epistles of such apostolic men as Clement and Polycarp ... should be enrolled with the apostolic Epistles, since their production was a continuation of the old apostolic procedure. The distinction or gap which we mentally interpose is an unhistorical one, based on the subsequent fact that some of them have been canonized, whereas others have not.[30]

But ought we to allow the canon to be discarded as an 'unhistorical' device? Let us grant that it is hard to defend the borderline decisions of the early Fathers: 2 Peter is undoubtedly a later work than 1 Clement, and the theological value of each will provoke some subjective weighing. But the existence of a borderline in the biological sciences, where the difference between plants and animals is blurred, does not mean that the distinction between botany and zoology is unscientific. The principle of canonicity, that some books are apostolic and therefore intrinsically different from others, was established in the second century, and ought not to be disregarded either because of the long disputes that followed about borderline cases or because of the lack of exact scholarship with which the debates were conducted. In adopting a canon the Christians of the second century were committing themselves to three affirmations: (1) that the heart of their gospel was a series of historic events; (2) that the apostles had been appointed witnesses to these events; and that (3) the New Testament is the primary record of the apostolic testimony. They therefore repudiated the charge

---

[30] P. Carrington, *The Early Christian Church* (Cambridge, 1957), i. 473. Even such a cautious and conservative scholar as E. Stauffer draws his evidence impartially from canonical and non-canonical writings because, notwithstanding his professedly Christocentric theology, he is concerned to delineate 'the sort of world in which the writers of the New Testament grew up' (*New Testament Theology* (London, 1955), 106).

that a canon was 'unhistorical'; it was their attempt to separate, within the body of tradition, written or oral, that which was primary and authoritative from that which was derivative and secondary.

1.2.3. *The Kerygmatic Approach*

In his inaugural lecture at Cambridge in 1935,[31] C. H. Dodd declared that one of the urgent tasks for New Testament scholarship was the reversal of the centrifugal tendency which had concentrated on the variety of the New Testament to the neglect of its unity; and he promptly set an example in his own writing.[32] It is worthy of note, however, that, although he argued that an outline of the apostolic preaching could be recovered from the epistles, and that certain passages of the Old Testament, read with a new and distinctively Christian principle of selection and interpretation, formed 'the substructure of Christian theology', he stopped short of asserting a common theology, recognizing that on the one foundation Paul, Apollos, and many others had built widely different superstructures.

Others, however, were less restrained. Alan Richardson started his work with the hypothesis that there was a common apostolic theology which underlies the books of the New Testament and can be reconstructed from them, claiming further that this hypothesis offered a more credible explanation of Christian origins than any other.[33] Such a quest had obvious attractions at a time when churches had abandoned the older, literalistic conception of biblical authority and were searching for a new one which would preserve the unity of the Bible and provide a foundation for ecumenical unity as well. But this fashion proved to be short-lived for obvious reasons. The attempt to discriminate in the New Testament between the central and the peripheral, the orthodox and the heretical, the treasure of God's word and the dispensable vessel that contains it, is as hazardous in practice as it is wrong-headed in conception. It is not, indeed, difficult to light upon details which appear to be dictated by conditions of first-century life in a Roman province: Jesus' instruction to the twelve to go on their mission barefoot (Luke 10: 4), Paul's advice to the women of Corinth

---

[31] C. H. Dodd, *The Present Task in New Testament Studies* (Cambridge, 1936).

[32] C. H. Dodd, *The Apostolic Preaching and its Development* (London, 1951²); cf. also *Gospel and Law: The Relation of Faith and Ethics in Early Christianity* (New York, 1951); and *According to the Scriptures* (London, 1952).

[33] A. Richardson, *An Introduction to the Theology of the New Testament* (London, 1968).

not to flout convention by leading public worship bareheaded (1 Cor. 11: 5), and the Presbyter's strictures on the limitation of hospitality (2 John 10). But to try to eliminate the historically contingent in order that the permanent may remain is to ignore the vital fact that *everything* in the New Testament is historically conditioned. The universal is always embedded in the particular. The achievement of Paul, which is entirely in keeping with his repudiation of Jewish legalism, is not that he provides us with a core of universal truth, let alone a universally valid system of dogma, but that he teaches us to think theologically about particular intellectual and ethical problems.

The temptation of those who look for a core of apostolic theology in the New Testament is to assume that it consists of any elements attested by two or three witnesses. But the nature of the New Testament literature should warn us to be hesitant about this. Paul refers to letters which have not survived and to conversations which were never recorded (1 Cor. 5: 9; 2 Thess. 2: 5). The author of Hebrews deliberately remains silent on certain elementary doctrines and regrets that his theme is circumscribed by the dullness of his hearers (6: 1–2; 5: 11). Jude never wrote his intended letter about 'our common salvation', which might have been immensely more illuminating than the inflammatory tract he subsequently bequeathed to us. The New Testament, in fact, contains by no means the whole of what the apostolic Church taught and thought, and much of its content we owe to the exigencies of controversy. If it had not been for flagrant disorders in Corinth, the New Testament might not have contained its only explicit reference to the Lord's Supper (1 Cor. 11: 23–6).

For the existence of a common *gospel* we have the express assurance of Paul (1 Cor. 15: 11). We may doubt, on the other hand, in view of the variety of wording in which this *kērugma* is expressed, whether at any time in the first century it was reduced to a stereotyped credal form. Many passages in the New Testament have been dubbed 'credal' or 'quasi-credal', but no two of them are identical. When Paul refers to the different buildings which Apollos and others are erecting on the one foundation which is Christ, he does not so much as hint that they ought to meet and produce an agreed statement, only that each will have to answer to God for his or her work (1 Cor. 3: 10 ff.).

Paul claims that his gospel is identical with that of the other apostles, but also that it came to him independently of them in an experience which nobody else shared; and from his letters we may well judge that this experience gave to his theology a quality and depth all of its own.

He alone in his enthusiasm for the Law had persecuted the Church. He alone had undergone the revulsion of feeling that came when he recognized that the Law, so far from leading him to God, had been a veil over his heart preventing him from seeing the glory of God in the face of Christ. He alone had transferred to the ascended Lord the devotion he had hitherto lavished on the Law. Modern theologians have made a career out of interpreting Paul, but the theology which had so individual an origin was, inevitably, hammered out into new and original shapes on the anvil of controversy which few of us can recover, sometimes with Jews or Jewish Christians whose background was rabbinic, apocalyptic, Hellenistic, or a mixture of all three, sometimes with those who had come to Christianity from the popular philosophies, cults, and clubs of Graeco-Oriental cosmopolitanism; and so intimately is it bound up with events that we cannot leave out from it an essential Paulinism and throw away the historical setting. All this is true, *mutatis mutandis*, of the other writers. For the rest, let it suffice that the Kingdom of God is the theological centre of the synoptic gospels, but not elsewhere; that Paul and John have much to say about God's love in sending His Son, while on this the synoptics, Hebrews, and 1 Peter are silent; that Paul, who believes in the theological significance of the earthly life of Jesus, betrays singularly little acquaintance with its details; that John the Seer does not, like John the Evangelist, portray Jesus as the Saviour of the World. It would appear then that there never was a time when anybody's belief consisted of the highest common factor of New Testament teaching.[34]

1.2.4. *The Author-by-Author Approach*

We thus return to the interrogation of witnesses. It is of course possible to interrogate them one at a time and to write a separate chapter on each. This way of writing New Testament theology has undeniable attractions. It has the initial advantage of attempting the possible. It also has the advantage of simplicity, since it is much easier to deal with the theological ideas of Paul or John consecutively, so that the full range of the author's thought can be seen as a whole. It has the advantage of dealing directly with evidence. For the only evidence we

[34] Tatian's *Diatessaron* was an attempt to reduce the four Gospels to a single coherent story, free from discrepancies. It had a long popularity, but in the end the Church decided that it needed the fourfold witness of the separate Gospels (cf. the discussion of B. M. Metzger, *The Early Versions of the New Testament* (Oxford, 1977), pp. 10 ff.).

have lies in the books themselves, and sound exegesis must always take precedence over speculative theories about origins and influences. It is true that for the full understanding of any utterance we need to know its context; but we have no knowledge of the context of any of the New Testament writings beyond what may be deduced from the study of them. Some light may no doubt be thrown on them by acquaintance with a variety of possible first-century backgrounds; but of all the competing backgrounds which have been proposed, for example, for Hebrews (Paul, the school of Stephen, the Samaritans, Philo, Qumran, Gnosticism, etc.) only a scrutiny of the epistle can determine which, if any, are relevent.

There is a practical difficulty that such a book would be dominated by Paul and John, since the Synoptic Gospels and the smaller Epistles could not by themselves yield chapters of comparable bulk and coverage. They would either be ignored, as they were by Bultmann, or they would be so grouped as to negate the fundamental purpose of the book.

But the real objection to this method is that it is the lazy way of doing it; it leaves all the most important work of collective comparison still to be done. We thus come to our approach to writing a New Testament theology.

1.2.5. *The Conference Table Approach*

(a) *The Method*

The presupposition of our study is simply stated: to write a New Testament theology is to preside at a conference of faith and order. Around the table sit the authors of the New Testament, and it is the presider's task to engage them in a colloquium about theological matters which they themselves have placed on the agenda. It might be objected that the presider cannot be sure exactly how many participants will attend the conference. There will probably be at least twelve: The four evangelists, Paul, the Pastor, the authors of Hebrews, James, 1 Peter, 2 Peter, and Jude, and John the Seer. But will Paul speak for 2 Thessalonians, Colossians, and Ephesians, or do we require one, two, or three extra seats at the table? Is Presbyter John, who wrote the Epistles, the evangelist or one of his disciples? This, however, is more a problem of visualization than of substance. The Gospel and Epistles of John undoubtedly come from the same Johannine circle, and the three disputed Pauline letters are the work either of Paul himself or of disciples with a profound understanding of his mind. What matters for our purpose is that every book, in so far as it has something to contribute, should be allowed a hearing.

A second question concerns the presider's role in the colloquium. However much the convener may desire to remain in the background and leave the panel of speakers free to speak for themselves, he or she cannot in fact hide behind the rules of parliamentary procedure, which dictate that the chair shall not at any time speak. The chair is bound to influence the discussion by the questions it puts on the agenda and by the order in which it calls on the speakers; nor can it evade the final responsibility of taking the 'sense of the meeting' and judging whether the discussion has indicated a common mind.

A third objection arises from the nature of the colloquium, for the members of our conference are dead. We may hold that they being dead yet speak; but can they say anything beyond what they have already said? We call them witnesses; but in addition to their evidence in the first instance, will they reply to cross-examination? Is it reasonable to picture them as entering into discussion? Should we not suspect that so fanciful a picture will disguise what is actually happening? These questions are so important that we must at once supplement the image of the conference table with another. The study of the New Testament, like any other historical exercise, entails a descent into the world of the dead.

In classical literature there are two stories of such a descent, which together provide a useful four-part paradigm of historiography. Odysseus (Homer, *Od.* 9), wanting a forecast of travels which would eventually lead him back to Ithaca, descends to Hades in search of the blind seer Teiresias; and there he slaughters a sheep, because the dead seer, being a shade, a flimsy, a mere carbon copy in the filing cabinet of eternity, cannot speak until animated by sacrificial blood. Aeneas (Virgil, *Aen.* 6) descends to the underworld to receive a foreview of the imperial grandeur of Rome; and he is warned that, whereas the descent is easy, the return journey is harder, since there are not one, but two exits, the ivory gate of false dreams and the horn gate of truth. From all of this we may derive four theses:

1. To descend into the past is to travel in an alien culture, with the traveller having to guard against two opposite temptations: the

temptation to modernize, to regard everything as though it were part of one's own familiar world, ignoring the underlying strangeness; and the more insidious temptation to archaize, to be so impressed by obvious superficial differences as to ignore the underlying similarity.[35] Readers of the New Testament are for the most part shielded from the full brunt of the culture shock by familiarity, by the unbroken tradition which links the Church of today with the Church of the first century, and by the degree to which New Testament teaching has interpenetrated their own culture. But this fact, so far from simplifying the historical task, merely blurs the issue. There is a further complication that the teaching of Jesus and his disciples, while couched in the language and thought forms of their age, was not the product of that age; it was no more part of their *Zeitgeist* than it is of ours.

2. The past is not accessible to us by direct observation, only through the interrogation of witnesses. History has indeed a factual content—stubborn, irreducible fact—but it comes to the historian not as fact but as evidence. We have said above that all historical sources are, in the last analysis, persons with whom to the best of his or her ability the historian must engage in conversation, and this is most obviously the case with the history of thought.[36] But the witnesses, like Teiresias, are dead; they need a sacrificial offering to bring them to life. To write a theology of Paul or John is to enter into dialogue with an ancient writer who does not even begin to speak until he has been animated by the life-blood of the historian's sympathy and imagination; and this can be achieved only by one who is in the same blood-group. Thus to write a New Testament theology is a daunting, perhaps impossible task. Anyone who is to give eleven or more blood transfusions must be a universal donor. Yet a scholar who is at home with Paul may not be equally at home with Hebrews, Revelation, or the Fourth Gospel.[37]

---

[35] 'The essence of the historical mind is the power of putting oneself into a different age and recognising not simply its differences from the present, but its essential affinities with the present' (J. Moffatt, *The Approach to the New Testament* (London, 1921), 173).

[36] 'Certain historians, sometimes whole generations of historians, find in certain periods of history nothing intelligible, and call them dark ages; but such phrases tell us nothing about those ages themselves, though they tell us a great deal about the persons who use them, namely that they are unable to rethink the thoughts which were fundamental to their life' (R. G. Collingwood, *The Idea of History* (Oxford, 1949²), 218–19).

[37] 'Bishop Gore once said to me that he paid visits to St John as to a fascinating foreign country, but he came home to St Paul. With me the precise opposite is true. St Paul is the exciting, and also rather bewildering adventure: with St John I am at home' (W. Temple, *Readings in St John's Gospel* (London, 1939), p. v). For a rather different reaction to John, cf. P. S. Minear, *John: The Martyr's Gospel* (New York, 1984), pp. ix ff.,

As the chair looks round the conference table and tries to fit a face and personality to each of the members, some will inevitably stand out more than others. If Luke is greeted as an old friend, Matthew may appear a comparative stranger.[38] Yet the task must be attempted. Everyone who regards the New Testament as authoritative has some preconceived notion, acknowledged or unacknowledged, about its unity; and it is therefore essential that from time to time the nature of that unity should be critically examined. Barth has defined dogmatics as 'the scientific test to which the Christian Church puts herself regarding the language about God which is peculiar to her'. By the same token New Testament theology is the periodic stock-taking by which a scholar tests the integrity and consistency of his or her exegesis. It is not a task which can be postponed until all the introductory and critical disciplines have completed their work. It is one individual's interim report from the apostolic conference.

3. But how may travellers in the past ensure that they return to the present through the gate of horn and not the gate of ivory? This is a question which has received much abstruse and recondite treatment under the grandiloquent title of hermeneutics. Fortunately, its complexities can be simplified by drawing two necessary, though much neglected, distinctions. First, we must be clear what kind of truth we are aiming at. If we consider any theological statement by Paul, for instance, there are two questions we may ask about it: 'Have I fully understood what he was intending to say? And was he speaking the truth when he said it?' Serious historians, and particularly historians of religion, are constantly aware that their work is raising questions of the second kind, but *qua* historian they are concerned only with questions of the first kind. Those to whom the Bible is a sacred book are particularly prone to disregard this distinction. They expect the Bible to say that which they may immediately accept as true, and the expectation may well prevent them from listening to what the Bible is actually saying. Even in ordinary conversation communication sometimes breaks down because we hear what we expect the other person to say instead of listening to what is being said. Second, to make the teaching of the New Testament intelligible to one's contemporaries is not the same thing as making it applicable to modern conditions and problems,

who speaks of his own 'repulsion' and 'allergies' to John, which 'have not been alleviated by either scholars or preachers'.

[38] It will become apparent that in many respects Matthew is the most puzzling book in the New Testament (see below, pp. 21, 195, 262).

and any attempt to elide the two activities is almost certain to result in falsity. The problem of the biblical historian is not, however, without analogy. Those who took part in the Second Vatican Council agreed afterwards that the most important result of the Council was the effect that it had on the participants; but how was that to be communicated to those who had not shared the experience?[39]

4. Odysseus and Aeneas both made their descent in order to learn about the future. To accept the past as one's own is to commit oneself to a destiny in keeping with it; and this is most emphatically so when the slice of the past one is considering consists of interpretations of a shared experience and of an offer of new life. The only thing to do with a life is to live it; and the ultimate test of a New Testament theology rests not in intellectual criteria but in the contribution it makes to the life of the Christian community.

Most of the problems surrounding our proposal have now been considered, but one last potential barrier needs to be removed. To describe the writing of a New Testament theology as the organization of a conference may seem for some a fantasy which ignores the fact that the authors could never actually have met to discuss anything. Yet this objection evaporates quickly, for our method is a pictorial, but none the less realistic, description of what goes on in a scholar's study. The student of the Fourth Gospel, for example, cannot be content to isolate the theology of John from that of the rest of the New Testament. Having asked a question of John and having received a provisional reply, one will turn to the other Gospels, Paul, Hebrews, and Revelation and put the same question to them. In other words we are setting the biblical writers discussing among themselves. Without some such attempt at comparison, one could hardly expect our work to be of much service to the systematic theologian.

(b) The Model

We shall now turn to the model for our approach. The first apostolic conference was held in Jerusalem less than twenty years after Pentecost, and it is appropriate that it should serve as a guide for the conduct of the conference we envisage. The full details of the meeting are far from clear, but certain facts emerge from Paul's description (Gal. 2: 1–10) with sufficient definiteness. Paul insisted on a private discussion between the five apostles, not because he set any store by ecclesiastical

---

[39] See Caird, *Our Dialogue with Rome, passim.*

office ('not that their importance matters to me: God does not recognize these personal distinctions'), but because these were the only
people he could trust to have the spiritual insight and perspicacity to
recognize the truth of the gospel when it came to them in an unfamiliar
guise. Paul's purpose in bringing about the meeting is clear: 'I laid
before them ... the gospel which I am accustomed to preach to the
Gentiles, to make sure that the race I had run, and was running,
should not be run in vain'. There are at least two points in this sentence
which require comment. When Paul speaks of his 'gospel', he is not
referring to what we have come to call the *kērugma*, the outline statement of the gospel story which Paul elsewhere tells us he received
from those who were Christians before him (1 Cor. 15: 3–10). His
gospel, as he has already assured the Galatians, came to him neither
from a human source nor through human mediation (Gal. 1: 11 f.). It
was given to him in his conversion, when he saw the Lord and was
convinced that he who had died under the curse of the Law had been
vindicated by God, and was now able to offer to those whose penalty
he had shared a share in his own victorious life. He was aware that
his gospel was concluded in terms quite different from those habitually
used by the other apostles, and that his proclamation that God justifies
the ungodly by their faith and not by their works had as a corollary
the equality of Jew and Gentile in the Church, which had not yet been
fully accepted in Jerusalem. When he speaks of striving in vain, we
can hardly suppose that he was ready to admit the possibility that his
whole conception of the gospel needed radically to be revised. The
apprehensions arose rather from his conviction that the Church into
which he had admitted Gentile converts had its roots in God's covenants with Abraham, was the Messianic people of God, and the heir to
His promises in the Old Testament, so that, if the mother Church in
Jerusalem failed to see the implications of the gospel as he saw them,
and refused to accept his converts as true sons of Abraham, his
missionary achievement would have received a serious setback.

The point at issue in this first conference, then, was the unity of
the Church, and it depended on the unity of the apostolic preaching.
It is of vital importance, both for our discussion of the unity of the
New Testament and for our discussions of church unity, that we
recognize the exact nature of the agreement reached by the apostles.
They did not draw up any creed or agreed statement of faith, nor did
they even attempt to reach unanimity. The Jerusalem apostles, Paul
tells us, 'added nothing to me', not because there was nothing to add,

but because there was no need to add it. They had heard enough to satisfy them. Whatever measure of agreement they achieved there was some outstanding difference of opinion, about which they agreed to differ. Peter and Paul were to go their own separate ways. But they could do this without any sense of radical division, because they had recognized that the same God was at work both in Peter's mission to the Jews and in Paul's mission to the Gentiles. On the basis of that recognition they were content to accept one another as colleagues and to shake hands on it.

Thus the New Testament itself provides a criterion for judging its own unity. The question we must ask is not whether these books all say the same thing, but whether they all bear witness to the same Jesus and through him to the many splendoured wisdom of the one God. If we are persuaded that the second Moses, the son of Man, the friend of sinners, the incarnate *logos*, the firstborn of all creation, the Apostle and High Priest of our calling, the Chief Shepherd, and the Lamb opening the scroll are the same person in whom the one God has achieved and is achieving his mighty work, we shall neither attempt to press all our witnesses into a single mould nor captiously complain that one seems at some points deficient in comparison with another. What we shall do is rejoice that God has seen fit to establish His gospel at the mouth of so many independent witnesses. The music of the New Testament choir is not written to be sung in unison.

It is part of the wisdom of God—utterly in keeping with the grace which uses the weak things to confound the things that are strong— that Christ is known to us only through the testimony of his witnesses; and because these witnesses were fallible human beings, conscious of their own limitations, we need to see Christ through many eyes if we are to see him at all. But do we not also need to see him through the eyes of the Old Testament writers ('their testimony points to me'— John 5: 40)? Ought not Mark, Paul, and John to sit down at the conference table with Moses and all the prophets? Ought we not to be writing a *biblical* Theology? The simple and final answer is that this is an academic impossibility: the modern Apollos cannot be equally learned in the scriptures of the Old and the New Testaments. But even if the task were within the compass of one person, there is a good reason why it ought not to be attempted. Before the advent of critical scholarship the Old Testament was read almost solely for its witness to Christ. Something no doubt was lost, but infinitely more was gained by the discovery that the prophet's main function was to speak the word of God to his own generation. For the first time in Christian history the prophets were allowed to speak for themselves, without having the 'pillars' of the New Testament adding anything to them. In all our efforts to interpret the Old Testament as Christian scripture this emancipation of the Old Testament must not be surrendered. It cannot be too often or too emphatically said that, if we read into the text of scripture something that the writer himself did not intend, we have no right to claim that we are putting ourselves under the authority of the word of God. When the author of Hebrews announced that the God who spoke to the fathers through the prophets was the same God who had spoken to a later generation in a Son, he was very far from claiming that what God said through the prophets was identical with what he said through the Son. 'From an historical point of view it is impossible to regard the statements of the Old and New Testament as being on one level without any distinction and by combining them together to produce a single theology of the Bible.'[40] In the heavenly Kingdom, we may be sure, Mark, Paul, and John will be found sitting at table with Abraham, Isaac, and Jacob. But in the earthly empire ruled by the Queen of the Sciences, Old and New Testament theology are separate and autonomous dominions.

And what of Jesus himself? Is he not our primary witness? According to Rudolf Bultmann, 'The message of Jesus is a presupposition rather than part of that theology itself.'[41] If by the theology of the New Testament we mean the ideas held by the various authors, this statement is obviously true, since Jesus lived, taught, and died before any of them set pen to paper. But if by the theology of the New Testament we mean the modern academic research into the ideas of the New Testament writers, then this statement puts the cart before the horse. The message of Jesus is not one of the data of New Testament study: we have only the message of Jesus according to Mark, or Luke, or Matthew, or John. Nobody has done more than Bultmann to force on our attention the critical questions which the gospel records raise: how much of the record comes from Jesus, how much from the early Church, how much from the evangelist? In the long run the answer we give to such questions will depend on the picture of Jesus that

[40] *Ebeling, 'Meaning of "Biblical Theology" ' ,* 220.
[41] R. Bultmann, *The Theology of the New Testament* (New York, 1951–55), 3.

emerges from our study of the New Testament as a whole. Research must begin with the documents and their theology and arrive only at the end of its course at the teaching of Jesus.

2.

The Divine Plan

2.1. THE WHOLE COUNSEL OF GOD

The focal point of the New Testament is an event which occurred on an April Friday sometime around AD 30. But no event is significant until it has been placed within a framework of interpretation, and on this there will undoubtedly be differences of opinion. Pilate, and other Romans after him, regarded the death of Jesus as a regrettable but necessary incident in the maintenance of law and order in a notoriously unruly province. Among Jewish leaders, the realists treated it as a condition of national survival (John 11: 50) or of the maintenance of law and order (John 19: 7), while the idealists, like the Pharisaic Paul, assumed, on strict religious principle, that divine retribution had fallen on one who had arrogated to himself the authority to break the Law and to teach others to break it, so that he had died under the curse which the Law pronounced on the convicted criminal (Gal. 3: 13; cf. Deut. 21: 23). The Christians were convinced that this death, together with the life which preceded it and the resurrection which followed, were 'the great things God has done' (Acts 1: 11), and argued in support of their case that the whole sequence of events was 'in accordance with the scriptures' (1 Cor. 15: 3). With a few exceptions,[1] this notion of fulfilment in one form or another pervades the New Testament, and it has long been agreed that it formed a part of the first apostolic preaching.[2] But what did these early Christians understand by it?

We allow Luke to open the discussion,[3] for he has provided us with

---

[1] It is present only by allusion in 1 Thess. and Jas., and not at all in 2 Thess., the Pastorals, and the Johannine Epistles.

[2] See C. H. Dodd, *The Apostolic Preaching and its Development* (London, 1951[2]).

[3] For the best recent works on Luke's theology see R. J. Cassidy, *Jesus, Politics and Society: A Study of Luke's Gospel* (New York, 1978); J. Jervell, *Luke and the People of God* (Minneapolis, 1972); R. Maddox, *The Purpose of Luke–Acts* (Edinburgh, 1982); D. P. Moessner, *Lord of the Banquet: The Literary and Theological Significance of the Lukan Travel Narrative* (Philadelphia, 1989); E. Schweizer, *Luke: A Challenge to Present Theology*

the fullest, most explicit and most consistent answer to this question. The two opening chapters of the Gospel are built up out of Old Testament allusions, and present to us a group of pious Jews, meticulous in their observance of the Torah (1: 6; 2: 22–4, 27, 39) and of the Temple worship, but waiting expectantly for 'the consolation of Israel' (2: 25; cf. Isa. 40: 1) and 'the redemption of Jerusalem' (2: 38). Zechariah is told that his son will be a new Elijah, to prepare Israel for the coming of God (1: 17; cf. 7: 27 and Matt. 4: 5–6; Ecclus. 48: 10) and at his birth proclaims that God has indeed come to bring the promised redemption, in fulfilment of prophecy and of his oath to Abraham (1: 68–79). Mary is told that her son is to sit on the throne of David and rule Israel (1: 32–3), and she responds as though she were herself the daughter of Zion (1: 46–55). Simeon declares his hopes fulfilled, not only for Israel but for the Gentiles (1: 30–2). The ministry of Jesus is introduced by the Baptist's announcement of the coming of God in universal salvation (3: 4–5; cf. Isa. 40: 4–5); by a genealogy which, in having the descent of Jesus through David and Abraham to Adam, indicates that he is to fulfil not only the purposes of God for Israel and its royal line, but the destiny of the human race; and by a programmatic claim that Jesus has inaugurated the great Jubilee, 'the year of the Lord's favour' (4: 18–19; cf. Isa. 61: 1–2). At the transfiguration Jesus talks with Moses and Elijah about the *exodus* (9: 31) he is about to accomplish in Jerusalem, and this choice of an unusual word for death, together with the sense of fulfilment implicit in the verb, depicts the crucifixion as the new Exodus, the promised act of divine redemption; and the voice from heaven designates Jesus 'my Son, my Chosen', with authority to speak in God's name (9: 31, 35; cf. Deut. 18: 15). Luke's four predictions of the fall of Jerusalem (13: 34–5; 19: 41–4; 21: 20–4; 23: 27–31) are all couched in language reminiscent of God's earlier judgements on His rebellious people; but they are not intended to cancel the hope of a national redemption to which Luke returns in his last chapter (24: 21; cf. 21: 28)—with a twice-repeated assurance that the crucified and risen Jesus is indeed

(London, 1982); C. H. Talbert, *Reading Luke: A Literary and Theological Commentary on the Third Gospel* (New York, 1984); and S. G. Wilson, *The Gentiles and the Gentile Mission in Luke–Acts* (New York, 1973). To these should be added the following commentaries: G. B. Caird, *St Luke* (Harmondsworth, 1963); E. E. Ellis, *The Gospel of Luke* (London, 1966); J. Fitzmyer, *The Gospel According to Luke*, 3 vols. (New York, 1981–6); I. H. Marshall, *The Gospel of Luke* (Exeter, 1978); and E. Schweizer, *The Good News According to St Luke* (London, 1984).

the divine agent to whom all the scriptures have pointed (24: 27, 49). All these claims are held together by Luke's frequent use of *dei* ('it is necessary') in connection with every aspect of the life of Jesus (2: 49; 4: 43; 9: 22; 13: 16, 33; 17: 25; 19: 5; 21: 9; 22: 37; 24: 7, 26, 44), and by his clear indication that the necessity was a scriptural necessity because Jesus found, and taught his disciples to find, in 'all the scriptures' the blueprint of his own ministry.

These themes are more openly exploited in Acts, where Luke is less constrained by the use of traditional material. Peter's speech at Pentecost (2: 14–36) makes the claim that the gift of the Spirit then experienced, and the offer of salvation which accompanied it, were foretold by Joel (2: 28–32), that David spoke with foreknowledge of the resurrection of Jesus (Ps. 16: 8–11) and of his enthronement as Messiah (Pss. 110: 1; 132: 11) and that the scriptures bore witness to the universality of God's salvation (Isa. 54: 19) and the urgent and universal need for it (Deut. 32: 15). But it also makes the point that Jesus was given over by the deliberate will and plan of God into the power of the Jewish people, who used heathens to kill him, so that the foreknowledge disclosed by prophetic voices in the Old Testament is but a piecemeal reflection of the comprehensive foreknowledge of God (2: 23). In Peter's second speech Jesus is the foreordained Messiah, destined to suffer, but also destined to bring about in Israel all that God had promised from the beginning; he is the prophet charged with authority to interpret the Law of Moses, and so to fulfil God's covenant with Abraham (3: 18–25; cf. 10: 42). The prayer of 4: 24–8 enlarges on this theme: the human actors in the drama of the Cross, rebels though they were against God and His Messiah, served but to carry out a plot which was not only pre-ordained, but was the plan of God the Creator. The speeches of Stephen in Jerusalem and Paul at Antioch make a fresh point, that God's plan of salvation has imposed a premonitory pattern on the whole of Israel's history, the one emphasizing the repeated cycle of unmerited grace and unresponsive obstinacy, the other the unbroken thread of promise leading from Abraham to Christ (7: 2–53; 13: 17–44). At the Jerusalem Conference James quotes Amos 9: 11–12[4] to prove that God's purpose in rebuilding the ruined house of David is to enable the Gentiles to seek the Lord (15:

---

[4] The fact that the quotation follows the LXX, which differs from the MT, raises historical problems but does not affect the significance of the passage for the theology of Luke, which in any New Testament theology is the real concern.

16–17). At Thessalonica Paul expounds the scriptures to prove that 'the Messiah had to suffer and rise from the dead' (17: 3), at Beroea he has the synagogue studying the scriptures daily to see whether they meant what he claimed (17: 11). He sums up his life-work in a farewell address to the elders of Ephesus with the extraordinary words, 'I never shrank from declaring to you the whole purpose of God' (20: 27), and this he could do because he was divinely appointed to know God's will (22: 14; 26: 16; cf. 10: 41). A final quotation from Isa. 6: 9–10 is used to prove that even the disbelief of the Jews had been built into God's purpose as a means of opening the gospel to Gentiles (28: 24–8).

This outline begs to be filled out with a rich variety of further detail. It will suffice, however, to show that Luke held a well-rounded theology, which, since he attributed it both to Peter and to Paul, he must have believed to be the common theology of the early Church. This theology may be summarized as follows:

1. The gospel story and its sequel (Acts) were events in which God was personally present and active.
2. The human characters in the story were actors in a drama with a pre-ordained plot of such power and flexibility that not only their obedience but their disobedience contributed to its ful- filment.
3. This plot was God's plan of salvation for Israel and through Israel for the world.
4. The plan of salvation was present in outline or in explicit promise in every part of the Old Testament.
5. This way of reading the Old Testament originated with Jesus who had understood God's plan from the beginning and had conducted his ministry in conformity with it.
6. In the light of the events in which God's plan had been put into operation the risen Jesus explained to the disciples the scriptural necessity which they had previously failed to understand.
7. Jesus' interpretation of the Old Testament had much in it that was offensive to his opponents and much that was puzzling to his friends, but it rested on theological convictions already held by pious Jews before his coming.

In the rest of this chapter we shall use the seven points of this Lucan scheme to put questions to the other New Testament authors about the framework and assumptions of their theology.

2.2. THE COMING OF GOD

There are those who would argue that the central theme of New Testament theology is Christology. Whether or not one should accept this claim depends largely on the definition of the term 'Christology'. If we mean by it that the centre of theology is Christ conceived as the ultimate revelation of God, what Christian could disagree? But if we mean debates about the divine and the human in the person of Christ, it is patently false. The New Testament is from beginning to end a book about God. And while Luke makes the coming of God the centre of his own theology, the other writers have much to say on this theme, albeit not quite as obviously.

In comparison with Luke's lavish and explicit treatment, for instance, Mark renders it, like the other themes he treats,[5] allusively and with extreme economy, so much so indeed that we might wonder whether the allusions were intended, were they not so numerous as to be mutually supportive. Thus Mark never says, in so many words, that the ministry of Jesus is the promised coming of God; but he everywhere *implies* it. His work (1: 2–3) opens with a hybrid quotation which identifies John the Baptist with the messenger of the covenant, the new Elijah (Mal. 3: 1; cf. 4: 5–6) and with the bringer of good news to Jerusalem (Isa. 40: 3), both of whom were to prepare for the coming of God. It has been held that Mark took the scriptural words from an anthology of proof texts, and had no interest in their original contexts.[6] In fact, however, his description of John shows that he believed him to be fulfilling the role of Elijah (1: 6; cf. 9: 11–13), and

---

[5] For recent studies of Mark's theology see, for instance, E. Best, *Following Jesus: Discipleship in the Gospel of Mark* (Sheffield, 1981); M. Hengel, *Studies in the Gospel of Mark* (London, 1985); M. D. Hooker, *The Message of Mark* (London, 1983); H. C. Kee, *Community of the New Age: Studies in Mark's Gospel* (London, 1977); J. D. Kingsbury, *The Christology of Mark's Gospel* (Philadelphia, 1983); M. Hengel, 'Literary, Theological and Historical Problems in the Gospel of Mark', in P. Stuhlmacher (ed.), *The Gospel and the Gospels* (Grand Rapids, 1991), 209 ff.; R. P. Martin, *Mark: Evangelist and Theologian* (Exeter, 1979); W. R. Telford (ed.), *The Interpretation of Mark* (London, 1985); and C. M. Tuckett (ed.), *The Messianic Secret* (Philadelphia, 1983). The commentaries of P. J. Achtemeier, *Mark* (Philadelphia, 1975); C. E. B. Cranfield, *The Gospel According to St Mark* (Cambridge, 1959), W. L. Lane, *The Gospel According to Mark* (Grand Rapids, 1974); and E. Schweizer, *The Good News According to Mark* (London 1971), are also to be consulted.

[6] In support of this view it may be argued that Mark 1: 2 has changed the pronoun of Mal. 3: 1 from the first person ('my face', *prosōpou mou*) to the second person ('your face', *prosōpou sou*).

he attributes the composite quotation wholly to Isaiah. Moreover, Isaiah 40–55 is the most likely Old Testament source of the word 'gospel'. There the herald is sent to Jerusalem with the good news that your God is here (40: 9), and that 'your God is King' (52: 7). In the Targum both of these are rendered, 'The Kingdom of your God is revealed'.[7] This was part of the evidence used by G. Dalman[8] to argue that in Jewish usage 'Kingdom' always meant 'sovereignty', never 'realm', and he pointed out that the Aramaic paraphrase was an instance of the reverential targumic practice of avoiding direct reference to the presence or activity of God. The Jesus of the Gospels regularly uses a wide variety of such reverential evasions,[9] so that we may be sure that the evangelists who recorded them were familiar with this style of diction. Thus Mark's summary of the preaching of Jesus, 'the time is fulfilled, the Kingdom of God has drawn near; repent and believe the good news' (1:15) is to be understood as an announcement of the arrival of God as King.

But did Mark believe this arrival to be present or future? Did he take the words of Jesus to mean that God was already present in the ministry of Jesus, asserting his sovereignty over a rebellious world? Or did he believe that God would shortly consummate His sovereignty in a final act of triumph? That Mark believed in a final triumph is not in doubt. The question is whether this is what Mark has in mind at 1: 15. The evidence may be summarized as follows:

1. Matthew and Luke record an unambiguous saying of Jesus that in the exorcisms of Jesus God is present exerting his sovereign power over the enemies of the human race (Matt. 12: 28; Luke 11: 20).[10]

2. The clause *ēngiken hē basileia tou theou*, taken by itself, is ambiguous: it can mean either 'the Kingdom of God has arrived' or 'the Kingdom of God is imminent'. But the ambiguity arises because the concept of nearness, spatial or temporal, involves in any language a varying degree of distance, which cannot be indefinitely extended, but which may diminish to vanishing point. In the ritual of the Temple, 'to bring near' is a technical term for laying an offering on the altar,

---

[7] Cf. B. D. Chilton, *God in Strength* (Friestadt, 1987).

[8] G. Dalman, *The Words of Jesus* (Edinburgh, 1902), 91–101.

[9] Ibid. 204 ff.

[10] In *The Parables of the Kingdom* (London, 1941), C. H. Dodd has shown that there is ample supporting evidence for the presence of the Kingdom in the ministry of Jesus (see further below, pp. 132ff., 366ff.)

not dumping it on the Mount of Olives. When Judas 'drew near' to kiss Jesus (Luke 22: 47) and the centurion 'drew near' to arrest Paul (Acts 21: 33), they could hardly have got closer. And when thieves 'draw near', the householder is worried not because they happen to be in the neighbourhood, but because they are digging through the wall. Similarly, in temporal usage, *ēngiken* may mean 'is coming shortly' (James 5: 8; 1 Pet. 4: 7); but it is also used as a synonym for *paresti* and means 'has arrived' (Lam. 4: 18 LXX). The REB correctly translates Matt. 26: 45 f. as 'the hour has come . . . the traitor is upon us', and Luke 21: 8 as 'many will come in my name, saying, "I am he" and "the Day is upon us" '; in each case the arrival of the person and the arrival of the crisis coincide. Luke carefully distinguishes the present and perfect tenses of the verb; his readers are to be sure that the destruction of Jerusalem has come but that, at a later date, their liberation is coming (Luke 21: 20, 28).

3. For the interpretation of Mark 1: 15 the opening clause is decisive, in spite of a minor ambiguity in the Greek word (*kairos*) for 'time'.[11] It may mean either 'the critical moment has arrived', or 'the preparatory period has run its course'.[12] It cannot mean that the critical moment is still some way off or that the preparatory period has a further indefinite time yet to run. We may therefore confidently translate: 'The time is over; the sovereign rule of God has come; repent and believe the good news.'

This conclusion is borne out by four other elements in Mark's narrative.

1. Mark records a saying of Jesus about slander against the Holy Spirit. What this may or may not have meant on the lips of Jesus is uncertain, but Mark adds a comment of his own which leaves his interpretation of it in no doubt (3: 28–9). Jesus said this because his critics had declared that he performed miraculous cures by the power of Satan. In this context 'Holy Spirit', as in the Old Testament, signifies God's presence powerfully at work in the world. The critics of Jesus, confronted by the presence in a miraculous cure, have attributed the result to Satan; and by such deliberate moral perversion they are in danger of disqualifying themselves from the divine mercy.

[11] Strictly speaking, *kairos* is the time *at which* something happens, while *chronos* is the time *during which* something happens. But the distinction is not consistently observed in biblical Greek, and the second of the two renderings given above is to be preferred.

[12] Cf. 2 Esd. 11: 44: 'The Most High has surveyed the periods he has fixed: they are now at an end, and his ages have reached their completion.'

2. Faced with a demand for a sign, the Marcan Jesus refuses with a sigh of exasperation and regret: 'No sign shall be given to this generation.' And here again, when we go back to the Old Testament antecedents of the pericope, the reason is clear. God's people, those who claim to know and love Him, ought to be able to recognize His presence when they see it, without external proof. And this is the nature of a sign; it is a demand for credentials. Thus in Mark's story (and its synoptic parallels) those who ask for proof of God's activity are merely showing that they are a wicked and adulterous generation, disqualified by their disloyalty from recognizing the presence of God when they see it. Those loyal to God will *know* if a prophet who comes in His name is indeed His true agent. Thus the repudiation of the sign in Mark is based on the assumption that in Jesus God is at work, and those who claim to be the servants of God ought to recognize that.

3. Mark's Gospel is punctuated, as R. H. Lightfoot[13] has pointed out, by notes of fear, but not the fear which people feel in the face of danger; rather it is the awe one experiences in the presence of the supernatural (cf. 4: 41; 10: 32; 16: 8).[14]

4. The dying protest of Jesus that God has deserted him implies that hitherto he had been continuously aware of God's presence (15: 34); and Mark knew, and would have his readers know, that at the point where God most *seemed* to be absent, excluded from His world by human rejection, He was most fully and effectively present.

It could be said, therefore, with its constant emphasis on the awe of those who encounter Jesus, that Mark's Gospel is the most numinous of the four. Matthew's Gospel, on the other hand, is the least numinous. Though he is editing Mark, Matthew lacks Mark's atmosphere, and though he shares much material with Luke, he does not have Luke's explicit theology of the divine presence. There are three reasons for this, one editorial, two theological:

1. As an editor Matthew has set out to produce a handbook of instruction for the Church of his own day,[15] and his whole manner therefore is didactic rather than impressive. In so far as Matthew speaks of fulfilment—one of his most recurring themes—he does so not in the service of a theology like Luke's which speaks of the fulfil-

---

[13] R. H. Lightfoot, *The Gospel Message of St Mark* (Oxford, 1950), 86–92.

[14] Cf. the modern exposition of Rudolf Otto, *The Idea of the Holy* (London, 1923).

[15] On this interpretation of Matthew's Gospel, see below, p. 34.

ment of the whole of the Old Testament or of 'the determinative counsel and foreknowledge of God' (Acts 20: 27), but rather his fulfilments are concerned with *details*: every jot and tittle of the ministry of Jesus has some predictive text for which he can go to the Old Testament.

2. While the general features of Matthew's theology remain a subject of continuing debate,[16] one thing which remains clear is his constant emphasis on fulfilment: Matthew concentrates on showing that details of the career of Jesus were foretold in the scriptures. He is interested less in the divine initiative than in the human response to it (and thus remains a reservoir for teachers of Christian ethics).

3. Christologically Matthew is interested less in Jesus as the channel of divine grace and presence than in his wielding of a plenary, delegated authority.[17] For Matthew, God is not personally present because everything has been handed over to Jesus. As we shall see below in Chapter 8, delegated authority is an essential element in

---

[16] Matthew remains the most difficult New Testament theologian to categorize. Among the best recent studies see G. Bornkamm, G. Barth, and H. J. Held (eds.), *Tradition and Interpretation in Matthew* (London, 1983[2]); R. A. Edwards, *Matthew's Story of Jesus* (Philadelphia, 1985); R. Guelich, *The Sermon on the Mount: A Foundation for Understanding* (Waco, Tex., 1982); J. D. Kingsbury, *Matthew: Structure, Christology and Kingdom* (London, 1976), and *Matthew as Story* (Philadelphia, 1986); J. P. Meier, *The Vision of Matthew: Christ, Church, and Morality in the First Gospel* (Ramsey, NJ, 1979); G. N. Stanton (ed.), *The Interpretation of Matthew* (Philadelphia, 1983), and *A Gospel for a New People* (Edinburgh, Clark, 1992). More specialist works, which none the less illuminate the theology of the evangelist, include B. R. Doyle, 'Matthew's Intention as Discerned by His Structure', *RB* 95 (1988), 386 ff.; F. J. Matera, 'The Plot of Matthew's Gospel', *CBQ* 49 (1987), 233 ff.; M. A. Powell, 'The Plots and Subplots of Matthew's Gospel', *NTS* 38 (1992), 187 ff.; G. N. Stanton, 'Matthew as a Creative Interpreter of the Sayings of Jesus', in Stuhlmacher (ed.), *The Gospel and the Gospels*, 257 ff.; and G. Strecker, 'The Concept of History in Matthew', in Stanton (ed.), *The Interpretation of Matthew*, 67 ff. One should also consult the older, but still relevant treatments of D. R. A. Hare, *The Theme of Jewish Persecution of Christians in Matthew* (Cambridge, 1967): R. H. Gundry, *The Use of the Old Testament in St Matthew's Gospel* (Leiden, 1967); K. Stendahl, *The School of St Matthew* (Philadelphia, 1968); and M. J. Suggs, *Wisdom, Christology and Law in Matthew's Gospel* (Cambridge, Mass., 1970). To these titles should be added the major commentaries, including W. D. Davies and D. C. Allison, *A Critical and Exegetical Commentary on the Gospel of Matthew* (Edinburgh, 1988); R. H. Gundry, *Matthew: A Commentary on His Literary and Theological Art* (Grand Rapids, 1982); and D. Hill, *The Gospel of Matthew* (London, 1972).

[17] This point is well illustrated by his editing of Mark's story of the paralytic. Mark 2: 12 says that the onlookers were amazed and praised God (for performing the cure through His agent), while in Matthew they were filled with awe and praised God for giving such authority to human beings (9: 8).

New Testament Christology; but elsewhere it is balanced by an equal emphasis on the presence of God in the person and activity of His delegate, so that we are never quite allowed to think that delegation entails remote control. At the beginning of his Gospel Matthew appears to be making this very point by drawing attention to the meaning of the name Immanuel—'God with us' (1: 23). But on the two occasions when he returns to this theme, it is to assert the continuing presence of Christ with his disciples (18: 20; 28: 20), not God; thus even this function has been delegated to Christ.

By contrast John makes the maintenance of this balance one of the main themes of his work.[18] On the one hand he has much to say about delegated authority. Jesus is the Son whom God has sent into the world (3: 17), vested with authority to speak His words (3: 35; cf. 7: 16; 8: 58; 12: 49–50), to complete His work (4: 24; 17: 4), to exercise jurisdiction (5: 22, 27), to grant eternal life (17: 2). Yet at the same time John constantly emphasizes that it is the function of Jesus to enable believers to see the unseen God (1: 18; 14: 9;[19] cf. 8: 19), he can do nothing by himself, but only what he sees the Father doing (5: 14).[20] And when he acts on God's authority it is not because God is remote and has left the discharge of His will to a delegate, but rather because 'He who has sent me is with me and has not left me alone' (8: 28). Believers are those whom the Father gives to Jesus or draws to him (6: 37, 44; 17: 6, 9). In bestowing on Jesus the glory of the

---

[18] On John's theology see J. Ashton (ed.), *The Interpretation of John* (London, 1986), and *Understanding the Fourth Gospel* (Oxford, 1991); W. H. Cadman, *The Open Heaven*, ed. G. B. Caird (Oxford, 1969); R. A. Culpepper, *Anatomy of the Fourth Gospel* (Philadelphia, 1983); C. H. Dodd, *Historical Tradition in the Fourth Gospel* (Cambridge, 1963), and *The Interpretation of the Fourth Gospel* (Cambridge, 1953); A. E. Harvey, *Jesus on Trial: A Study in the Fourth Gospel* (London, 1976); M. Hengel, *The Johannine Question* (London, 1989); R. Kysar, *John's Story of Jesus* (Philadelphia, 1984); B. Lindars, *Behind the Fourth Gospel* (London, 1971); S. Smalley, *John: Evangelist and Interpreter* (Exeter, 1978); and D. Moody Smith, *Johannine Christianity: Essays on its Setting, Sources and Theology* (Columbia, SC, 1984). See also the commentaries of R. E. Brown, *The Gospel According to John*, 2 vols. (New York, 1966); R. Bultmann, *The Gospel of John: A Commentary* (Philadelphia, 1971); B. Lindars, *The Gospel of John* (London, 1972); D. Moody Smith, *John* (Philadelphia, 1986); and R. Schnackenburg, *The Gospel According to St John*, 3 vols. (London, 1968–76). The works of J. L. Martyn (see bibliography) are also to be consulted.

[19] Dodd calls this 'the parable of the apprenticed Son' (cf. 'A Hidden Parable in the Fourth Gospel', *More New Testament Studies* (Manchester 1968), 30 ff.).

[20] The present tenses indicate that the reference is to the daily life of the earthly Jesus, not to any memories of a pre-existent state.

eternal *logos*, the Father is manifesting His own glory (11: 4; 12: 31). The deeds of Jesus show that 'the Father is in me and I in the Father' (10: 38), because 'it is the Father who dwells in me doing His own work' (14: 10). This same point constitutes the main argument of 1 John against a schismatic group who have denied the real humanity of Jesus (2: 22; 4: 2). And yet, as Raymond Brown[21] has noted, the author of 1 John agrees at many points with his opponents including their view that 'God is love' (4: 4), but denies their claim that they in some esoteric way share in God's life (1: 6), know Him (2: 4), and love Him (4: 20). Unless we recognize that the love of God has been spelt out in human terms in the life and death of Jesus, we cannot fill the word 'love' with any intelligent ethical content. 'Herein is love, not that we loved God, but that He loved us and sent His Son as the remedy for the defilement of our sins' (4: 10). Moreover, love cannot be known *ab extra*, i.e. studied objectively; it can only be known in the act of loving. Only those who, like Jesus, have allowed their lives to be channels for the divine love can be said to know either love or God. 'Everyone who loves is a child of God and knows God; the unloving know nothing of God' (4: 7–8). Faith is the ability to see, experience, and transmit the divine love; and this is the victory that defeats the world (5: 4). Thus we have a powerful claim not only that in Jesus we see one who was a channel for the redemptive love of God, but that that same call is integral to the Christian vocation, and without it no one can claim to have a knowledge of God.

On his own evidence, as well as that of Acts, Paul became a Christian when he was confronted by the risen Christ (1 Cor. 9: 1; 15: 8) and apprehended by him (Phil. 3: 12), so that from then on Christ became the centre of his life (Gal. 2: 20; Phil. 1: 21).[22] Yet he habitually described his conversion as an act of God. 'By God's grace I am what I am' (1 Cor. 15: 10). It was God who 'chose to reveal His Son in me' (Gal. 1: 15), who shone in his heart and enabled him to see 'the glory of God in the face of Jesus Christ' (2 Cor. 4: 6), who called him to be an apostle (1 Cor. 1: 1; Gal. 1: 1). He is Christ's captive, but continually walks in the triumphal procession of God (2 Cor. 2: 14). He is Christ's ambassador, but only because it is 'God who appeals to you through us' (2 Cor. 5: 20). Even his physical disability, his

---

[21] Cf. R. E. Brown, *The Community of the Beloved Discipline* (Ramsey, NJ, 1979), 131 ff.

[22] It is undoubtedly this feature of Pauline experience which has persuaded many theologians to treat Christology as if it were the centre of Christian theology.

'thorn in the flesh' sent by Satan to batter him into submission, was at the same time a gift of God to humble him and keep him dependent on God's grace (2 Cor. 12: 7). What Paul experienced in his own life he held to be true also of Jesus. It was God who in the fulness of time had sent forth His Son (Gal. 4: 4), who in Christ had been reconciling the world to Himself (2 Cor. 5: 19) and achieving what the Law had been too weak to achieve (Rom. 8: 3). In Christ God in all his fulness had chosen to dwell (Col. 1: 19; 2: 9). It was God who delivered him up to death (Rom. 3: 25; 4: 25; 5: 8) and raised him to life and victory (Rom. 6: 4; 1 Cor. 15: 15; 2 Cor. 4: 14; Gal. 1: 1; Phil. 2: 9). Paul is therefore confident that the faith of his converts also rests on the firm foundation of their experience of God (Gal. 3: 1–4). God has called them into the fellowship of His Son (1 Thess. 1: 4), rescued them from the domain of darkness, and brought them safely into the Kingdom of His Son (Col. 1: 13). And if in the common life of the Church they are called on to work out their own salvation, this is possible because in trembling awe they recognize the presence of God in their midst: 'It is God who works in you, inspiring both the will and the deed, for His own chosen purpose' (Phil. 2: 12–13; cf. Rom. 8: 26–8). Out of his own experience Paul was able to supply one notable instance of this principle at work; for in a crisis where divergent views might have split the Church, unity was secured when the Jerusalem apostles assented to Paul's claim that he held a commission parallel to that of Peter, because they recognized that the same God was active in the missionary work of both (Gal. 2: 7–8).

The author of Hebrews develops a number of distinctive themes,[23] and one of the most powerful is his contribution to our discussion at this point. Among human beings Christ has held by divine appointment a unique role in the plan of God (1: 2; 5: 5–6), which he has discharged with loyalty to the God who appointed him (3: 2). But he is also the Son through whom God has directly addressed His people (1: 1), speaking that piercing word which penetrates to the inner recesses of

---

[23] On the theology of Hebrews see, for instance, H. W. Attridge, *The Epistle to the Hebrews* (Philadelphia, 1989); P. Ellingworth, *The Epistle to the Hebrews: A Commentary on the Greek Text* (Grand Rapids, 1993); D. A. Hagner, *Hebrews* (San Francisco, 1983); L. D. Hurst, *The Epistle to the Hebrews: Its Background of Thought* (Cambridge, 1990); M. Isaacs, *Sacred Space: An Approach to the Theology of the Epistle to the Hebrews* (Cambridge, 1992); R. Jewett, *A Letter to Pilgrims: A Commentary on the Epistle to the Hebrews* (New York, 1981); W. L. Lane, *Hebrews*, 2 vols. (Waco, Tex., 1991); and B. Lindars, *The Theology of the Letter to the Hebrews* (Cambridge, 1991).

their being, leaving them naked and exposed to the God with Whom they have to reckon (4: 12–13). The severity of the Epistle has its source in the author's certainty of the richness and finality of that revelation. To be a Christian is to have an experience of God so powerful, so self-authenticating, that it is impossible to conceive what more God could say to those who have enjoyed it and then repudiated it (2: 1–4; 6: 4–6; 10: 26–31; 12: 25–6). But Jesus is not only the mediator of God's word to others; he is himself addressed by God. The Old Testament texts which the author applies to him are cited not as proof-texts or prophecies, but as statements made by God to His Son (1: 5–14).[24] They are, in other words, not only the terms by which the Christian is to understand Christ, but the terms in which Christ understood his own vocation. But the Old Testament is also a record of past experience of God. The cavalcade of the faithful in chapter 11 exemplifies the general principle that 'faith gives substance to our hopes and reality to what we do not see'. Their faith was in God's future, a confidence that He would keep His promise; they acknowledged themselves to be aliens in transit, travelling to a future city which God had in store for them; and they died without seeing the promise fulfilled. Yet their faith made real to them that which in the temporal order remained for them an object of hope, so that Moses could be 'resolute, as one who saw the invisible God' (11: 27).

The author of 1 Peter[25] shares with other New Testament writers the conviction that the Christian life is God's work from start to finish (1: 3–5), but he shows a particular interest in the relation of this to worship. The essence of worship is celebration, 'to proclaim the triumphs of him who brought you out of darkness into his marvellous light' (2: 9). Like Christian faith, Christian worship exists against a background of darkness which constantly threatens to engulf it. But worshippers are not just whistling in the dark to keep up their spirits. Out of the experience which they share with others it is acknowledged

---

[24] Cf. S. Kistemaker, *The Psalm Citations in the Epistle to the Hebrews* (Amsterdam, 1961), who demonstrates that the author of Hebrews is aware of the numerous verbal links between his psalm citations and their larger Old Testament contexts.

[25] On 1 Peter, cf. the recent treatments of D. L. Balch, *Let Wives Be Submissive: The Domestic Code in 1 Peter* (Chico, Calif., 1981); E. Best, *1 Peter* (London, 1971); J. H. Elliott, *A Home For the Homeless* (Philadelphia, 1981); J. N. D. Kelly, *A Commentary on the Epistles of Peter and Jude* (Grand Rapids, 1969); B. Reicke, *The Epistles of James, Peter and Jude* (New York, 1964); E. G. Selwyn, *The First Epistle of Peter* (London, 1946), and C. H. Talbert (ed.), *Perspectives on 1 Peter* (Macon, Ga., 1986).

with joy and wonder that in the dark God's light has shone, and is defying the darkness to extinguish it (John 1: 5; 12: 35–6; 2 Cor. 1: 20; Eph. 5: 13–14).

The Revelation[26] is written out of a profound religious experience which John, the author, seeks by powerful, evocative symbols to share with his readers. He sees his own banishment and the imminent martyrdom of his friends as part of the age-long battle between God and Satan. On the one side is the Church, pitifully weak and not very loyal, and on the other the grandeur and power of imperial Rome. John's confidence in the ultimate victory of God rests wholly on his conviction that in the death of Christ God has the decisive, archetypal victory, which will be repeated in the death of every martyr (3: 21), until Babylon the Great totters to her doom, drunk with the blood of God's people (17: 6; 18: 2–3). Behind every pang of human anguish, doubt, and despair, behind every catastrophe that shatters the godless world order, God's presence is felt. Yet even in John's vision God never appears in open view. His sovereignty, justice, and mercy are symbolized by throne, thunder, and rainbow. But otherwise (and thus John joins hands with 1 Peter), we see God's glory only as it is reflected in the worship of the heavenly choir.

2.3. THE PLAN OF SALVATION

The best commentary on Luke's claim that Paul disclosed to his converts 'the whole counsel of God' (Acts 20: 27) is found in the first three chapters of Ephesians, which are entirely devoted to this theme. 'God has made known to us His hidden design—such was His will and pleasure determined beforehand in Christ—to be put into effect[27] when the time was ripe: namely, that the universe [*ta panta*], i.e. all in heaven and on earth, might be brought into a unity in Christ' (1: 9–

---

[26] For full recent treatments of the theology of Revelation see for instance G. B. Caird, *A Commentary on the Revelation of St John the Divine* (London, 1985²); A. Y. Collins, *Crisis and Catharsis: the Power of the Apocalypse* (Phildadelphia, 1984); E. Schüssler Fiorenza, *The Book of Revelation: Justice and Judgment* (Philadelphia, 1985); J. P. M. Sweet, *Revelation* (Philadelphia, 1979); and R. W. Wall, *Revelation* (Peabody, Mass., 1991).

[27] So the REB translates *eis oikonomian*, following J. Armitage Robinson, who long ago observed that *oikonomia* does not necessarily mean 'dispensation' or 'stewardship' (*The Epistle to the Ephesians* (London, 1922³), ad loc. In classical Greek it also means the putting of something into effect, and this is the sense it has in all three instances of its usage in Ephesians (cf. also 3: 2, 9).

10). This purpose had already been at work in the world unrecognized, particularly in the history of Israel (1: 11–12); but it had from the beginning been God's intention that Gentiles should be included in its scope, and it is the breaking down of the barrier between Jew and Gentile in the family life of the Church that provides the solid ground for confidence that God can in the end reconcile all the warring and divisive forces that comprise the human world (2: 13–22). It is the function of the Church, by the unity of its life, to demonstrate to those forces 'the many splendoured wisdom of God' (3: 10).

In the exposition of this thesis no fewer than five synonyms are used: hidden design (*mustērion*), will (*thelēma*), pleasure (*eudokia*), purpose (*prothesis*), and wisdom (*sophia*).[28] The first of these, though originally a technical term of the mystery cults, had long since been taken into general currency to connote any secret deliberation divulged only to a privileged group; it was therefore the natural equivalent of the Hebrew *sōd* and the Aramaic *raz* when they refer to the secret deliberations of God.[29] The prophets had believed themselves to be God's oracles, through whom He communicated to Israel the secret purpose which He was currently implementing in their history (Amos 3: 7; Jer. 23: 18; cf. 1 Kgs. 22: 19–22), and one of the characteristics of a false prophet is that he had not stood in the counsel of God. But the prophets' vision rarely extended beyond the immediate historic crisis of their times. The contribution of the apocalyptists is that they correctly understood the secret with which they were entrusted to be the secret of universal history; and this is the predominant sense of the word *mustērion* in the New Testament.

There are three points in this treatment of God's eternal purpose which require special attention:

1. The purpose, not previously disclosed to the human race (3: 5), has been both revealed and put into operation in Christ; and, as we shall see below, revelation in the New Testament always involves these two elements. But there is no suggestion here, as there is elsewhere in the Pauline corpus, that this central role entails the pre-existence of Christ. This theme is totally absent in Ephesians. All that exists 'before the foundation of the world' is God and His purpose, though

---

[28] *Mustērion*: 1: 9; 3: 3 f., 9; 5: 32; 6: 19; *thelēma*: 1: 1, 5, 9, 11; 5: 17; 6: 6; *eudokia*: 1: 5; 2: 9; *prothesis*: 1: 11; 3: 11; *sophia*: 1: 8, 17; 3: 10.
[29] Cf. G. Bornkamm, '*Mustērion, Mueō*', *TDNT* iv. 802–28, and A. E. Harvey, 'The Use of Mystery Language in the Bible', *JTS* NS 31 (1980), 320 ff.

that purpose includes not merely the destiny of the human race but Christ's unique role in fulfilling it.

2. The purpose has been revealed to 'apostles and prophets' (2: 20; 3: 5). The function of an apostle is to bear witness to the earthly Jesus, and the function of a prophet, as speaking for the heavenly Christ, is to give an inspired interpretation both of the apostolic tradition and of the Old Testament; the fact that the two offices are held together by a single definite article (*tois hagiois apostolois autou kai prophētais*) indicates that their functions are not necessarily to be fulfilled by different individuals.

3. According to Luke, God's purpose operates even through the hostility and resistance of those who do not understand or accept it; and this is seen pre-eminently in the Cross. Of this there is nothing in Ephesians. Here the emphasis is rather that God gives a full understanding of His purpose to those who find salvation in Christ. The understanding, in other words, is not merely the means of its achievement, but is itself an integral part of the purpose. God in His wisdom intends the human race to share that wisdom (1: 15–19; 3: 4, 14–19; cf. Ecclus. 24), an observation which will have later ramifications for Christology.

In the rest of the Pauline corpus, this theme is everywhere assumed (e.g. Phil. 2: 13); and there are five passages in which it is expounded. In 1 Cor. 1–2 there is an extended contrast between the wisdom of the world and the wisdom of God: 'I speak wisdom with those who are ripe for it, not a wisdom belonging to this passing age, or to any of its governing powers, which are declining to their end; I speak God's hidden wisdom, his secret purpose (*mustērion*) framed from the very beginning to bring us to our full glory. The powers that rule the world have never known it; if they had, they would not have crucified the Lord of glory' (2: 6–8). What counts for wisdom in the old order, where knowledge, wealth, and birth are sources of power, is a system with its own interior logic, and those who are imprisoned in it have failed to see the wisdom of God revealed in the death of Christ. To them the Cross is folly and defeat, and in blind pursuit of their own worldly ends the ruling powers,[30] whether Jewish or Gentile, have combined to bring about the crucifixion, failing to see that in so doing they have composed their own downfall. What the world counts as weakness is the power by which God transforms even the hostility of

---

[30] On the identity of these powers, see below, pp. 102–107.

His enemies into an instrument of His own purpose. In keeping with this purpose God has called into His service those whom the world regards as nonentities to overthrow what the world regards as real (1: 28), and by the gift of His Spirit has enabled them to understand what remains hidden from the worldly mind (2: 10–16). Thus, as in Ephesians, the understanding of that purpose is a key element in its implementation.

This theme is carried a stage further in Rom. 8: 28–30, the true *locus* in Paul for a doctrine of predestination:

In everything the Spirit co-operates for good with those who love God and are called according to his purpose. Those he knew from the beginning he foreordained to be shaped to the image of his Son, that he might be the first in a family of many brothers; and whom He foreordained He also called, whom He called He also justified, whom He justified He also glorified.

Elsewhere in Paul the glory of the Christian is a hope for the future (Rom. 5: 2; 8: 18; 9: 23; 1 Cor. 15: 43; Phil. 3: 21; Col. 1: 27), occasionally an experience in the present (2 Cor. 3: 15), but never an accomplished fact. We must therefore conclude that the last of Paul's five verbs, like the others, is in the aorist tense (*edoxasen*) precisely because he is thinking of the whole process as having been completed in the eternal purpose of God.

In these two passages Paul's treatment of the divine purpose deals more with the means by which God attains His ends than with the ends themselves, about which Paul is reticent (see especially 1 Cor. 2: 9). This is equally true of Rom. 9–11. In the previous eight chapters Paul has established as the goal of God's plan of salvation the creation of a world-wide family in which Jew and Gentile have equal status. This goal has been rejected by the particularist Jew, who wishes no place in any universal commonwealth without a most-favoured-nation clause in its constitution. Paul has no doubt that such recalcitrance must attract divine retribution (cf. 1 Thess. 2: 16), but he has observed that it has had a beneficial effect in opening the gospel to the Gentiles, who would never have accepted a place in a solidly Jewish society; and he raises the question of whether Jewish rejection of the gospel would not actually have been willed by God as a means to a higher end.

Surely the potter can do what he likes with the clay. Is he not free to make out of the same lump two vessels, one to be treasured, the other for common use? But granted that it is God's will to give proof of His retributive justice[31] and to display His power, can it be that He has held His hand by showing great patience to receptacles for retribution fit for destruction, and has done so precisely in order to display the wealth of His glory on receptacles for mercy, which from the first He had prepared for glory? (Rom. 9: 21–3)

The context shows that the metaphor of the potter is not intended to refer to God the Creator, making at Creation one species, *homo sapiens*, followed by two subspecies, the saved and the damned. Paul in fact himself had once been one of the damned; he is no longer. It rather refers to God's ability to mould human lives for one purpose or another.[32] When a lump of clay resists the attempt to turn it into a work of art, an end in itself, the potter can still make it into a utensil, a means to an end. This helps us to understand Paul's apparently high-handed treatment of Pharaoh (9: 17–21). According to Exodus 9: 16, God raised up Pharaoh to be the villain in the drama of the Exodus, so that without his help the act of redemption on which Israel's religion was founded could not have happened. This then raises the objection: 'Why does God blame anyone, if no one can resist His will?' (9: 19). Now at one level Paul clearly believes that anyone can resist God's will, since he has just spent three chapters proving that sin and disobedience are not only possible but universal (cf. 3: 23); and at this level God wills that sin should be punished. The point Paul is making is that neither sin ('Pharaoh hardened his heart') nor its just retribution ('God hardened Pharaoh's heart') can thwart the purpose of God, but may indeed serve to promote it. It is moreover integral to Paul's argument that this purpose arises wholly from God's own merciful nature: 'For he says to Moses, "I will show mercy to whom I will show mercy and have pity on whom I will have pity".' Thus 'it does not depend on human will or effort, but on God's mercy' (9: 15–16). Paul's sole interest in God's 'elective purpose' (9: 11), or indeed in the concepts of election and predestination, is to assert the primacy of God and the sovereignty of grace (cf. 4: 16).

It is God's will that disobedience should be punished, but it is also His will to display His power, the wealth of His glory, in the salvation of the human race. Gentiles in the past have been prisoners of dis-

---

[31] Cf. 3: 25–6, where Paul claims that God has given proof of His justice in the death of Christ.

[32] Cf. 2 Tim. 2: 20–1, where it is possible for a household utensil to move from the kitchen to the china cabinet!

obedience, but now in entering the Church they have become recipients of mercy; the Jews in the past have been recipients of mercy, but now in rejecting the gospel they have become prisoners of their own disobedience. 'For in shutting all mankind in the prison of their disobedience, God's purpose was to show mercy to all humankind' (11: 32, REB).

Only in this way could the human race, in its stubborn pride, be persuaded that salvation is by grace alone. What is emerging from the apostle's agonizing over a pastoral and personal problem is the recognition that the expression 'the will of God' is ambiguous and must be understood at more than one level. The classic statement of this theme is the distinction drawn by John of Damascus (*de Orth. Fid.* ii. 29) between God's antecedent will or good pleasure (*eudokia*), which arises entirely from His own nature, and His consequent will or permission (*sunchōrēsis*) which arises from the acts of human beings. John of Damascus was here clearly building on New Testament foundations.

Paul had been brought up on the belief that the Torah was the full and final revelation of God's purpose, and at his conversion he came to see that an unwillingness to contemplate the secondary and provisional nature of the Torah had blinded him and other Jews to the new revelation in Jesus (2 Cor. 3: 13–15). Accordingly, in Galatians he reconsiders the place of the Torah in the purpose of God. In one sense the Torah is the whole Pentateuch (4: 21), and in this regard it contains an adumbration of God's purpose in the promise given to Abraham (3: 15–18). In another sense the Torah consists of Commandments given to Moses; and in this sense[33] it represents only the consequent will of God. It was added because of offences (3: 19),[34] it was a moral tutor to maintain discipline until God was ready to fulfil His promise (3: 23–4: 6). Paul even argues that the angels who attended God at Sinai were the real source of the Torah, and that this was why Moses was required as an intermediary (Gal. 3: 19); and

[33] This distinction between the two senses of God's will and the two senses of Torah is also set out clearly in Rom. 3: 21, where Paul claims that the righteousness of God is revealed *chōris nomou*, 'apart from law', 'though the Law and the prophets bear witness to it'.

[34] Even if we translate this phrase 'for the sake of offences', i.e. 'to make wrong-doing a legal offence' (REB), the main argument that the Law was given to restrain sin is unchanged, as is shown by the metaphors 'paedagogue' (3: 24) and 'trustees and guardians' (4: 2).

he concludes that the Torah neither represents nor modifies the original purpose of God. In Colossians we are told of 'the secret design hidden for long ages and through many generations but now disclosed to God's people', because 'the secret is Christ himself, in whom lie hidden all God's treasures of wisdom and knowledge' (1: 26; 2: 2). The ground for those assertions has been given in an earlier paragraph,[35] in which Paul[36] declares that Christ 'is the image of the invisible God' (1: 15), and by the one word 'image' he combines two of the most important themes of Old Testament theology. On the one hand, God created the human race to be His image, with supremacy over the rest of creation (Gen. 1: 27–8; Ps. 8: 6; cf. Col. 3: 10), so that in fulfilling the human destiny Christ has achieved pre-eminence over the universe. On the other hand, the personified Wisdom, the wisdom by which God has 'made all things' and 'fashioned humanity to be the master of His whole creation', is also sent to be the 'image of God's goodness' (Wisd. 7: 26; 9: 1–2; cf. Prov. 8: 22 ff.; Ecclus. 24: 1–23; Philo of Alexandria, *Leg. All.* i. 43; *de Conf. Ling.* 97); and Paul's hymn to the cosmic Christ is full of echoes of Wisdom's function as the plan and artificer of Creation. These two themes are held together by the fact that the wisdom which shone forth in Creation was also a divine attribute which God always intended to impart to the human race (Ecclus. 24: 7–10), so that the perfect human being is one in whom Wisdom resides, or as Paul puts it, 'God in all His fullness has chosen to dwell' (Col. 1: 19; 2: 9).

Mark's treatment of this theme is succinct but important. Once only does he use the word *dei* to indicate the necessity of Jesus' death (8: 31), and once only does he explain that it was a scriptural necessity (14: 21), adding that the contribution made by Judas to the denouement did not absolve him of responsibility for his treachery. The Marcan Jesus clearly has a sense of mission (1: 35; 2: 17); yet his words in Gethsemane, 'Your will, not mine, be done' (14: 36), might be construed merely as a prayer of resignation or an abandonment to the divine Providence, were it not that earlier he had rebuked Peter for failing

---

[35] Cf. G. B. Caird, *Paul's Letters from Prison* (Oxford, 1978), 176 ff.

[36] *Editor's note*: Despite the mood of current opinion, Caird remained convinced of the Pauline authorship of Colossians, and felt that it has many noteworthy similarities in language, style, and thought to Philippians (cf. T. K. Abbott, *A Critical and Exegetical Commentary on the Epistles to the Ephesians and Colossians* (Edinburgh, 1899), p. viii). For a defence of Pauline authorship, cf. E. Percy, *Die Probleme der Kolosser- und Epheserbriefe* (Lund, 1946).

to think God's thoughts and so tempting Jesus to stray from his true destiny (8: 33).

The will of God is, as we have seen, an ambiguous concept. It is interesting therefore to find the distinction between God's antecedent and His consequent will drawn, though without technical terms, in the Marcan debate about divorce (10: 1–9). Moses permitted divorce, and Jesus never for a moment suggests that he was wrong to do so; the Law of Moses is God's Law. But the commandment in question (Deut. 24: 1–4) was given in consequence of human hardness of heart, to protect the rights of women and the institutions of marriage and family. Jesus penetrates behind the positive Law to the intention of God the Creator that man and woman should live together in lifelong partnership. He is not initiating a new and harsher Law, but is insisting that the Torah will be wrongly interpreted unless it is constantly referred back to the intention of God who gave it. Similarly, he reminds his critics that 'the sabbath was made for man, not man for the sabbath' (2: 27); it was intended by God as a gracious gift, a release from the necessity of seven-day toil, so that anyone who so interprets the Law as to make the sabbath a burden, or to inhibit the free course of God's mercy, merely reveals his own ignorance of God and His purposes (see below, Chapter 8). In the light of these passages, and of the use of *mustērion* elsewhere in the New Testament, we can safely take 'the mystery of the Kingdom of God' (4: 11) to be God's secret plan for establishing His sovereignty over the world.

Matthew, in editing this chapter of Mark, perhaps intending a cross-reference to Dan. 2: 28, has altered the singular 'mystery' into a plural, though without changing the sense (12: 11). Later in the chapter (13: 34–5), to Mark's statement that Jesus never taught the crowd except in parables, he has added a proof-text: 'I will open my mouth in parables; I will utter things kept secret since the world was made' (Ps. 78: 2).[37] His readers are to understand that what is revealed in the parables to those who have the percipience to interpret them is God's eternal plan (cf. Luke 11: 50; 1 Pet. 1: 20; Rev. 13: 8; 17: 8), the plan whereby those who receive His blessing are to 'possess the Kingdom prepared for you before the world was made' (Matt. 25: 34).

The idea that the goal of God's purpose already exists ideally in

[37] According to the MT the psalmist proposed to 'expound the riddles of the past (*qedem*)'. But *qedem* can also mean 'beginning' (cf. Prov. 8: 23), and this is the way the verse was interpreted both in the LXX and by Matthew (or his source).

heaven, and that the means of its accomplishment has been determined from the beginning, is found also in 1 Peter. By the living and enduring word of God Christians have been given new birth (1: 3, 23), which entitles them to 'an inheritance which nothing can destroy or spoil or wither, kept for you in heaven' (1: 4–5); and the price of their redemption from the old life has been paid in 'precious blood, as of a lamb without mark or blemish, the blood of Christ, predestined before the foundation of the world and manifested in these last days for your sake' (1: 19–20).

There are close parallels in the Revelation, where the city, the final destiny of the redeemed, comes down out of heaven 'made ready like a bride adorned for her husband' (21: 2), the bridegroom is 'the lamb slain from the foundation of the world' (13: 8), and the redeemed are those 'whose names are written before the foundation of the world in the book of life' (17: 8; 21: 27). If his readers should mistake this for determinism, John disabuses them with the warning that names may be erased from the book (3: 5), and this warning is in keeping with the character of John's symbolism. John is using an apocalyptic convention, whereby everything that happens on earth has its heavenly counterpart, so that when he is called up to heaven, like a prophet summoned into the privy council of God, he is enabled to see symbols which correspond to earthly realities, past, present, and future. But the heavenly symbols are related to their earthly counterparts in two ways. Some, like the breaking of the seals (6: 1–17, 8: 1–5), are determinative, i.e. earthly events happen because God has so decreed. Others, like the war in heaven (12: 7–12) are descriptive, i.e. the heavenly events merely reflect what is happening on earth.[38] But even the determinative symbols do not necessarily express the antecedent will of God; many things happen only by permission. The seven-headed monster is 'allowed to make war on God's people and defeat them' (13: 8). The central symbol of God's true purpose is the scroll in the hand of the Creator, which contains His secret plan for imposing His sovereignty on a rebellious creation (4: 11–5: 1).

The opening sentence of Hebrews is commonly taken to be 'Christological'. Its subject, however, is God, and, like most Christological statements, it is in the first instance a statement about God and the

---

[38] An example of the second class is provided by 12: 7–11, where, as the heavenly chorus declares, Michael is able to drive his adversary Satan out of heaven; the real victory has been won by Christ on the Cross, and it is to be repeated in the victorious death of each of the martyrs.

place His eternal purposes have allotted to 'the Son, whom He appointed heir to the universe, through whom He created the worlds' (1: 2). Here, as in Colossians, the description of Christ in terms appropriate to the heavenly Wisdom has the effect of depicting him as the agent appointed both to reveal and to put into effect God's master plan. When, therefore, the author argues that 'it is not to angels that he has subjected the world to come' (2: 5), we can readily understand that the aorist (*hupetaxen*) refers to an act of God located, not in the course of past history, but in God's eternal decree. In creating the worlds or ages, God has decreed that the present age should be under the authority of angels, but not the age to come. For this statement the author can provide scriptural warrant:

> What is man that you remember him,
>   or the son of man that you have regard for him?
> You have made him for a short while lower than the angels,
> You have crowned him with glory and honour;
> You subjected (*hupetaxas*) all things under his feet.

> (Psalm 8: 6–8)

Using the LXX text,[39] the author assumes that the short time in which the human race is to be subject to angels corresponds to the present age, the angels being 'ministrant spirits sent out to serve for the sake of those who were to inherit salvation' (1: 14), and specifically the mediators of the Torah (2: 2). The age to come is included in the 'all things' (*panta*) made subject to humanity. But his first comment on this passage is, 'We do not yet see all things in subjection to man'. That which the psalm declares God to have done has not yet happened, except in so far as Jesus, the pioneer, is already crowned with glory and honour. It follows that the three aorist verbs ('made', 'crowned', 'subjected') must also have as their referent God's predestining purpose. What God has done in heaven is yet to be done on earth.[40] God's purpose was to bring 'many sons' to that glory of which the psalm speaks, and this purpose 'was in keeping with' (*eprepen*) the nature of

---

[39] The Hebrew has 'you have made him a little lower than God (*Elohim*)'.

[40] It is possible that this is the meaning of the clause 'your will be done' in the Lord's Prayer (Matt. 6: 10), which can mean (*a*) 'may your will be done both in heaven and on earth', (*b*) 'may your will be done by men and women on earth as it is done by the inhabitants of heaven', or (*c*) 'may your will, already done in heaven, be realized on earth'.

Him who is the ground and source of all that exists (2: 10–12).[41] Here the author of Hebrews comes very close to Paul: it all depends not on human effort or human will but on the eternal nature of God (Rom. 9: 16).

The Prologue of the Fourth Gospel, of course, presents us with one of the most towering problems of New Testament interpretation: Is the eternal *logos*, without which no created thing came into existence, to be understood as the cosmic reason of the Greek philosophers, or as the performative word of the Old Testament, which goes out from God in Creation, providence, judgement, and salvation to accomplish His purpose?[42] We may put the same question in a different form: does John intend the function of Jesus, as *logos* made flesh, to be the disclosure of an immutable truth to which men and women must respond and by which they are judged, or to be the agent of a purpose which will be revealed only in the course of its achievement? In spite of the weighty support of Bultmann[43] for the first interpretation, there are four good reasons for accepting the second.

1. Jesus in this gospel constantly speaks of doing the work or the will of God (4: 34; 5: 20; 9: 4) and dies with the triumphant claim that it is accomplished (*tetelestai*, 19: 30; cf. 17: 4).

2. In the frequent references to Jesus' 'hour' and by other allusive hints (2: 20; 3: 14; 6: 53; 7: 39; 8: 28; 10: 18), the Gospel points forward to the Cross as the climax of a pre-ordained process.

3. The hypothesis that the Fourth Gospel is to be interpreted wholly along the lines of 1: 18 and 3: 16–20, that by bringing the light of divine truth into the world Jesus divides the whole human race into those who belong to the light and those who belong to the darkness, leads only to despair; for as the story proceeds, believers fall away,

---

[41] For a fuller exposition of the argument of Hebrews on this point, cf. Caird, 'Son by Appointment'; L. D. Hurst, 'The Christology of Hebrews 1 and 2', in L. D. Hurst and N. T. Wright, *The Glory of Christ in the New Testament* (Oxford, 1987) 153 f.; B. Lindars, *The Theology of the Letter to the Hebrews* (Cambridge, 1991), 29 ff.; and M. E. Isaacs, *Sacred Space: An Approach to the Theology of the Epistle to the Hebrews* (Sheffield, 1992), 178 ff.

[42] For an extended discussion of this lengthy debate, see below, pp. 327–332.

[43] Bultmann's treatment of the question illustrates the weakness of the *Religionsgeschichtlich* method. His interpretation of the Prologue is dictated by the belief that it had a previous existence as a hymn. But even if this were true, what the hymn means in the Fourth Gospel is what John intends it to mean; and this we can discover only by reading his book.

leaving Jesus alone with the Twelve (6: 66), and finally even they desert him (16: 32), so that he alone is in the light and the whole world remains in the darkness. Bultmann's gospel is, in other words, no gospel at all.

4. Jesus not only reveals and implements the divine purpose; he *is* the purpose. For the union of the human and divine, which he displays in all his works and words in chs. 1–12, and which through the Cross he imparts to his disciples, and which they are to share with others and finally with the world, is the purpose for which God set the universe in motion: 'In the beginning was the purpose' (below, Chapter 8).

2.4. ISRAEL AND THE WORLD

We have seen that, according to Luke, the offer of salvation to the entire human race did not cancel the hope of a national salvation for Israel. It is now necessary to show that other New Testament writers agreed with him on three points: (*a*) the gospel was first offered to Israel; (*b*) it was subsequently opened to all humanity; and (*c*) the Church, with its mixed membership of Jews and Gentiles, could properly be assigned all the dignities and functions which had once pertained to Israel. But did they see the Church as Israel, or as the new Israel, as its continuation or as its replacement? Did they see Christianity as a new religion, in competition and conflict with Judaism, or as Judaism properly understood?[44] Had the Jewish people, by their failure to respond to the gospel, forfeited their unique place in the purpose of God? What difference did the fall of Jerusalem and the subsequent breach between Church and Synagogue make to the answers given to these questions after AD 70? And, above all, is the corporate nature of the Church something inherited from its Jewish origins (given the corporate nature of the Jewish nation), or is it a product of the voluntary principle inherent in the Christian's act of faith? As we shall see in Chapter 9, on the evidence of both Paul and Acts the early Church came only slowly and with difficulty to admit Gentiles. A famous critical problem lies in the background of this question. Although Mark has a statement by Jesus (13: 10) before his Passion that the

---

[44] Cf. E. P. Sanders, *Paul and Palestinian Judaism*, who asserts (p. 552) that the only quarrel Paul had with Judaism was that it was not Christianity. This assumes, of course, that Paul regarded Judaism as one religion and Christianity as another, hardly the only conclusion one may draw from the evidence.

gospel must be preached throughout all the world, and Matthew's Gospel ends with permission from the risen Jesus to 'go and baptise all nations and make them his disciples' (28: 19–20), and Acts begins with a charge from the risen Jesus to the apostles, 'You shall be my witnesses to Jerusalem, Judaea and the ends of the earth' (11: 18), nevertheless *no attempt is made in the first instance to go to the Gentiles*. And when Gentiles are admitted to the Church, the apostles require considerable persuasion that it is the right thing to do (cf. Acts 11: 1–18; 15: 1–29). This is borne out in the Paulines where Paul has to fight to establish his belief that Gentiles are to be admitted on equal terms with Jews without circumcision (Gal. 1–2). Why? One explanation is provided by J. Jeremias,[45] who suggested that Jesus found the blueprint of his mission in certain passages of Isaiah, Zechariah, and the Psalms, where God's coming act of salvation is depicted in two stages: first Israel would be rescued from pagan tyranny and restored to her proper holiness befitting God's people, and then the redeemed Israel would become a beacon or magnet, attracting all nations to the worship of the one God, because it would be plain that in it alone were true religion and the presence of God to be found (Isa. 2: 2–4; 49: 5–6; Zech. 8: 23; 14: 8–9). Jesus, in other words, believed that his own role was restricted to stage one (cf. Matt. 15: 22–8), since stage two could safely be left to the renewed Israel; and the Church followed his example until events and the guidance of the Spirit dictated otherwise. And this is the way Luke tells the story. Paul came to believe that instead of waiting for a converted Israel to bring in the Gentiles, it was God's will that the entry of Gentiles into the Church should be the means of bringing about the conversion of Israel (Rom. 11: 26). Meanwhile, Peter and James, convinced that it was right to admit Gentiles to the Church without circumcision (Gal. 2: 9ff.), were nevertheless still adhering to the prior claims of the mission to Israel. This divergence of policy was the subject of debate at the conference in Jerusalem, which ended with mutual understanding (although not without some recrudescences to the old view, Gal. 2: 1–10).

This reconstruction has the merit of making splendid and coherent sense of all the Pauline evidence, not to mention the evidence of

---

[45] *Jesus' Promise to the Nations* (London, 1958), 55 ff. Jeremias was taking up a point put forward more tentatively by J. Munck in his *Paul and the Salvation of Mankind* (1959) in its earlier German version (1946).

Luke–Acts. For Paul's theology, even at its most universalist, is deeply rooted in his Jewish past. Though the Jews have no advantage in being entrusted with the Law unless they keep it, it is a great advantage to have been 'entrusted with the oracles of God'—i.e. the Old Testament interpreted as God's plan of salvation (Rom. 3: 2). When Paul contrasts the old humanity of Adam with the new humanity of Christ, Adam's history is entirely a *Jewish* history which includes Moses and the Torah (Rom. 5: 12–21). Though 'in Christ there is neither Jew nor Greek' (Gal. 3: 27; Col. 3: 10), nevertheless Gentile Christians are 'grafted, like branches from a wild olive, onto a Jewish olive tree' (Rom. 11: 17). It is not enough for Paul to prove that Jew and Gentile are equally children of God; he must prove that they are equally children of Abraham (Gal. 3: 7; Rom. 4: 11–12). He can do this by showing that the difference between Isaac and Ishmael, between Jacob and Esau, lay not in physical descent, which all four shared, but in God's 'elective purpose' (Rom. 9: 11); yet he cannot leave the matter at that. To suggest that God has finally rejected His people because of their unbelief is to impugn the righteousness of God: 'God cannot go back on His own gifts and calling' (Rom. 11: 29). The whole argument of Romans 9–11 is designed to persuade Gentile Christians that God has not written Israel off: 'God has consigned all to the prison house of their disobedience, that He may have mercy on all' (Rom. 11: 32). Israel is to resume its status as God's people, when once it is prepared to share that status with Gentiles. Paul is well aware that this is a radical departure from the Judaism of his youth; but he is prepared to claim that it is Judaism *properly understood*. To insist on special privileges for Israel is to ascribe favouritism (*prosōpolēmpsia*) to God, the most grievous betrayal of justice even in a human judge (Rom. 2: 11; cf. Jas. 2: 9). 'The true Jew is he who is such inwardly, and true circumcision is of the heart, directed not by written precepts but by the Spirit' (Rom. 2: 29). And to deny that God is God of the Gentiles is to deny the monotheistic faith to which every pious Jew gave daily expression in the recitation of the Shema (Rom. 3: 29–30). Monotheism and universalism go hand in hand.

Mark's Gospel is written to answer the questions of a persecuted Church. Why must the followers of Jesus suffer? Why, if he was the promised Messiah, did he suffer, and why should Gentiles believe in him if his own people have rejected him? Mark answers these questions not by theological assertions but by a narrative in which the themes of misunderstanding, suffering, and triumph are subtly interwoven.[46] He has no doubt that Jesus is Messiah and Son of God (1: 1), or that these two titles are synonyms for 'King of the Jews' (15: 2, 9, 12, 18, 27). Jesus is king by divine appointment (1: 11), but the uncomprehending hostility of his enemies and the equally uncomprehending enthusiasm of his friends lead him inexorably to death. His closest friends misinterpret Messiahship in terms of privilege (8: 32–3; 9: 34). When he publicly admits to being Messiah and Son of God, his enemies take this to be blasphemy against God and treason against Caesar (14: 61–3; 15: 2–3). But in combining to remove a threat to the Jewish religion and the Roman state, they unwittingly fulfil the purpose of God by crowning, enthroning, and placarding Jesus as King of the Jews. It is on the Cross that he enters his Kingdom, and it is there that the veil of incomprehension which protected the presence of God from unhallowed approach is rent, so that the centurion, as a spokesman for the entire Gentile world, can say, 'This man was Son of God' (15: 37–9). As usual with Mark, the theology is all there, but only by implication.

While the Epistle of James continues to be a source of much discussion,[47] what remains clear is that it is addressed to the twelve tribes of the Dispersion by an author who sees himself as standing in the unbroken Jewish tradition of James of Jerusalem and who looks back to Abraham as 'our father' (2: 21); yet it is marked out as a Christian document by two mentions of Jesus Christ and by the author's obvious familiarity with his teaching. Likewise, 1 Peter is addressed to the Dispersion, but the majority at least of its recipients had been Gentiles (1: 14; 2: 10; 4: 3–4). Yet they too are encouraged to see themselves as descendents of Abraham and Sarah (3: 6). In the Epistle to the Hebrews Gentiles are never mentioned;[48] the author and his readers are at home in the Greek Old Testament and think of its heroic figures as 'our forefathers' (1: 1; 11: 1 ff). Even when the author is claiming

---

[46] Cf. Lightfoot, *The Gospel Message of St Mark*, who observes that predictions of the passion of Jesus, of the persecution of the disciples, and of the glory that lies beyond occur in close juxtaposition in chs. 8, 9, and 10; and that although the Passion of Jesus is told without theological comment (chs. 14–15), it is introduced by ch. 13 with its vision that lies beyond suffering and persecution (below, p. 255 f.).

[47] For recent general treatments of James, cf. the commentaries of M. Dibelius and H. Greeven, *James* (Philadelphia, 1976); and S. Laws, *A Commentary on the Epistle of James* (San Francisco, 1980).

[48] This is presumably why second-century editors thought it was addressed to 'the Hebrews'.

that Jesus has fulfilled the universal destiny of the human race (Ps. 8) by establishing a solidarity with his many brothers, the sons whom God is leading to their preordained glory, he assumes almost in passing that this solidarity is with 'the seed of Abraham' (2: 16). Yet the main argument of the Epistle is that the Old Testament repeatedly declares its own incompleteness and points forward to its fulfilment in the new covenant.[49] Those who take it seriously can find no abiding city in the old order to which it belongs, but must go outside that camp to Jesus in whom alone they have their permanent home (11: 13–14; 13: 13). These three writings all illustrate the point, which we have already seen in Paul's letters, that the early Christians regarded the Old Testament history as *their* history. But the weight which we attach to this evidence is bound up with the disputed questions of their date and milieu. For this assumption would be less significant in a Church still consisting mainly of Jews and more significant in a Church consisting mainly of Gentiles whose links with the Synagogue had been severed.[50]

Matthew by contrast demonstrably belongs to the later period, and at some points gives the impression that the destruction of Jerusalem was Israel's final forfeiture of her calling to be God's people. He particularly enjoys Mark's twofold description (1:23, 39) of the meeting-places as 'their synagogues' (4: 24; 9: 35; 10: 17; 12: 9; 13: 54; Mark 1: 23, 39), and alters the ending of the Parable of the Vineyard so that the displaced tenants, who in Mark's Gospel represented only the authorities, now represent the whole nation: 'The Kingdom of God will be taken away from you and given to a nation that yields the proper fruit' (21: 43). We might therefore draw the inference that he regarded the Church as a substitute for Israel rather than a continuation of it, a new structure built upon a new rock (16: 18). But in this Gospel first impressions are always misleading. For Matthew goes even further than Mark in assuring that Jesus was born to be King of the Jews (2: 2), and was to 'save his people from their sins' (1: 21). Moreover, he begins the mission charge to the Twelve

---

[49] Cf. G. B. Caird, 'The Exegetical Method of the Epistle to the Hebrews', *CJT* 5 (1959), 44–51.

[50] Compare the modern disputes between Roman Catholics and Protestants, or even among Protestant denominations, especially descendants of the Cavaliers and Roundheads. Though they share a common history, they interpret it differently. In Caird, *Language and Imagery of the Bible*, 207, the death of Charles I is instanced to show that no disputes are as acrimonious as those between people who share a common history and who disagree.

with an injunction not to go to Gentiles or Samaritans, but only to the 'lost sheep of the house of Israel' (10: 5–6; cf. 15: 24), and we have to explain what that prohibition is doing in a Gospel which ends with a commission to take the gospel to all nations (28: 19). We may argue that Matthew was the great synthesizer who included 'fossil' traditions simply because he found them in his sources; but since he can be shown to have edited Mark in the interest of his own theology; we have no reason to believe that he would have included anything which he flatly disbelieved. We may argue, with Jeremias, that Jesus' mission was restricted to Israel during his lifetime, and only subsequently extended; but that is not a fully satisfactory explanation of Matthew's editorial practice. For Matthew was not writing merely to tell a story about the past; he was providing a manual of instruction for the Church of his own day. The woes against the Pharisees serve not only to explain what contribution their faults made to the national tragedy which ended in the fall of Jerusalem; they also stand as a warning against any recrudescence of Pharisaism in the Church (23: 1–39). 'Let not you be called "Rabbi" '. Similarly the mission charge records not merely an episode in which Jesus was talking to his apostles; it was also intended as a guide for missionaries in Matthew's own day. He must therefore have intended its opening command ('Do not go to the Gentiles') as a reminder that Jesus was sent to be the saviour of the Jewish people, and that neither the Gentile mission nor the fall of Jeruselem had erased that first item on God's agenda. This view is confirmed by Jesus' promise to the Twelve: 'In the new world (*palingenesia*), when the Son of Man is enthroned in his majesty, you my followers will be enthroned as rulers of the twelve tribes of Israel' (19: 28).

There can be no doubt that the author of Revelation thought of himself and his churches as heirs to all the riches of the Old Testament, or that he regarded the Church as Israel. Among the enemies of the churches are 'those who claim to be Jews but are not' (2: 9; 3: 9). *True* Jews are in the Church. When John hears the roll of the martyrs called, he hears them enumerated as 12,000 from each of the tribes of Israel: but what he in fact sees is 'a throng, which no one could count, from every nation, tribe, people, and tongue' (1: 1–9). The Holy City is now the Church (11: 2), and Jerusalem, along with Sodom and Egypt, has become a symbol for the great city, by which the Church is persecuted. The new Jerusalem, which bears on its foundation the names of the twelve apostles, bears on its gates 'the names of the twelve tribes of Israel' (22: 12). Yet this is not just a transfer of old dignities to a new entity. John holds open the hope that Jewish persecutors of the Church who have been lured into 'the synagogue of Satan' may yet be admitted to the true Israel by him who holds the key of David (3: 9).[51]

John's Gospel has mistakenly been considered 'anti-Jewish'. In his theology the adversary of God is the world, which is at the same time the object of God's redemptive love. John has chosen to tell the story of Jesus as the controversy of God versus the world, and it was therefore inevitable that the part of the world should be played by Jewish actors. At the same time he makes it clear that 'it is from the Jews that salvation comes' (4: 22). It comes through union with Christ, but that union is symbolized in images traditionally associated with Israel (10: 11–16; 15: 1–6). A true child of Israel is one who recognizes Jesus as King of Israel, and has the faith to see 'God's angels ascending and descending upon the Son of Man' (1: 47–51). Caiaphas, intending an act of *Realpolitik*, unwittingly prophesies that Jesus 'would die for the nation, and not for the nation only but to gather together the scattered children of God' (11: 51–2). Even Pilate is God's agent in proclaiming Jesus 'King of the Jews' (19: 19–22). It is only by being the Jewish Messiah that Jesus can also be the Saviour of the world (4: 25–42).

2.5. ACCORDING TO THE SCRIPTURES

Luke's belief that God's plan of salvation could be read off from the Old Testament is not the only way that can be conceived whereby the early Christians could have justified their exegesis. To them fulfilment could have meant simply that the words of an Old Testament text fitted a New Testament situation—Isaiah might well have been addressing the contemporaries of Jesus (Mark 7: 6), and therefore could be deemed to have done so—or that a pattern of behaviour observable in the past had repeated itself in the present (Matt. 23: 29–32), or that an embarrassing circumstance could be explained away because a text could be found which predicted it (John 13: 18; cf. Psalm 4: 9). As Jews they had been accustomed to think of the Old Testament primarily as *halakah*, a revealed way of life; and a legal religion lends itself naturally to atomic exegesis. To them the Old

---

[51] Cf. G. B. Caird, *The Revelation of St John the Divine* (London, 1985²), 52 f.

Testament was scripture, inspired in all its parts, so that any citation from it, with or without reference to context or the intention of the human author, carried the full authority of a sacred text. Particularly in debate, any text was a good enough stick with which to bash an opponent.

Such observations were the basis of A. Rendel Harris's theory that the earliest literary activity of the Church was the gathering of proof-texts, to be used in defence of Christian claims about Jesus and in polemical debate with the Synagogue. He could point to the existence of such a collection in the time of Cyprian, and would have joined additional support from the discovery of similar collections at Qumran. His theory was designed to explain the widespread agreement in the choice of texts, and particularly in the combination of texts from diverse sources,[52] the attribution of texts to the wrong authors, and the existence of citations which do not exactly correspond either to the Masoretic Text or the LXX. It entailed the assumption that for the choice of proof-texts the events themselves provided the control, notwithstanding some evidence for the contrary view that events, or at least the details of them, were constructed out of the prophecies they were said to fulfil.

Harris, however, acknowledged that the polemical use of proof-texts implied a theology,[53] and he might well have added that polemical debate cannot be conducted except by contestants who have a great deal in common. Even the most legalistic Jewish exegesis rests on a theological belief that God has a purpose for Israel, and that the Torah is His revealed way of moulding them into a holy people. Moreover, the fact that many of the quotations used in the Qumran documents coincide with those used in the New Testament suggests that the selection was less haphazard than the atomic theory implies.[54] It is therefore improbable that the proof-text or atomic exegesis, as envisaged by Harris and his successors, was ever practised by Jew or Chris-

---

[52] The most famous instance of this is the combination of the 'stone' texts in 1 Peter 2: 4–8.

[53] 'As soon as we have sufficiently proved that a body of anti-Judaic testimonies was in existence before any of the books of the New Testament, we are in a position to draw some conclusions with regard to the primitive Christian theology' (*Testimonia*, ii (Cambridge, 1920), 101).

[54] Cf. J. A. Fitzmyer, 'The Use of Explicit Old Testament Quotations in Qumran Literature and the New Testament', in *Essays on the Semitic Background of the New Testament* (London, 1971), 5.

tian merely in the belief that the text in all its parts was sacred and inspired, apart from a larger conviction that it provided the key to the purposes of God.[55]

The inadequacy of Harris's theory to explain New Testament evidence was exposed by C. H. Dodd, who demonstrated that the questions in the New Testament from the prophetic books and the Psalter were not drawn from the whole range of available material, but from a limited number of passages, which were thus marked out as being in a special sense Christian scripture.[56] For instance, ninety of the psalms are not quoted at all, whereas seven different verses are quoted from Psalm 69;[57] of the twelve verses of Isaiah 53, eleven are quoted or alluded to;[58] and there are ten references to Zechariah 9–14.[59] Dodd concluded that the early Church went to the Old Testament armed with a principle of selection and interpretation, which, since it was presupposed by Paul, must have antedated all the New Testament writings. The passages Dodd thus identified he classified in three groups, each with its own plot.

1. In the apocalyptic eschatological scriptures (Joel 2–3, Zech. 9–14, Daniel) Israel is suffering oppression under sinister world powers, but is to be rescued by an intervention of God which 'takes the form of a judgment upon the evil things in history, and the establishment of a people of God through whom all nations will come under His everlasting and beneficent reign'.[60]

2. In the scriptures of the new Israel (parts of Hosea, Isaiah, and Jeremiah) rebellious Israel receives drastic punishment for her sins, but with the promise that beyond judgement lies restoration and renewal.

3. In the scriptures of the righteous sufferer (Isa. 40–66 and certain Psalms) Israel is called to undergo suffering in God's service, but with the assurance of ultimate vindication. Dodd argued that these

---

[55] 'the Priest [in whose heart] God set [understanding] that he might interpret all the words of his servants the prophets, through whom he foretold all that would happen to his people and [his land]' (IQpHab 2.9f.).

[56] *According to the Scriptures*; cf. also *The Old Testament in the New* (London, 1952).

[57] Matt. 27: 34; John 2: 18; 15: 25; Acts 1: 20; Rom. 11: 9 f.; 15: 3; Phil. 4: 3; Rev. 3: 5; 16: 1; 17: 8; 20: 12.

[58] Matt. 8: 17; Mark 9: 12; 10: 45; Luke 22: 37; John 12: 38; Acts 8: 32; Rom 4: 25; 8: 3, 34; 10: 16; Phil. 2: 7–8; Heb. 9: 28; 1 Pet. 2: 22–5; Rev. 5: 6, 12; 14: 5.

[59] Matt. 21: 5; 24: 30; 25: 32; 26: 15, 28, 31; 27: 9; Mark 14: 24, 27; Luke 21: 24; John 12: 14; 19: 37; Heb. 13: 20; Rev. 1: 7; 11: 2; 21: 6, 25; 22: 6.

[60] *According to the Scriptures*, 72.

scriptures were 'acutely interpreted along lines already discernible within the Old Testament canon itself or in pre-Christian Judaism', but that the application of them to Jesus was a piece of genuinely creative thinking, implying a claim that he had fulfilled the vocation of Israel.

> To have brought together, for example, the Son of Man who is the people of the Saints of the Most High, the Man of God's right hand, who is also the Vine of Israel, the Son of Man who after humiliation is crowned with glory and honour, and his victorious priest-king at the right hand of God, is an achievement of interpretative imagination which results in the creation of an entirely new figure.[61]

The prevalence of the pattern which Dodd detected in the scriptures most frequently cited in the New Testament need not surprise us when we recognize that it is the Exodus pattern, and that the deliverance from Egyptian bondage, together with the covenant which constituted Israel as God's elect and holy nation, was annually celebrated in the Passover. This archetypal rescue from slavery became the basis of confidence that God would redeem Israel from all other forms of tyranny (e.g. Pss. 77: 11–20; 130: 8), and the foundation of New Testament typology was laid by those prophets who depicted a coming act of divine deliverance as a new Exodus (e.g. Isa. 11: 12–16; 51: 9–10). It is also worthy of note that Dodd's canon within the canon included all these passages on which Jeremias relied for his theory about Jesus' attitude to the Gentiles.

There is one point, however, at which Dodd's thesis requires qualification. Granted that he was right about the principle of selection and interpretation which he called 'the substructure of New Testament theology', it does not necessarily follow that individual New Testament authors, in quoting from the passages in question, were doing so in order to express a common theology. B. Lindars, without dissenting from Dodd's fundamental conclusion, has shown that verses drawn from the same stock of passages could be used, often in a proof-text manner, for a variety of apologetic or polemical purposes.[62] Thus the fact that all drew on a common tradition of exegesis tends to suggest the hypothesis that all shared a common theological assumption; but this hypothesis can be substantiated only by the examination of each in turn, which unfortunately Dodd did not supply.

---

[61] Ibid. 109; cf. Dan. 7: 13 ff.; Pss. 80 and 110.
[62] *New Testament Apologetic* (London, 1961).

Throughout his Gospel Mark indicates that Jesus understood his vocation in Old Testament terms. In so doing he employs, on no fewer than six occasions, a composite quotation or reference. The Gospel opens with a hybrid quotation which identifies John the Baptist with the messenger of the covenant (Mal. 3: 1) and the herald of good news (Isa. 40: 3), both of whom were to prepare the way for the coming of the Lord. At Jesus' baptism the voice from heaven addresses him as the anointed Son of God (Ps. 2: 7), who is at the same time the chosen servant of the Lord (Isa. 42: 1). At Caesarea Philippi Peter hails Jesus as Messiah,[63] and he at once reinterprets his Messianic role in terms of the suffering of the Son of Man. On the mountain-top the heavenly voice echoes the words spoken to Jesus at his baptism (Ps. 2), but this occasion associates the role of Son with that of the prophet commissioned to speak in the name of God (Deut. 18: 15). In debate with the Jerusalem authorities Jesus himself raises a question about the relation between the traditional Davidic Messiah and the more exalted figure destined to sit at the right hand of God (Ps. 110: 1).[64] And finally, in answer to the High Priest's question at his trial, he openly claims to be Messiah and Son of God, but defines these terms in a composite quotation from Psalm 110: 1 and Daniel 7: 13. In view of Dodd's argument it is highly improbable that Mark originated any of these cross-references; but, since he includes six of them, it is even more improbable that he was passively taking over a tradition without being alert to its significance.

Apart from the claim (inherent in the opening genealogy) that Jesus was sent to fulfil God's promises to Abraham and David, and to complete the judgement and salvation of Israel begun in the Babylonian exile,[65] Matthew appears to add little to Mark. His eleven fulfilment quotations are not concerned with the grand design of Jesus' ministry but with its details: his birth (1: 22), events in his infancy (3: 5, 15,

[63] It has been conjectured that in the pre-Marcan tradition Jesus repudiated the title. This is not, of course, the view of Mark (cf. 1: 1; 14: 62; 15: 32); nor will it be obvious that it was Jesus' own view (below, pp. 309 f.).

[64] The general belief of the early Church was that Jesus was descended from David (Matt. 1: 1; Luke 2: 4; Acts 2: 30; Rom. 1: 3; 2 Tim. 2: 8; Heb. 7: 14; Rev. 5: 5; 22: 16). Mark shared this view (10: 48; 11: 10) and cannot therefore have believed that Jesus had repudiated the title. He is simply demonstrating that 'Son of David' is, of itself, a title inadequate to do justice to the full dignity and authority of the Messiah (cf. also below, pp. 309 f., 417.).

[65] Note the emphasis which Matthew's genealogy places on the Babylonian exile (1: 11–12).

17, 23), his Galilean ministry (4: 14), his healing of the sick (8: 17), his avoidance of publicity (12: 17), the misunderstanding he incurred (13: 14), his use of parables (13: 35), his moment of entry into Jerusalem (21: 4), and his betrayal (27: 9) were all foretold. Five of these quotations are loosely ascribed to 'the prophet(s)', though one is untraceable and another comes from the Psalter; one is wrongly attributed to Jeremiah; and in the last two instances the prophecy seems to have supplied details of the event which is said to fulfil it. Prima facie Matthew's usage bears out Harris's theory rather than Dodd's. On the other hand, Matthew is aware that four of his quotations come from Isaiah and one from Jeremiah, and we are bound to ask whether he was sensitive to their original contexts. Was he aware that the son whom God called out of Egypt was Israel (Hos. 11: 1), or that the children over whom Rachel wept were the captives on the way to that Babylonian exile already mentioned in his genealogy (Jer. 31: 15)? Did he read Isaiah 6–9 as a continuous narrative, so that the blindness of Israel, the coming of Immanuel, and the dawning of light on those who sit in darkness were all part of the one drama of salvation? One point at least is beyond doubt. The ostensible reason given for these quotations is often only a peg on which Matthew hangs the actual reason. He has no real interest in a Virgin Birth; after it is mentioned, he never develops the theme. What he does develop is the *name* of the child, with the curious comment that the prophetic name Immanuel ('God with us') is synonymous with the historical name Jesus ('God Saves'). Ostensibly he cites Isaiah 9: 1–2 and 42: 1–4 to explain the Galilean origin of Jesus and his avoidance of publicity, but in each case he quotes more than was needed for that purpose; Jesus appeared in Galilee because he was the bringer of God's light to the world's darkness, and he preferred to work incognito because he was the Servant of the Lord destined to bring justice and truth to the nations. In short, all the details of the life of Jesus were consistent with his commission to be the agent of God's purpose, since they could all be attested out of the programmatic scriptures.

Many of John's quotations, also, are of the proof-text variety, designed to authenticate details of Jesus' ministry and particularly of his Passion (7: 42; 13: 18; 15: 25; 17: 12; 19: 24, 36, 37). But these must be seen in the light of his more general claim that the scriptures as a whole are written about Jesus. He is the one 'whom Moses and the prophets wrote about' (1: 45). Scripture lays down that valid testimony requires at least two witnesses (8: 17), and Jesus can call scripture itself to be one of the witnesses that validate his claims (5: 39, 46). Whether the witness borne to Jesus comes from God, Jesus himself, his works, John the Baptist, the Old Testament, the Spirit, or the disciples (1: 7–34; 5: 31–8; 8: 14–18; 15: 25–7), its content is the same: Jesus is the incarnate *logos* sent by God to carry out His purpose.

Considering the frequency of his Old Testament quotations and the variety of terms for referring to God's cosmic purpose, it is surprising that Paul rarely makes a link between those two elements in his thought. He believed that God had 'announced the Gospel beforehand in sacred scriptures through His prophets' (Rom. 1: 2), and that 'Abraham had the Gospel preached to him in advance' (Gal. 3: 8), and that the Old Testament was the story of God's 'selective purpose' (Rom. 9: 11). But such explicit statements are few. The reason perhaps is that as a Pharisee Paul had been accustomed to read the scriptures as Law, and to identify that Law with the purpose of Creation, and that at his conversion he had discovered that this identification of the Law with the full and final revelation of God had blinded him to the presence of God in Christ (2 Cor. 3: 14; 4: 4). The scriptures had not brought him to Christ: rather God, through Christ, had opened his eyes to the true meaning of the scriptures. Hence, having denied that possession of the Law is any benefit to the Jew unless he keeps it, Paul can still claim that it is an advantage to be 'entrusted with the oracles of God' (Rom. 2: 7 ff.; 3: 2), i.e. the Old Testament read as the story of God's unfolding promise of grace and mercy. In Christ the righteousness of God is revealed 'quite independently of law', though 'the Law and prophets bear witness to it' (Rom. 3: 21). The Old Testament is a book of promises to which Christ is the 'Yes' (2 Cor. 1: 20), of types to which he is the counterpart (Rom. 5: 14), and of questions unanswered and visions unfulfilled; for did it not in sundry places confess that it had not the power to bring the human race to the obedience which in the name of God it required (Rom. 3: 19; 8: 3; cf. Gal. 3: 22)?

By contrast Hebrews is a book about the Christian use of the Old Testament. Its author's purpose is pastoral, but he achieves it by a sustained theological argument, designed to prove that what 'God spoke in fragmentary and varied fashion through the prophets' has now been fully revealed in the Son to whom by eternal appointment He has committed the achievement of His purpose for the human race. Since the majority of his quotations and allusions are from the

Pentateuch and the Psalter,[66] by 'the prophets' he must have meant the whole of the Old Testament.[67] It is prophetic partly because through it God still speaks to His people, but more particularly because it constantly draws attention to its own provisional and preparatory character ('in varied and fragmentary fashion', 1: 1). In it God addresses the man Jesus in terms more exalted than those used of the angels (the mediators of the old covenant—2: 2), because they are but 'ministrant spirits sent out to serve, for the sake of those who were to inherit salvation' (1: 14). Psalm 8 holds out a vision of human destiny which has remained unfulfilled until Jesus entered into the promised glory as leader and representative of the many sons whom God intends will share it with Him (2: 5–18). Psalm 95 contains a prospect of entering God's rest, which the old order could not make effective because it had not the power to elicit the response of faith ('the message was not mixed with faith in those who heard it', 3–4). Psalm 110 introduces a new and eternal order of priesthood, to take the place of the ineffective Levitical order (5–7). Jeremiah 31: 31 ff., in speaking of a new covenant, explicitly declares the old one to be obsolescent (8–10). Even the saints of the Old Testament, who by faith laid hold on God's future and therefore on the presence of the invisible God, confessed that they were seeking a city which was not to become accessible until the coming of Christ (11–12).[68]

This notion that the Old Testament revelation was not only incomplete, but was known to be incomplete, is expressed more succinctly in 1 Peter. The salvation of which both goal and means were pre-ordained[69] 'was the theme which prophets pondered and explored . . . to whom it was disclosed that the benefit of their ministry was not for their own time but for yours' (1: 10–12). Part of that benefit is that scriptural expectation provides an appropriately evocative language to describe the Christian community (2: 41) and the implications of faith for the individual believer (2: 21–5).

Such evocative use of scriptural language is so all-pervasive in the Revelation as to leave no doubt that John shared the same view, both

[66] Only four of his many Old Testament quotations are actually from the prophets (cf. Westcott, *Hebrews* (London, 1892), 474).

[67] Contrast Paul, for whom the whole Old Testament is *nomos*.

[68] For a fuller statement of the scriptural argument of Hebrews, cf. Caird, 'Exegetical Method', 44 ff.

[69] For the efficient and final cause as two ways of saying the same thing, see below, p. 337, n. 106.

about the fulfilment of prophecy in Christ and about its source in the eternal purpose of God. By allusion, myth, and typology he teaches his readers how to interpret their experience in the light of an eternal pattern in the ordering of history. Their imminent martyrdom is the climax of the long war between the sovereign purpose of God and the worldly forces which resist that purpose—a war in which the Cross is the decisive victory.

2.6. THE OBEDIENCE OF CHRIST

C. H. Dodd's thesis that the early Church came to the Old Testament armed with 'a principle of selection and interpretation' had an important corollary. The process he envisaged was 'a piece of genuinely creative thinking', which must have been the product of an 'originating mind'. It manifestly did not originate with any of the New Testament writers, since all, Paul included, assumed it without debate.[70] Rather than speculate about the existence of some forgotten genius, Dodd suggests that we should accept the evidence of the Gospels that 'it was Jesus Christ himself who first directed the minds of his followers to certain parts of the scriptures as those in which they might find illumination upon the meaning of his mission and destiny'.[71]

We have seen this to be the burden of Mark in which Matthew and Luke concur. Jesus knew himself to be the agent of a divine purpose to which scripture provided the blueprint, and he allowed that purpose to determine his cause; 'The Son of Man goes as it is written of him' (Mark 14: 21). Jesus was nurtured in the scriptures and drew both inspiration and guidance from them. Nevertheless, the opposition of his enemies and the incomprehension of his closest friends, to which all three evangelists bear witness, prove that he found in the scriptures that which no one else had hitherto found. The synoptists thus confirm Dodd's description of Jesus' exegesis as creative. He brought to the Old Testament a knowledge of God which had been fostered by it, but was not wholly derived from it (Mark 8: 33; Matt. 11: 25–7; Luke 10: 21–2).

It is on this last point that the Fourth Evangelist concentrates. Jesus

---

[70] It would run counter to the tenor of modern scholarly opinion to suggest that, even if it was invented by Paul, it could have percolated through him to all other writers of the New Testament. It is sometimes said that Mark, Heb., or 1 Pet. were influenced by Paul; but this could hardly be said of Matt.

[71] *According to the Scriptures*, 110.

has come to do the will of the Father who sent him (John 4: 34; 5:
30; 6: 38 ff.), and he knows this will not merely because he comes
from God, but because he lives his earthly life in close association
with the Father. He is indeed like an apprentice in the Father's workshop. 'The Son can do nothing by himself: he does only what he sees
the Father doing; what the Father does, the Son does. For the Father
loves the Son, and shows him all his works' (5: 19–20). What is true
of his deeds is true also of his words: 'What I heard from him I report
to the world' (8: 26), 'I speak what I have been shown by my Father,
and you speak what you have been told by yours' (8: 38), 'I do not
speak on my own authority, but the Father who sent me has himself
imparted to me what to say and how to speak' (12: 49). Since the
Johannine Jesus makes free use of the Old Testament in his teaching,
we may take it that the interpretation of scripture is included in what
he has learnt from the Father. The scriptures bear witness to him,
but only in confirmation of truths derived from elsewhere; mere
searching of the scriptures could not of itself have produced such
insight (5: 39).

We have already noted that Paul only rarely makes a link between
God's plan of salvation and the interpretation of the Old Testament.
When we add to this that he makes even scantier reference to the
earthly life of Jesus, it is hardly surprising that his letters contribute
nothing to our present theme. Only at two points does he mention
Jesus' knowledge of God's purpose, once when he contrasts his obedience with the disobedience of Adam (Rom. 5: 19), and once when he
celebrates his obedience even to the point of death, and a criminal
death at that (Phil. 2: 8). Paul's insistence that the salvation revealed
in the gospel is 'apart from law' (Rom. 3: 21) excludes the possibility
that he is thinking of Christ's obedience to the Torah; what brought
Christ to the Cross was his obedience to the redemptive purpose of
God, in which he was destined to take the central part.

The same may be said of Christ's obedience in Hebrews 5: 8,
although the treatment of the theme is quite different from Paul's.
Christ 'learned obedience'; that is to say, as qualification for his high-
priestly office he had to explore and experience to the full what, in a
sinful world, obedience to God entails. At this point there is no doubt
that the author is commenting on the earthly career of Jesus, with
particular reference to Gethsemane. Jesus, like any other high priest,
had been 'taken from among men and appointed their representative
before God' (5: 1); and the office was conferred on him by God, who

said to him, 'You are my Son; today I have begotten you', and (in another place) 'You are a priest forever according to the order of Melchizedek' (5: 5–6). These two verses are correctly interpreted as formulae of appointment, and are taken to be addressed by God to Jesus at the outset of his earthly ministry. From this we may infer that the earlier citation of Psalm 2: 7 and the catena of quotations which it introduces (1: 5 ff.) are also intended to be taken as formulae of appointment. According to this author, the Old Testament supplied not only the framework of ideas within which Jesus understood his own vocation, but the very terms in which God appointed him to it. No doubt he was aware that the passages he quoted had been written 'in former times' (1: 1), and believed that they enshrined a purpose which had existed in the predestining will of God before all worlds (1: 2). But the eternal decree, attested by the prophetic voice of scripture, had been renewed when God 'brings His firstborn into the world' (1: 6). Scripture moreover supplied the terms in which Jesus responded to and accepted his appointment (2: 12–13), as becomes abundantly clear in a later chapter (10: 5–7):

> That is why, at his coming into the world,[72] he says:
>
> 'Sacrifice and offering you do not desire,
>   but you have prepared a body for me.
> Whole-offerings and sin-offerings you take no delight in.
> Then I said, "Here am I, as it is written of me in the scroll,
>   I have come, O God, to do your will." '

The commentary which follows this quotation shows that the will of God which Christ thus undertook to perform was the removal by his sacrificial death of that sin which debarred the whole human race from access to the presence of God. In this respect, then, Hebrews appears to stand closer than Paul to synoptic theology.

2.7. THE OPENING OF THE SCRIPTURES

All four evangelists agree that Jesus used the Old Testament in a manner which was shocking to his opponents and mystifying to his adherents. Paul adds, out of his own experience of hostility to the gospel, that a veil of insensitivity lies over the minds of those who hear

---

[72] 'At his coming into the world' is best taken not to refer to birth but to the beginning of the adult Jesus' ministry.

a reading from the old covenant, which prevents them from seeing the glory of God in the face of Jesus Christ (2 Cor. 3: 14; 4: 3–6). How then did the early Christians come to understand the Old Testament as Jesus himself had understood it? Luke's answer is that the risen Jesus instructed them (24: 27, 44); and, in all the outline from which we started, this is the one point at which he receives no support from others.

Paul claimed that his conversion was an encounter with the risen Christ (1 Cor. 9: 1; 15: 8), in which Christ took hold of him (Phil. 3: 12) and made him an apostle (Gal. 1: 1). Yet whenever he refers to it as revelation, the agent of revelation is not Christ but God. It was God who had shone in his heart to give the light of revelation (2 Cor. 4: 6), God who had revealed his Son 'in me' (Gal. 1: 6). Elsewhere Paul ascribes the knowledge of God's wisdom, 'His secret purpose framed from the very beginning to bring us to our full glory', to a revelation by God through His Spirit (1 Cor. 2: 7–10). But only in one passage is this knowledge explicitly related to the interpretation of scripture. In his contrast between the written code which brought death and the life-giving dispensation of the Spirit, he argues that just as Moses removed the veil from his face when he turned to the Lord, so the veil of incomprehension which lay over the old covenant is removed only by turning to 'the Lord', the Spirit (2 Cor. 3: 6–17).

In Ephesians 3: 1–5 we are told that Paul's knowledge of the mystery, the purpose of God expounded in the two previous chapters, came to him 'by revelation', and that a similar revelation has been made to apostles and prophets 'by the Spirit'. It is far from clear whether in the case of Paul the revelation is to be identified with his conversion or with a subsequent experience of inspired illumination; and whether in the case of the apostles and prophets the revelation came from Paul or independently of him, and, if the latter, whether one occasion is meant or several. What the passage does not envisage, however, is instruction of the apostles by Christ prior to the sending of the Spirit.

In the Fourth Gospel it is one of the functions of the Paraclete, the Spirit of truth, to take the words and deeds of Jesus and interpret them to the minds and hearts of believers (John 10: 13–15), and this interpretation entails an understanding of the witness borne to Jesus by the scriptures. In his account of the cleansing of the temple John tells us that after the Resurrection the disciples recalled the words of scripture which formed a commentary on what Jesus had said and done (2: 17–21); and in his account of the triumphal entry he states that at the time the disciples did not understand that Jesus was fulfilling a prophecy, but 'after he had been glorified they remembered that this had been written about him, and that this had happened to him' (12: 16). Only when Jesus was glorified could they receive the interpreter Spirit (7: 39).

The author of 2 Peter, probably the least visible member of our conference table,[73] argues that the experience of the disciples at the transfiguration confirmed the message of the prophets, but adds that no prophecy admits of private interpretation. The prophets in all their human frailty were enabled to speak the words of God because they were inspired by the Holy Spirit, and it follows that the readers of scripture also must be guided by the Spirit. 'But Israel had false prophets as well as true; and you likewise will have false teachers among you' (2: 1). Claims of inspiration, both ancient and modern, must be tested, and security against error can be provided only by the collective experience and wisdom of the community in which the Holy Spirit is at work (2 Pet. 1: 16–2: 1).

2.8. A PEOPLE PREPARED

According to Luke, Jesus came to a people among whom there was already an attitude of expectancy. The other evangelists confirm this by their occasional references to a popular hope in the coming of a Messiah or a quasi-Messianic figure such as 'the prophet' (Mark 6: 4–6; 8: 28; 10: 47; 11: 9–10; John 1: 20–3; 4: 25; 6: 14; 7: 52). All the evangelists agree that the hope of a national salvation, which is well attested in Jewish sources, was heightened by the preaching of the Baptist, even though his emphasis was more on judgement than on the deliverance to follow.

Outside the New Testament there is ample evidence that many elements in the Lucan scheme were not merely pre-Christian, but current in Jewish thought in the time of Christ. The notion that God is working out a purpose in history, and that history may legitimately be written in such a way as to bring out a particular aspect or interpretation of that purpose, is at least as old as the Deuteronomic edition of

---

[73] For recent treatments of 2 Peter and Jude, cf. R. J. Bauckham, *Jude, 2 Peter* (Waco, Tex., 1983); Kelly, *Epistles of Peter and Jude*; and J. I. Snyder, 'The Promise of His Coming: The Eschatology of 2 Peter', D.Theol. dissertation, Basel, 1986.

Judges with its cyclic pattern of election–disobedience–humiliation–salvation (Judg. 2: 16–19); and it is variously exemplified in many of the psalms (e.g. 75, 106) and by later writers from the Chronicler to Josephus, including Jesus ben Sira (Ecclus. 44–50), the author of Wisdom (Wisd. 16–19), and the author of the Qumran Habakkuk commentary.

That world history is under the control of the one God and that all nations are subject to His judgement is the common belief of all the prophets (e.g. Amos 1–2, 9: 7; Isa. 10: 5 ff.; Jer. 1: 10), but it is to Deutero-Isaiah that we must turn for the most elaborate and consecutive exposition of the theme. The prophet announces the coming of God in power to end Israel's bondage, reminding his hearers that, as Creator, God holds human destiny in the hollow of His hand. Then follows a series of challenges directed to the pagan gods to enter into debate with the God of Israel, each side stating its case and adducing witnesses to prove which is in control of world history (41: 1 ff., 21 ff.; 44: 7 ff.; 46: 20 ff.). The decisive evidence is to be the accurate prediction of the future, and it is Yahweh's contention that current events, and specifically the use of the conquering Cyrus, have been foretold by Him long ago, because he is the First and the Last, able to 'reveal the end from the beginning' (46: 10). Whatever may have been implied in previous prophetic oracles, this is the earliest explicit statement that the purpose which Yahweh is pursuing in the history of the human race, with Israel at its centre, is the purpose for which the world was created.

A more domestic application of this theme is found in the descriptions of a personified Wisdom. In Proverbs 8: 22 ff. Wisdom, who is depicted as sharing the work of the Creator as His companion or master-builder, is a personification not only of the skill and knowledge entailed in Creation, but also of its purpose. Jesus ben Sira goes further and identifies this Wisdom with the Torah (Ecclus. 24: 10 f., 23); and from that point it is but a small step to the rabbinic belief that the Torah lay on the knees of God before the Creation, i.e. that the world was created in order that there might be a community to keep the Torah or Wisdom (below, Chapter 8).

The apocalyptic writers were heirs to both these developments. The prophets had believed themselves to be God's spokesmen, through whom He communicated to Israel the secret purpose which He was currently implementing in their history (Amos 3: 7; Jer. 23: 18), but the horizon of their vision had rarely extended beyond the immediate historical crisis of their times. The apocalyptic writers understood the secret with which they were entrusted to be the secret of universal history. Some gave expression to this by representing world history in a stylized framework, as in the case of the Apocalypse of Weeks (1 Enoch 93: 1–10; 91: 11–17) and the Book of Jubilees; and in each case the revealed pattern in said to be predestined because it is written on the heavenly tablets (1 Enoch 93: 2; cf. 81: 2; Jub. 3: 9–11; 6: 30–2; 17: 25; 28: 6; 32: 9–10; 50: 13). In the visions of Daniel, which more nearly concern us, the five-part statue (2: 31–2) and the four monsters that rise from the cosmic sea (7: 2–8) represent a succession of world empires; and the author's purpose in portraying them is to assure the victims of persecution that Antiochus Epiphanes (represented by the clay feet and the little horn) is only the last in a series of tyrannical powers, that all who wield such power derive their authority from God (2: 37; 4: 25), that God has always deposed rulers who have abused their delegated authority (5: 23–31), and that in a coming act of divine judgement world dominion is to pass to the saints of the Most High (7: 22, 26–7). The device of pseudonymity, whereby a second-century-BC author attributes his work to a sixth-century prophet, whatever may have been the origin of the literary convention, has the theological effect of giving confidence that the current crisis in national affairs has been foreseen by the divine wisdom and is therefore, in spite of appearances to the contrary, under the control of a benign providence. The martyrs are to understand that the Babylonian captivity of Israel has never really ended, but that the ancient prophetic promises of restoration remain firm nevertheless in the secure foundation of God's eternal will (9: 24–7); and that their present tribulation is but a part of the cosmic battle between the armies of God and forces of a godless world ruler which is destined to end in the victory of God (10: 13–21). A similar effect has been achieved by the author of 1 Enoch 1–36, who has taken the biblical description of Enoch as one who 'walked with God' to mean that he kept company with angels who instructed him in the long-distance plans which God had 'not for this generation, but for a remote one which is to come' (1: 2); and by the author of the Ezra Apocalypse, who has transformed the cosmic sea of Dan. 7: 1 into a symbol for the inscrutable purposes of God (2 Esdr. 13: 52).

E. Stauffer[74] has argued that 'the world of apocalyptic ideas is the

---

[74] E. Stauffer, *New Testament Theology* (London, 1955), 2.

one in which the New Testament writers were really at home'. It is questionable whether he was right thus to isolate apocalyptic from the general history of Jewish intertestamental thought, since it is far from clear that it ever existed in separation from the legal and Wisdom traditions, whether as a literary genre, as a movement of thought, or as the literature of a sect. The apocalyptists are as zealous as any Pharisee for the commandments of the Law (e.g. 1 Enoch 5: 4; 2 Esdras 3: 36); indeed, it is precisely because of their fidelity to the Law that Daniel and his companions are persecuted by Nebuchadnez-zar and Darius, and a comparison with 1 and 2 Maccabees shows that their story is meant to be read as a parable of the fidelity of the resistance movement under Antiochus Epiphanes. But the apocalyptists also lay great emphasis on wisdom: Daniel is a man to whom God has given wisdom (2: 11; 5: 11), and it is the wise who in the end are to shine like the bright vault of heaven (12: 3). The Similitudes of Enoch portray Wisdom looking for a home among human beings (1 Enoch 42: 1–2; cf. Ecclus. 24: 7–12; Prov. 9: 1–6) and finding it only in the Elect One (1 Enoch 49: 1–3), who is thus enabled to utter the secret wisdom of the Lord of Spirits (51: 3). In order to record his visions for posterity Ezra has to drink the cup of heavenly wisdom, and the books he then writes for the benefit of future generations are entrusted to none but the wise (2 Esdras. 14: 39–48).

In defence of Stauffer, however, it must be added that he defined apocalyptic as 'the old biblical tradition'. He correctly saw that the main emphasis of the apocalyptic literature lies not in the expectation of an imminent end to the world, but in a theology of history, in which 'the main theme' is the dramatic conflict between the *civitas dei* and the *civitas diaboli*, from primitive times right through to the end,[75] and the eschatology is but the reverse side of primordiality, i.e. the principle that the later course of history is implicit in its beginning. It is at least coming to be generally recognized that eschatology, whether in the prophetic writings, the apocalyptic literature, or the New Testament, has less to do with imminence than with confidence in the ultimate triumph of the purposes of God. For eschatology arises out of a clash between faith and fact. Faith asserts that God's sovereignty is over all the earth, and that in the exercise of it he has called Israel to serve Him as His holy people. Fact retorts that the world is dominated by pagan nations which do not acknowledge God's sovereignty,

[75] Ibid. 19.

and that Israel has conspicuously failed to live up to the demands of holiness. Eschatology is a defiant manifesto which declares, in the face of all realistic denial, that what is now held to be true in the purposes of God will become true in the experiences of His people and His world. And New Testament eschatology is the claim that in ways hitherto imperfectly grasped God has now acted in fulfilment of His purpose.

3.

The Need of Salvation

3.1. THE UNIVERSALITY OF SIN

The New Testament was written by those who had entered on a new life of freedom and dignity, opened to them by the forgiveness of sins, and who believed that their experience was offered to all human beings as God's universal answer to the world's universal need. 'God has consigned all to disobedience, that he may have mercy on all' (Rom. 11: 32); 'All have sinned and fall short of the glory of God' (Rom. 3: 23); 'The whole world is in the power of the evil one' (1 John 5: 19); 'In these sacrifices there is a reminder of sin year after year' (Heb. 10: 3); 'If you then, who are evil, know how to give good gifts to your children . . .' (Luke 11: 13); 'I wept much that no one was found worthy to open the scroll or to look into it' (Rev. 5: 4). The universality of sin, explicitly stated by these writers, is implied by all: for the primitive creed, which all shared, was that 'Christ died for our sins'.[1] To accept the new life by faith was at the same time to renounce the old by repentance. The light of glory which illumined the present and future cast a correspondingly dark shadow over the past from which they had emerged and the environment from which they were distinguished by God's grace. To them and to all people God had spoken His redeeming word, and to deny the need for that redemption was to call God a liar (1 John 1: 10).

This belief in the moral bankruptcy of the human race is expressed in a rich and varied vocabulary, which frequently we find grouped together in an admonitory list.[2] Such groupings suggest that the

---

[1] 1 Cor. 15: 3; cf. Matt. 26: 28; Mark 10: 45; Luke 24: 47; John 1: 29; Acts 10: 43; Rom. 5: 8; Gal. 1: 4; Col. 1: 14; 1 Tim. 1: 15; Heb. 10: 12; 1 Pet. 1: 18; 2: 24; 3: 18; 1 John 1: 7; 2: 2; Rev. 1: 5; 7: 14.

[2] See, e.g. Mark 7: 21 ff.; Rom. 1: 29–31 (the longest); 1 Cor. 5: 11; 6: 9–10; Gal. 5: 19–21; Eph. 4: 17–31; Col. 3: 5–10; 1 Thess. 4: 3–6; 1 Tim. 1: 9–11; 2 Tim. 3: 2–4; 1 Pet. 2: 1; 4: 3–4; and Rev. 21: 8. It will be noted in these passages that the vices greatly outnumber the virtues.

teachers of the early Church followed the practice of Greek schools and Hellenistic synagogues, where morality was inculcated by the memorizing of similar lists of vices and the corresponding virtues. The Christian writers, in fact, were by no means the first to paint a gloomy picture of human morals and manners. The ancient world had no lack of mentors to instruct its ethical ignorance or of critics to convict it of sin. But there were three ways in which the coming of Jesus sharpened the sensitivity of his followers to the general depravity around them.

1. The life and character of Jesus established a new standard of human goodness. He was 'the Holy and Righteous One', he 'who knew no sin', the 'lamb without blemish or spot', he 'who committed no sin, nor was guile found on his lips', 'in every respect tempted as we are, yet without sinning', 'holy, blameless, unstained, separated from sinners'; 'in him there is no sin'; 'and in him there is no false-hood'.[3] As the prophet Isaiah was abashed into confession by the vision of God's holiness (Isa. 6: 1 ff.), so Peter had been constrained, not merely by the wonder of Christ's miraculous power but by the greater wonder of his person, to say, 'Depart from me, for I am a sinful man, O Lord' (Luke 5: 8); and Paul, having been won over from blind incredulity to adoring faith by 'the light of the knowledge of the glory of God in the face of Jesus Christ' (2 Cor. 4: 6), knew by the same light that he and all others were falling short of that glory (Rom. 3: 23).

2. In spite of the protest of Job, Judaism had never adequately discriminated between sin and its consequences. The two Hebrew words *ḥatta'th* and *'awōn* were both used to express three related concepts: the iniquity, the guilt incurred by it, and the penalty visited on it.[4] The result is that, even in some of the great penitential psalms, it is not clear whether the psalmist's confession is the genuine recognition of a specific fault or simply an assumption that, since God is just, the disaster must have been deserved. In the Gospels Jesus leaves no doubt that some suffering could be the direct result of sin (John 5: 14; Mark 2: 5), but rejects the book-keeping type of religion which held that temporal rewards and punishments were dispensed by God according to individual merit (Matt. 5: 45; Luke 13: 1–5; cf. John

---

[3] Acts 3: 14; 2 Cor. 5: 21; 1 Pet. 1: 19; 2: 22; Heb. 4: 15; 7: 26; 1 John 3: 5; John 7: 18.

[4] For a useful summary of Hebrew words for sin, cf. N. Snaith, *The Distinctive Ideas of the Old Testament* (New York, 1974), 60 ff.

9: 3).[5] He thus opened the way for a repentance which was honest self-appraisal without self-pity. 'It is frequently difficult to distinguish between the Psalmist's sense of guilt because of his consciousness of sin, and his sense of guilt as the consciousness of calamity.'[6]

3. Paul had no difficulty in discovering passages in the Old Testament to illustrate his own belief in the universality of sin.[7] But during the period between the Testaments this belief had undergone a considerable modification. The pious Jews could not help recognizing the gulf which separated their moral standards from those of the pagan world around them. The Hasidim and their successors, the Pharisees, came to regard themselves as the righteous, and classified as 'sinners' the pagans and the renegade Jews who had come to terms with paganism.[8] This mood of self-congratulation received its first blow from John the Baptist, whose baptism of repentance required of all Jews, as a condition of their enrolment in the Messianic people of God, the same confession of sins and ceremonial cleansing as they had been used to impose upon a Gentile who wished to become a proselyte. But for the gospel writers it was Jesus' accusations against the Pharisees that first laid bare the sins of respectability. Criticisms of the Pharisees bulk large in the recorded teaching of Jesus,[9] partly, no doubt, because they reflect the continuing antagonism between Church and Synagogue, but partly also because, of all his contemporaries, this group most needed to be convicted of sin if they were to enter the Kingdom of God by the narrow door of repentance. Tax collectors and harlots needed no such reminder (Matt. 21: 31). Simi-

[5] Cf. the remark sometimes attributed to T. W. Manson: 'Jesus was never concerned about the genesis of evil, only its exodus.'

[6] See C. G. Montefiore's Hibbert Lectures, *Lectures on the Origin and Growth of Religion* (London, 1892), 515.

[7] Rom. 2: 24; cf. Isa. 52: 5; Rom. 3: 10; cf. Ps. 14: 1–2; 5: 9; 32: 1–2; 140: 3; 10: 7; Isa. 59: 7–8; Ps. 36: 1; Rom. 4: 7–8.

[8] This view has been resoundingly rejected by E. P. Sanders in his two most substantive works on the subject, *Jesus and Judaism* (Philadelphia, 1984) and the aforementioned *Paul and Palestinian Judaism* (Philadelphia, 1977). Sanders tries to show that Palestinian Judaism was neither anti-Gentile nor legalistic, but understood the Law as something given to those within the Covenant; if they were to keep the Law, it was not as a means of salvation but of 'staying in' (*Paul and Palestinian Judaism*, 517). For a full discussion, cf. G. B. Caird's review of Sanders' *Paul* in *JTS* NS 29 (1978), 540 ff.

[9] Cf. B. Lindars, 'Jesus and the Pharisees', in E. Bammel, C. K. Barrett, and W. D. Davies (eds.), *Donum Gentilicium* (Oxford, 1978), 51 ff.; R. J. Cassidy, *Jesus, Politics and Society: A Study of Luke's Gospel* (New York, 1978), and *Political Issues in Luke's Gospel* (New York, 1983); and below, pp. 386–393.

larly, when Paul sets out to convict the whole human race of sin, he can take for granted the corruption of the Gentile world, but he has to argue the inclusion of his fellow Jews within the general indictment (Rom. 2: 1–3: 20).[10]

3.2. THE UNIVERSALITY OF JUDGEMENT

Universal sin has its universal nemesis, here and hereafter. This is expressed in the New Testament in four ways. (1) The full and final retribution comes with God's Last Judgement (cf. e.g. Matt. 25: 31–45; Rev. 20: 11–15; 2 Cor. 5: 10). (2) Because Jesus, like the God he comes to reveal, can say 'I am the Alpha and Omega, the first and the last, the beginning and the end' (Rev. 22: 13), all that belongs to the final denouement of history has already become a present reality in him. (3) The judgement which he perfectly embodies has other partial, precursory embodiments in God's providential ordering of history. (4) Besides these outward forms of requital there is the inward effect of sin on the character of him or her who commits it, which, since it is ordained by God, must be reckoned as part of His judgement. As it is the nature of eschatology that the End constantly interpenetrates and informs the present, these various modes of retribution are never kept wholly separate by the New Testament, nor is it always certain which of them is in the forefront of a writer's mind. But for the sake of clarity it is worthwhile to attempt to distinguish them as far as possible.

1. According to Hebrews 6: 2, eternal judgement was one of the first principles of elementary Christian doctrine, and the consensus of the New Testament confirms this verdict.[11] John the Baptist, in proclaiming the imminence of the coming wrath, had compared it to the winnowing shovel in the hand of the farmer, ready to separate the wheat from the chaff—the one destined for the granary, the other for the bonfire (Matt. 3: 7–12; Luke 3: 7–17); and his preaching had let loose a flood of eschatological excitement which had lasted throughout

---

[10] So the prophet Amos, who in his first two chapters speaks of the sins of the other nations, but then finally rounds upon Israel, as opposed to the author of the Wisdom of Solomon, who in the last nine chapters provides a great nationalist vaunting of Israel and its history in comparison with the sins of the Gentiles.

[11] Mark 9: 43–8; Matt. 5: 21 f; Luke 10: 14; 11: 31–2; 12: 15; John 5: 28–9; Acts 10: 42; Rom. 2: 5–11; 2 Thess. 2: 5–10; 2 Tim. 4: 8; Heb. 10: 27; James 2: 13; 3: 1; 1 Pet. 1: 17; 4: 5; 2 Pet. 3: 7; John 4: 17; Jude 6; Rev. 20: 11–15.

the lifetime of Jesus and his disciples, who adopted John's vision of judgement with little alteration. Jesus spoke of the destiny of the impenitent as destruction (Matt. 7: 13) or as Gehenna (Matt. 5: 22).[12] Elsewhere in the New Testament we are given two good theological reasons for this belief. The first is that, when God's rule is consummated and His purpose complete, nothing can be admitted to His Kingdom which is a contradiction of His holiness, so that whatever then remains recalcitrant to His will can only be destroyed. This is the purpose of the lake of fire, which is the second death (Rev. 20: 14; 21: 8), of the last battle in which the enemies of God are overthrown (1 Cor. 15: 24–8), and of the earthquake which plays so prominent a part in apocalyptic vision,[13] because it 'indicates the removal of what is shaken in order that what cannot be shaken may remain' (Heb. 12: 27). An even more profound reason is that life flows from God, so that those who by their unbelief have turned their backs on him or by their conduct have disqualified themselves from access to him have, in effect, chosen 'eternal destruction and exclusion from the presence of the Lord' (2 Thess. 1: 9).[14]

Belief in a final judgement was accepted without question until the beginning of the second century, when the antinomian adversaries of the author of 2 Peter dismissed it as a 'cleverly devised myth' (1: 16). The author undertakes to prove the reality of the judgement by three proofs: that the apostles at the transfiguration saw a preview of the advent glory in which Christ would come to judge the world (1: 16–21); that God's past judgements of the ungodly were a matter of historical record (2: 4–10); and that the heretics bore, in their enslavement to vicious habits, the evidence of their own condemnation (2: 10–22). It is interesting to note that these three proofs correspond to the three ways in which we have claimed that the ultimate judgement is anticipated in the present.

[12] Cf. also Matt. 10: 28; Mark 9: 43, 45, 47; Luke 12: 5. *Ge Hinnom* ('the Valley of Hinnom') was the dump where the refuse of Jerusalem was consumed by fire. Hinnom was originally the site of Tophet—the altar (Isa. 30: 33) where parents burned their children as offerings to Molech and Baal (2 Chron. 28: 3; 33: 6).

[13] Cf. e.g. Hag. 2: 6; Jub. 1: 29; 4 Ezra 10: 25 ff.; 2 Baruch 59: 3; 1 Enoch 45: 1, and 1QH 3. 13 ff. O. Betz, 'The Eschatological Interpretation of the Sinai Tradition in Qumran and in the New Testament', *RQ* 6 (1967), 89 ff. gives a useful survey of the evidence.

[14] Cf. in particular S. G. F. Brandon, *The Judgment of the Dead* (London 1967); H. Bietenhard, 'Hell', etc., *NIDNTT* ii., 205 ff.; B. Reicke, *The Disobedient Spirits and Christian Baptism* (Copenhagen, 1946).

2. It is in the Fourth Gospel that we find the most explicit statements that the ultimate judgement has entered history in the person of Jesus. The present reality of that which in essence belongs to the End is expressed by the Johannine formula, 'the hour is coming and now is' (John 5: 25).[15] This eschatological hour is itself divided into two moments, for within the ministry of Jesus there is an hour which is 'not yet come' until it comes with the Cross.[16] There is accordingly a twofold judgement, the one brought about by the Incarnation, the other by the Cross. In his ministry Jesus is the Son of Man, to whom the Father has already entrusted the execution of judgement, by which human beings are assigned either to the resurrection of life or to the resurrection of judgement (5: 27–9). Judgement, it is true, is the result rather than the purpose of his coming (3: 17; 8: 15; 12: 47). In him the light of the eternal *logos* has entered the world, in order that men and women might 'not walk in the darkness but have the light of life' (8: 12); and they are judged by the response they made to this illumination (1: 4; 3: 18–19; 12: 46–50). Thus the first impression John conveys is that through the words and works of Jesus men and women are being sorted out into two classes, believers who already possess eternal life and unbelievers on whom the wrath of God rests. But as the process of sifting continues, the one class becomes smaller, and the other larger: Jesus is first left with the Twelve, doubtful even of their allegiance (6: 67), and is then deserted by them so that in the end he stands alone (16: 31); and the whole world, including the disciples, stands under the judgement of having rejected the light or of having received it with only a half-hearted faith. It is at this point that Jesus' hour arrives, when he must realize the judgement of God, not by executing it on others, but by bearing it himself. If their condition is such that they cannot come to the light and so join him where he abides in the bosom of the Father, he can join them where they are, under the judgement of God and in the death which is the wages of sin. 'Unless a grain of wheat falls into the earth and dies, it remains alone; but if it dies, it bears much fruit . . . now is the judgment of this world, now shall the ruler of this world be cast out; and I, when I am lifted up from the earth, will draw all men to myself' (12: 24, 31 f.). By accepting a death in which he could be identified with sinful

---

[15] *Not yet come*: 2: 4; 4: 21; 5: 25, 28; 7: 30; 8: 20. *Come*: 12: 23, 27; 13: 1; 16: 32; 17: 1 (5: 25 and 16: 32 contain both in paradoxical form). For parallels to the synoptic tradition, cf. S. Smalley, *John: Evangelist and Interpreter* (London, 1984) 188 n. 182.

[16] On this understanding of John's 'hour', see below, p. 79 f.

men and women, Jesus drew all into the unity of his own person, so that the judgement by light, under which the world stood utterly condemned, became instead the means of the world's salvation; and Satan, who appeared to have won a total victory, entitling him to claim possession of all unbelieving humanity, suffered instead a total defeat.

This theme, so intricately worked out in the Fourth Gospel, is not absent from the rest of the New Testament. In a lament over Jerusalem recorded by Luke, Jesus warns the city of her coming doom 'because you did not know the day of your visitation' (Luke 19: 44). We saw above that in the Old Testament the word 'visit' is used to describe the personal intervention of God, either to save or to punish; and the coming of Jesus is God's visit in both senses. To those who receive him, God 'has visited and redeemed his people' (1: 68), but those who will not have him as Saviour must have him as Judge. With this passage we may compare the many others in which Jesus is said to declare that people are judged by their response to the gospel, and that on their decision depends their eternal destiny.[17] This is a point made more explicitly in Hebrews 2: 2, where every transgression under the old covenant received a just retribution; 'How much less shall we escape if we neglect so great a salvation?'

The idea that the death of Christ was a judgement in which the powers of evil were condemned is found in Romans 8: 3, where the words 'he condemned sin in the flesh' mean, not that God declared sin to be wrong, but that he gave judgement against sin the tyrant and in favour of those who had been held in sin's bondage.

3. For Paul the Law was given to the Jews and conscience to the Gentiles, 'so that every mouth may be stopped, and the whole world may be held accountable to God' (Rom. 3: 19; cf. 2: 15; 1 John 3: 20). In 2 Corinthians 3: 7 ff. the Law is 'the ministration of condemnation and death'. It pronounces its curse on all who break it (Gal. 3: 10). Above all civil government has been instituted by God in order that criminals may be brought to justice, so that the magistrate may actually be described as an ordained minister of God 'to execute his wrath[18] on the wrong-doer' (Rom. 13: 1–7). In 1 Peter the Christians

---

[17] Matt. 10: 40 = Luke 10: 16; Matt. 10: 32 f = Luke 9: 26; Matt. 12: 39–42 = Luke 11: 29–32; Matt. 11: 21–4 = Luke 10: 13–15.

[18] Cf. E. Bammel, 'Romans 13', in E. Bammel and C. F. D. Moule (eds.), *Jesus and the Politics of His Day* (Cambridge, 1984), 365; C. K. Barrett, 'The New Testament Doctrine of Church and State', *New Testament Essays* (London, 1972), 1 ff.; M. Borg, 'A New Context for Romans 13', *NTS* 19 (1972–3), 205 ff.; F. F. Bruce, 'Paul and

of Asia Minor are commanded to be subject to the Emperor and his representatives, not only in the exercise of their God-given function of suppressing wrong and encouraging the right, but also when they exceed their proper jurisdiction by persecuting the innocent; for the fiery trial which the Church is to experience at the hands of the government is to be regarded as the onset of the Last Judgment, a judgement beginning 'with the household of God' (2: 13–14; 4: 12–17). The siege of Jerusalem and its destruction by Roman armies are described in the Lucan apocalypse as 'days of vengeance' and 'wrath upon this people'; and, although these days are undoubtedly regarded as a part of the eschatological future, they are brought about by historic circumstances and are expected to continue indefinitely, 'until the times of the Gentiles are fulfilled' (21: 20–4). The fall of Babylon, which from the heavenly point of view is accomplished by an angel pouring out the bowl of the wrath of God, has also to be worked out by earthly causes through the agency of the ten kings of the East who are expected to invade the Empire under the leadership of Nero redivivus (Rev. 16: 12–21; 17: 12, 16–17).

4. It remains to examine the psychological hardening and blinding effect which sin has upon the human personality, by which God has decreed that sin should become its own punishment. Three times in his analysis of Gentile unholiness Paul uses the expression 'God gave them up' (*paredōken*: Rom. 1: 24, 26, 28) to indicate that the catalogue of vices constitutes not the disease but only the symptoms of an idolatry that has repudiated the truth of God in favour of the futile thoughts and blind heart of paganism (Rom. 1: 18–25). If the human race should become corrupt, insisting on a truant independence, it shall therefore reap in corruption the consequences of its choice. Sometimes the same idea is presented in a more starkly Semitic form. In Exodus we read that Pharoah hardened his heart against the appeals of Moses, but also that God hardened Pharaoh's heart (Exod. 8: 15, 32; 9: 34); because it is God's decree that every refusal of His word shall make a person in future less able to hear and less able to obey. Similarly Isaiah is told, 'Make the heart of this people fat, and their ears heavy, and shut their eyes; lest they see with their eyes, and hear with their ears, and understand with their hearts, and turn and be healed' (Isa. 6: 10). The prophet's message was a call to repentance; but a rebellious

the Powers That Be', *BJRL* 66 (1983–4), 78 ff.; and R. Walker, *Studie zu Römer 13: 1–7* (Munich, 1966).

nation which rejected that call would hereby become confirmed in its rebellion, and the expected result of the preaching is therefore described as its (secondary) intention. Jesus is reported to have quoted this verse as a prediction of the outcome of his own mission, and there is no adequate reason to doubt the authenticity of the saying (Mark 4: 11 f.).[19] As an explanation of the use of parables the saying is indeed difficult, since it implies that the parabolic teaching of Jesus was more mysterious than his other teaching. But the word *parabolē* here does not mean 'parable' but 'riddle'. The pericope appears to have been misplaced by an editor who failed to realize that the word had more than one meaning. Jesus recognized that his preaching, like that of Isaiah, would either lead his hearers to repentance or harden them in their hostility (as it actually did), and in Semitic fashion accepted as the purpose of his mission its foreseen result. 'For judgement I came into this world that those who do not see may see, and that those who see may become blind' (John 9: 39). Paul also saw that a temporary hardening had come on a part of Israel, because, having heard the gospel, they had disbelieved it; but he has no difficulty in ascribing this result also to the predestining decree of God (Rom. 9: 18; 10: 16–21; 11: 25). Those who believe a lie, whether Jews or Gentiles, become progressively less able to recognize the truth: 'Therefore God sends upon them a strong delusion, to make them believe what is false, so that all may be condemned who did not believe the truth but had pleasure in unrighteousness' (2 Thess. 2: 11).

This spiritual condition is frequently described as death. From one point of view, as we have seen, death can be regarded as a physical event, the final annihilating verdict on sin pronounced by one who, 'after He has killed, has power to cast into Gehenna' (Luke 12: 5). But this final verdict only sets the seal on a long process. Those who embark on 'the way . . . that leads to destruction' must not object if they find themselves arriving at the only possible destination (Matt. 7: 13). 'Whatever one sows, that he will also reap. For he who sows to his own flesh will from the flesh reap corruption' (Gal. 6: 7–8). There are those 'whose end is destruction' (Phil. 3: 19), because 'their end will correspond to their deeds' (2 Cor. 11: 15). Such people are already 'dead in trespasses and sins' (Eph. 2:1); they are 'the perishing' (1 Cor.

---

[19] The genuineness of the saying is enhanced by the clear moral problem that Jesus' parabolic teaching intentionally blinded people (cf. Matthew's softened version (13: 15), in which the unbelief is simply a statement of fact).

1: 18; 2 Cor. 2: 15; 2 Thess. 2: 10) who will in the end receive death as wages (Rom. 3: 21, 23)—a recompense deserved and automatic. The idea that death came into the world through sin (Rom. 5: 12) presents a difficulty to the modern mind, which cannot accept as easily as Paul could the Jewish belief that Adam before the Fall was immortal (Wisd. 2: 23–4; 2 Esdras 3: 7; Bar. 17: 3; 23: 4). But the point which Paul is so rightly emphasizing is that for the human race, with all its immortal longings, made in God's image to enjoy everlasting fellowship with Him, death can never be a merely biological event. Sin separates the human race from God and death is the final severance. This is why 'the sting of death is sin' (1 Cor. 15: 56). The horror of death is not to die but to 'die in your sins' (John 8: 21, 74). Sin and death together are the negation of all that human beings, in their heart of hearts, know themselves to be, and under this double tyranny (Rom. 5: 14, 17, 21; 6: 12, 14) they live in anxiety, fear, and despair.

Two passages have been reserved for special treatment because it is a matter of dispute where they fit into the fourfold scheme. At the end of a vituperative attack on his fellow Jews—possibly the most anti-Jewish thing he ever wrote—Paul exclaims: 'The wrath has come upon them to the uttermost' (1 Thess. 2: 16). Those who have assumed that these words must refer to the destruction of Jerusalem have taken them to be evidence that the Epistle was written after AD 70 as an interpolation introduced *vaticinia ex eventu*, i.e. as a prediction employing a prophetic aorist to indicate the certainty of fulfilment. Others, on the equally fallacious assumption that the wrath of God in the New Testament is always future, have regarded them as a prophetic reference to the Last Judgement. But if we accept the verse as an authentic part of a letter written in approximately AD 50 and construe the past tense as a statement of fact, there are still two possibilities open to us. Paul may have been thinking either of the process of hardening and blinding that had come upon the Jews through their opposition to the gospel, or of the series of savage executions and massacres with which the Roman procurators had sought to control the rising tide of Jewish nationalism in the six years since the death of Agrippa.[20] On the whole the second interpretation is to be preferred;

---

[20] A useful treatment of the numerous massacres under the procurators (Fadus, Alexander, Comanus, Felix, Festus, Albinus, and Florus) is provided by R. H. Pfeiffer, *History of New Testament Times* (New York, 1949), 38–40, and S. Perowne, *The Later Herods* (London, 1958), 84–97.

for Paul is accusing the Jews, not of an inner disloyalty to be punished
by blindness and corruption of character, but of violence against the
Church repaid in the same coin by the violence of Rome.

When Paul declares that 'the wrath of God is revealed from heaven
against all ungodliness and wickedness of men' (Rom. 1: 18), the
natural interpretation of his words is that the wrath is identical with
the process of hardening which he goes on to delineate in the following
paragraphs. God reveals His wrath by condemning sinners to endure
the consequences of their own folly. The argument then is that, even
with the prospect of preaching in the capital city of the Empire, Paul
is not ashamed of the gospel, since in it God has let loose His saving
power into a world which desperately needs it, inasmuch as all people,
Jew and Gentile alike, are under wrath, under the judgement which
sentences them to imprisonment within their own wills and passions.
This interpretation, however, has been challenged on three grounds:

1. Sanday and Headlam[21] claim that the wrath in the New Testament
is always eschatological and translate the present tense (*apokaluptetai*)
as if it were a future. It is, of course, true that in Rom. 2: 5 Paul
speaks of a 'day of wrath when God's righteous judgment will be
revealed'. But the context there is quite against an exclusively eschatological concept of 'wrath'. For the Jews are accused of storing up wrath
against the day of wrath. All persons are debtors, to whom God is
regularly presenting a statement of their account, which he is always
prepared to write off on the ground of repentance, while the impenitent
are allowed to run up a long bill against the final day of reckoning.
God's wrath is a present reality which acquires a cumulative force
unless it is constantly converted into grace by repentence and forgiveness.

2. Others[22] have pointed to the parallelism between vv. 17 and 18
of Romans 1 and have asserted that the term *apokaluptetai* must have
the same value in each case, that Paul meant to say that the wrath of

---

[21] W. Sanday and A. C. Headlam, *A Critical and Exegetical Commentary on the Epistle to
the Romans* (Edinburgh, 1902⁵), ad loc.

[22] Cf. e.g. E. Käsemann, *Commentary on Romans* (Grand Rapids, 1980), 35 ('The
present tense [of *apokaluptetai*] has the same force as in v. 17. It relates to something
already present although not yet recognised, to something which only now comes to
light along with the gospel . . .') D. Guthrie, *New Testament Theology*, 102 n. 72; C. E. B.
Cranfield, *A Critical and Exegetical Commentary on the Epistle to the Romans* (Edinburgh,
1975), i. 109 f.; and C. K. Barrett, *A Commentary on the Epistle to the Romans* (New
York, 1957), 33, all make the same, or similar, points.

God as well as His righteousness was revealed only in the dispensation of the gospel. The wrath-process was indeed invisibly operative in the affairs of the human race ever since the Fall, but it only became visible to the eyes of faith, illumined by the gospel. On closer examination, however, this parallelism breaks down. For when Paul says that 'the righteousness of God is revealed', he does not mean that God's righteous character is disclosed as an eternal truth to the inquiring mind of the faithful, but that God's saving power has actively broken in upon the human scene. 'To be revealed' is the equivalent of 'to come into operation'; and one can hardly claim that a wrath process connected with the Fall has come into operation with the gospel.

3. K. E. Kirk[23] has a more radical form of the same argument, based on the two passages (Rom. 2: 4; 3: 25) in which God's attitude to sin before the coming of Christ is described as *anochē* (forbearance) and *paresis* (handing over). God's apparent indifference to sin so impugned His justice that he needed to indicate by the death of Christ His own righteous character and his wrath against sin. He cannot be said to have revealed his wrath against sin at the very time when he was allowing sin to pass unchecked. But Kirk's interpretation is open to the same objection as the previous one: it gives an inadequate meaning to *apokaluptetai*. It also ignores the nature of the divine wrath as Paul defines it in Romans 1. For the wrath of God is revealed not in a punishment which halts sinners in their tracks (that would certainly be a contradiction of *paresis*), but in a nemesis which fastens upon them the consequences of their error. The *paresis* which does nothing to halt the course of sin is identical with the wrath which compels the sinner to pursue his or her own way to its calamitous end.[24]

Dodd[25] has called attention to the wrath of God in the New Testament as an impersonal force, 'an inevitable process of cause and effect in a moral universe', with men and women 'receiving in their own persons the due penalty for their error' (Rom. 1: 27). For Dodd this process is built into the moral fabric of life and operates through natural agencies like disease and psychological hardening, and through

[23] K. E. Kirk, *The Epistle to the Romans in the Revised Version* (Oxford, 1937), 34 ff.

[24] Kirk has, however, drawn attention to a most important point of Pauline theology; that the wrath of God against sin is insufficient to establish His righteousness. God's righteousness must be more than a retributive justice, which leaves men and women defeated and sin victorious.

[25] Cf. C. H. Dodd, *The Epistle of Paul to the Romans* (New York, 1932) 22 ff.

human institutions like the state. Men and women can be called 'by nature children of wrath' (Eph. 2: 3), not because they are destined to wrath at the Last Day, still less because they are predestined to wrath—for the children of wrath include those who now have been saved by grace—but because the wrath-process has become a constituent element in their existence. Yet it is possible to overestimate the impersonal value of the wrath; for though the system of retribution may function as an inexorable and automatic law, the Jewish Law is of God's making and must be an expression of His mind and will. Paul does not hesitate to follow the impersonal expression—'the wrath of God is revealed' (1: 18)—with one which implies the personal activity of God—'God gave them up' (1: 24, 26, 28). Similarly, in Revelation the impersonal and the personal lie side by side. Babylon is twice said to have 'made all nature drink the wine of the wrath of her fornication' (14: 8; 18: 3; cf. 17: 2), where wrath is almost the equivalent of retribution. Yet elsewhere the wrath is the wrath of God, and once it is the wrath of the Lamb (6: 16).

The theological status of the wrath is part of a larger and perennial problem—how to reconcile God's will that all people should live with His will that sin should not go unpunished. 'It is not the will of my Father who is in heaven that one of these little ones should perish' (Matt. 18: 14). 'Unless you repent, you will all likewise perish' (Luke 13: 3, 5). 'God our Saviour who desires all to be saved and to come to the knowledge of the truth' (1 Tim. 2: 4). 'The Lord is not slow about His promise as some count slowness, but is forbearing to you, not wishing that any should perish, but that all should reach repentance' (2 Pet. 3: 9). Theologians in every age have felt that God's reaction to sin, since it is called forth by the human race's abuse of its freedom, cannot be as fundamental to God's character as His eternal purpose of grace. 'His anger is but for a moment; his favour is for a lifetime' (Ps. 30: 5). Philo believed that in His gracious dealings with the human race God works in a direct and personal manner, but delegates to the agency of His angelic powers the functions of government and punishment—'such duties as are not appropriate to God himself'.[26] With this we may compare the rabbinic saying, 'When God is angry, he says to the sinner who has provoked him, "you have caused me to take up a trade that is not mine",'[27] and Luther's exegesis

---

[26] Philo, *de Conf. Ling.* 36.
[27] Tahuma, quoted in C. G. Montefiore and H. Loewe, *A Rabbinic Anthology* (1960), 57.

of Isaiah 28: 21, in which God's 'alien work' is his wrath, behind which He hides His true nature of love.[28] Some of the rabbis attempted to resolve this problem by imagining conversations between the attribute of justice and the attribute of mercy, and there is a more elaborate medieval equivalent in the conversation of the four daughters of God, attributed (probably falsely) to St Bernard. Perhaps the most successful of all statements of the paradox is John of Damascus's distinction between the antecedent will or pleasure of God that all people should be saved and come to His Kingdom and His consequent will or permission that sinners should suffer punishment.

The New Testament writers were undoubtedly aware of the problem which has called forth such multifarious solutions. Paul, for example, draws a striking contrast between death which is the wages of sin, the automatic and ineluctable consequence, and eternal life which is the free gift of the Father to His children (Rom. 6: 23). We must, however, be quite clear what is meant by calling the wrath an impersonal process. It is to deny, first, that God experiences anger as an emotion and particularly that, when Jesus took upon himself the consequences of others' sins, God was 'angry' with him; and, secondly, that the punishment of sin is as fundamentally a part of God's purpose for the human race as the things He has prepared for those who love Him. But it is not to deny that the holy God sets His face uncompromisingly against evil.

3.3. THE EXPERIENCE OF SIN

What sin means to those who commit it may be seen most clearly reflected in the language of redemption: for justification, consecration, reconciliation, and redemption imply a guilt to be cancelled, a stain to be erased, an enmity to be dispelled, and a servitude to be abolished. It need hardly be added that these four metaphors do not connote four different experiences, but the four ways in which the one experience impresses itself, with varying emphasis, on different people.

1. *Guilt.* A sense of guilt involves the acceptance of responsibility for an action and an admission that the action was wrong; and without a sense of guilt there can be no sense of sin, neither can there be repentance and forgiveness. Before expounding the gospel Paul is at

---

[28] 'Alienum est opus eius ab eo, ut operetur opus suum' (Luther: *Lectures on Romans*, trans. and ed. W. Pauck (London, 1961), 241).

pains to prove, not merely that all are sinners, but that all are without excuse (Rom. 1: 20; 2: 1). For to be without excuse is to be eligible for pardon. He who forgives cannot excuse. To excuse is to deny either the offender's responsibility or the seriousness of the offence; to forgive is to do full justice to both and still to cancel the guilt. There is one passage where Paul appears to make excuses by denying his responsibility: 'It is no longer I that do it, but sin which dwells within me' (Rom. 7: 17–20). But what he is there describing is the paralysing effect of a guilty conscience. He could never have experienced sin as an inescapable bondage, unless at the same time his mind was assenting to the rightness of the Law which told him he was guilty. The fact that one cannot pay the debt does not absolve him or her from the obligation to do so. All are in the end answerable to the God who says, 'Turn in the account of your stewardship' (Luke 16: 2; cf. Rom. 14: 2; Heb. 13: 7; 1 Pet. 4: 5); and Jesus depicted the guilt of sin under the figure of the insolvent debtor whose debt was too large ever to be liquidated except by the magnanimity of the creditor (Matt. 6: 12; 18: 23–35; Luke 7: 41–3; 11: 4).

There are, of course, degrees of responsibility (Luke 12: 45–8). There is the sin of ignorance for which I am responsible because I should have known (Luke 23: 34). There is the sin of habit for which I am responsible because I ought to have resisted the original onset of temptation (Jas. 1: 14–15). And there are corporate sins for which I am responsible unless I actively dissociate myself from my environment (2 Cor. 6: 17; Rev. 18: 4) and disown my inheritance (Luke 11: 47–51).

2. *Stain.* Deep in the heart of the human race there is an instinctive aversion to dirt, disease, and death, and in almost every language the words which convey this abhorrence are used metaphorically to express and evoke a similar loathing for sin, and especially for the sins of sensuality and violence. The transference of this instinctive repugnance from the physical to the moral sphere is an important part of ethical education, for there is no deterrent so powerful as the horror of being unclean. The Jewish laws of cleanness and uncleanness, though they may have hindered the full concentration of this instinct upon moral offences, served nevertheless to keep it vividly alive, so that biblical language is rich in terms expressing a sense of contamination and a need for cleansing, which required only the clear moral insight of the recorded teaching of Jesus to direct them to their proper usage (Mark 7: 18–23). The unclean in Jewish Law was that which

disqualified one from participation in worship, so that he or she was in effect debarred from access to God; and the institution of sacrifice, at least in later Judaism, was largely concerned with the removal of this barrier (1 Sam. 6: 4; 1 Cor. 6: 9–10; Eph. 5: 5; Rev. 21: 27).[29] It is for this reason that the New Testament so constantly employs the language of sacrifice to declare the benefits of the Cross. A sense of pollution, whether of body or of spirit, implies an essential sanctity;[30] and the imperative need of those whom sin has defiled is that which can cleanse the conscience from dead works (Heb. 9: 14).

3. *Enmity.* Sin is also seen as an interruption of the human race's proper fellowship with God when it is called enmity or alienation (Rom. 5: 10; 8: 7; Col. 1: 21; Eph. 4: 18; John 15: 23 f.; Jas. 4: 4). 'No one can serve two masters; for either he will hate the one and love the other, or he will be devoted to the one and despise the other. You cannot serve God and mammon' (Matt. 6: 24 = Luke 16: 13; cf. 1 John 2: 17). This saying of Jesus is an example of a common Semitic idiom. The Semitic mind habitually thought in extremes and could tolerate no half-shades of compromise between white and black, good and evil, truth and falsehood, love and hate. To love the one was always to hate the other. If Jacob loved Rachel more than Leah, then Leah was hated (Gen. 29: 30 f.). Loving God above all earthly joys means hating father and mother (Luke 14: 26; cf. Matt. 10: 37). In a comparison of mundane attachments this hyperbole may seem extravagant, but nothing less is adequate to express the absolute demand of God for love and allegiance. 'Thou shalt love the Lord thy God'; and the one who withholds this tribute of loyalty and affection is a rebel. 'The mind that is set on the flesh is hostile to God, it does not submit to God's law' (Rom. 8: 7). 'Friendship with the world is enmity with God' (Jas. 4: 4). This permanent truth is accentuated by the coming of Jesus; for with him the Kingdom of God has broken in upon the citadel of Satan and an era has begun in which there can be no neutrality. 'He who is not with me is against me; and he who does not gather with me scatters' (Luke 11: 23); to be against Jesus is to be against God (cf. Acts 5: 39). 'He who hates me hates my Father also . . . now they have seen and hated both me and my Father' (John 15: 23–4).

---

[29] Cf. Kenneth Grayston, '*Hilaskesthai* and Related Words in the LXX', *NTS* 27 (1981), 640 ff., who shows that this is the real point at issue—the removal of contamination.

[30] See Lev. 17: 10–12, where the sanctity of all life is preserved by the taboo on blood, in so far as blood = life (but see below, p. 151, n. 28).

4. *Slavery*. 'Everyone who commits sin is a slave' (John 8: 34; cf.
Titus 3: 3; 2 Pet. 5: 18).[31] The moral disablement attendant upon sin
had received inadequate recognition in Greek and Jewish thought.
The Greeks were familiar enough with the idea of enslavement to
passion,[32] but tended to regard passion as the root of all evil, over-
looking the subtler and more radical sins of the spirit. The Hebrew
root *'bd* ('slave, servant') is never used in the metaphorical sense of
slavery to sin or passion, because it emphasized the service performed,
willingly or unwillingly, for a master, rather than the servitude involved.
The annual ceremony of the Passover, with its memory of liberation
from Egyptian bondage, was interpreted as a foreshadowing both of
God's constant providence in rescuing His people from trouble and
death, and of the last eschatological deliverence from oppression and
injustice; but only once in the Old Testament do we read of redemption from iniquity (Ps. 130: 8). The eighth-century prophets assumed
that it was within the capacity, even if it was not within the intention,
of Israel to respond to their calls to repentance; and the deeper insight
of Jeremiah (13: 23; 17: 9) which led him to conclude that the old
covenant had failed (31: 31–4), though it received a powerful echo
from Ezekiel (36: 25–32), made no lasting impression on the established religion, in which Israel's ability to keep the Torah was never
seriously questioned. Even John the Baptist, whose reverberating summons to repentance was matched only by his contemporaries' failure
to grasp their complete moral incapacity, belonged to the old order.[33]
It would be Jesus who first penetrated to the depths of the
heart-sickness which Jeremiah had discovered (below, Chapters 9
and 10).

3.4. THE ESSENCE OF SIN

Thus far we have dealt with sin as a universal fact, which brings in
its train a universal nemesis, and which in varying forms induces in
the human heart a sense of need. We have yet to ask what is the
essential nature of sin, seeing that it is not to be identified either with
moral degeneracy or spiritual malaise.

---

[31] *Hamartias* should probably be omitted with DbSyrSin and Clem. Alex.

[32] Plato, *Phdr.* 238e; Xenophon, *Mem.* 1. 6. 8.

[33] Cf. Luke 16: 16, where the phrase *mechri Iōanou* almost certainly means 'up to and
including John'; i.e. John is the last and greatest of the prophets of the old period.

1. For Paul the basic sin of the human race is 'holding the truth down in unrighteousness' (Rom. 1: 18). The context makes it clear that Paul is not talking merely about an intellectual atheism or agnosticism, but of a suppression of the truth which comes out in conduct.[34] The truth he has in mind is the truth about God, the truth which is written in the fabric of the universe, and which requires from human beings obedience and gratitude, which are the tribute of dependence. Paul is not in the least concerned to establish or to deny the possibility of natural theology, attainable by rational argument, independently of revelation. All theories on this subject, as Nygren[35] has shown, involve a deistic conception of God. What Paul affirms is an objective revelation of God, which the human race in fact has always suppressed. God's deity and power are inscribed, like an artist's signature, upon His handiwork; His decree that those who break the moral law shall suffer for it is built into the structures of life; and in conscience men and women have a faculty capable of apprehending the truth (1: 20, 32; 2: 15–16). All human beings in fact possess a knowledge of God and of His Law (1: 21, 32), but it has been thrust down into the recesses of their mind, so that only fitfully and in isolated cases does conscience guide them into right conduct and a true appraisal of their own innocence or guilt. In general, they have 'exchanged the truth of God for a lie' (1: 25); for the easiest way to evade the moral demands of God is either to deny His existence or to substitute for Him the figments of an idolatrous imagination. In all this Paul is thinking primarily of the Gentile world, for it was a Jewish axiom that 'the devising of idols was the beginning of fornication, and the invention of them the corruption of life' (Wisd. 14: 12); the futility of pagan thought and the degradation of pagan morals sprang alike from the great pagan lie, which they were even prepared to justify by intellectual arguments (*suneudokousin*, 1: 32).

The startling innovation in Paul's analysis of sin is that he turned the Jewish criticism of the Gentile falsehood against the Jews themselves. For Paul the Jew there was a lie at the root of the Jewish religion, which he had first lived and then seen through. But to Paul the Christian the Law also had, in the purposes of the God who gave it, some legitimate functions:

---

[34] Just as in the Old Testament the truth is not something to which one merely gives assent, but something one does (cf. Pss. 17 and 53).

[35] A. Nygren, *Commentary on Romans* (London, 1952), ad loc.

(1) After God's promise to Abraham, which embodied God's fundamental purpose of grace, the Law of Moses 'was added because
of transgressions' (Gal. 3: 17–19), to place Israel's life under
the restraint of discipline until the promise could be fulfilled in
Christ;

(2) 'Through the Law comes knowledge of sin' (Rom. 3: 20);

(3) 'Law came in to increase the trespass' (Rom. 5: 26), to exacer-
bate the human race's moral bankruptcy by converting ignorant
sin into knowing and wilful sin and so adding to the human
burden the incubus of a guilty conscience.[36]

Thus the Law was never meant to be God's final word to sinful
humanity. But Paul could remember how, as a Pharisee, he had prided
himself on possessing in the Law the whole counsel of God (Rom. 2:
17–20; Gal. 1: 14), and that pride had blinded him to the fuller and final
revelation of God in Jesus Christ. Like the Israelites in the wilderness
who had asked Moses to cover with a veil the fading glory on his face,
because they could not endure to contemplate the transience of the
covenant which it symbolized, he had refused to entertain the idea that
the Torah could be superseded; and it had become a veil over his heart,
by which Satan, 'the god of this world', had prevented him from seeing
the glory of God in the face of Jesus Christ (2 Cor. 3: 7–4: 6). Thinking
that through the Torah he had access to God, he had actually been so
ignorant of God as to fail to recognize His presence in the person of His
Son. His confidence in the Law had not been trust in God, but self-
confidence in his own ability to keep the commandments and to be found
blameless by their standards (Phil. 3: 6); and the righteousness he had
so diligently pursued had not been God's righteousness, freely bestowed
on men and women of faith, but a self-righteousness which is impervious
to the grace of God (Rom. 10: 1–3).

Thus the sins of Jew and Gentile alike can be traced to the same
source—the lie which refuses to acknowledge God as God. For God
is He upon whom all else depends, and the only path of life open to
human beings lies through the faith which is an acknowledgment of
utter dependence. To deny that dependence, either by substituting
for God other objects of worship or by attempting to satisfy God by

---

[36] This intended result of the Law is not to be confused with the unintended result
described in Rom. 7: 14, where the commandment actually becomes an incitement to
commit the sin it forbids—a process of distortion which Paul is careful to distinguish
from the true purpose of the Law.

one's own moral effort and merit, is to exchange the truth of God for a lie: 'Whatever is not of faith is sin' (Rom. 14: 23). Of both Jew and Gentile it can be said that 'God sends upon them a strong delusion, to make them believe what is false, so that all may be condemned who did not believe the truth but had pleasure in unrighteousness' (2 Thess. 2: 11).

The same conception of sin is prominent in the Johannine literature:

Why do you not understand what I say? It is because you cannot bear my word. You are of your father the Devil, and your will is to do your father's desires. He was a murderer from the beginning, and has nothing to do with the truth, because there is no truth in him. When he lies, he speaks according to his own nature, for he is a liar and the father of lies. But, because I tell you the truth, you do not believe me . . . He who is of God hears the words of God; the reason why you do not hear them is that you are not of God (John 8: 43–7).

Satan was a murderer from the beginning because, through the inherent falsehood of his nature, he was incapable of grasping the truth about God and told lies about Him, which brought death to Adam and Eve. The Jewish unbelief and antagonism to Jesus, culminating in a plot against his life, have betrayed a similar falsehood in the depths of their being. Ignorant of the truth of God, they fail to recognize it when they hear it from the lips of Jesus and see it embodied in his life. To those who have ears to hear, the word of God carries its own credentials, and everyone ought to have enough acquaintance with God to recognize its self-authenticating truth. Thus the Jews by their hostility to Jesus are confessing that they have 'exchanged the truth of God for a lie'. For the same reason in the Synoptic Gospels Jesus calls the sign-seekers 'an evil and adulterous generation' (Matt. 12: 39 = Luke 11: 29 = Mark 8: 12); an Israel that had remained loyal to her covenant vows would not have required proof of the divine origin of Jesus' message.

In 1 John we find the lie taking a specific form within the Christian fellowship. 'Who is the liar but he who denies that Jesus is the Christ? This is the Antichrist, he who denies the Father and the Son' (2: 22). The Gnostic antagonists of John, who have denied that the heavenly Christ can be identified with the human Jesus, upon whom he had temporarily descended, are deceived not only about the person of Jesus but about the nature of God. God is love (4: 15), but what this means can be apprehended only by those who have seen the divine love spelt out in human terms in the life and, above all, in the death of Jesus (3: 16, 4: 9). To deny that the self-sacrificing love manifested by the Cross was God's love is to admit a complete ignorance of God; to deny the Son is to deny the Father also (cf. John 8: 61). But this denial has ethical consequences: 'If anyone says "I love God" and hates his brother, he is a liar' (4: 20). Even the grudging of this world's goods to a brother in need discloses a heart unacquainted with love, and therefore with God (3: 17; 2: 4). For to know God is to know love with an intimacy that makes it the controlling spirit of life.

In the Revelation deception is the principal characteristic of the Dragon, 'the deceiver of the whole world' (12: 9), and of his earthly representatives, the Beast and the Harlot. The Beast claims human worship by being at every point a parody of divine truth; its title—'it was and is not and is to come'—is a travesty of the name of God (17: 8; cf. 1: 8); the head which received a mortal wound and yet lived is a caricature of the death and resurrection of Christ (13: 3; 17:11); its mark is an imitation of the Christian's sealing (13: 16; cf. 7: 3). So, too, the Harlot, with her worldly finery, is a parody of the other woman, clothed with the sun and crowned with the stars, who represents the Church. She is called a harlot because she has seduced men and women from the worship of God to the worship of luxury and wealth and 'corrupted the earth with her fornication' (19: 2). Throughout the book we are forcefully reminded by one symbol after another that evil wins assent only by presenting itself in the attractive vesture of good, and that 'Satan disguises himself as an angel of light' (2 Cor. 11: 14). In a world created by God evil must derive its existence and power from the corruption and distortion of original goodness; and this is the deception which underlies all sin.

2. From another point of view sin can be depicted as the human race's failure to be what God intended. 'All have sinned and are losing (or falling short of) God's glory' (Rom. 3: 23). According to a rabbinic legend Adam and Eve in the Garden of Eden had reflected in their faces the radiance of God, their outward aspect thus symbolizing the inner reflection of His holiness and love.[37] For to be made in God's image is to be a mirror to His perfection. When they sinned and were expelled from His presence, they were like mirrors turned from the light; the glory faded from their faces, as the innocence went out of their souls.

---

[37] For references cf. in general J. D. G. Dunn, *Christology in the Making* (London, 1980), 306 n. 15.

out of their souls. Sin is more than doing wrong acts: it is the loss of a perfection God meant the human race to have, a coming short of the highest standard of which it is capable. The full extent of the loss was apparent to those who, like Paul, had seen in Christ the image and glory of God (2 Cor. 4: 6) and who, under the influence of his Spirit, had begun to recapture the lost reflection (2 Cor. 3: 18).

This idea is expanded in many different ways by the various writers of the New Testament. In Mark, Peter is severely taken to task because 'you are not thinking the thoughts of God but the thoughts of men' (Mark 8: 33); for human beings are to think God's thoughts after Him, loving what He loves and willing what He wills. God 'called us to His own glory and excellence' in order to 'become partakers of His divine nature'; and this divine nature—though the phrase seems to smack of Greek metaphysics—can be attained only by the moral effort of those 'who have turned their backs on the corruption that is in the world because of passion' and seek to supplement 'faith with virtue, and virtue with knowledge, and knowledge with self-control, and self-control with steadfastness, and steadfastness with godliness, and godliness with brotherly affection, and brotherly affection with love' (2 Pet. 1: 3–7). In the Fourth Gospel the scene of human life has two levels, the heavenly and the earthly, *ta anō* and *ta katō*, and sin is to set the affections on *ta katō*. Men and women must, indeed, live in the world below, since they are *sarx* and can belong to the world above, the world of *pneuma*, only by the second birth (3: 3–6). But though they are in the world, they do not have to be of the world (8: 23; 15: 19; 17: 14, 16). To be of the world (*ek tou kosmou, en tōn katō*) is to be thoroughly at home in the world, to have one's horizons bounded by its concerns, to have one's aspirations limited by its satisfactions; it is to see only the things of earth and not through them to the heavenly realities of which they are the sacramental symbols (3: 1–12), to work for the food that perishes and not for that which endures to eternal life (6: 27), to love one's mortal life (*psuchē*) instead of rendering it up in sacrifice to God that it may be transmuted into life eternal (*zōē*, 12: 25), to seek the glory of human recognition rather than the glory of being united in love to the eternal God (5: 41–4). Paul makes use of a similar distinction between the realms of flesh and spirit. To live in the flesh is the common lot of all humanity, shared by Christ himself; but to live according to the flesh, to set the mind on the flesh, to do the works of the flesh (Rom. 8: 5–8; Gal. 5: 16–21), is to fall short of the glory of God.

In no book of the New Testament is this conception of sin as a failure to attain an appointed destiny more vividly worked out than in Hebrews. The author reminds his readers that according to Psalm 8 God made the human race a little lower than the angels, but crowned it (in His predestining counsels) with glory and honour, putting all things in subjection under its feet. The author's comment is that the human race has not in fact secured this position of pre-eminence, but that Jesus, crowned through his sufferings with glory and honour, has fulfilled the human destiny, and so has become the pioneer of salvation, leading the many to the glory which on their own account they had failed to achieve (2: 5–10). The Israelites in the wilderness failed through unbelief to enter into God's promised rest, and today, when the promise is still open, the same failure remains possible (3: 12–4: 11). The recipients of the letter are censured for having retained their childish faith instead of advancing to the *teleiotēs*, the maturity of Christian character (5: 11–14). The old covenant is said to have failed because it could not give to men and women that maturity or perfection which comes only through personal access to the inner presence of God (7: 11; 10: 1). When life is conceived as a pilgrimage to the city whose maker and builder is God, and the heroes of faith are people like Abraham, who went out not knowing where he was going, who refused to find a permanent home amid the things that are seen and temporal, who was prepared to sacrifice the son in whom all his paternal hopes and religious aspirations were concentrated, that he might receive him back by a better resurrection (11: 8–14), then virtue can be no static excellence, but only a courageous pressing forward to the goal of faith (6: 1; 12: 1–2); and the one great sin is to shrink back into destruction (10: 39).

3.5. THE THREEFOLD ADAM

In Pauline theology the archetypal sin is the sin of Adam. It is not easy to do justice to the complexity of Paul's thought on this point, since under the one term Adam he includes three related concepts which the modern theologian would wish to distinguish. Adam is the primeval human being, the progenitor of the human race, who grasped at equality with God (Phil. 2: 6; cf. Gen. 3: 5) by becoming the arbiter of his own standards of good and evil. Some modern scholars have assumed that the contrast in the Philippians passage is not between

Christ and Adam but between Christ and Satan.[38] But there are two insuperable objections to this theory. The first is that the pre-cosmic rebellion and fall of Satan, so familiar to readers of John Milton, plays little part in Jewish thinking about the problem of evil and none at all in biblical theology, where Satan, even when he is regarded as the enemy of God, still retains his original function as the one of the Sons of God charged with the function of public prosecutor in the divine law court; and in that guise he has his place in heaven until he is ejected by the atoning work of Christ.[39] The second objection is that the whole balance of Philippians 2: 5–11 depends on the reversal of Adam's conduct by the incarnation: Adam, being created in human form, grasped at equality with God; Christ, 'though he was in the form of God', stooped to accept equality with the human race. Christ cannot be said to have reversed the conduct of Satan: it was the human form he took, not the Satanic. Adam is thus Everyone, the typical human being whose story is constantly re-enacted, as all in fact make it their own—'as sin came into the world through one man and death through sin, so death spread to all because all sinned' (Rom. 5: 12). Adam is the sum total of humanity, bound together throughout the world and throughout the ages by the ties of racial solidarity, sharing a common nature and a corporate sinfulness. Thus human beings are involved in the sin of Adam in three ways, which we may call inclusion, imitation, and implication. By the concept of corporate personality the Hebrews thought of human personality as including that of one's posterity, so that the one name Jacob or Israel could be used both for the patriarch and for the nation which reckoned its descent from him, and Levi could be said to have paid tithes to Melchizedek because he was present in the loins of his ancestor Abraham (Heb. 7: 10); and in this sense the whole of humanity was included in the sinful act of their common ancestor. We all are our own Adam, committing sins which are 'like the transgression of Adam' (Rom. 5: 14), i.e. infringements of a known commandment; and all are therefore imitators of Adam. But the sin of the human race is something more than a series of broken commandments: it is a contagion which permeates the characters of individuals and the institutions of society, so that all, even

---

[38] See J. M. Furness, 'Behind the Philippians Hymn', *Exp.T.*79 (1967–8), 178 ff., who discusses, in addition to Satan, the other figures (Alexander, Heracles, Nero, Caligula) who have been thought to be the basis of the comparison.

[39] See below, pp. 107–109, together with G. B. Caird, *Principalities and Powers* (Oxford, 1956), ch. 2.

against their will, are implicated both in the general taint and in those corporate sins for which no one individually, but jointly everyone, is responsible. By imitation all add their quota to the common burden, and by implication all share the weight of it.

Like the Hebrew *adam*, the English 'man' has a variety of meanings, whether positive or negative; but, having inherited from the Greeks our analytical ways of thought, we endeavour to keep these meanings distinct and are suspicious of equivocation. But Hebrew thought proceeds not by analysis but by association. H. W. Robinson[40] has pointed out that along with the concept of corporate personality went a fluidity of thought which enabled the Hebrew writer to move freely from the individual as the embodiment of the group to the group as the extension of the individual. In his treatment of Adam Paul passes quite naturally from one meaning to another. Thus in Romans 7: 7–20 he describes in the first person, but in terms reminiscent of Genesis 3, the moral defeat of a divided personality. Just as the serpent took the commandment against eating from the tree of knowledge[41] and twisted it into a temptation which kindled into life and activity Adam's latent impulse to disobedience, so that he became subject to death, so in Paul's experience sin had converted the commandment against covetousness into a base of operations for a frontal—and fatal—assault upon his innocence. The prohibition had put ideas into his head which would not otherwise have occurred to him. The passage might be described as the autobiography of Adam, written by one who knows that he has been his own Adam, and who is aware that in some sense he is writing the autobiography of all members of the larger Adam,

[40] Cf. H. Wheeler Robinson, *The Christian Doctrine of Man* (Edinburgh, 1926³), 27 ff. More recently Robinson's 'mystical' idea of corporate personality has been challenged by J. W. Rogerson, 'The Hebrew Conception of Corporate Personality: A Re-examination', *JTS* NS 21 (1970), 1 ff., and J. R. Porter, 'The Legal Aspect of the Concept of Corporate Personality', *VT* 15 (1965), 361 ff.

[41] The Hebrew verb *yada*, 'to know', denotes three types of knowledge: (1) factual information, (2) intimate personal experience, and (3) determinative authority. Thus 'to know good and evil' could mean (1) to know what things are good and what things are evil, a knowledge which, so far from being a sin, is positively required of human beings (Deut. 1: 39; Isa. 7: 16); (2) A *first-hand* experiential acquaintance with good and evil, as when Paul speaks of knowing sin (Rom. 7: 7; 2 Cor. 5: 21; cf. Isa. 47: 8); and (3) the right to determine what things are good and what are evil (cf. Job 38: 33; Jer. 1: 5; Amos 3: 2; and Ezek. 37: 2), where the prophet's answer 'Lord, you know' really means 'Lord, that is for you to say' (cf. also Mark 13: 32; Matt. 11: 27). It is clear that only in the third sense is the knowledge of good and evil a divine prerogative which men and women ought not to usurp.

humanity. The personal reminiscence is unmistakable but because of the wider reference, both to the first Adam and to the universal Adam, it is not easy to say with certainty to what part of Paul's life the experience of frustration belongs. It is conceivable that Paul the Pharisee had suppressed a dissatisfaction with the Torah, which finally broke out, first in his vehemence against the Church, then in the violent upheaval of his conversion; but, in view of what he says elsewhere (Phil. 3: 6; Gal. 1: 14), it is hardly credible that at that time he would have acknowledged the existence in his life of a paralysing tension between the Law which he revered with his mind and the Law which controlled his actions. On the other hand, he cannot be describing his Christian experience, since the normative Christian life is expounded in the following chapter in quite other terms. The most probable explanation is that Paul the Christian is here laying bare, in the light of his new faith, the true nature of his old life under the Torah, and finding it typical of the existence of unregenerate humanity, from which, even now, he is delivered from day to day only by the indwelling Spirit of Christ.[42] (It has been suggested that there is a similar, implicit use of Adam typology in Romans 1, where the lapse of the Gentile world into sin is portrayed in terminology drawn to a large extent from Genesis 1.)[43]

To describe our common humanity Paul uses also a number of synonyms for Adam. He calls unredeemed human nature 'the old man' (Rom. 6: 6; Col. 3: 9; Eph. 4: 22) and 'the natural man' (*psuchikos*— 1 Cor. 2: 14; 15: 44, 46). The first of these terms is more derogatory than the second, always denoting a sinful life that must be renounced and not just outgrown. This use of *psuchikos*, on the other hand, is plainly derived from Genesis 2: 7, where God is said to have breathed life into Adam's dust so that he became a living *psuchē*. The *psuchikos*

---

[42] Rom. 7: 7–20 remains a subject of considerable discussion, with three views predominating as to its meaning: (1) A minority of interpreters have seen the passage describing the divided self of Paul the Christian who is caught between two worlds. (2) The majority of commentators have seen Rom. 7: 7–25 as Paul's retrospective understanding of his pre-conversion state in which 'the divided I' indicates his objective (but not necessarily subjective) misery outside of Christ. (3) Still others have maintained that Paul is in no way describing his own experience. For (1), cf. Cranfield, *Romans*, i, ad loc.; for (2) cf. W. D. Davies, *Paul and Rabbinic Judaism* (London, 1955) 24 ff.; J. Knox, *Chapters in a Life of Paul* (New York, 1950), 13 f.; and J. D. G. Dunn, *Romans 1–8* (Waco, Tex., 1988), 374 ff.; and for (3) cf. R. Bultmann, 'Romans 7 and the Anthropology of Paul', in S. M. Ogden (ed.), *Existence and Faith* (New York, 1960), 147 ff.

[43] Cf. M. D. Hooker, 'Adam in Romans 1', *NTS* 6 (1959–60), 297 ff.

anthrōpos is the living, sentient being that God created. But because God created Adam, not that he might live and die in his creatureliness, but that he might become a *pneumatikos*, capable of participating in the life to come, to remain merely *psuchikos* is to be earthbound and worldly. 'The spirit of man is the Lord's lamp' (Prov. 20: 27): and the *psuchikos* is one whose wick has never been touched by the divine flame (cf. John 12: 25; Jas. 3: 15; Jude 19). There is a similar ambivalence about Paul's use of the word 'flesh'. It is important to recognize that in his use of this word Paul is not employing the Greek distinction between body and soul, the material and the immaterial, but the Hebraic distinction between flesh which is the essence of human existence and spirit which is the being of God (Isa. 31: 3). 'The flesh' describes not humanity's material substance, but its psycho-physical organism; so that to be 'in the flesh' is exactly the same as to be 'in Adam'. But to live according to the flesh is to set one's mind on the flesh, to do the deeds of the flesh, to be controlled by worldly and selfish ends. There is no room here for any distinction between carnal sins and spiritual sins, for all are comprehended within the one term *sarx*. 'Now the works of the flesh are plain: immorality, impurity, licentiousness, idolatry, sorcery, enmity, strife, jealousy, anger, selfishness, dissension, party spirit, envy, drunkenness, carousing, and the like' (Gal. 5: 19–21).

It is characteristic of Paul's ethical teaching that the one who is 'under the Law', whether that law be the Torah or a pagan system of legalism, is nevertheless *psuchikos*. The mind may assent to the goodness of the Law, but the law of sin in the flesh is the controlling influence of life (Rom. 7: 21–3). To make people good was something that 'the Law, weakened by the flesh, could not do' (Rom. 8: 3). Ostensibly, it offered individuals a choice between life and death, the blessing and the curse: but because all had in fact sinned, the Law had become a dispensation of condemnation and death (2 Cor. 3: 7–11). One must live either by the Law or by the Spirit, and the one precludes the other (Rom. 8: 5–17; cf. Gal. 3–6).

3.6. THE SIN OF THE WORLD

Life in Adam involves also a contagion of sinfulness and a corporate guilt. 'Bad company ruins good morals' (1 Cor. 15: 33; cf. 5: 9; 2 Cor. 6: 14–7: 1). This is an idea to which the Synoptic Gospels contain a variety of allusions. Jesus speak of the leaven of the Pharisees and of

Herod (Mark 8: 15). He pronounces the sternest of warnings against the sin of causing others to sin: 'It is impossible that occasions for stumbling should not come; but woe to the one through whom they come!' (Luke 17: 1-2; Matt. 18: 6-7; Mark 9: 42).

In the Revelation the corporate sin of the human race is delineated under the figures of the Great City, the Beast, and the Harlot. In the forefront of his mind John, no doubt, identified such symbols with the Rome of his own day, with Domitian claiming the title *Dominus et Deus* and threatening persecution against those who denied him worship. But just because he uses symbols does not indicate that his meaning is exhausted by their immediate application. When he tells us that the Great City 'is allegorically called Sodom and Egypt, where their Lord was crucified', he is making Rome the legatee of all earth's sensuality since the destruction of the cities of the Plain, of all tyranny since Israel's Egyptian bondage, of an unbelief to equal that of Jerusalem (11: 8). The Beast has qualities drawn from each of the four beasts of Daniel's vision, the symbols of the four kingdoms under which Israel had suffered oppression, because it was the epitome of all worldly empires (13: 1-2). The Harlot is the quintessence of seductive luxury, and in her hostility to the people of God she is heir to the name of Babylon the Great (17: 4-5). The city, in fact, is not merely Rome, but Vanity Fair, the city of this world, which John believed had attained its final and most complete embodiment in the Roman Empire. About Rome John was partially mistaken, having failed, understandably, to appreciate her residual strength and grandeur; but we can learn much from his analysis of the spiritual, or unspiritual, realities which to this day underlie worldly dominion.

All that John the Divine depicts under his triple symbolism is by John the Evangelist designated 'the world'. John does not share Paul's concern for the physical universe; his world is the world of men and women, the organized system of life into which they are born (6: 14; 9: 5; 13: 1; 16: 21; 17: 11, 13). This world is God's creation (17: 5, 24), and, in spite of its essential transience (cf. 1 John 2: 15 ff.), it has been constantly irradiated by the divine light which men and women had only to apprehend in order to be given 'the right to become children of God' (1: 13). Their failure to receive the light and their preoccupation with earthly concerns has transformed the world into a system organized in neglect or defiance of God: 'The world knew him not' (1: 10; 17: 25). It has become in short, 'this world' (8: 23; 11: 9; 12: 25, 31; 13: 1; 16: 11; 18: 36), and those who are 'of this world' betray their affinities by their inability to recognize God in the words and works of his Son and to receive the Spirit of Truth (14: 17, 22). Out of the world Jesus chooses his disciples, and the world hates them as it has hated him (7: 7; 14: 27; 15: 18–19; 17: 14, 16). Yet the world remains throughout the object of the Father's redemptive love (3: 16) and, beyond judgement, the beneficiary of the Son's self-giving (4: 42; 12: 31–2; 17: 23).

3.7. PRINCIPALITIES AND POWERS

The institutional and even cosmic character of evil is presupposed in Paul's doctrine of angelic powers.[44] In its natural state the human race lives in bondage not only to sin, death, and the Law, but to a host of angelic beings, whose varied nomenclature indicates that all in common have been invested by God with a species of authority over the created order, though somehow the authority becomes corrupt and demonic. These powers include the guardians of the pagan state, the mediators of the Torah, and the angels who preside over the national order—the heavenly representatives of civil, religious, and natural law.

The theory that God had appointed an angelic guardian over every nation was Judaism's final solution to the problem of pagan religion (Deut. 32: 8–9).[45] Having attempted first to identify pagan gods with Yahweh and then to treat them as nonentities, the Jewish nation at last settled on a belief which denied their divinity but affirmed their existence and power. The gods were angels to whom the one true God had delegated His authority, so that His sovereign power, which He exercised directly and personally over Israel, the people who knew and acknowledged Him, was administered indirectly and impersonally over the rest of the world, where He was unknown and unheeded. But because these national angels had accepted the idolatrous worship of their subjects and had acquiesced in their immoralities and injus-

[44] A. Bandstra, *The Law and the Elements of the World* (Kampen, 1964); Caird, *Principalities and Powers*; W. Carr, *Angels and Principalities* (New York, 1981); H. Schlier, *Principalities and Powers in the New Testament* (New York, 1961); and W. Wink, *Naming the Powers* (Philadelphia, 1984), *Unmasking the Powers* (Philadelphia, 1986), and *Engaging the Powers* (Philadelphia, 1992).

[45] Cf. Deut. 32: 8 f. which the MT reads as, 'He fixed the borders of the peoples according to the number of the sons of Israel', a corruption of the text which originally read 'according to the number of the sons of God' (cf. Caird, *Principalities and Powers*, 5 n. 1).

tices, their rule had become a despotism which distorted, without obliterating, their divine commission, and from which men and women needed to be delivered into the freedom God had designed for them. Paul refers to these rulers in three different passages of 1 Corinthians. The 'rulers of this age, who crucified the Lord of glory' in ignorance of the divine wisdom, which had decreed that through the Cross they should be reduced to impotence, were not Pilate, Caiaphas, and Herod, but the angelic powers that stand behind the thrones of princes (2: 6–8); none of the earthly rulers could be said to have lost their authority because of their part in the Crucifixion, nor could they, at the time when Paul was writing, be described as *katargoumenoi* ('coming to nothing'); but both statements are elsewhere made about the spiritual powers (e.g. Col. 2: 15; 1 Cor. 15: 24). The angels over whom members of the Church are eventually to sit in judgement are those who preside over the administration of pagan justice, and into whose lawcourts the Corinthian Christians have been bringing their trivial quarrels, thereby belying their union with him who is to judge the world (6: 3). The angels to whom Christian women are asked to display deference by not appearing in public without a veil are those charged with the maintenance of the social order (11: 10).

Up to this point Paul stands firmly within the tradition in which he was reared. There are points in his epistles, however, which, though they have been thought capable of a milder interpretation, are best taken as evidence that he included among the demonic powers the angelic guardians and mediators of the Torah. For him, Jewish and Gentile Christians alike lived in servile obedience to the *stoicheia*, until Christ redeemed them, whether Jew or Gentile, from under the Law. He might be paraphrased, 'You (Gentiles), who were formerly enslaved to beings whom you erroneously supposed to be gods, are now wishing to impose upon yourselves certain regulations of the Jewish Torah; but in doing this you would be subjecting yourselves again to the very *stoicheia* from whose authority you have been delivered' (Gal. 4: 8 ff). The obvious deduction from this argument is that, in the case of the Gentiles, the *stoicheia* are to be identified with the astral gods of their former religion. Paul could call the polytheism of the Graeco-Roman world a regime of law only because in the centuries before Christ it had given a hospitable reception to the astrology of the Orient, which had transformed its hitherto capricious pantheon into an 'army of unalterable law'. His assumption that the Gentile Christians who wanted to be under the Torah were seeking to return to the very bondage from which they had been liberated is therefore a sure indication that he is using *stoicheia* in its astrological sense. But the Jews, too, had lived under the *stoicheia*, and in their case these must have been either the angelic guardians of the Torah or the Torah itself, who, like the pagan gods, exercised a derivative and secondary authority, which had become corrupt because it had been exalted into a place of primary and absolute importance. In Colossians Paul accuses a heretical group of living *kata ta stoicheia tou kosmou kai ou kata Christon* (2: 8). It is hardly adequate here to say that the *stoicheia* are the elementary principles of the human condition mentioned immediately before; rather they are rivals of Christ who are threatening to usurp the loyalty of his followers. For in the ensuing argument Paul seeks to demonstrate the folly of these heretics by reminding them that Christ is the head of every angelic rule and authority and that he has asserted his headship in the Cross, in which at one and the same time he has invalidated the legal bond of the Torah, with its sentence of death upon the convicted sinner, and has defeated the principalities and powers. In virtue of his victory Christians may be said with him to have died out from under the *stoicheia*. The *stoicheia* are, in fact, identified with the principalities and powers, i.e. the angelic representatives of the old legalism. It is not necessary to suppose, as some scholars have done,[46] that the heretics had worked out an elaborate Gnostic system, of the kind later denounced by Irenaeus, in which Christ occupied a place in a hierarchy of divine aeons or emanations which together constituted the *plērōma* or fullness of deity. Paul's language in this passage is not drawn from the vocabulary of heresy, but from his own theology; and the heretics may have been greatly surprised to read his description of their beliefs. All we are entitled to say about them is that they had adopted a religious asceticism, including elements from the Jewish ceremonial law (circumcision, sabbath and new moons, food laws). Paul accuses them of angel worship, not because they have established an idolatrous cult (he could hardly have treated them as continuing members of the Christian community in that case), but because all asceticism is a contempt for God's creative work, so that, whether they realize it or not, they have diverted to the angels of the Torah the worship due only to the Creator.

---

[46] For a succinct discussion of this view, cf. Caird, *Paul's Letters from Prison*, 160 ff. A fresh airing of the problem is provided by C. E. Arnold, *Ephesians: Power and Magic* (Cambridge, 1989).

The angels of Jewish and pagan law had also a relation to the natural order. This was clearly true of the astral deities; but there was a parallel belief, native to Israelite religion, that the stars were angels, the host of heaven assembled round the throne of God, and that the powers of nature were His ministering spirits.[47] A more important belief, attested both in the Old Testament and in later Jewish litera-ture, was that God had set Adam in authority over the whole creation, so that, when he sinned, the creation, deprived of its proper govern-ment, fell into anarchy and demonic control, from which it would be redeemed only by the coming of the Messiah.[48] Paul had thus inherited his belief that the whole creation was subjected to futility not through any fault of its own, but because God had determined that it should reach its proper perfection only under the lordship of the human race; and he was prepared to lay the world's bondage to corruption at the door of those principalities and powers which dominated the unredeemed life of men and women.

It is commonly assumed that the belief in the world's bondage to angelic powers is distinctively Pauline, and there can be no doubt that he developed it to its fullest expression. But there are many indications that the early Church as a whole shared his belief in the cosmic implications of the fall of Adam. Psalms 2, 8, and 110 were all freely used in the primitive preaching as Messianic *testimonia*, and all, thus interpreted, speak of the Messiah's triumph over the enemies of God. It is therefore unnecessary to imagine that 1 Peter 3: 22 ('who has gone into heaven and is at the right hand of God, with angels, authori-ties, and powers subject to him') is evidence of any Pauline influence.

Jude (v. 8; cf. 2 Pet. 2: 11) castigates his antinomian opponents for blaspheming the *doxai*, and the context makes it clear that he must be thinking of angelic guardians of the moral law, with a divinely ordained office similar to that of Satan; and this non-Pauline usage has interest-ing parallels in Philo.[49] In the apocalyptic sections of the New Testa-ment there are echoes of the Old Testament belief that when God

---

[47] Amos 4: 13 (cf. 9: 3 f.); Judges 5: 20; 1 Kings 22: 19; cf. Neh. 9: 6; Dan. 8: 9 ff.; Job 38: 7.

[48] Cf. Jer. 4: 23 ff., where creation returns to chaos; Jub. 3: 28 f. where through human sin the animals lost the power of speech and were driven out of Eden; and *Bereshith R.* 12–19, where the courses of the planets changed, the earth and heavenly bodies lost their brightness, and death came upon all living creatures.

[49] Philo, *de Spec. Leg.* i. 45; *Quaest Exod.* ii. 45; and in the Berlin Magical Papyrus 5025 (cf. K. L. Preisendanz, *Papyri Graecae Magicae*, i (Leipzig, 1928)).

judges the pagan nations he will judge with them their angelic representatives (Isa. 13: 10; 24: 12; 34: 4); the shaking of the powers of
heaven (Mark 13: 25; Heb. 12: 26 ff.), and the rolling up of the scroll
of heaven (Rev. 6: 14; 2 Pet. 3: 10) belong to this circle of ideas.
There are also two remarkable parallels to the Pauline insistence that
the powers of evil are located 'in the heavenlies' (Eph. 6: 12; cf. Col.
1: 16, 20; and Phil. 2: 11). Hebrews declares that the regular rites of
purification carried on in the earthly tabernacle, which was but a
shadowy pattern of the real heavenly Temple,[50] were a symbolic
reminder that in the long run the heavenly shrine itself required to be
purified by 'better sacrifices than these' (Heb. 9: 23). A similar idea
is conveyed by John's vision of the crystal sea in heaven. The origins
of this symbol are to be found in the creation myth of God's victory
over the primeval ocean dragon (Tiamat–Rahab–Leviathan),[51] the
element of disorder upon which God had imposed his sovereign
power. Israel's belief in the sovereignty of God was renewed by the
liturgical recital of this initial victory over the cosmic reservoir of evil,
but their realism had to admit that the victory was neither complete
nor final. It had been repeated at the Exodus, when God had smitten
the dragon and divided the sea to make a way for the redeemed to
walk on. But it would be brought to its consummation only at the New
Exodus when God would finally establish His Kingdom. Thus in the
Revelation the sea represents all that is recalcitrant to God's purpose,
all that blocks the human race's access to the throne of God. Out of
the sea arises the beast. Through the sea the martyrs must achieve
their Exodus before they can sing the song of Moses, and by the sea
the enemies of God, like the Egyptians before them, are engulfed.
The old tainted heavens must pass away with the old earth, because
in the new heaven and earth there is to be no more sea (21: 1).

The straightforward explanation of this convergent testimony to the
existence of evil in heaven is that the biblical writers never adequately
distinguished the literal heaven which is a part of the created cosmos
from the metaphorical heaven which is the eternal abode of God.[52] But
we cannot by so simple a device avoid the conclusion that to the New

---

[50] On the meaning of this idea, see below.

[51] Cf. for instance Pss. 74: 13–17; 87: 4; Job 7: 12; 9: 13; 26: 11–14; and Isa. 27: 1;
30: 7, as discussed by Caird, *Language and Imagery of the Bible*, 225 f.

[52] What e.g. is the relation between the heaven into which John was summoned by the
angel, the heaven he saw pass away, and the heaven from which he saw the city of God
descend?

Testament writers evil has a real existence to God, and that earthly sin carries implications which reach into the eternal order.

3.8. SATAN

The existence of evil in Heaven is most fully represented in the figure of Satan,[53] who is the personal embodiment of the paradox whereby the consequent will of God that sinners should be punished appears to conflict with His antecedent will that all should be saved and live in fellowship with Him. For Satan's primary function is to be the adversary of wrongdoers, but in pursuit of his duties he proves to be the adversary of God.[54] In the visions of Zechariah (3: 1) and in the prologue to the book of Job (1: 6 ff.), Satan is one of the sons of Elohim, a regular member of the heavenly council who discharged the duties of prosecutor with an enthusiasm for the divine justice. Yet even at this early stage of his history we can see where his one-sided emphasis on justice is to lead him. In both stories he is found arguing against God, whose holiness he is so anxious to defend. It cannot be said of *him* that he does not will the death of sinners, or that he is hoping that they would turn from their wickedness and live. He is a rigorous legalist, a prosecuting attorney, who must have a conviction, and who is satisfied only with a capital sentence. If the evidence does not give him a good case, he is prepared to manufacture new evidence by provoking Job into mortal sin. It is therefore no surprise to find that in the later Jewish literature he has added to his office of prosecutor the functions of *agent provocateur* and executioner.[55] The transformation of Satan, the angel of God's justice, into the Devil, the god of this world and enemy of God and all humanity, was no doubt accelerated by his

[53] Cf. e.g. Caird, *Principalities and Powers*, 31 ff.; M. E. Boismard, 'Satan selon l'Ancien et le Nouveau Testament', *Lumière et vie*, 15 (1966), 61 ff.; T. H. Gaster, 'Satan', *IDB* iv. 224 ff.; T. Ling, *The Significance of Satan* (London, 1961); J. M. Ross, 'The Decline of the Devil', *Exp.T.* 66 (1954–5), 58 ff.; and K. L. Schmidt, 'Luzifer als gefallene Engelsmacht', *Th.Z* 7 (1951), 161 ff.

[54] The Hebrew word *satan* means 'adversary', and is first used of the angel of Yahweh sent to reprove Balaam (Num. 22: 32), and of the foreign kings sent to execute divine judgement on the apostasy of Solomon (1 Kings 11: 14, 25). The function of Satan is a divine function; and, even when it devolves upon a single angel, the noun still retains the definite article.

[55] b.T. *Baba Bathra* 16ᵃ: 'Satan comes down to earth and seduces, then ascends to heaven and awakens wrath: permission is granted to him and he takes away the soul ... Satan, the evil impulse, and the angel of death are all one.'

identification with the ocean dragon of the creation myth and with the serpent of Eden (Wisd. 2: 24; Rev. 12: 9; 20: 2; Rom. 16: 20). But he was never to leave his original judicial duties, and heaven remains the scene of his operations, until the atoning work of Christ relieves him of his office (Luke 10: 18; Rev. 12: 9; 1 John 3: 8; Heb. 2: 14). In the Rabbinic writings he and Michael regularly appear as counsel for the prosecution and for the defence.[56]

In the New Testament Satan is still the lawyer. He is the legal adversary (*ho antidikos humōn*) whose attacks on the Christians are conducted in Roman courts of judicial inquiry (1 Pet. 5: 8). The conceited fall under his condemnation (1 Tim. 3: 6). He asks to have the Twelve, as formerly he had asked to have Job, confident that they too will learn from the midst of disaster to curse God to His face (Luke 22: 31). It is he who holds the power of death (Heb. 2: 14). And when he states his legal claim to the possession of the body of Moses, Michael, Moses' advocate, treats him with the courtesy due a fellow barrister (Jude 9). And when at last Michael expels him from heaven, he is disbarred because, through the atoning work of Christ, there is no place in heaven for the Great Accuser (Rev. 12: 7–12). If the prosecutor so urges his case that even the Judge of the human race finds himself in the dock, he must expect to find himself out of a job (John 12: 31–2). 'There is therefore now no condemnation for those who are in Christ Jesus . . . Who shall bring any charge against God's elect? It is God who justifies; who is to condemn?' (Rom. 8: 1, 33–4). The answer to Paul's rhetorical question is clear: not even Satan!

To the lawyer's gown Satan has added the insignia of dictator. All human beings have yielded to this seduction of the Tempter, have put themselves into the Prosecutor's power, and have incurred the sentence of the Angel of Death. 'The whole world is in the power of the evil one' (1 John 5: 19). He is 'the Prince of this world' (John 12: 31; 14: 30; 16: 11), the god of this world (2 Cor. 4: 4; cf. Eph. 2: 2; Acts 26: 18) by whom men and women are 'captured to do his will' (2 Tim. 2: 26). When Satan suggests that Jesus can attain to the world dominion for which he is destined only by using those Satanic methods which have been so successful in the establishment of other empires, because God has delivered over to him all worldly authority, Jesus refuses the gift without denying the claim (Luke 4: 6). He had no

---

[56] e.g. b.T. *Berak.* 46a; b.T. *Yoma* 20[a].

illusions about the extent of Satan's power. When the Pharisees accused him of casting out demons by the power of Beelzebul, the name ('Lord of the Mansion') evoked in his mind the picture of the strong man fully armed, guarding his palace. The world is Satan's fortress which he holds secure against all comers except him who comes in the name of the Lord. The chief evidences of his control over human life are bodily and mental illness, moral obliquity, and institutional corruption.

1. It was an important part of the preaching of the early Church that Jesus 'went about doing good and healing all that were oppressed by the Devil' (Acts 10: 38). All types of illness are included under this designation. Thus a crippled woman can be described as 'a daughter of Abraham whom Satan has kept in bonds for eighteen years' (Luke 13: 16). But the activity of Satan was particularly discovered in cases of demon possession, since he was 'the prince of demons' (Luke 11: 15). It is not to be imagined that in demon-possession we are dealing merely with a primitive medical diagnosis which has been outmoded by modern scientific discoveries. It is rather a spiritual diagnosis, which says of an affliction, 'An enemy has done this' (Matt. 13: 28). In Mark's Gospel the demons are regularly called unclean spirits, because the unclean includes all that has in any way evaded the control of the divine holiness. Paul also attributes human bodily ailments to Satan; for his 'thorn in the flesh, a messenger of Satan, to harass me' was almost certainly a chronic and recurrent illness (2 Cor. 12: 4). It is likely that he suffered a bout of this illness at Athens, and it was by this means that Satan repeatedly hindered him from returning to Thessalonica (1 Thess. 2: 18).[57] Paul believed, moreover, that the Church could, by a solemn anathema, hand an outrageous sinner over to Satan with disastrous physical consequences (1 Cor. 5: 5; cf. 1 Tim. 1: 20).[58] It is important to notice, however, that in Paul's interpretation both of his own illness and of the anathema, Satan remains 'God's Satan', operating only by divine permission (cf. Luke 4: 6; Rev. 13: 5) and unwittingly forwarding the divine purpose in the very act of resisting it (1 Cor. 2: 8).

---

[57] It is, however, just possible that this is a reference to Satan's political activities.

[58] While this may seem harsh, C. K. Barrett, *A Commentary on the First Epistle to the Corinthians* (London, 1968), 126, observes that handing the man over to Satan indicates the 'realm in which Paul himself [also] received Satan's attentions (1 Cor. 12: 7)'. Paul personally understood the buffeting which accompanies spiritual purification.

2. Satan's strongest hold over the human race is gained through moral lapse. He is 'the spirit that is now at work in the sons of disobedience' (Eph. 2: 2), and those who commit sin thereby confess themselves to be his progeny (John 8: 44; 1 John 3: 8, 10). He gains his foothold in their lives through their lack of self control (1 Cor. 7: 15), their anger (Eph. 4: 27), their conceit or their unpopularity (1 Tim. 3: 6–7), not to mention their gossip (1 Tim. 5: 15) and discord (1 Cor. 2: 11); in fact, through any heedless or unguarded conduct which exposes them to the flaming darts of temptation (Mark 4: 15; Jas. 4: 7; Eph. 6: 11, 12). In this way he takes possession of Judas (Luke 22: 3; John 6: 20; 13: 2, 27), Ananias (Acts 5: 3), and Elymas (Acts 13: 20), as before he had seized control of Cain (1 John 3: 12). Although in Thyatira there were apparently some who prided themselves on knowing 'the deep things of Satan', he does not normally solicit such open loyalty to himself. He is by nature 'the deceiver' (Rev. 20: 10) who 'disguises himself as an angel of light' (2 Cor. 11: 14). He tempts people to do wrong, not because it is wrong, but because it appears to be right.

3. Finally Satan operates through the corrupted institutions of Church and state. He uses the Mosaic law to blind the minds of the unbelieving (2 Cor. 4: 4). Through his machinations the Jews who have rejected the gospel have ceased to be Jews, properly so-called, and have become 'a synagogue of Satan' (Rev. 2: 9; 3: 9). There is, in fact, nothing in the world quite so destructive or quite so devilish as misdirected sincerity. By the same token Satan persuades human beings to make a god of the state and so converts it into a demonic power. It was the temple of the imperial cult that made Pergamum the place 'where Satan's throne is' (Rev. 2: 13). The totalitarian and persecuting origins of the Roman Empire are symbolized by the Beast, to whom 'the dragon gave his power and his throne and great authority' (Rev. 13: 2). By his activity the mystery of lawlessness is already at work, which will issue finally in the coming of Antichrist (2 Thess. 2: 3–12).

Most of the material in the New Testament concerning Satan appears in the form of myth; and it is a matter of some delicacy to determine how far the New Testament writers took their language literally. To many in the early Church Satan was undoubtedly a person; to others he may have been a personification.[59] For both alike, however,

---

[59] While Paul possibly pictured Satan as a person, he also was sophisticated enough to speak of personified Sin both as the Tempter (Rom. 7: 8) and as the Accuser who

it would be true to say that Satan was important at the very least because of what he symbolized. Despite the position we might take today on this issue, it may be said that Satan sums up in pictorial imagery all that the New Testament writers had to say about evil:

1. Evil is a real and virulent power, which cannot be explained away either as the adolescent growing pains of humanity or as the darkness in a Zoroastrian-like cosmic pattern of light and shade which is absorbed by the greater being of God (1 John 1: 5).

2. Evil is personal, and can exist only where there is a personal will in rebellion against God. In this respect the New Testament never uses Satan either to explain the origins of sin or to absolve human beings of responsibility for their sinfulness. It would be quite wrong to say that, if there had been no Satan, there would have been no sin. It would be true to say that, if there had been no sin, there could have been no Satan.

3. Evil, though human in its origin, is superhuman in its cumulative operation. It becomes a power which holds human life and society in abject bondage.

4. Evil is a perversion of goodness, and its power is the power of God. Satan is one of the Sons of God and holds his authority from God. 'The power of sin is the Law' (1 Cor. 15: 56).

5. Evil wins human assent by masquerading as good. 'Satan disguises himself as an angel of light' (2 Cor. 11: 14).

6. Evil is always the Enemy (Matt. 13: 28), against which the people of God must be prepared to fight, wherever it rears its head.

3.9. THE ANTICHRIST[60]

The name Antichrist is of Christian coinage, but the figure it denotes is of Jewish extraction. The name occurs only in the Johannine Epistles, where the Antichrist is said to have arrived in a heretical

---

loses his legal case by extending his prosecution of the human race to include the sinless Son of God (Rom. 8: 3).

[60] Cf. e.g. G. C. Jenks, *The Origins and Early Development of the Antichrist Myth* (Berlin, 1991); W. Bousset and A. H. Keane, *The Antichrist Legend* (London, 1896); E. Stauffer, *New Testament Theology* (London, 1955), 213 ff.; L. Sirard, 'La Parousie de l'AntéChrist: 2 Thess. 2: 3–9', *Studiorum Paulinorum Congressus* ii (Rome, 1963), 89 ff.; A. L. Moore, *The Parousia in the New Testament* (Leiden, 1966), and *1 and 2 Thessalonians* (London, 1969); and the commentaries on the Johannine epistles by Dodd (New York, 1946) and Bultmann (Philadelphia, 1973).

movement which was denying the reality of the incarnation (1 John 2: 18, 22; 4: 3; 2 John 7); but John clearly indicates that he is giving a new interpretation to a well-worn tradition. Traces of this earlier tradition are to be found in the desolating sacrilege, which Mark personifies by means of a masculine participle (*estēkota*, Mark 13: 14), in the 'man of lawlessness,' who is an incarnation of 'the mystery of lawlessness' (2 Thess. 2: 8), and in the Beast of the Revelation (Rev. 11: 7; 13: 1–4). All these are obviously variations on a single theme, and no explanation of any of them should be entertained which does not do justice to all. There are four types of explanations from which to choose: (1) The Antichrist is a purely mythological figure;[61] (2) The Antichrist is a mythological figure with a political counterpart in Roman totalitarianism; (3) The Antichrist is a mythological figure with a counterpart in the Jewish rejection of the gospel; and (4) The Antichrist, just because he is a mythological figure, was capable of being identified with a variety of historical counterparts. The fourth solution had a powerful advocate in W. Bousset, who cited patristic evidence to show that in later times, behind all written references to Antichrist, there was a continuous, esoteric oral tradition which did not have its origin in the New Testament;[62] and that among the Fathers opinion was divided almost equally between a Roman Antichrist and a Jewish one. For the later history of the Antichrist Bousset's theory is almost certainly correct. But within the limits of the New Testament we shall see that the political explanation predominated.

Five main streams of heredity compose the ancestry of Antichrist:

1. Like Satan, he certainly derives part of his character from the myth of the primeval dragon, the ocean monster which God had conquered at Creation (Ps. 74: 13–14), but whose final overthrow was reserved for the Day of the Lord (Isa. 27: 1). These dragons had already been identified with Pharaoh, King of Egypt (Ezek. 29: 3; 32: 2; cf. Isa. 51: 9) and with Nebuchadnezzar, King of Babylon (Jer. 51: 34), the two persecuting enemies of the people of God, and could therefore readily be further identified with persecutors of later days. In one of the Ras Shamra tablets this monster is described as a

---

[61] So H. Gunkel, *Shöpfung und Chaos in Urzeit und Endzeit* (Göttingen, 1921²), 171 ff.

[62] See Bousset and Keane, *Antichrist Legend*, and the references cited on p. 31. Sulpicius Severus is said to have received an oral tradition about the Antichrist from Martin of Tours (*Hist.* ii. 14): the esoteric character of the tradition is also suggested by Or. Sib. 10. 290 ('But not all know this, for not all things are for all').

'mighty one with seven heads',[63] and we are reminded that both the dragon and the beast in Revelation had seven heads and ten horns.[64]

2. Another line of the genealogy can be traced back to Gog of the land of Magog, whose attack on Israel was to be the last great outburst of the forces of evil before the establishment of God's everlasting Kingdom (Ezek. 35–9; cf. Joel 3: 9 ff. and Zech. 12–14, where the Last Judgement also takes the form of a battle). The prophet (whether Ezekiel or Ezekiel's disciple) evidently thought that the invasion would fulfil Jeremiah's prophecy of the coming of a foe from the North (Ezek. 38: 17), but this in itself does not account for his eschatological vision. For Jeremiah, like other pre-exilic prophets, had predicted the coming of heathen armies which would punish Israel for her infidelities; but Gog comes after the punishment and restoration of Israel, when through the redemptive activity of God the earth has attained a state of peace, and he comes not from Israel's historic enemies, but from beyond the horizons of the known world. He is the skeleton in the cosmic cupboard. He is in fact the symbolic expression of two beliefs: that the powers of evil have a defence in depth, out of which they can steadily reinforce themselves, so that no earthly order can ever find security from attacks from beyond the frontier, except in the final victory of God; and that, in a world where evil is so tenacious, there must be a final show-down before the consummation of God's reign.

3. Daniel's vision of the four beasts, representing four empires, whose beginning culminated in the reign of the little horn, and in his profanation of the temple by means of 'the abomination that makes desolate' (Dan. 7: 20; 8: 9–13; 9: 27; 11: 31; 12: 11), was originally evoked by Antiochus Epiphanes' attempt to Hellenize the Jews by the erection of an altar to Zeus Olympius in the Temple. But after the original crisis had passed the vision was reinterpreted as a prophecy that a similar profanation would immediately precede the establishment of God's Kingdom.

4. Two events in Roman history readily attached themselves to these older beliefs. One was Caligula's decree in AD 40 that his statue should be erected in the Holy of Holies in Jerusalem, a lunacy averted only

---

[63] See Alexander Heidel, *The Babylonian Genesis* (Chicago, 1942), 91.

[64] The ten horns clearly derive from Dan. 7: 7. For the Antichrist as dragon, see Or. Sib. 8. 68 and the patristic passages cited by Bousset and Keane, 144 ff.

by the courageous disobedience of the imperial legate and by Caligula's assassination. The other was Nero's suicide and the subsequent, extremely prevalent rumour that Nero redivivus was preparing to lead a Parthian invasion to destroy the Empire.[65]

5. Finally there were Jesus' predictions of the coming of false Christs and false prophets (Mark 13: 22). It was probably through the influence of this dominical saying that John's Antichrist bifurcated into a Beast, the false Christ, and a second beast, the false prophet (Rev. 13: 11; 19: 20; 20: 10).

In the light of all this we may now address ourselves to the three crucial passages. When Mark introduces the 'desolating sacrilege' with the cryptic parenthesis 'let the reader understand', he is clearly indicating his belief that the prophecy of Daniel was about to be fulfilled in an unparalleled tribulation inflicted on Judaea by Roman armies; and this belief may well have owed something to Caligula's aspirations to deity.[66] Similarly, the beast of Revelation, the epitome of Daniel's four beasts, is the worldly dominion which has found its last, greatest embodiment in Rome; and the head which has received a mortal wound and is healed, the head which is an eighth though it is one of the seven (17: 11), is Nero redivivus, possibly Domitian in the guise of a second Nero.[67]

Paul's 'man of lawlessness' is described as 'the son of perdition, who opposes and exalts himself against every so-called god or object of worship, so that he takes his seat in the temple of God, proclaiming himself to be God' (2 Thess. 2: 3–4). This is the Antichrist, whose advent will inaugurate 'the rebellion', the last uprising of the forces of evil against the Kingdom of God; but there can be no serious doubt

[65] Suet., *Nero* 40; Tac., *Hist.* ii. 8; Asc. Isa. 4; Or. Sib. 3; Dio Chrys., *Orat.* i. 314.

[66] Matthew's (24: 15) editorial alteration of Mark 13: 14 suggests that he at least took this view. It is true that he changes Mark's participle *estēkota* to the neuter *estos*, but this was probably for grammatical reasons, not because he wanted to change Mark's sacrilegious person to a sacrilegious object.

[67] Though all scholars agree with regard to this reading of the Beast, some have suggested that John superimposed it on an older Antichrist legend in which the Beast was a Jewish Antichrist. The reason given for this assertion is that in 11: 7 f. the Beast makes his first appearance in Jerusalem. But the words 'where their Lord was crucified' are as much part of the allegorical description of the city as the names Sodom and Egypt. The city in which the witnesses lie dead for three and a half days, visible to people of every nation, is the city of the passing world order, and the two witnesses represent the martyrs in every part of the Empire.

who it was that sat for the portrait. Writing less than ten years after Caligula's death, it is inconceivable that Paul should have used these words without intending a reference to the mad Emperor. 'The mystery of lawlessness', which would come to full expression in 'the man of lawlessness', had already given the world a preview of its character in Caligula. It was being contained by the Roman government, the power appointed by God for the restraint of evil (cf. Rom. 13: 1–7), and only with the collapse of civil government would it reach its full activity. In the end of Rome one can see a premonitory sign of the End.[68] This interpretation of the passage might seem to be open to the objection that it makes Rome the restrainer of Rome. The answer is that Paul uses mythological language precisely because it enables him to point beyond human beings and institutions to underlying realities, and in particular to the contradiction between its divine appointment and its demonic potentiality involved in every exercise of Roman imperial power. The Antichrist doctrine was not only an acknowledgment of the depth, the virulence, and the mystery of evil; it was also a pastoral idea of some importance, since it brought assurance to the victims of persecution that the atrocities they suffered were not outside the control of God's grand strategy. Perhaps we may add that it represented the only conception of progress entertained by the biblical writers. They believed that God's purpose was moving steadily to its consummation, but, in proportion as His cause prospered, it called forth a reaction from the powers of evil. Like a supersonic jet, which meets growing resistance until the breaking point at the sound barrier, God's purpose by its very success evokes a cumulative opposition, which reaches its height only at the crack of doom. 'The devil has come down to you in great wrath, because he knows that his time is short' (Rev. 12: 12).

---

[68] See e.g. 4 Ezra 5: 3, and Iren. *Haer.* 5. 26. The possibility that *to katechon* = *imperium*, while *ho katechon* = *imperator*, remains very attractive. On the other hand there is nothing to be said in favour of the theory that *ho katechon* = the apostle Paul. Granted that according to Mark 13: 10 the gospel must be preached 'throughout all the world' before the End, it would not be by preaching but only *by declining to preach* that Paul could be said to delay the final crisis.

3.10. THE UNFORGIVABLE SIN[69]

There is in the New Testament only one unforgivable sin—to put oneself beyond the reach of God's forgiveness. But this may be done in several ways: by an unforgiving attitude to others, by a denial of the Incarnation, by blasphemy against the Holy Spirit, and by a refusal to listen to the gospel.

1. 'If you do not forgive others their trespasses, neither will your Father forgive your trespasses' (Matt. 6: 12, 15; 18: 23–35; Mark 11: 25). This does not mean that human beings must earn God's pardon, that their forgiveness of others is a condition to be fulfilled before they can be entitled to the divine forgiveness. To be pardoned by God is to live no longer by one's merits but by His grace. Those who insist on dealing with others according to their deserts betray their own inability to comprehend the meaning of grace and therefore their incapacity to receive pardon. The forgiving spirit is a condition not of God's offer of pardon but of our receiving it. To refuse to forgive is to refuse to be forgiven. The elder brother must share the feast with the prodigal, not have one to himself.

2. To the author of 1 John the mortal sin, the sin of Antichrist, is to deny the reality of the incarnation (2: 22; 4: 2–3; 5: 16). God is love: but we know God only through recognizing His love at work in the incarnate life of Christ, through whose self-giving that same love becomes the directive principle of our lives. To deny that in the human life of Jesus the divine love has become incarnate is to cut oneself off from the saving knowledge of God and from the one source of love and life.

3. 'Truly, I say to you, all sins will be forgiven the sons of men, and whatever blasphemies they utter; but whoever blasphemes against the Holy Spirit never has forgiveness, but is guilty of an eternal sin' (Mark 3: 28–9).[70] The Marcan context of this saying provides a thoroughly satisfactory explanation of it. Jesus had been accused of casting out demons by the power of Beelzebul. By attributing what was obviously

---

[69] In addition to the standard commentaries on Mark, Hebrews, and 1 John, see O. E. Evans, 'The Unforgivable Sin', *Exp.T.* 68 (1956–7), 240 ff.; H. W. Beyer, '*blasphēmeō*', etc., *TDNT* i. 621 ff.; E. Lövestam, '*Spiritus Blasphemia': Eine Studie zu Mk. 3, 28f. par.* (Lund, 1968); and J. G. Williams, 'A Note on the "Unforgivable Sin" Logion', *NTS* 12 (1965–6), 75 ff.

[70] A different version of this saying stood in Q (Matt. 12: 31–2; Luke 12: 10), but the Marcan form is clearly original (below, p. 373).

a good act to the power of Satan, his critics were blunting their own faculty of distinguishing between right and wrong and running the risk of being unable thereafter to recognize goodness when they met it. To blaspheme against the Holy Spirit by calling His works evil is to deprive oneself of a standard of judgement for one's own life, and thus to become incapable of repentance.

4. In Luke's Gospel Jesus is repeatedly represented as urgently speaking of the judgement awaiting those who refuse to listen to the gospel (Luke 10: 12–15; 11: 29–32; 14: 15–24). The same note of urgency runs like a refrain through the Epistle to the Hebrews: 'How shall we escape if we neglect so great a salvation?' (2: 3); 'It is imposs-ible to restore again to repentance those who have once been enlight-ened, who have tasted the heavenly gift and have become partakers of the Holy Spirit, and have tasted the goodness of the word of God and the powers of the age to come, if they then commit apostasy' (6: 4–6); 'If we sin deliberately after receiving the knowledge of the truth, there no longer remains a sacrifice for sins, but a fearful prospect of judgment' (10: 26–7). God has spoken His final word in Christ. If men and women are not content with that, what more can He be expected to say?

Thus for the New Testament writers evil is a real and powerful entity, with a real and powerful grip not only upon human life but upon the entire cosmos. If help is going to come, it will have to come from the outside. It will have to come from God Himself.

4.

The Three Tenses of Salvation

'Now that we have been justified through faith, we are at peace with God through our Lord Jesus Christ, through whom we have access to that grace in which we stand, and exult in the hope of God's glory' (Rom. 5: 12).

'Freed from the commands of sin, and bound to the service of God, your gains are such as make for holiness, and the end is eternal life' (Rom. 6: 22).

'Were you not raised to life with Christ? ... You died, and now your life lies hidden with Christ in God. When Christ, who is our life, is manifested, then you too will be manifested with him in glory' (Col. 3: 1–4).

'The grace of God has dawned upon the world with healing for the whole human race; and by it we are disciplined ... to have a life of temperance, honesty, and godlinesss in the present age, looking forward to a happy fulfilment of our hope' (Titus 2: 11–13).

'Christ offered for all time one sacrifice for sins, and took his seat at the right hand of God, where he waits henceforth until all his enemies are made his footstool' (Heb. 10: 12).

Here we have five passages, each of which succinctly expresses the conviction, shared by other writers who have not provided so neat a summary of it, that salvation is a threefold act of God: an accomplished fact, an experience continuing in the present, and a consummation still to come.

But none of the New Testament authors ever attempts to provide a systematic discussion of this redemptive act. Rather they celebrate it, using a variety of metaphors, drawn from many fields of human activity, to record their grateful wonder at the mercy and power of God. Almost all of these terms can be used indiscriminately to refer to any one of the three tenses. Our modern logic might prefer to keep one set of terms for each part of the triad; e.g. justification for the accomplished fact, sanctification for the continuing experience, and glorification for the goal. But New Testament usage conforms to no such pattern. All that logic can claim is that there are differences of emphasis. Justification most often has a past reference, but it is also the status within which the Christian life is lived (Rom. 5: 21; Gal. 2: 21; Phil. 3: 9; cf. Jas. 2: 24 and 1 Cor. 6: 11—'Justified in the name of the Lord Jesus and by the Spirit of one God') before the eagerly expected final verdict (Gal. 5: 5). Glory tends to be associated with the future hope (Rom. 5: 2; 8: 18; Col. 1: 27; 3: 4; Heb. 2: 10; 1 Pet. 5: 1); but the glory of God has been revealed (2 Cor. 4: 6; Luke 2: 9; John 1: 14), has been attained by Jesus the pioneer (Heb. 2: 9), has been granted to the human race in his representative death (John 17: 22); and the Christian life is a transfiguration from one hidden glory to another (2 Cor. 3: 15; 1 Pet. 1: 8; 4: 14). Some of the emphases are unexpected: reconciliation, which we should expect to express the experience of restored personal relationships, more often refers to what has been achieved by the death of Christ (Rom. 5: 10; Eph. 2: 16; Col. 1: 20); though in one passage Paul proceeds directly from the one to the other (2 Cor. 5: 18–20).

The threefold pattern is best illustrated in the Pauline corpus; yet there is enough supporting evidence elsewhere to prove that this usage is no Pauline peculiarity. Christians have been saved once for all,[1] but they are also being saved, working out or reaping their salvation,[2] and look forward to a salvation yet to come (Rom. 13: 11; Phil. 3: 20; cf. Heb. 9: 28; 1 Pet. 1: 5). They have been set free,[3] but they have to live as free persons, standing fast in their new freedom (Gal. 5: 1; 2 Cor. 3: 17; cf. 1 Pet. 2: 16), while they wait for their final liberation.[4] They have been washed clean,[5] but the cleansing process continues (2 Cor. 7: 1; cf. Jas. 4: 8; 1 John 1: 7), until perfect purity is attained (Rev. 19: 8). The decisive victory over the powers has been won,[6] but

---

[1] Rom. 8: 24; 10: 10; 11: 11; Eph. 2: 8; cf. Luke 2: 30; 19: 12; 2 Tim. 1: 9; Titus 3: 5; Heb. 5: 9.

[2] 1 Cor. 1: 18, 15: 2; 2 Cor. 2: 15, 6: 2; Phil. 2: 12; cf. Acts 4: 12; 1 Pet. 1: 9, 3: 21, 4: 18.

[3] Rom. 6: 22; 8: 2; Gal. 4: 4–5; Col. 1: 13; cf. Luke 1: 68; John 8: 36; Titus 2: 14; Heb. 9: 12; 1 Pet. 1: 18; Rev. 1: 5.

[4] Rom. 8: 21; Eph. 1: 14; 4: 30; cf. Luke 21: 28.

[5] 1 Cor. 6: 8; Eph. 5: 26; cf. Heb. 1: 3, 10: 2; Rev. 7: 14.

[6] 1 Cor. 15: 54; Col. 2: 15; cf. John 16: 33; 1 Pet. 3: 22; Rev. 3: 21.

the war goes on[7] until no enemies are left to challenge the sovereignty of God.[8]

In making such a classification, however, we must be on our guard against a grammatical absolutism which ignores the ambiguities of the Greek tenses. It will not necessarily be the case that all past verbs refer to salvation as an accomplished fact and all future verbs to the final consummation. In all languages with a tense system the tenses have a prima facie reference, which we might here call the 'surface meaning'. But this can be overruled by other elements in the syntax or by the context. In the use of the historic present, for example, the tense is overruled by the narrative setting. We have already seen that events still future to the believer can be referred to in the aorist tense because they are conceived as already done in the predestining act of God. In Mark 1: 15 the perfect tenses ought (at their surface level) to refer to an event in the past with continuing effects in the present, but they have commonly been interpreted with reference to the future; and, although there is good evidence that this view is wrong, and that Mark intended the verbs to have their prima facie sense, the matter cannot be decided on grammatical grounds alone. In Mark 9: 1 the perfect tense refers to an event still future to Jesus, though past to certain observers who will look back at it.

The ambiguities of the future tense are more various and more hazardous. Greek has a verb *mellō*, whose sole function is to denote futurity, and in the New Testament it occasionally has this surface meaning (Mark 10: 32; Rom. 8: 38). But far more often it refers to that which is now present, though future from the point of view of the Old Testament which foreshadowed it. The Baptist is the Elijah to come (Matt. 11: 14), Jesus is the man who was to come, from the point of view of Adam with whom he is compared (Rom. 5: 14; cf. Acts 26: 22), the Law had a shadow of the good things to come (Heb. 10: 1; cf. Gal. 3: 23; Col. 2: 17); and in Hebrews 2: 5 the phrase 'the world to come' is deliberately ambiguous, since it is followed by a careful discussion of the extent to which the new world has come in the representative person of Jesus, but has not yet come in the general experience of humanity.

In the light of this usage we may observe a similar ambiguity in the

---

[7] Rom. 8: 37; Phil. 1: 30; Eph. 6: 12; cf. Jas. 4: 7; 1 Pet. 5: 8; 1 John 5: 4; Rev. 12: 10–11.

[8] 1 Cor. 15: 25; cf. Heb. 1: 13 and 10: 13; Rev. 17: 14; 19: 19.

phrase 'the last days'. The surface meaning, which many commentaries and translations take for granted, would appear to be 'the final period of world history'. But the phrase is commonly found in connection with prophecy, and in the Old Testament 'at the end of the days' has no more meaning than 'in the future'.[9] Thus, when the New Testament writers describe the events of their own time as happening 'in these last days' (Heb. 1: 2; Acts 2: 17), it may be that they intend no more than to identify their present with the future of the prophetic hope. On the other hand the Thessalonians clearly took Paul's reference to the final crisis with a literalness that he had not intended. Between these two extremes there were, no doubt, grades of interpretation. But the ambiguity is not resolved by a naïve assumption of temporal precision.

Another equally naïve and unjustifiable assumption is that, whenever salvation is referred to as future, the reference must be to the ultimate future, the final consummation. In some instances, to be sure, this will turn out to be so; but it is a sound rule that the future tense should be deemed to have an eschatological reference only where the context unambiguously requires it. In Mark's account of Jesus' reply to Caiaphas (14: 62), it could be that the coming of the Son of Man belongs to the end of history; but Matthew does not so understand his source, since in his version that possibility is overruled by the adverbial 'from now on', which firmly assigns the prediction to continuous experience: and this for Matthew and his readers was past and present as well as future. The point is further illustrated by a comparison between 1 Corinthians 15 and Romans 6. Both passages deal with what happens to the Christian after death, but in the one case it is the death of the body and in the other the death of the old Adam brought about by union with the crucified Christ. In 1 Corinthians 15, then, the future tenses may properly be called 'eschatological': 'As in Adam all die, even so in Christ shall all be made alive.' But Romans 6 has to do with the kind of life which the Christian is to live on earth: 'We died to sin; how can we live in it any longer?' (6: 2). It follows, then, that when Paul says, 'if we died with Christ, we believe that we shall also live with him' (6: 8), he is not talking about life after physical death, but about the life which the Christian lives in union with the risen Christ, which for him is future only from the point of view of the

---

[9] See F. Brown, S. R. Driver and C. A. Briggs, *A Hebrew and English Lexicon of the Old Testament* (Oxford, 1907), 31.

death which precedes it, and to which it is the logical sequel. It is therefore highly probable that the future tense in 6: 5 is also to be taken as a future of logical sequence: if it be true that baptism is the effective symbol of our union with Christ in his death, it will also be true that it is the symbol of union with him in his Resurrection. How else could it be possible that 'he who raised Christ Jesus from the dead will also give new life to your mortal bodies through his indwelling Spirit' (Rom. 8: 11)? How could Paul boast of 'always carrying in the body the death that Jesus died, in order that in my body should be made manifest the life that Jesus lives' (2 Cor. 4: 10; cf. Gal. 2: 20; Col. 2: 13)? By the same token the eschatological hope can be regarded as real only because it is grounded in present fulfilment (Rom. 5: 5; 2 Cor. 1: 7; Eph. 1: 18; Heb. 7: 19).

This grammatical excursion has been necessary because of the many attempts that have been made to simplify the New Testament teaching about salvation by giving to one of the three tenses a primacy over the other two. Some theories have so concentrated on the finished work of Christ as to leave little function for its sequel except the proclamation of what has been done once for all. In the existentialism of Bultmann the past event of the Cross has no saving value except in the believer's present decision of faith and in his or her encounter with the God who saves. The eschatological school has treated everything that happens before the end as proleptic. We continue to hear much of the tension between 'already and not yet' in the teaching of Jesus, as though the present were a mere link, itself void of significance, between the crisis of the Cross and the crisis of the Parousia. But the very fact that a case can be made for each of these positions is enough to show that all are forms of reduction which sacrifice something of the richness of New Testament thought. The wise course is to investigate the ways in which the New Testament writers themselves relate the tenses.

4.2. CHRISTIAN PROGRESS

The simplest way is to see the three tenses as stages in a process, begun, continued, and ended. One sort of progress takes place in the life of the individual Christian: 'The One who started the good work in you will bring it to completion by the Day of Christ Jesus' (Phil. 1: 6). Another is seen in the spread of Christ's influence throughout the world. Thus, in the prayer of John 17, Jesus prays first for himself, since the redemptive purpose of God is to be completed first in his representative person (vv. 1–5); then he prays for his immediate circle of disciples in whom the redemptive purpose first becomes operative (vv. 6–19); then for those who are to be brought to faith through their preaching (vv. 20–3); and finally for the whole world (v. 24).

The idea of progress is expressed in the New Testament by the use of metaphors from agriculture, building, athletics, and travel. When Paul used metaphors of growth he is almost always referring to the development of character (Rom. 7: 4; Gal. 5: 22; Phil. 1: 4). The new convert is an infant who must grow to maturity (1 Cor. 3: 1), and what holds for the individual holds also for the community which must attain to 'nothing less than the full stature of Christ' (Eph. 4: 13). When Paul declares that 'a man reaps what he sows', it might appear that he was interested only in the beginning and the end (already/not yet), but the context proves that the sowing he has in mind is a continuing process: 'Let us never tire of doing good, for if we do not slacken our efforts we shall in due time reap our harvest' (Gal. 6: 7–9). In two passages in Colossians the order of the verbs 'bearing fruit and growing' shows that the intended image is that of a tree which bears fruit one year before putting out new spurs for the year after: in one case (1: 10) insight into God's will produces fruit in conduct and leads to a fresh growth of insight; in the other (1: 6) the fruit of conduct leads to growth in the winning of new converts.

The portrayal of the Christian life as a growth from spiritual infancy to maturity appears to have been a commonplace of early Christian catechetical instruction (Heb. 5: 11–14; 6: 3; 1 Pet. 2: 2). In the Fourth Gospel, however, the bearing of fruit refers to the spread of the gospel. 'A grain of wheat remains a solitary grain unless it falls into the ground and dies; but if it dies, it bears a rich harvest' (12: 24); Jesus is alone 'in the bosom of the Father' (1: 18), and dies alone deserted by his friends (16: 32), but by his death he makes it possible for others to be where he is (14: 3); bearing fruit is for him the converse of being alone, and for the disciples it signifies the success of their mission to the world (15: 8).

This is also the main point of the synoptic parables of growth. Under the influence of a futurist eschatology and of Jülicher's arbitrary principle that a parable must have only one point of comparison, attempts have been made to argue that the sole point of these parables is the contrast between small beginnings and disproportionate results.

Even for a study of the teaching of Jesus these arguments are of dubious value, but for the theology of the evangelists they are utterly irrelevant. To Mark the Sower is a parable about the mysterious working of God's sovereignty, but also about the spiritual conditions which at any time militate for and against its triumph and the understanding of the gospel (4: 1–20). In the Seed Growing Secretly six words are devoted to the sowing, thirty-one to the process of growth, and thirteen to the harvest (4: 26–9). But it is the Mustard Seed that provides the decisive clue to the interpretation of all these parables. Even in Mark (4: 30–2) the birds that rest in the branches are a clear allusion to Nebuchadnezzar's dream tree (Dan. 4: 10–12), and Matthew (13: 32) and Luke (13: 19) make the allusion explicit by introducing the word 'tree' into the parable. According to Daniel the tree represents Nebuchadnezzar, or indeed any earthly agent to whom God entrusts sovereignty; God may give sovereignty 'to the humblest of men', but the right to exercise it depends on acknowledgment of the overruling sovereignty of heaven (i.e. God); and the birds roosting in the branches symbolize the world-wide extension of the delegated authority. In the parable the tree has become a symbol for God's own sovereignty, but its growth from small beginnings clearly depends on growing acknowledgment by the human race. Thus the climax of the parable is not an apocalyptic event at the end of world history, unrelated to what has gone before, but the success of a programme of world mission (cf. Mark 13: 10; 14: 9). To this we may add that in Matthew's parable of the Weeds interest is focused on the instructions the landowner gives to his servants for the care of the crop during its period of growth (13: 29–30).

Another metaphor, often found beside the metaphor of growth and even interlaced with it (1 Cor. 3: 5–14; Eph. 2: 20–1, 4: 12–15; 1 Pet. 2: 2–8), portrays the process of salvation as the erection of a building by God. Christ is either the foundation or the corner-stone, and believers find themselves built into the structure as living stones to form a temple for the worship of God (cf. Rev. 3: 12). Everything that is done in the Church must serve to build it up (1 Cor. 14: 12; Rom. 15: 12).

The earliest term used to describe the Christian movement was 'the Way' (Acts 9: 2; 19: 23; 22: 4), which could be conceived simply as a road of conduct to be travelled, but which came to signify the road leading to the Father and to be identified with Jesus (John 14: 4–6), and particularly with his self-surrender on the Cross (Heb. 10: 19–

20). Alternatively the Christian life was a race, requiring discipline and persistence, but leading to a victor's crown.[10]

We have already noted that such metaphors refer to more than one type of progress, and when we examine them more closely we observe that the progress is of four kinds: (1) numerical, (2) intellectual, (3) moral, and (4) social. (1) There must be numerical progress because, although salvation has been achieved once and for all in the representative person of Jesus and is universal in its scope, it becomes real and effective in human experience only in so far as it is appropriated by faith. If God's Kingdom is to be peopled, if Christ is to be the firstborn in a large family (Rom. 8: 30; Heb. 2: 10), the gospel must be preached to all the world,[11] to every nation, language, and race (Rev. 7: 9). (2) There must be intellectual progress because, although the truth of God, His redemptive love, and His plan of salvation, has been revealed once for all, believers need to grow, individually and corporately, in their understanding of it.[12] Because the old life from which they have been rescued was characterized by blindness and futility, the new life demands a constant renewal of the mind,[13] a constant advance in knowledge, wisdom, and discernment.[14] (3) There must be moral progress, because salvation is deliverance from sin. Christ has once for all offered to God the obedience God required (Rom. 5: 19), but that obedience must be reproduced in his followers in a life that befits their calling,[15] a life of discipline,[16] a life of effort (2 Pet. 1: 5–8; 3: 2), a steady advance to perfection.[17] (4) If there must be social progress, it is for one simple reason: men and women are social beings, and can live the new life only in a new order. Christ has inaugurated a new creation (2 Cor. 5: 17; Gal. 6: 15), a new humanity (Eph. 2: 15; Col. 3: 10), which will one day come to its full realization (Eph. 4: 13; 2 Pet. 3: 13; Rev. 21: 1, 2, 5). Christ has won a victory over the powers

[10] 1 Cor. 9: 24; Phil. 3: 13–14; Gal. 5: 7; 1 Tim. 6: 12; 2 Tim. 4: 7; Heb. 12: 1–2.
[11] Mark 13: 10; Matt. 28: 19; Acts 1: 8; John 15: 8; 1 Cor. 9: 19; 2 Cor. 2: 14.
[12] John 8: 32, 16: 13–15; Rom. 15: 8; 1 Cor. 4: 2; 1 Tim. 2: 4; Titus 1: 1; 1 Pet. 1: 22; 1 John 3: 19.
[13] Rom. 8: 6; 12: 2; 1 Cor. 2: 16; Phil. 2: 5; Col. 3: 2, 10.
[14] Rom. 16: 19; 1 Cor. 2: 6; 14: 20; Eph. 1: 17; Phil. 3: 8, 10, 12; Gal. 1: 9; 3: 16; Jas. 3: 15, 17.
[15] Rom. 6: 22; Gal. 5: 22; Eph. 5: 9; Phil. 1: 11; Heb. 12: 11; Jas. 3: 18.
[16] Rom. 5: 3–4; 1 Cor. 9: 24–7; Heb. 12: 5–11; Jas. 1: 3–4; 1 Pet. 1: 13–16.
[17] Matt. 5: 18; John 17: 23; Phil. 3: 12; Eph. 4: 13; Heb. 5: 12; 6: 1; 7: 11, 19; 9: 9; 10: 1, 14; 12: 33; Jas. 2: 22.

which control the old order (John 16: 33; Col. 2: 15; 1 Pet. 3: 11; Rev. 3: 21), but he must continue to reign until his sovereignty is universally acknowledged (1 Cor. 15: 25; Heb. 10: 12; Rev. 11: 15).

4.3. THE PRESENCE OF THE TRANSCENDENT

The New Testament writers are not, however, content with such a simple, linear approach. Though God acts in history, He transcends it. He is the Eternal One, the One in whom past, present, and future cohere; and His dealings with His creatures are informed by that coherence. He is the Alpha and the Omega. And wherever His presence becomes real to men and women, there they confront the Beginning and the End. Just as creation is not merely an initial act but an ongoing process, and the story of the fall of Adam relates not simply to what happened once but to what happens in the life of every human being, so the myth of the end symbolizes not only the final consummation, but that which is decisive or ultimate at any critical period of history.[18]

The author of Hebrews leaves no doubt about his commitment to history and to the Jesus of history: Jesus was 'sprung from Judah' (7: 14), he lived an earthly life (5: 7), and died 'once for all' in the sequence of earthly events (7: 28; 9: 12, 26, 28; 10: 10). But he believed that by obedience to God's will Jesus had turned that death into a sacrifice which could be offered to God (10: 10), that the sacrifice was offered 'through eternal spirit' (9: 14), in the heavenly sanctuary (9: 24), and that it effected 'an eternal deliverance' (9: 12; 5: 9). Thus the historical event of the Cross is taken up into the eternal order. Jesus is appointed by God to a High Priesthood in perpetuity (5: 6; 6: 20; 7: 3), but he does not exercise it on earth (8: 4). He holds it in virtue of 'an indestructible life' (7: 16); and his self-offering does not need to be repeated because 'he remains forever' (7: 24). 'That is why he is able to save absolutely those who approach God through him: he is always living to plead on their behalf' (7: 25). He has thus become the eternal contemporary, 'the same yesterday; today and forever' (13: 8). Through him believers become recipients of a Kingdom which does not belong to the transient world of created things, but to the unshakeable realm of the transcendent (12: 28).

[18] See J. A. T. Robinson, *In the End, God* (London, 1950), *passim.*

The same interpenetration of the temporal by the eternal is signified in the Johannine phrase, 'a time is coming and now is':[19]

In very truth, anyone who gives heed to what I say and puts his trust in him who sent me has hold of eternal life, and does not come up for judgment, but has already passed from death to life. In truth, in very truth I tell you, a time is coming, indeed it is here already, when the dead shall hear the voice of the Son of God, and all who hear shall come to life. For as the Father has life-giving power in himself, so has the Son, by the Father's gift (John 5: 24–6).

Here 'a time is coming' refers to the immediate future when Lazarus leaves the tomb, to the continuous experience of the Church (cf. 1 John 3: 14), and to the ultimate future of the Last Judgement (5: 29); but the time is already here because Jesus is the embodiment of the eternal *logos*, is the resurrection and the life (11: 25), and can say 'Before Abraham was I am' (8: 58).

With these two authors there is a possibility that their thinking on this subject has been affected by ideas derived from Greek philosophy, either directly or through the Hellenistic Synagogue, and that they cannot therefore be regarded as typical of early Palestinian Christianity. No such suspicion can attach to the author of Revelation, in whose work the tenses of salvation are more thoroughly interfused than in any other. For him the name of God is not I AM; it is 'Who is and was and is coming' (1: 4).[20] He is the Alpha and the Omega (1: 8), and this is a title He shares with the victorious Christ (22: 13), so that to meet him is to encounter the Beginning and the End. John sees the Lamb take from the hand of God the scroll of destiny, and immediately hears the whole redeemed creation join in the worship of the heavenly choir (5: 13). He sees the conquerors sealed for their great ordeal and at once emerging from it into heavenly bliss (7: 1–17). He sees Michael defeat Satan in a war in heaven, and leaves us in some doubt whether the earthly reality that corresponds to this vision is the death of Christ which already comprehends the victorious death of the martyrs, or the death of the martyrs in which Christ wins again his own victory (12:

---

[19] 4: 23; 5: 25; 16: 32. See C. H. Dodd, *Interpretation of the Fourth Gospel* (Cambridge, 1953), *passim*.

[20] This is clearly an adaptation of the LXX rendering of the divine name in Ex. 3: 14—*ho ōn* (cf. Wisd. 13: 1), and it might be argued that Greek influence comes to bear on John at this point. But his recasting of 'the Name' emphatically dissociates it from the Greek, 'static' concept of eternal reality.

7–12). The fall of Babylon is contemporaneous with the death of the martyrs at her hand (14: 8). And the new Jerusalem descends out of heaven from God not only before and after the millennium, but wherever martyrs win their crown (3: 12).

John's visions are seen against a background of heavenly worship; and it is in the setting of worship that his theology is best understood; for his book begins on the Lord's Day and ends in Eucharist. He believed in a final coming of the Lord, but he believed that this universal coming was constantly anticipated in the coming of Jesus to the individual believer (3: 20) or the local church (2: 5; 3: 3), and week by week he had known the prayer *Maranatha*, 'Come, Lord Jesus', to be answered in the eucharistic coming of him who is the First and the Last. In the Pauline churches, eucharistic worship had this same time-transcending quality. In sharing the bread and the cup they would 'proclaim the death of the Lord until he comes'. Past and future bent their frontiers to meet in the liturgical present.

Moreover, in this respect the worship of the Pauline churches had Jewish antecedents. In the Passover the Jews relived the Exodus, in confident anticipation of the Exodus to come. They celebrated the New Year festival as the day on which God judges the human race.[21] In the psalm cycle which celebrates the kingship of Yahweh (Pss. 93, 95–9), the Lord who asserts His sovereignty at the beginning over the waters of chaos and at the end in universal judgement, lays claim to the loyalty of His people 'today', which the author of Hebrews correctly understands as the day of invitation and opportunity (3: 13).

Such thoughts, however, are not confined to a liturgical context. When Paul refers to the Spirit as 'firstfruits' (Rom. 8: 23) and as a 'down-payment' (2 Cor. 1: 22; 5: 5; Eph. 1: 14), both metaphors make it clear that the continuing experience of salvation is not different in kind from the final inheritance.[22] How indeed could it be otherwise if salvation, here and hereafter, is life in the presence of God, the free access of the child to the Father (Rom. 8: 15, 23)?

Paul's teaching on justification should be seen in the same light. It is now agreed that the verb 'justify (*dikaioō*), together with its cognate

---

[21] b.T, *RH* 16a.

[22] In 1 Cor. 15: 23 Paul uses the metaphor of 'first-fruits' to stress the solidarity between Jesus and those who constitute the final harvest (cf. Rom. 11: 16). The other term, *arrabōn*, has, in many modern translations, been misconstrued as 'guarantee'. A guarantee is nothing more than a firm promise. But *arrabōn* is a commercial term for the first instalment of an agreed price (cf. J. Behm, '*arrabōn*', *TDNT* ii. 475).

adjective and noun (*dikaios*, *dikaiosunē*), is a forensic metaphor. In the earthly court a judge, faced with two litigants, justifies one, declaring him to be in the right, giving judgment in his favour. A successful litigant is therefore *dikaios*, he has right on his side; and *dikaiosunē* is not a quality inherent in his character, but the status accorded by the verdict of the court. In the heavenly lawcourt the question at issue is whether one has done that which God requires. From the precedent established in the case of Abraham, Paul argues that what God requires is not compliance with commandments but belief that God will keep His promises. Abraham believed God, and God gave the ruling that his faith constituted righteousness. Similarly, anyone who believes that in Christ God has kept His promises (including the promise to Abraham) is declared to be in the right. As we have seen, Paul uses this metaphor mainly in speaking of the initial act of faith by which a person becomes a believer and a member of the believing community. But it would be a caricature of Paul's theology to suppose that after initiation God's requirement changes, so that His verdict is pronounced on some other ground.[23] The Christian life is a life of faith from start to finish (Gal. 2: 20; Phil. 3: 9; Rom. 1: 17); for faith is the only proper response to grace, and to live by any principle other than faith is to fall away from grace (Gal. 5: 4).

4.4. THE KINGDOM OF GOD

It is extremely fortunate that the Greek *basileia* is an ambiguous term which comprehends the three possible senses: sovereignty, reign, and realm. And these three are logically so inseparable that it is no surprise to find the New Testament writers moving freely from one sense to another, and even exploiting the ambiguity. There continues to be a prolonged debate on the time reference of the phrase 'Kingdom of God', 'thoroughgoing eschatology' maintaining that the Kingdom belongs wholly to the final consummation, 'realized eschatology' that it is present in the ministry of Jesus, and 'inaugurated eschatology' that what happened in Jesus was but the beginning of a process. The

---

[23] For righteousness as status see Rom. 5: 19, where the obedience of the one establishes a new legal status for the many. While the opinion of most scholars is now that justification is a forensic metaphor, a few have not yet disengaged themselves from an ethical meaning of *dikaios* and *dikaiosunē*. An example of the latter group is J. A. Ziesler, *The Meaning of Righteousness in Paul: A Linguistic and Theological Enquiry* (Cambridge, 1972).

fact that substantial evidence could be marshalled in support of all three schools strongly suggests that the Kingdom is subject to the same three-tense structure as other terms we have examined, and that in this debate 'eschatological' is a tautology, signifying nothing more than that, in the Kingdom of God, God is King. One reason for the proliferation of conflicting opinions has been the almost universal practice of using the Synoptic Gospels as a quarry for material to be used in a conjectural reconstruction either of the teaching of Jesus himself or of the teaching of the primitive Church, without first ascertaining what the expression meant to the evangelists themselves: and for this reason the Synoptic Gospels will here be left until the last.

Paul uses the expression once in a context which leaves no doubt that he has in mind a transcendent realm beyond death and history: 'Flesh and blood cannot inherit the Kingdom of God' (1 Cor. 15: 50; also 2 Tim. 4: 1, 18; 2 Pet. 1: 11). It is therefore likely that this is also the case in three other instances where he speaks of inheriting the Kingdom (1 Cor. 6: 9, 10; Gal. 5: 21; but see also Eph. 5: 5). Elsewhere, however, he assumes that the Christian is already living in the Kingdom: 'The Kingdom of God is not a matter of talk but of power' (1 Cor. 4: 20); 'The Kingdom of God is not eating and drinking, but justice, peace and joy in the Holy Spirit' (Rom. 14: 17). To be a Christian is to live under God's sovereignty, implemented by the power of the Spirit; and Christians must accordingly 'live lives worthy of the God who calls you into His Kingdom and glory' (1 Thess. 2: 11). Paul's colleagues are his fellow workers in the service of the Kingdom of God (Col. 4: 11). At the same time the Christian lives within the Kingdom of Christ: God 'received us from the domain of darkness and brought us into the Kingdom of His dear Son' (Col. 1: 13).[24] By exalting Jesus to His own right hand God has decreed that all things should be subject to him, entrusting to him His own sovereignty: and he must reign until that subjection is complete and that sovereignty is universally acknowledged (1 Cor. 15: 24–8).

The same pattern is to be observed, with variations, in John's Revelation. John begins by exploiting the ambiguity of *basileia*. Christ, he tells his readers, 'has made of us a Kingdom, priests to his God and Father' (1: 6). This certainly includes the idea that they have become

---

[24] Cf. Rom. 5: 17–21 (cf. 1 Cor. 4: 8), where those who previously were under the reign of death established by the one individual Adam are assured that they will henceforth share both the life and the reign of the one individual Christ. The future tense in both v. 17 and v. 19 is a future of bifocal consequence.

subject to God's kingly rule, for the throne of God's universal sovereignty is the symbol which dominates John's later version, in which God is continually referred to as 'He who sits on the throne'. But when John repeats the phrase it is clear that it means something more. 'You have made them a Kingdom and priests for our God and they shall reign on earth' (5: 10). They are to be not merely subjects of God's sovereignty but agents of it, a royal dynasty. This promise receives its fulfilment in the millenial reign of Christ (20: 6), and again in the new Jerusalem (22: 5), but John cannot have intended it to be confined to the ultimate future. Whatever may be the relation of the millenium to the earthly experience of the Church, it cannot, in view of the kaleidoscopic nature of John's imagery, be one of mere chronological succession. For he addresses his book to his contemporaries who are his partners 'in the ordeal and sovereignty and endurance which are ours in Jesus' (1: 9). Just as the Cross was for Jesus an enthronement, so it is in their martyrdom that his followers become agents of the divine reign, the means by which God the King overcomes the resistance of a rebellious world. They are the two witnesses, the two sons of oil, on whom have devolved the functions of the anointed king and the anointed priest (11: 3–4; cf. Zech. 4: 14). At the death of the martyrs, which is their victory over the Great Accuser, the heavenly choir raises the hymns of triumph: 'Now is the hour of victory for our God! Now His power and sovereignty have come, and the rightful reign of His Christ' (12: 10). The sovereignty of God has come, but not for the first time or for the last. It has come in archetypal fashion in the victory of Christ (3: 21), and it will come in its fulness only when 'world sovereignty has passed to our Lord and to His Christ' (11: 15; cf. 19: 6).

As already noted, in Hebrews the Kingdom stands for the unshakeable presence of the transcendent in the midst of a world liable to be shaken by the earthquake of God's judgement (12: 28). With this we may compare the one occurrence of the term in the Fourth Gospel (3: 3, 5). To see the Kingdom of God, to enter it, to be born of the Spirit, and to have eternal life are interchangeable descriptions of the one experience of salvation which is to become available to enquirers like Nicodemus only when Jesus has been 'lifted up' (3: 15). Jesus is indeed already King of Israel (1: 50; 12: 13, 15; cf. 20: 31), but not in the only sense his enemies could understand. His sovereignty (18: 36) is not derived from the military strength and popular acclaim on which worldly political power depends; it is derived from God who has entrusted to His Son the exercise of His own kingly authority.

We have also seen that in his chapter of parables Mark treats the Kingdom as a process, which began when Jesus proclaimed the arrival of God the King. Occasionally, Mark (like Paul) uses 'the Kingdom of God' to refer to that eternal life beyond death which is the goal of the process (9: 47; 14: 25). Elsewhere entry into the Kingdom is synonymous with following Jesus. 'Whoever does not accept the Kingdom of God as a child can never enter it' (10: 15). 'How hard it is for the wealthy to enter the Kingdom of God' (10: 23).[25] The question which is here at stake is not the distance of the Kingdom from the present, but the distance of a potential disciple from the Kingdom (12: 34). In yet another sense Jesus is a king who has not yet entered on his royal status (10:37), whose coronation occurs only when the places on his right and his left are occupied by those to whom they have been assigned (15: 17, 27). But that is not to say that Mark thought Jesus had to die in order to bring in the Kingdom.[26] The proclamation of Jesus was not, like John's baptism, an 'advance notice' of forthcoming events. Rather it was in obedience to the demands of the Kingdom that Jesus went to the Cross.

Besides Mark, Matthew, and Luke had a common source (or sources) which laid all the emphasis on the presence and activity of the Kingdom in the ministry of Jesus. It contained two sayings which identified John the Baptist as the greatest person who ever lived outside the Kingdom, the end of the old order of Law and prophets (Matt. 11: 11; Luke 7: 28; Matt. 11: 12–13; Luke 16: 16), which had given place to the new order of the Kingdom.[27] Evidence that the Kingdom is exerting its power is to be seen in the healing ministry of Jesus (Matt. 12: 27–8; Luke 11: 20) and of the disciples (Luke 9: 2; 10: 9). But by contrast the opponents of Jesus are criticized because they neither enter the Kingdom nor allow others to do so (Matt. 23: 13;

[25] The future tenses, here translated by 'can' and 'must', are gnomic futures, expressing a logical consequence attendant on a fulfilled or unfulfilled condition (cf. Rom. 5: 7). Luke has shown that he understands them so by altering the second to a present.

[26] As an example one may cite R. H. Fuller's treatment of Mark 9: 1: 'The event referred to can only be the final coming of the Kingdom . . . Whatever the difficulties, there can be no doubt that it implies the coming of the Kingdom of God as a future event' (*The Mission and Achievement of Jesus* (London, 1954), 27 f.). Here 'future' is clearly used as a synonym for 'final'.

[27] Whether in the second of those passages the Kingdom is said to be grasped by those of force or ravaged by those of violence, it must be regarded as a present reality.

Luke 11: 52). The Kingdom operates like leaven (Matt. 13: 33; Luke 13: 21) and lays claim to a radical obedience (Matt. 6: 33; Luke 12: 31).

To what he has taken from his sources Luke adds some distinctive points of his own. In a number of editorial passages he describes Jesus as proclaiming the good news of the Kingdom of God (4: 43; 8: 1; 9: 11, 60). When we encounter this expression again in Acts, it is clearly shorthand for the gospel as God's act of salvation, with Jesus at its centre, fulfilling the purpose of God adumbrated in the Old Testament (8: 12; 20: 25–8; 28: 23, 30–1); and we can safely assume that Luke intends it to have the same sense throughout.[28] Luke lays particular emphasis on the place of Israel in the reign of God. The Kingdom is in the first instance God's rule over Israel, and consequently God's rule through Israel over the world. The story begins with a promise for Jesus that 'the Lord God will give him the throne of his ancestor David, and he will be King over Israel forever' (1: 32–3), and ends with his legacy to the disciples: 'Now I vest in you the kingship which my father vested in me: you shall eat and drink at my table in my Kingdom and sit on thrones as judges of the twelve tribes of Israel' (22: 29–30). These two references to kingship are firmly linked to the main teaching about the Kingdom of God by the opening paragraph of Acts (1: 3–8).

Over a period of forty days he appeared to them and taught them about the Kingdom of God ... They asked him, 'Lord, is this the time when you are to establish once again the sovereignty of Israel?' 'It is not for you to know about dates or times', he answered, 'which the Father has set within his own control. But you will receive power when the Holy Spirit comes upon you; and you will bear witness to me in Jerusalem, across all Judea and Samaria, and to the ends of the earth.'

Here the date of the final denouement is known only to God, not because it has been arbitrarily fixed in advance and then kept secret, but because it will come only when God is ready for it (cf. Luke 19: 11; 17: 20–5). But in the meantime the sovereignty of God and the kingship of His Christ are to be made an earthly reality through the testimony of the apostles, confirmed by the activity of His Spirit.

Prominent among the evidence that has been cited for the essential

---

[28] There is a significant editorial change in 18: 29, where Luke alters Mark's 'for my sake or for the Gospel' (10: 29) to 'for the sake of the Kingdom of God'.

futurity of the Kingdom is the clause in the Lord's Prayer, 'Your Kingdom come'. In Luke's shorter form (11: 2) this might be taken to be a prayer for the final triumph of God's reign, though the Lucan evidence we have examined points firmly to the conclusion that Luke himself understood it to have a multiple reference to the future progress of that reign through the preaching of the gospel and the work of the Spirit. Matthew has provided the short prayer with an interpretative gloss, 'your will be done on earth as in heaven', which leaves no room for doubt that he understood the prayer in the same way as Luke: God's reign is present and active on earth wherever there are human agents obedient to His will. It is true that Matthew shows more interest than do the other evangelists in the final crisis of history (13: 40, 49; 19: 28; 24: 3; 25: 31; 28: 20) and is the only one to introduce the word *parousia* into his record (24: 3, 27, 37, 39), even on occasion speaking as though entry into the Kingdom were the final reward of the righteous (7: 21–2; 25: 34). But such passages are balanced by an equal interest in the presence of the Kingdom in the ministry of Jesus and the life of the Church. The parables of the Treasure and the Pearl (13: 44–6) represent the Kingdom as immediately accessible to a single-minded quest, and the parable of the Two Sons indicates that the opportunity is already being grasped by unexpected candidates (21: 31–2): 'Tax-gathers and prostitutes are entering the Kingdom of God ahead of you.' The parables of the Two Debtors (18: 23–5) and the Hired Hands (20: 1–16) depict the way in which the reign of God operates in a world where there are wrongs to be forgiven and work to be done. Those who make themselves eunuchs by renouncing marriage do so in the service of the Kingdom and not just to win the Kingdom as a heavenly reward (19: 12). A comparison of the two versions of the parable of the Great Banquet (Matt. 22: 1–14; Luke 14: 16–24) shows that Matthew's version has been elaborated by the introduction of a punitive military expedition; but the intrusive verse proves that Matthew thought of the banquet as happening on earth in the course of history. Above all there is Matthew's editorial addition to Mark's parable of the Wicked Tenants: 'I tell you, the Kingdom of God will be taken away from you, and given to a nation that yields the proper fruit' (21: 43). Israel has forfeited its ancestral claim to be the subject and the agent of God's reign. When to all this we add Matthew's preoccupation with doing the will of God (7: 21; 12: 50; 21: 31; 20: 42; cf. 5: 19; 7: 24; 23: 3; 24: 46), not as a remote eschatological prospect, but as an immediate required response to

God's offer of forgiveness and love, we can see that he has maintained the temporal ambiguity of the Kingdom as fully as any other New Testament writer.

5.

The Fact of Salvation

5.1. THE ONE AND THE MANY

Having guarded ourselves against any one-sided reduction of the three-tense structure, we look now more closely at each of the tenses in turn, beginning with the strong emphasis of the New Testament on salvation as an act of God fully achieved. Jesus has finished his course (Luke 13: 32), has completed the work which God gave him to do (John 4: 34; 5: 36; 17: 4; 19: 30), has died to or for sin once for all (Rom. 6: 10; 1 Pet. 3: 18), has once for all offered himself to bear the burden of human sin (Heb. 7: 27; 9: 28), to abolish or remove sin (Heb. 9: 26; 10: 10), and to secure for himself and others entry into the eternal sanctuary (Heb. 9: 12). Elsewhere in the New Testament a belief in this finished work, though not so explicitly stated, is constantly implied by the use of aorist tenses and the inseparable connection of salvation with the life, death, and resurrection of Jesus.

Although in other respects it is self-evident that God's salvation is not complete, it can be spoken of in this way because it is seen to be complete in the representative figure of Jesus, who embodies human destiny. He is the one who has acted and suffered in the place of (*anti*), or on behalf of (*huper*),[1] the many (Mark 10: 45; Rom. 5: 19; Heb. 2: 9; 9: 28). In contexts which deal with the historic setting of Jesus' ministry, the many are identified as the Jewish nation, though always with wider implications (John 11: 50–2; Heb. 2: 16); but where the universality of the gospel is at stake the many become 'all' (2 Cor. 5: 15; 1 Tim. 2: 6), or 'the world' (John 6: 51). Far more often the application is personal: he died for us,[2] for our sins (1 Cor. 15: 3;

---

[1] For helpful discussions of *anti* and *huper* cf. C. F. D. Moule, *An Idiom Book of New Testament Greek* (Cambridge, 1971²), 63 f., 71; and M. J. Harris, Appendix to *NIDNTT* iii. 1179 f., 1196 f., with the bibliography on pp. 1214 ff.

[2] Rom. 5: 8; Gal. 3: 13; Eph. 5: 2; 1 Thess. 5: 10; Heb. 6: 20; 1 Pet. 2: 21; 1 John 3: 16.

2 Cor. 5: 21; Gal. 1: 4), for us all (Rom. 8: 32), or for me (Gal. 2: 20).

Such a consensus raises two questions: granted that the one has done for the many that which they could not do for themselves, what is it that he has done, and by what right has he done it? The second question must be reserved for later discussion (below, Ch. 8), since any convictions about the person of Christ which may have emerged in the early Church were inferences from its experience of atonement. But to the first question there are four conceivable types of answer, all well represented in the New Testament, concerning what the one may do for the many:

1. that which they cannot and need not thereafter repeat, but need only accept in faith and gratitude;
2. that which they must subsequently acknowledge to have been done in their name, in such a way as to include them in the doing of it;
3. that which they must subsequently appropriate in their own experience;
4. that which they must subsequently do for others.

It has long been customary to describe the redeeming work of Christ as vicarious and to use other, more specific terms to distinguish the four types of vicariousness. On the surface, 'substitution' might appear to be a suitable title for (1), 'representation', 'inclusion', or 'incorporation' for (2), 'leadership' for (3), and 'example' for (4). There is no harm in the use of such terms, provided that we treat them as nothing more than convenient short-hand, and do not turn them into labels for conflicting theories or doctrines of atonement.[3] Most debates on this subject have been attempts to prove that one of these formulations is correct and the rest wrong, or that one is primary and the others

---

[3] One term, however, notwithstanding its use in the AV, must be discarded from the start. There was not in 1611, nor is there today, any justification for the use of 'propitiation' in this connection. 'Propitiate' is a transitive verb which requires a personal object, and which entails a change of attitude in the person propitiated. But in the New Testament atonement in all its forms has its origin in the unchanging purpose and love of God. If we are true to New Testament evidence, we shall not frame any sentence about atonement or salvation with Jesus as its subject which could not equally have God as subject. The only exceptions, more apparent than real, are sentences which speak of Jesus' obedience to the will of the Father and understanding of His purpose. The continued use of 'propitiation' in theological debate is more the waving of a partisan flag than an aid to understanding.

derivative, or that one is the mature, developed form to which the others are elementary and inadequate approaches. We shall find, on the contrary, that all four are irreducibly complementary and inter-locking, that the New Testament writers move with great freedom from one to another, and that the New Testament teaching will be misrepresented if any one of them is emphasized at the expense of the rest.[4]

Passages classified under (4), for instance, are not the less profound or the less central for being called exemplary, since they include those which trace atonement to its source in the love of God. We must therefore be cautious about drawing hard-and-fast distinctions between the objective and the subjective. For, although there are no conditions attaching to God's free gift of salvation, there are substantial conditions attached to the reception of it and the belief in it.[5]

Having laid this groundwork, we may now examine how the New Testament writers work out this fourfold scheme under the following heads: revelation, atonement, breaking sin's power, inauguration, and solidarity or identification.

5.2. REVELATION

For the New Testament writers Jesus is Saviour, first, because he is the bringer of revelation. Revelation is an intricate concept, constructed of three main strands, all integral to salvation. The first is the mediation of God's presence and activity, since salvation first and foremost con-sists in the knowledge of God and in access to Him. But equally important is the disclosure of the truth about God's character, purpose, and methods, together with the exposure of those false beliefs and lies about God which are inherent in the nature of sin. And since salvation is the gift of a new life to be lived here and hereafter in response to God's grace and authority, there must also be a clear delineation of that life, its privileges and its obligations.

One of the distinctive features of the Synoptic Gospels is the degree to which revelation is emphasized in the teaching of Jesus. And here it is ironic that Mark, who records less of the teaching than do Luke

---

[4] On the Atonement cf. e.g. G. Aulén, *Christus Victor* (New York, 1969), and M. Hengel, *The Atonement* (London, 1981).

[5] For the distinction between merit and capacity, see C. F. D. Moule, *Essays in New Testament Interpretation*, 278 ff. For a statement of a similar point in terms of existentialist philosophy, cf. R. Bultmann, *Theology of the New Testament*, i. 322.

or Matthew, lays the greatest stress on his role as teacher. Jesus instructs his disciples about the nature of God's sovereignty (4: 1– 32), and about the methods by which God intends to implement it (8: 27–38; 10: 35–45). He enters into controversy with the authorities, and particularly with the Pharisees, not simply because he disagrees with them in detail, but because he is at odds with them about what it means for Israel to be God's holy people, and therefore about the nature of God's own holiness. To them holiness is something to be hedged round with protective regulations; but to Jesus it is absurd to tremble for the ark of God's holiness, which is a dynamic force bursting into the world of Satanic wickedness to rescue the helpless, stronger than any influences which might contaminate it (2: 15–17; 3: 22–7). Mark is particularly impressed by the authority of Jesus (1: 22, 27), which is derived partly from his commission (1: 11; 2: 10), and partly from his obedient acceptance of his own role in the redemptive plan of God (9: 4; 10: 45; 14: 35), and the gospel reaches its climax in the centurion's recognition that, in accepting the Cross, Jesus has revealed himself to be Son of God (15: 39).

The Marcan Jesus is reticent about the fatherhood of God (below, Chapter 9). Only four times does he apply the title 'Father' to God (8: 38; 11: 25; 13: 32; 14: 36), and three of these refer to his own unique status. To him the fatherhood of God is not a doctrine to be proclaimed, but a relationship to be explored in understanding, trust, and obedience.[6] To this Matthew and Luke add that it is a relationship to be shared with others. 'I thank you, Father, that you have hidden these things from the wise and learned, and revealed them to the simple . . . No one knows the Son but the Father, and no one knows the Father but the Son, and those to whom the Son may choose to reveal Him' (Matt. 11: 25–7; Luke 10: 21–7). This is not to be taken as a denial that anyone else has ever believed in God's fatherhood or addressed him as Father, a denial which would be absurd in view of Old Testament evidence and Jewish practice. It is rather a claim that Jesus has experienced the divine fatherhood with such intensity and fulness that only he can adequately impart to others the knowledge of it. The Lord's Prayer is the instruction by which Jesus conveys to his disciples what it means to address God as Father, as he himself has done: and the repercussions of it are felt throughout the New Testa-

---

[6] See T. W. Manson, *The Teaching of Jesus* (Cambridge, 1945), 113, and below, pp. 400–404.

ment (cf. esp. Rom. 8: 15; Gal. 4: 6; 1 Pet. 1: 17). The key to the interpretation of the prayer lies in its first petition, 'hallowed be your name'. This may be construed either as a reverential passive, asking God to act for the manifestation of His holiness,[7] or as a true passive, asking that God's holiness may receive recognition and response among men and women; and the probability is that the ambiguity is intentional and covers both senses, and that all the other clauses are governed by the same duality. He who learns from Jesus to pray as Jesus himself prays must ask God to reveal himself as Father, to reveal His holiness, His sovereignty, His providence, His forgiveness, His redemptive power; and true worshippers must at the same time offer themselves to be both the recipients and the agents of that revelation.

John's Gospel is expressly concerned with the revelation of the unseen God (1: 18). By revelation he means us to understand the unfolding of a purpose which becomes known only in the course of its achievement; but conversely, since that purpose includes human understanding of the character and ways of God, it can be achieved only in the disclosure of it. What the Johannine Jesus reveals is that he himself is the content of the revelation he brings. By the incarnation of the *logos* God has taken the human being Jesus into union with Himself, so that all that was formerly predicated of the *logos* can now be predicated of him. He is the light of the world (8: 12; cf. 1: 4), the Father has granted him to have life in himself (5: 26; cf. 1: 4), he has manifested his possession of celestial glory (2: 11; cf. 17: 5). All his words and works, and particularly those works which John calls signs,[8] demonstrate that the Father has sent him (5: 36), that the Father abides in him and he in the Father (10: 38; 14: 10–11), and that he and the Father are one (10: 30). If they are to be set free from sin, believers need to know the truth and that truth is embodied in Jesus (8: 32, 35; 14: 6). Eternal life is to know God and Jesus whom he has sent (17: 3). Yet confronted by that truth even the most intimate friends of Jesus can hardly be said to believe (16: 31). Something more has to be both achieved and revealed in the Cross before saving faith becomes possible.

In the ancient world the lawcourt was the one institution devoted to the quest for truth: the truth of any matter was to be established

---

[7] See G. B. Caird, *Language and Imagery of the Bible*, 28 ff.

[8] For an extended treatment cf. R. T. Fortna, *The Gospel of Signs* (New York, 1970), and C. H. Dodd, *Interpretation of the Fourth Gospel*, 289 ff.

on the evidence of two or three witnesses (Deut. 19: 15), and the verdict turned not so much on the production of external clues as of the credibility of the witnesses.[9] John gives his story a forensic setting. In the case of God versus the world witnesses were called to prove the truth of God's indictment against the world and of the gospel which offers to the world salvation from the sentence it has incurred (5: 31–9; 8: 13–18; 10: 25). Yet John is aware that all these witnesses together are not enough to win the case. Only when, through the death of Jesus, the Advocate comes who is the Spirit of truth, will He be able to take the teaching of Jesus and the story of his life, death, and resurrection, and so bring them home to the hearts and consciences of men and women as to convince the world that it has been wrong (16: 7–11). So by the double witness of the apostles and the Spirit, the truth is to be confirmed.[10]

The author of 1 John is confident that in Christ a definitive revelation has been given: eternal life has been made visible because the love of God has become incarnate (1: 1–3; 2: 22; 4: 2). Yet this conviction has been challenged by a powerful splinter group, whose departure has left loyal believers shaken and wondering how they can be sure that they are right and the others wrong.[11] John's answer is that only those can be assured of the objective reality of the incarnation who in some measure have experienced the same love, not merely as beneficiaries, but as channels of it. 'Everyone who loves is a child of God and knows God, but the unloving know nothing of God. For God is love and His love was disclosed to us in this, that He sent His only son into the world to bring us life. The love I speak of is not our love for God, but the love He showed us in sending His son as the remedy for the defilement of our sins' (1 John 4: 7–10). There are no conditions attaching to God's revelation of truth as to His gift of salvation, but there are conditions attached to our capacity to accept the gift and to know the truth; and those conditions are both spiritual and moral. 'If anyone says "I love God", while hating his brother, he is a liar' (4: 20). Incarnation and atonement are not facts but convictions which have to be reached on credible evidence, and the credibility

---

[9] See A. E. Harvey, *Jesus on Trial* (London, 1976), and A. A. Trites, *The New Testament Concept of Witness* (Cambridge, 1976), 78 ff.

[10] The principle of double witness is differently understood in Acts, where the testimony of the apostles is confirmed by the Spirit in deeds of power (Acts 5: 32; cf. Heb. 2: 3–4).

[11] On this splinter group cf. above, p. 37.

is proportionate to the capacity of the believer. It follows, then, that revelation, though essential to salvation, is not self-sustaining, unless God can with it remove the obstacles to faith and create the conditions for it. In this respect the Epistle reflects an insight already provided in the Gospel, 'The teaching that I give is not my own; it is the teaching of Him who sent me. Whoever has the will to do the will of God shall know whether my teaching comes from Him or is merely my own' (John 18: 16–17). Jesus is a perfect channel for the divine revelation because he is wholly subservient to the divine purpose; but the belief that this is so, that in him the divine purpose has taken human form, makes sense and is credible only to those who in some degree have the capacity and intention to share his obedience.

According to Hebrews the revelation given to past generations was fragmentary in comparison with the word spoken in Jesus Christ, not merely because that word was complete and final, but because it was the fulfilment of promise, the reality of which the old order had but a shadowy outline (1: 1; 8: 5; 10: 1). God's word is living and active; performative as well as revelatory (4: 12). There were, to be sure, in the past men and women of faith, but their faith was in God's future, in His promised act of salvation, and they had not yet, as have Christians, received what had been promised (11: 39–40). Of past generations in general, and the wilderness generation in particular, it could be said that they had received the gospel promise, but that it 'did no good because it was not mixed with faith in those who heard it' (4: 2). The reason why Jesus was able to become the mediator of a better and more effective covenant was that he not only 'offered for all time one sacrifice for sins' (10: 10), but was able also to elicit the faith that this was the true significance of his death; he was 'the author and perfecter of faith' (12: 2).[12] James Denney said of the author of Hebrews that he believed in 'a finished work of Christ, a work finished in his death, something done in regard to sin once for all, whether any given soul responds to it or not'.[13] But Denney could not have said, and would

---

[12] That Jesus is 'the author and perfecter of faith' is normally understood to mean that Jesus himself is in no way the focus of faith—he only points the way to faith in God. The obvious contrasts are then drawn with Paul's idea of 'faith-union' and 'in Christ'. See however D. Hamm, 'Faith in the Epistle to the Hebrews: The Jesus Factor', *CBQ* 52 (1990), 270 ff., who argues cogently that in Hebrews faith is Christologically focused in a very Pauline way.

[13] J. Denney, *The Death of Christ* (London, 1902), 225. But see also pp. 119 ff. and 140 f. for Denney's distinction between fact and theory.

not have wished to say, 'whether *any* soul responds to it or not'. An objective atonement is incredible if it is presented independently of the power of Christ to elicit faith that it is so. Salvation may be acheived as a free gift of God, but it is not a thing, an object to be transferred from donor to beneficiary; it is a life to be lived, a right of access into a presence, a relationship with God. Thus to receive enlightenment (6: 4; 10: 32), to acknowledge the truth (10: 26), entails more than an initial response; it entails a persistent exercise of moral judgement in adherence to that which has once been accepted as true (3: 6, 14; 10: 23). For although the gospel provides milk for spiritual infants, it is solid meat for grown men and women 'who have their faculties trained by long use to discriminate between good and evil' (5: 14).

The Apocalypse is primarily a revelation about the imminent future, but it is grounded in a revelation contained in the gospel story, 'the word spoken by God and attested by Jesus Christ' (1: 2, 9). Jesus is the 'faithful witness' because in his death he has revealed God's way of dealing with evil (1: 5; 3: 14; 19: 11), and therefore by his death he has won the right to break the seals on God's scroll of destiny, disclosing the purpose it contains and bringing it into operation (5: 9). For this reason 'the testimony of Jesus is the Spirit that inspires the prophets' (19: 10), those who like John are called to follow the example of Jesus at the risk of life and liberty. Here, as in the Fourth Gospel, the words 'witness' and 'testimony' have their original forensic sense.[14] Jesus bore his testimony in the court of Pontius Pilate (cf. 1 Tim. 6: 13). John himself has been sentenced by a Roman judge, and he writes for martyrs who face the same prospect; but he writes to assure them that on their evidence the verdict of the earthly tribunal will be reversed in the heavenly court of appeal, where the truth is established before the great white throne (20: 11).[15]

Many of the themes we have noted elsewhere are developed in his own idiom by Paul. Sinful humanity had been blinded to God's truth, either because its passions had rendered its mind futile (Rom. 1: 21) or because its preoccupation with the demands of law had cast a veil of incomprehension over its heart (2 Cor. 3: 14; 4: 4). It was 'ignorant of the righteousness that comes from God' (Rom. 10: 3). But Christ is the image of God who by reflecting God's glory (2 Cor. 4: 4–6)

---

[14] Cf. Trites, *New Testament Concept of Witness*, 154 ff.

[15] On the heavenly court's reversal of Satan's verdict, cf. G. B. Caird, *The Revelation of St John the Divine* (London, 1985²), 154 f.

has made visible the invisible God (Col. 1: 15). Above all Christ's death reveals the love of God, its boundless extent and its unmerited costliness: 'God gives proof of His love to us in that while we were still sinners Christ died for us (Rom 5: 8; cf. 2 Cor. 2: 7–8, where forgiveness is defined as the assurance of unwavering love). 'The love of Christ constrains us, once we have reached the conclusion that one man died for all, and therefore all died' (2 Cor. 5: 14–15). These two sentences make it plain that, when Paul says 'I have been crucified with Christ' (Gal. 2: 20; cf. Rom. 6: 6), he is not referring to his conversion or to the subsequent experience which he variously describes as dying daily (1 Cor. 15: 31) or putting to death all that is earthly (Col. 3: 5), but to an event which happened on Golgotha long before he himself was aware of it. Christ's death for all involved the death of all; and when he died, all died. Yet this is not a fact, but a conclusion of type (2) which has to be reached by those who are prepared to commit themselves to the death of their old nature and the beginning of a new life under the constraints of Christ's love. Paul himself takes no credit for having reached this conclusion. What happened at his conversion was that 'God revealed His son in me' (Gal. 1: 16); the Creator said, 'Let there be light' (2 Cor. 4: 6).

Paul reserves his most systematic treatment for the revelation of God's righteousness (Rom. 1: 17). This includes 'God's way of righting wrong' (NEB), but much more besides. Paul is here expounding the age-long problem of the theist, the problem of theodicy, to provide a triumphant demonstration of the wisdom and power of God. 'Shall not the judge of all the earth do right?' (Gen. 18: 25; cf. Rom. 3: 6). The duty of earthly judges or rulers is to see justice done (2 Sam. 15: 4, Deut. 16: 20); to ensure that wrongdoing does not pay (Job 31: 18) and so to rid Israel of wickedness (Deut. 1: 17); to rescue the helpless (Ps. 72: 13–14; Isa. 1: 17; Luke 18: 3); to show impartiality in their judgments (Deut. 1: 17; Ps. 58: 2; Prov. 24: 21–3); and to be consistent with their own established practice and the demands of the covenant (2 Chr. 19: 9; 1 Sam. 11: 5).[16] Paul is aware that God's righteousness might be impugned on any of these four counts. In the past He had shown a forbearance which had allowed sin to go unpunished and unrestrained (Rom. 2: 4; 3: 25–6). He had given the human

---

[16] The *mishpat* of the king, for example, appears to have been the declaration of a policy to which he could be expected to adhere (1 Sam. 10: 27). Cf. 'the law of the Medes and Persians' (Dan. 6: 8), which the king could not alter at his own discretion, even to meet hard cases.

race up to the consequences of its own folly (Rom. 1: 24, 26, 28), leaving it enslaved and helpless to free itself from the sin to which it had surrendered (Rom. 6: 16). By His election of Israel he had given some Jews the impression that they would receive preferential treatment just because they were Jews, possessing the Law and the external mark of circumcision, whether or not they were true Jews, obedient to the Law and having the inward circumcision of the heart (Rom. 2: 11–29). Yet, if God were to treat all alike, what would become of His covenant? The above four principles of justice seem, to mere human wisdom, so mutually conflicting that God could not satisfy one without violating another. But not to God's wisdom! By allowing Christ to die for the human race that death which all owe to the Law they have broken (Rom. 6: 10; 7: 4–6), God has shown with what seriousness He regards sin, and has at the same time provided an escape from its bondage: 'While we were still helpless, Christ died for the wicked' (Rom. 5: 6). God has given 'proof that He is both just and the vindicator of anyone who has faith in Jesus' (Rom. 3: 26). He has shown that 'there is no discrimination between Jew and Greek, because the same Lord is Lord of all' (Rom. 10: 12)—yet without forgetting His promise to His ancient people, Israel. 'Has God rejected His people? I cannot believe it! . . . God never goes back on his gifts and calling' (Rom. 11: 1, 29). It is precisely by the inclusion of Gentiles in His covenant of grace that God means to liberate the Jewish people from the prison of their national self-righteousness (Rom. 10: 3). Small wonder that the revelation of God's righteousness leaves Paul breathless with adoration: 'O the depth of God's wealth and wisdom and knowledge. How unsearchable his judgments, how untraceable his ways!' (Rom. 11: 36).

5.3. ATONEMENT

Under this heading the New Testament writers treat Christ as Saviour because he has borne sin's guilt, removed sin's taint, and broken sin's power.

5.3.1. *Bearing of Guilt*

In the Old Testament it was confidently expected that guilt would be cancelled by forgiveness. 'In the fulness of your mercy blot out my misdeeds. Wash away all my guilt and cleanse me from my sin' (Ps.

61: 12). Yet in the New Testament the cancellation of guilt is uniformly associated with Jesus, and commonly with his death. 'It is through him that forgiveness of sins is proclaimed' (Acts 13: 38; cf. Luke 1: 77; 24: 47); 'God was in Christ, reconciling the world to Himself, not entering its sins in the record book' (2 Cor. 5: 19). God's vindicating of His righteousness is effective through faith in Jesus Christ (Rom. 3: 22), and through union with him all offences are forgiven (Col. 2: 13; cf. Eph. 4: 32). Sins are forgiven for his sake (1 John 2: 12; cf. 1: 9; 3: 5), and from him Christians derive the authority to pronounce God's pardon (John 20: 33). His blood was shed 'for the remission of sins' (Matt. 26: 28), and the New Covenant, as Jeremiah predicted, is founded on that remission (Heb. 10: 18).

These early Christians never asked, as their modern counterparts sometimes do, why God could not simply forgive, why pardon had to be tied to the life and death of Jesus. To forgive sin by fiat would be to ignore it, to treat it as though it did not exist; like cancelling traffic offences by abolishing the rules of the road. The early Christians experienced forgiveness first and then tried to explain how it had come to them, and their explanations varied. To Luke, Jesus was the friend of sinners, who brought salvation to them through his transforming friendship; if in the end he was 'numbered among transgressors' (22: 37), this was but the logical outcome of the role he had chosen, the price exacted by an uncomprehending world from one who had dared to let God's forgiveness loose into the world.[17] But to other writers the heart of the matter was that the innocent had died in place of the guilty: 'Christ died for sins once for all, the just for the unjust, to bring us to God' (1 Pet. 3: 18). 'Christ was innocent of sin, and yet for our sake God made him one with human sinfulness' (2 Cor. 5: 21). 'Sin is lawlessness, and Christ appeared, as you know, to remove sins, being himself innocent of sin' (1 John 3: 4–5). But whose place did Jesus take on Good Friday? Mark's answer is, as usual, in story form. Jesus was executed by order of a Roman official on a charge of leading or inciting insurrection against the rule of Rome, and he died between two brigands,[18] members of the Jewish resistance movement, who were

---

[17] Luke omits the only two verses of Mark which explicitly give atoning power to the death of Jesus (10: 45; 14: 24), and in the speeches in Acts he presents the death of Jesus as an act of human sin which is reversed by God in the resurrection.

[18] It is utterly misleading to call them 'thieves' (*kleptai*, cf. Matt. 6: 19 f.; Luke 12: 33, 39). They were *lēstai*, or *to lēstrikon*, the name given by Josephus to the movement which he calls 'the fourth philosophy'. Luke records a conversation between Jesus and one of

guilty of the charge of which he was innocent. Before he was sentenced, the Jerusalem mob had been asked to choose between him and a killer called Barabbas, a member of the Liberation Front, whose murderous activities were dictated by religious and patriotic principles. The authorities who handed Jesus over to Pilate and the crowd who called for the release of Barabbas were not members of the underground, but they showed by their actions where their sympathies lay.

At this point we must allow Paul to join the discussion. 'I have been crucified with Christ: the life I now live is not my life, but the life which Christ lives in me: and my present bodily life is lived by faith in the Son of God, who loved me and gave himself for me' (Gal. 2: 19–20). No doubt Paul intended what he said of himself to be universally applicable, but it arose out of his own experience. Before his conversion he had not been a sinner in any conventional sense. A Pharisee educated in the strictest tenets of the Jewish religion, proud of his national inheritance, proud of his own reputation for rectitude, deeply committed to the maintenance of high moral standards, sure that in the Law he possessed the very substance of knowledge and truth, he had persecuted Christians in the confidence that in so doing he was doing the work of God: Jesus had been a menace to all that he held most dear, and the menace had revived in the nascent Church. If it be true that Jesus died for such as Paul, then the one thing certain is that the sins he bore included the sins of sincerity. Paul's autobiography provides an important commentary on Mark's story. Christian tradition has regrettably accustomed us to think of those who brought about the Crucifixion as villains; but if we observe them through the eyes of Paul, we get a different view. 'I bear them witness that they have a zeal for God, however unenlightened' (Rom. 10: 2). No doubt they had their faults and fallacies, but each in his own way was a sincere person, honestly trying to do what was right in the interest of religion and national survival. But in all the annals of human vice, no power is as destructive or demonic as perverted sincerity.

It took the Cross, interpreted as the vicarious bearing of guilt, to pierce the armour-plate of Paul's self-congratulation. It proved that when he had been most confident of serving God, he had been God's enemy; and it had revealed a love great enough to kill the enmity (Rom. 5: 8; 2 Cor. 5: 18–21). 'What room then is left for human pride?

---

his companions which makes explicit what is implicit in Mark: 'We are paying the price for our misdeeds, but this man has done nothing wrong' (23: 41, REB).

It is excluded. And on what principle? The keeping of the Law would not exclude it, but faith does' (Rom. 3: 27). His conversion[19] had convinced him that Jesus was alive, and that his resurrection was God's vindication of all he had stood for. It followed therefore that his death under the Law and the curse which the Law pronounces on flagrant violators of it (Gal. 3: 13; 4: 4–5)[20] must have been vicarious, that Jesus had identified himself with sinners where they were, in sin and under God's annihilating judgement, in order that they might be identified with him in his risen, vindicated life. God's verdict of justification, then, which cancels guilt, is pronounced on those who have faith in Christ; and faith is the acceptance of the identification he offers. 'He was delivered up for our misdeeds and raised for our justification' (Rom. 6: 25). 'There is no condemnation for those who are in Christ Jesus . . . who will be the accuser of God's chosen ones? It is God who justifies; who then can condemn?' (Rom. 8: 1, 33). With such a faith Paul felt no option open to him but to allow Christ to live out the rest of his curtailed life in the person of the one whose place he had taken. 'The life I live is not mine, but the life Christ lives in me' (Gal. 2: 20). That is not the voice of mysticism,[21] but the acknowledgement of a debt of love which only love can repay.

In the Johannine literature the guilt of sin is symbolized by the Great Accuser (above, chapter 3). In the Revelation the running commentary of the heavenly chorus leaves no doubt that the victory of Michael over Satan is a lawcourt victory of defence[22] over the pros-

[19] On Paul's conversion, cf. C. Dietzfelbinger, *Die Berufung des Paulus als Ursprung seiner Theologie* (Neukirchen-Vluyn, 1985); J. Dupont, 'The Conversion of Paul and Its Influence on His Understanding of Salvation by Faith', in W. Gasque and R. Martin, *Apostolic History and the Gospel* (Grand Rapids, 1970), 176 ff.; J. Gager, 'Some Notes on Paul's Conversion (Its Influence on His Theology)', *NTS* 27 (1981), p. 697 ff.; S. Kim, *The Origin of Paul's Gospel* (Grand Rapids, 1981); and J. D. G. Dunn, '" A Light to the Gentiles": The Significance of the Damascus Road Christophany for Paul', *Jesus, Paul, and the Law* (Philadelphia, 1990), 89 ff.

[20] Cf. Caird, *Principalities and Powers*, 91, who includes Gal. 3: 13 with the other Pauline texts (Phil. 2: 8; 2 Cor. 8: 8; Rom. 8: 3; 2 Cor. 5: 21) which link Christ with 'the corporate unity of mankind' under the control of the rulers of this age.

[21] Cf. A. Schweitzer, *The Mysticism of Paul the Apostle* (London, 1953²). Despite its 'faded glory' today, Schweitzer's work remains important, and should not be understood apart from the extraordinary circumstances in which it was written (cf. S. Neill and T. Wright, *The Interpretation of the New Testament 1861–1986* (New York, 1989) 404 n. 3).

[22] The mixing of legal and martial metaphors found in Rev. 12: 7 ff. is familiar enough: cf. 'We will submit this to the arbitration of battle.'

ecution which is made possible because Michael's clients have been represented in the earthly contest by Jesus, whose victory embodies theirs (12: 7–9). It is in him they have their ordeal (1: 9), in his blood their robes are made white (7: 14), and by that same blood they win their victory over the Accuser and the blessing for those who die in the Lord (14: 13).

In the Fourth Gospel there are constant reminders of the vicarious character of Jesus' death. He is 'the Lamb of God who takes away the sin of the world' (1: 29), he must be 'lifted up' before he can bestow life (3: 14), he gives his flesh for the life of the world (6: 51), he lays down his life for his sheep (10: 11) and for his friends (10: 13), and in ironical fulfilment of Caiaphas's cynical argument from expedience, he dies 'not for the nation alone, but to gather together the scattered children of God' (11: 52). But there are also constant reminders that without that vicarious death the coming of Jesus would be an aggravation of the world's guilt rather than an absolution of it. He comes to bring light into the world, only to find that the world prefers its concealing darkness (3: 19). He comes to give sight to the blind, only to be condemned as a sinner by those who think they see (9: 39–41). Their rejection of him, and particularly of his words and deeds which express God's redeeming purpose, is the ultimate recapitulation of the world's guilt and lowers that guilt inexorably upon them (15: 24–6). That, and no less, is the sin which the Lamb of God must take away; for the world in all its hostility to God is still the object of His saving love (3: 16).

The death of Jesus is at one and the same time the judgement and the salvation of the world. 'Now is the judgment of this world; now shall the prince of this world be driven out. When I am lifted up from the earth, I shall draw all men to myself' (12: 31–2).[23] The rejection of Jesus has shown that the world is in Satan's power (8: 40–4). Through his earthly minions such as Judas (13: 2), Satan sets out to kill Jesus by bringing him to trial on a capital charge. But Jesus is innocent (18: 38; 19: 4, 6). Satan, the prosecutor, has no claim over him (14: 30);[24] he secures the death sentence in the earthly court, but loses his case in the higher court of heaven. From that court he is drummed out, losing his claim not only over the innocent Jesus, but

[23] Cf. G. B. Caird, 'Judgement and Salvation: An Exposition of John 12: 31–2', *CJT* 2 (1956), 231 ff.

[24] Perhaps the point would be best conveyed by the modern colloquial phrase, 'he has nothing *on me*'.

over the guilty world, for the death he has engineered has drawn the whole human race into union with Jesus. But what has been objectively achieved in a representative death must be subjectively appropriated in individual faith. It is accordingly the task of God's advocate, the Spirit of Truth, to convince the world that it has been wrong:[25] wrong about sin in its condemnation of Jesus; wrong about righteousness, in that the resurrection has proved right to be on his side rather than theirs; and wrong about divine judgement, because when the human race is on trial in the person of Jesus the verdict goes against its Accuser (16: 8–11).

5.3.2. *Removal of Taint*

Another image, that of sin as taint, takes us out of the imagery of the lawcourt into that of the temple. Old Testament ritual was based on a double distinction 'between sacred and profane, between clean and unclean' (Lev. 10: 10). That which was clean might be used by God or human beings, while that which was unclean was fit for neither. Clean things or persons might, by the appropriate ritual, be either profaned, i.e. released for common use, or consecrated, i.e. made over to God. Those who for any reason had become unclean were debarred from the sanctuary until the taint had been removed (Lev. 12: 4; Num. 8: 19).[26] Sin was an uncleanness which not only barred the sinner from access to God (Pss. 19: 12; 51: 2; Prov. 20: 9; Isa. 6: 7), but threatened also to contaminate the land (Num. 35: 33). The purpose, then, of atoning sacrifice was to remove the taint of individual and national sin from sanctuary, altar, people, and land (Lev. 16: 19). As the author of Hebrews remarks: 'According to the Law, it might almost be said, everything is cleansed by blood, and without the shedding of blood there is no forgiveness of sins' (9: 22).[27] How sacrifice achieved this

---

[25] C. K. Barrett (*The Gospel According to St John* (Philadelphia, 1978²), ad loc.) agrees that this is the natural interpretation, but thinks it disqualified on the ground that the verb *elegchō* must have the same sense as in 8: 46. No amount of ingenuity, however, can make that sense fit this passage, and Barrett proves this by constantly lapsing into the sense he had rejected. In the New Testament *elegchō* has a wide variety of related senses, and there is no reason for John to be tied to only one of them.

[26] Cf. the thorough discussion of David P. Wright, *The Disposal of Impurity: Elimination Rites in the Bible and in Hittite and Mesopotamian Literatures* (Atlanta, 1987).

[27] It is highly probable that the author is here echoing the words of the Last Supper (cf. Matt. 26: 28, which also speaks of inaugurating a covenant by the spilling (or pouring) of blood for the forgiveness of sins).

result nobody seems to have asked. But around the institution of sacrifice there gathered four associated ideas which help us to understand what it meant to those for whom it was the central symbol of worship: (1) communion, (2) offering, (3) power, and (4) commemoration.

1. Sacrifice was communion because 'the life of a creature is the blood' (Lev. 17: 11), and within the symbolic unity of the one surrendered life God and people are brought together, and their covenant bond is first established, then renewed (Exod. 24: 6–8). Often sacrifice was conceived as a shared meal in which God and people were united, and it was essential to the sin-offering that the priests, as representatives of the people, should eat it in the sacred precincts (Lev. 10: 17).

2. Sacrifice was an offering made to God, not as payment, let alone as bribe, but as the tribute of loyalty and dependence presented to the divine majesty by a grateful and admiring people. It was required that the offering be 'without spot or blemish' (Lev. 4: 3), a token of the perfect self-offering which the worshipper would give if he or she were able.

3. Sacrifice was a release of power, since blood stood for life[28] (Lev. 17: 11), and whatever was consecrated communicated its holiness to anything that touched it (Lev. 6: 17–18).

4. In the annual sacrifice of the Passover, Israel commemorated her liberation from Egyptian bondage (Exod. 12: 14).[29] It is impressive to find all four of those associations explored by the New Testament writers in their use of sacrificial imagery. Believers are consecrated by 'the blood of the covenant' (Heb. 10: 29; cf. Mark 14: 24; John 17: 17, 19; 1 Cor. 11: 25), made partners with Christ (1 Cor. 10: 16–21) and given access to God (1 Cor. 6: 11; Rev. 22: 14). Christ is the Lamb 'without spot or blemish' (1 Pet. 1: 19; Heb. 9: 12; cf. John 1: 29), who has presented himself to God in order that his Church too may be without blemish (Eph. 5: 2, 26–7). He owes his priesthood

---

[28] There is, of course, a long-standing debate on this point, usually framed between 'non-conservatives' and 'conservatives', as to whether for the Hebrews spilling of blood meant (1) release of life, or (2) death. For (1), cf. V. Taylor, *The Atonement in New Testament Teaching* (London, 1945), 92 ff., and *Jesus and His Sacrifice* (London, 1937), 125 ff. For (2), cf. L. L. Morris, 'The Biblical Use of the Term "Blood" ', *JTS* NS 3 (1952), 216 f.; *The Apostolic Preaching of the Cross* (Grand Rapids, 1965³), 112 ff.; and R. V. G. Tasker's bowdlerized version (London, 1951) of Denney's classic, *The Death of Christ.*

[29] Through the phenomenon known as *anamnesis* those who 'remember' an event actually relive it.

and the efficacy of the sacrifice he offers 'not to a system of earth-bound rules, but to the power of an indestructible life' (Heb. 7: 10). And in the Eucharist the Church commemorated its Paschal redemption (1 Cor. 5: 7; 11: 24).[30]

Paul is sparing in his use of sacrificial terminology. He reminds the Corinthians that to possess the Kingdom of God means entering God's holy presence from which the unclean are debarred; but they 'have been washed, consecrated, justified through the name of the Lord Jesus and the Spirit of our God' (1 Cor. 6: 11). His solitary and controversial[31] use of *hilastērion* (Rom. 3: 25) is undoubtedly drawn from the vocabulary of sacrifice and designates the death of Christ as God's way of dealing with sin's defilement; but it occurs in a passage where Paul piles up metaphors drawn from diverse spheres of human experience—lawcourt, slave-market, temple—without attempting to indicate how they are related. More frequently he uses the phrase 'the blood of Christ' (Rom. 3: 25; 5: 9; 1 Cor. 10: 16; 11: 25, 27; Eph. 1: 7; 2: 13; Col. 1: 20), by which he means his life laid down in sacrifice; and here, as we shall see later in this chapter, the emphasis is on the union established by the life-blood of the victim.

In Hebrews, by contrast, temple[32] imagery predominates, because to this writer religion consists in access to God. This is evident in his frequent use of the verbs 'approach' (4: 16; 7: 25; 10: 1, 22; 11: 6; 12: 18, 22) and 'draw near' (7: 19; cf. also 10: 19).[33] Christ has made purification for sins (1: 3), has 'offered himself once for all' (7: 27), has 'offered for all time one sacrifice for sins', has 'suffered outside the gate to consecrate the people by his own blood' (13: 12). The old system purported to provide such cleansing and hallowing of the defiled, but since it could not cleanse the conscience (9: 13–14; 10:

[30] On the Paschal associations of those passages, cf. C. K. Barrett, *A Commentary on the First Epistle to the Corinthians* (London, 1968), 128 f., 266 f.

[31] Cf. for instance C. H. Dodd, *The Bible and the Greeks* (London, 1954²), 94; D. Hill, *Greek Words and Hebrew Meanings* (London, 1967), 41 ff.; C. E. B. Cranfield, *A Critical and Exegetical Commentary on the Epistle to the Romans*, i ad loc.; J. D. G. Dunn, *Romans 1–8*, ad loc.; F. Büchsel, '*hilaskomai*' etc., *TDNT* iii. 320 ff.; and L. L. Morris, 'The Meaning of *hilastērion* in Romans 3: 25', *NTS* 2 (1955–6), 33 ff., and *The Apostolic Preaching of the Cross* 144 ff. Dodd argued for 'expiation' as the correct translation of *hilastērion* (cf. NEB), while Morris, with most conservative evangelicals following him, argued for 'propitiation'.

[32] While it is true that the author concentrates entirely on the Old Testament tabernacle, it may be assumed that in the back of his mind stands the contemporary Jewish temple.

[33] *engizō*, 7: 39; *proserchomai*, 4: 6; 7: 25; 10: 1, 22; 11: 6; 12: 18, 22.

2), it in fact provided only a shadowy outline of the reality that was to come (8: 5; 10: 1). Under that system the way to God was barricaded, because only the High Priest could enter the Holy of Holies, and he only on the Day of Atonement; but Christ has entered the real sanctuary, of which the earthly tabernacle was but a prefigurement, a shadowy sketch-plan,[34] and has opened the right of entry to all (9: 6–14; 10: 19–25). At the same time, however, Christ is said to have borne the sins of many (9: 28), and to those who were familiar with the ritual for the Day of Atonement there might seem to be some inconsistency in this elision of sin-bearer and sin-offering. For on the Day of Atonement the High Priest was instructed to take two goats, one of which was to be consecrated to God as sin-offering, while the other, the scapegoat, was to be ceremonially loaded with the sins of the people and driven out into the desert. The sin-bearing goat was unclean and could not therefore be offered to God. But these two images had already coalesced in the prophetic vision of the Servant of the Lord, of whom it was said that 'the Lord laid upon him the guilt of us all', but also that he 'made himself a sacrifice for sin' (Isa. 53: 6, 10). The Servant could fulfil both roles because what he was to offer to God was his willingness to atone for the sins of others by being their scapegoat. This is precisely the climax to which the argument of Hebrews leads, for 10: 5–10 makes it clear that the perfect sacrifice is obedience to God's purpose of redemption.

In 1 Peter also (2: 19–24) Christ is depicted as the scapegoat Servant of the Lord, but the extensive cento of quotations from Isaiah 53 omits any mention of sin-offering. Instead of being the one sacrifice for sin, Christ's sin-bearing is held up as an example for all Christians, slaves in particular. Wrongdoing carries the uncleanness of a contagious disease, and the voluntary acceptance of undeserved suffering is the disinfectant by which it is to be put out of circulation. With this we may compare Mark's frequent use of the word 'unclean' in connection with diseases cured by Jesus, which are clearly intended as a paradigm of his redemptive ministry, and are linked by the parable of the doctor (2: 15–17) with social disease, and so with the lethal hostility which Jesus incurred by his curative friendships. Matthew's explicit quotation of Isaiah 53: 4 (Matt. 8: 17) seems curiously less profound than Mark's more allusive treatment of the theme.

---

[34] 'Sketch-plan' remains the best translation of *hupodeigma* in Hebrews, which does not mean, and never has meant, 'copy' (*contra* RSV, NEB, and virtually all modern

In the Revelation, in spite of the pervasive use of temple imagery and of the symbol of the slaughtered lamb, sacrificial language is rare; and when it does occur, it is always, through the common element of blood, interfused with the language of victory. The martyrs have 'washed their robes and made them white in the blood of the Lamb' (7: 14). But they are also the conquerors, who by the blood of the Lamb have vanquished the Great Accuser (12: 11); white is the colour of victory as well as purity. John clearly believes in some sort of vicariousness. The death of the martyrs was in some way included in the archetypal death of Jesus; yet the efficacy of his blood did not exclude, but rather required, the shedding of their own, and when at the end Jesus appears as the victorious horseman, it is with their blood that his robe is stained, not with that of his enemies (19: 11). Thus the sacrificial motif that appears to be uppermost is the release of power. The victory of Christ has released a power which enables the martyrs to win their victory: 'They follow the Lamb wherever he goes' (14: 4). His testimony is the spirit that inspires Christian prophets to confirm it with their own.[35]

In all this evidence there is not a trace of anything that could be called a sacrificial theory of atonement.[36] These writers use the metaphor of sacrifice imaginatively and in conjunction with other metaphors which serve to define its scope. They use the metaphor, not because they imagined that a detailed study of the sacrificial system would explain the Cross, but because all the aspiration to purity, all the commitment to holiness, all the quest for access to the divine presence which that system had attempted to express were now embodied in the one inclusive act of self-consecration. This is what we find also in the Gospel and first Epistle of John. When the Baptist hails Jesus as 'the Lamb of God who takes away the sin of the world' (1: 29), it is fruitless to scour the Levitical rulebook to see whether the reference

commentaries on Hebrews (cf. L. D. Hurst, 'How "Platonic" are Heb. 8: 5 and 9: 23 f.?', *JTS* 34 (1983), 156 ff.).

[35] Cf. M. E. Boring, 'The Apocalypse as Christian Prophecy', *SBL Seminar Papers 1974*, 43 ff.; and D. Hill, 'Prophecy and Prophets in the Revelation of St John', *NTS* 18 (1971–2), 401 ff.

[36] Cf. Colin Gunton, *The Actuality of Atonement: A Study of Metaphor, Rationality and the Christian Tradition* (Edinburgh, 1989), together with 'Christ the Sacrifice: Aspects of the Language and Imagery of the Bible', in L. D. Hurst and N. T. Wright (eds.), *The Glory of Christ in the New Testament* (Oxford, 1987), 229 ff. Gunton's work should be read in conjunction with Aulén, *Christus Victor*; Hengel, *Atonement*; and F. W. Dillistone, *The Christian Understanding of Atonement* (London, 1984).

is to either of the victims of the Day of Atonement (both of which were goats) or to the Paschal lamb (which was not a sin-offering).[37] This lamb was the epitome of all sacrifice. The wine of the gospel replaces in overwhelming plenty the water of the old rituals of purification (2: 1–10).[38] Jesus washes his disciples' feet, ostensibly as an object lesson[39] in humble service, but also as a symbol of the cleansing power of his death, as appears from his warning to Peter that he will understand what is being done for him only when he has seen the reality that underlies the symbol (13: 1–15). Jesus has been 'consecrated and sent into the world by the Father' (10: 36), but it is in his death that he consecrates himself for the sake of the disciples and the world to which they are sent (17: 19). This weaving of sacrificial motifs into the intricate pattern of his tapestry is in keeping with John's use of the Old Testament, which is as often comprehensive as it is precise (e.g. 1: 45; 5: 39; 6: 45; 7: 38, 52; 20: 9).[40]

The sacrificial language of 1 John has been thought to be more traditional than that of the Gospel, but it is no less fully integrated into the fabric of the author's thought. Christians are 'cleansed from every sin by the blood of Jesus' (1: 7), who is 'the remedy for the defilement of our sins, not ours only but the sins of all the world' (2: 2; 4: 10). But this cleansing is related in thoroughly Johannine fashion to the common life, that life which is shared with the Father and his Son Jesus Christ (1: 3), and to the redemptive love of God which can be known only by being shared (4: 7–12).

5.3.3. *Breaking Sin's Power*

The idea of the breaking of sin's power is depicted by the use of two closely allied metaphors, the redemption or liberation of slaves and the defeat of an enemy. From one point of view sinners themselves

---

[37] Cf. C. K. Barrett, 'The Lamb of God', *NTS* 1 (1955–6), 210 ff.; Dodd, *Interpretation of the Fourth Gospel*, 230 ff.; and J. Jeremias, '*amnos*', etc., *TDNT* i. 338 ff.

[38] In addition to the standard commentaries on John, cf. the exhaustive study of M. Hengel, 'The Interpretation of the Wine Miracle at Cana: John 2: 1–11', in Hurst and Wright (eds.), *The Glory of Christ in the New Testament*, 83 ff., and the vast amount of literature cited there.

[39] Here the word for 'pattern', *hupodeigma*, clearly indicates that which is to be *followed* (see above, p. 153, n 34, on Heb. 8: 5 and 9: 23).

[40] On John's use of the Old Testament, cf. C. K. Barrett, 'The Old Testament in the Fourth Gospel', *JTS* 48 (1947), 155 ff.; F.-M. Braun, *Jean le Théologien; Les Grandes traditions d'Israël et l'accord des Écritures selon le Quatrième Evangile* (Paris, 1959–72);

may be regarded as the enemy whose hostility to God's purpose needs to be broken down (Acts 5: 39; 13: 10; Rom. 8: 7; Col. 1: 21; Jas. 4: 4). According to 1 Peter God's way of putting 'ignorance and stupidity to silence' was exemplified in the refusal of Jesus to repay wrong with wrong: 'When he was abused, he did not retort with abuse, when he suffered he uttered no threats, but committed his cause to the one who judges justly' (2: 15, 23; 3: 9). Retaliation wins a victory for wrongdoing, by recruiting the victim into the army of hatred and violence. Wrong propagates itself by chain-reaction, and can be stopped in its career only by someone who absorbs it and lets it go no further. The author of 1 Peter no doubt had in mind the tradition which Mark preserves of Jesus' silence at his trial (14: 61; 15: 5). Whether this tradition was derived from historical memory or from the typological use of Isaiah 53 as a portrait of Jesus, unprotesting like a sheep led to the slaughter, is a question of interest to those engaged in the quest for the historical Jesus, but which makes no difference to Mark's theology, where the centurion becomes the speaker for all whose resistance has been broken by non-resistance (15: 39).

It was Paul, however, whose experience as a persecutor constantly reminded him that, when he had supposed himself to be God's most zealous servant, he had in fact been God's enemy (Gal. 1: 13f.); and it is perhaps because of this unique background that he alone describes the redemptive work of Christ in terms of reconciliation.[41] 'If, when we were God's enemies, we were reconciled to Him through the death of His Son, how much more, now that we are reconciled, shall we be saved by his life!' (Rom. 5: 10). 'God was in Christ reconciling the world to Himself . . . in Christ's name, we implore you, be reconciled to God' (2 Cor. 5: 19–20). There are two striking points in Paul's treatment of this theme. The first is that, although he is well aware that reconciliation is the restoration of personal relationships between two parties, he speaks of it throughout as an act of God accomplished

---

E. D. Freed, *Old Testament Quotations in the Gospel of John* (Leiden, 1965); and G. Reim, *Studien zum alttestamentlichen Hintergrund des Johannesevangeliums* (Cambridge, 1974).

[41] See James Denney, *The Christian Doctrine of Reconciliation* (London, 1917); E. Käsemann, 'Some Thoughts on "The Doctrine of Reconciliation in the New Testament"', in J. M. Robinson (ed.), *The Future of our Religious Past* (New York, 1971), 49 ff.; and R. P. Martin, 'Reconciliation and Forgiveness in Colossians', in R. J. Banks (ed.), *Reconciliation and Hope: New Testament Essays on Atonement and Eschatology* (Exeter, 1974), 90 ff.

in Christ's vicarious death, quite independently of human response. He does not say that Christ's death opened up the possibility of subsequent reconciliation; subsequent events are covered by the indicative 'we shall be saved' and by the imperative 'be reconciled', but both are consequent on a reconciliation achieved 'while we were still God's enemies'. Moreover the reconciliation was universal in its scope; it encompassed 'the world'. 'Through him God chose to reconcile the whole universe to himself, everything in heaven and on earth, making peace through the shedding of his blood on the Cross' (Col. 1: 12).

The second point is that Paul in all these passages apparently has nothing to say about reconciliation between individual human beings. The omission is significant, not because Paul is uninterested in human relationships, but on the contrary because he *assumes* that those who are reconciled to God will be reconciled to one another. Only in Ephesians is the assumption spelt out, in a passage which picks up and explains the former point also (2: 14–16). Christ's identification of himself with the human race on the Cross was a royal proclamation that hostilities were over, but because the reconciliation with God was effected in his 'single body', nobody could profit by it without sharing it with all others. In this way, across every division of hatred, antagonism, distrust, and suspicion that separates human beings from one another, of which the division between Jew and Gentile in the early Church was the most pressing instance, he had 'made the two one'.

More commonly sin in one or other of its many forms was the enemy; the human race needed to be set free not only from the individual slavery of habit and deeply entrenched attitudes, but also from the corporate slavery of sin embedded in the practices, institutions, conventions, and ethos of the old order. A source of vivid metaphor lay ready to hand in the story of the Exodus, the liberation of Israel from slavery in Egypt, which through its communal commemoration in the Passover had long been a symbol of redemption from oppression by tyrannical powers and from the national sin which, as the prophets taught, had incurred that oppression as its divine retribution (Ps. 130: 7–8). In this context 'redemption'[42] was already a metaphor, drawn from the practice of buying the release of a slave by payment of a ransom (Lev. 25: 47–9); but since at the Exodus from Egypt no money

---

[42] Cf. J. F. A. Sawyer, *Semantics in Biblical Research: New Methods of Defining Hebrew Words for Salvation* (Naperville, Ill., 1972), 36, 40; D. Hill, *Greek Words*, 49 ff.; H. Ringgren, '*ga'al*', etc., *TDOT* ii. 350 ff.; and R. E. Nixon, *The Exodus in the New Testament* (London, 1963).

changed hands, the notion of price was not necessarily implied in the metaphorical usage, as Deutero-Isaiah points out in his repeated assurances that God is Israel's redeemer (Isa. 52: 3). Hence in the New Testament redemption (*lutrōsis, apolutrōsis*)[43] signifies liberation, without any closer link with its etymology. Luke uses these terms of the long-awaited liberation of Jerusalem (1: 68; 2: 38; 21: 28; 24: 21), and in Paul and Hebrews they denote emancipation from the trammels of an obsolete system.[44]

There are, indeed, five passages in which the death of Christ is described as a ransom, a means of winning freedom for the many (Mark 10: 45; Matt. 20: 28), for the whole human race (1 Tim. 2: 6), for those who have been slaves to any kind of wickedness (Titus 2: 14), or to the empty folly of their traditional way of life (1 Pet. 1: 18). It is important to note that when ransom terminology is used in conjunction with sacrificial imagery, as at 1 Pet. 1: 18–19, it does not thereby become sacrificial. But in Titus and 1 Peter elements in the context ('people marked out for his own' (Titus 2: 14), 'gird up the loins' (1 Pet. 1: 13), 'sojourning' (1 Pet. 1: 17)) make it clear that the Exodus is in view, and this conclusion gains support from the prevalence of Exodus imagery throughout the New Testament.

The Exodus background is important when we come to ask how the New Testament writers could conceive of the Cross as a liberation. For the ancient Israelites freedom was achieved by escape from the territory of the tyrant into a land not under his control; and the idea of migration to a place where new life can begin underlies all New Testament teaching on redemption. 'He rescued us from the domain of darkness and brought us away into the Kingdom of his dear Son' (Col. 1: 13). Matthew's story of the descent of the infant Jesus into Egypt and his return is a parable of his rescue of God's people from their Egyptian bondage (2: 13–15).[45] According to Luke, Jesus on the mountain of Transfiguration spoke with Moses and Elijah about the 'exodus' he was to accomplish, the one word doing double service for death and deliverance (9: 31). The Gentile Christians of Asia Minor have been redeemed out of the ignorance and folly of paganism (1 Pet.

[43] Cf. Hill, *Greek Words*, 66 ff.; and J. Schneider and C. Brown, 'Redemption', *NIDNTT* iii. 189 ff.

[44] *Lutrōsis*, Heb. 9: 12; *apolutrōsis*, Rom. 3: 24; 8: 23; 1 Cor. 1: 30; Col. 1: 14.

[45] On this passage cf. R. H. Gundry, *Matthew: A Commentary on His Literary and Theological Art* (Grand Rapids, 1982), 33 f., and G. M. Soares-Prabhu, *The Formula Quotations in the Infancy Narrative of Matthew* (Rome, 1976), 216 ff.

1: 14, 18). The martyrs of Revelation escape from the great city whose allegorical name is Egypt and, after crossing the sea of glass, sing the song of Moses and the Lamb (Rev. 11: 8; 15: 2–3). Members of the Johannine community have 'migrated out of death into life' (John 5: 24; 3: 14).

A new home may be regarded as an objective fact, but it entails a new allegiance. 'You have had time enough in the past to do all the things that people want to do in the pagan world' (1 Pet. 4: 5). The old master must be renounced if the new one is to be acknowledged. 'Emancipated from sin, you have become slaves of righteousness . . . freed from the commands of sin, and bound to the service of God . . . in Christ Jesus the life-giving law of the Spirit has set you free from the Law of sin and death' (Rom. 6: 18, 22; 8: 2). Paul links this idea with the theme of death and resurrection. Because Christ has identified himself with all who lived in the old order, under the tyranny[46] of sin, death, and law, and has died their death, they are now free to be identified with him in the new life of his resurrection. 'We know that our old humanity has been crucified with Christ, for the destruction of the sinful self, so that we may no longer be slaves of sin, because death cancels the claims of sin' (Rom. 6: 6 f., REB). Paul is not arguing that Christians cannot do anything wrong, but simply that they have been placed in a new situation where the old order no longer dictates the pattern of their life.

With this last passage we may compare two others. 'When anyone has endured bodily suffering he has finished with sin' (1 Pet. 4: 2). 'No one who abides in his sins has either seen Him or known Him . . . No one born of God commits sin: for God's nature abides in him, and he cannot sin because he is born of God' (1 John 3: 6, 9). The argument in 1 Peter turns on allegiance: anyone who has chosen to undergo persecution rather than join in pagan immorality has taken his or her stand, and is done with the old life. The position adopted in 1 John appears more extreme, but the appearance is belied by the explicit statement that any Christian who claims to be without sin is a liar (1: 8; 2: 1–2). Here too the point is that persistence in sin is totally out of keeping with the new life.[47] The difference between the three writers is that they are combating three different temptations

---

[46] Note the use of the words 'reign' (*basileuō*, Rom. 5: 14, 17, 21; 6: 12) and 'control' (*kurieuō*, Rom. 6: 9, 14; 7: 1).

[47] A statement of obligation or ideal as though it were a fact of experience is a familiar enough turn of expression. Cf. 'Pupils in this school do not cheat!'

for the redeemed to return to the security of the Egyptian fleshpots. Paul's hypothetical opponent holds that the old religion of law cannot be abandoned without grave threat to moral standards. 1 Peter is written to dissuade Christians from buying immunity from persecution by making themselves at home in their pagan environment. 1 John is written against a schismatic sect who have boasted that their religious experience is so intense as to put them beyond the restraints of ethical obligation.

Closely allied to the idea of emancipation is that of victory over an oppressor.[48] Here the impetus came partly from the ancient myth of God's past, present, and future victory over the forces of chaos, and partly from the Christological use of Psalms 2 and 110 with their promise that the Messianic king is to reduce the enemies of God to subjection.[49] Whether the oppressor is Satan (Mark 3: 27; Luke 22: 53; Acts 26: 18; Heb. 2: 14; 1 John 3: 8; Rev. 12: 9), the world (John 16: 33; 1 John 5: 4), sin and death (Rom. 6: 9), or the cosmic powers and authorities (Col. 2: 12), there is general agreement that Jesus on the Cross has won the archetypal, inclusive victory in which believers may share because of the bond that unites them with their Lord. 'Thanks be to God who gives us the victory through our Lord Jesus Christ' (1 Cor. 15: 57). 'Overwhelming victory is ours through him who loved us' (Rom. 8: 37). 'I have conquered the world' (John 16: 33). 'To the conqueror I will grant a seat beside me on my throne, as I myself conquered and sat down beside my Father on his throne' (Rev. 3: 21).

5.3.4. *Inauguration: The New Age*

The themes of the previous section together cover the negative, backward-looking aspect of salvation, the cure of disease, the repair of damage, the removal of obstacles. But a theology which did nothing but look back to the city of destruction would share the monumental sterility of Lot's wife. The New Testament writers are uniformly positive and forward-looking. We might observe how regularly statements

---

[48] Cf. Aulén, *Christus Victor*; G. B. Caird, 'The Descent of Christ in Ephesians 4: 7–11', in F. L. Cross (ed.) *Studia Evangelica*, 2 (1964), 535 ff.; C. F. D. Moule, 'Reflections on So-Called "Triumphalism" ', in Hurst and Wright (eds.), *The Glory of Christ in the New Testament*, 219 ff.; and the trilogy of W. Wink, *Naming the Powers*, *Unmasking the Powers*, and *Engaging the Powers* (Minneapolis, 1984–92).

[49] Cf. B. Lindars, *New Testament Apologetic* (Philadelphia, 1961), 139 ff.

of belief in an objective, once-for-all atonement are followed by a purpose clause, descriptive of new opportunity. 'By baptism we were buried with him and lay dead, in order that, as Christ was raised from the dead in the splendour of the Father, so also we might set our feet upon the new path of life' (Rom. 6: 4; cf. 2 Cor. 4: 11, 15; 5: 21; John 3: 15; 17: 19; Heb. 9: 14; 1 Pet. 3: 18; Rev. 1: 5–6). In the death of Christ the love of God has been manifested, but only in order to be shared (1 John 4: 7–11). 'Finis' has been written across the old regime of law (Rom. 10: 4), but only in order that the proper aims of the Law might be fulfilled by another order (Rom. 8: 2–4). The taint of sin has been removed to open access to the throne of grace (Heb. 4: 16). Slaves have been set free to become sons (Gal. 4: 4–5). The passing of the old age is the beginning of the new (1 Cor. 10: 11, Heb. 9: 26).

Paul expresses his belief in a new beginning in a variety of ways. Jesus is the inaugurator of a new covenant, sealed by his sacrificial death (1 Cor. 11: 25; 2 Cor. 3: 6; Gal. 4: 24). By his resurrection he has become the second Adam, the head of a new humanity (1 Cor. 15: 45–9; cf. Rom. 6: 9; Eph. 2: 15; 4: 24; Col. 3: 9–10), and in that capacity he has become 'a life-giving Spirit', so that the life he now leads may be manifested in the mortal bodies of his followers (2 Cor. 4: 10; Rom. 8: 11). 'Through the Law I died to the Law in order to be alive for God. I have been crucified with Christ; the life I now live is not my life, but the life which Christ lives in me' (Gal. 2: 19–20). In other words Christians have been brought to life together with Christ and share in his resurrection (Eph. 2: 5–6; Col. 2: 12–13; 3: 1). Paul frequently refers to the old order as 'this age' or 'this world', but he agrees with John (15: 19; 18: 36) that Christians no longer belong to it: Christ 'gave himself for our sins, to rescue us out of this present age of wickedness' (Gal. 1: 4), so that for them the new age has already come into existence, and with it a new world. 'When anyone is united to Christ, there is a new world; the old order has gone, and a new order has already begun' (2 Cor. 5: 17). Citizens of the new world must abandon their conformity with the old one and undergo a 'renewal of the mind' (Rom. 12: 2; Col. 3: 10).

The idea of the new covenant, which by Christian definition has its origin in the synoptic tradition (Mark 14: 24; Luke 22: 29), is fully exploited in Hebrews.[50] In predicting the establishment of a new

---

[50] A useful summary of the covenant concept in Hebrews is provided by E. A. C. Pretorius, '*Diatheke* in the Epistle to the Hebrews', *Neotestamentica* 5 (1971), 37 ff.

covenant, Jeremiah had pronounced the first one obsolescent because of its ineffectiveness (8: 13). The old covenant, together with its Law, priesthood, and sacrifices, provided only a shadowy outline[51] of what was to come. Jesus has become mediator of that 'better covenant, legally secured by better promises' (8: 5–6), and his death is to be regarded as the inaugural sacrifice of the new order (9: 18–26).[52] The saints of the Old Testament had shown, by turning their backs on the present and putting their trust in God's future, that they were strangers and pilgrims on earth looking for a homeland,[53] the city whose architect and builder is God. But that heavenly city has now become an earthly reality: 'You have reached Mount Zion and the city of the living God . . . and Jesus the mediator of a new covenant, whose sprinkled blood has better things to tell than the blood of Abel' (11: 10, 16; 12: 22–3).

John has nothing that corresponds to Paul's doctrine of the second Adam, but like Paul he portrays Jesus as the giver of life to the dead. 'As the Father raises the dead and gives them life, so the Son gives life to whom he will' (5: 21). Anyone who believes in him 'has already crossed from death to life' (5: 24; cf. 1 John 3: 14). But that transit is possible only when Jesus, by his own death and resurrection, has opened the way (14: 2–6). The object of his coming is that others 'may have life and have it in all its fulness' (10: 10); but that life is himself and becomes accessible only in his self-giving (11: 25; 14: 6). 'Unless you eat the flesh of the Son of Man and drink his blood you can have no life in you' (6: 53).

The Johannine writings share with 1 Peter (1: 3, 23) and James (1: 18) an image of new beginning which is not found in Paul[54]—that of rebirth. To those who respond to the *logos* in the person of Jesus God gives the right to become children of God (John 1: 13), but they realize

---

[51] On this translation see above, p. 153, n. 34.

[52] For the view that Heb. 9: 18 ff. is referring to the inaugural sacrifices of the covenant rather than the yearly Atonement ritual, cf. L. D. Hurst, *The Epistle to the Hebrews: Its Background of Thought* (Cambridge, 1990), 38 ff.

[53] This motif was brought to the fore in 1939 by E. Käsemann's *Das Wandernde Gottesvolk* (ET, *The Wandering People of God* (Minneapolis, 1984)). Unfortunately the book is marred by the view that Hebrews was written against a Gnostic background, a viewpoint rejected now by most scholars, including Käsemann himself.

[54] Paul is obviously familiar with this turn of speech, for when he speaks of himself as having become a father to others (1 Cor. 4: 15; cf. Gal. 4: 19; Phil. 2: 22), he is certainly thinking not simply of their personal relation to himself, but of their conversion. Yet he never speaks of conversion in itself as a rebirth.

that right only by being born from above (3: 7), and that heavenly birth, by water and spirit, depends on the lifting up of Jesus, which is both his death and his exaltation (3: 14; cf. 8: 28; 12: 32). A son should take after the father, and to be born of God is to become like him (1 John 2: 29; 3: 9), to become part of the heavenly family (5: 1–4), and above all to share God's love (4: 7).

We began this chapter by asking what it is that Christ is believed to have done. But when we consider salvation as a new beginning, it is evident that the emphasis shifts to what he has *become*. He has become second Adam and life-giving Spirit, the firstborn of a large family, and has been awarded a name above all names (1 Cor. 15: 45–7; Rom. 8: 29; Phil. 2: 9). He has become the merciful and faithful high priest, the source of eternal salvation, the mediator of the new covenant, and it is through the blood of the eternal covenant that he is the great Shepherd (Heb. 13: 20; cf. 1 Pet. 2: 25; John 10: 15). Like a grain of wheat, he has by dying become the bearer of harvest (John 12: 24). He has won the right to open the scroll of destiny (Rev. 5: 15). He has become Messiah, Lord and King (Acts 2: 36; Rom. 1: 4; 8: 34; 1 Cor. 15: 25; Eph. 1: 20; Col. 3: 1; Heb. 1: 3; 1 Pet. 3: 22; Rev. 3: 21).

5.3.5. *Solidarity, Identification*

When we look back at all Jesus is said to have accomplished or become, it is evident that at every point it is contingent on his establishing some sort of identification with the beneficiaries. In common experience the natural forms of solidarity are family and nation; and the importance of both in Israelite tradition is too obvious to require illustration. But in both instances that same tradition recognized the need for the strengthening of the natural bond by other means. Kinship might be disowned (Deut. 33: 14; Isa. 63: 16), and therefore the acknowledgment of it had to be encouraged by moral or legal service (Deut. 21: 17). The right and duty of redemption in cases of slavery, debt, or alienation of family property, as well as in the responsibility for levirate marriage, lay with the next of kin, so that the one word *go'el* did double service for redeemer and kinsman (Lev. 25: 49; Deut. 25: 5–10): but the legal possibilities of exemption from the responsiblity made the acceptance of it a matter of choice (Ruth 3–4). One brother might go surety for another, accepting responsibility not only for his safety but for his misdeeds (Gen. 44: 32–3), and a wife might do the same for her husband (1 Sam. 25: 24). But in addition the ordinary principle was built into the structure of the family through the institution of marriage, in which by free choice on both sides, whether of the couple themselves or of their parents, a new solidarity was established, so that the two became 'one flesh' (Gen. 2: 24). There are also proverbial warnings that a friend or neighbour may be of more help than a relative (Prov. 18: 24; 27: 10).

By means of tracing its genealogy and descent from Abraham through the twelve patriarchs, the nation could be regarded as an extended family. But here too kinship was never regarded as self-sufficient; it had to be reinforced. The nation had been brought into existence at Sinai by an act of covenant, which entailed choice on God's side and acceptance on Israel's (Exod. 19: 4–6);[55] and at each renewal of the covenant the people were required to confirm their decision (Josh. 24: 22; 2 Kings 23: 3).

Just as the life of the family was thought to be embodied in the head of the household, so that whatever he did, his family and even his descendants were included in the doing of it,[56] so the life of the nation was embodied in the king. Thus in both national and in family affairs the principle of kinship, which gives to the concept of solidarity its imaginative realism and evocative power, was always interfused with the principle of choice, which supplies its personal and moral quality. But the element of choice was present in two other ways also. The path had always been open for a non-Israelite to join the holy people by becoming a *ger* or proselyte, and the book of Ruth stood in the canon of scripture as a reminder that David himself had a Moabite great-grandmother, and that the native Israelite, dependent on God's unmerited grace, was no more than a *ger* without permanent right of tenure in the sight of God (Ps. 39: 12).[57] At a later stage, when Isaiah's warning that only a remnant would survive God's judgement had been transformed into a promise that the true Israel would always be rep-

---

[55] On the covenant in Israel cf. R. E. Clements, *Prophecy and Covenant*; D. R. Hillers, *Covenant: The History of a Biblical Idea* (Baltimore, 1969); G. E. Mendenhall, *Law and Covenant in Israel and the Ancient Near East* (Pittsburgh, 1955), and 'Covenant', *IDB* i. 714 ff.; J. Pedersen, *Israel: Its Life and Culture*, i (Atlanta, 1991), 263 ff.; and J. Hempel and L. Goppelt, 'Bund', *RGG*³ i. 1512 ff.

[56] Thus the author of Hebrews can argue that, when Abraham paid tithes to Melchizedek, his descendent Levi was 'in Abraham's loins' (7: 9 f.).

[57] On 'the stranger' (*ger*) in Judaism, cf. D. L. Lieber, 'Strangers and Gentiles', *Encyclopaedia Judaica* 15 (New York, 1971–2), 419 ff.; and S. McKnight, *A Light to the Gentiles* (Philadelphia, 1991), 11 ff.

resented by a faithful remnant, it became clear that membership of the remnant was not a matter of birth but of loyalty, and debates began to arise between rival factions as to who were the true sons of Abraham.

All these motifs are exploited by the New Testament writers as they attempt to expound the relationship of believers to the vicarious achievement of their Lord. In view of the emphasis they place on the fatherhood of God, it is not surprising to find a widespread use of the ideas of family solidarity. But at the outset of the story John the Baptist had renewed the Old Testament warning that birth alone does not guarantee membership in the family of God (Matt. 3: 9; Luke 3: 8). Accordingly we find Jesus in Mark's Gospel claiming to be the centre of a new style of family circle, united in obedience to God (Mark 3: 35), in Matthew's Gospel insisting that loyalty to himself should take precedence over that due to parents (Mark 10: 37, cf. Luke 14: 26),[58] and in Luke's Gospel justifying his own identification with the lost sheep of the house of Israel by a parable in which the Pharisaic elder son who disowns his brother proves himself totally out of touch with the mind of his father (Luke 15: 25–32). According to Paul the role of Christ as Son is 'that he might be the eldest among a large family of brothers' (Rom. 8: 29). John the Evangelist, who never uses 'Son' of Christians, but exclusively of Jesus, 'the only begotten Son', nevertheless finds another way of expressing the bond of kinship: 'Go to my brothers and tell them, "I am now ascending to my Father and your Father, my God and your God"' (John 20: 7). John the Seer has a vision of a woman in heavenly splendour and a dragon who fails to devour her male child at his birth and goes off 'to wage war on the rest of her children' (Rev. 12: 1–6, 17). But the theme of family solidarity is most fully worked out in Hebrews 2: 10–14, where it is combined with the supplementary images of the pioneer who blazes the trail for others to follow (6: 20) and the consecrating priest who represents the worshipping congregation in the presence of God, and the emphasis is not just on the ties of kinship, but on the willingness of Jesus to acknowledge the responsibilities they entail.

The metaphorical use of marriage as a means of establishing a new union is adumbrated in synoptic parables (Mark 2: 19; Matt. 22: 10; 25: 1), further explored by Paul (2 Cor. 11: 2), John (3: 29), and the

---

[58] Matthew's addition of the possessive 'our' to the first word of the Lord's Prayer should probably be regarded as an indication of family solidarity.

Revelation (19: 6–9; 21: 2, 9; 22: 17), but fully worked out only in Ephesians 5: 25–32, where the emphasis is placed on the bond created by the self-giving love of Christ. It is also in this Epistle (3: 14–15) that we find the remarkable description of God as 'the Father from whom every family in heaven and on earth takes its name' (i.e. 'is brought into existence'). This comes as the climax of an argument that God's plan of redemption is to bring the universe into a unity in Christ (1: 10) and that by the exercise of his fatherhood He brings family unity into existence where before there was none, a unity which can be seen in his bringing of Jew and Gentile into union with Christ and therefore with one another. 'Through him we both have access in one spirit to the Father' (Eph. 2: 18).

The universal application of the metaphor of kinship is hinted at in Luke's genealogy, where by tracing the descent of Jesus through David and Abraham to Adam he indicates that as Messiah Jesus is bound by family ties not only to Israel but to the human race (Luke 3: 38). This is the point also of Paul's more elaborate comparison between Adam and Christ (1 Cor. 15: 22; Rom. 15: 12–21). The natural solidarity of all humanity in Adam, which Paul regards as a fact of experience which requires little demonstration, and which the individual has no choice but to accept, is made the basis for the possibility of a new, voluntary solidarity in Christ, established by God's free act of grace on the one side and the human response of faith on the other.

Kinship, however, takes on an added significance when it is seen as an expression of national unity, embodied in the person of the king. For any Jew the archetypal kingship was the reign of David, and the story of that reign points to a function of kingship other than the exercise of autocratic power which, according to the New Testament, Jesus renounced. The king did not merely rule Israel; he *was* Israel. In the studies of sacral kingship in the Old Testament and the Ancient Near East which we associate with the 'Myth and Ritual' school, all the emphasis was placed on the position of the king as the agent or representative of God.[59] But sacral kingship had another side to it, which was no less prominent in ancient Hebrew thought. As Roland de Vaux[60] has put it, 'It is a common idea among primitive peoples

[59] Cf. for instance S. Mowinckel, *The Psalms in Israel's Worship* (Oxford, 1962), i. 55 ff.; A. R. Johnson, *Sacral Kingship in Ancient Israel* (Cardiff, 1967²); and S. H. Hooke (ed.), *Myth, Ritual, and Kingship* (London, 1958).

[60] R. de Vaux, *Ancient Israel* (London, 1965), 110.

that the king embodies the good estate of his subjects: the country's prosperity depends on him, and he insures the welfare of his people.' A. S. Tritton[61] speaks of 'the national significance of the king's person'. A calamity to the king was a national disaster; and he accordingly draws the conclusion that 'the question whether certain of the penitential psalms are individual or national is beside the point; it is the king, the people's representative, who speaks for the nation'. Pharaoh exemplifies this solidarity between king and people when he confesses to Moses, 'I and my people are in the wrong' (Exod. 9: 27), when the people had done nothing except what was included in the act of their royal representative. It is exemplified further by Jehoiada's covenant (2 Kings 11: 17), and by many of the royal psalms (see especially Pss. 18: 50; 20 : 7–9; 63: 11). A. B. Davidson once said that 'in Zech. 9: 9 Zion's king shares the character of the saved people',[62] which leads us to the important corollary that the king is not so much the bringer of salvation as the recipient of it on behalf of the nation.

A king, then, is one whose actions are such that his subjects are included in the doing of them, and his calamities are such that his subjects are included in the suffering of them. The full implications of this are brought out by the story of David in greater detail—beginning with his installation. 'Now all the tribes of Israel came to David at Hebron and said to him, "We are your own flesh and blood [Heb. 'bone and flesh'] . . ." And the Lord said to you, "You shall be shepherd of my people Israel; you shall be their prince." All the elders of Israel came to the king at Hebron; there David made a covenant with them before the Lord, and they anointed David king over Israel' (2 Sam. 5: 1–2). The solidarity of prince with people, of shepherd with flock, is grounded on divine appointment, on the bond of kinship, and on the reinforcing bond of covenant; and in the ensuing wars with the Philistines, when David's life was in danger, 'his officers took an oath that he should never again go out with them to war, for fear that the lamp of Israel might be extinguished' (2 Sam. 21: 17). Before long the further bond of loyalty is invoked. In opposition to David, Absalom is anointed king, and a messenger reports that 'the hearts of the men of Israel are after Absalom' (*opisō Abessalom*, LXX)—or, as the REB has it, 'The men of Israel had transferred their allegiance to Absalom' (2 Sam. 15: 13). As soon as the rebellion has been suppressed, a

---

[61] *ERE* vii. 726 f.
[62] *HDB* iv. 123.

quarrel arises between Israel and Judah over the right to escort the king home. To the claim of Judah that the king is their near kinsman, the people of Israel reply: 'We have ten shares in the king; and, what is more, in David we are senior to you' (2 Sam. 19: 43). This retort appears absurd until we recognize that 'in David' was to the speakers interchangeable with 'in Israel', and that in Israel Judah was only the fourth of the sons of Jacob. Almost at once, however, Sheba ben Bichri calls them to renounce their loyalty in a new rebellion: 'What share have we in David? We have no lot in the son of Jesse' (2 Sam. 20: 1). And the death of David is not the end of the story; for a generation later the cry of Sheba is renewed by the ten tribes in their rebellion under Jeroboam ben Nebat (1 Kings 16: 12). This unity of the nation, and the embodiment of its welfare and salvation in David's anointed person, imprinted itself on the Jewish mind as an abiding hope through the centuries (Hos. 1: 10–11; 3: 4–5; Ezek. 34: 12–13, 22–3).

Mark opens his Gospel with an unequivocal statement of his thesis: Jesus is Messiah.[63] Moreover, for Mark 'Messiah' means 'King of Israel'. He is certainly not one of those writers who believes that Jesus' command of silence at Caesarea Philippi was tantamount to rejection of the title Peter accorded him. It is as the King of Israel, and claimant to the throne of Israel, that Jesus is arraigned, condemned, and cruci-fied. The Roman soldiers salute him sarcastically as 'King of the Jews', and Pilate causes that title to be nailed to the Cross. But this is an alien address, such as only a Gentile would use. The Jewish crowd, even though it is in mockery and rejection, use his correct style: 'Let the Messiah, the King of Israel, come down from the cross' (Mark 15: 32). Mark is as sensitive to irony as is John, though he does not find it so necessary to rub it in. For him, Jesus is the King of Israel, and therefore Son of God, precisely because he does *not* come down. We may thus conclude that, whatever other significance 'Son of God' may have for Mark, it is a title of royalty, but one which, because in the Old Testament it was used not only of the king (2 Sam. 7: 14; Ps.

---

[63] The textual difficulty of 1: 1—whether or not to include the phrase 'the Son of God', a Marcan synonym for the Messiah—is well known. Some weighty manuscripts exclude it (cf. C. E. B. Cranfield, *The Gospel According to Saint Mark* (Edinburgh, 1959), ad loc). But the claim both at the beginning of the story (1: 11) and at the end (15: 39) indicates that the question is ultimately theological, not textual. Mark's Gospel is *from beginning to end the gospel of Jesus Christ the Son of God*. Thus, even if 'Jesus Christ' is taken to be a proper name and not a title, the longer text of Mark 1: 1 may be taken to be genuine.

2: 7), but also of the nation (Exod. 4: 22; Hos. 11: 1), could carry the overtures of unity between king and people.

For Mark the king is also Son of David and Son of Man. It is true that Mark appears to call the first of these terms into question. 'How can the scribes maintain that the Messiah is Son of David?' (Mark 12: 35). The simple answer is that the scribes are right to maintain this, and that they could cite pages of scripture to prove it: they say that the Messiah is Son of David because that is what 'Messiah' means. It is true that the prophecies of Zechariah speak of two 'sons of oil', the anointed king and anointed priest (4: 14), and that these two figures appear side by side not only in the documents of Qumran, but also in the imagery of Revelation (11: 4). It is true also that it has become fashionable to talk loosely of Jewish expectations of a variety of 'Messianic figures' or even 'quasi-Messianic figures'. But for this there is not a shadow of linguistic warrant.[64] Certainly to the writers of the New Testament 'Messiah' and 'Son of David' were synonyms (below, Chapter 8). The Davidic descent of Jesus is widely attested, and the attestation can have had no other function than to support his claim to Messiahship. Moreover, Mark can hardly be deemed to deny it. For the Marcan Jesus cites David's appropriation of the shewbread as precedent for his own sovereign freedom, accepts the title of 'Son of David' from Bartimaeus by commending his faith, and makes no objection to the hosannas of the pilgrims, 'Blessings on the coming kingdom of our father David' (Mark 2: 25–6; 10: 46–52; 11:10). What he rejects, therefore, with the hyperbole characteristic of all Semitic debate, is the notion that 'Son of David' is all the Old Testament has to say on the subject.

But the 'Son of David' pericope contains a further contradiction not so easily resolved. Jesus appears to be laying claim to a royal status higher than that of David. 'David himself calls him "Lord" (*Kurios*); how can he also be his son?' Yet in Mark 10: 42 ff. Jesus refuses to construe his kingly role in terms of lordship. It is the rulers of the Gentiles who lord it (*katakurieuousi*) over their subjects. In such a monarchy the king is lord and all his subjects, from the least to the greatest, from slave to minister of state, are servants. But Jesus and his associates are not to be the recipients but the givers of service.

---

[64] Cf. in particular M. de Jonge, 'The Use of the Word "Anointed" in the Time of Jesus,' *NT* 8 (1966), 133 ff., who points out that before the time of Christ 'we hardly find any occurrence of the absolute use of the term "the Messiah", i.e. without a following genitive or possessive pronoun'.

Here then is a paradox, that he whom David (and therefore scripture) hails as lord, he whom God enthrones at His own right hand, himself abjures any such dignities.

There are two ways of resolving this paradox, one wrong and the other right. The wrong way is to see lordship at the right hand of God as a promotion achieved through humble service, much as the boss might start life on the factory floor, or the theatre director work his way up from being assistant to the stage carpenter. The right way is to see that the career of service chosen by Jesus is the only greatness recognized in the sight of God. At this point there is a close affinity between Mark and the so-called hymn of Philippians 2: 6 ff., where the exaltation of Jesus and the bestowal of the name 'Lord' are not the reversal of earthly humility and servanthood but the enthronement of them.

If kingship is to be so drastically reinterpreted, however, does it make sense to continue harping on the title as Mark does? This is a question which C. F. D. Moule asks. 'The crucifixion must once and for all have extinguished absolutely any literal hopes that Jesus might become the King of Israel.'[65] Because his interest is in the question of origins, Moule concludes, quoting O. Cullmann, that 'the early Church believed in Christ's Messiahship because they believed that Jesus believed himself to be Messiah'.[66] Without wishing to disagree with this conclusion, one might be uneasy about the way it is reached, since there seems to be a suggestion that Jesus in his lifetime was content to abandon to the 'National Liberation Front'[67] any literal idea of kingship and to interpret his own role in some non-political, pietistic sense. This was not the view of Mark. And M. Hengel[68] has argued persuasively that the synoptic writers were deliberately trying to reproduce a pre-Easter point of view.

We shall see below that the phrase 'Son of Man' in the context of the teaching of Jesus is a complex and much-debated question. But in the Marcan context four points are beyond question: (1) it is a self-designation of Jesus; (2) it is a title of royalty; (3) it is derived from Dan. 7: 13 (cf. Mark 14: 62); and (4) Jesus habitually preferred it to the title 'Messiah' as a more accurate expression of what he understood by his own kingly role. In the book of Daniel the human-

---

[65] C. F. D. Moule, *The Origin of Christology* (Cambridge, 1977), 33.
[66] Ibid 34.
[67] On this phrase see below, p. 357.
[68] Cf. M. Hengel, *The Atonement* (Philadelphia, 1981).

like figure is a symbol comparable with the four beasts that precede it, which stand both for the four successive empires and for the kings in whom the imperial power was vested. The Son of Man is explicitly said to stand for the saints of the Most High, but the way was open for the symbol to be given an individual, representative interpretation (below, Chapter 9), and this is the way it was taken, not only in the Gospels but in 4 Ezra 13 and 1 Enoch 37–71. There is therefore a strong prima facie case for arguing that Mark intended his four titles of royalty together to point to Jesus as the embodiment of the new Israel, and this impression is borne out by his handling of them.

The first open proclamation of Jesus as Messiah is followed by a warning that the Son of Man must come to royal power through suffering, which entails certain death for him and the risk of death for his followers; anyone who disowned Jesus in his self-surrender will be disowned by the Son of Man in the triumph that follows. Thus for Mark to acclaim Jesus as Messiah is to make an affirmation not merely about him, but also about the Israel he embodies; and in a divided Israel it is also to raise the question of loyalty. Every Israelite must decide whether he has a share in the king, a lot in the Son of David. This is what the Marcan conversation of Caesarea Philippi concerns:

Anyone who chooses to give me his allegiance [*opisō mou elthein*] must set self aside; he must take up his cross and follow. Anyone who chooses to save his life shall lose it. But anyone who will lose his life for me and for the gospel shall save it. What can anyone gain by winning the whole world and forfeiting his life? What can he give to buy his life back? Whoever disowns me and my teaching in this treacherous and sinful age, the Son of Man will disown when he comes in the glory of his Father with the holy angels (Mark 8: 34–8).

Peter has hailed Jesus as Messiah, though he does not yet understand the term as Jesus understands it and God intends it. Of course Jesus could save his life if, like David, he withdrew from the battle into obscurity, but that would be to lose his life as Messiah, the life which God promises here and hereafter to those who obey him. He could fall in with popular expectation and pursue the course of world dominion, but that also would be to lose his life, to quench the lamp of Israel. And what holds for him also holds for his followers. The prospect is forbidding, but the alternative is more forbidding; it is to forfeit a place in the Israel of God. When the king renders his account to God, justice requires that he should disown those who on earth have disowned him. The Son of Man must be able to vouch for the saints of the Most High. Hence the request of James and John to be allowed to share the royal dignity of Jesus is not refused, but is countered with a warning that any share in the role of Jesus must be a share in his cup and baptism, and that greatness among his followers is meant to be construed not in terms of domination but of service, since redemptive service is the vocation of the Son of Man (Mark 10: 35-45).

Finally, in the upper room, the Son of Man knows that he is to be betrayed by one of his disciples and disowned by all of them. And if those who have disowned Jesus on earth are to be disowned before the judgement seat of God, who then can be saved? We appear to be confronted by a shepherd in danger of losing not one sheep out of a hundred, but the whole flock, by a king whose subjects have renounced their allegiance, by a Son of Man with no saints to represent. And it is here that Mark brings his readers to that further function of kingship which we have already noted: the king must redeem. 'He shall have compassion on the needy and the poor; he shall save the lives of the poor; from oppression and violence he shall redeem their lives and precious shall their blood be in his eyes' (Ps. 72: 13-14).

We have also seen that in Israel's code of civil law the right and duty of redemption, whether from slavery or the alienation of property, lies with the next of kin. Because he is bound to them by ties of kinship, the king has the responsibility of redeeming any among his people who have no other legal recourse and are in need of redemption. But where can there be greater need than when the whole nation has forfeited its life in rebellion against their king? Mark has already told us that Jesus had compassion on the crowd because they were like sheep without a shepherd (6: 34). Divine justice demands that he should disown those who have disowned him; but divine compassion demands that he accept the duty of redemption, even at the cost of his own life. Thus Jesus refuses to disown them, and instead makes a new covenant with them which is to be sealed by his death (14: 17-25).

The dilemma which faces the Marcan Jesus is precisely that which the prophets attribute to God Himself. 'Back they shall go to Egypt, and the Assyrian shall be their king: for they have refused to return to me ... bent on rebellion as they are. Though they call on their High God even then he will not reinstate them. How can I give you up, O Ephraim, how can I surrender you, O Israel?' (Hos. 11: 5-8). It is also, incidentally, the dilemma that Paul faces in Romans 3. The whole world is reduced to silence under the judgement of God, and justice requires the sentence of condemnation; but that would be a defeat for the purpose of God. In the *hilasterion* of the Cross the righteousness of God is demonstrated, because there justice and mercy are reconciled and proof is given that God is 'both just and the justifier of anyone who has faith in Jesus' (3: 25f.).

When we understand that the Marcan Jesus gives his life as a ransom, not merely for those who are unable to redeem themselves, but for those whose lives are forfeit because, whether by rejection, denial, or desertion, they have declared that they have no share in the king, it may at first appear that 'substitution' is the most adequate descriptive term. But its inadequacy becomes apparent only when we recognize that the one who gives his life as a ransom for the many is also the king of Israel, who by divine appointment, by kinship, and by covenant, is entitled to act as the embodiment of his people, and who by his share in the divine compassion refuses to disown even those who have disowned him. Whatever he does is a corporate act, so that they are included in the doing of it. If then we find Jesus occupying the position that, according to the scriptures, had always been intended for Israel,[69] this need occasion no surprise, since this was the role which the king of Israel could be expected to discharge.

With one great exception Matthew, in spite of his emphasis on Jesus as king and saviour of Israel, has nothing to add to Mark on the representative function of kingship.[70] The exception is Matt. 25: 31 ff., where 'the King' describes the suffering of his followers as having been done also 'to me', a statement difficult to explain apart from the Old Testament antecedents seen above. Luke makes two significant additions: Jesus was baptized in the midst of a general baptism of 'the whole people', thus identifying himself with a national response to John's summons to repentance; and it was this that called forth the approval of the voice from heaven (3: 21–2; below, Chapter 8), while at the Last Supper the covenant which Jesus makes is a royal covenant with the Twelve in their capacity as the symbolic representatives of a renewed and restored Israel (22: 29–30; cf. Matt. 19: 28).[71]

[69] Cf. C. H. Dodd, *According to the Scriptures* (London, 1952), 114 ff.

[70] The identification expressed in Matt. 10: 40–2 (cf. Mark 9: 37; Luke 10: 16; and John 13: 20) rests on the different principle of delegation.

[71] The original text of Luke 22: 15 ff. lacked the Marcan reference to 'covenant-blood'. The arguments of Jeremias in favour of the shorter text in the 1st ed. of his *Die Abendmahlsworte Jesu* (Göttingen, 1935, 42 ff) have never been refuted, even by Jeremias himself in the 3rd ed. of the same work (ET 1960).

For some reason that has never been adequately explained, Paul makes little use of the Messiahship of Jesus. He refers to Jesus as king rarely (the exceptions being Rom. 8: 34; 1 Cor. 15: 25; Eph. 1: 20; Col. 1: 15; 3: 1). He believes that Jesus was descended from David *kata sarka* ('according to the flesh'), and that from the Jewish nation who are his kinsmen *kata sarka* comes the Messiah *kata sarka* (Rom. 1: 4; 9: 3, 5); but in his normal usage *christos* has become a proper name. We cannot therefore treat his characteristic expression *en christō* as though it means 'in the Messiah'.[72] Nevertheless the concept of national solidarity is fundamental to all Paul's thinking about the relationship between Jesus and believers. It is not enough for him to prove that Gentiles equally with Jews can, in union with Christ, be regarded as sons of God; he must prove that they are sons of Abraham (Gal. 3: 8, 26). It is true that his case depends on the argument that to be a son of Abraham is not a matter of physical descent but of sharing Abraham's faith (3: 7), but the point is that he is not thereby content to regard the physical solidarity of the old covenant as a metaphorical model for the true spiritual solidarity of the new, as he does in the contrast between physical circumcision and true circumcision (Rom. 2: 28–9; Col. 2: 11). He finds it necessary to argue that the voluntary principle, God's free choice and the free human response of faith, was integral to the existence of Israel from the start. As debating points Paul's two resorts to scriptural authority in Galatians are of dubious cogency; but as illustrations of the working of his mind they are clear enough. He first argues that God's promises were made 'to Abraham and to his seed', and that, since the word 'seed' is singular, it must refer to Christ (3: 15–16). Behind the grammatical absurdity[73] lies the valid point that 'seed' in this sense is a collective noun, so that, once Paul has concluded on other grounds that Christ is the fulfilment of God's promises, the application of this term to Christ

[72] In any case this expression is almost without exception used in contexts dealing with life in the Christian community, and not with the initial representative event in which believers were included. The only possible exceptions are Rom. 3: 21; 8: 2; 1 Cor. 1: 2; Gal. 2: 17; and Eph. 1: 20.

[73] Paul's point remains difficult to appreciate by modern canons of exegesis. Since the promise is to the 'seed' (*to spermati*) of Abraham, and not to 'seeds' (*tois spermasin*), the promise must have been of Christ. But *to spermati* is already plural. A useful treatment of the problem is provided by E. E. Ellis, *Paul's Use of the Old Testament* (London, 1957), 70 ff. Ellis points to various rabbinic texts which show that Paul's exegesis was not unusual in his day, concluding that 'the true significance of Paul's usage lies in the argument running throughout the chapter' (p. 71).

shows that he thinks of him as the embodiment of a national identity. In the following chapter (4: 22–31) Paul argues that by physical descent Ishmael was as much a son of Abraham as Isaac, and that only God's promise dictated that Isaac should be the patriarch of God's people, while Ishmael went out to join the Gentiles. The two boys and their mothers are therefore symbolic representatives, Ishmael and Hagar of those whose claim that membership in the people of God rests on descent, Isaac and Sarah of those whose claim rests on faith in God's promise. But there are two loopholes in the argument: (1) the son of a concubine does not compete on the same level with the son of a wife; and (2) this case does not cover those who have no claim to descent from Abraham. The first loophole Paul plugs in Romans 9: 6–13 by adding the case of Jacob and Esau, one of whom becomes patriarch while the other goes out to join the Gentiles. The second objection he covers by citing the promise to Abraham 'in you shall all the Gentiles find blessing' (Gal. 3: 8),[74] which he takes to mean that it was always God's intention that Gentiles should be incorporated into the national unity of Israel. In spite of his emphasis on the equality of Jew and Gentile in Christ (Gal. 3: 28; Col. 1: 10), Paul does not hesitate to remind Gentiles that the corporate unity into which they have been brought is of Jewish origin: they are branches of a wild olive grafted on to the stock of Abraham (Rom. 11: 17–18), fellow citizens with the Jewish foundation members of the divine commonwealth (Eph. 2: 19).

To approach Paul's doctrine of the corporate Christ in this way is to avoid the excesses of those who have concentrated on his figurative use of the word 'body' and have mistaken vividness of imagery for 'ontological realism', that is to say, a relation between Christ and the believer that is somehow less than personal. The origins of Paul's usage are still in dispute, but the three possible sources, each of which may have contributed something to his thought, all point in the same direction. If he drew the idea from his pagan environment, we know that there 'the body' was already a symbol of political unity, as is seen in the fable of Menenius Agrippa.[75] If behind the term body (*sōma*) we

---

[74] It is an interesting conjecture that this scriptural use of it may have been one of the sources of Paul's preposition in the phrase *en christō*.

[75] According to this fable the fictitious Menenius Agrippa convinced the plebeians (who had seceded from Rome) to return by telling them the parable of 'The Belly and the Limbs'.

are to detect the Hebrew 'flesh' (*basar*), that was a term signifying kinship, both of the family and of the nation. If Paul developed his usage out of the tradition of Jesus' eucharistic words, then his editing of those words is illuminating. In the Marcan version there is a parallelism of body and blood; but in Paul's version it is between body and covenant, the corporate unity established by the symbol of broken bread defined by the symbolism of the cup as a covenant between Jesus and the people of God.[76]

In 1 Peter the main symbol of unity is the spiritual temple in which believers are living stones and Christ the corner-stone (2: 4–6; cf. Mark 12: 10; Acts 4: 11; 1 Cor. 3: 16; Eph. 2: 20; Rev. 3: 12).[77] But this symbol is at once reinterpreted in terms of a new national unity: 'You are now the people of God, who once were not his people.'

The author of Hebrews shared with the rest of the early Church the belief that Jesus as Messiah was enthroned at the right hand of God (1: 4), but he had his own way of confirming what we have found about the representative function of kingship. In Psalm 110 the king is addressed by God as High Priest 'in perpetuity in the order of Melchizedek'; and a High Priest also has a representative function. 'Every High Priest is taken from among men and appointed their representative before God . . . he is called by God, as indeed Aaron was. So it is with Christ' (5: 1–5). Aaron and Melchizedek are symbols for two radically different styles of representation. It is the duty of the Aaronic High Priest once a year to enter the Holy of Holies to make atonement on behalf of the people. His function may well be described as substitutionary, and that is the measure of its failure and of God's intention that the old order should possess no more than a shadowy skeleton of the real thing. For the Holy of Holies is a symbol for the presence of God from which the people are permanently debarred, which they may enter only in his representative person. Christ, by contrast, is High Priest in perpetuity, not only because he has entered the eternal sanctuary of which the earthly was only a shadowy sketch,

---

[76] On the Lord's Supper in the New Testament, see below, pp. 225–32.

[77] Cf. 1 Cor. 3: 16 ff.; 6: 19; (by implication) 2 Cor. 6: 16; 1 Pet. 2: 4 ff.; Eph. 2: 19 ff. Moule, *Origin of Christology*, 89 ff., denies that Jesus is ever depicted as the new temple in the New Testament. For helpful studies on the general question, cf. R. J. McKelvey, *The New Temple* (Oxford, 1968); H. W. Turner, *From Temple to Meeting House: The Phenomenology and Theology of Places of Worship* (New York, 1979); B. Gärtner, *The Temple and Community in Qumran and the New Testament* (Cambridge, 1965); and I. H. Marshall, 'Church and Temple in the New Testament', *TB* 40 (1989), 203 ff.

but also because he is representative of his people after the fashion of a pioneer, who opens the way for others to follow (6: 20; 10: 18; below, Chapter 8).

The fusion of the roles of king and priest is characteristic also of the Revelation, though it is there directed to a very different purpose. Christ is hailed at the outset as the ruler of earthly kings and appears in the vestments of priesthood. But the dual role is to be shared with his followers, whom he has made 'a royal house of priests to his God and Father' (1: 6; 5: 10). As the two 'sons of oil' the martyrs are to win afresh the victory which Christ won on the Cross (11: 4) and so to contribute to his final victory (11: 15); but it is by virtue of the shedding of his blood that they become conquerors (12: 11).

Like Mark, John tells us that he wrote his Gospel in order to prove that Jesus was the Christ (20: 31), and we can be sure that he is not using the title in any esoteric Christian or quasi-Gnostic sense, because at his first appearance Jesus has been designated Messiah and King of Israel (1: 41, 49). He depicts Jesus as the temple which must be destroyed before it can be raised again (2: 18) and as the vine of Israel, to which his disciples must remain united as branches (15: 1–8). But in his fullest exposition of the theme of solidarity, though he does not use the word priest, he uses priestly language. 'For their sake I now consecrate myself that they too may be consecrated in the truth' (17: 19). At the beginning of the prayer Jesus prays, 'Glorify your Son', and we may well ask why he should want to receive that which he has possessed and manifested all along (1: 14; 2: 11). The answer is that he is praying as representative of his people. He does not ask that the glory should be conferred directly on them; it must be given to him as their representative in order that he may impart it to them (17: 22; below, Chapter 8).

John shares with Paul and the author of Revelation one further insight into the bond of unity which links Jesus with his followers: it is a bond of love. Whatever symbols of solidarity may be drawn from the wide arena of human experience, this is the essence of the reality they symbolize. 'God gives proof of His love toward us in that while we were still sinners Christ died for us' (Rom 5: 8). 'The love of Christ constrains us, once we have reached the conviction that one died for all, and therefore all have died' (2 Cor. 5: 10). 'He loved me and gave himself up for me' (Gal. 2: 20). 'To him who loves us and freed us from our sins with his own life's blood ... be glory and dominion for ever and ever. Amen' (Rev. 1: 5–6). 'If you heed my command, you will dwell in my love, as I have heeded my Father's commands and dwell in his love ... There is no greater love than this, that a man should lay down his life for his friends' (John 15: 10, 13).

6.

The Experience of Salvation

6.1. NEWNESS OF LIFE

The ongoing process of salvation is the progressive appropriation in the experience of believers, individual and corporate, of all that had been accomplished once for all in the representative and inclusive person of Christ. As they believed that God had been in Christ working out His plan, so they believed that God was present in their midst, acting in and through them to carry His plan to its consummation. Since the New Testament authors wrote not only to record their convictions about the past and their hopes for the future, but above all to deal with the pastoral needs of the present, it is hardly surprising that almost everything they wrote had a reference to this central concern. Yet whatever the immediate need, they do not allow us to forget that it offers an occasion for a fresh experience of God.

Through all the varieties of emphasis there runs the one dominant theme of life: rich, full, abundant, and free, a pulsating and irrepressible vitality. To be a Christian is to enter the service of the living God, 'who gives life to the dead and calls into being what does not yet exist' (Rom. 4: 17);[1] it is to be united with him who died and came alive again, so that his new life might be manifested in the mortal bodies of his followers;[2] it is to receive the life-giving Spirit (John 6: 63; 7: 39; Rom. 8: 11; 2 Cor. 3: 6), to be enabled to walk in a new path of life (Rom. 6: 4; Gal. 5: 25). In all this there are implications for the life that awaits beyond death, to which we shall turn in the next chapter; but the primary interest is in the present, in a new mode of being alive, and in the moral consequences which this entails for those who participate in it. 'If the Spirit is the source of our life, let the Spirit also direct our course' (Gal. 5: 25).

[1] Cf. also Matt. 16: 16; John 6: 57; Acts 14: 15; Rom. 9: 26; 2 Cor. 3: 3; 6: 16; 1 Thess. 1: 9; 1 Tim. 3: 15.
[2] Rom. 14: 9; 2 Cor. 4: 11; 13: 4; cf. John 14: 19; 1 Cor. 15: 47; Gal. 2: 20; Phil. 1: 21; Col. 3: 3; Heb. 7: 8; 10: 20; Rev. 1: 18; 2: 8.

This theme is explicitly stated in the Fourth Gospel. The believer 'has eternal life', 'has already crossed over from death to life', has heard the voice of the Son of God and come to life; and this has happened because 'as the Father has life in himself, so He had granted to the Son to have life in himself' (5: 24–6). The gift of life is nothing less than the life of the risen Jesus which he lives in those who are united to him by faith: 'I am coming back to you . . . because I live, you too shall live; then you will know that I am in my Father and you in me and I in you' (14: 18–19). This life consists in the knowledge of God, as He has been revealed by Jesus (17: 3), and is therefore not to be construed as other-worldly or narrowly spiritual. As the ministry of Jesus has made plain, it comprehends and interpenetrates the whole earthly life of the human race. 'I have come that they may have life, and may have it in all its fulness' (10: 10). When the *logos* became flesh, the love and purpose of God entered into the 'stuff' of earthly existence; 'In him was life, and the life was the light of [i.e. designed for] men' (1: 4).[3] It is for this reason that Jesus insists that 'the bread of God which came down from heaven and gives life to the world' is his own flesh (6: 33, 51). It is himself he gives, in all the concrete reality of the human life that his contemporaries have seen and known. 'As the living Father sent me, and I live because of the Father, so the one who eats *me* shall live because of me' (6: 57, emphasis added).

The moral implications of this are drawn out in 1 John. 'This life was made visible; we have seen it and bear our testimony; we here declare to you the eternal life which dwelt with the Father and was made visible to us' (1: 2). The life thus made visible is offered to believers so that in them it may be made visible again; they can do nothing with it except live it, and the proof that it has been offered and received lies in the quality of their own lives. 'We for our part have crossed over from death to life; this we know, because we love our brothers . . . Christ laid down his life for us, and we in turn are

---

[3] This punctuation of v. 3 f. is dictated both by the theology of the Gospel and by the structure of the Prologue. The alternative punctuation ('that which came to be in him was life') would imply that the revelation of the life and light of the *logos* in Jesus was neither unique nor new, but had all along been available to the human race in every part of the created order. In the Prologue, the reference to the Baptist is decisive; he came to bear witness not to the light shining throughout the ages in every creature, but to the light seen for the first time in the one to whom it is John's sole function to point (1: 29–34; 3: 27–30; 5: 33–5); see W. H. Cadman, *The Open Heaven* (Oxford, 1969), 15 ff.).

bound to lay down our lives for our brothers. But if anyone has enough to live on, and yet when he sees his brother in need shuts up his heart against him, how can it be said that the divine love dwells in him?' (3: 14–17).

What is explicit in John is implicit in the narratives of the Synoptic Gospels. The evangelists wrote to place the life and teaching of Jesus on record, but in such a way that the record might illumine, inform and inspire the life of communities created by the story in its oral form. Whether in Mark's brooding over a luminous mystery, in Matthew's dialectic exposition of a law which transcends law, or in Luke's lyrical portrait of a transforming friendship, the story opens for its readers a world of new possibilities; and it does this through a form of teaching which fuses an impossible ideal with an immeasurable gift, through miracles which drive back the encroachments of mortality, through parables which in the daily life of men and women make translucent the activity of God. The readers already believed that the central figure of this story had risen from death, but this belief was credible to them because of the impression made by him on his first disciples and communicated by them to others: 'It could not be that death should hold him in its grip' (Acts 2: 24). Luke's sequel to his Gospel starts with a statement that Jesus, after his death, gave ample proof that he was alive (Acts 1: 3), and the proofs continue throughout the rest of the book. It is the living Jesus who pours out the Holy Spirit (2: 33), whose name has power to heal (4: 10; 9: 34), who turns the arch-persecutor into the greatest of missionaries (9: 4–5). He is the Prince of Life (3: 14), the first title given to the new movement of his followers is 'this life' (5: 20), those who accept the gospel are granted 'life-giving repentance' (11: 18), and those who reject it judge them-selves unworthy of eternal life (13: 46). Luke punctuates his narrative with summaries which draw attention to the awe and wonder, the power and purpose, the free confidence and unaffected joy, the one heart and soul, which characterized the new community which rose triumphantly over opposition and disaster.

Paul's letters too reverberate with vitality: eagerness (Rom. 1: 15) and exultation (Rom. 5: 2–3), confidence (2 Cor. 5: 6, 8; 7: 16; 10: 1–2) and plain-speaking (2 Cor. 3: 12; 7: 4; Phil. 1: 20; Philem. 8), open-handed generosity (2 Cor. 8: 2), steady growth towards an incomparable glory (2 Cor. 3: 18; Rom. 8: 18), and life which flows from the power of God and transcends human weakness (2 Cor. 12: 9; 13: 4; cf. Rom. 15: 13, 19; 1 Cor. 2: 4; 4: 20; Phil. 3: 10; Col. 1:

11; 2: 29; 1 Thess. 1: 5). The Pauline corpus contains over forty references to joy, an exuberance reflected also in Paul's style. He is fond of words expressing wealth and abundance: the riches of God's goodness (Rom. 2: 4), glory (Rom. 9: 23; Phil. 4: 19; Col. 1: 27), and wisdom (1 Cor. 1: 5; 2 Cor. 6: 10; 8: 9; 9: 11; Col. 2: 8), by which believers are enriched, the abounding grace which engenders increasing hope, love, generosity, gratitude, and good works (Rom. 5: 15; 15: 13; Phil. 1: 9; 2 Cor. 8: 2; 9: 8, 12; 1 Cor. 15: 58). He particularly delights in compounds of *huper*, the superlative increase of faith (2 Thess. 1: 3), superabounding glory, joy, grace, power, and love (Rom. 5: 20; 2 Cor. 3: 10; 7: 4; 9: 14; Eph. 1: 19; 2: 7; 3: 19), transcendent power, glory, and revelations (2 Cor. 4: 7, 17; 12: 7), a knowledge of Christ outweighing loss (Phil. 3: 8), a peace that surpasses comprehension (Phil. 4: 7), a love that gives overwhelming victory (Rom. 8: 37).

A similiar assumption is to be found elsewhere in the New Testament. Christians have access to the throne of grace, to the inner sanctuary of God's presence, to the city of the living God (Heb. 4: 6; 10: 19; 12: 22), because they are represented by a High Priest who holds office, not by earthly succession, but 'by the power of an indestructible life' (Heb. 7: 16). They have been 'brought to new birth by the word of truth' (Jas. 1: 18), 'begotten again to a living hope ... through the living and enduring word of God', and are 'transformed with a joy too great for words' (1 Pet. 1: 3, 8, 23). And in the letters to the seven churches of Asia, written in the name of him who was dead and came to life again, the greatest danger attaches to the church which has lost its early love, which has a name for being alive though it is dead, which is neither hot nor cold (Rev. 2: 4, 8; 3: 1, 16).

6.2. WORSHIP

Second only to the theme of life is the theme of worship. It is, to be sure, muted in Matthew,[4] and almost absent from Mark. But in the Lucan writings it is pervasive. The Gospel begins and ends in the

---

[4] Matthew's Gospel refers three times to the praise of God (5: 16; 9: 18; 15: 31; cf. Mark 2: 12). It records the homage of the Magi (2: 8–11), and five times introduces the verb *proskunein* into a story from Mark, usually as a substitute for some Marcan equivalent (8: 12; 9: 18; 14: 33; 15: 25; 20: 20). In view of its use of the same verb in 28: 9, 17, it may have intended throughout to make allusive preparation for the Church's worship of Christ in his own day (but see 18: 26). Otherwise its apparent lack of interest in worship casts some doubt on G. D. Kilpatrick's theory that the Gospel is the product of prolonged *liturgical* use of Mark (*The Origins of the Gospel According to St Matthew*

temple, and hymns both human and angelic at the nativity provide its
theological setting. The prayers of Jesus (3: 21; 5: 16; 6: 12; 9: 18,
28; 11: 1; 22: 41) are balanced by the praise to God which he elicits
from others, the crowd at Nain, the crippled daughter of Abraham,
the Samaritan leper, Bartimaeus, and the Roman centurion (7: 16; 13:
13; 17: 15; 18: 43; 23: 47). In Acts the common life of the Church,
its courage under persecution, and the direction of its mission are
all set in a context of worship (2: 42–7; 4: 24–30; 10: 9, 33; 11: 18;
13: 2).

The Fourth Gospel achieves the same effect by its frequent mention
of Jewish festivals (2: 13, 23; 4: 45; 5: 1; 6: 4; 7: 2–14, 37; 10: 22;
13: 1; 18: 28; 19: 14).[5] The truth adumbrated in the Jewish worship
is now fully embodied in Jesus. He is the true temple, the bread from
heaven, the water and light of life, the true shepherd of his people,
the true vine, the true Paschal Lamb; and it is of this truth that he
speaks to the Samaritan woman. 'The time is coming, and is already
here, when true worshippers will worship the Father in Spirit and in
truth' (4: 22).[6]

To the author of Hebrews religion consists in access to God, and
he expresses this conviction partly by the use of temple imagery, partly
by the repetition of the words 'approach' (4: 16; 7: 25; 10: 1, 22; 11:
6; 12: 18, 22) and 'draw near' (7: 19; 10: 25). To enter God's presence
is no doubt an end in itself, the chief end of human existence, but it
is also the means by which the worshipper is consecrated (2: 11), made
fit for the service of God (9: 14), and enabled to worship God as He
would be worshipped (12: 28).

1 Peter, which begins with blessing and ends with doxology, also
shares with Hebrews the theme of access. 'Come to him, the living
stone, rejected by men but in God's sight choice and precious, and
let yourselves be built as living stones, into a spiritual temple; become
a holy priesthood; to offer spiritual sacrifices acceptable to God
through Jesus Christ.' The community of believers is to fulfil the

---

(Oxford, 1946)). K. Stendahl's theory that it was produced by a learned school of
Christian Scribes (*The School of St Matthew and Its Use of the Old Testament* (Philadelphia,
1968) better fits the didactic character of the work—although it remains a theory still
far from proven.

[5] It is quite possible that these references have a further significance, whether for
chronology or for the structure of the Gospel. But this does not affect their primary,
theological bearing.

[6] Cf. the brief but useful discussion of R. Mayer, 'Feast', *NIDNTT*, i. 628 ff.

functions of temple, priesthood, and nation, by proclaiming in the life they lead 'the triumphs of him who has called you out of darkness into his marvellous light' (2: 4–9).

The Revelation of John begins on the Lord's Day and ends in Eucharist. At the centre of his vision is He who sits on the throne, yet the enthroned figure is never described. He is symbolized by the throne of sovereignty, the rainbow of mercy, and the thunders of judgement. Otherwise we are allowed to see Him only as He is reflected in the worship of His heavenly court. The choir throughout provides an interpretative chorus to the unfolding drama of salvation; and to the worship of heaven is added the worship of earth. The prayers of God's people are brought as incense to the heavenly altar (8: 3–4). Christ has redeemed people of every race and nation, and has made them 'a royal house, to serve as priests of his God and Father' (1: 6; 5: 10). But in this book the royal and priestly offices of Christ which devolve on his followers are fulfilled in the witness they have under persecution. Those who cross the fiery sea of martyrdom in a new Exodus sing the triumphal song of Moses and the Lamb (15: 3–4), which turns in due course into a victory song over the fall of the enemies of God (19: 2). Yet even in his vision of judgement John has room for the larger hope that, with the fall of the great city, the whore Babylon, the nations of the world, whom she has enslaved and seduced to her worship, will learn the fear of the Lord and turn to the worship of the God of heaven (11: 13). On the other hand John himself comes near to the idolatry which his book condemns. Twice he tells us that he fell prostrate at the feet of his escorting angel to worship him, and twice he earns the rebuke, 'No, not that. I am but a fellow servant with you and your brothers who bear testimony to Jesus. It is God you must worship' (19: 10; 22: 9). The essence of idolatry is to attribute infallibility and ultimate worth to that which is derivative and secondary, to that which is not God.

Paul's references to worship are rich and varied, considering that they are for the most part incidental to his immediate purpose. Just as sin is a locating of ultimate worth in the wrong place, a failure to give glory where glory is due (Rom. 1: 21), so the faith of Abraham, which God declared to be righteousness, consisted in acknowledgment of God's glory, in the firm conviction that God was able to keep His promises (Rom. 4: 20–1). Christian faith goes a step beyond this, for it is the conviction that in Christ God has kept His promises. 'He is the "Yes" pronounced over all God's promises; that is why it is through

Jesus Christ that we say "Amen", and so give glory to God' (2 Cor.
1: 20). The Christian life is from start to finish the response of worship
to God's grace and glory (Phil. 1: 11), the incense offered to God by
Christ to complete his own sacrifice of obedience (2 Cor. 2: 15), the
service of God inspired by the Spirit (Phil. 3: 3). Paul can hardly speak
of the gospel without bursting into thanksgiving. Yet true worship
cannot be restricted to words. The glory of God is the criterion of all
truly Christian conduct (1 Cor. 10: 31). Paul's readers are to serve
God with their bodies (1 Cor. 6: 20), to offer to him their whole selves
(Rom. 12: 1–2). The quality of their common worship must display
to all comers that 'God is truly among you' (1 Cor. 14: 25). Their
common life is to be distinguished by a mutual acceptance which
transcends all divisions (Rom. 15: 7), by the same attitude of mind
which led Christ to renounce his rights and dignities in humble self-
giving, and so to be exalted to the highest place that heaven affords,
'to the glory of God the Father' (Phil. 2: 5–11).

6.3. THE SOVEREIGNTY OF GRACE

Paul's running battle with Judaizers and his insistence that justification
is on the ground of faith alone served a single purpose: to maintain
the primacy of grace. God's promise to Abraham had to be on the
ground of faith so as to establish its character as sheer grace.[7] God's
election could not be based on merit; otherwise grace would cease to
be grace (Rom. 11: 5–6). As a Jew Paul had no doubt believed in the
grace of election, but Pharisaic zeal had overlaid that belief with
national and personal pride. It was his conversion that recalled him to
what he should always have known to be true, that enabled him to
look back on his Jewish past, outwardly a history of blindness and
rebellion, and to see it as a manifestation of prevenient grace (Gal. 1:
15–16); to claim that although in the face of God's judgement and
God's mercy alike Jew and Gentile stand on equal footing, it was all
the same a great advantage to have been entrusted with the oracles of
God (Rom. 3: 2); to recognize the lavishness of God's provision for
His ancient people (Rom. 9: 4–5). It was the death of Christ and his
own encounter with the risen Lord that persuaded him of the majesty
of that grace which could turn an enemy into a friend (Rom. 5: 10),

---

[7] 'The promise was made on the ground of faith in order that it might be a matter
of sheer grace' (Rom. 4: 16a, REB).

could deal effectively with human sin and alienation (Rom. 3: 24; 4: 4–5), and could open for the human race a new beginning (Rom. 5: 15–21; cf. 2 Cor. 5: 17).

Yet all this was only a beginning; for it was God's intention that 'through the act of the one, Jesus Christ, grace might establish its reign' (Rom. 5: 21). Through him believers 'have secured access to the grace in which we stand' (Rom. 5: 2). Paul's quarrel with the Judaizers was not over his interpretation of the Cross as God's act of salvation (with which they largely agreed), but over his claim that grace must govern every aspect of Christian life (2 Cor. 1: 12). Whether from fear of Jewish reprisals (Gal. 2: 14; 6: 12), to gain personal ascendancy (Gal. 6: 13)—as Paul suggests in the heat of controversy or out of a genuine moral concern[8]—or from a belief in the permanent validity of the Law, they wanted to produce a synthesis of Law and gospel. Paul argued that the Law exercises its authority only over the old life, the Adamic life which in the representative figure of Jesus had been nailed to the Cross; thus to invoke its authority over the life which Christians enjoyed in union with the risen Christ was to nullify the grace of God (Gal. 2: 21); and to fall away from grace was to be severed from Christ (Gal. 5: 4).

Paul's severity towards any hint of the insufficiency of grace had two causes. The first is his conviction that grace is ethically powerful. God has done and is doing by grace what He never did, and never intended to do, by law. 'What the Law could not do, because our sinful nature robbed it of all potency, God has done ... so that the requirement of the Law may be fulfilled in us, whose conduct, no longer controlled by our sinful nature, is directed by the Spirit' (Rom. 8: 3). The Law had adumbrated the life of holiness, but it could not produce it. Paul is never in any doubt that the people of God must be a holy people. To be saved is to live with God, and those who live with God must be holy; they must reflect His character. But true holiness is always God's free gift, never a human achievement. In confirmation Paul can point to his own life, with its manifest change from what he once had been to what he now was (1 Cor. 15: 10; Gal. 1: 13–15, 23; Phil. 3: 3–11). But he can point to a similar change in others (2 Cor. 3: 2–3; Rom. 11: 30; Col. 1: 21; 3: 7; Eph. 2: 1–6).

---

[8] The attack on Paul, which he indignantly rebuts (Rom. 3: 8; 6: 11), seems to have arisen from a suspicion that his emphasis on justification by faith alone, apart from law, entailed a lack of concern for moral standards.

God's power is most obviously effective when working through human weakness. 'He has chosen things low and contemptible, mere nothings, to overthrow the existing order' (1 Cor. 1: 28). On the other hand, Paul knew from experience how hard it is for human pride to surrender to the inexorability of grace. As a Pharisee he had always wanted to excel (Gal. 1: 14; Phil. 3: 5–6), and as a late-comer on the Christian scene he had striven to prove himself second to none (1 Cor. 15: 10; 2 Cor. 11: 5). He therefore resented his 'thorn in the flesh', which sapped his energies and restricted his achievement; and he had to learn that this was God's way of keeping him humble and dependent on God's all-sufficient grace (2 Cor. 12: 7–10). If the great protagonist of grace himself needed to be taught such a lesson, his stringent warnings to others could hardly be wasted.

It is not, however, to be supposed that Paul regarded grace as one alternative to either moral constraint or moral effort. Grace and love exercise an inner constraint far more compelling than the external constraints of law. 'The love of Christ compels us, when once we have reached the conclusion that one died for all, and therefore the whole human race has died; and his purpose in dying for all was that those who live should no longer live for themselves, but for him who for their sake died and rose again' (2 Cor. 5: 14). To live apart from grace is to experience frustration and helplessness (Rom. 7: 7–25). Only the operations of grace can direct human effort to its proper goal. The Philippians can 'work out their own salvation' because 'it is God who works in you, inspiring both the will and the deed, for His own chosen purpose' (Phil. 2: 12–13). But by the same means Paul can attain the excellence to which he aspired: 'In my labours I have outdone them all—not I, indeed, but the grace of God working within me' (1 Cor. 15: 10). Being a Christian is nothing less than sharing the work of God (2 Cor. 6: 1).

Life under grace, then, involves transformation, and it begins with a transformation of the mind (Rom. 12: 2; cf. 1 Cor. 2: 14; 2 Cor. 3: 18; Phil. 2: 5; Col. 3: 10). Christian faith is the conviction that, by the grace of God, the death and resurrection of Christ were inclusive (2 Cor. 5: 14). The old life is dead, crucified with Christ (Rom. 6: 6; Gal. 6: 19), and a new life lies open, in union with the risen Lord. In Romans 6: 1–11 Paul uses a past tense to refer to union with Christ in his death, and a future to refer to union with him in his resurrection; and it has sometimes been assumed that he therefore regarded the one as a fact and the other as no more than a hope, however confident.

But this is a shallow travesty of Paul's argument, which turns from first to last on the style of life which the believer is to live here and now. Union with the crucified Jesus is no more a fact than union with the risen Christ; both are convictions about the inclusive nature of Jesus' own death and resurrection, and the second is logically entailed in the first. 'You must therefore regard yourselves as dead to sin and alive to God, in union with Christ Jesus' (6: 11). It need hardly be said that Paul is not encouraging his friends to indulge in pious make-believe, but to live their lives on the assumption that both convictions are true.

A profound change of attitude to one's own life affects inevitably one's attitude to others. If my being a Christian depends from start to finish on God's free work of grace, then I must be prepared to recognize that same work of grace in my fellow Christians. 'With us therefore worldly standards have ceased to count in our estimate of anyone; even if once they counted in our understanding of Christ, they do so no longer' (2 Cor. 5: 16). Paul is here gently castigating his Corinthian critics for concentrating on what is visible and transient, and so failing to recognize that his physical frailty conceals an inner life which is in the process of daily renewal and transfiguration (2 Cor. 3: 18; 4: 16–18). It is the same sort of spiritual percipience that he urges on the Philippians when he tells them to work out their own salvation, and to do it 'in fear and trembling' because they recognize the presence and activity of God in one another and in the corporate life of the community (Phil. 2: 12–13). A generosity of judgement capable of recognizing the grace of God is the more necessary because God's gifts take many forms. Paul frequently uses *charis* of a gift which he believed to be peculiar to himself—his commission to be apostle of the Gentiles (Rom. 1: 5; 12: 3; 15: 15; 1 Cor. 3: 10; Gal. 2: 9; Eph. 3: 7–8; Phil. 1: 7), and it was a gift which laid on him an inescapable obligation (1 Cor. 9: 16–17). But others had their different gifts, all essential to the well-being of the Church; and none was without his or her particular endowment (1 Cor. 12–14).

Where grace reigns, there is the Kingdom of God. This phrase, so common in the dominical tradition, is rare in Paul.[9] It is on the other hand facile to conclude that in the early Church, and especially in the

---

[9] The term 'kingdom' occurs relatively seldom in Paul's letters (cf. Rom. 14: 17; 1 Cor. 4: 20; 6: 9, 10; 15: 24, 50; Gal. 5: 21; 1 Thess. 2: 12; 2 Thess. 1: 5; Col. 1: 13; 4: 11; and Eph. 5: 5).

thought of Paul, Christ takes the place of the Kingdom as the centre of the gospel. Paul's occasional use of the expression shows that the concept was well known to him, though he had other ways of expressing it. 'The Kingdom of God is not a matter of talk, but of power' (1 Cor. 4: 20). 'The Kingdom of God is not eating and drinking, but righteousness, peace and joy, inspired by the Holy Spirit' (Rom. 14: 17). Paul shared with the rest of the early Church the belief that the risen Christ was enthroned at God's right hand (e.g. Rom. 8: 24; Col. 3: 1), i.e. that God had entrusted to Jesus the exercise of divine sovereignty. Only at the end would Christ hand the sovereignty back to God the Father (1 Cor. 15: 24). In the meantime believers have been transferred from the domain of darkness into the Kingdom of God's Son (Col. 1: 13). *De facto* Christ rules over those who accept him as Lord and yield their hopes to him in faith and obedience. But *de jure* he rules over the world; he is destined to reign until he has reduced all rival powers to subjection (1 Cor. 15: 24–5; cf. 2: 6–8), until every tongue confesses that he is Lord (Phil. 2: 11).

It is at this point that Paul gives us a glimpse of the social and political implications of his ethical teaching. Since he was writing for small communities living in a predominantly pagan society, with little chance of influencing the patterns of Graeco-Roman life or the affairs of state, his letters could give the impression of being personal and 'churchly' in their dominant interest. But to enter the Kingdom is not to join a society shut off from the world. It is to enlist in the service of a king engaged in the task of bringing the whole world under the sovereignty of God. It cannot, however, be too strongly stressed that the king who sits enthroned at God's right hand is not a different person from the Jesus of the gospel story. He has not left behind the character and methods of his earthly life in order to wield in heaven an autocracy which on earth he had renounced. It is not Jesus, but the concept of sovereignty that has changed. The renunciation of rights and dignity, the humble self-surrender which led Jesus to the Cross, these God had declared to be the only greatness recognized in heaven, the only forms of authority by which the world can be brought to acknowledge the one true God; and only in so far as believers arm themselves with that attitude of mind can they serve as agents of God's ultimate victory (Phil. 2: 6–11).

Notwithstanding his emphasis on grace, and on faith as the sole ground of justification, there are passages where Paul seems to hold that God's final verdict will depend on conduct (Rom. 2: 5–10; 1 Cor.

6: 9–10; 2 Cor. 5: 10; 11: 15; Gal. 5: 21; 6: 7–8; Eph. 5: 5). Such passages are not to be explained away as 'fossils' left over from a pre-Pauline theology; he would not have written so often in this way if the idea had been foreign to his own thinking. It is important to give utterances of this kind their full value, since we shall find a similar juxtaposition of apparently conflicting ideas elsewhere in the New Testament. The inconsistency, however, is superficial. Divine grace does not cancel, but rather enhances, human responsibility. Grace is God's will and power to refashion human lives according to His own pattern, and faith is trust in His ability to enable men and women to do their part, combined with a willingness to submit to His transforming skill. Justifying faith is without conditions, but it is not without consequences: 'The only thing that counts is faith active in love' (Gal. 5: 6); and there are some forms of conduct which cast doubt on the reality of faith.

On this point there is no disagreement between James and Paul, only a slight variation of emphasis.[10] According to James, God is 'a generous giver' (1: 5), the source of 'every perfect gift' (1: 17), who has provided the means of a new birth (1: 18), who has 'chosen those who are poor in the eyes of the world to be rich in faith and to inherit the Kingdom He has promised to those who love him' (2: 5). The spirit which God has implanted within the human race has desires which may tend towards quarrelsome envy; but the grace God gives to the humble is strong enough to triumph over them (4: 1–6). The only proper response to God's grace is a humble faith which accepts the free offer of access to God's presence: 'Come close to God, and he will come close to you' (4: 7). But a living faith will spontaneously prove its vitality in conduct; otherwise it is but a corpse (2: 17–26).

The kingship of Christ is one of the *leitmotifs* of Hebrews,[11] but always with a reminder that the nature of his sovereignty has been revealed in his earthly career. He has been exalted to royal status, far above angels and his companions, because he had been the bringer of salvation (1: 3, 8, 13), united by sympathy and suffering with the people whom he represents as priest and king (2: 10–18); because his

---

[10] Cf. A. Schlatter, *Der Glaube im Neuen Testament* (Darmstadt, 1963), 323 ff.; M. Dibelius and H. Greeven, *A Commentary on the Epistle of James* (Philadelphia, 1976), 174 ff.; and L. Goppelt, *Theology of the New Testament* (Grand Rapids, 1981–2), ii. 209 ff.

[11] While kingship is never in Hebrews openly discussed (as is priesthood), it is implicit in the royal psalm citations of ch. 1 and in the figure of the priest-king Melchizedek. See S. Kistemaker, *The Psalm-Citations in the Epistle to the Hebrews* (Amsterdam, 1961).

self-giving has qualified him once for all to be the mediator of a new covenant (8: 1–6; 10: 12), because he 'endured the Cross, making light of its disgrace' (12: 2). In all this, however, he showed himself to be 'the effulgence of God's glory and the stamp of God's very being' (1: 3). It was by the grace of God that he tasted death on behalf of all (2: 9). It was in keeping with God's character that he should qualify for this role by vicarious suffering (2: 10). The throne which he shares with God is not a terrible throne but a 'throne of grace', to which his followers can at all times come with confidence 'to receive mercy and the timely help of grace' (4: 16), grace which alone should govern their conduct (13: 9). Even the passages of pastoral severity contribute to this theme (2: 1–4; 3: 12; 4: 1, 11; 6: 4–6; 10: 26–31; 12: 16–17), since they are occasioned by the author's belief in the finality of grace. For those who sinned and were justly punished under the Law, there still remained in store the gospel of grace. But if they should slip away from that gospel, turn their backs on the privileges once enjoyed, insult the Spirit of grace, and renounce their birthrights, what more could God be expected to offer? Can God provide yet another sacrifice for sin (10: 26), another way into the eternal Kingdom for those who will not have it as a gift (12: 28)? Here, then, as in Paul, faith is the confidence that God can be trusted to keep His promises (10: 23); but in place of the Pauline contrast with meritorious works we find a strong emphasis on the need for persistence in the face of opposition and discouragement.[12]

The followers of Christ are defined in Hebrews by a series of present participles as 'those who approach God through him' (7: 25; 10: 1; 11: 6; cf. 4: 16), 'those who obey him' (5: 9), 'those who are being sanctified' (2: 11; 10: 14). They are bidden to seek 'the holy life without which no one can see the Lord' (12: 14); but this can be achieved only by sharing in God's own holiness (12: 10). God above is holy, and the dilemma of sinners is that they are debarred from the only source of holiness. But Christ has taken the sinner's part: 'The sanctifying priest and those who are being sanctified are all of one stock; and that is why he does not shrink from calling them his brothers' (2: 11). He is the bringer of sanctity because he has opened up a way into God's presence (10: 19–20), and because he has himself entered the eternal order his help is eternally available: 'He is able to save for all time those who approach God through him; he is always

---

[12] Cf. e.g. 6: 11 f.; 10: 23, 32 ff.; 12: 1 ff.; and 13: 13 ff.

living to plead on their behalf' (7: 25). The obedience they offer to him is thus the obedience of faith, but it is also the acceptance of the holy life which faith entails. They are to let themselves be borne along towards maturity (6: 3), that wholeness which the old covenant had never been able to bestow (7: 19; 9: 9; 10: 1).

In the Petrine and Pastoral Epistles grace is for the most part a formal word, used either in greeting or as a general term for the whole dispensation of the gospel (1 Pet. 1: 10; Titus 2: 4). The same might be said of the Fourth Gospel, since grace appears there only in the Prologue (1: 14, 16, 17). But here appearances are misleading. We have seen that in Paul's treatment of this theme the terms grace and love can be interchangeable. By concentrating on God's love John is able to explore the idea of mutuality, and so to bridge the gap between grace and conduct. In his own fashion John emphasizes the priority of God's love no less strongly than Paul; it is love for a blind, rebellious, and undeserving world (3: 16–20). But it is also the love which has subsisted eternally between God and the *logos* (17: 24), and into this reciprocity of love Jesus has entered, when in him the *logos* took flesh: the Father loves the Son (3: 36; 5: 20), and the Son dwells in the Father's love and returns it (15: 10; 14: 31). But to dwell in the Father's love is to share His love for the world, to love those whom the Father has loved, to keep the Father's commands; and into this mutuality of love and obedience believers are invited. 'As the Father has loved me, so I have loved you. Dwell in my love. If you heed my commands, you will dwell in my love, as I have heeded my Father's commands and dwell in His love' (15: 9–10). But nobody can be merely a recipient of God's love; he or she must also be a channel for it. 'This is my command to you: love one another' (15: 17); through that mutual love the universal love of God is to reach out to the world (17: 23). 'I have made known your name to them and will make it known, so that the love you had for me may be in them and I in them' (17: 28).

The First Epistle of John emphasizes even more strikingly both the primacy of God's love and its ethical implication. 'Everyone who loves is a child of God and knows God, but the unloving know nothing of God. For God is love . . . the love I speak of is not our love for God, but the love He showed us in sending His Son as the remedy for the defilement of our sins . . . If we love one another God dwells in us, and His love finds its perfection in us' (4: 7–12). God's love is experienced not in the reception of it, but in its transmission; and it reaches its full expression when, through its archetypal expression in Jesus, it becomes active in the lives of His people.

The Revelation reaches a similar conclusion, but by a very different route: it recreates the concept of sovereignty. God is 'the Lord God omnipotent' (1: 8, and seven other times); and what is revealed to John is that the omnipotence consists not in the coercion of limitless power, but in the persuasiveness of invincible love. In the middle of the heavenly throne he sees 'a Lamb with the marks of slaughter upon it' (5: 6), 'the Lamb slain from the foundation of the world' (13: 8).[13] The symbol of the slaughtered Lamb controls all the other symbolism of the book, since only the Lamb has the right to break the seals on the scroll of the divine purpose; and it is by his death that he has won the right (5: 5, 9).

Jesus first appears as king and priest, who shares his royal and sacerdotal functions with his redeemed followers (1: 5–6); they are to reign with him on earth (5: 10). But it soon appears that he has come to the throne by conquest over God's enemies, that his victory is the Cross, and that it is by the same power that his followers are to win their victory and share his throne (3: 21; 12: 11). Retaliation and the use of worldly weapons to oppose or restrain aggression and injustice are a victory for the seven-headed monster of world power, a success for the great whore who seduces the world to the pursuit of her own methods of attaining them. Only those who 'follow the Lamb wherever he goes' (14: 4), who meet the world's evil as Jesus met it, whose lives are a testimony to his forgiving, sacrificial love, contribute to God's ultimate victory. 'This is the hour of victory for our God, the hour of His sovereignty and power, when his Christ comes to his rightful rule. For the accuser of our brothers is overthrown . . . By the sacrifice of the Lamb they have conquered him, and by the testimony they bore; no love of life made them shrink from death' (12: 10–11).

Mark's Gospel is a narrative commentary on the opening proclamation of Jesus that the reign of God has come. From the start he summons others to join him (1: 16–20), and as the story unfolds we are led to see that following Jesus is synonymous with entering the Kingdom, i.e., enlisting in the service of God the King (10: 17–31). We are shown at the same time the nature of the Kingdom they are

---

[13] The Greek can, of course, be translated, 'all whose names have not been written from the foundation of the world in the slaughtered Lamb's book of life'. But the phrase 'from the foundation of the world' is naturally taken with the participle 'slaughtered', which immediately precedes it.

called to serve. This is first disclosed in Jesus' persistent ministry to human need, his release of men and women held in Satan's bondage (3: 22–7). It had been thought that the main obstacle to Israel's life as a holy people under God's reign was foreign domination; but the real restriction comes from the region of a more sinister power (5: 9); as for Rome, it is possible to pay Caesar his due without at all detracting from what is due to God (12: 13–17). It had been thought that the holiness of Israel would be contaminated by unclean contact, whether with unclean things or with unclean people; but the only contamination that matters comes from the heart and can be cured only by a miracle of grace (7: 1–23; cf. 10: 27). It had been thought that God's redemption would be limited to Israel, but even during the earthly ministry of Jesus there were signs that God's sovereignty was about to break out of the protective fortress which had become its prison (7: 24–30; 11: 11; 13: 10; 14: 9). It had been thought that God's reign would be a reign of law; but Jesus had insisted that the Law must be interpreted in the light of the purpose of love and mercy it was intended to implement and enshrine (2: 23–3: 6; 10: 1–8). Above all God's sovereignty dictates its own way of overcoming evil: Jesus himself must suffer, and his followers must be ready to lose their lives in the service of the gospel (8: 31–7). By frequent references to the disciples' lack of understanding Mark prepares us for their final desertion in the hour of crisis, but the covenant which Jesus makes with them on the eve of his death is the guarantee that, through his death and resurrection, their commission will be renewed. Their failure serves to reinforce the point that Mark has already made: the Kingdom is God's work of grace. The success of the harvest may depend on the soil into which the seed falls (4: 1–20), but the growth does not come from human effort: 'A sower scatters seed on the land; and he goes to bed at night and gets up in the morning, and the seed sprouts and grows—how, he does not know' (4: 26–7).

Matthew's Gospel has too readily been classified as legalistic and antithetical to the Pauline theology of grace, perhaps even written in criticism of Paul. There are indeed passages which, read as proof-texts in isolation from the rest of the book, might give the impression that right conduct, even perfect conduct, is demanded as a condition of salvation (5: 20; 7: 21–3; 22: 11–12). We must remember, however, that some of these passages have synoptic parallels, and therefore derive from a pre-Matthaean tradition (cf. Luke 6: 46), that we have some passages of similar import in Paul, and that Matthew has a truly

Semitic way of setting antithetical ideas in parallel, without attempting to explain away the apparent contradiction.[14] The stringency of Matthew, as of Paul, is set in a controlling context of grace. He takes over the Marcan framework and systematically, by alteration, comment, and addition, removes Mark's ambiguities. The Kingdom of God is present as God's free gift to the needy (12: 28), good and bad alike (22: 10; cf. 13: 47), and it is those who have no claim to deserve it that are least inhibited from entering it (21: 31). Mercy is its keynote, not only as a divine attribute, but as a moral imperative (9: 13; 12: 7; 23: 23). Those who have been forgiven must forgive, even to the point of meeting massive wrong with equally massive non-retaliation (18: 12–35, especially vv. 21–2). Such altruism can be expected of them because they have the continuing presence of Jesus in their midst (18: 20; 26: 64; 28: 20). The Kingdom is his Kingdom, and in it he restrains the moralistic fervour and unquenched spirit of his servants from attempting to distinguish between wheat and weeds (13: 24–30, 36–43); when the time for that comes, there will be many surprises (19: 30; 20: 16). The master engages labourers to work in his vineyard, but pays them what his own generosity dictates, not merely what they have earned; and those who insist on their deserts have no right to complain if that is all they receive (20: 1–16).

Matthew's handling of Peter is particularly instructive. He is the typical disciple, speaking for the rest in their grasping for comprehension (15: 15; 16: 16–23; 17: 4, 24; 18: 21; 19: 27; 26: 35). The truth about Jesus comes to him only by revelation from God (16: 17). His attempt to walk on the water is a parable of the life of discipleship— through lack of faith the disciple sinks in the storm unless supported by the ever-present Jesus (14: 28–33). And into the story of Peter's denial Matthew has inserted a significant cross-reference to an earlier saying of Jesus which Mark gives in a radically different form. In the Matthaean mission charge Jesus had said: 'Whoever denies me before men I will deny before my Father in heaven' (10: 33; cf. Mark 8: 38). Matthew picks up both the verb and the preposition in his description of Peter's denial: 'He denied before all' (26: 70). Peter was the first to fall under the strictures of Jesus' judgement, and deserved to be

[14] The disciples are instructed to do their good works in public (5: 16), but are warned not to be like the hypocrites with their public piety (6: 2–6, 16–28). They are not to judge others (7: 1–5), but must withhold their pearls from those whom they judge to be pigs. On parataxis as a form of Semitic style, see G. B. Caird, *Language and Imagery of the Bible*, 117 ff.

disowned before God; yet he had been restored to his place as first among the apostles.

In view of all this, we need to look afresh at the passages of moral stringency, and particularly at the paragraph in the sermon in which it is concentrated (5: 17–20). There are three points to be noted. The first is that the eternal viability here accorded to the Law and the prophets must be understood in the light of 7: 12 and 22: 40, where it is enshrined in the golden rule and in the commandment of love to God and neighbour (cf. Rom. 13: 8–10). The second is that the righteousness which exceeds that of scribes and Pharisees is defined in the six antitheses which follow (5: 21–48), in which Jesus takes one commandment after another and presses it beyond the range of overt action to cover inner attitudes and traits of character. It is not enough for one to refrain from perjury; Christians must be so fundamentally honest that 'Yes' and 'No' always mean what they say; the very sugges- tion that, if they were not on oath, they would be free to lie comes from the Devil. Outward conduct is determined by the disposition of the heart, just as the quality of the fruit is determined by the state of the tree (7: 17–20; 12: 33–6; 15: 15–20). What is required, therefore, is a more radical change than could ever be achieved by an intensified legalism (below, Chapter 9). The third point is that 'to enter the Kingdom', though it is a phrase of deliberate and comprehensive ambi- guity, has its primary reference to entering on the life of discipleship in the service of God. Those who enter through the narrow gate will subsequently find themselves on the equally narrow road that leads to life (7: 13–14). But the stringency is laid upon them precisely because they are to be agents of God and mirrors of His limitless goodness (5: 68). People are to see their good works and acknowledge that they have come from God (5: 16). As children of God they are to take after their Father and be a credit to Him (5: 45).

Luke's Gospel presents no such complications. To him the King- dom is God's reign of grace, a free gift to His little flock (12: 32), already recording its victory over the kingdom of Satan in the exorcisms of Jesus and the mission of the seventy (11: 20; 10: 17–18). The banquet is ready, and the only disqualification is preoccupation with other claims (14: 15–24). The Kingdom belongs to those whom the world accounts deprived—the poor, the hungry, the sorrowful, and the unpopular—those, in short, who are aware of their need and are ready to allow God to fill it (6: 20–6). Its dominant characteristic is a love which does not retaliate, seeks no reward, is not censorious;

because this love is a determined commitment to the true interest of others, undeterred by hostilities, unlimited by a valuation of deserts, rooted in the nature of God (6: 27–38). Such love is engendered only in response to grace: great love comes of great forgiveness (7: 41–3). Nevertheless grace imposes its own obligation, and aspirants to discipleship must count the cost (9: 57–62; 14: 26–33), since they are accepting an unlimited liability (7: 7–10) which takes precedence over all human loyalties.

In Acts, grace is but one of the terms Luke uses to indicate that the life of the Church and the progress of its mission are under the direction of God. Stephen is 'full of grace and power' (6: 8). One congregation after another is exhorted to 'remain in the grace of God' (13: 43; cf. 20: 32). The apostles themselves are not in control: it is enough for them to be able to recognize the grace of God when they see it at work (11: 23), to be commended to the grace of God when they set out on their travels (14: 26), and to testify to that grace by the fulfilment of their task (20: 24).

6.4. THE IMITATION OF CHRIST

For every modern Christian who has read the monkish instructions attributed to Thomas à Kempis there must be millions who are familiar only with the title of the book and regard that as a full and adequate description of the Christian life. To be a Christian is to be like Christ, to respond like his first disciples to the invitation, 'Follow me.' This popular assumption appears to have wide support in the New Testament. 'Bend your necks to my yoke, and learn from me' (Matt. 11: 29). 'Come, follow me' (Mark 10: 21; cf. Matt. 8: 22; Luke 9: 59). 'I have set you an example' (John 13: 15). 'Follow my example as I follow Christ's' (1 Cor. 11: 1). 'You followed the example set by us and by the Lord' (1 Thess. 1: 6). 'We must . . . run with resolution the race for which we are entered, our eyes fixed on Jesus' (Heb. 12: 2). 'This is the very nature of your calling, because Christ suffered on your behalf, and thereby left you an example; it is for you to follow in his steps' (1 Pet. 2: 22). 'They follow the Lamb wherever he goes' (Rev. 14: 4).

The popular devotional tradition has turned such quotations into a general and comprehensive ethical principle. Yet even at this level there are formidable difficulties. 'Do you know about the life of Jesus?' is a legitimate question. Yet even the evidence we have depicts a life too narrowly circumscribed to provide an example of conduct for all the varied activities of any particular time. As far as we know, Jesus did not marry or have children. He had no vote. He lived in an agrarian society. He knew nothing of industry, let alone modern technology and science. He never travelled more than eighty miles from his home town. Moreover, not all the incidents recorded in the Gospels are typical. One person is told to sell everything and follow Jesus (Mark 10: 20), but another who offers to follow him is told to go home (Mark 5: 19). Luke makes the selling of possessions into a general rule (12: 33), but does not apply it to the wealthy women who provided for Jesus and his disciples 'out of their own resources' (8: 3), or to Joseph of Arimathea who was clearly a person of substance (23: 50).

Our concern, however, is with a more primary question: What did the New Testament writers themselves understand by the imitation of Christ? For what purposes did they appeal to it? Did they intend it to have universal application and, if so, did it in any sense include a share in Christ's redemptive task? How did they relate it to the teaching of Jesus so that his followers might imitate God (Matt. 5: 48; Luke 6: 36; cf. Lev. 19: 2; 1 Pet. 1: 15), should think God's thoughts after Him (Mark 8: 33), and should be children who take after their Father (Matt. 5: 45; Luke 6: 35)? And how could such teaching be consistent with the belief that the attempt to be like God was the primal sin (Gen. 3: 5; Isa. 14: 14), which Christ reversed by his act of renunciation (Phil. 2: 6)?

Paul reminds the Thessalonians that his initial preaching to them was 'not in mere words but in the power of the Holy Spirit', and congratulates them on being imitators of himself and of the Lord, because they received that preaching as a call from God and responded to it with trust and obedience, undeterred by the hardships they thereby incurred at the hands of a hostile society (1 Thess. 1: 4–7). At Corinth 'the strong party' has written a letter to Paul describing the bracing, if not to say abrasive, line they had been taking over various matters of behaviour, appealing for support to Paul's own doctrine of Christian freedom, and inviting his agreement. He urges them to be sure that their conduct will redound to God's credit, that it will not give offence inside or outside the Christian community, and that they are acting in the interest of others and not to promote their own self-importance. In this way they will follow his example as he follows Christ's (1 Cor. 10: 31–11: 1).[15] In writing to Rome he enlarges on his instructions to Corinth. 'Those of us who have a robust conscience must accept as our own burden the tender scruples of the weak, and not consider ourselves. Each of us must consider his neighbour and think what is for his or her good and will build up the common life. For Christ too did not consider himself . . . Accept one another as Christ accepted us' (Rom. 15: 1–3, 7).

The impression we get from these three passages is confirmed by those in which Paul speaks of the mind of Christ. In dealing with the party divisions at Corinth he declares that their jealousy and strife are proof that the Corinthians are still *sarkikoi*, immature and devoid of insight. 'One who is unspiritual refuses what belongs to the Spirit of God: it is folly to him; he cannot grasp it, because it requires spiritual discernment . . . We, however, possess the mind of Christ' (1 Cor. 2: 14, 16). Christians must allow their minds to be remade after the model of Christ: 'Then you will be able to discern the will of God, and to know what is good, acceptable, and perfect', and in particular to understand the mutual interdependence of those who are 'limbs and organs in the one body of Christ' (Rom. 12: 2–5). It is noteworthy that in every passage where Paul speaks of the mind of Christ, or of the mind which Christians ought to have through their union with Christ, there is some reference both to insight and to the unity of the Church. 'You have discarded the old nature with its deeds and have put on the new nature, which is constantly being renewed in the image of its Creator and brought to recognise God; and in it there is no question of Greek and Jew, circumcised and uncircumcised, barbarian, Scythian, Slave and free; but Christ is all and in all' (Col. 3: 10 f.). The reason for this is explained in the long, continuous argument of Phil. 2: 1–11. The 'hymn' which celebrates Christ's resignation of all claim to heavenly rights and dignity, in order to identify himself with the human race and be the obedient agent of God's purpose, has an ethical preface and an ethical sequel. In the preface the Philippians

---

[15] The letter from Corinth also made the claim that it was better for a Christian to remain celibate, and so to follow the good example of Paul. It is significant that Paul in reply makes no reference to the example of Jesus. Celibacy, he argues, is admirable, but only for those whom God has equipped for it. 'Everyone has the gift God has granted him, some one way, some another' (1 Cor. 7: 7). Similarly Matthew, by his triple use of the pejorative 'eunuch', makes it clear that he regards marriage as normal, and celibacy as abnormal, whether caused by congenital defect, human violence, or renunciation in the service of the Kingdom (19: 10–12).

are told to put the rights, needs, interests, and well-being of others before their own: 'Let this attitude of mind be the mark of your common life, your life in Christ Jesus.' In the sequel they are told to emulate the obedience of Jesus, working out their communal salvation in that trembling awe which goes with the recognition that God is at work in their midst. The love which shows itself in self-abnegation is not only the true source of unity; it also provides a true insight into the character of God. It was *because* he was 'in the form of God',[16] *because* he was obedient to God's purpose of love, that he chose to act as he did; and for the same reason ('therefore') God has accorded to him the fullest conceivable acknowledgment. Adam's[17] desire to be like God was not merely a sin of presumption; it was a sin of idolatry, because the God he wanted to be like was a God made in the image of his own self-seeking.

In Pauline usage, then, the imitation of Christ comprises three related themes: the ability to discern the presence and purpose of God, an attitude of mind which subordinates personal interest to the service of that purpose and therefore to the needs of others, and a trust in God that remains constant in the face of hostilities and menace. And these are the themes which we shall find repeated elsewhere.

For the author of Hebrews, Jesus is the pioneer who has blazed the trail for others to follow (6: 20; 2: 10; 12: 2). It is a path of faith and obedience, a path of constancy which remains faithful to God's calling in the face of suffering and death: 'Think of him who submitted to such opposition from sinners; that will help you not to lose heart or grow faint' (12: 3). It is a path which leads to maturity or perfection, which Jesus, no less than his followers, needed to attain. In the case of Jesus, perfection included the completeness of his qualifications to be the representative of the human race. It was as pioneer that he must become perfect through sufferings (2: 10). He must be like his

---

[16] 'Though he was in the form of God' (RSV) gives quite the wrong impression, implying that God himself, or one who shared God's nature, could be expected to act otherwise.

[17] For the parallel between Adam's choice and that of Christ, see especially O. Cullmann, *The Christology of the New Testament* (London, 1963), 181; J. Murphy-O'Connor, 'Christological Anthropology in Phil. 2: 6–11', *RB* 83 (1986), 25 ff.; W. D. Davies, *Paul and Rabbinic Judaism* (London, 1948), 41 f.; M. D. Hooker, 'Philippians 2: 6–11', in E. E. Ellis and E. Grässer (eds.), *Jesus und Paulus* (Göttingen, 1975), 160 ff.; C. K. Barrett, *From First Adam to Last* (1962), 69 ff.; Robinson, *The Human Face of God*, 163; and J. D. G. Dunn, *Christology in the Making* (London, 1980), 114 ff.

siblings in every respect (2: 17), and because of that likeness he could never be free of the temptation to abandon his calling (4: 15).[18] 'Son though he was, he learnt obedience in the school of suffering, and, once perfected, became the source of eternal salvation for all who obey him' (5: 8–9). It was not that he needed to be coerced into obedience; always ready to obey (10: 8), he had to learn through experience, in the process of obeying ('the school of obedience'), what it meant, with all the pressures and antagonism of the world upon him, to be an obedient Son to the heavenly Father. For the Christian perfection means following Jesus on the path he has opened and finding that it leads to the presence of God (10: 19 f.).[19] The mature Christian, accordingly, is one 'whose faculties are trained by constant use to discriminate between good and evil' (5: 14). But such discrimination will lead him or her, like Moses, to consider the stigma that rests on God's Anointed greater wealth than the treasures of Egypt (11: 26), and to join Jesus outside the camp of the old order, 'bearing the stigma that he bore' (13: 12).[20]

In 1 Peter the imitation of Christ is invoked repeatedly and solely in connection with innocent suffering. Those who are persecuted for their faith have 'a share in Christ's sufferings', provided that in other respects they are innocent of offence (4: 13–16; cf. 3: 16–18; Rom. 8: 17; Phil. 3: 10). But innocent suffering is also commended even where loyalty to the faith is not at issue. Slaves are told that if they endure with fortitude undeserved suffering meted out by a harsh master, this 'is a fine thing in the sight of God'. It is indeed the very nature of their Christian calling; and this can only be because they are bearing wrong without resistance. Resentment or retaliation is inimical to God's grand strategy for the defeat of evil. To this extent it must be said that those who share Christ's sufferings share also in this redemptive quality.

This is the point which is hammered relentlessly home in the Revelation. Those who 'follow the Lamb wherever he goes' (14: 4)

---

[18] The traditional rendering of this clause as 'tempted in all points as we are' is simply false; but happily it is also a mistranslation of the Greek.

[19] See D. Peterson, *Hebrews and Perfection* (Cambridge, 1982), 153 ff.

[20] Cf. also 11: 26, where Moses is said to have embraced, 12 centuries before Jesus, 'the stigma of the Christ' (RSV), or better, 'the stigma that rests on God's Anointed' (REB). The reference is either to Ps. 89: 51 (88: 50 ff. LXX) or Ps. 69: 9 LXX. The author almost certainly knew both passages, and understood the stigma not as prophetic of Jesus only, but as that which rests upon all who are consecrated to the task of God.

are not the full membership of the churches, but the conquerors to whom a special promise has been addressed in each of the seven letters, the specially chosen troops in the army of the Lamb, through whose martyrdom he is to win afresh the victory of the Cross. They are the vast army whom John has seen emerging from the great ordeal, with palms of victory in their hands, ascribing their victory to the Lamb; and they are the armies of heaven who at the end accompany the victorious Christ (7: 9–17; 19: 14).

When Mark records the command to follow Jesus, he uses two near-synonyms, the one signifying allegiance (1: 17),[21] the other companionship and a shared task (2: 14; cf. 10: 21).[22] In due course it emerges that the one who has given the command is the Messiah, the King of Israel, and that the way of life he embodies is therefore God's ordained purpose for His holy nation; and Peter is rebuked for failing to recognize this, and for acting as Satan's agent to seduce Jesus from his course (8: 27–32). At this point Mark puts his synonyms into double harness: 'Anyone who decides to become my loyal supporter must leave self behind; he must take up his cross and follow me' (8: 34). Jesus is the leader of a national movement which, although itself peaceful and non-violent, is certain to evoke violent resistance from those who see the national destiny in terms of security, prosperity, independence, and power.

Matthew and Luke add their commentary to this Marcan outline by emphasizing the national implications of Jesus' ministry (Matt. 1: 21; 2: 2; Luke 1: 17, 32, 54, 68; 2: 25, 38) and the temptations to interpret his Messiahship along the lines of popular expectation (Matt. 4: 1–10; Luke 4: 1–12). They also have one saying in common which requires that the claims of discipleship shall take precedence over every other allegiance, however sacred (Matt. 10: 38; Luke 14: 27). Matthew alone has the invitation, 'Take my yoke upon you and learn of me' (11: 29). It is significant that he places this immediately after the great thanksgiving: 'No one knows the Son but the Father, and no one knows the Father but the Son and those to whom the Son may choose to reveal him.' What the disciples must learn from Jesus is how to know God as Father and how to conduct their lives as the Father's children. Notwithstanding the strain of the Gospel's ethical

---

[21] On this meaning of *opisō*, see above, p. 167.

[22] Cf. 3: 14, where the task ('sent out to preach') is coupled with Jesus' personal need ('to be with him').

teaching and the demand for self-abnegation, the yoke is easy for those who have learned from Jesus to feast on the Father's love.

It is hardly surprising that this passage has been regarded as a synoptic link with the Fourth Gospel. There Jesus is the light of the world: 'No follower of mine shall wander in the dark; he shall have the light of life' (8: 12). Those who possess the light know where they are going, and they become 'sons of light'—i.e. sources of light to others (12: 35–6). It is a striking fact that, although in this Gospel great stress is placed on the commands of Jesus, he never gives any except the one commandment of love (15: 12). His commands are not general rules, but orders which he gives day by day to those who dwell in his love, just as he has day by day followed the directions of his Father (5: 19–20). Those who have the light of life will know where to go: 'My sheep listen to my voice; I know them and they follow me' (10: 27); and those who follow find that he leads them to the place where he himself is, in the bosom of the Father (12: 26; cf. 1: 18; 10: 38; 14: 11). Yet John too is aware that there is a price to be paid. 'Where I am going you cannot follow me now, but one day you will' (13: 36). Peter cannot follow Jesus yet because Jesus is going to the Cross where he must bear alone the burden of the world's hatred, when even his closest disciples have deserted him. Only when by his death he has drawn the whole human race, including Peter, into union with himself can Peter travel the road of sacrifice (21: 18–19).

Underlying these differences of approach and style is a remarkable consensus. To follow Jesus or to follow his example turns out to be, as popular tradition has held, the higher road, that particular morality which the gospel imposes on the Christian. But such a morality does not consist in conformity to any stereotyped pattern; it consists rather in learning from Jesus an attitude of mind which comprises sensitivity to the presence of God and to the will of God which is the only authority, a constant submission of personal interest to the pursuit of that will in the well-being of others, and a confidence that, whatever the immediate consequences may appear to be, the outcome can safely be left in God's hands.

6.5. IN CHRIST AND THE SPIRIT

To leave the outcome in God's hands could of course sound like a form of fatalism. With such a view the New Testament writers have little in common. If God is involved in the process, it is because He is working in them to will and to do His good pleasure (Phil. 2: 12–13; cf. Rom. 8: 26–8). Not through the external authority of blind decree or human hierarchy or written word, but through the continued activity of God in the hearts of men and women does Jesus live out his truncated life: 'Christ in you, the hope of glory' (Col. 1: 27).

But if Paul can speak of Christ being in the believer, he is more accustomed to speak of the believer being in Christ.[23] Here, however, we need to guard against two misunderstandings: (1) The phrase 'in Christ' has too often been treated as something mystical, a purely spiritual form of union located deep in the soul, that thing which can barely be understood or expressed. In fact for Paul 'in Christ' expresses something objective and phenomenally human—the incorporation of believers into the new humanity. Paul believed that Christ had become 'the last Adam' (1 Cor. 15: 45–7; 2 Cor. 5: 17). Before that time all men and women had belonged to the old race of Adam, dominated as it was by sin, death, and the powers of darkness. Even Christ in his earthly life belonged to the old Adam. It is only by virtue of the resurrection that he becomes the last Adam. Having been born the image of the man of dust, he is now the heavenly man, and all those 'in him' belong to the new creation, in which none of the old conditions any longer apply (1 Cor. 15: 45; 2 Cor. 5: 17). (2) 'In Christ' has frequently been taken to indicate that Paul has replaced God with Christ as the centre of his religion.[24] Where once there was theology there is now Christology. But just as 'the Spirit' had previously been a way of talking about God manifesting himself in effective action and power, with no separate entity intended, so with life in Christ. God, the indwelling Christ, and the indwelling Spirit are all one and the same. Therefore in Romans 8: 8 ff. 'in the Spirit', 'the Spirit of God dwelling in you', and 'Christ in you' are interchangeable expressions (cf. 2 Cor. 3: 16–18, where the term *kurios* appears to indicate all three members of the Trinity).[25]

---

[23] Cf. e.g. A. Deissmann, *Die neutestamentliche Formel 'In Christō Jesu'* (Marburg, 1892), for a totally subjective view of the phrase, and its critique by A. Schweitzer, *The Mysticism of St Paul* (London, 1953²) 33 ff.; F. Neugebauer, 'Das paulinische "en Christo"', *NTS* 4 (1957–8), 124 ff., E. Schweizer, 'Dying and Rising with Christ', *NTS* 14 (1967–8), 1 ff., and A. Wickenhauser, *Pauline Mysticism* (Edinburgh, 1960), provide further discussion of the phrase.

[24] Cf. e.g. A. Deissmann, *The Religion of Jesus and the Faith of Paul* (London, 1923); J. Fraser, *Jesus and Paul* (Abingdon, 1972); and J. Klausner, *From Jesus to Paul* (Boston, 1944). For other opinions, cf. H. J. Schoeps, *Paul* (London, 1961), 276 ff.

[25] Similarly in 1 Cor. 15: 45–7, in contrasting Adam and Christ, Paul claims that, whereas the first Adam became a living soul, the last became a life-giving Spirit. Once

Closely related to the phrase 'in Christ' is Paul's unique image of the body, which in his letters has a constantly varying emphasis. In 1 Corinthians 12: 12–27 he is concerned with the multiplicity of functions required within an organic unity, in Romans 12: 4–5 with the mutual interdependence of Christians, in Colossians 1: 18 with the common dependence of Christians on their head, and in Colossians 1: 24 with an extension of Christ's life and character. We have seen (p. 175) that it is not clear from what source Paul drew this picture of the Church; but most probably it proceeded from the idea that Christ, like the human body, exemplifies multiplicity in unity. But Paul certainly had in mind also the parallel between the body of Christ which is the Church and the body which is the eucharistic bread: 'Because there is one loaf, we who are many are one body, for we all partake of the same loaf' (1 Cor. 10: 17). When he comes to write of the disorders at the Lord's Supper, he accuses the Corinthians of 'not discerning the body', because, in disregarding the poorer members of the Church they had failed to see in the sacramental loaf the symbol of their unity in Christ (1 Cor. 11: 29; see below).

God's activity in the lives of His followers is also seen as the work of the Spirit. In the New Testament the Spirit is always an eschatological gift, a portent of 'the last days'. For Paul the Spirit is the guarantee or down-payment of our inheritance (2 Cor. 1: 22; 5: 5; Rom. 8: 23, Eph. 1: 14), to the author of Hebrews 'the powers of the age to come' (Heb. 6: 4 f.), in 1 Peter the possession of those who follow Christ's suffering to glory (1 Pet. 4: 14), and in Revelation the Spirit of prophecy which allows the martyrs to bear their witness triumphantly (Rev. 11: 3). In the Fourth Gospel the coming of the Paraclete virtually replaces the Parousia (14: 3), while in Acts the speech attributed to Peter links the coming of the Spirit foretold by Joel to the eschatological crisis brought about by the ministry of Jesus (Acts 2: 17 f.).

In the light of such powerful associations it is hardly surprising that from the Church's inception the Spirit was seen as the primary motivating power underlying Christian experience. But just as in pre-Christian times the Spirit's activity was progressively moralized until it almost became synonymous with the divine Wisdom, so in the New Testament a similar development takes place within a shorter time-

---

again we have an apparent confusion of the persons of the Trinity. But here the explanation is simple: Paul's first acquaintance with the Christ he came to acknowledge as Lord was on the road to Damascus, and it was there that he met him as 'a life-giving Spirit'.

frame. In the accounts of earliest Christian history the Spirit is once again connected with power (Acts 1–2, Heb. 2: 4), with manifestations of healings, tongues, prophecy, etc. (Paul and Luke agree that this will continue; see below). It is Paul[26] who is first responsible for highly moralizing the Spirit's activity. In his earliest letter he sees the Holy Spirit manifesting Himself in power (1 Thess. 1: 4). Paul understood that the human spirit is designed to be the vehicle or transmitter of the Spirit of God (cf. Prov. 20: 27: 'The Spirit of a person is the candle of the Lord'). But he also knew from the Old Testament that not every phenomenon is evidence of the Spirit of God. Just as Jeremiah said much on distinguishing true from false prophets, so for Paul the spirits must be tested (1 Cor. 14: 29, 32; cf. 1 John 4: 1). In 1 Corinthians 12–14 the manifestations are even ranked, with love the highest and tongues the lowest. Just so in Galatians 5: 22: there Paul represents both the earliest and the highest degree of moralization of the Spirit's activity.

As a sphere of life Paul contrasts the Spirit with the flesh in a number of ways. Whereas the flesh is a source of weakness which lays men and women open to the attacks of sin (Rom. 7: 5–25), the Spirit is the power of God which supplies the dynamic for the new life. The gifts and graces of the Christian life are produced as spontaneously by the Spirit as fruit grows on a tree (Gal. 5: 22). Of particular importance is the Spirit as the fountain of all genuine conviction (1 Cor. 12: 3), especially the conviction that God is a Father who calls His errant creatures to be His children and to live as members of His family (Gal. 4: 6; Rom. 8: 14–17). It is the Spirit which has sent the cry '*abba*' into their hearts, a spirit not of bondage but of freedom—one of the chief characteristics of Paul's treatment of the Spirit. Paul frequently contrasts the Spirit of adoption with the Spirit of slavery. Those who live under the Law are slaves, because the authority which governs their lives is an external rather than an internal authority. For the Christian, however, 'The Lord is the Spirit, and where the Spirit of the Lord is, there is freedom' (2 Cor. 3: 17). Here, as we have seen, Paul, in three verses (vv. 16–18), shifts the word 'Lord' from

---

[26] The literature on Paul's view of the Spirit is predictably enormous. See in particular W. D. Davies, 'Paul and the Dead Sea Scrolls: Flesh and Spirit', K. Stendahl (ed.), *The Scrolls and the New Testament*, 157 ff.; J. D. G. Dunn, *Baptism in the Holy Spirit* (London, 1970), *passim*, and *Jesus and the Spirit* (London, 1975), 205 ff.; D. Hill, *Greek Words and Hebrew Meanings* (London, 1967), 265 ff.; and R. Scroggs, 'Paul: *Sophos* and *Pneumatikos*', *NTS* 14 (1967–8), 33 ff.

God, to Christ, to the Spirit, then back again to Christ, and finally (v. 18) again to the Spirit. He can do this because as a sphere of life within which the Christian experiences the ongoing process of salvation, the Spirit is paramount and all-inclusive. Thus if Paul strenuously resisted any attempt to make the Mosaic code obligatory for Christians, it was because he saw the ethics of law and the ethics of liberty as totally incompatible. It is true that he recognized the validity of certain external guides to ethical decision: the words of the Lord (1 Cor. 7: 10), the pattern of traditional teaching (Rom. 6: 17), the usage of the churches (1 Cor. 11: 16; 14: 33), but none of these constituted a legal code or a substitute for the renewed mind. 'I give my opinion as one who by the Lord's mercy is trustworthy' (1 Cor. 7: 25). 'We have the mind of Christ' (1 Cor. 2: 16).

But Paul was not content to think of the Spirit as merely an experience of the inner person. For him the Spirit also produces outward signs,[27] and these are fourfold:

1. Fellowship (*koinōnia*). For Paul, ties of sympathy which bind the minds of individual Christians are the products of the fellowship which the Spirit creates. Paul thus fervently hopes that the individual churches should not settle their disputes by argument and divisiveness but by achieving a common mind under the guidance of the Spirit (Phil. 2: 1 f.; 2 Cor. 13: 13; Rom. 15: 5 f.; 1 Cor. 1: 10; 2 Cor. 13: 11, Phil. 1: 27; 2: 1 f.).

2. Glossolalia or tongues. Those who were endowed with this gift were popularly supposed to be speaking foreign languages (Paul himself may adopt this interpetation in 1 Cor. 14: 21).[28] But, despite his belief that it is one of the gifts of the Spirit which assists Christians in their intercessions with God, Paul rates it fairly low in its value to the Church in so far as it does not build up the body. As one who himself possessed the gift in abundance (1 Cor. 14: 18), Paul understands it as a profound religious experience (1 Cor. 14: 2), but these utterances should never be given free rein at the expense of order and discipline (1 Cor. 14: 2, 14, 16, 19).

[27] Cf. e.g. Dunn, *Jesus and the Spirit*, 205 ff., and E. E. Ellis, 'Spiritual Gifts in the Pauline Community', *NTS* 20 (1974), 128 ff.

[28] Cf. R. H. Gundry, 'Ecstatic Utterance', *JTS* 17 (1966), 299 ff. For the view that glossolalia for Paul indicates a non-human, heavenly language, cf. Dunn, *Jesus and the Spirit*, 244, and C. K. Barrett, *A Commentary on the First Epistle to the Corinthians*, (London, 1968), 299. On the difficulty of arriving at any certainty, cf. S. D. Currie, 'Speaking in Tongues', *Int.* 19 (1965), 274 ff.

3. Prophecy. Just as the function of the Old Testament prophets was to speak the word of the Lord, so through His Christian prophets God communicates with the churches. Pre-eminently for Paul this means inspired preaching (1 Thess. 1: 5; 1 Cor. 2: 4). Along with such preaching went *paraklēsis*—'the moral strengthening which comes from the presence and guidance of those who are strong in faith'.[29] This word and the corresponding verb (*parakaleō*) occur frequently in Paul's letters (cf. e.g. Rom. 15: 4; 2 Cor. 1: 3 f.; 7: 4, 6).

4. Signs and wonders. Paul not only ascribes these powers to the energy of the Spirit, but in one place actually questions the right of all those who wish to call themselves apostles unless their claims are attested by 'the signs of an apostle' (1 Cor. 12: 2)—a phrase which certainly covers miracles, though it may include other things as well (1 Cor. 12: 9–10, 28–30; Gal. 3: 5; Rom. 15: 19; Heb. 2: 4).

This Pauline emphasis on the outward working of the Spirit takes a somewhat different turn in his impassioned argument in 2 Cor. 3–5. Paul has been under criticism from those who have come from the outside (probably Palestine) with introductory letters from apostles of weighty authority. Paul's response to the Corinthian church is startling: 'You are my letters of testimonial' (3: 2). Integral to his argument is the claim that the work of the Spirit should be visible in them. The Spirit is transforming them into the image of Christ from one stage of glory to another, and this, he says, should be obvious to everyone. But in chapter 4 he has to admit that it may not after all be that obvious. The outward person is in a state of decay, which is to be expected, since he or she has to die eventually. But the inner person is being renewed from day to day. Such a process will eventually yield an eternal weight of glory, provided we look at things unseen rather than things seen (4: 17 f.). This argument Paul concludes in 5: 7 by saying that Christians walk by faith, not by sight—a comment which in turn qualifies his earlier statement that the Corinthians are his letters of testimonial. 'Your life is hid with Christ in God' (Col. 3: 3).

Virtually the same point is made in 1 Cor. 12–14, where for Paul the gifts and the fruit of the Spirit are contrasted. The gifts—prophecy, tongues, knowledge, healings—important as they may be for the building up of the body, are external to the person, and thus transitory, whereas the fruit—'faith, hope, love'—are internal, working silently in the deep recesses of the human character. For this reason the fruit,

[29] E. G. Selwyn, *The First Epistle of St Peter* (London, 1946), 262.

unlike the gifts, survives into the next age, inasmuch as the fruit makes up what the person is, now and forever.

Luke,[30] no less than Paul, emphasizes the role of the Spirit in Christian experience, although his emphasis takes the form of dramatic narrative rather than personal teaching. In Luke's Gospel the Spirit is at work from the very beginning. The Spirit fills John the Baptist in his mother's womb (1: 15), comes upon Mary (1: 35), inspires Simeon (2: 25–32), descends upon Jesus bodily at his baptism (3: 22), leads Jesus into the wilderness (4: 1), and drives out demons (4: 33 ff.; 8: 2, 33, etc.). When Jesus returns from his temptation 'in the power of the Spirit' (4: 1), he publicly proclaims himself the fulfilment of the promise of the Spirit in Isaiah 61: 1 f. (4: 16 ff.), while later he is said to have 'rejoiced in the Spirit' (10: 21). In Acts, Jesus continues his work, for there the Spirit is the Spirit of Jesus.[31] The risen and reigning Lord has poured out his Spirit upon his disciples, and through the Spirit he exercises his authority over them (2: 33; cf. Eph. 4: 8). Every new development in the story is brought about by the guidance of the Spirit. Stephen is made a deacon because he is recognized as being filled with the Spirit, and by the Spirit he is empowered to speak in his hour of need (6: 3, 10). The Spirit directs the missionary work of Philip and Peter (8: 29, 39; 10: 19 f.) and overcomes the initial hostility of the Jerusalem Christians to the admission of Samaritan and Gentile converts (8: 17, 10: 44). By the power of the Spirit Barnabas recognizes the Gentile mission at Antioch to be proper (12: 23 f.). It is the Spirit who separates Paul and Barnabas for their mission (13: 3), achieves a consensus at Jerusalem (15: 28), and persuades Paul and Silas to make the evangelistic leap from Asia to Europe (16: 6 f.).

To a remarkable degree Luke's understanding of the outward manifestations of the Spirit resembles Paul's, and may therefore be treated under the same four heads.

1. Fellowship (*koinōnia*). To belong to Christ, to receive the Spirit, and to be a member of the Church are different but inseparable aspects of the same experience, with the Spirit the creator of unity and fellow-

---

[30] On Luke's view cf. J. D. G. Dunn, *Jesus and the Spirit* (London, 1975), 157 ff., and G. W. H. Lampe, 'The Holy Spirit in the Writings of St Luke', in D. E. Nineham (ed.), *Studies in the Gospels* (Oxford, 1955).

[31] Cf. F. D. Bruner, *A Theology of the Holy Spirit* (London, 1970), 156: 'Luke's first sentence makes clear an intention of his entire book: the Spirit is not to be dissociated from Jesus. The Spirit *is* Jesus at work in continuation of his ministry.'

ship. Community of possessions is the outward symbol of an inner community of thought and purpose, and both are the product of the Spirit (Acts 2: 42; 4: 31 f.).

2. Glossolalia. Tongues are for Luke a common experience in the early Church (Acts 10: 46; 19: 6). His account of Pentecost has been much scrutinized by critics who have claimed that he has changed an occurrence of glossolalia into a linguistic miracle, a reversal of Gen. 11: 7–9 (cf. Acts 2: 61). But Luke was not the only one to see this as foreign speech (cf. 1 Cor. 14: 21), and if he has at all heightened the narrative he inherited (which is far from certain), it was for a theological purpose. Representations of every nation are brought under the scope of the gospel because this was the fulfilment both of the prophecy of Joel 2: 28 (Acts 2: 17) and of Jesus' promise that his followers would be 'imbued with power from on high' (Luke 24: 49).

3. Prophecy. Like Paul in 1 Cor. 12–14, Luke mentions tongues and prophecy together (Acts 19: 6), ostensibly because both constituted inspired speech, the only difference being that prophecy could be understood by the listener. Prophecy is seen in the famine prediction of Agabus (Acts 11: 28) and (again like Paul) in the use of *paraklēsis*, which is said to be the work of the Spirit (Acts 9: 31).

4. Miracles. Luke's narrative in Acts is packed with signs and wonders.[32] It is not our purpose here to defend what might appear to be an excessive preoccupation; we need only observe that this phenomenon is discussed and accounted for by Paul in a way which presents no clear conflict with what Luke might have said had he been pleased to offer his own opinion.

The Fourth Gospel[33] has its own distinctive contributions to make to the theme of the Spirit. The abiding presence of the Spirit is in the first place attributed to Christ alone (John 1: 32 f.), which

---

[32] According to Dunn, *Jesus and the Spirit*, 190, '[Luke] shares the enthusiast's desire for tangibility in spiritual experience . . . the Spirit is most clearly seen in extra-ordinary and supernatural phenomena, and in Acts is hardly visible anywhere else.' Accordingly, Dunn views Luke's presentation of the Spirit as 'fairly crude'.

[33] Cf. e.g. C. K. Barrett, 'The Holy Spirit in the Fourth Gospel', *JTS* NS 1 (1950), 1 ff.; R. E. Brown, 'The Paraclete in the Fourth Gospel', *NTS* 13 (1966–7), 113 ff.; Bruner, *Theology of the Holy Spirit*; G. M. Burge, *The Anointed Community: The Holy Spirit in the Johannine Tradition* (Grand Rapids, 1987); G. Johnston, *The Spirit-Paraclete in the Gospel of John* (Cambridge, 1970); A. R. C. Leaney, 'The Johannine Paraclete and the Qumran Scrolls', in J. H. Charlesworth (ed.), *John and Qumran* (London, 1972), 38 ff.

distinguishes him from past prophets and leaders. It is transferred to the Church only after his glorification (John 7: 39; 14: 7). Water is the symbol of the abiding presence (John 4: 14; 7: 38; possibly 3: 5), in contrast to Mark 1: 8 and parallels, where the Baptist distinguishes water and the Spirit.

As with Luke in Acts, John is keenly interested in the movement of the Spirit. In the old period Haggai 2: 5 and Isaiah 63: 10–43 had referred to the moving tabernacle and not to the temple with its static, localized conception of God's presence. John 1: 14, *eskēnosen en hēmin* ('tabernacled among us'), implies that this mobile presence was continued by the dwelling of the Spirit in the Church. Wherever the Church journeys it has the Spirit which guides it as a company of pilgrims towards its heavenly destination. The Spirit blows wilfully and indiscriminately (John 3: 8), and neither at Jerusalem nor at Gerazim is true worship to be offered (4: 23). The freeing of the Spirit from all earthly locations takes place only in God's presence which Jesus imparts.

For this writer, God can only be worshipped in God who is Spirit and truth (4: 24). Once again we find ourselves on the threshold of the doctrine of the Trinity. So that the human race can worship God there must be a descent of God's love in His Son (objective), but that descent can only be accomplished through the descent of the Spirit, which is as much a veiling as a revelation; and after the Resurrection there comes a new revelation of God within which one is given new eyes to see and ears to hear the fulness of the objective revelation and enter into the eternal truth of the gospel. 'The *logos* became flesh and we beheld his glory' (John 1: 14). John's Gospel is the story of the life and ministry of Jesus in the light of the teaching of the Spirit-Paraclete, who enables men and women to penetrate the incognito and see in the human Jesus an eternal revelation of the love which unites the Father and Son, in which union the Spirit makes believers partakers of the same. John's term 'Paraclete', derived from the verb *parakaleō*, in earlier usage had meant one 'called in' to give support, in the sense of a pleader or advocate of an accused person. In John's usage, however, the function of the Paraclete is not that of an intercessor or pleader for the disciples before God (*contra* comparisons sometimes made between John and Hebrews on this point), but that of a helper towards their discernment of the self-revelation of the Father in his own human–divine person. He is 'the Spirit of Truth' (14: 17) 'who shall teach you all things, and bring to your remembrance all that I have said' (15: 25 f.; cf. 16: 12–15). Here the meaning of 'all things' is to be governed by the second half of the saying. It is not that the revelation that Jesus accomplished on earth was incomplete. The Paraclete would bring them to the knowledge of the union of Jesus with the Father by recalling to their minds everything that the historical Jesus had said and done. By the joint testimony of the disciples and the Spirit of Truth to the fact and meaning of the Cross, those who never saw Jesus will come to find in him the saving act of God (20: 29). Thus in every age the believing Christian is the contemporary of Christ.

The personal distinctness of the Spirit is also clearer in John than it is in Paul or Luke. God is the perfect communion or *agapē* of the Father with the Son in the Spirit, into which communion men and women are somehow to be raised; but because of human sin and failure there must first be the descent of the Son, and then the descent of the Spirit, who interprets the Son's descent to make his history present to every age.

In the rest of the New Testament there are scattered but instructive references to the work of the Spirit. In Hebrews believers are made 'partakers of the Holy Spirit' (6: 4), just as earlier they were said to be 'partakers of Christ' (3: 14). The Spirit is linked with 'signs, wonders and miracles and gifts ... distributed according to His will' (2: 4), an echo of 1 Cor. 12: 11, where 'the Spirit apportions to each one individually according to His will'. The Spirit's role in biblical revelation is also stressed (3: 7; 10: 15), and it may be through the Spirit that Christ offered himself in sacrifice to God (9: 14). When we turn to 1 Peter we find the Spirit as 'the Spirit of Christ' (1: 11; cf. Rom. 8: 9, Gal. 4: 6, Phil. 1: 19) who inspired prophetic prediction of the sufferings of Christ (cf. 2 Pet. 1: 21), sanctifies Christians (1: 1), energized Jesus to rise again (3: 18; cf. 1 Tim. 3: 16), and rests upon those who are being persecuted (4: 14).

As to be expected, the Revelation provides us with the most theologically imaginative and poetic description of the Spirit's activity. In 1: 4 the Spirit is represented by the seven spirits (cf. 3: 1; 4: 5; 5: 6), a symbol clearly pointing to the fulness of His activity and power. Possibly John here alludes to the sevenfold spirit which was to rest upon the Messiah (Isa. 11: 2), but more probably to Zechariah 4, where the prophet describes a candelabrum (Israel) with seven lamps ('the eyes of the Lord which range over the whole earth'), a vision which leads him to the conclusion, ' "Not by might or power, but by my Spirit," says the Lord of hosts.' John's kaleidoscopic imagery is especially rich in 3: 1, 4: 5, and 5: 6, where the Spirit is associated with seven stars, seven flaming torches, and seven eyes.

The Spirit in Revelation is pre-eminently the Spirit of prophecy. Each letter to the seven churches ends with a warning to heed 'what the Spirit says', a clear identification of Christ with the Spirit as He speaks through his prophetic representative. And it is only through a series of Spirit-inspired trances that John is enabled to witness the remarkable events he describes (1: 10; 4: 2; 17: 3; 21: 10; 22: 17).

In attempting to summarize this evidence, we need only note the way in which all of these writers show a remarkable agreement that the Spirit is Christ's way of remaining permanently with his people, the Church, and that He signifies God Himself as He descends into the common world to make His activity felt in new and dramatic ways. Thus most of our New Testament witnesses provide additional raw material for what will later be known as the Church's doctrine of the Trinity.

6.6. IN THE CHURCH

6.6.1. *Christ and His Church*

Any modern scholar who attempts to let the New Testament writers discuss what they believed about the Church faces a double difficulty. The literature on the subject is enormous and the linguistic problems acute. Not only does the Greek term *ekklēsia* have a complex semantic history of its own; the English word 'church', and its equivalents in other modern languages, come to us loaded with centuries of debate which have rendered them blunt tools for accurate theological exchange. In attempting to allow our conference members to speak for themselves, interpreters must be aware that they are probably viewing the subject through the spectacles of their own upbringing. The most that can be hoped is that into the grinding of those spectacles goes enough scholarly accuracy to correct any sectarian astigmatism.

We allow Paul to open the discussion. And to modern dogmatic theologians, in whatever tradition they stand, it will commonly come as a shock to be reminded that the term *ekklēsia* does not occur in Paul's letter to the Romans before the final chapter of greetings. This letter, rightly regarded as the fullest and most massive exposition of Paul's theology, can apparently dispense not only with the word, but largely with the concept. There is a great deal here about Christ's relationship with believers, but nothing about his relationship with the Church.

Even to formulate such a distinction, however, is to become aware how modern it sounds, how utterly out of keeping with Pauline usage. Here statistics are important. In the eight letters[34] which are our first concern, Paul uses *ekklēsia* forty-six times. In all but four of these he unambiguously refers to the local church (twenty are in the plural, and at least twelve denote the church gathered in regular assembly). Three others have to do with Paul's persecution of the Church (1 Cor. 15: 9; Gal. 1: 13; Phil. 3: 6)—apparent metonymy, with 'church' meaning 'Christians'. This leaves only one usage that is wider than local in its reference (1 Cor. 12: 28), and even this occurs in a context in which the local reference is predominant.

Over against statistics is to be set the fact that the word Paul chooses to designate the local communities of Christians is *ekklēsia*. And while the action of coming together is certainly included, it is unlikely that Paul's meaning is exhausted by the English word 'assembly'. Eight times it is qualified as 'the Church (or churches) of God', and this in itself should be enough to show that he is using it with the full theological weight it has acquired in the LXX as *a designation of the people of God*.[35] In this sense there can be only one *ekklēsia*, and this is even more obviously true when the Old Testament ideology of the people of God is seen to have its fulfilment in Christ. If Paul can regularly use *ekklēsia* in the plural, it is because the one *ekklēsia* is truly present in every company of believers. The distinctions we have been taught to make between the Church and the churches, the universal and the local, the invisible and the visible, have no foundation in Pauline usage.[36]

This conclusion is amply borne out by the evidence of synonyms. It was the local church of Corinth which Paul had betrothed to Christ as a pure virgin (2 Cor. 11: 2). It was these same Christians of Corinth who, with their varied functions, constituted Christ's body (1 Cor. 12: 27). Because they sat at the one table sharing the common eucharistic

---

[34] Rom., 1 and 2 Cor., Gal., Phil., 1 and 2 Thess., and Philem.

[35] This is denied by J. Y. Campbell, 'The Origin and Meaning of the Christian Use of the Word *Ekklēsia*', *Three New Testament Studies* (Leiden, 1965), 41–54, and I. H. Marshall, 'The Biblical Use of the Word *Ekklēsia*', *ExpT.* 84 (1973), 359 ff. See also R. Banks, *Paul's Idea of Community* (Grand Rapids, 1980), 34 ff.

[36] Cf. Banks, *Paul's Idea of Community*, 36 f.

meal, though many they were one loaf, one body (1 Cor. 10: 17), they were the temple of God in which the Spirit of God had His dwelling (1 Cor. 3: 16–17). Christ does not have many brides, many bodies, many temples. It is typical of Paul's ecclesiology that the universal exists only in the particular.

While Paul always conceives the relationship of Christ to the believer as an intensely personal one ('He loved me and gave himself up for me', Gal. 2: 20; 'By God's grace I am what I am', 1 Cor. 15: 9), the relationship is also a corporate one, but only because those who belong to Christ of necessity belong to one another (Rom. 12: 5; 1 Cor. 1: 13; 12: 12).

Thus for Paul the Church is the community of believers, and this is true even if the Church is seen as the new Israel. Membership in the old Israel might appear to be a matter of descent and race, though Paul in fact argues powerfully that it was from the start a matter of God's elective purpose with individuals responding in faith. Membership in the new Israel rests also on God's gracious calling and human response. Paul is therefore giving a definition of the Church when he writes: 'To the Church of God at Corinth, saints by God's calling, dedicated to Him in Christ Jesus' (1 Cor. 1: 2).

When we turn to Colossians, there are two obvious changes. What in Paul's earlier letters was the simile of the body has now become a metaphor; and *ekklēsia* is twice used of the universal Church without any immediate local reference. The second of these passages is notoriously difficult. 'This is my way of helping to complete, in my poor human flesh, the full tally of Christ's afflictions still to be endured, for the sake of his body [*sōma*] which is the Church [*ekklēsia*]' (1: 24). Whatever else may be said, there can be no doubt that here the Church is being treated as an extension of the life and character of Jesus, although this impression is conveyed more by the word 'Christ' than by either *sōma* or *ekklēsia*. Paul cannot mean that the sufferings Jesus endured on the Cross were incomplete, or that Christians need to supplement his saving work; nor does he elsewhere use the term 'affliction' (*thlipsis*) of the Cross. 'Christ' here must be the corporate Christ, who lives on in the Church, and whose continuing life conforms to the original pattern of suffering, glory, death, and resurrection. Thus, as in the earlier Pauline letters, the body of Jesus is the human, empirical, suffering Church, whose sole heavenly counterpart is Christ himself.[37]

---

[37] On the 'corporate Christ', see also above, pp. 175, 205.

The other passage is the so-called Christological hymn of 1: 15–20, where the description of Christ as 'head of the body' is part of a general hymn on the pre-eminence of the 'cosmic Christ', in whom God has brought to realization His purpose of elevating the human race to be the lord of all creation and of uniting all things under its authority (see above, Chapter 2).

This same theme is worked out in greater detail in Ephesians. 'He put the universe in subjection beneath His feet, and to the Church which is His body gave him as head over the universe, the complete embodiment of Him who is in the process of filling the universe to the full' (1: 22–3). We saw above that the purpose of God is that the whole creation should become permeated with His own nature, and this He is achieving in three stages: Christ has already been endowed with the divine nature in all its fulness; he has been given as God's gift to the Church, in order that the Church may be the first sharer of that fulness; and through the Church He intends to communicate the same fulness to the rest of creation.

Later in Ephesians (4: 11–16) the image of the body is combined with two others, the building and the marriage. The Church is indeed the body of Christ; but it is a body in the process of building, with all its perfection and completeness still lying in the future. We have seen that one of the dangers of the image of the body is that it should be taken literally, with the result that the relationship between one member and another, between the members and the head, is conceived as less than personal. The image of the marriage (5: 25; cf. Rev. 19: 7–9) supplies the needed corrective. Christ treats the Church as his own body, not because the distinction between the two is obliterated in some sort of physical fusion, but because he loves the Church, just as in the unity of a mutual wedded love husband and wife become one.

Among the synoptic writers this heading will inevitably concentrate on Matthew, for the simple and clear reason that his is the only Gospel in which the word *ekklēsia* occurs. As with the Fourth Gospel, to a great extent we must use bifocal vision in interpreting Matthew, since everything he wrote was intended both as a record of the historic life of Jesus and as instruction to the Church of his own day.[38]

---

[38] Cf. G. D. Kilpatrick, *The Origins of the Gospel According to St Matthew* (Oxford, 1946), for whom the liturgical background of the Gospel serves as 'a focus or channel' (p. 140) for the historical elements of the book.

It is of course Matthew who has given us the one famous passage (16: 17–19) which, more than any other, continues to divide modern Christians. The Protestant–Roman Catholic debate, however, may be temporarily left on one side, until we have a theological context in which it can be understood. Apart from this famous crux, the chief question at issue concerns the significance of the Twelve. Do they represent the whole Church that is to be, with the sayings addressed through them to all Christians? Or do they represent an ordained ministry within the Church? If we assume that the number twelve contains a symbolic reference to the twelve tribes of Israel (cf. 19: 28), are the Twelve appointed to rule over the new Israel? Or are they to be the new Israel in nucleus? Is the mission charge of 10: 5 ff. (not to mention the larger charge of 28: 19 f.) addressed to all Christians, or only to the ordained ministry?

The place to begin to look for an answer to such questions is chapter 18, with its discourse on church order and discipline. According to the evangelist the discourse was spoken to 'the disciples'; but this in itself hardly settles the matter. Mark systematically draws a distinction between 'the Twelve' and 'the disciples', with the second phrase always meaning the larger body from which the Twelve were chosen. Matthew frequently uses the word 'disciple' when he obviously means 'the Twelve'. We cannot therefore be quite sure from his introduction exactly whom he supposed to be the recipients of this collection of sayings. We must, however, assume that he intended the whole discourse for the same recipients. Now there are some parts of it which must have been intended by him for the Church as a whole. The paragraph (vv. 13–17) about how to deal with an offending member, whose offence is in the last resort to be reported to the *ekklēsia*, cannot have been designed solely to settle quarrels on the episcopal bench. The parable of the Two Debtors (vv. 23–34) cannot have been included at this point because Matthew thought the ordained ministry peculiarly liable to an unforgiving spirit. These two passages at least must have been addressed to the *whole body of believers*. But does it not therefore inescapably follow that the material which links the two passages is also addressed to the Church at large? It is to the whole community of believers that the authority to bind and loose is given, together with the promise that their prayers will be answered. They wield Christ's own authority, not by delegation from an absentee master, but because he is present in their midst. 'Where two or three are gathered together in my name, there I am among them' (18: 20).

Since the promise of the presence of Christ is here demonstrably made to the *ekklēsia*, however small, we are justified in deducing that this is also true of the promise of Immanuel with which the Gospel opens (1: 23), and of the similar promise with which it ends. 'All authority in heaven and on earth has been committed to me. Go forth therefore and make all nations my disciples . . . And be assured, I am with you always, even to the end of time' (28: 18–20). Here again there is no delegation of authority. Jesus himself is to be present, acting in and through those who preach, baptize, and teach in his name. 'To receive you is to receive me, and to receive me is to receive the One who sent me' (10: 40). At the Great Assize the nations will be judged by the treatment they have meted out to Christ in the person of his brothers and sisters. 'Anything you did for one of my brothers here, however, humble, you did it for me' (25: 40). Because Jesus is present in and identified with the humblest member of the Church, no grades or distinctions can be allowed within its fellowship. 'You must not be called "rabbi", for you have one Rabbi, and you are all brothers. Do not call anyone on earth "father"; for you have one Father, and He is in heaven. Nor must you be called "teacher"; you have one Teacher, the Messiah' (23: 8–10).

The Matthaean passage in which Peter is called 'the Rock' (16: 17–19) continues to vex commentators. Here we are not raising the question of the authenticity of that passage as a teaching of Jesus.[39] Our concern is with the theology of Matthew, for whom it is beyond dispute that his Gospel consistently accords to Peter a greater pre-eminence than he enjoys even in the supposedly Petrine Gospel of Mark. If we confine ourselves to the intention of Matthew, the only matter that remains in doubt is whether he regarded Peter as a single, historical, irreplaceable person or as the holder of an office in which he might have successors; and on that question, it would appear that Matthew himself provides little guidance. In the light of our previous discussion, however, two comments are clearly in order: (1) The right of binding and loosing, here given to Peter, is subsequently given to the whole company of disciples, so that, whatever this right may entail (and on

---

[39] Cf. e.g. M. Wilcox, 'Peter and the Rock', *NTS* 22 (1975), 73 ff.; J. A. Emerton, 'Binding and Loosing—Forgiving and Retaining', *JTS* 13 (1962), 325 ff.; and B. Meyer, *The Aims of Jesus* (London, 1979), 185 ff. According to Meyer, 'though few gospel texts have been branded unhistorical more emphatically than Matt. 16: 17–19 has been, the evidence favours both its historicity and the originality of its placement in the Caesarea Philippi scene' (186).

that one would be brave to venture an opinion), Peter must hold it as *primus inter pares*. (2) Whatever function may be assigned to Peter, the building of the Church remains the work of Jesus himself: 'On this rock I will build my Church.'

It would seem that Paul and Matthew are in the closest agreement about the relationship of Christ to his Church. For a summary of their teaching one could do no better than to go outside the New Testament to the letters of Ignatius. For the gospel of Ignatius is Matthew's gospel, and the hero whom he most reveres, imitates, and quotes is Paul. 'Wherever the bishop is to be seen, there let the congregation be, just as wherever Christ Jesus is, there is the Church in all its fulness' (*Sm.* 8: 2). For the second part of this statement Ignatius has the full support of his two great mentors. In the first part he goes a little beyond them—but only a very little. When we find that the Ignatian bishop was still the pastor of a local congregation, that his chief function was the preaching of the gospel and the administration of the Eucharist, and that Ignatius regarded him as the focus of unity for the common life of the fellowship over which he presided, we may well accept his definition in its entirety as an epitome of the New Testament teaching. Where Jesus is faithfully preached and faithfully received, whether by the spoken word or in the acted gospel of the sacraments, where the Spirit is at work to sanctify, direct, and unite, where believers share a common life of love and service, which they derive from their crucified and risen Lord, there Christ is present constituting his followers the Church of the living God.

As usual this emphasis is carried forward in the Revelation through the use of vivid imagery. The glorified Jesus holds in his right hand the stars (1: 16) and walks among the lampstands, both symbols of the churches. And it is of paramount significance that Jesus is *among* the lamps. As for Paul and Matthew, for John, Jesus is no absentee Christ, residing in heaven until his Parousia, meanwhile exercising his authority over the churches by remote control through their celestial representatives, the angels. Christ is present with the worldly congregations of his people, and whatever else John has to say about the coming of Christ must be understood in the light of this fact.

Jesus is he who will 'come in and have supper' with his followers (3: 20), an invitation which has a strong eucharistic flavour. Week by week, past and future meet in the sacramental Now, in which the crucified and risen Lord makes his presence known to his disciples in the breaking of the bread. Yet it is not the Lord's Supper to which

John is ultimately directing his readers' interest. He is using language ripe with eucharistic associations to depict a coming of Jesus even more personal and intimate than that which is found in the corporate worship of the Church.

These images are supplemented with another, that of the Church as the woman who gives birth to the Messiah (ch. 12). But here the birth is not the nativity; it is the Cross, 'the agony of her labour' (v. 2), the suffering endured by the loyal people of God as they wait for their anointed king. The woman is allowed to escape 'to a place prepared for her by God' (v. 6). To those whose eyes are fixed only on what is seen on earth the Church is a vulnerable human society; but to those with eyes to see what is unseen and eternal, the Church is inviolate to the assaults of Satan himself.

Elsewhere John depicts the Church as the bride of the Lamb (19: 7 f.), an image which has strong Old Testament roots (Hos. 2: 5; Isa. 1: 21; Jer. 2: 2; cf. Eph. 5: 32). From all this we may conclude that John's depiction of Jesus and his Church is as intimate and personal as anything which may be found in Paul or Matthew.

In the rest of the New Testament there is nothing quite like this emphasis on the presence of the risen Jesus, although the writers have their own distinctive contributions to make. The author of Hebrews never describes the Church as the body of Christ. It is Jesus' brethren (2: 11), God's house (3: 2–6), the wandering people of God (4: 1–11), and the company of people for whom Jesus as priest makes sacrifice (4: 14–5: 10; 7: 26–9: 28). As nomads looking for a better city which is to come (13: 14), they have already approached Mount Zion (12: 22) in fear and trembling. But it would be wrong to claim that for this author Christ is not personally related to his followers. He sympathizes with them in all their weakness (4: 14 f.), and they have been made partakers of him (3: 14). They share his insult (11: 26) and have an altar from which the old covenant priests have no right to eat (13: 14). Such images are as warm and personal as anything to be found in Matthew or Paul.

This is not the case in 1 Peter, where the author tends to rely on stock metaphor. Believers are living stones built into a spiritual house, with the cornerstone Christ (2: 4–6). Those who were once 'no people' have become God's people (2: 10), and have become 'a chosen race, a royal priesthood, a holy nation, God's own people' (2: 9). Here there is nothing of Jesus' presence with the Church which is so strongly portrayed in Paul and Matthew.

When we allow the Fourth Gospel to join the discussion, prima facie we face a misconception that has tended to skew the picture. It is frequently claimed that John's Christology is more 'individualistic' than Paul's, lacking the Pauline emphasis on the corporate Christ.[40] There is some truth to this claim, of course. John uses the preposition *en* (14: 20; 15: 5; 17: 21–3) to denote a relationship of mutuality in a way subtly different from the usage of Paul. But are mutuality and individualism inseparable bedfellows? If, in the thinking of John, the person of Christ was such that a multiplicity of individuals could have a mutual relationship with him, and thereby be drawn into unity not only with him but with God and with one another, can we seriously suppose that John thought of that person in individual terms? A vine and its branches (15: 1–5), while obviously employing a different image from that of the body, may certainly be seen as just as incorporative as anything found in Paul. The tables might even be turned on this argument by claiming that of the two writers it is *Paul* who is the individualist; for whereas in the Fourth Gospel Jesus is the Saviour of the world (3: 16), to Paul he is the one 'who loved me and gave himself for me' (Gal. 2: 20). Paul and John are in fact individualistic at precisely the same point, in their insistence that the relationship of Christ to the Christian becomes real, operative, and effective through faith, which is an individual act of acceptance, loyalty, and obedience. The many have not in advance authorized the one to act as their representative; their part is to recognize in retrospect that what he has done was done in their name, so as to include them in the doing of it.

If, as it will be claimed below, the starting point for New Testament Christology is the Cross, then the question of whether John, like Paul, believed in a corporate Christ needs to be reframed. The real question is whether John believed that in the Cross the salvation of the world has been achieved in such a way that believers could subsequently acknowledge that they had been included in Christ's vicarious death. And the evidence we have already considered would lead us to answer strongly in the affirmative.

---

[40] Cf., e.g., C. F. D. Moule, 'The Individualism of the Fourth Gospel', *NT* (1962), 171 ff.

6.6.2. *Sacraments*

The New Testament sacraments are symbolic acts like those of the Hebrew prophets. When Jeremiah broke a pitcher in the valley of Hinnom (Jer. 19), his act was not merely a dramatic symbol of the coming destruction of the city, but that which helped to accomplish what it represented. And if the prophets believed their symbolism to be effective, it was because it was a visible preaching of the word of God, and the word of God is always effective. In the same way the sacraments of baptism and the Lord's Supper were seen to be a visible preaching of the word which God had uttered in His Son. God had pledged to those who accept the gospel and receive the Spirit new life and membership in the Messianic community. Of this baptism and the Lord's Supper were symbolic, and because God is always true to His promises, the sacraments conveyed that which they symbolized. This Hebraic understanding of the sacraments is confirmed by 1 Peter, where newly baptized converts are described as 'begotten again . . . through the living and abiding word of God' (1 Pet. 1: 23; cf. Jas. 1: 18; Acts 2: 41; 16: 32 f), and by Paul, for whom the Lord's Supper is a preaching of Jesus' death (1 Cor. 11: 26).

(a) Baptism[41]

It was John the Baptist who provided the Jewish *Tebilah* with a new meaning and urgency by requiring that Jews should also submit to a baptism of repentance for the remission of sins as an initiation into the new Israel. Mark, Q, and Acts understand this as the beginning of the Christian gospel (Mark 1: 8; Matt. 3: 11; Luke 3: 16; Acts 1: 5). Luke in particular stresses that baptism was practised from the day of Pentecost (Acts 2: 38; cf. 3: 19, 10: 43). This emphasis is supported by Paul, for whom it is obvious that all Christians will be baptized at conversion. 'We were buried with him in baptism, and

---

[41] On the subject in general, see K. Aland, *Did the Early Church Baptize Infants?* (London, 1963); K. Barth, *The Teaching of the Church Regarding Baptism* (London, 1948); G. R. Beasley-Murray, *Baptism in the New Testament* (Grand Rapids, 1962); G. Bornkamm, 'Baptism and New Life in Paul (Romans 6)', in *Early Christian Experience* (London, 1969), 71–86; O. Cullmann, *Baptism in the New Testament* (London, 1950); Dunn, *Baptism in the Holy Spirit*; W. F. Flemington, *The New Testament Doctrine of Baptism* (London, 1948); J. Jeremias, *The Origins of Infant Baptism* (Naperville, Ill. 1963); G. W. H. Lampe, *The Seal of the Spirit* (London, 1967²); A. Oepke, '*baptō*' etc., *TDNT* i. 529–46, and '*louō*', *TDNT* iv. 295–307; and R. Schnackenburg, *Baptism in the Thought of St Paul* (New York, 1964).

were dead, so that as Christ was raised from the dead in the splendour of the Father, so also we might walk in newness of life' (Rom. 6: 4; cf. Gal. 3: 27; 1 Cor. 1: 13; 6: 11; 12: 13). This idea receives a more developed treatment in Col. 2: 11 f., where the water of baptism is clearly the symbol of divine judgement, with the initiate voluntarily accepting that death which is God's sentence upon sin. But since Jesus died that very same death (Rom. 6: 10), baptism is also a symbolic union with him in *his* death and resurrection (Rom. 6: 3–5; 2 Cor. 5: 14). The old nature dies, to be replaced by the new humanity of the risen Lord. Thus for Paul, baptized Christians no longer live in that old order in which the principalities and powers exercise their sway, nor to which they owe any further loyalty. In baptism Christians have accepted a solidarity with Jesus which carries with it a share in his supremacy over all other representatives of spiritual authority.

It is in this context that we should understand Paul's apparent comparison of baptism with circumcision in Col. 2: 11. There, in replying to the 'philosophers' who were insisting that circumcision was the only true form of initiation into Christianity, Paul claims that true circumcision is not literal but metaphorical ('made without hands'); it is not the removal of flesh from the body, but the surrender of the impenitent heart (cf. Rom. 2: 28 f.; Phil. 3: 13). True circumcision is not minor physical surgery, but major spiritual surgery, the excision of the old Adam; and this is accomplished at baptism. We shall probably also see a Pauline allusion to baptism in Colossians 3: 9–10, where Paul speaks of putting off the old nature and putting on the new (cf. Gal. 3: 27, where all who have been baptized into Jesus have 'put on' Christ). For Paul baptism is the prophetic symbol of the new nature, which is not the product of human moral effort, but of the creative handiwork of God.

Outside the Pauline corpus there are only a few scattered allusions to baptism. John 3: 5 uses baptismal language to refer to the new life opened up to people of faith by the coming of Jesus (below). The Pastorals refer to 'the good confession in the presence of many witnesses' (1 Tim. 6: 12), a probable baptismal allusion (although Titus 3: 5, 'the washing of regeneration', is less certain). Hebrews 10: 22 f. speaks of 'hearts sprinkled and bodies washed', a phrase which clearly illustrates how in some quarters baptism was felt to touch every aspect of the human person. The plural 'baptisms' in Hebrews 6: 2, on the other hand, is difficult as a reference to Christian baptism, and may have some other referent. And in one of the most obscure passages in the New Testament, 1 Peter 3: 18–21,[42] the author compares the Christian's experience at baptism to Noah's flood. Baptism is 'not the washing away of bodily dirt, but the appeal made to God by a good conscience', which is made possible by the resurrection life of Christ (v. 21). The workings of this author's mind are hardly obvious here; possibly he is drawing a parallel with two aspects of the Genesis flood account, salvation through water and new creation.

Baptism in the New Testament is also strongly connected with the gift of the Holy Spirit. The tradition of the descent of the dove at the moment when Jesus came out of the water (Mark 1: 10; Matt. 3: 16; Luke 3: 22; John 1: 31–3) could not help but suggest that the gift of the Spirit should come to Christians through the same rite as it had to him (1 Cor. 12: 13; Acts 2: 38; 9: 17 f.; 19: 1–6). The case of Cornelius, in which the Spirit came first and baptism followed (Acts 10: 47 f.), was an exception to the normal pattern (Acts 2: 38) that the Spirit followed baptism.

The laying on of hands was also part of the rite of baptism and the Spirit's bestowal, although the connection between the three is never really explained (Acts 8: 8–17; 9: 17 ff.; Heb. 6: 2).

As for the question of *who* should administer baptism or the laying on of hands, the New Testament is completely indifferent. The one thing which may be ruled out is that either was a monopoly of the apostolate.

A final difficulty which concerns the New Testament theologian involves whether or not it should be given to infants. Those who have argued that baptism should be administered only to those who are capable of a conscious form of faith point to those texts in which baptism follows a faith-confession on the part of the initiate.[43] Those on the other hand who favour the baptism of infants point to instances where whole households were baptized (Acts 16: 15; 1 Cor. 1: 16), and to Paul's statement in 1 Cor. 7: 14 that infants are 'holy' (*hagios*) due to the presence of at least one believing parent.[44]

In fact both positions may be regarded as partly right and partly wrong. In the first century baptism was administered exclusively to converts, who were then baptized with their whole household. But

---

[42] The best discussion of the passage remains that of B. Reicke, *The Disobedient Spirits and Christian Baptism* (Copenhagen, 1946).

[43] Cf. Beasley-Murray, *Baptism in the New Testament*, for the fullest expression of the 'adult' or 'believers' ' position.

[44] Cf. Cullmann, *Baptism in the New Testament*, for an equally comprehensive statement of the infant baptism point of view.

children born to parents already Christian were not baptized in infancy or later in adulthood, because they had already been born into the household of faith.

Despite the note on which we began, a final qualification concerns the modelling of Christian baptism on the baptism of Jesus rather than that of John. For anyone familiar with the story of Jesus' baptism it would be natural, even without an explicit command from Jesus himself,[45] that the gift of the Spirit should come through the same rite in which it came to him (Mark 1: 9–11 and parallels; cf. John 1: 33), and that those who were admitted to the fellowship of the Christian community should be baptized with his baptism. If converts were baptized 'in the name of the Lord Jesus' (Acts 8: 16; 19: 5) or 'in the name of Jesus Christ' (1 Cor. 1: 10, 13), it was because in his name remission of sins and salvation was offered to them, and they were therefore introduced into a form of union with Christ.

It is further significant that the synoptic writers portray Jesus as regarding his baptism as a symbolic inauguration into servanthood and death (e.g. Luke 4: 8; 12: 50; Mark 10: 38 f.). It is therefore likely that when Paul says that baptism is a putting on of Jesus crucified, he is not innovating, but interpreting. What Jesus had seen as a symbol of his own death in prospect, Paul saw as the Christian's identifying with Jesus' death in retrospect.

(b) The Lord's Supper[46]

Whatever battles have been waged over New Testament texts concerning baptism will seem mild when compared with those which continue to be waged over the Lord's Supper. Once again it is remarkable how

---

[45] The majority viewpoint is still that the baptismal formula of Matt. 28: 19 represents a later view than that of Jesus (cf. for instance E. Schweizer, *The Good News According to Matthew* (London, 1976), 513f.; D. Hill, *The Gospel of Matthew* (London, 1972), 362; and Kilpatrick, *Origins of the Gospel of Matthew*, 128 f.).

[46] The literature is massive, only a fraction of which will include the following: O. Cullmann and F. J. Leenhardt, *Essays on the Lord's Supper* (Richmond, 1968); A. Farrer, 'The Eucharist in 1 Corinthians', in *Eucharistic Theology Then and Now*, SPCK Theological Collections (London, 1968), 15 ff.; B. Gärtner, *John 6 and the Jewish Passover* (Lund, 1959); A. J. B. Higgins, *The Lord's Supper in the New Testament* (London, 1952); J. Jeremias, *The Eucharistic Words of Jesus* (Oxford, 1955); H. Lietzmann, *Mass and Lord's Supper* (Leiden, 1979); R. P. Martin, *Worship in the Early Church* (London, 1975[2]); I. H. Marshall, *Last Supper and Lord's Supper* (Exeter, 1980); C. F. D. Moule, *Worship in the New Testament* (London, 1961); E. Schweizer, *The Lord's Supper According to the New Testament* (Philadelphia, 1967); V. Taylor, *Jesus and His Sacrifice* (London, 1965[6]),

all the disputants have been equally assured that the Bible is on their side. Here exegesis has usually been dictated by the exigencies of controversy based upon the proof-text method which has been now almost universally discarded. We have thus been bequeathed a polemical vocabulary of exaggeration and depreciation, the influence of which is difficult to escape. There are, on the other hand, good reasons why this topic should be approached with more temperance than has been exercised in the past.

The most striking and inexorable fact is that there is only one explicit mention of the Eucharist in the New Testament (1 Cor. 11: 17 ff.), and it makes a curious contrast with the frequent references to baptism. There is no eucharistic teaching in Acts, 1 Peter, the Pastorals, Hebrews, or Revelation.[47]

We could, of course, conjecture with the Form Critics that the description of the Last Supper in each of the Synoptics was preserved and moulded by liturgical tradition;[48] but they contain no command to repeat the rite, except in the suspect longer text of Luke.[49] And if it were not for the Pauline passage, we should certainly read this pericope as an account of what happened once, on a particular night, at the end of the life of Jesus. The reference to the cup and bread in 1 Cor. 10: 4 ff. is undoubtedly eucharistic, but we can assert this only because we interpret it in the light of the following chapter; and a similar observation may be made about the use of 'flesh' and 'blood' in John 6: 51 ff.

Above all, our investigation notes two remarkable omissions: the Eucharist is not included among the marks of the Church's unity in Eph. 4: 4–6; and the Epistle to the Hebrews, in its elaborate exposition

---

114 ff., 175 ff., 201 ff., 236 ff., and 'The New Testament Origins of Holy Communion', in *New Testament Essays* (London, 1970), 48 ff.

[47] It may be conjectured that the breaking of bread mentioned three times in Acts (2: 42, 46; 20: 7) was eucharistic. But the breaking of bread at Emmaus was an introduction to an ordinary supper, and the two disciples who recognized Jesus when he did it are not said to have been present at the Last Supper. Moreover, Luke uses his most thoroughly eucharistic formula for an occasion when the participating company consisted of pagan sailors (Acts 27: 35).

[48] Cf. e.g. W. Marxen, *The Lord's Supper as a Christological Problem* (Philadelphia, 1970), and 'The Lord's Supper: Concepts and Developments', in H. J. Schultz (ed.), *Jesus in His Time* (Philadelphia, 1971).

[49] Cf. G. B. Caird, *The Gospel of St Luke* (London, 1968), 237 f.; V. Taylor, *The Passion Narrative of St Luke* (Cambridge, 1972), and the survey of the question in J. Green, *The Death of Jesus* (Tübingen, 1988), 35 ff.

of the story of Melchizedek in Genesis 14, uses every other detail except the bread and wine which Melchizedek brought out for Abraham.[50]

Paul's evidence encourages us to find the prototype for the Eucharist in the actions and words of Jesus at the Last Supper. The most obvious discrepancy among the sources is that the Synoptic Gospels identify the Last Supper with the Passover, whereas John does not. Jeremias[51] has provided a few persuasive reasons for accepting the synoptic dating. Now while this is essentially a historical question, and has no direct bearing on our enterprise, it has important implications for New Testament theology; for if Jeremias is correct, we may be forced to ask further probing questions: Why did the annual celebration of the Passover become a weekly celebration of the Eucharist? Is the Passover merely the setting for the inauguration of a wholly new rite? Or should Paschal associations be assumed in the interpretation of the Eucharist (only Luke's version of the eucharistic words makes explicit reference to the Passover)? Here the justification for the use of sacrificial terms in connection with the Eucharist will to some extent be dependent on the answer given to these questions.

But the New Testament theologian as always needs to be scrupulously critical. Ideas which modern scholars are accustomed to associate with the Eucharist occur regularly in the New Testament in dissociation from it. Even the word *eucharistia* is never used sacramentally. The verb *eucharistō* occurs in all four accounts of the Last Supper, but is more commonly used of thanksgiving over ordinary meals or of thanksgiving in general. *Koinōnia* is used eucharistically in 1 Cor. 10: 16, but elsewhere denotes the fellowship created by the Holy Spirit, while in Acts 2: 42 it is actually listed as a characteristic of the Christian life distinct from the breaking of bread. Above all, the New Testament knows nothing of a specifically eucharistic presence. The presence of Jesus is closely linked with the preaching of the gospel, the experience of the Spirit, and the common life of the Christian community. It is no doubt possible to show that what later came to be known as the

[50] R. Williamson, 'The Eucharist and the Epistle to the Hebrews', *NTS* 21 (1975), 300, uses the silence regarding the Eucharist in Hebrews as evidence of an anti-eucharistic tendency on the part of the writer and his community. While some may object to the argument from silence, at least it shows that the celebration of the Lord's Supper may not have been as woven into the fabric of early Christian practice as is often assumed.

[51] Cf., Jeremias, *Eucharistic Words of Jesus*, 89 ff.

Eucharist fits into this pattern, but there is no evidence that it was regarded as central to the thought or to the worship of the early Church.

We have seen that 1 Cor. 11: 17 ff. is the passage on which all our knowledge of the Eucharist in the apostolic age depends. But we must begin by admitting that there is one important point at which we do not fully understand it. Nobody has yet proposed a plausible rendering for the difficult verb *diakrinō* in v. 29. Traditionally translated 'if he does not discern the body', it has been taken to refer to a failure to recognize either the eucharistic body under the elements of bread and wine, or the ecclesiastical body in the assembled community. The difficulty with both these interpretations is that nowhere else in Greek literature does *diakrinō* mean 'to recognize', and this sense hardly fits the second occurrence of the word at v. 31 ('we shall not be *judged*').[52]

If, however, ignoring the lexical difficulties, we persist in the traditional rendering of the verb as 'discern', we should probably adopt the suggestion of C. F. D. Moule[53] that the theme of judgement is integral to the interpretation of the sacrament. Because the eating and drinking are a commemoration of the Lord's *death*, worthy participants take their stand with all who are united with the crucified body of their Lord, under the judgement which he bore for them. Unworthy participants evade that saving judgement only to share God's judgement on the world (i.e. on those who were responsible for the crucifixion). The attitude which 'fails to distinguish the body' (i.e. that which fails to see under the tokens of broken bread and shared cup the crucified body in which all Christians are made one with their Lord and therefore with one another) is the same as the attitude which fails to 'distinguish ourselves' (i.e. to see ourselves as sinners whose judgement Christ has borne). But it must be granted that even this interesting proposal does not wholly eliminate the problems of the passage.

Whatever doubts may arise over this question, there are some positive theological points to be made about the passage as a whole.

1. Paul finds the warrant for the celebration in what Jesus did and said 'on the night of his arrest'. These words are so emphatic that

---

[52] Cf. Barrett, *First Corinthians*, 274 ff.

[53] C. F. D. Moule, 'The Judgment Theme in the Sacraments', in W. Daube and W. D. Davies, *The Background of the New Testament and Its Eschatology* (Cambridge, 1956), 464 ff.

they must be taken to govern the meaning of the whole. The words Paul attributes to Jesus mean that Jesus, with his own hands, passed the bread and the cup to his disciples, in which case the broken bread and shared cup were prophetic symbols pointing forward to the reality of Calvary. To Paul and his churches they are commemorative symbols pointing back to the same historic event. Thus we may repeat the similarity we have noted to baptism: what the Last Supper is to the Cross in prospect the Lord's Supper is to it in retrospect.

2. In Paul's account, as in the others, the parallel to 'bread' is not 'wine' but 'cup'. Elsewhere in the recorded words of Jesus the cup is the symbol of his own crucifixion (Mark 10: 38; 14: 36).

3. The word over the bread and the word over the cup both contain the Greek copula *estin*. The fact that Aramaic, like Hebrew, possesses no such copula should warn us against building a metaphysic on one word. But the argument can be overstated. Aramaic is just as capable as any other language of predication, even without the use of a copula, and can therefore say in its own way what is here said in Greek. A more significant point is that predication does not necessarily signify the identity of subject and predicate. There are many other logical connections which may be expressed by the same form of words. Here it should be obvious that Paul does not identify the cup with the new covenant. It follows therefore that in his version of the saying the copula has the value of 'symbolizes' or 'represents'.

Paul's sidelong allusion to the Eucharist in 1 Cor. 10: 14 ff. is part of a long argument about the propriety of eating meat which had been slaughtered at a pagan sacrifice. The context supplies an adequate key to his terminology. Just as pagans drink the cup and eat from the table of those demons whom they call gods and so become partners of those gods, just as Jews by eating sacrifices become partners of the altar, so Christians by drinking the cup and eating the broken bread become partners in the body and blood of Christ, i.e. in his atoning death. Here too Paul emphasizes that there is no automatic efficacy. The Israelites in the wilderness had typological anticipations of the Christian sacraments, yet they came under the annihilating judgement of God. 'If you feel sure you are standing firm, beware! You may fall!' (10: 12).

This passage is crucial for New Testament theology, in so far as it demonstrates how easily Paul's mind moves from 'the blood of Christ' and the 'body of Christ' to that body which is the Church. 'Because there is one loaf, we, many as we are, are one body; for it is one loaf of which we all partake' (10: 17). All who share the one loaf are united to one another because they are united to Christ. It demonstrates that the fluidity of imagery which characterizes Paul's theological writing is better suited to the evocative atmosphere of worship than to the precise definitions of systematic theology.[54]

The evidence of the Fourth Gospel is often misinterpreted. This is largely because it is another New Testament writing which must be read through bifocals. Through the distant lens we see events in their historic setting in the life of Jesus (e.g. the constant reference to the hour which has not yet come, 2: 4; 8: 20). Through the near lens we see the same events illuminated by sixty years' theology—instruction from the Spirit of Truth (16: 14). In addition to this is the problem that some have thought John to be a sacramentalist,[55] and have detected references to the sacraments in every chapter, whereas to others he has been an antisacramentalist,[56] guarding against superstitious and magical abuse.

There are two places only where a sacramental allusion is unde-niable, in chapters 3 and 6. The contrast between natural and spiritual birth in 3: 3–5 did not require a reference to water, and the contrast between the manna given by Moses (the Torah) and the manna from heaven which is Jesus did not require a reference to blood. If John has Jesus speak of rebirth by water and Spirit and demand that the Jews should drink his blood as well as eating his flesh, he is clearly using sacramental language. But is he doing more than this? It would be difficult to maintain that the subject of the discourse with Nico-demus was baptism or that the subject of the sermon at Capernaum was the Eucharist. The Johannine Jesus is using sacramental language to talk about experiences which at a later stage came to be associated with the sacraments: in the one case the new life opened up to people of faith by the coming of Jesus, and in the second case the Incarnation as the source of the new life.[57]

The climax of the discourse at Capernaum comes when Jesus asserts that he himself is the true manna from heaven (John 6: 51), where John uses the word 'flesh' rather than 'body' because he is making a

---

[54] A point made by L. W. Hurtado, *One God, One Lord* (Philadelphia, 1988).

[55] Cf. O. Cullmann, *Early Christian Worship*, pt. 2.

[56] Cf. R. Bultmann, *The Gospel of John* (Philadelphia, 1971), 234 ff., 677 ff.

[57] Cf. S. S. Smalley, 'Liturgy and Sacrament in the Fourth Gospel', *EQ* 29 (1957), 159 ff., and *John: Evangelist and Interpreter* (London, 1984), 206 ff.

deliberate cross-reference to 1: 14. Jesus did not pre-exist either as bread or flesh, but as *logos*; but it is only as flesh, i.e. in his full humanity, that he can give himself. Thus to eat the flesh of the Son of Man is to believe in the incarnation and to accept its benefits.

When the Jews then ask, 'How can this man give us his flesh to eat?', this is no captious question. For he cannot do so until he has been crucified. He is the *logos* incarnate, and already it is possible for men and women to penetrate his incognito and believe that he has come from God; but it is not yet possible for them to have the saving faith that can appropriate the benefits of his coming in the flesh. Nobody can come to him without being drawn by the Father (v. 44), and that process of drawing has not yet begun (12: 32). At this point therefore Jesus declares, 'Unless you eat the flesh of the Son of Man and drink his blood you can have no life in you'. Here we cannot improve on Westcott's[58] understanding that 'by the "flesh" in this nar-rower sense we must understand the virtue of Christ's humanity as living for us, and by the "blood" the virtue of his humanity as subject to death.' The believer must be made partaker of both. The Son of Man lived for us and died for us, and communicates to us the effects of his life and death as the perfect human being. Without this com-munication of Christ men and women can have 'no life in themselves'. Whatever language Jesus may use about his self-giving, it is himself he gives. He is himself the bread of life. The terms 'flesh' and 'blood' are therefore not to be understood literally, but as synecdoche, with the part standing symbol for the whole.

This is a point which John himself underlines. Jesus is the *living* bread. It is as a living person that he addresses the crowd and offers himself. Admittedly they cannot receive the gift until he has died. But his is a life which death cannot extinguish. 'As the living Father sent me, and I live because of the Father, so he who eats me shall live because of me' (v. 57). It is his living self he gives, not part of his dead body. 'The Spirit alone gives life: the flesh is of no avail; the words I have spoken to you are both spirit and life' (v. 63). The unbelief of the crowd arises precisely from their literalism. Like pagan critics of Christianity in the third century, they assume that Jesus is talking of cannibalism and find the idea understandably repulsive.

All this applies with equal strength when the passage is given its secondary, eucharistic application. It is the living Christ who is present

---

[58] B. F. Westcott, *The Gospel According to St John* (London, 1887), 106 f.

in his own person to give the living bread which is himself, the incarnate *logos*. The reality of his presence and the reality of his gift are guaranteed not by the tokens of bread and wine, but by the words with which the significance is imparted to them. 'The words which I have spoken to you are both spirit and life' (v. 63). 'Your words are eternal life. We have faith, and we know that you are the Holy One of God' (v. 69).

6.6.3. *Lack of Organization*

A third outstanding feature of the Church according to the New Testament writers is its relative lack of organization. It is characteristic of life in the Church that all members share not only in the ministry of Christ but in each other's ministry as it is expressed in spiritual gift or gifts. Paul himself holds a unique office, and he seldom tires of mentioning the *charis* given to him, the special privilege of his apostolate. There are many missionaries, but only one 'Apostle to the Gentiles' (Rom. 1: 5; 11: 3; 12: 3; 15: 15; 1 Cor. 3: 10; Gal. 2: 9; Eph. 3: 2, 7, 8; Phil. 1: 7). Yet he never seems to regard his apostolate as being in itself a mediation of the presence of Christ. If he, as apostle, mediates that presence it is not in virtue of an office, but in virtue of a function—the preaching of the Gospel. 'Christ did not send me to baptize but to proclaim the Gospel; and to do it without relying on the language of worldly wisdom, so that the fact of Christ on his Cross might have its full weight' (1 Cor. 1: 17). 'Even if I preach the Gospel, I can claim no credit for it; I cannot help myself' (1 Cor. 9: 16).

Paul's low-keyed approach seems for some time to have prevailed. But when he and the other apostles disappeared, and the growing threat of false prophecy and heresy became apparent, the later New Testament writers had eventually to face the issue of Church order. We have seen that Matthew puts together in one paragraph sayings which bear on the theme of discipline (18: 15–20), and these he clearly understood to be addressed to the Church as a whole. In Paul's own writings we find reference to 'government' (*kubernēsis*, 1 Cor. 12: 28) and those who 'bear rule' (1 Thess. 5: 12; Rom. 12: 8), while he opens his letter to the Philippians with a greeting to the 'rulers' (*episkopoi*, 1: 1).

Elsewhere the New Testament writers speak of elders (*presbuteroi*, Acts 20: 17), leaders (*hēgoumenoi*, Heb. 13: 7, 17, 24), and deacons (*diakonoi*, Acts 6: 1 ff., 20: 24, 21: 19, 2 Cor. 5: 18, Phil. 1: 1). It is now fairly certain[59] that *episkopoi, presbuteroi,* and *hēgoumenoi* are synonyms, while *diakonoi* usually refers to those charged with menial tasks such as waiting on tables and distributing financial help (Acts 6: 1 ff.; cf. 1 Tim. 3: 8 ff.).

The Pastoral Epistles are concerned especially with Church order, but they approach it with a different concern in mind. The Pastor is anxious about the moral and spiritual qualifications of those who would be appointed to the office of elder. The Pastorals refer once to the practice of *dokimasia*—enquiry into an individual's character and gifts before appointment to office (1 Tim. 3: 10). But even here Luke, Paul and the Pastorals agree that *presbuteroi* and *episkopoi* are interchangeable terms. It is true that the Pastorals depict Paul as commissioning Timothy and Titus to act as Paul's representatives in the appointment of a ministry for the churches. But, apart from the obvious problem of the letters' authenticity, Timothy and Titus are here viewed as ambassadors with a roving commission rather than permanent residents of any local church.

Other leaders are mentioned in the exhaustive statement of Ephesians 4: 11: 'And it is he who has given some to be apostles, some prophets, some evangelists, some pastors and teachers, to equip God's people for work in His Service, for the building up of the body of Christ' (REB). This list is an extremely helpful summary of the division of labour in the first century according to spiritual gifts. Generally these terms are functional, focusing on specific activities rather than offices.

In other points of Church order we find a thundering silence. If Paul hardly mentions the organization of the Church it is for one clear reason: an organism does not need to be organized. For him the striking fact about the Christian community was the spontaneous emergence of a common life in people of multifarious backgrounds and interests, transcending differences of race, class, and sex, but allowing for divergence of capacity and function (Gal. 3: 28; 1 Cor. 12: 4–11). There is no evidence that the New Testament writers saw the administration of the sacraments as the monopoly of any ministerial office, or that ordination involved the laying on of apostolic hands.

Those who were to be ordained might be ordained by an apostle (2 Tim. 1: 6) or by a presbytery (*presbuterion,* 1 Tim. 4: 14); but on any other feature the New Testament is silent. It is true that the

---

[59] Cf. G. B. Caird, *The Apostolic Age* (Essex and London, 1955), 149 ff.

Church in the New Testament period falls heir to the old Israelite term 'royal priesthood' (1 Pet. 2: 9, Rev. 1: 6). But no individual Christian is ever called a priest, and sacerdotal language is used only once to describe a distinctively ministerial function, when Paul in a violent metaphor claims to have been called to 'a priestly administration of the Gospel of God, that the sacrificial offering of the Gentiles may be acceptable, sanctified in the Holy Spirit' (Rom. 15: 16).

The reason for this fairly uncomplicated pattern is clear. The later New Testament writers were concerned to keep intact their inheritance from the apostles, and preserved unaltered until the end of the century the simple and democratic form of ministry which the apostles had originated.

6.6.4. *Abolition of Discrimination*

The final outstanding feature of the Church discussed by the New Testament writers is the requirement of the abolition of all forms of discrimination. For them the Church is one because Christ is one. We here again concentrate mainly on Paul, for the simple fact that the unity of the Church is one of his most recurrent themes. Faced with the self-assertive factions at Corinth, he asks, 'Is Christ divided?' For him those who find divisions tolerable even for a moment only display how little their thinking and attitudes have been transformed by the Spirit of Christ (1 Cor. 1: 13; 3: 1). But the most serious threat to Church unity that Paul faced came from the segregation of Jewish and Gentile Christians, the one group claiming to be bound by loyalty to an ancestral tradition, the other standing pat on a new-found freedom. Paul answers the threat, not with a statement of obligation or of hope, but with an assertion of fact. Divisions belong with the old, unredeemed humanity which died with Christ on the Cross (Gal. 6: 14 f.; cf. Eph. 2: 14, 16).

If Paul was a passionate advocate of liberty, this liberty must be one in which Jew and Gentile share. Paul had a vision of one Church, in which Jews and Gentiles were fellow heirs of the old covenantal promises realized in Jesus. Thus when his fanatical followers claimed him as their leader, he sharply rebuked them; and when news came to him that others were preaching Christ so as to cause him personal distress, he could rejoice that, one way or another, Christ was being proclaimed (1 Cor. 1: 12–17; Phil. 1: 16–18).

It was on the principle of Church unity that Paul took his stand in the dispute at Antioch which he records in Gal. 2: 11 f. There he fiercely rebukes Peter for compromising the Gentiles' freedom by compelling them to adopt Jewish habits. For Paul, that there should be two separate communions within the one church at Antioch was unthinkable. Those who belong to the one body must be able to partake of the one loaf. Christ could not be divided.

The same emphasis is also seen in one of Paul's most important statements on the status of women. 'Through faith you are all sons of God in union with Christ Jesus. Baptized into union with him, you have all put on Christ as a garment. There is no such thing as Jew and Greek, slave and free, male and female; for you are all one person in Christ Jesus' (Gal. 3: 26 ff.). Christian liberty pertains to all who are baptized into union with Jesus and has a direct and transforming effect on their social relationships. Since Paul clearly intends the three pairs in his list to be treated in parallel, his meaning must be located in that which is common to all three. And the one thing the three pairs have in common is that they denote the three deepest divisions which split the society of the Roman world. For Paul such divisions, typical rather than exhaustive, have no place in the thought or practice of those who are united with Christ.

Elsewhere the idea of a Christian society unspoiled by divisions of religion, culture, language, or social status is found in Colossians 3: 10 f. 'You have discarded the old nature with its deeds and have put on the new nature, which is being constantly renewed in the image of its Creator and brought to know God. There is no question here of Greek and Jew, circumcised, barbarian, Scythian, slave and free: but Christ is all, and is in all' (Col. 3: 10 f.). In Galatians the phrase 'male and female' had been an echo of Genesis 1: 26, a text which undoubtedly meant much to Paul (cf. 1 Cor. 11: 7); but here Genesis is given an entirely new emphasis: the creation of the human race in God's image does not belong to the dawn of history. It does not even belong to the more immediate past when Jesus inaugurated the new creation. It is an ongoing process, in which men and women are themselves summoned to an active participation. They must so frame their conduct as to allow room for a constant renewal which finds its primary expression in a growing insight into the character and purpose of God. In other words, Paul expects the Christian community to grow in its understanding of the faith and its practical implications. He thus allows for the possibility, even likelihood, that some of his ethical instructions will one day appear out of date.

This is particularly true of certain comments Paul makes in 1 Cor. 7, 11, and 14 on the role of women in the Church. 'For this case ought the woman to have power on her head because of the angels' (11: 10) has, of course, yielded a plethora of interpretations,[60] but here Paul is alluding to the angels as representatives and guardians of the old, pagan world order which is shortly to come under judgement (cf. 6: 3). The authority (*exousia*) which a woman should wear on her head, whether it be a veil or her own natural covering, is not to be worn in response to an unchanging natural decree, but only out of deference to the accepted conventions of the society in which she lives. Similarly in 1 Corinthians 7 the decision to postpone or refrain from marriage is based on the exigencies of the moment, not on any lasting theological necessity. Even the apparently misogynist comment of 14: 34 f. is best explained as a culturally determined form of behaviour (incessant chatter) or as a non-Pauline gloss.[61]

The same principle governed Paul's relations with the church of Jerusalem. Although he asserted that his gospel and his apostolic authority had come to him independently of the other apostles, it seems never to have occurred to him that either he or his converts should live independently of those who were in Christ before them. The collection for the needy Christians of Jerusalem which Paul organized throughout the churches he had founded was undertaken in the hope that it would make both givers and receivers aware of their common membership in Christ. For the Gentiles it was to be the acknowledgement of a debt of gratitude, the acceptance of responsibility for the

---

[60] A much fuller discussion of this evidence is found in G. B. Caird, 'St Paul and Women's Liberty', *BJRL* 54 (1972), 268 ff., and G. Osborne, 'Hermeneutics and Women in the Church', *JETS* 20 (1977), 337 ff.

[61] On the difficulties surrounding such texts as 1 Cor. 7: 1–9; 11: 3–10; and 14: 34 f., see Caird, 'Paul and Women's Liberty', 270 f., 276 ff.; M. D. Hooker, 'Authority on her Head: An Examination of 1 Corinthians 11: 10', *NTS* 10 (1963–4), 410 ff.; Barrett, *First Corinthians*, ad loc.; and W. J. Martin, '1 Corinthians 11: 2–16: An Interpretation' in W. W. Gasque and R. P. Martin (eds.), *Apostolic History and the Gospel* (Exeter, 1970), 231 ff. For the role of women in general in the New Testament, cf. E. Schüssler Fiorenza, *In Memory of Her* (New York, 1983); K. S. Keener, *Paul, Women, and Wives* (Peabody, Mass., 1992), especially 19 ff.; A. J. Malherbe, *Social Aspects of Early Christianity* (Philadelphia, 1983); W. A. Meeks, *The First Urban Christians: The Social World of the Apostle Paul* (New Haven, Conn., 1983); D. P. Nystrom, 'Not Many Wise, Powerful, or Noble: The Sociology of Primitive Christianity', Ph.D. dissertation, University of California, Davis, 1992; G. Theissen, *The Social Setting of Pauline Christianity: Essays on Corinth* (Philadelphia, 1983); and B. Witherington, *Women in the Earliest Churches* (Cambridge, 1991).

wider community to which they belonged, the realization of their equal status in the commonwealth of Israel; to the Jerusalem church it was to be a proof that the Pauline churches had really been brought into subjection to the Gospel of Christ, and for both it was to be a token of unity.

The other New Testament writers preserve a strangely similar pattern. Mark tells of the rending of the temple curtain, and he leaves little room for doubt that to him this is a figurative description of the effect of the crucifixion, closely parallel to the assertion in Ephesians that on the Cross Jesus demolished the dividing wall between Jew and Gentile (Eph. 2: 14), or to the picture drawn in Heb. 10: 19 f. of the crucified Jesus opening up a new and living way through the Temple curtain into that heavenly presence of which the Holy of Holies was but a shadowy symbol. The Epistle of James furthermore castigates those who would show any form of discrimination within the worshipping Church (2: 1–7).

An interest in the unity of Jesus' followers intense enough to rival that of Paul is found in the Fourth Gospel. Too often the modern ecumenically minded exegete has allowed the dominant ethos of this writer to be dictated by the words in the prayer of ch. 17: 'That they may all be one, as we are one' (v. 21). Wrenched from their context in the prayer, however, these words give the impression of a Johannine Jesus who regarded unity as a remote goal, faintly glimpsed in the mists of a far horizon. But in John's theology, as in Paul's, the union of the disciples with Jesus is achieved on the Cross. It is by dying that he, like a grain of wheat, ceases to be alone and bears a rich harvest (12: 24). It is in being lifted up from the earth that he draws the whole human race to himself (12: 32). Unity, then, is his gift to his followers: 'The glory you gave me I have given to them, to make them one as we are one' (17: 22). The gift, to be sure, requires a human response: it is a gift of life, and the recipients must live it, making their unity and mutual love visible in the eyes of the world. Not the least part of the apostolic commission is that the world is to be won for Christ by observing the unity of his followers: 'Then the world will know that you sent me, that you have loved them just as you have loved me' (17: 23).

7.

The Hope of Salvation

Christians, said Paul, do not need to grieve for their dead as do others, who have no hope (1 Thess. 4: 13). Now at first blush this might seem an ungenerous, not to say ill-informed, estimate of non-Christian religion. Surely the prevailing gloom of the first century, so well attested by its surviving epitaphs, ought not to have made Paul forget that many Jews believed in the resurrection of the just and many Gentiles in the immortality of the soul, or in an escape from mortality by initiation into one of the numerous mystery cults. If we look beyond Paul's immediate environment to the whole history of religion, then from many parts of the world and from many periods of history comes ample evidence that God has put 'immortal longings' into the human heart. Nevertheless, Paul's claim that the Christian alone has hope is not nonsensical if one makes a proper distinction between hope and desire. The *Oxford English Dictionary* defines hope as 'desire combined with expectation'. The word has, to be sure, like its counterparts in other languages, often been used to denote either a baseless optimism or a vague yearning after unattainable good. But if hope is to be genuine hope, it must be founded on something which affords reasonable grounds for confidence in its fulfilment. It must have a basis.

The ostensible basis for Christian hope in the New Testament is the resurrection of Jesus.[1] And here we need briefly to review what the New Testament writers have to say about the Easter event itself.

---

[1] On the resurrection of Jesus cf. e.g. R. H. Fuller, *The Formation of the Resurrection Narratives* (London, 1971); C. F. D. Moule (ed.), *The Significance of the Message of the Resurrection for Faith in Jesus Christ* (London, 1968); H. Grass, *Ostergeschehen und Osterberichte* (Göttingen, 1964); B. Rigaux, *Dieu l'a ressuscité. Exégèse et théologie biblique* (Gembloux, 1973); U. Wilckens, *Resurrection* (Atlanta, 1978); Pheme Perkins, *Resurrection* (New York, 1984); Rowan Williams, *Resurrection* (Cleveland, Ohio, 1982); and Peter Carnley, *The Structure of Resurrection Belief* (Oxford, 1987). For a useful recent survey of the literature, cf. Colin Brown, 'Resurrection', *NIDNTT* iii. 281 ff.

It is well known that the earliest New Testament account of Jesus' resurrection is found not in the Gospels, but in the letters of Paul, particularly 1 Corinthians 15. There (v. 3) Paul mentions a tradition he had received from the earliest Church which included a list of eyewitnesses to the resurrection. It has sometimes been said[2] that Paul shows no knowledge of, or belief in, the story of the empty tomb, and that for at least two reasons: (1) Paul mentions only the recorded appearances of Jesus, including the appearance to himself; (2) he emphasizes that the resurrection body is not a body of flesh but a spiritual body or a body of glory (1 Cor. 15: 44; Phil. 3: 21). But a closer reading shows that Paul clearly presupposed the empty tomb. For Paul Christ was 'buried' (v. 4). Since for Jews a dead person will naturally be buried, the statement is hard to explain unless something unusual had happened to the one who had been buried. Paul goes on (vv. 42 ff.) to distinguish between the physical body of this life and the spiritual body to come, and having said that flesh and blood cannot inherit the Kingdom of God, he explains that the spiritual body must come out of the physical body by a process of transformation. 'We must all be changed' (v. 51). It is the corruptible, physical body, not a disembodied spirit, which must put on immortality (v. 53); and it is clear that the argument turns on the belief that the body of Jesus had already undergone such a transformation.

To all this might be added the simple fact that no Jew would have used the word 'resurrection' to describe an afterlife in which the physical body was left to the grave.[3]

The accounts of the empty tomb and the resurrection appearances in the Gospels are therefore only making explicit what is already implicit in Paul. The emphases and details of the Gospel accounts of course differ, and it is unlikely that they could ever be harmonized so as to provide one thoroughly consistent, neatly articulated account.[4] The Marcan, Matthaean, and Johannine traditions stress the post-

---

[2] Cf. the discussion of Williams, *Resurrection*, 100 f. C. K. Barrett, *A Commentary on the First Epistle to the Corinthians* (London, 1968), commenting on 15: 4, says 'if he was buried, and was subsequently seen alive outside his grave, the grave must have been empty, and may well have been seen to be empty' (p. 340).

[3] So S. H. Hooke, *The Resurrection of Christ as History and Experience* (London, 1967), 5 ff., and R. H. Fuller, *Formation*, 17. Fuller cites Isa. 26: 19, Dan. 12: 2, and 1 En. 92: 3 as examples.

[4] 'Divergences in detail are ... such as one would expect from independent and excited witnesses' (B. M. Metzger, *The New Testament: Its Background, Growth, and Content* (Nashville, 1983), 127).

resurrection Galilean appearances (although Mark has only the promise),[5] whereas for Luke the appearances are limited to the vicinity of Jerusalem. The reason for Luke's emphasis is clearly theological: while he allows time for the post-resurrection Galilean phase (Acts 1: 3), he makes Jerusalem the centre of activity in order to stress the Jewish roots of the future Gentile mission.

And yet, these differences notwithstanding, there remain interesting convergences between the accounts. Luke 24: 13–43, for instance, has a close resemblance to John 20: 3–29, and both are almost certainly dependent upon allied streams of oral tradition.[6] Both narratives agree that Jesus appeared in a bodily form not subject to normal physical limitations, and both go out of their way to show that Jesus' body was corporeal. We can probably discern three possible motives behind this emphasis, particularly as it is found in Luke:

1. The first motive was historical. Luke had inherited from the Aramaic-speaking Church a tradition in which Jesus eats and drinks with his disciples after the resurrection (Acts 10: 36–43).

2. The second motive was apologetic. Whereas the Greeks tended to think of reality in terms of abstractions and universal truths, the Semitic mind saw reality as particular and concrete. The highly material splendours of the new Jerusalem in the Revelation (21: 2 ff.) indicate that it is a place not of rarified spirituality but of 'solid joys'. To any Jew a disembodied spirit could only seem a ghost, not a living being; and since Jesus' enemies would certainly try to explain away the claims of the disciples by arguing that they had seen a ghost, an apologetic motive may be assumed.

3. The third motive was theological. The early Christian heresy of Docetism, which claimed that the divine Christ descended upon the human Jesus at his baptism and left him just before the crucifixion, is most likely the problem underlying the accounts of Luke, the Fourth Gospel, and the Epistles of John, all of which vividly wish to claim that the risen Christ and the flesh-and-blood Jesus are one and the same. The Epistles and Gospel of John certainly contain polemical references to this aberration (1 John 2: 22; 4: 2 f.; John 1: 14; 6: 53;

---

[5] Most scholars now recognize that Mark 16: 9–20 is not part of the original Gospel.

[6] See in general E. Osty, 'Les points de contact entre le récit de la passion dans saint Luc et dans saint Jean,' *RSR* 39 (1951), 146 ff.; P. Parker, 'Luke and the Fourth Evangelist', *NTS* 9 (1962–3), 317 ff.; and M.-É. Boismard, 'Saint Luc et la redaction du quatrième évangile', *RB* 69 (1962), 185 ff.

20: 24–9), and it is possible that for this reason Luke also wished to identify the risen Christ firmly with the flesh-and-blood Jesus.

It is well known that for Rudolf Bultmann the resurrection is to be understood in the New Testament as a completely 'private' event in the lives of Jesus' followers, in the same sense that Isaiah's vision (Isa. 6: 1 ff.) or Buddha's illumination under the bo tree were private events. It did not happen independently of the early Church's faith which later spoke of it.[7]

Now while it is clearly not the purpose of the New Testament theologian to become embroiled in arguments for the historicity of the resurrection, which are properly found in dogmatic and apologetic works, we must ask whether this is what the New Testament writers themselves claim. And here the various accounts suggest precisely the opposite of Bultmann's understanding. For Paul, Mark, Luke, Matthew, and John the resurrection is to be believed not because it had happened to the early Christians, but because it had happened to Jesus. It was the event which created the faith, not vice versa.[8]

And yet the New Testament writers do not stop with saying that the resurrection was an event which happened to one man, on a particular morning, in AD 29 or 30. They go on to claim that it was the anticipation of something to come in the future which will have implications for the whole human race. 'God not only raised our Lord from the dead; he will also raise us by His power' (1 Cor. 6: 14; cf. 15: 12–20; 2 Cor. 4: 14; Rom. 8: 11). 'Praise be to the God and Father of our Lord Jesus Christ, who in His mercy gave us new birth into a living hope by the resurrection of Jesus Christ from the dead' (1 Pet. 1: 3). 'Because I live, you too shall live' (John 14: 19). 'To the conqueror I will grant a seat beside me on my throne, as I myself conquered and sat down beside my Father on his throne' (Rev. 3: 21). Death did not have the final word over Jesus, and therefore Christians may equally expect that one day they will be raised to the same kind of incorruptible glory.

But who knows where or when? From the days of the earliest Christian

---

[7] Cf. 'The New Testament and Mythology', in H. W. Bartsch (ed.) *Kerygma and Myth* (London, 1972), 39 f. A similar position is put forward by W. Marxen, 'The Resurrection of Jesus as a Historical and Theological Problem', in Moule, *Significance of the Resurrection*, 15 ff.

[8] See again the judicious and balanced treatment of Brown, 'Resurrection', esp. 292 ff.

Church to the present, attempts to answer this enormous double question have led the enquirer into the dark and tangled wood called New Testament eschatology. Those seeking a way out have been often assured that there are at least three beams of light by which their steps may be guided: (1) The first Christians were almost, if not quite, unanimous in expecting an imminent Parousia of Jesus. (2) They thought that they had the authority of Jesus for this expectation. (3) It did not happen. Now it will be our contention that the only one of the three which provides any real illumination is the third. Ever since Johannes Weiss[9] and Albert Schweitzer[10] replaced the Cross with eschatology as the centre of New Testament theology, it has been generally accepted that either Jesus expected an imminent End, and was wrong, or the early Church so thoroughly misunderstood him as to attribute to him this erroneous belief. It is hardly too much to say that eschatology has been the greatest single obstacle to the quest for the historical Jesus (below, Chapter 9). Because of eschatology Schweitzer himself ended with a Jesus 'who comes to us as One unknown, without a name',[11] speaking to us out of a discredited world-view. Because of eschatology Bultmann found himself forced (though far from unwilling) to demythologize the New Testament and leave us only with the bodiless grin of existentialism.[12] Even Dodd,[13] who spoke more sense than most on the subject, granted that the early Church had misunderstood Jesus and recast his teaching in the mould of Jewish apocalyptic. Kümmel,[14] rejecting Dodd's solution in favour of the belief that Jesus himself was mistaken, grappled with the theological implications of early Christian eschatology, only to emerge with a solution of his own indistinguishable from Dodd's. And later Hans Conzelmann[15] was to argue that Luke totally transformed the primitive tradition he received, substituting for eschatology a theology of world history which opened up an indefinite future for the Church. The existence of such radically differing solutions indicates that the next

---

[9] J. Weiss, *The History of Primitive Christianity* (ET, New York, 1937), and *Jesus' Proclamation of the Kingdom of God* (Philadephia, 1971).

[10] A. Schweitzer, *The Quest for the Historical Jesus* (London, 1954).

[11] Ibid. 403.

[12] R. Bultmann, 'The New Testament and Mythology'.

[13] C. H. Dodd, *The Parables of the Kingdom* (London, 1941), *passim*.

[14] W. G. Kümmel, *Promise and Fulfilment: The Eschatological Message of Jesus* (London, 1957), esp. 151–5.

[15] H. Conzelmann, *The Theology of St Luke* (London, 1960).

question to be put on the conference table concerns the very nature of eschatology itself.

7.2. THE MEANING OF 'ESCHATOLOGY'

'Eschatology' is a nineteenth-century German term which was introduced into English as early as 1845. Its classical definition is found in the *Oxford English Dictionary* (1891 and 1933): 'The department of theological science concerned with the four last things, death, judgement, heaven and hell.' In this sense 'eschatology' deals with the ultimate destiny of the individual. Since the beginning of this century, however, the word has been used in the sense we all now take for granted, to cover the biblical teaching about the destiny of the world and the working out of God's purposes in and through his holy people.[16] These two distinct types of eschatology may be called 'individual' and 'historical'. The second sense of the word was undoubtedly imported into France and England from Germany, and through the influence of Weiss and Schweitzer it soon ousted the original sense from its primacy and almost from the study of theology itself. Schweitzer himself attributed the use of the word in its national and cosmic sense to Reimarus, the erratic genius of the eighteenth century who taught that Jesus was a revolutionary who tried to bring in the Kingdom of God by force, only to be thwarted by the refusal of the Jewish nation to join in the rebellion.[17] The historic is almost the only kind of eschatology we find in the Old Testament—hardly surprising when it is remembered that almost all the books of the Old Testament were already written before the Jews achieved a belief in an afterlife (below). It is regrettable, however, that the one word ever came to be used to cover two such divergent forms of future hope, for its use has almost inevitably led to the quite baseless assumption that the finality which attaches to death, judgement, heaven, and hell must be characteristic also of

---

[16] In I. Singer *et al.* (eds.), *The Jewish Encyclopaedia* (New York, 1901–6) v. 209, Kaufmann Kohler wrote: 'Jewish Eschatology deals primarily and principally with the final destiny of the Jewish nation and the world in general, and only secondarily with the future of the individual: the main concern of Hebrew legislator, prophet, and apocalyptic writer being Israel as the people of God and the victory of His truth and justice.'

[17] H. S. Reimarus (1694–1768) is best known for his defence of deism and the posthumous publication by Lessing of his *Fragmente eines Urgenannten* (*Fragments by an Unknown Author*). Cf. Schweitzer, *Quest*, 13 f., and the most recent edition of the *Fragments* by C. H. Talbert (Philadelphia, 1985).

national eschatology, and therefore to an intolerable kind of literalism in the interpretation of the imagery used by prophet and apocalyptist to describe the Day of the Lord. The complexity of the issue is exacerbated in the New Testament, since by this time both Jews and Christians hold a well-established belief in life after death. It is therefore not always easy to tell whether we are dealing with national or individual eschatology, and, as the Church moved more and more away from its original Palestinian setting into the Gentile world, there must have been a tendency to reinterpret the national in terms of the individual.

The distinction between the two senses is well illustrated by a passage in the Revelation of John:

When he broke the fifth seal, I saw underneath the altar the souls of these who had been slaughtered for God's word and for holding to the testimony. They cried aloud, 'How long, sovereign Lord, holy and true, is it to be before you pass sentence and avenge our blood on the inhabitants of earth?' Then each of them was given a white robe, and they were told to wait patiently for a little while longer, until the roll of their brothers should be complete, those who were to be killed in Christ's service as they had been (Rev. 6: 9–11).

The question 'how long?' takes us straight to the heart of all eschatology, whether personal or national; for, as we have seen, eschatology arises out of the clash between faith in a benevolent purpose of God and the harsh facts of a ruthless world. 'If only we knew,' say the martyrs, 'where it is all going to end.' But the point is that these martyrs are given a double answer to their question. First, 'each of them was given a white robe'. These robes are unquestionably the symbol of eternal life; they have already been promised to the conqueror, along with other symbols of heavenly bliss, in the letters to the seven churches; and in the next chapter John is to see the white-robed throng of victorious martyrs led by the Good Shepherd into the green pastures beside the still waters of the spring of life. But the gift of immortality is not in itself an adequate answer to the cry of the martyrs. They have died for God's word, and no theodicy can justify their death except the triumph of the cause for which they gave their lives. It is for the vindication of God's justice within earthly history that they are 'told to wait patiently a little while longer'. The initial victory of God over the powers of evil has been won by Christ on the Cross. But that victory must be repeated over and over again in the victory of the conquerors, and only when the full tally of martyrs is complete will the final victory be won.

That during the formative period of Jewish eschatology the Hebrew people had no belief in the afterlife is a fact which can hardly be overstressed. Sheol, like the Hades of the Greeks, was the land of the dead, the final dumping-ground, and was usually associated with such terms as death, oblivion, darkness, the grave, and the pit. Its inhabitants were shades, wraiths, pale photocopies relegated to the subterranean filing cabinet.[18] The individual only survives via a good name and progeny. It was *national* survival that counted; and as late as the second century BC Jesus ben Sira still understood the reward of pious Jews to be the continuance of their children 'within the covenants, where their name lives for ever' (Ecclus. 44: 12–14).

When belief in an afterlife finally began to emerge, it was as a by-product of a belief in a new age of world history dawning for the nation of Israel. The idea of resurrection, which we automatically associate with personal immortality, was first used by Hosea and Eze-kiel figuratively of a national revival, and only four centuries later did it come to be used literally by Daniel of the resuscitation of the right-eous dead, who would need their bodies to join in the glorious future of the nation, to which God had at last entrusted world dominion (Dan. 12: 2). Through the doctrine of the remnant another element of individualism was injected into the national hope, because it became a matter of individual faith and loyalty who did and who did not belong to the holy people of God. This dawning perception of the worth of the individual to God, often associated with Jeremiah, achieves full expression in some of the later psalms, the idea now being that the righteous have a communion with God that even death cannot destroy. When the author of the Wisdom of Solomon claims that 'the souls of the just are in God's hand . . . for though in the sight of men they are punished, they have a sure hope of immortality . . . because God tested them and found them worthy to be his' (3: 1–5), he may be using language borrowed from the Hellenistic world,[19] but his ideas are a bequest from his Jewish ancestors.

Yet in spite of a number of such points of contact, personal escha-tology and national eschatology must remain distinct, and much of our

---

[18] According to Ezek. 32: 22–30 the dead in Sheol are arranged in nations. Cf. also the beginning of Homer's *Iliad*, which depicts the bodies of the soldiers littering the field of battle while their shades are in Hades.

[19] The Greeks, no longer content with the drabness of the classical Hades, came under the influence of the philosophers to believe that the body is a tomb and the earth a prison house from which the pious soul must strive to escape at death.

difficulty with New Testament eschatology arises out of a confusion between the two. The situation is not helped by the fact that even within each of these two separate types, New Testament eschatology exhibits a bewildering variety. If we restrict ourselves to personal eschatology, what are we to make of the promise to the penitent thief, 'Today you shall be with me in Paradise' (Luke 23: 43), which appears to conflict so strikingly with the doctrine that Jesus himself rose on the third day, and also with the widespread belief that the dead sleep until the resurrection at the last day? We cannot avoid the difficulty by demoting Paradise to the status of a waiting room, for then the promise would be less, not more, than the thief had asked. In any case we have the parable of Dives and Lazarus (Luke 16: 19–31) to reckon with; for they appear to be already assigned at death to their respective destinations of torment and bliss. When we turn to the Epistles of Paul, we receive the general impression that the resurrection of the body is to take place only at the last trumpet. Yet in his first letter he can say that whether we wake or sleep we shall be alive with Christ (1 Thess. 5: 10), and in his last letter he can speak of being ready to depart to be with Christ (Phil. 1: 23; below). In the Revelation there is the passage already mentioned, in which the martyrs are given the white robes which equip them for eternal life in the celestial city. Yet at a later stage in the story, after they have waited the 'little while longer', they are said to be the only ones to participate in 'the first resurrection', which enables them to share the millennial reign of Christ (20: 4–6).

This handful of examples will be amplified below, but at this point it may serve to illustrate the problem. In the past there has been a tendency to treat these varieties of eschatology as evidence either for a steady growth from primitive *naïveté* to ultimate sophistication, or for a decline from a hypothetical norm, the teaching of Jesus, which the early Church—whether from weakness of intellect or through a misguided zeal for applying that teaching to a new *Sitz im Leben*— totally misunderstood.

But rather than treating eschatology as just one of the doctrines of the creed or of the departments of Christian theology, we should think of eschatological language as capable of being adapted to many purposes. If we define an *eschaton* as that beyond which nothing can conceivably happen, it is no doubt proper to imagine an *eschaton* both for the individual and for the world. But at least 90 per cent of what we have come to call 'eschatology' in the Bible has nothing to do with an *eschaton* in this strict sense; it is rather the use of eschatological language to describe something quite different. It belongs not with the doctrines of Creation, Sin, Atonement, and the Church, but rather with metaphor, parable, typology, allegory, and myth.

We have by now noted on a number of occasions the device of metaphor, where language is transferred from one situation to another. Words or ideas intended literally in the first situation are to be taken non-literally in the second. Thus terms which would be literal in the lawcourt, the slave-market, or the battlefield may mean something new when used to express the death of Christ. What is not so commonly recognized is that there are other, more complex forms of linguistic transference than metaphor. It is possible for language which is typical of one situation to be transferred to another in such a way that it is literally intended in both. It is also possible for language which is already metaphorical in the source situation to be used to illustrate or interpret quite a different situation. A prime example of these three kinds of transference is derived from the language of the Eucharist. When Mark (6: 41) tells the story of the feeding of the 4,000, he says of Jesus, 'taking the seven loaves and giving thanks he broke and gave . . .' It is generally agreed that this is an intentional use of euchar-istic language, though it is employed to describe an event which is not a eucharist; and the breaking, the giving, and the eating are literal in both cases. When John (Rev. 3: 20) is told to write to Laodicea, 'Here I stand at the door knocking; if anyone hears my voice and opens the door, I will come in and have supper with him and he with me', he is using words reminiscent of the literal supper of the Eucharist in a metaphor to describe an analogous but highly individual and personal encounter with the heavenly Christ. And, as we have already seen when the other John (6: 53) has Jesus say, 'Unless you eat the flesh of the Son of Man and drink his blood, you do not have life in your-selves', he is talking not about the Eucharist, but about belief in the incarnation. Language which is already metaphorical in its eucharistic setting is being used to describe a response of faith which is logically anterior to any participation in the Eucharist. Such language may be described, at the risk of pleonasm, as 'transferred metaphor'. In pre-cisely the same way the highly metaphorical and symbolic language of eschatology can be used by transference to describe all sorts of other experiences and situations.

Before looking at examples of eschatological language being used by transference in a non-eschatological situation, we need first to guard ourselves against a very obvious line of attack. It might be said that we are committing an anachronism, attributing to the first century an understanding of the mechanics of language which is comparatively modern.[20] The writers of the New Testament were unlettered people who had never heard of Ricœur, Bréal, or Wittgenstein, and they took their picture language, and especially their eschatology, with simple literalness. This is no 'straw man' argument. The whole of Bultmann's essay on 'demythologizing' was based on the assumption that the early Christians were unaware of the mythological nature of the universe in which they lived. Yet the idea that Jesus had only the inadequate linguistic tools of his time—metaphor and picture language[21]—open to him to express his understanding of life is an insufferably patronizing attitude which betrays more ignorance of the nature of language than it ascribes to Jesus. It assumes that we in our lofty superiority have a kind of language which is free from the baby-talk of metaphor and pictorial imagery. And yet, when we consider the mastery of Jesus over parable, hyperbole, irony, and other figures of speech, it is incredible that he should have been ignorant of the nature of the language he was using. Paul, too, regularly warns his readers that he is speaking by way of human analogy, lest they should be tempted to take him literally. And John of Patmos gives a similar warning that the city whose name is Sodom and Egypt, where the Lord was crucified, is an allegory, in case, like so many modern commentators who ignore his warning, they should imagine that he means Jerusalem. Of course, there were plenty of people in the first century who took literally what others meant figuratively, but such people are not unknown in the twentieth century, even among the ranks of biblical scholars.

A fuller answer to this objection can, however, be provided by a study of the use of myth. Here 'myth' means what the anthropologist means by myth: a story about the remote past in order to explain the facts, practices, and beliefs of the present and to provide imagery

---

[20] *Editor's note*: This criticism has on occasion been made in reviews of Caird's own work. Cf. for instance M. F. Wiles in *JTS* NS 33 (1982), 199: 'I suspect that Professor Caird is inclined to modernize the intention of the ancient writers, but there is no easy way to determine whether or not this is the case.' A similar statement is made by C. F. D. Moule in his review of Caird's *Paul's Letters from Prison*, in *JTS* NS 28 (1977), 162. There Caird's 'demythologizing' of the principalities and powers is thought to be 'too rational'. In response to this Caird would have certainly replied that twentieth-century people chronically underestimate the rationality of writers such as St Paul.

[21] Cf. *ERE* v. 384: 'Perhaps to Him there was open only the inadequate language of His time—metaphor and pictorial imagery.'

whereby each succeeding generation may interpret and express its experience.[22] A good example is the seven-headed dragon of Revelation 12. This dragon has its origin in the Creation myth, known to us from Babylonian and Canaanite sources as well as from the Old Testament. We have seen this device used in the Exodus motif, wherein the language of the Creation myth is regularly used to describe historical situations. Deutero-Isaiah applies it both to the Exodus and to the return from Babylonian exile: let the arm of the Lord which cut Rahab in two at Creation, and again at the Red Sea to make a path for the redeemed, do it again to bring about a new Exodus (51: 9–11). Ezekiel identifies the ocean dragon with Pharaoh (29: 3) and Jeremiah with Nebuchadnezzar (51: 34). The figurative language which is proper to the Creation story is therefore used in connection with any crisis of history in which the writer detects a new victory of God over the forces of chaos. The dragon is a true myth precisely because he is capable of wearing any number of human faces. Similarly when Nero had coins struck bearing his head irradiated, he was claiming to re-enact the myth of Apollo, the sun god, and to be leading the human race in its age-long battle against the powers of darkness. Mythological language thus forms the exact counterpart to what should be said about eschatological language. If language and imagery proper to the story of the beginning of history can be used to interpret and give theological significance to events happening within the course of history, there is no reason why language and imagery proper to the story of history's end should not be used by a similar transference. The Old Testament writers were well versed in this type of language. Jeremiah, for example, had a vision in which he saw the whole earth return to primeval chaos: 'I saw the earth—there it lay, waste and void, the sky, and its light was gone. I saw the mountains totter before my eyes, and all the hills rocking to and fro. I saw—and not a man was there, the very birds of the air had fled' (4: 23–5). Another prophet had a vision of Paradise restored, the wolf keeping company with the lamb and the leopard with the kid (Isa. 11: 1–9). Yet neither of these visions has anything to do with the end of the world. The one is a vivid prediction of an invasion of Judah by foreign armies, the other an idealized picture of an earthly kingdom, in which justice still needs to be administered and the rights of the poor protected. The classic description of the

[22] As defined, for instance, by Joseph Campbell in his numerous works, the last of which was *The Power of Myth* (with Bill Moyers) (New York, 1988).

Day of the Lord, found in Isaiah 13, begins: 'The Day of the Lord is coming, cruel in its fury and fierce anger, to make the earth a desert and exterminate its sinners. The stars in the sky and their constellations shall withhold their light; the sun shall be dark at its rising, and the moon shall cease to shine. I will punish the world for its evil and the wicked for their sin.' At first glance this might appear to be both cosmic and final; and yet, when we read on, we discover that what the prophet expects is the invasion and destruction of the Babylonian Empire by the armies of the Medes. Turning from prophecy to apocalyptic, we find a difference of literary convention, but no difference of theological content. The book of Daniel was written in time of persecution, and the only end its author was interested in was the one he refers to in his last chapter: 'When the shattering of the power of the holy people comes to an end, all this will be completed' (Dan. 12: 7). The lesson of the book, which Nebuchadnezzar has to learn the hard way, is that 'the Most High controls the kingdom of men and gives it to whom He chooses' (4: 17, 25, 32). When the prophet sees the throne of judgement erected, this is not the end of the world, but the climax of history, in which world dominion is to pass from the bestial and tyrannical oppressors by whom it has been exercised into the hands of the saints of the Most High, represented by that symbolic figure, 'one like a son of man' (7: 9–27; below, Chapter 9).

7.3. THE PAROUSIA AND ITS IMMINENCE

Having cleared away some of the confusion which surrounds the word 'eschatology', we may now turn to the question of Jesus' future coming—his Parousia. And it is clear that the New Testament writers believed in a decisive and consummate intervention of God in history. Christians are to 'wait expectantly for the revealing of our Lord Jesus Christ' (1 Cor. 1: 7), who is to be 'revealed from heaven with his mighty angels in blazing fire', and who will 'do justice upon those who refuse to acknowledge God and upon those who will not obey the gospel of our Lord Jesus Christ' (2 Thess. 1: 7 f.). 'For at the trumpet of command the Lord himself will descend from heaven; first the Christian dead will rise, then we who are left alive shall join them, caught up in the clouds to meet them in the air' (1 Thess. 4: 17). 'Then comes the End, when he hands over the Kingdom to his God and Father' (1 Cor. 15: 24). 'Listen! I tell you a mystery; we shall not all die, but we shall all be changed, in the twinkling of an eye, at the last trumpet' (1 Cor. 15: 51 f.). 'Then the lawless one will be revealed, whom the Lord Jesus will slay with the breath of his mouth, and annihilate by the radiance of his coming' (2 Thess. 2: 8). 'So Christ, who was offered once to bear the sins of many, will appear a second time, not to deal with sin but to save those who are eagerly awaiting him' (Heb. 9: 28).

Less numerous, but equally striking, are those passages which appear to lend support to the view that Jesus, or the early Church (or both) believed that his historical consummation would take place within their own lifetime. 'Before you have gone through all the towns of Israel the Son of Man will have come' (Matt. 10: 23). 'There are some of those standing here who will not taste death before they have seen the Kingdom of God having come with power' (Mark 9: 1). 'Jesus said, "I am; and you will see the Son of Man seated at the right hand of the Power and coming with the clouds of heaven"' (Mark 14: 62). 'It is time for you to wake out of sleep, for deliverance is nearer to us now than it was when first we believed' (Rom. 13: 11). 'The Lord is near' (Phil. 4: 7). 'O Lord, Come!' (1 Cor. 16: 22). 'For soon, very soon, he who is to come will come; he will not delay' (Heb. 10: 37). 'You must be patient and stout-hearted, for the coming of the Lord is near' (Jas. 5: 8). 'The end of all things is upon us . . . The time has come for the judgement to begin: it is beginning with God's own household' (1 Pet. 4: 17).

The excitement which such statements would arouse among the earliest Christians is now difficult to recreate. During the first century events were continually happening which, either within Judaism or the ministry of Jesus, inexorably fostered a surge of expectancy. Does Caligula's intention to set up his statue in the Jerusalem Temple imply that Daniel's 'desecrating horror' (2 Thess. 2: 1–12) is at hand? Do 'wars and rumours of wars' in Palestine suggest that God's wrath is finally descending on the children of disobedience (1 Thess. 1: 16)? Is persecution of Christians the first instalment of the Last Judgement, which begins at 'the household of God' (1 Pet. 4: 17)? Does the fall of Jerusalem mark the beginning of the wedding-banquet of the Son of God (Matt. 22: 7)? Is Domitian's demand to be worshipped the rise of Antichrist against God's Kingdom (Rev. 13)?

These are difficult questions which require careful answers. And perhaps the best place to begin is with Paul's experience in Thessalonica. In what are probably the earliest New Testament writings Paul is faced with the dilemma that his Greek converts cannot understand the Jewish idea of history. To the predominantly Gentile church at Thessalonica the question of the time of the Parousia was a source of such confusion that he had to produce two letters in quick succession to deal with it. In his first letter Paul claimed that the Day of the Lord would come without warning, at any moment, 'as a thief in the night' (1 Thess. 5: 2); in his second letter he cautions his readers to temper their frenzy of excitement with the knowledge that the Day would not come immediately, but only after 'the rebellion' (2 Thess. 2: 3). Some modern interpreters[23] have been so perturbed by this apparent contradiction that they have denied the authenticity of 2 Thessalonians, and can we doubt that the church at Thessalonica was equally confounded? How can two such seemingly irreconcilable views be held by any rational, sane person?

The same question presents itself elsewhere in Paul's writings. He asks the church at Rome, for instance, to

remember how critical the moment is. It is time for you to wake out of sleep, for deliverance is nearer to us now than it was when first we believed. It is far on in the night; day is near. Let us therefore throw off the deeds of darkness and put on our armour as soldiers of the light. Let us behave with decency as befits the day: no revelling or drunkenness, no debauchery or vice, no quarrels or jealousies! Let Christ himself be the armour you wear; give no more thought to satisfying the bodily appetites (Rom. 13: 11–14).

Those who take this passage with pedantic literalness find proof that for Paul the Parousia was so near it would happen in his own lifetime. But this reading cannot but do violence to the paragraph as a whole. Certainly 'our deliverance' or 'salvation' takes place at the Parousia, i.e. the dawning of day. Before then it is night, and night is the time for sleep. Since their conversion Paul and his friends have been slum-

---

[23] The first writer to deny the authenticity of 2 Thess. on the basis of its eschatology was apparently J. E. C. Schmidt. ('Vermuthungen über den beyden Briefe,' repr. in W. Trilling, *Untersuchungen zum zweiten Thessalonicherbrief* (Leipzig, 1972), 159 ff.). More recently C. Masson, *Les Epîtres aux Thessaloniciens, à Philemon* (Neuchatel, 1957), and G. L. Holland, *The Tradition that You Received from Us* (Tübingen, 1988), 91 ff., have advanced the same position. According to Holland, the author of 2 Thess. has reinterpreted Pauline eschatology 'into a more systematic and overtly apocalyptic form' (p. 127). But see also the thorough examination of R. Jewett, *The Thessalonian Correspondence: Pauline Rhetoric and Millenarian Piety* (Philadelphia, 1986). Jewett concludes that 'the evidence concerning the authenticity of 2 Thessalonians is equivocal, with the likelihood fairly strongly on the side of Pauline authorship' (16 f.).

bering, having set the alarm clock for an hour before dawn. But now the clock is waking them to the dawning of day. Paul had already told the Thessalonians that Christians are 'children of day' and 'children of light', and so did not belong to night or darkness (1 Thess. 5: 4–5). In Romans 13 Christians are not being asked to wake up and discard their nocturnal existence for the first time; they are being asked to recall that watchfulness to the allures of this age is to be expected of children of the light. What then can 'our deliverance is nearer to us now than it was when first we believed' mean? There are two possible ways of taking the comment: (1) The darkness which is nearly over equals the old pagan order which Paul believed is approaching its doom, and is hence more dangerous than ever in its final agony. Thus Christians need not fear trials and persecution during this period of pagan opposition; it is not permanent, and deliverance is progressively coming nearer. (2) 'Deliverance' means final salvation, which can come only when the gospel has been preached universally, when the human race has been allowed time to repent, and when the image of Christ has been built up fully in the Church. Either (1) or (2) makes reasonable sense, but perhaps we should maintain a slight presumption towards (2), the more traditional view, in which case Paul is saying that enough progress has been made to assure the Christian that history *is* moving towards its divinely appointed goal and that the struggle against the principalities and powers in not futile.

It has similarly been held that 1 Corinthians 7 contains views about marriage which result from Paul's belief that the time is too short for such fleshly frolics.[24] There are three expressions which lend support to this interpretation: 'a time of stress like the present' (7: 26), 'the critical time will not last long' (7: 29), and 'the form of this world is passing away' (7: 31). But, again, such comments are capable of two interpretations: (1) Paul is here saying that the end of the world is imminent. (2) In a period when the old regime is beginning to disintegrate, Christians must expect some unpleasant death pangs. Our decision in this case depends on what meaning should be given to 'this world', an expression Paul elsewhere uses of the old order which has now been superseded. Those considering marriage (7: 27–8), fathers with young daughters (7: 36–8), and slaves longing for freedom (7: 21) should not be ultimately concerned with their present status.

---

[24] Cf. the authorities cited by A. L. Moore, *The Parousia in the New Testament* (Leiden, 1966), 114 f.

Yet Paul's 'asceticism' is strangely half-hearted. His one controlling idea is that Christians should be 'free from anxiety'. It is not just that marriage distracts one from full-time ministry. Christians might spare themselves the sort of anxieties which married people are likely to encounter in times of duress (7: 28). The one appeal he never employs is that they should be ready for the Parousia. 'In saying this for your own good I have no wish to keep you on a tight rein; I only want you to be free from distraction in your devotion to the Lord' (7: 35, REB).[25]

Those who have found Paul's comments on this point difficult to resolve into a coherent picture have had similar problems with Mark's Gospel. Mark contains an entire chapter (13) in which he discusses the premonitory signs which will precede the day of the Son of Man, and the chapter ends with the warning (vv. 35–7): 'Begin watching now, for you do not know when the time will come.' Some have explained the apparent tensions in the chapter as the result of botched editing, others (e.g. L. Hartman[26] and L. Gaston[27]) as the product of a prophetic tradition which was constantly applying and reapplying the words of Jesus to new situations so as to make Mark 13 more a repository of later Christian prophetic utterances than a single, unified dominical discourse. If Mark's Gospel, on the other hand, is seen as the product of a Hebrew mind, whether Jesus' or Mark's, which is not uncomfortable with the juxtaposition of incompatibles, the

[25] Barrett, *First Corinthians*, 178, speaks of 'social and mercantile institutions' which have 'no permanence'. B. W. Winter ('Secular and Christian Responses to Corinthian Famines', *TB* 40 (1989), 86 ff.) argues similarly (and persuasively) that Paul's views regarding marriage in 1 Cor. 7: 25 ff. are dictated by uncertainty brought about by an imminent local famine. The mood of recent scholarly opinion is clearly against taking 1 Cor. 7 as indicating an imminent 'end of the world', as that phrase is normally understood.

[26] L. Hartman, *Prophecy Interpreted: The Formation of Some Jewish Apocalyptic Texts and of the Eschatological Discourse, Mark 13 par.* (Lund, 1966).

[27] L. Gaston, *No Stone on Another: Studies in the Significance of the Fall of Jerusalem in the Synoptic Gospels* (Leiden, 1970). More recent works dealing with apocalyptic should also be consulted in their relevant sections, including the following: D. C. Allison, *The End of the Ages has Come* (Philadelphia, 1985); G. R. Beasley-Murray, *Jesus and the Future* (London, 1954), and *Jesus and the Kingdom of God* (Grand Rapids, 1986); R. W. Crown, 'The Non-Literal Use of Eschatological Language in Jewish Apocalyptic and the New Testament', D. Phil. thesis, Oxford, 1986; D. Ford, *The Abomination of Desolation in Biblical Eschatology* (Washington, DC, 1979); T. J. Geddert, *Watchwords: Mark 13 in Markan Eschatology* (Sheffield, 1989); R. H. Hiers, *Jesus and the Future* (Atlanta, 1981); J. Marcus and M. L. Soards, *Apocalyptic and the New Testament* (Sheffield, 1989); and D. Wenham, *The Rediscovery of Jesus' Eschatological Discourse* (Sheffield, 1984).

interpreter may be a good way along the narrow path that leads to understanding.

Part of our problem as logical moderns remains this: Mark 13 opens with a prediction of the destruction of the Temple, and the disciples ask when this is to take place. Jesus then apparently answers them with an irrelevant discussion of the end of the world. But what if in this national catastrophe his disciples may see the coming of the Son of Man to whom God has entrusted authority over the nations (cf. Dan. 7: 22; John 5: 27; 1 Cor. 6: 27)? The other famous contradiction of the chapter, in which Jesus seems to know that the End will come within a generation, but God alone knows the day or the hour (13: 30, 32), has led the pedants to assure us that Jesus knows generally the year in which the world will end, but not whether it will be a Wednesday or a Thursday or in the morning or afternoon.[28] But could Jesus (or Mark for that matter) have said anything so incredibly trivial?

Two writers in particular have helped us to see that the answer must tend towards the negative. R. H. Lightfoot[29] has observed that the chapter ends with the parable of the Absent Householder, who may return at evening, midnight, cock-crow, or dawn. He then explains that Mark has used these same four watches of the night to highlight the ensuing Passion story. Evening is the time of the Last Supper, when Judas is caught unaware that the Devil is overtaking him (14: 17). Midnight is the hour when Jesus finds his three disciples napping and repeats the warning to 'watch' (14: 32). Cock-crow is the hour of Peter's denial (14: 72). And dawn is the hour when the whole nation is asleep as its Messiah is delivered over to the Gentiles (15: 1). Now Mark certainly believed in a final denouement of history when God, the householder, would demand from His servants a reckoning; but he sees all the issues of that *ultimate* crisis of history foreshadowed in the crucial moments of the story of Jesus. Thus His followers must be on watch constantly; the master comes at an hour they do not expect, and in a manner they do not expect. Lightfoot's treatment would be worth reading for that percipient comment alone; it throws a flood of light on the eschatological language of the New Testament.

The second writer, A. L. Moore,[30] has demonstrated that the alleged

---

[28] A view taken, for instance, by G. R. Beasley-Murray, *Jesus and the Future* (London, 1954), 261 f.; see also *A Commentary on Mark 13* (London, 1957), 107 f.

[29] R. H. Lightfoot, *The Gospel Message of St Mark* (Oxford, 1950), 48 ff.

[30] Cf. Moore, *Parousia*, 131 ff. (A similar analysis is found in J. Wenham, *Christ and the Bible* (London, 1972), 67 f., and R. T. France, *Jesus and the Old Testament* (London, 1971), 227 ff.).

inconsistency between v. 30 and v. 32 in fact results from a misreading of Mark 13. He bases this on two points, one grammatical, one structural. First he shows that the word *tauta* ('these') in the phrase *tauta panta* ('all these things') in v. 30 must refer back to the same word *tauta* in v. 29, in so far as no new referent is given. But to what does *tauta* in v. 29 refer? The answer is provided by v. 28: 'Now from the fig tree learn its lesson: when its branch becomes tender, and puts forth its shoots, you know that summer is near'. For Moore 'these things' in v. 29 ('Even so, when you see *these things* come to pass, know that he is nigh, even at the doors') must therefore refer to the *signs* of the End, not the End itself, or even the End as well: the whole point of the verse is that when you see the signs coming to pass, then you know that the End is *near*.

Moore's second point concerns the structure of the chapter, which begins with two questions: 'When will these things be? And what shall be the sign when they are to be accomplished?' In Mark these two questions are then given four answers: 'When will be the end?' is expanded to include '*What* will be the end?', while 'What will be the signs?' is expanded to include '*When* will be the signs?' We are therefore left with the following structure:

5–23: 'What are the signs?'
24–27: 'What is the End?'
28–30: 'When will be the signs?' (with parable)
31–37: 'When will be the End?' (with parable)

This argument is illuminating. But should we not also here see 'the End' as bifocal? Moore's point needs to be wedded to Lightfoot's. The signs of the End (earthquakes, wars, famines, persecution, the ravaging of Judaea, the appearance of false prophets and Messiahs, and the falling of stars from heaven) will come upon Jesus' own generation. God is constantly calling His servants to account, and therefore the End is constantly impacting upon the present. But the date of the End is a secret which God keeps only to Himself, for the very good reason that only He can decide when He will be ready for it (cf. Acts 1: 8; 2 Pet. 3: 3–8). We may consequently see the End of Mark 13: 24–7 as having two levels of meaning: on one level the destruction of Jerusalem is the End; on another level it points to the End.[31]

---

[31] On the whole New Testament theologians have failed to recognize not only that it was a function of prophetic eschatology to present historical crises in the light of God's final judgement of history, but also that to describe any event as eschatological is also to make a statement about the End. The ultimate may illumine the present, but the

Of the New Testament writers Luke's treatment is clearly the most complex, and therefore deserves the most detailed consideration. We have seen that he opens his Gospel with a group of pious Jews who are looking for 'the restoration of Israel' (2: 25) and 'the liberation of Jerusalem' (2: 38), and with songs which celebrate the prospect of a national deliverance. It ends with Jesus reassuring two disciples that their hope 'that he would be the one to liberate Israel' (24: 21) was not unfounded. The Gospel in between is interspersed with warnings, framed in language drawn from Jeremiah and Ezekiel, that Jerusalem will be levelled by Roman armies, and that this will be God's judgement for their failure to 'recognize the moment when God was visiting them' with one last offer of peace (19: 41–4; 21: 20–4; 23: 27–31). Hans Conzelmann has argued that Luke has here 'historicized' the original eschatological Gospel, a case which rests mainly on Luke 19: 11: 'He went on to tell them a parable, because he was now close to Jerusalem and they thought the reign of God might dawn at any moment'. 'The thought in 19: 11 and the consequent meaning of the following parable show that Luke is aware he is contradicting a part of Christian tradition.'[32] To Conzelmann it seemed evident that by 'they' Luke meant not the bystanders who heard Jesus' conversation with Zacchaeus, but the whole Christian Church from Pentecost to his own day. But the verse, even if we do not take it exactly at its face value, might just as well mean that Luke fully understood and agreed with the Christian tradition and was confident that those who expected an imminent dawning of the Kingdom had misunderstood it. A more balanced treatment of Luke's theology is that of S. G. Wilson,[33] although he also fails to grasp this point. Jesus, so Wilson tells us, did not expect a mission to the Gentiles because he 'believed that his hope would be fulfilled in the apocalyptic events of the End-time'. Mark retains the eschatological setting of the proclamation to the Gentiles, but sees it as 'a historical process which must be completed before the End comes'. 'Luke makes the final and perhaps inevitable break, by severing even the eschatological connections.'[34] What needs to be questioned here is the contrast, so often made, between apocalyptic

known will also throw light upon the unknown. If Jesus was the centre of God's decisive eschatological act whereby He established His Kingdom in the midst of history, then Jesus will also be the centre of God's final act.

[32] Conzelmann, *The Theology of St Luke*, 135.

[33] S. G. Wilson, *The Gentiles and the Gentiles Mission in Luke–Acts* (Cambridge, 1973).

[34] Ibid., 57.

or eschatological events on the one hand, and historical events on the other. An unhistorical event is a contradiction in terms, since history in this sense is simply the succession of events, and after history ends there can be no more events. If events happen, even if they are assigned to a period which we choose to call the End-time, they are 'historical'. The careful distinction, therefore, between the expectations of Jesus, Mark, and Luke evaporates, and with it Luke's supposed 'historicizing' of an originally eschatological tradition.

The point is amplified in ch. 21. Luke's version of the Marcan discourse ends (21: 36) with instructions to the disciples to pray that they may have strength to escape 'all these things', and it is a reasonable assumption that for him 'all these things' in v. 36 covers the same set of events as 'all things' in v. 32. But from the Parousia and final consummation of the Kingdom there could be no escape, nor can we imagine an intelligent writer suggesting that Jesus' disciples should be taught to pray for any. The disciples were to pray that they might survive the historical crises of persecution and the siege of Jerusalem; and these, according to Luke, were the events which Jesus declared would happen before a generation has passed away. Here Luke is drawing on the long series of predictions in the Old Testament regarding the Day of the Lord, which was to be a day of both vengeance on God's enemies and salvation for the downtrodden nation of Israel. In Luke's adaptation, however, the scenario is vastly different: the *true* Israel is now the Church, and Jerusalem, rather than expecting divine vindication, finds itself judged with the enemies of God. The Gentiles must first visit God's wrath on Jerusalem before they themselves are visited with the heavenly judgement, and only when both events are past can the Church look for its salvation ('look up and raise your heads, for your redemption is drawing near', 21: 28).

As we have seen for Mark the false Messiahs (13: 6) were the first of the many signs of the approaching siege and destruction of Jerusalem. Luke makes this more explicit by attributing to these harbingers the words, 'The time is at hand' (21: 8), and denouncing them as false prophets. In this way the second half of Mark's paratactic dilemma[35] (i.e. the fall of Jerusalem *is* the End, *but the End is not yet*) is made clearer by Luke: the final crisis of history (Mark's 'that day or that hour', 13: 32) is not identical with what Jesus said would happen within a generation, and anyone who proclaims the End to be imminent

---

[35] On parataxis see below, p. 262, n. 38.

is false. Mark's indeterminate interval between 13: 30 and 13: 32 is amplified by Luke as 'the times of the Gentiles', a distinct echo of Daniel's prophecy, wherein God has bestowed upon a Gentile kingdom the power to visit havoc upon Israel for a time, two times, and half a time (12: 7). Here the distress of the Gentiles (Luke 21: 25 f.) is described in mythological terms. 'The roaring of the sea and waves' is the primeval deep out of which God brought order at Creation—it is the site of all opposition to God (cf. Rev. 13: 2) which is still to be subdued in God's ultimate victory. The powers of heaven (v. 26) are the celestial bodies, equated in antiquity with oriental and Graeco-Roman deities, which were perceived by Israel as angelic delegates (Deut. 32: 8). The convulsion of the heavenly powers therefore does not so much point to the destruction of the material cosmos as the replacing of pagan imperial power with its preordained and victorious counterpart, 'the Son of Man'.

That Luke is using historical persecution as a lens through which to view God's ultimate judgement—and vice versa—is further indicated if we compare ch. 21 with 17: 30-7 and 12: 35-48. We find in 17: 20-4 Jesus saying that 'the Kingdom of God is not coming with observable signs, nor will they say, "Lo, it is here", or "There!" For behold, the Kingdom of God is in the midst of [or within][36] you' (vv. 20 f.), a statement followed by the apparently contradictory claim that 'as the lightning flashes and lights up the sky from one side to the other, so will the Son of Man be in his day' (v. 24). Once again the paratactic dilemma presents itself. On the one hand the Kingdom is already present; on the other hand it and the Son of Man will come with all the subtlety of a lightning flash. No sentries will herald its approach. Just as in the time of Noah and Lot the tranquil pursuits of everyday life led to a complete indifference to the impending day of cataclysm which was to engulf them, so the days of the Son of Man will be climaxed by a day which will intrude upon normal human activities, so that of boon companions one will be trapped while the other will survive (vv. 26-37). Thus we would have no problem in construing v. 24 for what prima facie it appears to be, a picture of the *eschaton*, were it not for the warning of vv. 20 f.—a warning made even more stringent by vv. 31 f. The sudden occupation of a military foe may lead to emergency evacuation tactics, but they would not

---

[36] The ambiguity of *entos* in this passage is well known (cf. G. B. Caird, *The Gospel of St Luke* (London, 1968), 197).

have much significance if the emergency in question is the universal Parousia of the Son of Man. Again, what seems to be in view is the imminent siege and destruction of Jerusalem. Was the editor of Q wrong to introduce these two sayings (20 f., 31 f.) into a context which concerns the Parousia, with Luke further blundering by failing to see the problem? Or is it possible that in Luke's mind, as in the mind of Jesus and Mark before him, the judgement on Jerusalem and the Last Judgement are inseparably linked, so that the historic crisis embodies the eschatological crisis, with Luke believing that Jesus was challenging Israel to confront a choice of eternal importance, a choice between fulfilling or forfeiting her calling as God's holy nation?

Such a hypothesis gains conviction if we recall the Old Testament prophecies noted above (Jer. 4: 23–6 and Isa. 13: 6; cf. Ezek. 20: 3; Joel 1: 15; 3: 14; Obad. 15, and Zeph. 1: 7) which saw in the historical crisis the point at which the circle of eternity intersects the line of time, the moment when Israel was facing in all their finality the questions of life and death. The Old Testament prophets were able to see one picture of the impending future coalesce with another of the ultimate future, resulting in a unified stereoscopic vision of divine judgment. Are we to exclude Jesus, Luke and Mark from such company?

If the Day of the Son of Man and fall of Jerusalem were for Luke indissolubly intertwined (cf. 12: 40), it should be at least conceivable that Luke 17: 26–29 was meant to have the same double reference. It is worth noting that in neither of the instanced ancient disasters does Jesus say anything about the notorious sins of the people concerned; it was their complacent disregard of coming calamity which brings about the downfall of the contemporaries of Noah and of Lot. Here, as we have seen above, it is not God's judgement on individuals which is involved, but a collective judgement on historical civilizations.

Luke further shows how well he understood the teaching of Mark (and Jesus?) by introducing into this section the reference to the Son of Man's rejection (v. 25). The rejection of Jesus by Israel set into motion a process which could be terminated only with 'the Day of the Son of Man'; and could the judgement be far behind? The descent of vultures upon a camel dying in the desert could not be more automatic (v. 37).

Working backwards to 12: 35–48, we find Luke's picture taking on even greater definition. There he records a number of admonitions to the disciples to be on the alert for a coming crisis, the advent of the Son of Man: they are to tuck their long robes into their belts in case sudden and strenuous action is required; they are like loyal servants waiting up all night in case their master should suddenly appear after an extended trip. They must not be caught napping, nor are they to be like the householder caught by surprise when the thief burrows through the clay walls of the house (cf. Mark 13: 33 ff.).

The fact that Luke follows this passage with one about the approaching end of Jesus' life (vv. 49–50) and another about the judgement which is presently to engulf the nation Israel shows that in Luke's mind these three themes could not be separated. Jesus was looking to one great test involving death for himself, the final examination of his disciples, and judgement on Israel; and this three-pronged event, against all human perceptions, was to be the final victory predicted in Daniel 7: 13 and 27, whereby world empire would pass by confiscation to the Son of Man, the symbol of God's true people.

This makes considerable sense if one considers the probabilities of Jesus' own life. Jesus may well have had much to say about his own return and the final denouement of history, but it is hard to imagine him asking his disciples during their lifetime to watch night and day for a crisis which could not happen at the very least until some time after his death. If, on the other hand, the moment of the final and fatal act of official hostility to his work was unknown, it would make sense that he should constantly be telling his friends that the clash, in which they would probably also be implicated, could happen at any moment, that moment when Israel would seal its own fate. Lightfoot's reading of Mark 13 thus has as much value for the understanding of Luke's Gospel as for Mark's. By inserting Peter's question ('Lord, are you telling this parable for us all?'), Luke makes Peter the spokesman for the Christians of his own day; they are not to engage in useless speculation about dates. They rather are to be busy and loyal servants (cf. Acts 1: 7–8). Once again what is allusive and thematic in Mark is made explicit in Luke.

Of the four Gospels, Matthew's is, at first blush, the most resistant to such an explanation. Writing long after AD 70, he, more clearly than the others, is editing the tradition of Jesus' teaching to the needs of his own day. Of the four, he alone uses the term *parousia* ('coming') and the phrase *sunteleia aiōnos* ('the end of the world', 13: 39, 40, 49; 24: 3; 28: 20). And, as Dodd has shown,[37] parables which in their original context illuminated the crisis provoked by Jesus' ministry are

[37] See Dodd, *Parables*, 115 ff.

now made to refer to the final judgement, with Mark's question about the destruction of the temple broadened: 'When will this happen? And what will be the sign of your coming (*parousia*) and the end of the world' (24: 3)?

Before we attempt to grapple with Matthew on this point, it may be worth remembering that on all counts he is the most elusive of all the major contributors to the New Testament, and the difficulties of his Gospel are by no means confined to eschatology. To note just a few examples, his Gospel is the most Jewish and also the most anti-Jewish. Yet it is he, not the Gentile Luke, who constantly explains Semitic forms of diction in order to make them intelligible to Gentiles (e.g. Matt. 12: 28 = Luke 11: 20; Matt. 10: 37 = Luke 14: 26). He ends with a command to make all nations disciples of Jesus, but includes a chapter, apparently designed as a manual for missionaries, which begins with a command to go only to Jews. Christians are to let their light shine in public, so that the good they do may be seen (5: 16); but they are to do their acts of piety, including acts of kindness to others, in private so that only God will see them (6: 2–6, 16–18). They are to pass no judgement on anyone (7: 1), but must avoid throwing their pearls to those they judge to be pigs (7: 6). On a missionary journey they are to give without charge, but to expect their keep (10: 8–10). It is, of course, possible to give a long, precise, and boring proof that each of these pairs is complementary and mutually corrective; but that is not Matthew's way, nor was it the way of Jesus before him. However uncomfortable the modern rationalist may feel with the Hebrew method of simply juxtaposing two apparently contradictory ideas side by side, it has one great advantage: it does not conceal the fact that, when all explanations are exhausted, the problem of balance remains.[38]

In keeping with these tendencies, Matthew is also far from being a thoroughgoing literalist in his eschatology. He firmly believed, as did the other writers of the New Testament, that the Kingdom of God had already arrived in the ministry and person of Jesus (cf. e.g. 12: 28; 21: 31). Moreover he has altered Mark's version of Jesus' reply to the High Priest (Mark 14: 62) by adding the words *ap arti*, 'from now on' (26: 64). These two words leave no doubt that he thought of the coming of the Son of Man on the clouds of heaven as a *continuous*

[38] On parataxis as a feature of Semitic style, cf. G. B. Caird, *The Language and Imagery of the Bible* (Essex and London, 1980), 117–21.

process which would begin with the crucifixion.[39] Matthew's emphasis on the Last Judgement (e.g. 25: 31–46) is therefore to be seen as the product not of a dominating interest in the end of the world, but of an awareness singularly like Mark's, in which the Last Judgement is constantly impacting upon the present in both offer and demand. Could a Gospel which begins with the birth of one called Immanuel, 'God with us' (1: 23), and ends with the promise, 'I am with you to the end of the world' (28: 20) leave us in any doubt on this point? Finally, we should remember that if Matthew, not to mention the other New Testament writers, had taken his eschatology with a strict literalism, one would have expected the fall of Jerusalem in AD 70, unaccompanied by a Parousia, to be an emergency of the first order for Christian theology. But there is no sign that in fact it was so.[40]

In the Fourth Gospel there is nothing that could be construed as an imminent Parousia, since the End is so totally identified with Christ that eschatology is transposed into Christology.[41] One by one John takes the terms which were traditionally associated with the Last Day, and shows how they have found their total fulfilment in the incarnate life of Jesus. He is the light of the world, in whose presence everyone stands already before the judgement seat of God. He is the life; to believe in him is to make the journey from death to life eternal. He is the resurrection, through whom death is drained of its power. He is the incarnate *logos*: in him the eternal purpose of God is revealed and implemented. The *logos* goes forth from God and does not return to him void: 'I have finished the work which you gave me to do' (17: 4). This concludes the logical process which began when Jesus said, 'The time is fulfilled' (12: 23). Only God is the First and the Last; and to say that the life of Jesus was an eschatological event is to say that God was in Christ. Thus for John the 'glory' of Jesus is not something still to come at the Parousia; it is the state of being caught up into God's redemptive purpose. John still believed in the Last Day,

---

[39] Is it not in the light of *ap arti* (26: 64) that the strange saying of Matt. 10: 23 ('Before you have gone through all the towns of Israel the Son of Man will have come', REB) is to be understood?

[40] This becomes clear in Matt. 24: 29. Whatever 'immediately' means there, the one thing it *cannot* mean is that the Parousia was understood by Matthew to take place directly after the fall of Jerusalem in AD 70.

[41] In John's theology Jesus is 'the resurrection and the life' (11: 25). That which the Jews had conceived 'eschatologically' happens with the appearance of the Son and the sending of his Spirit into the world.

that it was near ('It is the last hour', 1 John 2: 18) and did not know what it would bring.[42] But it could bring with it nothing that had not been already accomplished when Jesus proclaimed that redemptive love had achieved its end. 'It is accomplished' (19: 30). For John that is the Kingdom, the power, and the glory forever.

The author of Hebrews, by contrast, tells his readers that 'the Day is drawing near' (10: 25), the 'coming one' will come 'very soon', and will not delay (10: 37–8), and that Jesus will appear again 'for those who are eagerly expecting him' (9: 28). But, as with the other New Testament writers, the imminence of the Parousia is hardly a controlling factor. There is a sense of overwhelming urgency, to be sure; but the urgency derives not from any belief in the nearness of the Parousia; it comes from the finality of the word which God has spoken in Christ. For this writer 'the world to come' which is his 'theme' (2: 5) has already arrived, and we should seriously mistake his meaning if we imagined that for him this world was still future. We do not indeed see all things subject to the human race; but we do see Jesus crowned with glory and honour as the pioneer and representative of his many brothers (2: 9–10). Christians have tasted the powers of the age to come and have reached Mount Zion, the city whose architect and builder is God. This author uses the verb *mellō* with all its future implications because he in thinking of the new age from the point of view of the Old Testament which predicted it. 'The Law had a shadow of the good things which were to come' (*tōn mellontōn agathōn*, 10: 1; cf. 9: 11).[43]

The same pattern occurs in James. The rich have piled up wealth 'in the last days' (5: 3), and the coming (*parousia*) of the Lord is near. But when James urges his readers to remain steadfast because the judge stands at the door, and reminds them that they have heard of 'the patience of Job and the end [*telos*] of the Lord [i.e. what the Lord did for him in the end]', it is reasonable to assume that he thought the end to be at hand for them in exactly the same sense as it had been for Job.

---

[42] John 6: 39 f., 44, 54; 12: 48; 1 John 2: 18; 3: 2.

[43] On the eschatology of Hebrews see for instance, C. K. Barrett, 'The Eschatology of the Epistle to the Hebrews', in D. Daube and W. D. Davies, *The Background of the New Testament and its Eschatology* (Cambridge, 1956); L. D. Hurst, *The Epistle to the Hebrews* (Cambridge, 1990), 24 ff.; R. Williamson, *Philo and Hebrews* (Leiden, 1970), esp. 424 ff.; and B. Lindars, *Theology of the Letter to the Hebrews* (Cambridge, 1991), *passim*.

Similarly for the author of First Peter 'the end of all things is at hand' (4: 7). But the salvation which is now 'in readiness' 'will be revealed at the end of time' (1: 5), a revelation of 'glory' whose time is not specified (1: 11; 4: 13; 5: 1, 10). Christ has already been made manifest, also 'in the last time' (1: 20).

The author of Revelation was expecting the end of the world no more than were the other New Testament writers.[44] He was expecting persecution in which he saw the embodiment of the final judgement of God. In the midst of this trial Christ the Judge would come either to remove the lampstand of the faithless community or to reward the conqueror with a place in the City of God. The whole intention of the rich and varied imagery of his heavenly drama was to nerve Christians for their coming ordeal by helping them to see the indispensable contribution that their martyrdom would make to the grand strategy of God's war against the forces of the Abyss. The choice which faced the Christian in the Roman lawcourt was whether he or she was to belong to the earthly city, whose permanent characteristic is that it 'goes to perdition', or to the heavenly city, whose permanent characteristic is that it 'comes down out of heaven from God' (21: 10). The fall of Babylon and the coming of the heavenly city are imminent future events in so far as they are involved in the decision of the martyr to accept his or her share in the victory which overcomes the world.

It is in this vein that the author's two references to the parable of the midnight thief should be taken. To the church of Sardis the heavenly Christ sends the message: 'If you do not wake up, I shall come upon you like a thief, and you will not know the hour of my coming' (3: 3). This is one of a number of conditional warnings in the letters. 'If you do not repent, I shall come and move your lamp from its place' (2: 5). 'Repent: otherwise I shall come and make war on you with the sword of my mouth' (2: 16). 'I have given her time

---

[44] Sometimes scholars who make this point arrive at the right conclusion by the wrong means. D. Hill, for instance, distinguishes apocalyptic from prophecy and assigns Revelation to the latter. Following von Rad, he argues that 'for the apocalypticists the events of their own time were not a locus of divine action . . . the present age was meaningless and evil, and would be swallowed up and destroyed in the End-Time. The prophetic *Heilsgeschichte* on the other hand speaks, not of the termination of history, but of its fulfilment through God's disclosure of himself in history' (*New Testament Prophecy*, 74). But by the consent of almost all scholars the two best known apocalypses remain Daniel and Revelation, and they were written to set a historic crisis in the light of God's final judgement. That such an intention was different from that of the prophets is far from clear.

for repentance, but she refuses to repent of her fornication; so I am making her take to her bed and bringing severe pain on her lovers, unless they renounce what she is doing' (2: 21 f.). In each case the threat is contingent on a failure to repent or wake up. It cannot therefore be what we would call the Second Advent. Jesus does not say, 'I am coming in any case, and if you are asleep I shall take you by surprise.' *It is the coming, not the surprise, that is conditional.* 'If you do not wake up, I shall come.' This coming of the Risen Lord for discipline is therefore not a world-wide coming, but one which is as particular and private to the church concerned as is his coming in grace and friendship to those in Laodicea who open to his knocking. The one coming is described in eucharistic language, the other in eschatological.

Later in the book there is a second reference to the midnight thief in the prophecy of Armageddon. The orthodox approach to eschatology has found this verse so intolerable that one editor after another has either excised it from the text or quarantined it as an eccentric parenthesis.

Then I saw coming from the mouth of the dragon, from the mouth of the monster, and from the mouth of the false prophet three foul spirits like frogs. They were demon spirits able to work miracles, and they went out to the kings of the whole world to muster them for battle on the great day of God Omnipotent. See how I come like a thief! Blessed is the man who stays awake and keeps his clothes by him, so as not to be seen walking naked and ashamed! So they mustered the kings to the place called in Hebrew Armageddon (16: 13–16).

The court flattery, the lying propaganda, and above all the idolatrous religion of Rome are to become demon spirits spreading beyond the frontiers of the Empire and producing a reaction which will cause the fall of the imperial city, Babylon the Great. And in this crisis, as in many another, Christians are to see the coming of their Lord. Jesus had warned his disciples that the last days of Jerusalem would come with a suddenness which would allow no time for those taking a nap on the roof to go downstairs for their belongings, or those working in the fields to go home for their coats (Mark 13: 15 f.). In the same vein the heavenly Christ warns his followers to be ready for the last days of Babylon: 'Blessed is the one who stays awake and keeps his clothes by him.' It is of course a spiritual wakefulness that is demanded; the danger is not that they will be caught napping by foreign invasion, but that they will fail to see in it the coming of the Lord. He comes like a thief because the manner as well as the hour of his coming is unexpected.

And finally, in the latest document of the New Testament, the author is faced with scoffing literalists who do not understand that one day or a thousand years are the same in the patient purposes of God (2 Pet. 3: 8–9).

7.4. INDIVIDUAL ESCHATOLOGY

7.4.1. *The Redemption of the Body*

We have allowed the New Testament authors to discuss the universal aspects of salvation, but this is not the whole story. Salvation must also extend to the individual. And for Paul, the earliest New Testament writer to discuss the resurrection of Jesus, the most obvious aspect of salvation which is still to come is the redemption of the body. Here we concentrate totally on Paul, for the simple reason that this is one of his unique contributions to the conference table.

After his conversion Paul accepted the early Church's account of what happened to Jesus on Easter Sunday and rapidly built it into the structure of his theology. He believed that when Christ left the tomb his physical body was transformed into a spiritual or glorious body (Phil. 3: 21), just as a seed when planted in the ground dies and is given a new body (1 Cor. 15: 36–8). So too the Christian must undergo a future transformation. In 1 Corinthians this is envisaged as happening suddenly, 'in a flash, in the twinkling of an eye' (1 Cor. 15: 52). A slightly different picture of the process emerges in the second letter, where Paul assures his readers that the Christian life is a steady transfiguration into the likeness of Christ. This metamorphosis goes on through a daily renewal of the inner nature, even as the outward appearance is decaying (2 Cor. 4: 16). Some modern interpreters would have been happier if at this point Paul had said that the outer husk drops away and leaves the inner self unhampered by its weakness. But the Jew did not believe that human beings consist of an immortal soul entombed for a while in a mortal body. What happened to the body happened to the person. If there is to be eternal life, then this lowly body of humiliation must be changed even as Christ's has been.

The New Testament writers have often been accused of treating human beings as brands plucked from the burning and the world in general as a grim vale of soul-making, with the brilliant achievements of human labour, skill, and thought as nothing more than the expendable backdrop for the drama of redemption. This was hardly the view of the Hebrews of the Old Testament. We have seen that most of the books of the Old Testament were written at a time when the Hebrew people had no belief in an afterlife for the individual. For them life meant this life. Like the God of the Creation story, they looked at the world, and behold, it was very good. Their eschatology was concerned with the vindication in history of the truth and justice of God and of His purpose for Israel and the world. The end they looked for might be described as a new heaven and a new earth, but this was figurative language, and what they meant was the present heaven and earth renewed by the transfiguring radiance of God. Their belief in an afterlife for the individual was grafted somewhat uneasily on to the older and more earthly hope.

Paul's views on this point were partly the result of this Jewish background, and partly the result of his own experience. We saw above how his critics at Corinth had tried to use his battered, unimpressive physical condition to undermine his authority, implying that if he were a real apostle God would take better care of him. Paul counters this charge by making capital of his weakness, notwithstanding his old horror of decay inherited from a Greek background. The critics, he claims, are basing their judgement on what is visible and transient (2 Cor. 4: 18), just as he had once judged Christ by outward and worldly standards; but when on the Damascus Road he saw the glory of the Son of God revealed, he was never again able to view any human being on the same superficial basis (2 Cor. 5: 16). The Christian life is therefore a steady process, the goal of which for the believer is to be transformed into the image of Christ from one stage of glory to another (2 Cor. 3: 18); or, as he puts it elsewhere, 'to experience the power of the resurrection, and to share his sufferings, in growing conformity with his death, if only I may finally arrive at the resurrection of the dead' (Phil. 3: 10). In the latter passage resurrection, sufferings, and death are not seen as episodes in the story of Jesus, nor as future experiences in which Christians are one day to share, but as forces present in the Christian life now (otherwise Paul would hardly have put resurrection *first*). It is his belief in, and hope of, the resurrection which forms the starting point of all Christian experience. Such knowledge, on the other hand, might well lead to pride; thus to protect against it God has provided that the transformation be concealed within 'an earthenware vessel', a perishable body subject to pain and decay (2 Cor. 4: 7, cf. 12: 7–9); it is a treasure hid with God in Christ (Col. 3: 2; cf. 2: 3). Later God will clothe Christians with a new body, corresponding to the secret, inner life which God has built up within them and ready to be put on like a suit of clothes. This is so that when we appear before him we will not be 'naked' (*gumnos*), i.e. bodiless. While to the Greek this might be expected, to the Jew it is unthinkable.[45]

As to *where* this resurrection life is to be lived, Paul's thinking may have undergone some development. When he wrote his earliest letter, he gave no hint concerning the question; believers, whether dead or alive at the coming of Christ, would be caught up to meet him in the air (1 Thess. 4: 17). But years later in his letter to Rome he gives the impression that the life everlasting is to be lived on a transformed earth. It is likely that between the two writings he had wrestled with the question of the relation of the human physical body to the physical cosmos of which it is a part, and had concluded that the redemption of the body was unthinkable apart from the transformation of the universe as a whole (Rom. 8: 18–25). Paul shared the commonly held view that the subhuman creation had been involved in the fall of the human race; the ground had been cursed for Adam's sake, and, deprived of its proper control, nature had become red in tooth and claw. Thus for Paul the whole natural order is subject to the law of decay. The human body, which links the human race with animals that are perishing, must therefore be transformed 'by the power which enables Him even to subject all things to himself' (Phil. 3: 21). Paul here alludes to Psalm 8 (Rom. 8: 20[46]—cf. 1 Cor. 15: 26; Eph. 1: 22), where God's purpose is that the universe should be subject to humanity. Paul's whole doctrine of the End, and his vision of a universe redeemed, whatever minor factors may have contributed to it, is in the main a logical development of his belief that Christ is the second Adam, the one who truly reflects God's rule over the cosmos (Col. 1:

[45] On 'naked' in 2 Cor. 5: 3 cf. Jean Héring, *The Second Epistle of Saint Paul to the Corinthians* (London, 1967), 37: 'Never at any time did the Apostle envisage taking possession of the glory-body before the parousia. This is precisely why the state intermediate between death and resurrection is characterized as "nakedness".'

[46] At first blush Rom. 8: 20 does not appear relevant to Ps. 8. Yet who is the 'subjector' (*hupotaksanta*)? Humankind, Satan, and God are possibilities (cf. W. Sanday and A. C. Headlam, *A Critical and Exegetical Commentary on the Epistle to the Romans* (Edinburgh, 1902), 208, and G. W. H. Lampe, 'The New Testament Doctrine of *Ktisis*', *SJT* 17 (1964), 458). But that the subjection is performed 'in hope' is decisive—God must be the subjector, which makes Rom. 8: 20 almost certainly an echo of Ps. 8: 6.

15 ff.). Paul was certainly not dependent in this view on any literalistic interpretation of Genesis 1 and 2; there did not actually have to be a time when Adam exercised that dominion over all creation which he now attributes to Christ. All he needed to believe was that God had deliberately left creation incomplete, in order that it might be completed by the co-operation of the human race, His image in this world, and that with the coming of Christ this co-operation had become a genuine possibility. In this astonishingly modern view of the relation of human beings to their cosmic environment, they are part and parcel of the created order and must be saved in their integrity if they are to be saved at all.

A large part of our difficulty with New Testament eschatology continues to be caused by our attempts to force it into an alien dogmatic mould. Along this line it may be surprising to note that there are few, if any, passages in the New Testament that promise that people will go to heaven when they die. It is true that their inheritance or treasure or new life is frequently said to be laid up for them in heaven; but those who inherit a fortune do not have to live in the vaults of their father's bank in order to enjoy it.

For Paul the 'down-payment' (*arrabōn*)[47] of this future inheritance is the Spirit which God has given the Christian, a spirit not of slavery but of sonship, crying, '*Abba*, father' (Rom. 8: 15; Gal. 4: 6). This enables the Christian to enter into the relationship which Jesus has with God as Father: Jesus is leading many sons to His own glory (Rom. 8: 19), although we groan along with the rest of the universe waiting for it to happen. The truly surprising feature of Paul's theology on this point is not the groaning of the universe[48] but the equation of sonship with the redemption of the body (Rom. 8: 23).

Elsewhere Paul relates the future redemption of the body to the resurrection of Christ by an appeal to the Jewish calendar: Jesus has been raised from the dead, the 'firstfruits of them that sleep' (1 Cor. 15: 20). The imagery is drawn from the ecclesiastical year which began Nissan 1 (late March), with the first festival, Passover (Nissan 15) coinciding with the first of the eight days of Unleavened Bread. On the third day of the eight the priests offered a wave offering of the first sheaf of the harvest, and seven weeks later they celebrated the

---

[47] On this term see above, p. 128 n. 22.

[48] See above, p. 105, for the Jewish view that the whole universe fell with Adam. This shows that on this point Paul was not innovating.

ingathering of the grain harvest at Pentecost. Paul's vivid analogy, in which the Church is living between Passover and Pentecost, with the firstfruits already offered but the harvest yet to come, might naturally give rise to imminent expectations: Passover had happened, and now Pentecost is not far off. But in another sense Pentecost *had* happened. The imagery was not intended to produce a logical conceptual unity such as we might insist upon today. The Spirit came, in accordance with the scriptures; and this was also an event of the last days (cf. Acts 2: 16 ff.)

7.4.2. *Death and Eternity*

One of the great perplexities surrounding the future hope in the New Testament is the fact that alongside the traditional Jewish belief in the resurrection of the body at the Last Day lie statements which seem to imply that the future life begins immediately at death. In Mark 12: 18 ff. Abraham, Isaac, and Jacob already enjoy eternal life in the presence of God. According to Luke 16: 19 ff. the future punishment and reward of the rich man and Lazarus, respectively, are experienced at a point when there is still the opportunity for messengers of warning to be sent to living relatives. As we have seen, the difficulty of harmonizing the promise to the penitent thief ('Today you shall be with me in Paradise', Luke 24: 43) with the traditional Jewish expectation of 'a resurrection of good and wicked alike' (Acts 24: 15) is not eased by demoting Paradise to the status of a waiting room. And when John of Patmos looks under the heavenly altar and sees the souls of those who have suffered for their testimony, and hears their plea for vindication, he gets a twofold response. All the martyrs are to be given a white robe, the token of eternal life, but the final triumph of the cause for which they died must be delayed until the filling up of the full tally of those who are to die in God's cause. Here entry into the presence of God and the partaking of 'the springs of the water of life' (7: 17) are not delayed until the final denouement of history.

The problem presents itself in its most acute form in Paul, who appears to speak in both ways, sometimes in the confines of a single letter. It has already been noted that in Philippians 3: 20 f. Paul expresses belief in a future bodily transformation at the day of Christ. But in the same letter his desire is 'to depart and be with Christ; that is better by far; but for your sake there is greater need for me to stay on in the body' (1: 23). And in his second letter to the church at

Corinth, in a discussion ringing with echoes of his earlier comments in 1 Corinthians 15 concerning the future resurrection, he says, 'We know that as long as we are at home in the body we are exiles from the Lord . . . We are confident, I repeat, and would rather leave our home in the body and go to live with the Lord' (2 Cor. 5: 6–8).

This dilemma has led interpreters to extremely diverse solutions. Philippians 1: 23, for instance, has been construed variously to mean: (1) Paul thinks that he would experience a special bodily translation, as had happened in the case of Enoch and Elijah. (2) He is thinking of the particular reward reserved only for martyrs. (3) He is not thinking of life after death but of the identity with Christ in martyrdom. (4) He is thinking of a bodiless intermediate state in which the dead wait for the final resurrection. (5) In true Hebrew fashion he is using parataxis, in which mutually irreconcilable views are held without any attempt to reconcile them.

Such views are obviously not of the same weight. With reference to (1), for instance, if Paul were thinking of a special case, whether himself alone or the category of martyrs, it is hardly likely that he would have addressed his comments to the entire Corinthian church in the first person plural ('We are confident . . .', 2 Cor. 5: 6–8).[49] Nor does it make much sense that he would have viewed the sleep of death as *far better*, or that Christians who are slumbering in their tombs are 'with Christ', who has long since left the tomb.

There is one other option to consider before we dissolve into exegetical despair. Paul may have thought of death in a very real sense as sleep. When one is asleep time is, from our conscious perspective, suspended. The next thing one is consciously aware of is waking. Along the same lines after falling asleep in death the next thing the Christian is aware of is the Day of Christ. Thus it could be equally true that one enters the presence of Christ at the moment of death and that this is experienced by everyone simultaneously.

Such a potentially ingenious solution to the problem of relating time and eternity should not be dismissed by twentieth-century sophisticates as too 'modern'. If the apostolic conference finds itself at an impasse on this point, perhaps it should allow a voice from the gallery to enter the discussion. While younger than the New Testament writers and not in their canonical league, the writer of 2 Esdras has an interesting solution to the problem we are considering:

---

[49] It also runs counter, incidentally, to Paul's emphasis on salvation *sola fide*.

I said, 'But surely, lord, your promise is to those who are alive at the end. What is to be the fate of those who lived before us, or of ourselves, or of those who come after us?'
He said to me, 'I will compare the judgment to a circle: the latest will not be
too late, nor the earliest too early.' (2 Esd. 5: 41 f.)

The idea is that in a circle all points on the circumference are equidistant from the centre. Could one ask for a better analogy to the problem of death and resurrection, in which every person's death is equidistant from the Day of the Lord?

7.5. HISTORICAL ESCHATOLOGY

7.5.1. *The Maturing Purpose of God*

We saw above that the New Testament writers held firmly to the idea that one day God will again intervene in human history and that this intervention is inextricably interlocked with the Parousia of his Son. But also bound up with this idea is the belief that before the final crisis God will regather the nations into a unit. The claim, expressed in a number of ways, has perhaps its most explicit treatment in Acts 1: 8, where the gospel must first be preached 'in Jerusalem, Judea and Samaria, and to the uttermost parts of the earth'. This agenda, when broken down, involves the reunion of North and South (the salvation of Israel as a whole), to be followed by the salvation of the Gentile nations.

The first element, the reunion of Israel and Judah, cannot be said to be a Lucan creation, since it has strong Hebrew roots:

Then the people of Judah and of Israel shall be reunited and shall choose for themselves a single head . . .
For the Israelites shall live many a long day without king or prince . . . but after that they will again seek the Lord their God and David their king (Hos. 1: 11; 3: 4–5).

As a shepherd goes in search of his sheep when his flock is dispersed all around him, so I will . . . bring them out from every nation, gather them in from other lands, and lead them home to their own soil . . .
I will save my flock . . . then I will set over them one shepherd to take care of them, my servant David (Ezek. 34: 12–13, 22–3).

It is now well known that the intertestamental literature shows a bewildering variety and even a discrepancy of belief about almost every aspect of the Jewish eschatological hope;[50] but the one element which appears with remarkable constancy is the gathering of the scattered people of God into a single unified nation, as in the time of David.

Luke's idea (Acts 1: 8) that 'the uttermost parts of the earth'—the Gentiles—must also be brought within the scope of redemption, and Paul's affirmation that in the end God will have mercy 'upon all' (Rom. 11: 32), are well anticipated in the Hebrew scriptures. The Jews of Jesus' day held to a wide variety of beliefs and hopes about the ultimate destiny of the Gentile nations, but there was one school of thought, particularly represented in the prophets Isaiah and Zechariah, which declared that the Gentiles would have a place in God's final Kingdom. But their inclusion was not to be brought about by any missionary activity on the part of the Jews, not by any gradual process of making individual converts to Judaism, but rather by a mighty act of God in the last days. When the Day of the Lord arrived, and Israel would be restored to the righteousness and dignity proper to her calling as the holy people of God, Jerusalem would become a truly holy city, in which God could be expected to dwell, and from which the voice of authority could issue to the world; then the redeemed nation would act as a beacon, drawing all nations to Jerusalem to join in the worship and service of the one true God.

> In the end the mountain of the Lord's house
> shall be firmly set above all other mountains,
> raised higher than the hills.
> All nations will come streaming to it;
> many peoples will come and say:
> 'Come! Let us go up to the mountain of the Lord,
> to the house of the God of Jacob,
> so that he may teach us His ways,
> and we may walk in His paths.
> For from Zion comes teaching with authority,
> and the Lord speaks His word from Jerusalem'.
>
> (Isa. 2: 2–3)

> I made him a witness to all races,
>   a prince and instructor of peoples;
> and you in turn shall summon nations you do not know,
> and nations that do not know you shall come running to you.
>
> (Isa. 55: 4–5)

[50] A point tellingly made by Morton Smith in his discussion of the Qumran evidence ('What is Implied by the Variety of Messianic Figures?', *JBL* 78 (1959), 66 ff.).

In those days ten men out of nations speaking every language will seize hold of the robe of a single Jew and say: 'We will go with you, for we have heard that God is with you' (Zech. 8: 23).

It is understandable, then, that after the death and resurrection of Jesus the members of the Jerusalem church should be described by Luke as seeing their immediate task to be the winning of Israel to an acceptance of its proper role as God's nation. 'Repent therefore and return to God, so that your sins may be blotted out, that God may grant you a period of recovery, and that He may send the Messiah appointed for you, Jesus, who must remain in heaven until the time for the universal restoration of which God spoke through his holy prophets in days of old' (Acts 3: 19–21). The winning of the Gentiles, so Luke believed, belonged to that universal restoration which would begin just as soon as Israel had accepted the demand and invitation of the gospel.[51]

This viewpoint in Acts 1: 8 is virtually reproduced in one, though not the only, interpretation of 1 Peter 1: 10–12, where Christian prophets were devoting their attention to discovering the date and circumstances of the Parousia, when it was revealed to them that the gospel must first be preached to the Gentiles. In Ephesians the same intention is developed to such as extent that the Parousia entirely drops out of sight. Mark's Gospel, with its long description of eschatological events culminating with the coming of the Son of Man, contains the warning that 'the Gospel must first be preached to all nations' (Mark 13: 10), a passage strangely omitted by the Gentile Luke. And Paul, expounding his claim that the Jews, despite their unbelief, have not been ultimately rejected, takes pains to underscore that it is only after the inclusion of the Gentiles that Israel will be regrafted into the olive tree of God's people (Rom. 11: 16–32).

7.5.2. *The Redemption of the Powers*

We have seen how Paul's cosmic vision would not allow him to divorce his vision of the future of the human race from a belief in the redemption of creation as a whole. But this must of necessity also include the principalities and powers. At times Paul's hope is depicted in terms of conquest, an idea undoubtedly not of his own creation. The wide-

[51] Cf. S. G. Wilson, *Gentile Mission*, who, some reservations notwithstanding, on the whole finds Munck's reconstruction compelling.

spread use of Psalm 110: 1 (with its companion companion Psalm 8) which was emphasized by Dodd indicates the theme to have been already present in the early Church before Paul wrote his Epistles.[52] In Paul's earlier letters he was satisfied that these powers should be defeated and destroyed. Writing in AD 50, only ten years after Caligula had threatened to erect his statue in the Jerusalem Temple, he saw the Roman *imperium* as the incarnation of a mystery of lawlessness which would finally manifest itself in a man of lawlessness, whom Jesus would slay with the breath of his mouth (2 Thess. 2: 3–12). The rulers of this age who had been behind the Cross were being reduced to impotence, and in the end would be destroyed, together with the human race's final enemy, death (1 Cor. 2: 6–8; 15: 24–6). As he benefited from its administration in many parts of the world, however, Paul came to have a more profound appreciation of the Roman Empire, so that when he wrote Romans he could speak of the divine ordination of its authority without qualification (Rom. 13: 1–7). The Empire with its capital at Rome and its colonies dispersed throughout the provinces suggested to him the image of a divine commonwealth with the Jerusalem above as capital and every church on earth a colony of heaven (Phil. 3: 20). Thus in his later letters when he had worked out the cosmic dimensions of the crucifixion, and had come to see the salvation of the human race as the centre of a cosmic redemption, Paul could see even the heavenly powers as within the redemptive scope of God (Phil. 2: 10). In Christ was the origin and goal of their being, and thus in Christ was the hope of their restoration to the place which God had ordained for them in His eternal purpose. 'In him all things were created, in heaven or on earth, visible and invisible, whether thrones or dominions or principalities or authorities—all things were created, through him and for him . . . in him all the fulness of God was pleased to dwell, and through him to reconcile to himself all things, whether on earth or in heaven, making peace by the blood of his Cross' (Col. 1: 16–20).

---

[52] To this it may be added that the exorcism stories of the Gospels probably loom so large in the synoptic narrative because they indicated to the pagan world that Jesus had authority over the principalities and powers.

7.4.3. *The City to Come*

As to the nature of the life to come, the New Testament writers are reticent about giving details, preferring rather to provide powerful images. For those who have known poverty and hunger it is the great feast (Rev. 19: 9); for those who have borne the burden and heat of the day it is a sabbath rest (Heb. 4: 10); for saintly worshippers it is the vision of God (Matt. 5: 8); for faithful servants it is the joy of their Lord (Matt. 25: 21); and for those who cannot rise upon the wings of faith to anticipate the future hope in imagination, it is 'what eye has not seen, what ear has not heard, what has not entered into the human heart, the things that God has prepared for them that love Him' (1 Cor. 2: 9).

Within this variety one of the most developed images is that of the city.[53] For the New Testament writers, if the life to come is to be no mere expectation of survival—a prospect most have regarded as a threat rather than a promise, the only exceptions being the ancient necromancer and the modern spiritualist—it must contain life of such transcendent quality that it is beyond the power of death to destroy it, a life of love to God and our neighbours. It is, in short, a social life, and it is found only by losing ourselves in service to God and one another. No conflict appears to have existed between the individual and the social hope; for the New Testament writers human beings can fulfil their personal destiny only by taking their proper place in the new society.

For the author of Hebrews the city to which the people of God have come is 'Mount Zion, the city of the living God, the heavenly Jerusalem . . . the full concourse and assembly of the firstborn who are enrolled in heaven' (Heb. 12: 22–3, REB). Although it is a heavenly and eternal city, it is also a place which is related in a very intimate and special way to the world of earth and time. The city is but another name for the new order which has already broken in upon the old, not by way of negation or contradiction, but by gathering up the past with all its shadowy anticipations into the final perfect consummation.

Likewise John the Seer depicts the human future not as a loose collection of individual souls but as a vibrant, functioning society. He ends his work with a double climax, and it is one of the peculiarities

---

[53] Gal. 4: 25 f.; Heb. 11: 10, 16; 12: 22 ff.; 13: 14; Rev. 3: 12; 21: 2, 10 ff.

of his prophecy that its principal eschatological symbols (the court scene, the wedding, and the battles) have a double fulfilment, first within history before the millennium and then beyond history in the new heaven and earth. At first reading we may receive the impression that, while the millennium is the vindication of God's purposes within history, the new heaven and earth are discontinuous with the old ones which have been rolled up like a scroll. But this is to take the imagery too literalistically. For we are told that into the New Jerusalem shall be brought the wealth and splendour of the nations, though nothing unclean may enter it (21: 26–7). Not only are the gates of the city open on all sides to receive the numberless company of its citizens, but everything of real worth in the old heaven and earth, including the human achievements of inventive, artistic, and intellectual prowess, will find a place in the eternal order. For John this is meant to include a share in the joy with which God rejoices over His creative works. Thus if human beings have been created not only to appreciate but to complete the work of God, they need not appear empty-handed when they enter into that joy.

8.

The Bringer of Salvation

'In the beginning, before all creatures, God begat a certain rational power from Himself, who is called by the Holy Spirit, now the Glory of the Lord, now the Son, again Wisdom, again an Angel, then God, then Lord and *logos*.' Thus in one sentence Justin Martyr identifies Jesus with all the modes of divine revelation in the Old Testament.[1] In doing this he thought he was following to their logical conclusion two lines of thought which he found in the New Testament. The first was the belief in the pre-existence of Christ. 'In the beginning was the *logos*. . . and the *logos* became flesh and dwelt among us' (John 1: 1, 14). 'Being in the form of God . . . he emptied himself' (Phil. 2: 6–7); he was the effulgence of God's glory and the very image of His substance (Heb. 1: 3); he had glory with the Father before the world was (John 17: 5); before Abraham was, he could say 'I am' (John 8: 58). The second line of thought was that by which quotations from the Old Testament which originally were intended to apply to God were referred to Christ. The author of 1 Peter uses of Christ words which were first spoken of the Lord of Hosts (1 Pet. 3: 15; Isa. 8: 13). The Epistle to the Hebrews refers to Christ a psalm originally spoken in praise of the Creator (Heb. 1: 10–12; Ps. 102: 25–7). And Mark begins his Gospel with a double quotation, drawn partly from Malachi 3: 1 and partly from Isaiah 40: 3: 'Behold, I send my messenger before your face, who shall prepare the way before you. The voice of one crying in the wilderness, "Prepare the way of the Lord, make his paths straight".' The messenger and the voice crying in the wilderness are identified with John the Baptist, whose function it was to prepare the way for Jesus. But in both Old Testament passages the task of the herald was to prepare the way for God himself. In using

---

[1] *Dialogue with Trypho*, 61.

these quotations, therefore, Mark is declaring his faith that the coming of Jesus was the coming of God.

What qualifications did Jesus possess that these writers could make such claims for him? Or, framed in terms of the question we asked in Chapter 5, by what right has Jesus done what he has done? One way to approach the question, of course, is to assume simply that it is a matter of who Jesus is, leaving aside the question of what he does. Those of this persuasion will make the all-embracing question of christology *'Cur deus homo?'* The incarnation is taken to be a datum, guaranteed by the word of scripture and the Church creeds, and it is asked why it had to happen and how the early Christians came to believe in it.[2] Others might insist against all such speculative interpretations that the Cross is the centre of New Testament theology, and that the conclusions of the earliest Christians about the person of Jesus were inferences drawn from the fact of the atonement. And indeed if within little more than a generation after his death worshippers were hailing Jesus as the image of the invisible God, the offprint of His character, and the incarnate *logos*, it must have been because they had first seen him as the one 'in whom our release is secured and our sins forgiven' (Col. 1: 14), who 'offered for all time one sacrifice for sins' (Heb. 10: 12), and who could claim to have finished the work God had given him to do (John 17: 4).

New Testament Christology should start from where the first disciples of Jesus started. They first knew him as a man, and whatever other staggering affirmations they may have later come to make about him, they never ceased to think of him as a man. The first growing point in their thinking about him was undoubtedly the resurrection, but what mattered was that it was the resurrection *of the crucified*. It was the work which they believed had been accomplished on the Cross which set them to asking the question, 'Who could have accomplished such a great work?' 'By what right has he done it?' Any other view, such as treating the person of Jesus as a revealed truth in its own right, is bound to throw the New Testament teaching out of focus. And here it must be said that distinguished scholars like Westcott—

---

[2] This is the line adopted, for example, by D. Guthrie, in *New Testament Theology* (Downers Grove, Ill., 1981), in which the chapter on the person of Christ occupies 188 pages, and the chapter on his saving work 78 pages, largely devoted to a defence of the words 'substitution' and 'propitiation' as tools of interpretation. Atonement is therefore treated as a corollary to belief in the divinity of Christ: 'The early Christians were not merely interested in who Jesus was, but also in his activity' (p. 431).

not to mention radicals who make no profession of orthodoxy—have failed to follow the route of the earliest disciples. Put another way, using the principle so well laid down by James Denney,[3] it is fatal for Christology to begin with Christology.

8.2. DEVELOPING FROM THE BEGINNING

But knowing where to begin is not the only challenge faced by those who attempt to reconstruct the Christology of the New Testament writers. At a time when theologians seem bent on fighting once again the Christological battles which led to the uneasy truce of Chalcedon,[4] the New Testament theologian of all people must do everything possible to ensure that the primary documents are allowed to speak with their own voice, without modern theological fashions distorting or even replacing that voice. And in the realm of Christology, the most fashionable—and distortive—belief of modern times has been that of chronological development. How often is it stated, almost as an axiom, that whole sections of the New Testament may be regarded as 'late', 'secondary', and 'theological', while others are 'early', 'primitive', and 'historical'? This is not to suggest that there was no growth in the early Church's thinking about Jesus; for where there is life, there is growth, and the apostolic age was a period of ebullient vitality. But no sooner is the word 'development' used than a process of suggestion sets in. Development in other spheres of activity or experience denotes the change from child to adult, from simplicity to sophistication; and it is all too easy to slip into the unquestioned and largely unfounded assumption that this was the course of New Testament thought also. We have seen how the same may be said of the word 'primitive'. When we speak of the 'primitive Church', we correctly mean the Church of

---

[3] J. Denney, *The Death of Christ*, 1–10.

[4] Cf. e.g. Hans Küng, *Um Nichts als die Wahrheit: Deutsche Bischofskonferenz contra Hans Küng, eine Dokumentation*, ed. W. Jens (Munich, 1978); Walter Kasper, *Jesus the Christ* (London, 1976); John Hick (ed.), *The Myth of God Incarnate* (London, 1977); Michael Green (ed.), *The Truth of God Incarnate* (London, 1977); Michael Goulder (ed.), *Incarnation and Myth: the Debate Continued* (London, 1977); the majority of the articles in L. D. Hurst and N. T. Wright (eds.), *The Glory of Christ in The New Testament* (Oxford, 1987); and A. J. Malherbe and W. A. Meeks (eds.), *The Future of Christology* (Philadelphia, 1993); M. de Jonge, *Christology in Context* (Philadelphia, 1988); *Jesus: The Servant Messiah* (New Haven, Conn., 1991); and *Jesus: Stranger from Heaven and Son of God* (Missoula, Mont., 1977); and B. Witherington, *The Christology of Jesus* (Philadelphia, 1990).

the earliest days after the resurrection of Jesus. But the word 'primitive' also tends to carry associations of crude, naïve, and untutored beginnings, which readily intrude upon our assessment of early Christianity. That Christian doctrine had a primitive stage in this second and pejorative sense is an assumption we bring to the study of the New Testament, hardly a conclusion we derive from its evidence.

Behind the bondage imposed by such words lies the postulate that all development must be as logical as Euclid. We consequently tend to assign anything that looks simple, elementary, or unreflective to an early stage in the process, and anything that looks complex, advanced, and profound to a later stage. But there is no conversion table which enables us to exchange a logical sequence for a chronological one. The Pastoral Epistles, thought by most New Testament scholars to be later than Paul and written by his admirer, often appear theologically naïve in comparison with the undisputed Pauline writings.[5] The First Epistle of Clement was probably written in the same decade as the Fourth Gospel and the Revelation, and by one who had read the Epistles of Paul and the Epistle to the Hebrews; yet Irenaeus (*Haer.* iii. 3) is surely indulging in hyperbole when he points to it as a signal monument of apostolic Christianity.

Perhaps the most arresting piece of evidence is to be found in the work of Luke. Anyone who thought it a profitable enterprise to classify the New Testament writers according to the height of their Christology would have to say that Mark's Christology is higher than Luke's. It is, of course, true that Luke habitually prefers his non-Marcan sources to Mark; but we cannot use this preference to explain away his use of Mark. Luke is a theologian in his own right, and his theology is his own, however much he may have derived from authentic sources. In Mark and Q, 'Son of God' is a high Christological title, but in Luke Jesus is Son of God because he can trace his descent back to Adam. Luke's interest from start to finish is in the human Jesus, 'a man singled out for you by God' (Acts 2: 22), and 'anointed with the Holy Spirit and power' (Acts 10: 38). Moreover, although Luke's sources contained a number of references to the prevalent belief of the early Church in a corporate Christ (e.g. Acts 9: 4; 22: 7; 26: 14), Luke's

---

[5] In his study of *Church Order in the New Testament* (ET London, 1961), E. Schweizer actually cites Matthew, Luke, and the Pastorals as evidence for the thought and practice of the pre-Pauline *Urgemeinde*.

Jesus, whether on earth or exalted in heaven, remains an individual.[6] Also, as we have seen, Luke omits from his Gospel any sayings which give atoning significance to the Cross, presumably because he regarded the whole life and ministry of Jesus as God's saving act; and he has consistently tried to clarify Mark's apparently futurist eschatology.[7]

Most statements of Christological development made this century continue to rest on an optimistic programme of reconstruction which has relied upon four main assumptions:

1. 'Hellenistic' theological elements are to be treated as secondary and late when compared with those which are 'Jewish' and 'Palestinian'.

2. 'Functional' statements concerning Jesus—those which focus on what he *does*—are to be treated as 'low' and thus earlier, while 'ontological' statements—those which focus on who he *is*—are 'high' and later.

3. The tracing of an idea in the New Testament to a source—whether Christian or non-Christian—will bring us closer to an understanding of that idea.

4. Any element in the gospel tradition which can be shown to correspond to the theology or practice of the Christian community cannot be properly attributed to the earliest period—that of Jesus himself.

These assumptions, which in some quarters still enjoy the status of dogma, are in fact the product of outdated ideas and imprecise distinctions, and need to be called into serious question at each point.

1. Any rigid distinction between Palestinian and Hellenistic Judaism, and therefore between Palestinian and Hellenistic Christianity, is now seen to be based on two fallacies: that the Mishnah is normative for first-century Palestinian Judaism, and that Philo is normative for the Judaism of the Diaspora. Qumran has given the *coup de grâce* to the first of these. As for the second, we have it on the evidence of Philo himself that there were at least three types of Jew in Alexandria in his day—the literalists, the progressives and the middle-of-the-road people like Philo himself;[8] and we also know that the Diaspora syna-

---

[6] So C. F. D. Moule, *The Phenomenon of the New Testament* (London, 1967), 36 ff. The same point is often made for the Christology of Hebrews.

[7] See above p. 257–61, and Caird, *Language and Imagery of the Bible*, 266.

[8] For the literalists cf. *de Somn.* i 120; *de Conf. Ling.* 14; for the progressives cf. *Migr.* 16: 89; and for the whole subject cf. H. A. Wolfson, *Philo* (Cambridge, Mass., 1968[4]), i. 57–73.

gogues maintained close touch with Jerusalem, and that there were
plenty of Hellenists living in Jerusalem and throughout Palestine.

2. We saw above that there is no heightening of Christology when
we move from a Jewish Christian setting, where the relation of Jesus
to God is expressed in terms of function, to a Gentile Christian setting,
where it is expressed in terms of status or origin. 'The Jewish evidence
about "Messiahship" is decisive. The *function* of the Messiah is a Divine
function; his bringing in the "Kingdom of the Heavens" is God's own
bringing in of His own Kingdom; the Messiah's action in history is
starkly identified again and again with God's own action in history.'[9]
This attitude is perhaps best exemplified in the Fourth Gospel, which,
for all its thin Greek veneer, stands firmly in the same Jewish tradition:
it makes and can make no higher claim for Jesus than that the Father
has entrusted him with the doing of His own work, and has given him
authority to pass judgement, because he is the Son of Man (John 5:
17–27).

3. The treatment of the New Testament as a patchwork of ideas
drawn from Jewish and pagan sources tends to obscure the evidence
that it is a new and coherent unity. Parallels to the New Testament
in other literatures and religions are in themselves no evidence of
dependence; and, even where dependence can be proved, the fact
remains that to trace a word, an idea, or a practice to its origin helps
us very little to explain what it means in its new setting. Whatever
scholars might claim concerning the pre-Mosaic origins of the Jewish
Passover, it tells us nothing about the Christian Eucharist. Bultmann
has informed us that the Prologue to the Fourth Gospel had a previous
existence as a Gnostic hymn,[10] and for all we know he may be right.
But even if this could be proved beyond reasonable doubt, it would
be a fact of singularly little importance to the commentator on the
Gospel. What the hymn meant to its supposed Gnostic author may
provide an interesting exercise for the antiquarian. But for the exegesis
of the Gospel all that matters is what it meant to the evangelist; and
this we can discover only by reading the Gospel.

4. Is it reasonable to countenance the existence of a community
whose beliefs and teaching at no point coincided with those of its
founder? We shall treat this question more fully in Chapter 9. But at

[9] G. Dix, *Jew and Greek* (Westminster, 1953), 80 (cf. above, p. 13). A similar point
is made by R. N. Longenecker, *The Christology of Early Jewish Christianity* (London,
1970), 2 ff.

[10] Cf. R. Bultmann, *The Gospel of John: A Commentary* (Philadelphia, 1971), 20 ff.

this point we may say that it is hardly surprising that even Bultmann could not apply such a criterion consistently. On the evidence of the Epistles, eschatology was clearly one of the dominant interests of the early Church and therefore the one element in the teaching attributed to Jesus which is most unmistakably marked out for the critical axe; yet this is one of the few elements which Bultmann declares to be undoubtedly authentic.[11] The whole approach so obviously dissolves into arbitrary subjectivity that it ought to have been abandoned long ago.

In the end all proposals of doctrinal development carry within them inherent dangers, most notably the danger of over-simplification. This, on the other hand, is not to suggest that something else should take their place, only that the modern cult of methodology or hermeneutics should never be allowed to take the place of the study of the New Testament. It is therefore incumbent upon us to look at the evidence of New Testament Christology with as few presuppositions as possible, if only to see where that evidence might lead us.

8.3. THE QUALIFICATIONS OF JESUS

If we return to our original question (what qualifications did Jesus possess in order to do what he has done?), we will sooner or later have to face the traditional division of Christological statements in the New Testament into the categories of the human and the divine. And there is certainly nothing illegitimate in such a division, so long as the New Testament writers are allowed to speak for themselves, without later theological and philosophical formulations distorting the picture. We begin therefore where the first disciples of Jesus began: with the humanity of Jesus.

8.3.1. *Humanity*

In outlining their understanding of the humanity of Jesus, the New Testament writers make three rather dramatic claims: Jesus is fully human, perfectly human, and he identifies fully with sinful humanity in its need.

---

[11] By 'eschatology', of course, Bultmann meant 'myth': the naïve historical Jesus must be retranslated into a 'modern', existentialist framework.

(a) *Full Humanity*

Why should one person be thought qualified to die for an entire race? For the New Testament writers the answer to that question is clear: such a person must fully belong to the race for which he is dying. There are essentially two ways this is established by the writers. The first, an appeal to the facts of Jesus' human experience, focuses on history. The second, an appeal to Psalm 8, focuses on scripture.

Human Experience

Jesus' human experience is described by the writers in several significant ways. First, and most conspicuously, he was *born*. 'But when the time had fully come, God sent forth his Son, born of a woman, born under the Law' (Gal. 4: 4). The New Testament writers agree that Jesus went through the normal channels of conception, pre-natal development, and childbirth. *Or do they?* What of the Virgin Birth? Here, of course, some attention must be given to the theological dimensions of this idea, without getting embroiled in questions of historicity.[12]

In fact the idea of the Virgin Birth had no place in the apostolic preaching recorded in Acts. Mark and the Fourth Gospel could relate the story of Jesus' birth without mentioning it, though both have a hint of a Jewish rumour that Jesus was born out of wedlock (Mark 6: 3; John 8: 41). John is interested only in spiritual birth of which physical birth is a parable (3: 3–7).[13] For Paul, belief in the divinity of Jesus is assured (Phil. 2: 5–11), but he also maintains that in entering this world by the normal channel of birth Christ had taken upon himself humanity with all its horrors (Gal. 4: 4; Rom. 8: 3; 2 Cor. 5: 21; Gal. 3: 13; Phil. 2: 7). For Paul, new creation begins at Jesus' resurrection. And we have seen that in Revelation 12: 2–5 the birth

---

[12] Valuable studies on the Virgin Birth and its historical and theological implications include those of R. E. Brown, *The Birth of the Messiah* (London, 1977); H. von Campenhausen, *The Virgin Birth in the Theology of the Ancient Church* (London, 1964); P. S. Minear, 'Luke's Use of the Birth Stories', in L. E. Keck and J. L. Martyn (eds.), *Studies in Luke–Acts: Essays Presented in Honor of Paul Schubert* (London, 1968), 111 ff.; W. Pannenberg, *Jesus: God and Man* (London, 1968), 141 ff.; and V. Taylor, *The Historical Evidence for the Virgin Birth* (Oxford, 1920).

[13] See also 1: 13, which, despite the textual variant of b Irenaeus (Lat.) and Tertullian, is normally accepted as referring to the divine birth of Christians, not of Jesus (with C. K. Barrett, *The Gospel According to St John*, ad loc., and *contra* J. Marsh, *The Gospel of St John* (Baltimore, 1968) ad loc.).

of the Messiah occurs, but his mother is not Mary but the Jerusalem above who is our mother—i.e. the Messianic community (cf. Gal. 4: 26). The author is expounding Psalm 2, and the birth of the Messiah is meant to convey not the nativity but the Cross, which is simultaneously the moment of his enthronement. It is also significant that nowhere in the New Testament is Psalm 2: 7 ever used of the nativity.

Turning to Matthew and Luke, it is quite clear that the former believed in a Virgin Birth. He appears to have understood the term *parthenos* in Isaiah 7: 14 in the restricted sense of 'virgin'. But here we must be careful. Matthew's Gospel, as we have seen, is the Gospel of 'God with us'. 'Where two or three are gathered together in my name, there I am in the midst of them' (18: 20); 'Lo, I am with you always, even until the end of the age' (28: 20). The Jesus of Matthew is no absentee Lord; his authority is to be exercised in person. It is therefore likely that Matthew records the Virgin Birth at the beginning of his Gospel not because he is particularly concerned to establish that Jesus was born of a virgin, but rather because he wants his readers to know the prophecy that Jesus' name shall be Immanuel, 'God with us'.

It is hardly too much to say that the Virgin Birth is as peripheral to Luke's story as it was to the other New Testament writers. He appears to have believed in it—although he makes no use of the Isaiah prophecy—but his belief is not expressed by his use of the word *parthenos* (1: 27), which is probably best translated 'girl'.[14] There are two verses in Luke's Gospel which imply a Virgin Birth (1: 34; 3: 23), and in both the belief is merely hinted at. If one takes away these two verses the account reads like the story of a normal human birth, supernatural only because God has chosen it as His means of delivering His people. Joseph is the father of Jesus (3: 23; 4: 22), and it is through Joseph that Jesus is said to have descended from David (1: 27; 2: 4; 3: 31). For Luke, Jesus is the Son of God, but this title links him with Adam (3: 38), and his sonship is therefore a facet of his humanity. Luke ultimately is concerned to emphasize that Jesus began his status of sonship at birth by a new creative act of that same Holy Spirit which at the beginning brooded over the waters of chaos. It is this new creation which is the real miracle of Jesus' birth and the real theme of Gabriel's announcement and Mary's response of wonder (1: 26–

---

[14] So REB; *contra* Brown, *Birth of the Messiah*, 299 ff.

55); and the supernatural nature of the event is unaffected by the question of whether Jesus had one human parent or two.

We have here only skimmed the surface, and the question of the Virgin Birth will remain a subject of debate among historians, dogmatists, and apologists for as long as the Church continues. But from the New Testament theologian's point of view, the sole concern is that neither Matthew nor Luke regarded this event as in any sense a qualification of Jesus' humanity.

The next means by which the New Testament writers spell out Jesus' humanity is by stressing that he participated in the normal experiences of mortal life. He 'grew in wisdom and stature, and in favour with God and man' (Luke 2: 52). The extraordinary idea that the child Jesus *grew in wisdom*, coupled with the even more remarkable claim that God's favour (*charis*) towards Jesus developed as he grew, was later found to be intolerable by philosophically oriented theologians who inherited the Greek idea of the unchangeableness and impassibility of God. But the notion that God changes and remains the same is a thoroughly Hebrew tension which is consistently maintained by the New Testament writers.

There are strong hints in the Gospels that Jesus nourished his spiritual life through scripture and by attendance at the synagogue, just as any other Jew would have done. It has too often been assumed that Jesus' communion with God must have been closer than that of others because it was of a different species; that he had spiritual advantages which put him into a different category from his followers. It is more likely that regular attendance at the synagogue and regular reading of the scriptures had a large place in his life. He was not the architect of his own destiny, but as a master builder he followed faithfully the blueprints which he found in the writings of the scriptures.

The synoptics portray Jesus as displaying the full range of human emotions. He suffered hunger, thirst, fatigue, anger, sorrow, disappointment, pity, joy, exhilaration. He was tempted. He had a small circle of intimate friends for whom he felt both affection and need. He prayed to God for guidance (Luke 7: 9; Mark 4: 40). There were limitations to his knowledge (Mark 13: 32). He asked people their names. He was amazed at their faith—or lack of it (Luke 7: 9; Matt. 8: 10; Mark 4: 40).[15]

---

[15] J. R. Michaels, *Servant and Son* (Atlanta, 1981), 163 ff., suggests that it was the Syro-Phoenician woman's witty reply to Jesus' comment about Gentiles and 'dogs'

What is perhaps most intriguing is that the two Gospels which portray Jesus in the most numinous and supernatural terms also most strongly emphasize his complete humanity. For Mark, Jesus is the Son of God (e.g. 1: 1; 14: 62), but is recognized as Son only in his humiliation (15: 39). In the Fourth Gospel, Jesus' anointing as King is his anointing for burial, and his crown is a crown of thorns (12: 3, 7; 19: 2). In Mark, Jesus' miracles are in some sense dependent on faith (5: 34; 9: 19, 29; 10: 52), while the Fourth Gospel, which Bultmann has characterized as Docetic and Gnostic, portrays a Jesus who is completely dependent on his heavenly Father for authority and daily instructions. For John, Jesus is aware that God has willed that in him the *logos* should take flesh, but this does not mean that he has a memory of pre-existence. In 16: 12–15, furthermore, the function of the Paraclete is the exposition of the historic facts of Jesus' life, not an exercise in philosophical Christology.

And finally, against all who would claim that we must not 'psychologize' Jesus, it must be asserted that, for the New Testament writers, Jesus' human experience is essential to the proclamation of the gospel.[16]

Psalm 8

We have seen that one of the most influential Old Testament texts for the theology of the New Testament is Psalm 8,[17] and that the author of Hebrews opens his discourse with a catena of scriptural quotations about the relative positions of Jesus and the angels. The point of this extravaganza appears only in the second chapter, where the author has clearly adopted the Jewish eschatology of the two ages, assuming furthermore that Psalm 8 is a description of humanity, not just in empirical fact, but in the eschatological intention of God.[18] During the first age God had set the human race under the authority of angels,

(Mark 7: 24 ff.) that may have advanced his understanding of the Gentiles' place in God's plan. But see below, pp. 395.

[16] Cf. G. N. Stanton, *Jesus of Nazareth in New Testament Preaching* (Cambridge, 1974), for whom the human life of Jesus occupies a significant place in the early Church's preaching.

[17] It is a merit of D. Juel's *Messianic Exegesis* (Philadelphia, 1988) that it devotes no consideration to Ps. 8. The implication is that Ps. 8 was not understood Messianically in early Judaism or Christianity.

[18] For useful treatments of Ps. 8 in Hebrews see for example S. Kistemaker, *Psalm Citations*, 16 f.; B. Lindars, *New Testament Apologetic* (Philadelphia, 1961), 168 f.; J. A. T. Robinson, *The Human Face of God* (Philadelphia, 1973), 159 f.; B. F. Westcott, *The Epistle to the Hebrews* (London, 1889), 42 f.; and Hurst, 'The Christology of Heb. 1 and 2', in Hurst and Wright (eds.), *The Glory of Christ in the New Testament*, 153 f.

including the angelic mediators and guardians of the Torah (2: 2), which, together with its whole system of priesthood and sacrifice, the epistle shows to be obsolescent. It was only designed by God to be provisional and preparatory (1: 14; 10: 1). The angels of the old regime, under whose control men and women must live 'for a little while', were never addressed by God in the exalted terms reserved for the human race; they were 'ministering spirits, sent out to serve for the benefit of those who were to inherit salvation'. The new age, the age of salvation and fulfilment, God has put under the authority of humankind. Already in the predestining decree of God the human race is crowned with glory and honour, with all things subdued to its control. The author goes on to comment that we do not yet see humanity in this position of universal authority, so that in this sense 'the world to come' (2: 5)[19] is still to come. Yet in another sense it is already present, for 'in Jesus ... we do see one who for a short while was made lower than the angels, crowned now with glory and honour because he suffered death, so that, by God's gracious will, in tasting death he should stand for us all' (2: 9). Only with Jesus' death and resurrection did the new order begin to break in upon the old. Only then did he become the head of a new humanity, the first of many brothers and the pioneer leading many sons to glory (2: 6 f.), taking to himself not angels but the sons of Abraham (2: 16), qualified by sympathy to represent them in the presence of God as their great High Priest (4: 14 f.; 6: 20; 7: 26; 8: 1; etc).

Paul also quotes Psalms 8 and 110 in a single passage (1 Cor. 15: 25–7). Here, as in Hebrews, Psalm 8 is interpreted eschatologically. God has decreed that the Christ should exercise authority over the whole universe, and this decree is now in the process of realization. He is already king *de jure*; should he not also reign until he is king *de facto*? The difference between this passage and Hebrews is that here the angels of the old order are being identified with the enemies who need to be subdued, the principalities and powers, the elements of this present world. There might, indeed, seem to be a second difference. We might suppose that Paul was treating Psalm 8 Messianically—not as a description of the destiny of the human race, now fulfilled in some representative fashion by Jesus, but as a Messianic

---

[19] The world 'to come' (*mellō*) of Heb. 2: 5 is ambiguous, referring either to the future from the standpoint of the author or that of the recipients of the old covenant. In the latter case it would indicate 'the good things which *have* come' (9: 11, reading *genomenōn*—with p46 B D etc.—not *mellontōn*).

prophecy of the unique glory of the reign of Christ.[20] But this is in fact not so. For this passage forms an integral part of Paul's comparison between the old, corporate humanity of Adam and the new, corporate humanity of Christ. As the sequel (vv. 45 ff.) shows, it was only at the resurrection that Jesus became head of the new, second, heavenly, and spiritual humanity. Until that point, like other human beings, he had borne the image of Adam, the man of dust, and had been subject to the angels of the old order, living under the Law and under the dominion of the human race's last enemy (cf. Gal. 4: 4; Rom. 6: 9).

For Paul, the spiritual does not come first; the animal body comes first, *then* the spiritual. 'The first man was made of the dust of the earth: the second man is from heaven. The man made of dust is the pattern of all those of dust, and the heavenly man is the pattern of all those of heaven. As we have worn the likeness of the man made of dust, so we shall wear the likeness of the heavenly man' (1 Cor. 15: 46–9). We have seen how, in Romans 8, Paul is concerned with the fulfilment of Psalm 8, and it is likely that C. H. Dodd was justified in seeing a further allusion to the same psalm in Phil. 3: 21: 'He will transfigure the body belonging to our humble state, and give it a form like that of his own resplendent body, by the very power which enables him to make all things subject to himself';[21] cf. also Col. 1: 15 ff. What Paul is saying, therefore, tends to reverse our conception of things: *if it does not happen to the human race, it cannot have happened to Jesus.*

The first Epistle of Peter has little to offer in the way of Christology, but it is worth noting the one passage in which there is a composite allusion to Psalms 8 and 110, which speaks of Jesus being at the right hand of God, after angels, authorities, and powers had been made subject to him (3: 22). If we had not already found three instances in which these two psalms were combined, we might fail to notice the combination in the present case. And yet it is there, and we have not the slightest reason to suppose that it is borrowed from Paul. It has been claimed that the difficult passage to which this verse forms the conclusion was an early credal hymn. Whether this is true or not, it certainly presupposes an exegesis of these two psalms which is older than the author of the Epistle, since he takes it wholly for granted.

The Fourth Gospel contains few quotations from the Old Testa-

---

[20] A view held for instance by R. N. Longenecker, *Biblical Exegesis in the Apostolic Period* (Grand Rapids, 1975), 181 n. 62, where Paul's 'Christological' interpretation of Ps. 8 is distinguished from the 'anthropological' interpretation of the author of Hebrews.

[21] C. H. Dodd, *According to the Scriptures* (London, 1952), 33.

ment, and might therefore seem to be an unpromising field in which to pursue our investigation. On the other hand, one of its most characteristic themes is the glorification of the Son of Man; and it may be worth asking whether Psalm 8 is not one of the several scriptural texts which have moulded the evangelist's thought on this point. The glorification or exaltation of Jesus is the Cross: it is there that he receives a new access of glory ('Glorify me . . . with the glory which I had with you before the world began', 17: 5). But we have to remember that this eternal glory of the *logos* had already been imparted to the man Jesus at the incarnation, 'glory such as belongs to an only Son' (1: 14); and that he had manifested this glory constantly in the signs which comprise his ministry (2: 11). Why then does he pray for that which he already possesses? The answer is that in the Fourth Gospel, as in Paul and Hebrews, the Cross is the moment when the humanity of Jesus ceases to be individual and becomes corporate. 'And if I am lifted up from the earth, I will draw all men to myself' (12: 32). Jesus prays as the representative of all who by the Cross are to be drawn into the unity of his person. 'The glory you gave to me I have given to them, that they may be one, as we are one' (17: 22). The glorification of the Son of Man turns out to be not his individual triumph only, but the fulfilment of the human destiny, its crowning with glory (Ps. 8: 5),[22] though it must be added that John has given to the term 'glory' a deeper significance than it had before.[23]

(b) Perfect Humanity

The New Testament writers were painfully aware that the noble vision of the psalmist never reached its realization. The 'man' and 'son of man' of Psalm 8 of course bears some relationship to the figures of Adam and Eve, who were created 'in God's image' (Gen. 1: 26). But is one created in God's image thereby perfect? In the case of Adam and Eve, this was obviously not the case: they fell. Being fully human, they were not perfectly human. A perfect human would appreciate fully the height, depth, and length of what it means to live in the presence of God, no matter what the vicissitudes of life may bring. And to the question of what such a being might be like, the New Testament writers dare an answer. Jesus is the perfect human.

---

[22] On the plausibility of Ps. 8 and Dan. 7 lying behind the Johannine Son of Man sayings, see W. H. Cadman, *The Open Heaven* (Oxford, 1969), 41.

[23] So C. H. Dodd, *Interpretation of the Fourth Gospel* (Cambridge, 1953), 206 ff.

Once again we allow Luke to open the discussion. We have already noted the claim in Peter's Pentecost speech which declares that death could not hold Jesus. The reason for this is provided in an extended quotation from Psalm 16: 8–11, where Peter is said to argue that, although David was the author, he cannot be the 'I' of the psalm, since David in fact died and was buried. David was writing prophetically, putting himself in the place of his descendant, the Messiah. The Messiah, though a human, mortal king of David's lineage, would be delivered from death because his whole life would be lived in the presence of God, and that presence alone would be his guarantee of ultimate felicity. Unlike Adam, who had hidden himself from God in the garden (Gen. 3: 8), Jesus in the garden had sought his Father's presence (cf. Mark 14: 35). In other words to live continually in the presence of God is for Luke that perfection of humanity which is pleasing to God.

There is nothing in the Epistles of Paul comparable to this, except the two passages in which he speaks of the obedience of Jesus (Rom. 5: 19; Phil. 2: 7–9). The second of these passages clearly asserts that the exaltation of Jesus was the consequence of his lifelong obedience. We must be careful, however, not to allow a residual legalism to distort Paul's meaning. He is not saying that the human race, having failed to satisfy the demands of God by its own merits, can satisfy them vicariously by sharing in the merits of Christ. The obedience of Jesus is held up as an example for believers to follow, and, so hotly and constantly does Paul repudiate the idea that human standing with God depends on merit, we are bound to conclude that this is true even of Christ. He too must have lived by grace and grace alone.[24] His obedience was offered not to the demands of law but to the demands of love. It was a willing participation in the divine purpose of redemption. Therefore Paul also believed that the human life of Jesus was lived in close communion with God. It had always been the purpose of God that men and women should live face to face with the divine perfection and reflect it in their own character; and the disastrous consequence of sin was that it removed them from the divine presence and so cut them off from the source of the glory they were designed to bear—

---

[24] *Editor's note*: This comment shows Caird's clear affinity with the Lutheran rather than the Reformed tradition. According to the latter, Jesus lived in perfect obedience to the demands of the Law (cf. C. E. B. Cranfield, 'St Paul and the Law', *SJT* 17 (1964), 43 ff., and R. N. Longenecker, 'The Obedience of Christ in the Theology of the Early Church', in R. Banks (ed.), *Reconciliation and Hope* (Exeter, 1974), 142 ff.).

'all have sinned and lose the glory of God' (Rom. 3: 23). This glory had been restored in Jesus, not only in the splendour of his risen power (2 Cor. 4: 6), but also in the incognito of his earthly obedience (1 Cor. 2: 8).

This theme receives a fuller treatment in Hebrews. The main argument of the Epistle is that the Old Testament is not only an incomplete book, but a book aware of its own incompleteness, full of warnings to the readers not to make themselves at home in it or see it as their abiding city. One of the inadequacies of the old regime of the Law, with its system of priesthood and sacrifice, is that it did not have the power to lead its adherents to their destined perfection (10: 1; 7: 11; 8: 5, 19; 9: 9). Perfection in this Epistle clearly has some moral content, but it is not to be identified simply with moral goodness. For three times we are told that Jesus himself, 'dedicated, innocent, undefiled, separated' as he was (7: 26), still had to become perfect (2: 10; 5: 7–9; 7: 28). The meaning which lies on the surface of all three passages is that, if Jesus was to be the pioneer of human salvation, he must be like men and women in every respect, exhausting all the possibilities of human temptation and suffering, following to its end the path of obedience to God. By this means he was 'made perfect', i.e. fully qualified for his task. But underlying this is an even more important idea. If Jesus is to be the pioneer, he must open up a new road which others will be able to follow. He must therefore have no powers at his disposal which are not also available to them. 'He who consecrates and they who are consecrated are all of one' (2: 11). They are derived from one stock and must draw their sanctity from the one source, which is God. Hence the author puts into the mouth of Jesus the words of Isaiah: 'I will keep my trust fixed on him.'[25] Like his followers, Jesus must live by faith and prayer, discovering by personal experience what it means to be utterly obedient to God, and, even in face of the terrors of Gethsemane, to leave the results in the hands of God.

With the theme of perfection goes the theme of access. 'Nothing was brought to perfection by the Law, but by the introduction of a better hope, by which we draw near to God'[26] (7: 19; cf. 4: 14–16; 7:

---

[25] Cf. H. W. Attridge, *The Epistle to the Hebrews* (Philadelphia, 1989), 91, for whom 'the citation is . . . an allusion to that which above all is or ought to be the characteristic of all God's children, their faithful reliance upon God'.

[26] For D. Peterson, *Hebrews and Perfection* (Cambridge, 1982), 187, 'the writers adopted this terminology [of perfection] as a means of expressing the absolute effectiveness of Christ to fulfil the divine plan of bringing "many sons to glory" '.

25; 10: 1, 22; 12: 18, 22). The human race reaches perfection only through standing in the presence of God. The old regime had failed because it taught that only the morally fit may enter the divine presence; and so the way to God was barricaded as long as the old system lasted. The new regime teaches that God is Himself the only source of moral fitness and offers open access to God on the grounds of faith alone. But the corollary of such a remarkable claim is that Jesus himself must have derived his goodness from the divine presence. The right of approach to the throne of grace carries with it all that men and women can hope or desire, including both holiness and eternal life. Thus, for this author, as with Paul and Luke, eternal life does not consist merely in living forever; it consists in living with God.

Those who dislike this argument may, of course, counter it with the assertion that the author, like the Apostle John (below), thought of Jesus as from first to last a heavenly being, without drawing any distinction between his eternal and his temporal existence.[27] But against all such crypto-Docetism the author would clearly have asserted that the earthly life of Jesus was paramount and provided the indispensable foundation for any claims that might be made on his behalf. The earthly Jesus does not come 'trailing clouds of glory' from any pre-incarnate status; nor is there a single one of his dignities which he is said to hold in virtue of a heavenly origin. Through testing he *became* superior to the angels and *inherited* the loftier name (1: 4). And if we find this disturbing, the fault may lie in ourselves, not in our sources.

The idea of perfection through testing is also prominent in the synoptic accounts of Jesus' temptation.[28] Can one who is totally good truly be tempted as are others? To this question the Synoptic Gospels

[27] E. F. Scott, *The Epistle to the Hebrews: Its Doctrine and Significance* (Edinburgh, 1922), 151 ff.

[28] See in particular E. Best, *The Temptation and the Passion: The Markan Soteriology* (Cambridge, 1965); B. Gerhardsson, *The Testing of God's Son (Matt. 4: 1–11 and Par.)* (Lund, 1966); J. B. Gibson, 'The Traditions of the Temptation of Jesus in Early Christianity', D.Phil. thesis (Oxford, 1992); U. W. Mauser, *Christ in the Wilderness* (London, 1963); P. Pokorny, 'The Temptation Stories and their Intention', *NTS* 20 (1973–4), 115 ff.; H. Riesenfeld, 'The Messianic Character of the Temptation in the Wilderness,' in *The Gospel Tradition* (Philadelphia, 1970), 75 ff.; J. A. T. Robinson, 'The Temptations', in *Twelve New Testament Studies* (London, 1962), 53 ff.; and G. H. P. Thompson, 'Called–Proved–Obedient: A Study in the Baptism and Temptation Narratives of Matthew and Luke', *JTS* 11 (1960), 1 ff. T. W. Manson's classic *Servant Messiah* (esp. p. 57) should also be consulted for its treatment of the temptation from the perspective of servanthood.

supply an answer: *yes, and more so.* Here the idea is that one who resists a temptation understands its strength more than one who submits during the first assault. If for the synoptic writers Jesus never felt tempted to do the things that moderns might view as anti-social or immoral, his temptations were not thereby less real or powerful. Those who are tempted are usually tempted to do things which are not ugly but attractive; and the subtlest, most diabolical temptation is to do that which seems to be good, but is not. One who feels called to liberate the downtrodden and bring in a reign of justice and peace would be vulnerable to three kinds of temptation: to let the good take the place of the best, to pursue God's goals by means foreign to God's nature, and to force God's hand by taking short-cuts to success. And it is these three which constitute the backbone of the Q temptation narrative (Matt. 4: 1–11; Luke 4: 1–13).

Each of the temptations is portrayed as aiming not at a point of weakness but at the reservoir of Jesus' power—his compassion, his commitment, his faith. And each Satanic suggestion is countered with a passage from Deuteronomy (8: 3; 6: 13; 6: 16), indicating a parallel between Jesus' experience in the desert and the similar terrain of the Sinai peninsula. Recalling the divine authority given at the baptism, Jesus replies by asserting his humanity: 'If you are the Son of God . . .'; 'It is written, "Man shall not live by bread alone".' Putting himself under the authority of the Word of God, the Synoptic Jesus understands that to worship God and to serve his fellow human beings is his true and irrevocable calling.

Luke adds his own curious note that Satan left him 'until a more convenient time' (4: 13). While the Synoptics depict Jesus as having won a victory, they also portray the same temptations as plaguing him during his ministry (cf. Mark 8: 33), culminating in Gethsemane: 'Father, remove this cup from me . . .' (Mark 14: 36). That this request is followed by the addendum, 'Nevertheless not what I will, but what you will', indicates that the Jesus of the Synoptics never ceases to obey the Father in whose presence he continually lives.

The Fourth Gospel highlights the obedience of Jesus, but in a way curiously different from the Synoptists. Here, of course, we appear initially to be in unpromising territory, in so far as the commonly held opinion continues to be that the evangelist barely discriminates between the pre-existent *logos*, the historical Jesus, and the glorified Christ. And yet John never uses 'Son' of the pre-existent *logos*, only of the incarnate *logos*, the human Jesus (below). It is accordingly the historical Jesus who is said to be 'in the bosom of the Father' (1: 18; cf. REB—'nearest to the Father's heart'). When Jesus declares that 'no one ever ascended to heaven except the one who descended from heaven, the Son of Man who is in heaven' (3: 13), he is not the glorified Christ speaking literally about what will later be called the ascension,[29] but the earthly Jesus speaking figuratively about the communion with God which he already enjoyed at the moment when he was conversing with Nicodemus (3: 13). Similarly, when he claims to speak only what he has seen or heard from his Father,[30] this is not to be construed as memory of a precosmic existence as *logos*. His whole earthly life has been a continuous process of watching and listening to his Father. The clearest evidence for this is found in the so-called 'parable of the Apprenticed Son': 'A son can do nothing by himself; he does only what he sees his father doing: what the father does, the son does. For the father loves his son and shows him all that he is doing' (5: 19–20). Here is a picture of a human father instructing his son in his own trade and sharing with him all his professional secrets, and through the lens of this picture from daily life may be seen the relation between Jesus and God. So complete is the mutual understanding of this partnership that everything Jesus says or does is at the same time the word or deed of God. It is a partnership of mutual love (15: 9–10) and mutual indwelling (10: 38; 14: 11). On the side of Jesus it is characterized by humility, obedience, and total dependence; yet so totally is his person laid at the disposal of the Father's purpose that the divine truth, light, and glory can be manifested through him to the world. The important point for John's theology is that all this applies also to Jesus' possession of eternal life. 'As the Father has life in himself, so also he has granted to the Son to have life in himself' (5: 26). For Jesus, as later for his disciples, eternal life is not the sequel to bodily death, nor is it a matter of endless duration. It is a quality of existence derived from communion with God, from the fact that he is in the Father and the Father in him.

---

[29] 'The descent of the Son of Man is one way of describing his origin in God . . . His ascent to heaven is His coming, under the guidance of the Spirit, to a knowledge of that origin and of its implications for mankind. . . . He had seen and constantly saw God, and therefore could reveal him and bear testimony to the heavenly things' (Cadman, *Open Heaven*, 30). This is preferable to all those attempts to delineate precisely the historical moment in Jesus' ministry when the ascent/descent may be said to have taken place.

[30] 3: 11, 31–2; 8: 26, 28, 38, 47; 12: 49; 14: 10.

It was one of the weaknesses of the older, dogmatic approach to the Fourth Gospel that it could not provide any reasonable explanation for the descent of the Spirit on Jesus.[31] Why should the incarnate *logos* need in addition the power and guidance of the Spirit? It is absurd to suggest that John included this episode, without attempting to assimilate it into his own theology, simply because it came to him in the tradition. He omitted too many important elements of the tradition for that to be plausible, including the temptation, the transfiguration, the Last Supper, and the baptism, to which the descent of the Spirit was always an adjunct. There must be a theological explanation, and John does not fail to provide it. In the farewell discourse (chs. 14–16) the disciples are told that the crucifixion will establish an objective union between Jesus and themselves, but that they will have to wait for the coming of the Paraclete, the Spirit of Truth, before they can enter into a subjective apprehension of what has happened (16: 13).[32] In the same way the incarnation established an objective union between the *logos* and the individual humanity of Jesus. But the man Jesus needed the guidance of the Spirit to lead him to a subjective awareness of this fact. He had to attain, in the reality of spiritual experience, to a knowledge of God, which in his case was at the same time self-knowledge. It was true of him, as later of his disciples, that only when he came to see himself as he truly was did he also see the Father.

These very different writers are therefore in agreement about one central affirmation: that the man Jesus already possessed, during his earthly career, a life over which death had no power, an indestructible, eternal life, because he lived in such close union with God that, without any loss of identity, his human personality was taken up into the divine.

---

[31] This difficulty has led some to find in the baptism the point of union of the *logos* with the human Jesus (cf. e.g. F. Watson, 'Is John's Christology Adoptionist?' in L. D. Hurst and N. T. Wright (eds.), *The Glory of Christ in the New Testament* (Oxford, 1987), 113 ff.; and R. H. Fuller, 'Christmas, Epiphany, and the Johannine Prologue', in M. L'Engle and W. B. Green (eds.), *Spirit and Light: Essays in Historical Theology* (New York, 1976), 63 ff. (Cf. also Fuller's 'Lower and Higher Christology in the Fourth Gospel', in R. T. Fortna and B. R. Gaventa (eds.), *The Conversation Continues: Studies in Paul and John* (*Fest. J. L. Martyn* (Nashville, 1990), 363).

[32] For a more comprehensive statement of the idea, see above, pp. 211 f., and J. A. T. Robinson, *The Priority of John* (London, 1985), 352 ff., esp. 387 f.

(c) Sinful Humanity

One who is fully and perfectly human might well realize the vision of Psalm 8. But how could one also be said to save others? A perfect being would be, and might well feel, superior to those who have not risen to such standards; and it is on this point that the New Testament writers are very precise in making an additional and astounding claim about Jesus: he identified with the human race not where it should be, but where it *is*.

This is, of course, most clearly seen in the synoptic accounts of Jesus' baptism. But why be baptized at all? Baptism implied a request for pardon from God, and the New Testament unanimously affirms that Jesus was sinless (e.g. Acts 3: 14; 2 Cor. 5: 21; 1 Pet. 1: 19; Heb. 7: 26; John 8: 46). In the recorded teaching of Jesus there is no hint that he ever had a sense of separation from God. The searing indictments of empty formalism attributed to him prevent us from believing that he would have undergone baptism unless it held an enormous significance. Why, then, would he have done it? The answer provided by the Synoptic writers is that Jesus knew he had a public calling, and that John had previously demanded repentance of all Israelites. Living among those of unclean lips, he must stand with them in their movement towards God. If he was to lead them into the Kingdom of God, he himself must enter it by the only door open to them. If he was to be their King, he must be numbered with the transgressors before he could see the fruit of the travail of his soul (Isa. 53: 11–12; cf. Luke 22: 37). The words 'you are my Son' at the baptism are therefore meant to be seen not only as a commission from God; they are God's own approval of Jesus' decision to share the predicament of His people. 'Yes—this is what it means to be my Son, my Anointed, my Servant.' Refusing to accept the dichotomy of sinlessness and obedience, the Jesus of the Synoptics receives the ultimate accolade.

This same theme is pursued by Luke in Acts. We have seen that the idea found in Peter's Pentecost speech that the life, death, and resurrection of Jesus took place according to 'the deliberate will and plan of God' (Acts 2: 23) is hardly peculiar to the Lucan writings. But in them it has a peculiar theological purport. The Jewish scriptures are cited to show that all things have happened 'by the deliberate plan and foreknowledge of God' (Acts 2: 23). In his Gospel, too, Luke makes frequent use of the verb *dei* to show that the whole ministry of

Jesus was controlled by a divine and scriptural necessity. On the other hand, it has been frequently remarked that the speeches in Acts assign no atoning significance to the Cross, and the inference used to be drawn that this was no part of the most primitive *kērugma*, but was the product of later theology. But there are two good reasons for rejecting this specious conclusion. Paul explicitly states that 'he died for our sins according to the scriptures' was part of the tradition he had received (1 Cor. 15: 3). We have also seen that in his Gospel Luke omits the two Marcan sayings which interpret the Cross as a ransom or a covenant sacrifice (Mark 10: 45; 14: 24). Though he is the only evangelist to quote Isaiah 53 in the Passion narrative (22: 37), the verse he quotes says nothing of the Servant as scapegoat or sin-offering. It is likely therefore that the omission of the atoning death from the speeches in Acts is also due to the editorial activity of Luke. How then are we to account for this apparent contradiction, that Luke plays down the atoning effect of the Cross, but that he insists that it happened in accordance with the plan of God? The obvious answer is that Luke believed that the atoning work of Jesus ought not to be concentrated on Calvary. From the moment of the Annunciation it could be said that God had 'visited and redeemed his people' (1: 68). The whole ministry of Jesus was the promised coming or visit of God (7: 16; 19: 44). Jesus could bring salvation 'today' to the house of Zacchaeus, because he carried with him the saving presence of God (19: 9). If at the end he was crucified between two criminals, it was because he had all along chosen to be numbered with the outlaws.

This theme is carried a stage further by Paul. In fact no New Testament writer makes more explicit statements of the total identification of Jesus with sinful humanity. 'Christ was innocent of sin, and yet for our sake God made him one with human sinfulness' (2 Cor. 5: 21; Gal. 3: 13; Rom. 8: 3; Gal. 2: 20). The most striking expression of this conviction is found in the so-called Christological hymn in Philippians, which provides the main Pauline evidence for the relation of Jesus to God: 'He assumed the nature of a slave' (2: 7). The order of the clauses rules out the possibility that Paul is here thinking of Jesus as Servant of the Lord. The servile form was what he assumed at the incarnation, not a role he chose to fulfil during his earthly ministry.[33] In becoming human he accepted servitude to all the varied

[33] The aorist *ekenōsen* ('emptied') is probably to be construed as a constative, referring to *a definite point in time*. We are therefore left with the unanswered (and unanswerable) question of when, if the choice to assume the form of a slave is to have taken place *in*

powers of evil which haunted the individual and corporate life of humanity and, by constant obedience to God, broke their control over himself and others.

We have seen that in the rest of the New Testament there is nothing that exactly corresponds to Paul's simile or metaphor of the body. But the idea of corporate solidarity can be just as real and vivid when it is expressed in terms of personal relationship, and those terms have the added advantage of not being liable to literalistic misinterpretation. We have noted that in Hebrews the perfecting of Jesus required that he should undergo the whole range of human temptation and suffering. The purpose of this is not only to ensure that he was fully and perfectly human, but also that he was fully qualified by personal experience to sympathize with the ignorance and error of sinful men and women (2: 17–18; 5: 2). Because of this experience he 'does not shrink from calling them his brothers' (2: 12); they are 'the children whom God has given me' (2: 13), and he 'takes them to himself' (2: 16). The whole elaborate argument about Aaron and Melchizedek turns on the duty of the High Priest to be the representative of men and women before God (5: 1).

Writers who ought to have known better[34] have made unfavourable comparisons between Hebrews and Paul or the Fourth Gospel, on the supposition that in Hebrews the atoning work of Jesus is never grounded in the love of God. It is, of course, true that the word *agapē* is not used, except twice to denote a Christian virtue (6: 10; 10: 24). But must we be slaves to the concordance on this point? The theology of Hebrews might well be subtitled 'Atonement by Sympathy'; and the sufferings of Jesus which qualified him to be a sympathetic High Priest are said to have had their source in the character of God. 'It befitted God . . . in bringing many sons to glory, to make the pioneer of their salvation perfect through suffering' (2: 10).

The Fourth Gospel by contrast depicts the earthly Jesus as is 'in the bosom of the Father'. His whole life is spent in watching and listening to his Father and in doing His work (or rather, in allowing the Father to work through him). 'It is the Father who dwells in me doing His own work' (14: 10). And yet the Jesus of the first half of the Gospel is a lonely figure, the only Son (*monogenēs*) who goes where

Jesus' human lifetime, this could have taken place. It is better to posit the act of choice *before* his human lifetime began.

[34] See e.g. V. Taylor, *The Atonement in New Testament Teaching* (London, 1945), 165.

others cannot follow him, demonstrating in every act his unique relationship with God. How then can he be said to identify with his followers? The answer is that his relationship to men and women is concentrated wholly in the Passion. We are told, certainly, that he has loved his disciples all along; but it is only when he loves them to the uttermost that they can 'have part with him' (13: 8), only then that he goes to prepare a place for them, so that they may be where he is— in the bosom of the Father (14: 2). 'And when I am lifted up from the earth, I will draw all men to myself' (12: 32). At this point in the Gospel each term which has been used to describe the unique interrelationship of Father and Son is put to new service in describing the analogous relationship of Jesus and believers: glory and love, life and truth, abiding and sending, mutual indwelling and mutual knowledge. It hardly needs to be added that all this issues from the love of God for the world (3: 16), which Jesus shares, and of which he has become the perfect mediator. Into the eternal love which subsists between God and the *logos* is taken up first the individual humanity of Jesus, then those who by the Cross are drawn into his inclusive humanity, then those who believe through their testimony, and finally the world. For John, as with the other writers we have surveyed, the identification of God with his fallen creatures is total.

8.3.2. *Divine Agent*

But if for the New Testament writers God is fully identified with His creatures, does that also mean that He is fully present with them? In one sense the answer must be 'yes'. For the New Testament writers His presence is often seen in dramatic interventions on the human stage. In another sense, however, as A. E. Harvey points out, God cannot be spoken of as *fully* present, for the simple reason that he is *God*. He is, among other things,

a devouring fire, one whom to see is to die, the Lord of heaven and earth whose holiness is such that his creatures, for their own sake, cannot encounter him face to face . . . It is a necessary attribute of God that his creatures cannot see him and expect to survive . . . God therefore makes use of intermediaries in his dealings with us . . . acting and speaking in one way or another as God's representatives, God's 'agents'.[35]

---

[35] A. E. Harvey, 'Christ as Agent', in Hurst and Wright (eds.), *The Glory of Christ in the New Testament*, 243.

The concept of agency is an essential and undeniable element of New Testament theology. To Jesus God has delegated His own authority, and it is only in him that the full divine authority and presence may be felt. There can be no 'higher' Christology than one which transfers to Jesus the role of Old Testament divine intermediaries who in one way or another represent God to His creatures: prophet, priest, Son of David, Messiah, Son of God, Servant of God, *logos*, wisdom, and Lord—each contributes in one way or another to the elaborate mosaic which will later be called New Testament Christology.

(a) Prophet

If, as we have seen, it is fundamental to the faith of Judaism that in the working out of His purpose God has enlisted the help of His creatures, those creatures must know something at least of the purpose they are called to assist. They must be able to read of it in the books God has written—the books of Creation and Providence. And it is here that the prophets found their distinctive vocation. The prophets were interpreters who, by their special commission and the spiritual gifts that go with it, were able to translate the language of divine action into the language of human speech.[36] God speaks the creative word which effects His will in the realms of nature and history, and, as he speaks, the prophet overhears. 'Surely the Lord God will do nothing without taking his servants the prophets into his secret' (Amos 3: 7). The prophets are those who stand in the Privy Council of the Lord (Jer. 23: 18). Because they know what God is intending, they can explain to Israel what its part should be in the events of their time.

But this is not to imply that the function of the prophet was purely interpretative. Often the prophetic word, like the divine word it mediated, created history. Isaiah was influential as a statesman at the court of kings. Jeremiah's commission was to let loose into the world the powerful divine word which would settle the destiny of nations;

---

[36] Competent introductions to Hebrew prophecy include those of E. W. Heaton, *The Old Testament Prophets* (Harmondsworth, 1976); H. H. Rowley, 'The Nature of Old Testament Prophecy in the Light of Recent Study', in *The Servant of the Lord and Other Essays on the Old Testament* (Oxford, 1965²), 95 ff.; R. de Vaux, *Ancient Israel* (London, 1965), 384 ff.; W. Brueggemann, *The Prophetic Imagination* (Philadelphia, 1978); A. Blenkinsopp, *A History of Prophecy in Israel* (Philadelphia, 1983); K. Koch, *The Prophets* 2 vols. (Philadelphia, 1983–4); D. L. Petersen, *The Roles of Israel's Prophets* (Sheffield, 1981); J. Barton, *Oracles of God* (London, 1986); and R. R. Wilson, *Prophecy and Society in Ancient Israel* (Philadelphia, 1980).

and only when it was spoken would events move inexorably in the direction of triumph or disaster. The prophecies of Jeremiah, Ezekiel, and Second Isaiah were instrumental in bringing about the return from Babylon which they predicted. In such instances the prophet not only interpreted but shared in the activity of the divine word. This performative force of the prophetic word was aptly conveyed by symbolic acts. When Isaiah went naked and barefoot for three years (Isa. 20) he was giving solid reality to God's sentence of doom on Egypt and Ethiopia. When Jeremiah smashed his pitcher in the valley of Hinnom (Jer. 19: 1–13), he was providing something more than a sermon illustration; it was the publication of a divine warrant authorizing the destruction of Jerusalem.[37]

But prophecy, despite its value, had an equally great liability. One of the worst problems which plagued Israel throughout its history was false prophecy. How does one distinguish the true prophet from the false? Tests were required, and one of the oldest is found in Deuteronomy 13: 1–3; there God has allowed the possibility of error about His word in order to provide a test of loyalty, to which people are expected to respond by the use of their own critical judgement. The quest for an absolute standard of authority is an illegitimate one, a deliberate evasion of God's test. With this conclusion Amos was in agreement: 'The lion has roared; who is not afraid? The Lord God has spoken; who can help but prophesy?' (Amos 3: 8). Those who have heard the lion's roar need no second warning; those who have heard the authentic word of God ask for no confirmation. Jeremiah, too, defines the true prophet as one who has stood in the Council of Yahweh (23: 18). Such a definition speaks volumes about the inner certitude of the prophet, but provides no external standard of discrimination. Prophets are to use their own faculty of moral judgement to distinguish the word of God from ideas of merely human origin,[38] and their hearers must use the same faculty to distinguish true prophecy from false.

It is usually said that after the period of Ezra and Nehemiah the Jewish people were aware that the voice of prophecy had ceased in Israel, and they were therefore forced back into concentrating on the

---

[37] On such prophetic symbolism see below, p. 306.

[38] A point made most forcibly by Robinson, *Human Face of God*, 173, who demonstrates that in the Fourth Gospel the complaint against Jesus' unbelieving audience is that they, unlike himself, cannot distinguish the authentic words of God because of their moral failure, not because of any lack of divine prerogatives.

written word.[39] When we enter the New Testament period, however, we are brought from the word embodied in the text back to the living, prophetic word. We are first warned of the return of prophecy when we are told that the word of God came to John the Baptist (Luke 3: 2), as it had come to the prophets of old. It is, however, pre-eminently in the ministry of Jesus that the return of prophecy is seen,[40] and this is spelt out by the New Testament writers in two ways: (1) in his attitude to the scriptures of the Old Testament; (2) in the conduct of his ministry.

1. It would be wrong to say either that the Jesus of the Gospels put himself under the authority of scripture or that he exercised authority over it. He put himself under the authority of God's sovereign reign, which he found mediated to him in the scriptures, but he used the scriptures for this purpose with prophetic discrimination. He went to the scriptures armed with a principle of selection and interpretation in which Psalm 110 was a better guide to the Messianic calling than 2 Samuel 7 (Mark 12: 35–7), Genesis 2 was to be preferred to Deuteronomy 24 for marriage guidance (Mark 10: 1–10), and the Levitical rules of cleanliness were but a pointer to a need for inner purity (Mark 7: 15; Matt. 23: 25–6). Where the Pharisees saw in scripture only divine Law, Jesus looked deeper and discovered a divine purpose, to which a more radical obedience was due than any law could elicit, and in the light of which all other interpretations of scripture must be judged. The sabbath Law, for instance, must not be so administered as to frustrate the gracious purpose it was ordained to serve (Mark 2: 23–8; 3: 1–6; Luke 13: 10–17; 14: 1–6; John 5: 19–21; 7: 23; 9: 16; below). In his acceptance of the sovereignty of God's purpose Jesus showed his likeness to the prophets; but, whereas they spoke of that purpose 'in fragmentary and varied fashion' (cf. Heb. 1: 1), he knew himself to be entrusted with the whole counsel of God (Matt. 11: 25–7).

2. The Gospel accounts of Jesus' public ministry conform strongly

---

[39] For a contrary view cf. A. E. Harvey, *Jesus and the Constraints of History* (Philadelphia, 1982), 58.

[40] Jesus as 'prophet' is a New Testament category recognized by virtually all New Testament theologians and commentators. So, for instance, L. Goppelt, *Theology of the New Testament* i. 165 ff.; J. D. G. Dunn, *Christology in the Making*, (London, 1980), 137 ff.; O. Cullmann, *The Christology of the New Testament* (London, 1963), 13 ff.; M. Borg, *Jesus: A New Vision* (San Francisco, 1987), 156 ff., 172 ff.; and C. K. Barrett, *The Holy Spirit and the Gospel Tradition* (London, 1966), 94 ff.

to the Jewish prophetic office (cf. Luke 7: 16; Mark 6: 14–16; 8: 28; Matt. 21: 10 f.; John 6: 14) because they portray him as asking his hearers to use the inner faculty of moral judgement to tell if his prophecy is true or false. 'Why do you not judge what is right for yourselves?' (Luke 12: 57). 'If anyone wills to do God's will, he shall know whether my teaching is from God or whether I am speaking on my own authority' (John 7: 17). When asked for an external sign to authenticate his ministry, he answers that 'an evil and adulterous generation asks for a sign, and no sign shall be given to them' (Mark 8: 11–13; Matt. 12: 39; cf. Luke 11: 29–30).[41]

Many of Jesus' controversies with the religious authorities are represented as reflecting his return to the old prophetic emphasis on justice and mercy over cold religious formalism. And when he is said to have broken bread and handed it to his disciples, we have seen that it was a symbolic act like that of Jeremiah and the pitcher, with one significant difference: more than symbolizing his forthcoming death on their behalf, it was making over to them the benefits of that death. And in that sense he had clearly gone beyond the prophets.

(b) Son of David, Messiah

By the time of Jesus the royal terms 'Son of David'[42] and 'Messiah'[43] had become virtually synonymous. The first arises from the Jewish belief that there would never be lacking a son to sit upon the throne of David, and the New Testament provides abundant evidence of this hope. 'The Lord God will give to him the throne of his ancestor David' (Luke 1: 32; cf. 1: 68 and 2: 4). 'Son of David, take pity on us' (Matt. 9: 27; cf. 15: 22; Mark 10: 47; Luke 18: 38). 'Can this be the Son of David?' (Matt. 12: 23). 'Does not the scripture say that the

[41] Matthew and Luke, of course, differ on the interpretation of Mark's 'no sign' (below, p. 361).

[42] On Son of David see in particular E. Lohse, '*huios David*', *TDNT* viii. 478 ff.; J. A. Fitzmyer, 'The Son of David and Mat. 22: 41–6 (and Par.)', in *The Dynamism of Biblical Tradition* (New York, 1966), 75 ff.; and W. Wrede, 'Jesus als Davidssöhn', *Vorträge und Studien* (Tübingen, 1907), 147 ff.

[43] Helpful modern discussions of Jesus as Messiah remain T. W. Manson, *The Teaching of Jesus* (Cambridge, 1945) and *The Servant Messiah* (New York, 1953); W. Manson, *Jesus the Messiah* (London, 1943); J. D. G. Dunn, 'The Messianic Secret in Mark', *TB* (1970), 92 ff.; and N. Dahl, *The Crucified Messiah and Other Essays* (Minneapolis, 1974), *Jesus in the Memory of the Early Church* (Minneapolis, 1976), and *Jesus the Christ* (ed. D. Juel) (Minneapolis, 1991). The standard New Testament Christologies (Cullmann, Fuller, Hahn, etc.) should also be consulted.

Messiah is of the family of David?' (John 7: 42). Jesus is 'descended from David according to the flesh' (Rom. 1: 3), 'risen from the dead, descended from David' (2 Tim. 3: 8), 'the root of David' (Rev. 5: 5; 22: 16), and 'the true one, who has the key of David' (Rev. 3: 7).

Similarly the term 'Messiah' (Greek *Christos*), originally meaning 'anointed', for the New Testament writers becomes a title. The Messiah is to be born at Bethlehem (Matt. 2: 3–5). Some think John to be the Messiah (Luke 3: 15; cf. John 1: 4). Jesus accepts the term from Peter, although reinterpreting it in terms of the suffering Son of Man (Matt. 16: 13–20; Mark 8: 27–30; Luke 9: 24). During the last week of his life Jesus accepts a demonstration of Messianic proportions (Mark 11: 1 ff.; Matt. 21: 1 ff.; Luke 19: 29 ff.), with the donkey apparently an allusion to Zechariah 9: 9–10. The Fourth Gospel preserves the Aramaic form (*messias*) along with its Greek equivalent (John 1: 41; 4: 25). John's readers are to believe that 'Jesus is the Christ, the Son of God' (20: 31; cf. 1 John 2: 22; 4: 3; cf. also 2 John 7). In Acts and Paul Jesus is likewise 'the Christ' (2: 36; 4: 26; 5: 42; 8: 5, 12; 9: 22; 10: 36, 38—and, by implication, Rom. 9: 5). To these references may be added the dozens of times in the New Testament the term 'Christ' is used as a proper name for Jesus.

But if these two titles were important in the New Testament period it was largely because they carried associations with David. We have seen that historical memory is highly selective and interpretative. The popular tradition of Israel, conveniently forgetting the barbarity and disreputable incidents of David's reign, focused upon those elements which appealed to the political and religious aspirations of each succeeding age. It was David who had united the tribes of Israel as never before, in a unity which, after the death of Solomon, they were never to know again. It was the kingship of David and his successors which was also believed to be a sort of replica or reproduction of the kingship of God. Indeed God was spoken of as King because the human king seemed to provide one of the best mental pictures by which could be grasped the unseen and mysterious being of God. Such anthropomorphic images, while dangerous when taken literally, are also capable of producing remarkable results in the way of religious and moral progress.[44] Gradually for Israel the sovereignty of God, derived as it was from the human institutions of monarchy, transformed its picture of what a human king ought to be.

[44] For a thorough discussion, cf. Caird, *Language and Imagery of the Bible*, 172 ff.

Thus was born the hope of the Messiah. In the Temple worship were the psalms, while in the synagogues the reading of the prophets was a constant reminder of the royal dignity of David which must one day be revived. It went without saying that the restoration of Israel and its king could be accomplished only by a great intervention of God. But even in the most exalted expressions of hope the Messiah never ceased to be a mortal human being who would reign over an earthly kingdom.

The hope of a Messiah was from start to finish a political hope. But we should make a tragic mistake to stop here. The political hope was always part of a larger, more important hope in the coming of the Kingdom of God. We have seen how in one sense this phrase means that God is eternally King, and that His Kingdom is an everpresent spiritual reality on this earth. But His sovereign power, justice, and holiness had not yet been clearly manifested in the history of men, women, and nations. The existence of tyrannical and idolatrous empires, trampling on the rights and liberties of smaller nations like Israel, was a denial of God's justice, and even Israel's own way of life was an affront to His holiness. Israel's hope in the coming Kingdom arose out of this clash between its faith and the hard facts. God was King; yet the world was not yet subject to His sovereignty; but in the end God, through His chosen agent, would assume His sovereign power and reign openly, to the confusion of the ungodly and the vindication of the oppressed.

It has, of course, been said that shortly before the Christian era many Jews abandoned the traditional expectation of an earthly Messiah descended from David in favour of a belief in a heavenly Messiah, a divine being who was to descend from heaven to earth to save God's people at the end of the present age. This theory has now, for good reasons, been abandoned.[45] The same may be said for the view that some sectarian groups held to a belief in two Messiahs, one priestly and one lay.[46] What is clear is that belief in the political Messiah, whom

---

[45] 'Nowhere in the whole range of Old Testament prophecy, pre-Christian apocalyptic and Gospel teaching, is the word "descend" used of the Messiah', (T. F. Glasson, *The Second Advent: The Origin of the New Testament Doctrine* (London, 1945), 168). Cf. also Dunn, *Christology*, 22.

[46] For persuasive studies on this subject cf. C. T. Fritsch, 'The So-Called Priestly Messiah of the Essenes', *Jaarbericht van het vooraziatsch-Egyptish genootschap Ex Oriente Lux*, 6 (1967), 242 ff.; A. J. B. Higgins, 'Priest and Messiah', *VT* 3 (1953), 321 ff.; and L. Silberman, 'The Two "Messiahs" of the Manual of Discipline', *VT* 5 (1955), 77 ff. For a summary of the question, cf. L. D. Hurst, *The Epistle to the Hebrews: Its Background of Thought* (Cambridge, 1990), 47 ff.

God would send as a human king of the house of David to re-establish on earth the power and economic prosperity which Israel had enjoyed in the reign of David, is seen in the enthusiasm with which the Jews followed one revolutionary leader after another,[47] and sometimes this enthusiasm was fanned into a kind of nationalistic frenzy.

If, despite the danger of encouraging such beliefs, the New Testament does not shy away from ascribing to Jesus the role of Messiah, it is because in several ways he clearly corresponds to the ancestral figure of David. Just as David represented God to the people of Israel, so Jesus represents God to those who see in his face the glory of the Lord (2 Cor. 3: 18). Just as David *was* the people of Israel and represented them before God, so Jesus incorporates the people he has come to save. This is made especially clear in Acts, where the title 'Christ' is given to Jesus in virtue of his resurrection (2: 36). The mere fact that a dead man had risen from the grave could not have won for him the right to the title of Messiah. It was because Jesus had died and risen *as Israel's representative* that he was now thought to reign over God's people at the right hand of God.

To all this we need add only two more points. Contrary to the claim of Wrede,[48] there is no reason to believe that Jesus—or his disciples for that matter—could not have spoken of him as Messiah before his death. Leaving Jesus' own view aside for now, this is hardly to suggest that the term 'Messiah' would have had for his interpreters one clearly defined meaning. For Mark, Peter's confession at Caesarea Philippi (Mark 8: 27–30; Matt. 16: 13–20; Luke 9: 18–21) is clearly intended to be as much a discovery of the true nature of Messiahship as it is a claim about Jesus. The ambiguous word 'Messiah' is being defined by the known quantity, Jesus. For the other New Testament writers, the raising of Jesus from the dead is similarly God's stamp of approval on Jesus' interpretation of Messiahship, not in terms of nationalistic power, but in terms of service and death.

The phrase 'Son of David' is equally capable of ambiguity, as is made clear from Mark 12: 35–7 (cf. Matt. 22: 41–6, Luke 20: 41–4). There Jesus asks the question, 'How can the scribes say that the Christ is the Son of David? . . . David himself calls him Lord; so how

---

[47] A sedulous account of revolutionary leaders from Judas the Galilean to Bar Kochba is provided by R. Pfeiffer, *History of New Testament Times* (New York, 1949), 35 ff.
[48] See W. Wrede, *The Messianic Secret* (London, 1971), *passim*.

is he his son?' Certainly the New Testament evidence considered above does not allow us to conclude that Jesus was denying (or that Mark thought he was denying) the equation; he did not need to be told that the scribes had ample scriptural authority for the teaching he ascribed to them. What he was suggesting is that 'Son of David', like 'Messiah', is an equivocal term and that the traditional equation did not exhaust its significance. Taken by itself, it is inadequate, for the scriptures contains clues that the expected agent of God will be a far more elevated figure who, rather than merely sitting on David's throne, will share the throne of God.[49] But that his enthronement would have nothing to do with nationalistic pride was a concept which in the end Jesus was unable to convey to a nation plunging headlong towards the conflagration of AD 66–70.

(c) Servant

Another 'title' often assigned to Jesus by modern writers on the New Testament is 'Servant of God'.[50] But again we must proceed with more than usual caution, in so far as neither Jesus nor the evangelists use it, nor are scholars agreed that it is even a category for the New Testament theologian. Certainly when we come back to the conference table, we find surprisingly little discussion on this point. Was the 'Servant of the Lord' an important feature of the writers' thinking? Or is one dealing here with a creation of modern scholarship? Prima facie the evidence is far from obvious.

The Jewish background of the theme is extremely wide. The term *ebed* occurs approximately 800 times in the Old Testament, and was the common term for slaves and prisoners of war. But a king's subjects, no matter how exalted, are also his servants, and the word could therefore refer even to high officers of state (cf. the modern expression 'ministers of the Crown'). To worship a deity is also to serve him (as with e.g. Baal, 2 Kings 10: 19–23), and therefore any worshippers of God are thereby His servants as well.

Since the end of the last century we have been accustomed to speak of four passages known as 'the Servant Songs' (Isa. 42: 1–4; 49: 1–

---

[49] See above, pp. 169 f.

[50] With the literature cited below one should also consult T. W. Manson, *Servant Messiah*; C. F. D. Moule, *The Phenomenon of the New Testament* (London, 1967), 82 ff.; C. F. North, *The Suffering Servant in Deutero-Isaiah* (London, 1956²); E. Lohse, *Märtyrer und Gottesknecht* (Göttingen, 1963²); and E. Lohmeyer, *Gottesknecht und Davidssöhn* (Göttingen, 1953²).

6; 50: 4–9; and 52: 13–53: 12) (occasionally a fifth song is added, 61: 1–3). The fourth song is the longest and most powerful, and it is the one which has most often been thought of in connection with Jesus. As a whole the Songs present a successive picture of election, suffering, and vindication. The Servant is chosen by God to bring the unrepentant nation of Israel back to Him (42: 1, 49: 5). Having been instructed by the Lord (50: 4) that he should be a light to the nations and the agent of judgement and salvation to the ends of the earth (42: 1–4), he learns that he is to achieve this only through his suffering (53: 4–10). His appearance is unprepossessing (52: 14; 53: 1–9), and in his own defence he remains silent (53: 7). He suffers and ultimately dies (53: 8, 9). But it is revealed that this suffering and death are not on account of his own sins, but for those of others, the 'many' (*polloi*, 53: 12 LXX); he bears the punishment which belonged to the people, and through his suffering and intercession on their behalf (53: 12) they are acquitted of the charge against them. Finally, God raises him from the dead and exalts him, giving him a universal sovereignty (52: 13–15; 53: 12). The question raised by these passages for New Testament theology is simply stated: What role, if any, did they play in the formation of the earliest Christian portraits of Jesus? For centuries Isaiah 53 has been read by Christians as a direct prophecy of the life and sufferings of Jesus. Part of the current scepticism no doubt results from the rehabilitation of the Jewish scriptures as speaking to their own time and having their own meaning, apart from any Christian fulfilment. But some writers have gone further. M. D. Hooker and C. K. Barrett have claimed that the New Testament has no 'Servant Christology'; it on occasion makes use only of a Servant *theme*, represented throughout the Old Testament and which is linked to Israel and her representative figures, but with no specific connection with the Isaianic Servant.[51] These writers reacted largely to the arguments of Jeremias,[52] who had seen the Servant as a major influence on the self-understanding of Jesus and on the theology of the New Testament writers. Hooker in particular saw the Gospel references cited by Jeremias as unable to bear the weight he placed upon them.

[51] M. D. Hooker, *Jesus and the Servant* (London, 1959); C. K. Barrett, 'The Background of Mark 10: 45', in A. J. B. Higgins (ed.), *New Testament Essays* (Manchester, 1959), 1 ff., and *Jesus and the Gospel Tradition* (London, 1967), 35 ff.

[52] J. Jeremias and W. Zimmerli, *TDNT* v. 654–717 (published separately as *The Servant of God* (London, 1957)).

For some Barrett and Hooker have settled the issue.[53] But for others
'it is hard not to believe that somewhere in the background Isaiah 53
has influenced the ideas of vicarious suffering found in the Gospels'.[54]
'In her strenuous rejection of influence from Servant texts' Hooker
has 'underplayed the importance of such passages'.[55] B. D. Chilton, in
a penetrating examination of the Isaiah Targum, finds there a pre-
Christian interpretation of the Servant as Messiah, making more plausible the notion that the Servant was already, by the time of Jesus, a
significant figure for first-century Judaism.[56] Others continue to produce persuasive arguments for the Servant as a decisive influence on
the Gospel narratives, which may go back to Jesus himself.[57] Such
assessments augur a rehabilitation of the Servant in scholarly opinion
which may reopen some form of the case of Jeremias.

Of the New Testament writers Luke is the only one who actually
uses the term *pais theou* for Jesus (Acts 3: 13, 26 and 4: 27–30).
Although lexicographers tell us that *pais* may mean 'son' or 'servant',
Acts 3: 13 is by unanimous consent an allusion to Isaiah 52: 13 (the
glorification of the Servant), while 4: 27 refers to Isaiah 62: 1 (the
anointing of the Servant); therefore Luke may reasonably be said to
reflect a 'Servant Christology', at least in these two places.[58] To this
must be added Acts 8: 32 f., where Luke explicitly refers to Isaiah 53:
7 f. in his story of Philip and the Ethiopian eunuch, and records the
view that Jesus is the one who fulfils the prophecy (without saying
how). When we turn from Acts to Luke's Gospel, we find Luke opening Jesus' ministry in Nazareth with a quotation from Isaiah 61: 1 f.
And, as already noted, Luke is the only Gospel writer explicitly to
apply a verse from Isaiah 53 to the death of Jesus (Luke 22: 37, quoting
Jesus). But here, as elsewhere in Luke's writings, an opportunity to
expound the atoning significance of the death is passed over; it is not
why Jesus dies which interests Luke, but *where*: 'He was numbered

---

[53] So e.g. E. P. Sanders, *Jesus and Judaism* (Philadelphia, 1984), 332, who dismisses
Jeremias's entire view by the simple expedient of citing Barrett.

[54] C. Rowland, *Christian Origins* (London, 1985), 176.

[55] D. Juel, *Messianic Exegesis* (Philadelphia, 1988), 129.

[56] From a large body of work one might cite *The Glory of Israel: The Theology and
Provenience of the Isaiah Targum* (Sheffield, 1982), and *A Galilean Rabbi and His Bible*
(Wilmington, Del., 1984), 57 ff.

[57] Cf. e.g. Harvey, *Constraints*, 23 ff., 141, 149, and B. Meyer, *The Aims of Jesus*
(London, 1979), 217, 234 f., and 240.

[58] Cf. J. E. Ménard, '*Pais Theou* as a Messianic Title in the Book of Acts', *CBQ* 23
(1961), 14 ff.

among the transgressors'. This is in harmony with the emphasis in his Gospel that Jesus is the friend of sinners, the sick, and the outcasts. Once again for him Christology takes a back seat to another concern.

While the Lucan Servant references are well agreed upon, with Mark the situation is less than certain. Those who see the Servant figure as an influence on Marcan Christology invariably find allusions at 10: 45 ('For the Son of Man came not to be served, but to serve, and to give his life a ransom for many'), 14: 24 ('This is my blood of the covenant, poured out for many'), 1: 9–11 (where at Jesus' baptism the voice appears to conflate Ps. 2: 7 with Isa. 42: 1), and in the passages in which Jesus sees his sufferings as a divine necessity (8: 31; 9: 31; 10: 33 f., all of which use the term *dei*).[59]

Mark 10: 45 remains a magnet for controversy, both with regard to its authenticity and its purported Servant allusions. The question of authenticity will be determined largely by the presuppositions of the interpreter. But it is also true that there are prima facie no reasons why a figure such as Jesus could not have read the straws in the wind and seen the likelihood of his own death, and then offered his interpretation of that death out of his understanding of the scriptures, including the Targum of Isaiah 52 f. As for the purported Servant allusions, we cannot here enter into the technicalities of the debate, except to say that in 10: 45b *dounai tēn psuchēn autou* ('to give his life'), *lutron anti* ('a ransom for') and *pollōn* ('many') are echoes of terms or ideas found in Isaiah 40–55.[60] Barrett and Hooker placed too much

---

[59] It is correctly noted by M. Casey, ('The Original Aramaic Form of Jesus' Interpretation of the Cup', *JTS* 41 (1990), 11 n. 26) that *dei* has no close equivalent in Aramaic. But, as C. C. Caragounis, *The Son of Man* (Tübingen, 1986), 198, notes, the fourfold use of *dei* in the Greek text of Daniel (2: 28, 29 [twice], Theodotion 2: 45) is important for Mark's usage in so far as it involves Nebuchadnezzar's dream about the first of the four kingdoms to be eclipsed by the kingdom of the Son of Man. While Caragounis goes too far in assuming that Jesus would have used, or known, the term *dei*, it may be taken as a faithful representation of his meaning: the Danielic 'shall be,' which concerns the immutability of God's purposes for the kingdoms of this world, is therefore a 'must be' which cannot be overruled by the wishes of mortals.

[60] Cf. R. H. Fuller, *Foundations of New Testament Christology* (London, 1965), 153 ('It should be taken as firmly established that Isa. 53 is constitutive for Mark 10: 45b and 14: 24'). (Fuller, however, traces this usage to the early Church, not to Jesus.) See also Cullmann, *Christology*, 65; R. T. France, *Jesus and the Old Testament* (London, 1971), 110 ff.; P. Stuhlmacher, *Reconciliation, Law, and Righteousness: Essays in Biblical Theology* (Philadelphia, 1986), 27 ff.; and S. Kim, *The 'Son of Man' as the Son of God* (Grand Rapids, 1983), 38 ff. Kim's work, while suspect in its assessment of 'the Son of Man' (cf. J. D. G. Dunn, *Jesus; Paul and the Law* (Philadelphia, 1990) 103 n. 43), provides strong evidence in favour of the Isaianic allusions (the same may be said of France,

emphasis on *verbal* links, and not enough on the *allusive* way in which Servant-related themes interfuse Mark's account. Thus while 'we have no more than possible allusions to Isaiah in the sayings tradition',[61] this is precisely what we should expect at least from Mark, for whom exactitude of reference is alien to his atmosphere.

The other New Testament writers contain scattered references to the Servant Songs. Matthew, taking over Mark's material, adds two formula quotations which cite Isaiah 53: 4 (8: 17) and 42: 1–4 (12: 18–21). In the Fourth Gospel the Baptist says of Jesus, 'Behold the Lamb of God, who takes away the sin of the world' (1: 29), which some see as a reference to Isaiah 53: 7. Others tentatively trace John's use of *hupsō* ('lift up') to Isaiah 52: 13. And the evangelist himself explicitly quotes Isaiah 53: 1 as having been fulfilled by Jesus (12: 38). Pauline references to the Servant are often detected at 1 Cor. 15: 3; Rom. 4: 25; 5: 19; 2 Cor. 5: 21; and Phil. 2: 5–11. Except for the last all of these passages have a serious claim to be Servant allusions. And 1 Peter contains a very deliberate reference to Isaiah 53: 9, 7, 5 at 2: 21–5 (cf. especially v. 24), with a further allusion likely at 3: 18.

Of some importance is Hebrews 9: 28–10: 10, although the point has been obscured by the arbitrary chapter division. Many see in Hebrews 9: 28 a reference to the offering of the Isaianic Servant 'for the sins of the many';[62] but what is noteworthy is the exposition which follows, in which that offering is explicated in terms of a *willing* sacrifice (unlike the animal offerings). Here we may see a relatively early interpretation of Isaiah 53 in which Jesus, through the help of another Old Testament text, Psalm 40, is seen to have added a *volitional* element to the Isaiah passage which in its original setting is not openly taught.[63]

From all of this we may draw six clear conclusions.

1. There is a surprising paucity of Servant references in the New Testament in proportion to what one might expect. We should therefore maintain that *there is no 'paidology', no developed doctrine of the Servant* which exercises a distinct or dramatic influence on New Testa-

---

although his overall argument is somewhat undermined by his insistence that the Isaiah passages show a belief in a substitutionary atonement).

[61] Juel, *Messianic Exegesis*, 130.

[62] See e.g. G. W. Buchanan, *To the Hebrews* (Nashville, 1972), 155.

[63] It is not clear from the text whether the figure who suffers does so through deliberate choice or through a quiet aquiescence to overwhelming forces.

ment Christology. The writers on the whole did not look to Isaiah 53 to make sense of Jesus' death; they had other means of doing that.

2. The fact that the Servant Songs had comparatively little effect on the New Testament writers does not thereby diminish the influence these texts might have had upon Jesus. It is possible that Jesus has not been fully understood on this point. Allusions to Daniel 7 are even more sparing in the New Testament than are Servant allusions. But, as with Servant allusions, when they occur in the Gospels (e.g. Mark 14: 62),[64] they occur at dramatic moments.

3. Isaiah 53 was most likely the text which forced early Christians to re-think traditional ideas of Messiahship in the light of Jesus' Passion and resurrection. But it is just as likely that Jesus knew the Targum of Isaiah 53, and what is feasible for the Aramaic-speaking Church is equally feasible for the Aramaic-speaking Jesus.[65]

4. Mark 10: 45b and 14: 24 may be reasonably accepted as examples of a Servant Christology. Those who have difficulty with this have not fully appreciated a central feature of Mark's technique, his *deliberate allusiveness*. The usage of Daniel 7, which Hooker regards as important for Mark's Christology, falls into this pattern.

5. The theme of suffering followed by vindication, so graphically portrayed in Isaiah 53, elides well with the Son of Man theme in Jesus' teaching (see below). But to those who would trace all the elements of suffering and vindication in Mark's Passion predictions to Daniel 7 it must be said that the evidence will be better served if we see Jesus modifying the triumphalism of Daniel by wedding it to the concept of a rejected and vindicated Servant[66] or a suffering Messiah[67] (Mark 10: 45a *and* b).

6. No discussion of the Servant in the New Testament should conclude without inquiring what was in the original prophet's mind. Who was *his* Servant of the Lord? Was he thinking of Israel (cf. Isa. 49: 3), a remnant within Israel, or only one person, the Messiah?

---

[64] Cf. Hooker, *Son of Man*, 163 ff.

[65] 'The citation of the relevant passages in Isaiah by followers of Jesus who were familiar with the Targumic tradition is quite explicable. That Jesus himself used such language as he faced death for claiming (explicitly or not) to be God's messiah is also a possibility which ought to be held open' (Chilton, *Galilean Rabbi*, 200).

[66] Juel, *Messianic Exegesis*, 133.

[67] So Chilton: 'the Targum offers no support for anything like a "suffering servant" motif in early Judaism of which Jesus might have availed himself, but it does speak of a messianic servant commissioned by God whose ministry involves at least the risk of death' (*Galilean Rabbi*, 200).

Champions of all three theories continue to come forward, and it is probable that each contains a degree of truth. We have seen how for the Semitic mind the group had a collective personality which could be embodied in an individual, and the individual was bound up with the life of the group. Israel, the remnant, and the Messiah were three different facets of the same truth. Certainly the prophet knew that God would bring salvation through His servant Israel, and he knew also that God can save by many, by few, or by only one.

But he was uncertain of the response. How many would answer? If scholars today continue to debate these questions, it is perhaps because the prophet himself did not know. It was as though he was publishing an advertisement: 'Wanted, Servant of the Lord: all applicants welcome', accompanied by a 'job description'. Undoubtedly aware that empirical Israel was too far gone in its lassitude and lack of vision to respond, he was forced to use ancient figures, Moses and Jeremiah included, as the models for the portrait he was painting.

A 'situation vacant' approach may answer some questions, but it raises others even more disturbing. How would Jesus have interpreted the Servant's death? Would he have seen it pointing only to himself, or to himself and his followers? Would he be dying on their behalf, on behalf of Israel, or on behalf of the whole world? Such questions, on the other hand, in the end may be indivisible; particularism and universalism are seldom entirely exclusive concerns. What is clear is that the debate will go on, with the identity of the Servant in its original context and in its later applications an enigma shrouded in a mystery.

(d) Son of God

In the phrase 'Son of God' we once again find an expression of considerable ambiguity which is often used as if it were a term of precise definition. Learned battles are waged over the background and meaning of the phrase,[68] with no sign of an end to hostilities. Questions abound. Is it a phrase rooted in the Hebrew concept of Israel and its king? Or was it the Hellenistic divine man (*theios anēr*) who sat for the

---

[68] The standard works on Christology (Cullmann, Dunn, Fuller, Hahn, etc.) are on this point adequate; but special studies should also be consulted, in particular O. Michel and O. Betz, 'Von Gott gezeugt', in W. Eltester (ed.), *Judentum, Urchristentum, Kirche: Festschrift für J. Jeremias*, BZNW 26 (1964), 3 ff.; G. Wetter; *Der Sohn Gottes* (Göttingen, 1916); M. Hengel, *The Son of God* (London, 1975); R. Bauckham, 'The Sonship of the Historical Jesus in Christology', *JTS* 31 (1978), 245 ff.; and B. Witherington, *The Christology of Jesus* (Minneapolis, 1990).

portrait? Does it focus mainly on Jesus' divinity, or his humanity? Is it a term of likeness to God or of difference from Him? Are these correct distinctions?

The fact that such questions can be asked makes it clear that we are dealing with an ambiguous phrase which has a wide and varied history. In pagan cultures a 'Son of God' was a human being who had been generated by one or more of the gods and who could therefore be called a *theios anēr*. The emphasis was upon the physical aspects of the generation and the subsequent miraculous powers of the hero.[69]

The *theios anēr* question continues to be much debated.[70] But in our context we may safely say that sufficient grounds now exist for seeing those studies which would trace the New Testament concept of sonship to such pagan speculation as falling utterly wide of the mark.[71]

There continues to be considerable debate over whether, in the Jewish writings, 'Son of God' was a Messianic 'title' in the time of Jesus.[72] The phrase occurs in pseudepigraphic literature (e.g. Ezra Apocalypse 7: 28 f.; 13: 32, 37, 52; 14: 9) as a designation for the Messiah, but the dating of such material continues to be precarious (below). On the other hand 4Q Florilegium is certainly pre-Christian, and there 'Son of God' in 2 Sam. 7: 14 is another description of the Branch of David.[73] This could mean that 'Son of God' was in the first century just beginning to emerge as a Messianic title; but it is also a slender thread on which to hang any thesis.

In the Old Testament 'Son of God' has two usages. It is used metaphorically of either the nation (Exod. 4: 22; Hos. 9: 1) or the Israelite king (2 Sam. 7: 14; Ps. 2: 7). Therefore it could easily have led to its application to an ideal monarch, as embodying in himself

---

[69] Cf. G. Theissen, *Urchristliche Wundergeschichten* (Gütersloh, 1974), 262 ff., 279 ff. (as cited in Hengel's *Son of God*, 31 n. 60); and D. L. Tiede, *The Charismatic Figure as a Miracle Worker* (Missoula, Mont., 1972).

[70] Cf. Hengel, *Son of God*, 31 ff.; L. Bieler, *Theios Anēr: Das Bild des 'göttlichen Menschen' in Spätantike und Frühchristentum*, 2 vols. (Vienna, 1935–6); and C. H. Holladay, *Theios Anēr in Hellenistic-Judaism: A Critique of the Use of this Category in New Testament Christology* (Missoula, Mont., 1977).

[71] Cf. J. D. Kingsbury, 'The "Divine Man" as the Key to Mark's Christology—the End of an Era?', *Int.* 35 (1981), 243 ff.

[72] Cf. M. de Jonge, 'The Use of the Word "Anointed" in the Time of Jesus', *NT* 8 (1966), 132 ff.

[73] So 4QFl 1: 11–12, combining the same two passages with Ps. 2: 7. According to Fuller, *Foundations*, 32, '4QFl shows that the title "Son of God" *was just coming into use as* a messianic title in pre-Christian Judaism' (italics his).

the ideal relation of Israel to God and to the world.[74] It never indicates
a relationship with God resulting from divine conception, but through
election the carrying out of divine work and strict obedience to God
who elects.[75] Likewise in the New Testament sonship conveys the
Hebraic idea that Jesus is the 'true representative of God, the one
who truly embodies what [God] is and does, and in whom [God's]
authority is vested'.[76] Unlike the prophets, who never perfectly represented Yahweh, Jesus is God's Son because he is totally 'like' God;
likeness indicates parentage.

The Jewish concept of agency (below) is also important in this
context. In his teaching, prophetic actions, and consummate obedience, the Son acts as God's agent on earth. It is as if, in his words
and actions, God himself is personally present.[77]

We discuss the sonship of Jesus in the Synoptic Gospels elsewhere,
so here we need offer only a bare summary of the material. Jesus is
Son at the beginning of Mark's Gospel (1: 1), the baptism (Mark 1:
11 = Matt. 3: 17 = Luke 3: 21–2), the temptation (Mark 1:
12 ff. = Matt. 4: 3, 6 = Luke 4: 3, 9), Peter's confession (where 'son'
is linked with 'Christ', Mark 8: 29 = Matt. 16: 16 = Luke 9: 20), the
transfiguration (Mark 9: 2 ff. = Matt. 17: 1 ff. = Luke 19: 28 ff.),
(by implication) in the parable of the Vineyard (Mark 12: 1–
12 = Matt. 21: 33–43 = Luke 20: 9–19), and in other passages
in which Jesus refers to himself simply as 'the Son' or to God as
'Father'.

When we turn to Paul it is clear that he speaks of Jesus as Son in
numerous contexts (for instance Gal. 2: 20; 4: 6; Rom. 1: 4; 8: 29;
1 Cor. 1: 9; and 2 Cor. 1: 9) in such a way as to indicate that he is
thinking primarily of the human Jesus. Indeed, it is the Spirit of God's
Son which has sent the same Spirit into the hearts of his followers,
crying, '*Abba*, Father', an idea which bears comparison with the synoptic understanding of sonship as something which Jesus shares with his
followers.

This could be challenged of course by the Pauline claim of Galatians
4: 4 that 'when the time had fully come, God sent forth His Son, born
of a woman, born under the Law', or Romans 8: 3, which speaks of
God as 'sending His own Son in the likeness of sinful flesh'. Such

---

[74] Dodd, *Interpretation of the Fourth Gospel*, 253.

[75] O. Cullmann, *Christology*, 52.

[76] Robinson, *Human Face of God*, 152.

[77] Cf. Harvey, *Constraints*, 154 ff.

statements certainly look as though Paul is talking about the pre-incarnate Christ, not the human Jesus.

But again we proceed with caution. We have seen that it is one of the fundamental beliefs of Judaism that God sends agents to do His work, and a concordance study of LXX verbs for 'send' (*apostellō*, *exapostellō, pempō*) and the noun 'sent one' (*apostolos*) indicates the range of usage,[78] most of which concerns a messenger who becomes the full representative of the commissioner, acting with equal authority. When the LXX uses *apostellō* and *exapostellō* approximately seven hundred times, the objects of the commissioning are nearly always human beings or angels. Within the former category are the prophets, whom God sends to His people. It is therefore clear that being sent by God hardly *requires* that we are dealing with the concept of personal pre-existence. The commissioning of the agent may even be pre-natal, as in the case of Jeremiah (1: 5); but that does not mean that Jeremiah personally pre-existed.

The main difficulty emerges when we attempt to relate this fact to the incarnation. In addition to Galatians 4: 4 the New Testament contains several statements to the effect that God sends forth His Son, with the normal destination of the sending, stated or implied, 'the world'. The time (if time is the correct word) of the sending is at or before birth, and we are faced with the problem of whether this language is saying anything different from what God did with Jeremiah. Our vision may be obstructed by the fact that Paul clearly believed in Christ's divinity and pre-existence (although the pre-existent Christ is never said to be 'sent' in Phil. 2: 5–11 or 2 Cor. 8: 9). Thus the question remains: For Paul, does 'Son of God' focus on Jesus' humanity, or his divinity?

One answer of course could be *both*. But there are two forms in which this answer could be understood, one helpful, the other unhelpful. The unhelpful form is to say that Paul made absolutely no distinction between the various stages of Christ's existence. But that does not stand up to the evidence. Paul never thinks, for instance, of either the pre-existent Christ or the incarnate Christ as an object of worship. This is a dignity which he attains only by the resurrection (Rom. 1: 4, Phil. 2: 9–11). In spite of his heavenly origin, Christ possesses no

---

[78] Cf. e.g. Judg. 6: 8, 14; Ezek. 2: 3; Jer. 1: 7; Mal. 4: 5, Matt. 23: 34 (with reference to prophets); Ps. 107: 20 (with reference to God's word); and Ps. 57: 3 (with reference to God's mercy). Rengstorf's extensive treatment (*TDNT* i. 408 ff.) should also be consulted.

static divinity; he has a real and developing history. He is in the form of God; he assumes human form, not in any temporary or Docetic sense, but permanently; and as a man he passes through death and resurrection into new life. Then and only then does God bestow on him the exalted title of Lord (Phil. 2: 9) and makes him the recipient of all worship. Then, and only then, does he become 'a life-giving spirit' (1 Cor. 15: 45), able to dwell in others as God has dwelt in him (Rom. 8: 9–10; 2 Cor. 3: 17). Nor is his history finished: there remains the final crisis of his Parousia (above, Chapter 7).

The helpful form is to say that Paul arrived at his most elevated conception of Jesus precisely by taking seriously his true humanity, and that he never had any problem over the relation of Jesus' two natures because God for him had created the human race for just that union of the human and the divine which Adam had failed to achieve and which was exemplified in Jesus. Thus for Paul Jesus *was more not less truly human* because 'in him dwells the whole fulness of deity bodily' (Col. 2: 9). This is not to deny the uniqueness of Jesus. Paul believed that only in union with him can men and women 'put on the new nature, which is being renewed in knowledge after the image of its Creator' (Col. 3: 10). They become children by adoption (Gal. 4: 4–7; Rom. 8: 14–17).

The same linking of sonship with Jesus' earthly life is found in Hebrews, although it is a point difficult to find acknowledged in most commentaries. It is usually said that the Epistle opens with a reference to the eternal Son, to his place in God's eternal plan, to his activity in Creation, revelation, and providence (1: 1–3a); then and only then comes a brief mention of his earthly life (1: 1–3b), leading to his consequent exaltation to heavenly dignity (1: 3c); and the impression made by the first sentence is confirmed when to Jesus is transferred a psalm which in the original Hebrew was addressed to God the Creator (1: 10–12).

But this view involves a number of difficulties, the most important being that it does not precisely represent what the author says. The Epistle does *not* begin with a reference to the eternal Son; it begins with a contrast between what God has said in the past through the prophets and what He has now, in these last days, said through Jesus. Here, as in Paul, 'the Son' is a title for the human Jesus. It is he whom God appointed heir to the universe and who has now by his heavenly exaltation entered upon that inheritance. Moreover, in one passage after another where the title is used, the idea of appointment is present in the context. In contrast to Moses who was faithful in God's household as servitor, Jesus was faithful as Son 'to God who appointed him' (3: 1–6). Admittedly we might here claim, as in 7: 28 and 8: 3, that Jesus was already God's Son, and that the appointment mentioned was to the high priesthood. But we saw above that this option is hardly open to us in the comparison between Aaron and Christ in 5: 4–6, in which the author of Hebrews interprets Psalm 2: 7 just as a modern Old Testament scholar would do, as a formula of appointment to the royal status of 'Son', and assumes in the light of the second quotation, Psalm 110: 1–4, that this appointment carries with it the further office of priest in perpetuity.

Thus Christ ranks higher than the angels because, by God's decree, he holds a superior appointment; and this theme is sustained throughout chapter 1 in the whole sequence of the seven quotations. But the workings of this author's mind in the construction of the sequence are not always obvious. The third quotation asserts that Jesus' status as Son entitles him to the homage of angels, but it has a longer introductory formula than the others, and one which, though clear enough in meaning, is obscure in motive. The title 'firstborn' poses no problem to those who know the Psalter: 'And I will appoint him my firstborn, highest among the kings of earth' (Ps. 89: 27). Jesus' appointment to sonship (and thus to 'the highest place that heaven affords') rests on an eternal decree, reiterated (*palin*) by God when Christ appeared on earth, even though the full implications of his status would be realized only when he had qualified for it by his earthly career.

John's Gospel has its own distinctive contribution to the theme of sonship. Jesus is 'the *only* son' (*monogenēs*; 1: 14, 18;[79] 3: 16, 18; cf. 1 John 1: 9), indicating that for John there were no other sons in the same sense in which Jesus was Son. Jesus also refers on numerous occasions to 'my Father' in a way which clearly distinguishes his sonship from the sonship of others—cf. 20: 17, 'I ascend unto my Father and your Father, and my God and your God'.

It is also clear that, as with the term *logos* (see below), John is drawing on a body of Christian tradition in his use of the term. But

---

[79] Most early manuscripts (B C 33 boh pesh Gnostics Irenaeus Clement Origen) read *monogenēs theos* at 1: 18 instead of *monogenēs huios*, and the former is therefore preferred by many commentators. But the evidence of Clement and Irenaeus makes it clear that *monogenēs theos* arose *after* the Fourth Gospel had already gone into circulation. *Huios*, incidentally, conforms to John's usage elsewhere (1: 14; 3: 16, 18; cf. 1 John 4: 9), and is therefore to be preferred.

he also associates 'Son' more than once with the title 'Messiah' or 'Christ' (1: 45; 4: 42; 20: 31), thus allowing each term to contribute something to the understanding of the other.

More acute problems arise if 'Son' is seen as interchangeable with John's *logos*. Throughout the body of the Gospel Jesus is never called *logos*, nor is the pre-incarnate *logos* ever spoken of as 'Son'. For John the Son is what the *logos becomes* by virtue of the incarnation. This is made most clear at 17: 5, where the Son prays for the glory he had with God before the world was founded. It would be nonsense for the Son to pray for a glory which was already his eternally, even for a glory which might be manifested in his lifetime, since according to John he has been manifesting the glory of God all along in the signs (1: 14; 2: 11). The 'glory' of the Son which he had with God in the beginning must mean the inclusive humanity of Jesus which is going to be activated in the Cross. 'Unless a seed falls to the ground and dies, it abides alone: but if it dies, many will be born in its name' (12: 24). Indeed, if without support from the Gospel, we were to ascribe sonship to the pre-cosmic or pre-incarnate *logos*, we would blunt the very point John is attempting to make: that it is the humanity of Jesus which is the perfect expression of what God intended when His *logos* created the universe. Jesus was the only one who could express and disclose the ultimate end which God has for men and women: that they should become His children (1: 12).

The expressions 'I and my Father are one' (10: 30; 17: 11, 22), 'I am in the Father and the Father is in me' (14: 10 f.; 10: 38; 17: 21), and the claim that he is God's Son (10: 36) are variations on the same theme. (Note also that the sonship in 10: 36 is qualified two verses later so as to mean, 'the Father is in me and I am in the Father', a claim made of Christians in 17: 21 ff.)

Of major significance is John's parable of 'the Apprenticed Son', which we have already had reason to note. Here Jesus depends utterly upon the Father for his daily instructions. The human son who is constantly 'listening to' and imitating the father in the workshop may even explain some of the more difficult instances of Jesus' apparent divine consciousness in John, particularly that found at 8: 58 ('Before Abraham was, I am'). The parallel between the 'listening' Son of God and those ancient prophets 'to whom the word of God came' (10: 35) also does not escape our notice.

This is hardly to exhaust the meaning of Sonship for John. That he can use it in tandem with 'King of Israel' (1: 49) guards against our adopting too narrow definitions. And at the very least such passages should warn us that John, like the synoptic writers, Paul, and the author of Hebrews before him, has not lost the royal and national associations inherent in the Old Testament phrase 'Son of God'. Certainly John precludes us from supposing that he intended the term *christos* in a purely Christian or even quasi-Gnostic sense, completely divorced from its Jewish origins. In fact, it would not be going too far to say that, whatever extra sense 'Son of God' may have had for this writer, it is first and foremost a title of royalty. The strong emphasis on the kingship of Jesus which Dodd discovered in the Fourth Gospel, and which he believed to be bedrock tradition,[80] is not for that reason to be excluded from John's own theology.

In the rest of the New Testament, the sonship theme does not play a pivotal role. James does not mention it, in the Petrine literature it is mentioned only twice (1 Pet. 1: 3; 2 Pet. 1: 17), and in the Revelation the theme is almost totally eclipsed by the image of Christ as the Lamb.

The best summary for the phrase 'Son of God' in the New Testament is twofold: (1) It always, or nearly always, refers to the human Jesus who is God's ultimate agent on earth, bearing His full authority, and making His presence immediately felt. (2) It is an expression of supremely exploitable ambiguity. Depending on its context, it can connote absolute dependence, supreme authority, agency, mutuality, uniqueness, or the identification of the one with the many. And therefore, as a pre-packaged 'title' which can be homogenized and used at any point to elucidate New Testament Christology, it is virtually useless.

(e) Priest

Our final title given to Jesus is that of priest.[81] And here of course we are dealing prima facie with Hebrews. As with his other themes, the starting point of the writer's thinking is the exposition of an Old

---

[80] See C. H. Dodd, *Historical Tradition in the Fourth Gospel* (Cambridge, 1953), *passim*, esp. 215 ff.

[81] On Jesus as priest see, in addition to the standard commentaries on Hebrews, Cullmann, *Christology*, 83 ff.; T. W. Manson, *Ministry and Priesthood: Christ's and Ours* (London, 1959); and D. Peterson, *Hebrews and Perfection* (Cambridge, 1982). Peterson's work, which in other respects is a penetrating examination of one of the most difficult problems raised by Hebrews, falls into the error of attempting to pin-point the exact historical moment when Jesus' priestly ministry began (191 ff.). For Peterson Jesus' priesthood begins at the Cross, with everything going before 'preparation' for priesthood.

Testament passage, Psalm 110. Psalm 110 describes the enthronement of a king who is to reign until all his enemies are subdued, but who is also a priest in perpetuity according to the order of Melchizedek. The psalm was written at a time when the temple cultus was in the hands of the Levitical priests, who claimed to trace their descent back to Aaron.[82] Why then should the psalmist dream of the day when God would institute a new order of priesthood? Why indeed, unless he felt the present order to be deficient? 'If perfection had been attainable . . .' (7: 11 ff.). It is important to recognize that throughout his treatment of Melchizedek our author is concerned solely with the exegesis of Psalm 110. He carries us back to the story of Genesis 14 not to compose a fanciful and allegorical midrash on that chapter after the manner of Philo,[83] but rather because the author wished to answer a very modern question: What did the words 'priest for ever after the order of Melchizedek' mean to the psalmist who wrote them? The author clearly believed (and had dominical authority for believing) that the psalm was a Messianic prophecy and that the psalmist, feeling the need of a new priesthood to mediate between God and the human race, found the prototype of that priesthood in the shadowy figure of the priest-king Melchizedek, who, at the dawn of Israel's history, had stood 'on the Godward side of Abraham',[84] so that through him Abraham was enabled to draw near to God. But even this does not satisfy our elusive exegete. He is fascinated with every detail of the text, no matter how minute. Why should the psalmist imagine that Melchizedek, of all people, could provide the symbol of an eternal priesthood? The answer he supplies is that no doubt the psalmist deduced this from the fact that Melchizedek is the only character in Genesis who is not provided with parentage and genealogy.[85] Thus the allegorical

This of course denies to Jesus precisely the kind of priesthood which Melchizedek exemplified—a priesthood of life upon earth.

[82] On the background of Ps. 110 cf. D. Hay, *Glory at the Right Hand*, 19 nn. 1 and 2. For its subsequent usage in Judaism cf. ibid. 21 ff., and Juel, *Messianic Exegesis*, 137 ff. On Melchizedek specifically, cf. F. L. Horton, *The Melchizedek Tradition* (Cambridge, 1976).

[83] Cf. Philo, *Leg. All.* 3. 79 ff., where the name Melchizedek, as a type of the *logos*, is treated allegorically, a point often drawn between Philo and Hebrews (see e.g. G. H. Gilbert, 'The Greek Element in the Epistle to the Hebrews', *AJT* 14 (1910), 531).

[84] Cf. A. Nairne, *The Epistle of Priesthood* (Edinburgh, 1913), 160 ff.

[85] It is by now well known that the terms *apatōr* and *amētōr* are found in pagan texts for the miraculous birth of deities (for a useful summary of the pagan evidence, cf. J. M. Thompson, *The Beginnings of Christian Philosophy* (Washington, DC, 1982), 119).

exegesis of Genesis, which scholars have thought to be typical of the mentality of this author,[86] turns out in fact not to be an exercise in which he indulges in his own person, but one which he attributes, probably correctly, to the psalmist, in his attempt to understand what processes of thought led the psalmist to make the staggering assertion that the priestly order of Aaron must give place to a new order of Melchizedek.

But if we think we have now exhausted the significance of the priesthood theme in Hebrews, we will be badly mistaken. For the author of Hebrews between the ineffective institutions of the old Israel and the effective work of Jesus there are also real and meaningful parallels. Jesus is the great High Priest, and the author is at some pains to show that there was a real correspondence between his office and that of Aaron. Both were chosen from among human beings, both were appointed to bring offerings for sin, both were qualified by sympathy to represent the ignorant and wayward, and both were ordained to office by God. But it is not enough at this point to invoke the magic word 'typology', as though we could explain everything by calling Aaron a 'type' of Jesus. For Jesus as High Priest is related not only to Aaron but to Melchizedek, and related in a totally different fashion. The words which the Epistle uses to denote these relationships are 'sketch' (*hupodeigma*)[87] and 'shadow' (*skia*) in the case of the Aaronic priesthood and the cultus for which it was responsible, and 'likeness' (*homoiotēs*) in the case of Melchizedek.

The Jewish sacrificial system had 'but a shadow of the good things to come instead of the true form of these realities' (10: 1). The priesthood had all the outward trappings of true priesthood, but not the essential quality of enabling men and women to draw near to God. The sacrifices had the appearance of true sacrifices, but not the power

Those who claim that they refer in Hebrews to miraculous generation include H. W. Montefiore, *The Epistle to the Hebrews* (London, 1964), 119; Michel, *Hebräer*, 162 f.; and M. de Jonge and A. S. van der Woude, '11Q Melchizedek and the New Testament,' *NTS* 12 (1965–6), 301–26. The simplest objection to this view is that if Melchizedek was seen by the author of Hebrews as superhuman, his arguments for the superiority of Melchizedek to Abraham and Levi become altogether otiose.

[86] This stubborn view, maintained almost unanimously throughout the first half of the twentieth century, is given its most thorough exposition by S. Sowers, *The Hermeneutics of Philo and Hebrews* (Richmond, Va., 1965). Sowers's work should not be read apart from R. Williamson, *Philo and Hebrews* (Leiden, 1970). Williamson does not directly confront Sowers, but his work has devastating consequences for the arguments Sowers presents.

[87] On this term see above, p. 153 n. 34.

to purify the conscience from dead works. For the author the ancient priesthood and sacrifices were only shadow pictures of reality; but they also prepared men and women to appreciate the reality when it appeared in Jesus Christ.[88] God spoke to the fathers in the ancient ritual in order that they might become familiar with a picture language without which they could neither apprehend nor convey the full scope of His later work of salvation.

It is different with Melchizedek, of whom it is said that 'resembling the Son of God he continues a priest for ever' (7: 3). His priesthood was no mere shadow, but partook in some degree of the reality of the priesthood of Christ. It was a genuine anticipation. For in Jesus, we are told, 'another priest arises in the likeness of Melchizedek, who has become a priest, not according to a legal requirement concerning bodily descent but by the power of an indestructible life' (7: 15 f.). That is to say, Melchizedek represents a 'natural' priesthood which depends not upon heredity or outward appointment but on the inner, spiritual resources of human character. Melchizedek, neither inheriting nor inaugurating any priestly succession, blessed Abraham, and through him Abraham drew near to God. Melchizedek, then, is the prototype of a natural priesthood. But here the word 'natural' does not imply any distinction between nature and grace. The distinction is that between what people are in their own essential character and what they are by appointment, succession, and office.

The author would not wish to claim that throughout the whole Old Testament period Melchizedek was the sole representative of the order of natural priests, nor indeed that such natural priesthood is necessarily incompatible with priesthood of office. Certainly we are shown a cavalcade of men and women of faith who throughout this entire period 'endured as seeing Him who is invisible' (11: 27). Must we not add that a priest who possessed that faith which is 'a secure grasp of the objects of hope and a guarantee of things not yet seen' (11: 1)[89] could

---

[88] This argument bears a distinct similarity to that of Paul in Gal. 3: 24 f.: there the Law acts as a tutor or guardian (*paidagōgos*) until Jesus came, at which time it is no longer necessary.

[89] 'Only in reference to the future do the two halves of the definition [11: 1] become identified' (A. H. McNeile, *New Testament Teaching in the Light of St Paul's* (Cambridge, 1923), 256). That Heb. 11: 1 is to be interpreted in the light of 11: 3 is becoming increasingly recognized (Cf. Williamson, *Philo and Hebrews*, 37 ff., and E. Käsemann, *The Wandering People of God* (Minneapolis, 1984) 37 ff). According to Käsemann, the concept of faith in Heb. 11 is suffused with the notion of hope in the future.

have penetrated behind the shadows of the cultus and led others in some measure at least into the presence of God? The point, however, is that in Melchizedek, whether he be one person or a whole order of priests, the psalmist appears to recognize the existence of a priesthood radically different from that of Aaron, and to look for its full realization in God's Messiah.

While not using the term 'priest', the Fourth Gospel makes its own striking contribution to the theme. The prayer of chapter 17 has traditionally been known as 'the high-priestly prayer'.[90] It is of course true that only at one point in it does John use priestly language, but that may be enough. 'For their sake I *consecrate* myself, that they too may be consecrated by the truth' (17: 19). Like the king, the High Priest stood before God as the representative of his people, and his consecration embodies, symbolizes, and guarantees theirs. Even so, in Zechariah's vision, the High Priest Joshua stood before God 'wearing filthy clothes', which the prophet expressly identifies as 'the guilt of the land'; and God's command that Joshua be reclothed in clean garments is the prophetic symbol and guarantee of a national deliverance (Zech. 3: 1–10). The Johannine Jesus prays for glory (17: 5) not for himself, but as the royal and priestly representative of the people of God.

8.3.3. *Bearer of the Divine Word/Wisdom*

Another qualification of Jesus explored by the New Testament writers is his role as the bearer of two divine attributes: *logos* and wisdom. Both have been dealt with extensively in recent literature, and both require careful handling.

(a) Logos

The term *logos* continues to be a source of notorious ambiguity.[91] Here much of the problem results from the curious phenomenon that for the Hebrews qualities or activities of God are often pictured as

---

[90] This is perhaps brought to the fore best by E. Käsemann in *The Testament of Jesus* (London, 1968). But while his book continues to assume the status of a semi-classic, Käsemann's inheritance of certain of Bultmann's presuppositions regarding the Gospel (notably the idea that John's Jesus is Gnostic and Docetic) continues to bring it into question.

[91] In addition to the standard commentaries and New Testament theologies, see Dodd, *The Interpretation of the Fourth Gospel*, 263 ff., 318 ff.; B. Klappert, 'Word', *NIDNTT* iii. 1114 ff.; J. A. T. Robinson, *Twelve More New Testament Studies* (London, 1984),

having an almost independent existence apart from Him. Human words, for instance, once uttered, are like messengers, sent out to perform the task of which they speak; and as messengers they may be of two kinds, according as their task is performed or neglected. On the one hand, there are words which are only wind (Job 16: 3), words which cannot stand up (Isa. 8: 10), but fall to the ground (1 Sam. 3: 19). In all probability these are the idle words of which Jesus said that men and women must give account on the Day of Judgement (Matt. 12: 36). They are idle, not because they are spoken in a thoughtless moment, but because they do not accomplish the things they talk about. On the other hand, there are words which produce results, which are established, verified, or performed, words which go out and do not return empty-handed.[92]

By contrast with human words the word of God is always active, always equally His utterance and His act, always performative. But the same concreteness attaches to His word as to human words. His word is sent out as a messenger to perform His will (Isa. 9: 8; 45: 23; 55: 11).

Because of the concrete quality of the Hebrew language, which accorded to the uttered word something like independent existence, the word of God was always on the point of personification. The word which is sent against Jacob and alights upon Israel, the word which is like a fire and a hammer, the word which runs swiftly to do God's bidding, has every semblance of an angelic messenger. But the prophets never took the final step. It was the Wisdom tradition which eventually personified the creative and providential activity of God, and it naturally chose the title of Wisdom, not that of the Word (below, pp. 333 ff.).

The phenomenon of giving attributes or activities of God an existence apart from Him should be understood as part of a wider and more typically Hebrew development of thought, which begins in the oldest Hebrew scriptures and comes to maturity in the intertestamental and rabbinic literature. This is the use of reverential evasions for the divine name. An extreme belief in the holiness of God made it undesirable that His name or person should be mentioned in too close proximity to human affairs, and writers therefore resorted to circumlocution

65 ff., 171 ff. and *The Priority of John* (1985), *passim*; and R. Schnackenburg, 'Logos-Hymnus und johanneischer Prolog', *BZ* 1 (1957), 69 ff.

[92] For examples cf. Caird, *Language and Imagery*, 20 ff.

as a form of linguistic insulation. Even in the early strands of the Pentateuch the belief that the divine presence was with Israel is expressed by means of such terms as the angel (Exod. 14: 19), the Name (Exod. 23: 21), and the face of God (Exod. 33: 14). Ezekiel carries the practice to an extreme when, in his determination to avoid saying that he saw God, he uses three such buffer terms: 'This was the appearance (*mareh*) of the likeness (*demuth*) of the glory (*kabōd*) of the Lord' (Ezek. 1: 28; cf. 1 Sam. 15: 1; Zeph. 2: 5; 1 Kings 13: 18). But it is in the Targums that the full flowering comes, with the use of the terms *memra* (word), *shekinta* (presence), and *yeqara* (glory). Wherever the scriptures suggest that God came into close contact with human beings, the Targums insert one or more of these terms, often regardless of syntax. If the Hebrew says that God spoke, the Targum says 'the *memra* of God spoke'; if the Hebrew says that God dwelt among Israel, the Targum says 'the *shekinta* dwelt'; and if the Hebrew says 'they saw God', the Targum says 'they saw the *yeqara* of God'.[93]

All four Gospel writers present the preaching of Jesus as a declaration of a new divine act, the act to which all the hopes of the prophets had been directed. Just as God spoke at one and the same time through the events of Hebrew history and in their interpretation by the prophets, so He spoke both in the events of the ministry of Jesus and in the interpretation of them by Jesus and his followers. But this was one of the major differences between Jesus and the prophets. The word which the prophets preached was given them from above, and the events were not of their own making; the word which Jesus preached was himself, and the event his own coming. He preached the sovereignty of God as much through his actions as through his words, and word and action were part of the redemptive activity of God. 'If by God's finger I cast out demons, that proves that the Kingdom of God has arrived among you' (Luke 11: 20). Like the prophets, he used symbolic acts, but his acts were, in a deeper sense than theirs, a part of what they symbolized.

When Jesus reinterpreted the Law of Moses, his authority is not presented by any of the Gospel writers as the prophetic 'Thus says the Lord', but the personal 'I say to you'. The individuals called into allegiance to the gospel are called into allegiance to himself as its

---

[93] Cf., e.g. Targ. Jer. on Gen. 3: 9, Exod. 13: 18; Targ. Onk. on Gen. 20: 3; Exod. 17: 7; 24: 10; 29: 45; Deut. 31: 17; and for the combinations of the two terms Targ. Jon. on Isa. 6: 5; 40: 22.

centre (Mark 8: 35; 10: 29). When he set out to seek and save the lost, people found in him the embodiment of the divine mercy. And when he abandoned his parabolic teaching and 'spoke the word openly', it was to speak of his own death (Mark 8: 32). For these writers, in Jesus the act of God and the prophetic word had become one. We have moved beyond synaesthesia[94] when Luke claims to base his Gospel on the evidence of those 'who from the beginning were eyewitnesses and ministers of the Word'.

A similar view is to be found in the Pauline tradition, where the word of God is a newly revealed mystery, and the mystery is Christ (Col. 1: 25–7; Eph. 3: 1–12). Where the word of Christ dwells richly in all wisdom, there Christ is himself present through faith (Col. 3: 16; Eph. 3: 17). In 1 Peter, to be begotten again to new life by the resurrection of Jesus Christ is to be begotten by the living, abiding word of God (1: 3, 23). Hebrews opens with the statement that Jesus is the final and complete utterance of God (1: 1–4). In 1 John, the word of life is the gospel, but the gospel not only heard as a message, but seen and handled in the person of Jesus (1: 1). And the victorious horseman of the Apocalypse bears the title 'the Word of God' (Rev. 19: 13).

It is of course the Fourth Gospel to which most modern readers will turn as the primary New Testament text depicting Jesus as the incarnate Word. But is 'word' the only, or even the best, term with which to translate John's *logos*? How shall we render this all-important term? Translators who know their Greek proficiently continue to produce learned arguments for various options.[95] But ultimately it is a question of conceptual background rather than that of simple word-for-word translation.

One could for instance try to find the background in Greek philosophy, as so many early Christian apologists used to do. The term was introduced to philosophy by Heraclitus,[96] and taken up and given more general currency by the Stoics, who taught that *logos* was the active principle of form or rationality which entered into the passive principle of matter and gave it meaning and purpose. Of course nobody today

---

[94] Synaesthetic metaphor, the transfer of one of the senses to another (e.g. 'the word that Isaiah the Son of Amos *saw*' , Isa. 2: 1; cf. Gen. 15: 1; 1 Sam. 3: 1; 9: 27; Jer. 2: 31; Ezek. 11: 25; Ps. 147: 19) is common to most languages (cf. Caird, *Language and Imagery*, 146 f.).

[95] The various possibilities are well canvassed by C. K. Barrett, *The Gospel According to St John* (Philadelphia, 1978), 127 ff.

[96] Hippolytus, *Haer.* 9. 9.

supposes that the Fourth Evangelist had ever read Heraclitus or Chrysippus; but through popularizers such as Posidonius, Stoic terminology had, to a certain extent, become a part of everyday speech. 'The term *logos* must have been as familiar in educated circles as "evolution" was a generation ago, or as "relativity" is today.'[97] It is possible also that through the work of Philo of Alexandria[98] its use had spread throughout the synagogues of the Hellenistic world. In his work *On the Creation of the World* Philo treats the two Creation stories in Genesis as accounts of two distinct acts, corresponding to the two Platonic worlds of ideas and matter. The first Creation in seven days is compared to the plan of a city which exists only in the mind of the architect; and this is identified with *logos*. The second Creation reproduced imperfectly in matter that which already existed in the mind of God; and into physical humanity God breathed *logos* as its spiritual nature. There is clearly some affinity here with Johannine thought.[99]

Which background, the Hebrew or the Greek, underlies the Johannine prologue is a source of debate which has no end in sight. Ultimately, however, the choice may not have to be an exclusive one. It was not beyond the capacity of the Fourth Evangelist to produce a synthesis between the *logos* of the Greeks, which gave meaning to the universe, and the prophetic *dabar* which gave purpose to human history.[100] Standing at the crossroads of two worlds, it is possible that John was attempting to explain an idea which at its foundation was Jewish but in a way that would stimulate the intellectual ferment of the sophisticated Greek mind. But, as Sir Edwin Hoskyns has reminded us, the Evangelist also had behind him sixty years of Christian theology, and it is this Christian background that is probably decisive for the understanding of Johannine theology.[101]

---

[97] In W. F. Howard, *The Fourth Gospel in Recent Criticism and Interpretation* (London 1955), 160.

[98] Philo in particular describes the *logos* as 'begotten by the Father of the universe', and calls him 'His eldest son and His first-born' (*de Conf. Ling.* 63, 146; cf. *de Agric.* 51). Likewise the Father begat the *logos* and made him the unbreakable bond of the universe (*de Plant.* 8, 9). The *logos* is also said to be God's 'name' (*de Conf. Ling.* 146), and the name of God is 'the interpreting *logos*' (*Leg. All.* 207). In *de Cher.* 36 the *logos* is regarded as 'the ruler and steersman of all'.

[99] In *de Op. Mundi* 19 and 24 f., Philo argues that the *logos* was God's own perfect blueprint for the world which he planned before he actually made the world.

[100] Cf. Barrett, *St John*, 32, for whom Hellenistic and Hebraic influences have been 'fused into a unitary presentation of the universal significance of Jesus'.

[101] E. C. Hoskyns and F. N. Davey, *The Fourth Gospel* (London, 1947²), 162 f.

In the main part of his Gospel John uses the term *logos* much as it is used in the rest of the New Testament. To abide in Jesus men and women must abide in his word (8: 31; cf. 15: 7). To keep his word is the equivalent of believing in him (6: 47; 8: 51); and those who believe in him have God's word abiding in them (5: 38). It is entirely consonant with the general practice of John to take into his vocabulary a word which has already won its place in the theological terminology of the Church, and in one instance, or two at the most, to use it as a title for Jesus.[102] We have therefore a strong likelihood that *logos*, like the other Christological titles, grew out of language which the Church had already brought into use to describe Jesus and the gospel. In this usage God's word was always purposive, and His purpose was always ready to be spoken.

Thus we come to the central question: how is John 1: 1f. to be translated? And here one thing is certain: the idea that the *logos* and God are identical—gained only by taking the last clause *in vacuo*—is ruled out by the second clause. In fact both may be held in logical tension by offering the solution that *logos* for John primarily means 'purpose'. 'In the beginning was the purpose, the purpose in the mind of God, the purpose which was God's own being.' It is surely a conceivable thought that God is wholly identified with His purpose of love, and that this purpose took human form in Jesus of Nazareth.

While all of this is significant, we should never be allowed to forget the uniqueness of John's contribution. He has taken the revolutionary step not only of personifying the *logos* but of saying that it is now permanently and fully with us. In Jesus God has taken the whole human race up into unity with the *logos*, in order that ultimately the human race should share the same purpose. The *logos* has come forth from God and has not returned to Him empty-handed. 'I have finished the work you gave me to do' (17: 4).

---

[102] John especially uses in this way words synonymous with the gospel or for Christianity, a point best appreciated if one considers other titles used for Jesus: 'the Bread of Life' (6: 35); 'the Light of the World' (8: 12); 'the Door' (10: 9); 'the Good Shepherd' (10: 11); 'the Resurrection and the Life' (11: 25); 'the Way, the Truth, and the Life' (14: 6). All these terms have a history of Christian usage, traceable through the Epistles and the Synoptic Gospels, not to mention the Fourth Gospel itself; and two of them, 'the Life' and 'the way', had already been used as names for the Christian movement (Acts 5: 20; 9: 2; 19: 9, 23; 22: 4; 24: 14, 22).

(b) Wisdom

Closely related to God's purpose is His Wisdom.[103] To the Hebrews God alone is wise, and He therefore is the sole source of wisdom. Any human wisdom that is worthy of the name comes from Him. But this idea of the imparting of divine wisdom is a complex one which requires careful analysis. When we say of human teachers that they impart their 'wisdom' to their pupils, we may mean either or both of two things: that they train their pupils to think with the same sort of understanding and discernment as they do, or that they transmit to their pupils the content of their own thoughts. God's wisdom has the same dual aspect. When God imparts wisdom to human beings, He may be bestowing something of Himself, and in this sense the gift of wisdom is closely allied to the gift of God's Spirit. In the other sense the gift of wisdom may be a body of revealed truth. In later Judaism there was a strong tendency to emphasize the second aspect and to identify wisdom with the Law of Moses. And one of the interesting things that happens in the New Testament is that the proper balance between the two is restored.

Because human beings may record their wisdom in a book, it was easy for the Scribes to conceive of God's wisdom as something which bodies forth from him with a quasi-independent existence of its own. Thus it came about that they were able to personify Wisdom, both as a heavenly being, actively participating in Creation and Providence at God's side, and also as a mother figure presiding over the religious education of the human race (Prov. 8–9; Ecclus. 24: 23, 25; Wisd. 7–10). There is not the sightest justification for treating this as anything more than a figure of speech, a literary device which gave forceful expression to what God in His wisdom has done. Yet it is also true that Wisdom is more than a personification of a divine attribute. Wisdom is created by God, just as the wise mind may be said to create the wise thought.

---

[103] The best treatments of Wisdom remain those of J. L. Crenshaw (ed.), *Studies in Ancient Israelite Wisdom* (New York, 1976); W. D. Davies, *Paul and Rabbinic Judaism* (London, 1955), 147 ff.; M. Noth and D. W. Thomas (eds.), *Wisdom in Israel and in the Ancient Near East* (Leiden, 1955); G. von Rad, *Old Testament Theology* (New York, 1962), i. 418 ff. and *Wisdom in Israel* (Nashville, 1972); R. B. Y. Scott, *The Way of Wisdom in the Old Testament* (New York, 1971); and R. E. Murphy, 'Wisdom in the Old Testament', in D. N. Freedman (ed.), *The Anchor Bible Dictionary* (New York, 1992), vi. 930 ff.

> The LORD created me the beginning of His works
> before all else that He made, long ago.
>
> (Prov. 8: 22)
>
> Before time began He created me,
> and I shall remain for ever.
>
> (Ecclus. 24: 9)

For the Hebrews Wisdom was the master plan or purpose of God which underlies the universe, giving it coherence and meaning.

By a slight shift of imagery this cosmic figure becomes the Lady Wisdom of a more local scene, the hostess who presides over an academy of gracious living and who invites young patrons to take part in the educational talk of her salon. Hence for all her cosmic functions she stands fundamentally for a way of life, so that she can even be identified with the Torah, the Law of Moses (Ecclus. 24: 23).

It may hardly be surprising therefore that Wisdom is also depicted as looking for a permanent home among human beings:

> Among them all I looked for a home:
> in whose territory was I to settle?
> Then the Creator of the universe laid a command
>   upon me;
> my Creator decreed where I should dwell.
> He said, 'Make your home in Jacob;
> find your heritage in Israel.'
>
> (Ecclus. 24: 7–8)

When we come to the New Testament, it should be even less surprising that the earliest Christian theologians should come to think of Jesus as Wisdom's embodiment. The author of Hebrews opens with an orotund acclamation of what God has said in His Son, which clearly echoes the portrait of the personified Wisdom from Wisdom 7: 26. The fact that the author does not consider it necessary to explain, elaborate, or even justify such language strongly suggests that this way of thinking about Jesus had long become traditional in the theology of the Church. It is therefore a plausible hypothesis, though hard to test, that the pre-existent Wisdom is closely allied to the idea of God's eternal purpose and consequently contributes as much to the cosmic functions of the *logos* in the Prologue to the Fourth Gospel as does the idea of God's word (Heb. 1: 10–12).

But the writer who makes the earliest and most comprehensive use of this concept is Paul. He begins by contrasting what the world falsely regards as wisdom with the true Wisdom of God, kept hidden from all eternity, but now disclosed and put into effect in Christ. This Wisdom is God's plan for the human race, and therefore for the whole universe of which men and women are intended to be the centre and crown. To know God's Wisdom is the same thing as knowing His mind, and this in turn is the same thing as knowing the mind of Christ (1 Cor. 1: 19–2: 16). As a Pharisee, Paul had believed that God's whole Wisdom was enshrined in the Torah, and that ethical behaviour consisted in obeying its commandments. Paul the Christian gave to Christ the central position he had once accorded to the Law, and his one principle of human behaviour was to have the mind of Christ (cf. Phil. 2: 5). It will therefore be seen that Paul has tipped the balance away from Wisdom as a body of revealed truth into the direction of Wisdom as a divinely imparted attitude of mind.

Paul's most distinctive contribution to this theme is in his letter to the Colossians, where he designates Christ 'the image of the invisible God, the first-born of all creation' (1: 15). What Paul's argument requires is that Christ should be accepted as the true image, and therefore the true revelation of the unseen God, precisely because he is '*adam*' as God had always intended '*adam*' to be (Gen. 1: 26). He *is* the human race, in whom the divine Wisdom has taken up permanent residence. But here, as frequently elsewhere, Paul's mind leaps ahead of the argument. Where we should have expected him to say 'because in him the divine wisdom came to dwell', Paul actually says, 'because in him the complete being of God came to dwell' (1: 19). Christ is himself God's whole secret plan; for 'in him lie hidden all God's treasures of wisdom and knowledge' (2: 2).[104]

Two important riders to Colossians are added by Ephesians, which opens with an orotund benediction expounding God's cosmic purpose to gather the universe into unity in Christ. Not only is it true that Christians have been given the wisdom to understand this purpose; it is part of the purpose that they should be enabled intelligently to co-operate with it. Christ himself is both the revelation and the agent of God's plan, and those who are drawn into union with him find themselves sharing both his functions. The empirical ground for belief in God's universal purpose is found in the fact that in the Pauline

---

[104] On Col. 1: 15 ff. see also above, p. 46.

churches the barrier of hatred between Jew and Gentile has been demolished and the two made into a single new humanity in union with Christ (2: 14–16). Where this most intransigent hostility has been overcome, there can be confidence in God's power to reduce all the warring forces of the universe to harmony.

Since for Paul it is the duty of the Church to proclaim, not only by word of mouth but in the unity of its common life, the reconciling power of Christ, we come to the second idea peculiar to Ephesians. It is God's purpose that 'through the Church the wisdom of God in all its varied forms might be made known to the rulers and authorities in the realms of heaven' (3: 10). The variegated wisdom of God embraces in its redemptive purpose not only individual men and women, but the corporate life of humanity with all its principalities and powers, all those shadowy spiritual forces which preside over the structures of power and authority and regulate or constrict the social, economic, political, and religious life of organized humanity. They also are to be brought, through the agency of the Church, under the unifying influence of Christ.

To this must be added a number of passages where Paul appears to make an arbitrary, allegorical use of the Old Testament, in so far as he is exploiting in the interest of his Christian theology a familiar rabbinic device of exegesis. In 1 Corinthians 10: 1–4 we hear the echoes of a rabbinic legend that the well of Moses (Num. 21: 16–18) became a rock which rolled along with Israel through the wilderness, which made sense to the rabbis because to them the rock stood for God's wisdom, already identified with the Law of Moses. But for Paul it was not to the Law but to Christ that men and women were to turn to find the whole counsel of God.[105]

In Hebrews by contrast the Law was only a shadowy pattern of the good things to come (8: 5; 10: 1); it prefigured those things which belong to the New Covenant. But here also the life and death of Jesus and his exaltation over the universe are something which God intended from the beginning. Christ is 'the image of the invisible God' and was 'appointed heir to the whole universe' (1: 2). Yet this rank is his, not in virtue of some pre-cosmic divine existence, but as the pioneer of human salvation, destined to lead God's many children to glory. He

---

[105] Cf. Davies, *Paul and Rabbinic Judaism*, 148: 'Conformity to Christ, his teaching and his life, has taken the place for Paul of conformity to the Jewish *Torah*. Jesus himself— in word and deed or fact—is a new *Torah*.'

has indeed his part in Creation and providence, but as the goal to which the whole process is directed. It used to be thought that the world-view of Hebrews was Platonism, mediated by the Hellenistic Judaism of Philo. But if its author was under any philosophical influence whatever (an exceedingly dubious assumption), it might as well be argued that there is something distinctly Aristotelian about a theology in which the final cause operates as efficient cause also.[106]

This role of Wisdom, as we have seen, also helps to explain one of the more vexatious passages in the Epistle. In Hebrews 1: 10–12 the author is quoting Psalm 102: 25–7 (101: 25–7 LXX) so as to make the human Jesus the bearer of the whole purpose of Creation. If this is difficult to accept today, it is probably because we tend to forget how easy it was for a Jewish theologian to combine the idea of a pre-existent Wisdom with a doctrine of simple humanity. For whatever cosmic functions Wisdom and Torah might acquire, each remained essentially a code of human conduct, a design for living which had the merit of being identical with the design of the whole universe. And if the same Wisdom which was with God in the beginning, which traversed the arc of the firmament and plumbed the recesses of the Abyss, had come to take up her residence in Israel (Ecclus. 24: 3–12), Israel, by obeying the Torah, was fulfilling not only God's purpose for the human race but for the whole creation. It was God's good pleasure that in human beings His wisdom should find a dwelling. This way of approaching New Testament theology has one great advantage: it disencumbers us from one of the more celebrated problems of classical Christology. In the debates which followed in succeeding centuries one of the major questions was, 'How could Jesus Christ be both human and divine without either a diminution of his Godhood or absorption of his humanity?' For the New Testament writers this question simply did not arise. The union of the human and the divine which had been achieved in Jesus was nothing less than that which God had intended from all eternity to be the destiny of the human race.

---

[106] Aristotle's four causes were the following: (1) the efficient cause which brings things into being; (2) the formal cause which is their essential nature; (3) their final cause or purpose; and (4) the matter of which they consist. The first three are merely different ways of saying the same thing, and in *Metaph.* 12. 7. 1072^{b}3 Aristotle can speak of *Kinei hōs erōmenon*: God as prime mover by reason of being the goal to which all things are drawn.

8.3.4. *Lordship*

According to Luke the earliest Christians believed in Jesus not only as Messiah but as Lord (Acts 2: 36; 10: 36).[107] The term *kurios* had been used by the Septuagint writers to translate the Hebrew *adōn*, often in connection with 'king' (cf. *kurie basileu* for *adoni hamelek* in 1 Sam. 24: 9 and 2 Sam. 13: 33 LXX). 'My Lord the King' was a normal form of address for Hebrew royalty, and what had been suitable for Saul or David was therefore eminently appropriate for the Messianic king to come. But it also had been used by the Septuagint translators to render the tetragrammaton, the divine name YHWH. After the exile this name was never uttered in public worship, partly from reverence, partly from fear that it might be heard and profaned by Gentiles. Wherever it occurred in the sacred text the reader substituted *adonai*, 'Lord'. When the Septuagint was produced the translators followed this practice and used the term *kurios*, which gave rise to the Latin translation *Dominus* and the English 'Lord'. But *kurios* had a long and diverse history as a divine title in pagan cults.[108] It is not remarkable therefore that very early it became acceptable for Jesus, supplying a climate in which Christian devotion to him could grow.[109]

The confession 'Jesus is Lord' was undoubtedly pre-Pauline, and was possibly the normal form used in baptism (1 Cor. 12: 3; Rom. 10: 9; 2 Cor. 4: 5; Phil. 2: 11; cf. Acts 19: 5) and Eucharist (1 Cor. 11: 23). James, the leader of the church at Jerusalem bore the title 'the Lord's brother' (Gal. 1: 19; cf. 1 Cor. 9: 5). Certainly the idea that at the resurrection Jesus took his seat at the right hand of God was derived from an ancient testimony that the Messiah was also addressed as 'Lord';[110] and there are grounds for believing that Jesus regarded lordship as an accurate description of his own vocation (Mark

---

[107] For Christ as *kurios* see (in addition to the standard New Testament theologies) W. Bousset, *Kyrios Christos* (Nashville, 1970); Fuller, *Foundations, passim*; F. Hahn, *The Titles of Jesus in Christology* (London, 1969), 68 ff.; W. Kramer, *Christ, Lord, Son of God* (Naperville, Ill., 1966); Longenecker, *Christology of Early Jewish Christianity*, 120 ff.; J. C. O'Neill, 'The Use of *Kyrios* in the Book of Acts', *SJT* 8 (1955), 155 ff.; I. H. Marshall, *Jesus the Saviour* (London, 1990), 197 ff.; E. Lohmeyer, *Kyrios Jesus: Eine Untersuchung zu Phil. 2: 5–11* (Darmstadt, 1961²); and L. W. Hurtado, *One God, One Lord: Early Christian Devotion and Ancient Jewish Monotheism* (Philadelphia, 1988).

[108] Cf. W. Foerster and G. Quell, '*kurios*', etc., *TDNT* iii. 1039 ff.

[109] See esp. Hurtado, *One God, One Lord*, 104 ff.

[110] On Ps. 110: 1 see in particular Hay, *Glory at the Right Hand*, 19 nn. 1 and 2, and Juel, *Messianic Exegesis*, 137 ff.

9: 11–13; 12: 35–7; Matt. 11: 14). The Aramaic-speaking community, furthermore, commonly used the prayer *Maranatha*, which meant either 'our Lord comes' or 'O Lord, come' (1 Cor. 16: 22; cf. the *Didache* 10: 6).[111]

All of this indicates that the Aramaic *mar* and its Greek equivalent *kurios* were used in the early Church as a means of elevating Jesus to the status of an object of worship.[112] To share God's throne is to share His attributes. Paul's own habit of praying to Jesus (2 Cor. 12: 8) is paralleled in Luke's account of the prayer of the dying Stephen (Acts 7: 59 f.). For Paul 'calling upon the name of the Lord' appears to refer to Jesus, and he assumes it to be the normal Christian response to the proclamation of the gospel (Rom. 10: 13; 1 Cor. 1: 2).

The term *kurios*, on the other hand, contains a note of distinct ambiguity, and there are at least two points at which we must proceed with our usual caution:

1. *Kurios* could mean simply 'master' and be used of anyone from the master of a household to the ruler of a nation; and already in New Testament times it had acquired the usage which it has in modern Greek as a polite form of address—'Sir' (cf. Mark 9: 24; Luke 5: 12; etc.).

2. Most commentators agree that in Phil. 2: 9 f. 'the name which is above every name' given to Jesus is *kurios* (cf. Acts 2: 36). But this cannot be viewed as compromising Paul's essential monotheism. With the possible exception of Romans 9: 5[113] he does not appear to have taken the step of calling Jesus God. Even if Jesus could be said to be 'in the form of God' (Phil. 1: 2) and 'equal with God' (Phil. 2: 6)— even if 'the highest place that heaven affords' belonged to him by right—yet in the end he must hand over his sovereignty to God, 'so that God may be all in all' (1 Cor. 15: 28).[114] In Philippians as elsewhere

---

[111] *Maranatha* may be vocalized either as *Marana-tha* ('Our Lord, come!'), or *Maran-atha* ('Our Lord comes!'). The former is the more likely.

[112] Cf. C. F. D. Moule, *The Origin of Christology* (Cambridge, 1977) 36 ff.; Hurtado, *One God, One Lord*, 106; and Longenecker, *Christology of Early Jewish Christianity*, 121 ff.

[113] B. M. Metzger, 'The Punctuation of Rom. 9: 5', in *Christ and Spirit in the New Testament* (Cambridge, 1973), 95 ff.

[114] In commenting on this passage Cullmann, *Christology*, 225, actually speaks of the 'end' of Christ's lordship, as does J. Héring, *The First Epistle of St Paul to the Corinthians* (London, 1962) (168: 'the final extinction of the dignity of *Kurios*')—although for Héring this does not involve 'the loss of His nature as the Son of God and the Image of God, which he has had since His pre-existence'.

Jesus remains subordinate to God the Father. The ultimate acclamation of Jesus is not an end in itself, but completes the purpose for which the cosmos was created, to mirror forth the glory of God. This use of *kurios* without requiring a flat equation with God is perhaps most evident in 1 Cor. 8: 6, where Paul appears to have taken over the *Shema* ('Hear, O Israel, the Lord is our God, the Lord is One', Deut. 6: 4) and given it a new complexion: 'For us there is one God, the Father, from whom all being comes, towards whom we move; and there is one Lord, Jesus Christ, through whom all things came to be, and we through him.' The deliberate distinction of 'Lord' from 'God' in this passage is, at the very least, striking.

If in the end Jesus is termed 'Lord' by the New Testament writers, it is not because they are offering any ontological statements involving an inherent deity. It is because, like the other titles we have already discussed, it is an essentially functional idea of agency and delegation.[115]

8.3.5. *Pre-Existence*

The final means by which Jesus is said to be qualified to bring salvation is by having a pre-cosmic existence. And yet again we must proceed with caution. While Jewish antecedents explain much of the terminology used in John, Paul, and Hebrews to describe the pre-existence of Christ, we have seen that there is all the difference in the world between a pre-existent personification and a pre-existent person. Wisdom, e.g., was never the latter. From where, then, did the idea arise that Jesus pre-existed as a person?[116]

In attempting to answer this question, there are three dangers we must initially guard against. The first is to assume that, as with 'pre-existent', the terms 'eternal' and 'eternity' may be invoked with self-evident clarity. But here it is all too easy to assume that 'time' is characteristic of 'earth' and 'eternity' of 'heaven', and that pre-

---

[115] Even D. Guthrie admits this. For him, 'Lord' conveys the meaning that 'the same *functions* assigned to God are assigned to Christ' (*New Testament Theology* (Downers Grove, 1981) 301, italics mine).

[116] On the pre-existence of Christ in the New Testament, cf. e.g. R. G. Hamerton-Kelly, *Pre-existence, Wisdom and the Son of Man* (Cambridge, 1973); F. B. Craddock, *The Pre-existence of Christ in the New Testament* (Nashville, 1968); Robinson, *Human Face of God*; G. B. Caird, 'The Development of the Doctrine of Christ in the New Testament', in N. Pittenger (ed.), *Christ for Us Today* (London, 1968), 75 ff.; J. Hick (ed.), *The Myth of God Incarnate*; M. Goulder (ed.), *Incarnation and Myth: The Debate Continued*; and K.-J. Kuschel, *Born Before All Time?* (New York, 1992).

existence and post-existence belong to heaven—whatever may be thought of the 'interlude' of earthly life. We have seen that the New Testament writers were not naïve prisoners of mental pictures inherited from the Old Testament. Their theology began and ended with God; heaven, eternity, life, and holiness are to be found with Him. They have no separate existence.[117]

The second danger is that the pre-existence of Christ may be explained by the notion that Jesus pre-existed as a man. Reitzenstein's[118] theory that the New Testament belief in the pre-existence of Christ was derived from a Graeco-Oriental *anthropos* myth—'the heavenly man'—has for good reasons few surviving advocates today. Much of his evidence was drawn from later Christian deviations; and in Philo's *De Opificio Mundi* and the Hermetic Tractate *Poimandres*, both of which are demonstrably the product of speculation on Genesis 1, the heavenly man is a cosmological figure used to explain the creation of the human race, not a soteriological figure used to bring about its salvation. But the important point is that, even if the biblical writers had been acquainted with such speculation about 'a heavenly man', they would emphatically have dissociated themselves from it. We saw earlier that for Paul 'the man from heaven' is second, not first, in time. To be sure, the Fourth Gospel speaks of the Son of Man as having come 'down from heaven' (3: 13; 6: 62); but if we press this form of language to the point of insisting that he must have pre-existed as a man, we shall find ourselves in deep trouble. For later in this Gospel Jesus claims also to be the living bread which came down from heaven, and then goes on to explain that this bread which he gives for the life of the world is his flesh (6: 33, 41, 50, 51, 53). Jesus cannot be thought to have pre-existed as bread, still less as flesh. Flesh is what the *logos* became at the incarnation, and in John's vocabulary flesh means humanity. In any case we have John's unequivocal statement that Jesus pre-existed as *logos*, and that the *logos* was God.

The third danger is best deferred until the following point has been made. The tractate *Bereshith Rabbah* opens with a paragraph, based on Proverbs 8: 30, in which the Torah is said to be the blueprint which

---

[117] A question originally raised by J. A. T. Robinson's *Honest to God* (London, 1963) in a rather strident and provocative manner. One may wish to consult his more considered and sedate treatment of the same subject in *The Human Face of God* and the posthumously published *The Priority of John* (London, 1985).

[118] Cf. R. Reitzenstein, *Das iranische Erlösungsmysterium* (Bonn, 1921), 115 ff., and *Die hellenistischen Mysterienreligionen* (Bonn, 1927³), 168 ff.

God consulted when making the world. This interpretation was much older than the midrash in which it occurs, and indeed was almost certainly known to Paul. There is therefore no need to detect Greek influence. It is more likely that in his interpretation of the Genesis Creation stories Philo was following an older rabbinic tradition than that which the rabbis were borrowing from Philo. For the identification of the Torah with the personified Wisdom first occurred on Palestinian soil, in the writings of Jesus ben Sira of Jerusalem,[119] and it was this that set the rabbis thinking about pre-existence. In two places in the Babylonian Talmud we are told that seven things existed before the Creation (the Torah, repentance, Paradise, Gehenna, the throne of glory, the Temple, and the name of the Messiah), and in each case a biblical proof-text is provided.[120] This use of proof-texts might suggest that we are dealing merely with the extravagances of rabbinic exegesis; but if we turn to *Bereshith Rabbah*, we find evidence of genuine theological reflection. For there we are told that, of all the things which preceded the Creation, only the Torah and the throne of glory were actually created, while the rest had simply been decided on by God. We may have here another example, however embryonic, of the distinction later drawn by John of Damascus between the antecedent will of God (what God wills of His own nature) and His consequent will (what He wills because of human sinfulness). Certainly repentance and Gehennah could be said to pre-exist only in so far as God foreknew the fall of the human race; and it is likely that the pre-existence of Paradise and of the Temple should be fitted into the situation in which sin had to be dealt with, whether by rewards and punishments or by sacrificial atonement. But the Torah and the reign of God belong to God's absolute and unconditional purpose. According to the rabbis, it was in order to have a race of beings capable of obeying the Torah that God set the creative process in motion. But if our suggestion is correct, then it follows that *all* pre-existent things could be said to exist, in one mode or another, within the purpose of God.

Neither the Fourth Gospel nor Hebrews ever speaks of the eternal

[119] Ecclus. 24: 23, 25: 'All this is the book of the covenant of God most High, the law laid on us by Moses, a possession for the assemblies of Jacob. It sends out Wisdom in full flood like the river Pishon . . .' (REB).

[120] *Pes.* 54a; *Ned.* 39b. The proof texts are: Prov. 8: 22; Ps. 90: 2–3; Gen. 2: 8; Isa. 30: 33; Ps. 93: 2; Jer. 17: 22; Ps. 72: 17. For the most authoritative survey of opinion from Lightfoot to the present, cf. R. P. Martin, *Carmen Christi* (Cambridge, 1967).

logos or Wisdom in terms which compel us to regard it as a person. If we are in the habit of crediting them with such a belief in a pre-existent person, and not just a pre-existent purpose, it is because we read them in the light of Paul's theology. Paul alone attributed to the pre-existent Jesus a personal act of *choice*. 'You know how generous our Lord Jesus Christ has been: he was rich, yet for your sake he became poor' (2 Cor. 8: 9). 'He did not think to snatch at equality with God, but made himself nothing, assuming the nature of a slave' (Phil. 2: 6–7). Attempts have been made from time to time to suggest that Paul in Philippians is talking about the human Jesus, with his 'emptying' simply a reversal of the act of Adam.[121] These arguments have not, to be sure, won many converts,[122] and the traditional interpretation—normally, and with justification, identified with the name of Lightfoot[123]—continues to be preferred. But this will in turn lead us to an astonishing conclusion: the highest Christology of the New Testament is also its earliest.

We are now in a position to state our last *caveat*. If Paul alone articulated and understood the pre-existence of Jesus as personal, we may be tempted to think that by tracing the origin of his belief to a source in his thinking, whether the pre-existent Wisdom, or rabbinic exegesis such as is found in 1 Cor. 10: 3–4,[124] we have both understood and explained it. Here it may be wiser to accept Paul's own claim that at times he was the recipient of a new and extraordinary revelation. But if we are pressed to provide an explanation, we will undoubtedly be led back to the person of Jesus. It was the person of Jesus which brought Paul to his remarkable claim. Paul has often been, quite unjustly, accused of having little or no interest in the earthly life of Jesus. But it was because in the earthly life of Jesus the eternal purpose of God had appeared as a person that Paul and others after him found it impossible to imagine his pre-cosmic existence as anything other than personal. And thus, while the pre-existence of Christ may be

---

[121] Cf. for instance J. Murphy-O'Connor, 'Christological Anthropology in Phil. 2: 6–11', *RB* 83 (1976), 25 ff.; Robinson, *Human Face of God*, 162 ff.; and Dunn, *Christology*, 114 ff.

[122] For surveys see L. D. Hurst, 'Re-enter the Pre-Existent Christ in Philippians 2: 5–11?' *NTS* 32 (1986), 449 ff., and C. A. Wanamaker, 'Philippians 2: 6–11; Son of God or Adamic Christology', *NTS* 33 (1987), 179 ff. N. T. Wright provides a full-length discussion in *The Climax of the Covenant* (Philadelphia, 1992), 56 ff.

[123] J. B. Lightfoot, *Saint Paul's Epistle to the Philippians* (London, 1878), ad loc.

[124] So for instance E. E. Ellis, *Prophecy and Hermeneutic in Early Christianity* (Tübingen, 1978), ch. 14.

described in language borrowed from Wisdom or Torah, the new wine of the gospel has burst the linguistic skins into which it has been poured.

9.

The Theology of Jesus

9.1. FOUR CARDINAL ERRORS

Having examined what the New Testament writers believed about the crucial matters of the Christian faith, we now return to the question posed at the end of our first chapter. What of Jesus himself? Where does *he* fit into the picture? Can we be sure that he even existed? There are rumours abroad that the records of his earthly life are unreliable. And the fact that these rumours arise partly out of the Church's attempt to be honest about its own origins, not to claim more than the evidence will support, hardly allays the doubts and restores confidence.

There are indeed those who would argue that the historical Jesus has no place in a theology of the New Testament.[1] And if we are honest, if we are determined to pursue our model of the apostolic conference, it cannot be denied that they have a point. Where would Jesus fit into such a scheme? Ought we to *try* to fit him in? Or should we leave a chair at the conference table empty, as at the Passover the Jews do for Elijah?

Such questions are weighty, and deserve an answer, however unsatisfactory the answer may be to any one individual or theological school. The answer we shall propose here is that in one sense Jesus is indeed present at the conference, but not in an obvious or obtrusive way. We might add that those who disagree with this claim will have legitimate reasons for concluding this book at the end of Chapter 8. For them, what follows will be an addendum, an afterthought to the subject of New Testament theology. Those who wish to continue, on the other hand, may do so with another idea in mind: that in the teaching of

[1] See e.g. the arguments of Robert Morgan, 'The Historical Jesus and the Theology of the New Testament', in L. D. Hurst and N. T. Wright (eds.), *The Glory of Christ in the New Testament* (Oxford, 1987), 187 ff.

Jesus, as recorded in the four Gospels, we can see both the starting point and the goal of New Testament theology.

Such a suggestion of course leads us on to what is perhaps the ultimate question: what were the *steps*, the *process*, by which the Church advanced, within a generation, from memories of Jesus of Nazareth, whom friends and followers had known as a man, outwardly at least like themselves, to a belief in a cosmic Christ, who might properly be worshipped alongside God the Father, without doing violence to an essential monotheism, and whose death is in some sense vicarious for the whole human race? Was this process a development, in which external influences were no more than a stimulus to the unfolding of that which was fully present in germ form from the beginning? Or was it a mutation into a new species, a syncretism in which the external elements predominated over the meagre contribution of historical memory?[2] In the history of scholarship since Wellhausen to the present the initiative has lain with those who adopted the second view, the probability with those who, always somewhat defensively, have adopted the first.

Now it may be said, no doubt with the wisdom of hindsight, that this dichotomy need never have occured, because it arose from the beginning out of four errors of method:

1. The first error has been to assume that the Jesus of history was a different person from the Christ of the Church's faith. Those who have pressed the distinction between the historical and the theological in this way have only succeeded in rendering the New Testament unintelligible. The theology of the New Testament is no mere epiphenomenon superimposed upon the history; it is part of the chain of cause and effect which prompted all the characters in the story, Jesus included, to say what they said and to do what they did.

The antithetical approaches which one may take to this issue are well exemplified by two classic works, published one year apart, nearly a century ago: Wrede's book on the Messianic secret, *Das Messiasgeheimnis in den Euangelien* (1901), and Denney's examination of *The Death of Christ* (1902). Wrede's book, of course, has long been accepted as the charter of those who believe that the Church of the Epistles invented the Jesus of the Gospels.[3] Denney's book moves in

---

[2] A distinction made by C. F. D. Moule, *The Origin of Christology* (Cambridge, 1977) 1 ff.

[3] Cf. esp. p. 131.

the opposite direction by making a powerful and eloquent case that Jesus was the founder of the Christianity which is common to the Gospels and the Epistles. For Wrede the unity of the New Testament was arbitrary and factitious,[4] with the canonical segregation of its books from other ancient literature an offence to the historian. For Denney, in establishing the canon the Church did nothing more than give recognition to an existing and organic coherence.[5]

Deciding which approach is correct will ultimately lead the inquirer into the quest for the historical Jesus. And those who believe that in the life and teaching of Jesus God has given a unique revelation of His character and purpose are committed by this belief, whether they like it or not, whether they admit it or not, to that quest. Without the Jesus of history the Christ of faith becomes a Docetic figure, a figment of pious imagination, who, like Alice's Cheshire cat, ultimately disappears from view. There remains no person about whom we have any evidence.

The New Testament writers, on the other hand, put enormous weight upon the actuality of the events they describe. 'We cannot give up speaking of the things we have seen and heard' (Acts 4: 20). 'This is supported by an eyewitness, whose evidence is to be trusted' (John 19: 35). The Fourth Gospel uses a blind man to convey that approach to simple fact which always triumphs over dogmatic theorizing: 'All I know is this: once I was blind, but now I see' (John 9: 25). Luke's Gospel begins with the claim that the author was 'following the traditions handed down to us by the original eyewitnesses' (Luke 1: 2). Those aspiring to apostleship were required to have been eyewitnesses (Acts 1: 21–2). And the terms *euaggelidzō* and *kērussō* connote the proclamation of news, not an invitation to a mystical, creative experience.

The Form Critical school, on the other hand, has often insisted that the Gospels are not biographical, in so far as the early Church was interested in the heavenly Christ rather than the Jesus of history. But the more one thinks about this claim the more it is shown up for what it is. Granted that the earliest Christians believed that they had

[4] See W. Wrede, *Über und Methode der Sogennanten neutestamentlichen Theologie* (1897, ET Robert Morgan, in *The Nature of New Testament Theology* (London, 1973), 68–116), and H. Boers, *What is New Testament Theology?* (Philadelphia, 1979), 45 ff.

[5] 'The books did not come together by chance . . . it would be truer to say that they gravitated toward each other in the course of the first century . . . and imposed their unity on the Christian mind, than that the church imposed on them by statute' (p. 3).

in their midst the heavenly Christ, the evidence equally demonstrates that they knew well that his character was known to them only through their memories of the earthly Jesus; and the First Epistle of John was written to demonstrate that it was heresy to think otherwise (1 John 1: 1–2).

This is not to imply that the early Church was uninterested in religious experience. But it understood, in a way which many modern scholars have not, that experience is the point at which theology is grounded in history. All such experience would be illusory unless it was accompanied by a rational confidence in the objective reality of that which has occasioned it; it must be grounded in the existence of something which is independent of the experience itself.

2. The second error, closely related to the first, is to treat Christology as though it is exclusively a question about Jesus' relationship to God, in traditional terms a question about his deity. To begin with such a question palpably ignores the equally pressing and fundamental question of his relationship to the human race. In the first instance this may be seen as a distinctively Pauline theme, on the ground that Paul alone explicitly formulates the concept of the corporate Christ in whose representative person all humanity has died and risen. But the same concept is implicitly present elsewhere in the belief that Jesus' death is of universal significance. But what must Jesus have been like to justify the enormous confidence that his death had universal validity? What understanding of his own mission and person may we attribute to him if that confidence is to be anchored in historical reality? Such questions are too often ignored by those who make the primary focus of Christology the relationship of Jesus to God.

3. The third error is normally associated with the name of Rudolf Bultmann. In 1926 Bultmann wrote: 'Critical investigation shows that the whole tradition about Jesus which appears in the three Synoptic Gospels is composed of a series of layers which can on the whole be clearly distinguished.'[6] Having stripped off the Hellenistic layer, which owes its origin to the Gentile communities in which the Gospels were actually written, we are left with Palestinian material, where again 'different layers can be distinguished, in which whatever betrays the specific interests of the church . . . must be rejected as secondary'.[7]

---

[6] R. Bultmann, *Jesus* (Berlin: Deutsche Bibliothek, 1926); E.T. *Jesus and the Word* (London, 1934), 17.
[7] Ibid. 12 f.

But the interests of Jesus and those of the early Church were hardly so mutually exclusive that what may be ascribed to the one must be denied to the other. Bultmann's principle, however, has a certain negative force. If in the tradition something survives which corresponds to the interests of the early Church, it is false logic to suppose that it cannot therefore be a genuine teaching of Jesus. But if we find in the tradition a large body of material which has no direct relation to the life, needs, and interests of the primitive Church,[8] then we have every right to assume that we are in touch with solid historical fact. We shall be suggesting in this chapter that the Gospels contain a large amount of material which links the ministry and teaching of Jesus to the history, politics, aspirations, and destiny of the Jewish nation. Here we need only say that early in the history of the Church the gospel broke out from its Jewish cocoon to become a universal faith. The Jewish nation was regarded as a persecuting opponent, against which the Church had to defend itself; and the idea that this nation had once occupied the forefront of the gospel message, though it was never wholly forgotten, slipped quietly into the background. The result is that the evangelists record the facts at which we shall soon be looking, but without evincing any special interest in them. They record, for example, that among the Twelve one was a member of the Jewish resistance movement (Luke 6: 15; Acts 1: 13), while another belonged to the group of 'Quislings' who had taken service under the government and were hated for fraternizing with the enemy (Mark 2: 14; Luke 5: 27); yet they never so much as hint at the personal strain that must have been generated when these two were thrown regularly into each other's company. They record the death of John the Baptist, but it is Josephus, not Mark, who provides the political explanation of that tragic event.[9] They tell us of the release of Barabbas, 'who had committed murder in the insurrection', without any reference to that series of violent revolts, suppressed with a growing ruthlessness, which is the history of first-century Judaism. But if we admit that the evangelists were

[8] For a somewhat dated but still important summary of how little overlap exists between the concerns of the early Church and those current in Jesus' lifetime, cf. B. S. Easton, *The Gospel Before the Gospels* (New York, 1928), 40 f.

[9] *AJ* 18. 109–19. According to Josephus, John was beheaded by Herod because he feared a revolt by the Nabateans, who were sympathetic to John's denunciation of Herod's marriage to Herodias as incestuous (cf. B. Reicke, 'The Historical Setting of John's Baptism', in E. P. Sanders (ed.), *Jesus, the Gospels, and the Church* (Macon, Ga., 1987), 209 ff.).

largely indifferent to Jewish politics, this hardly means also that Jesus shared their indifference.

4. The final and most destructive error is to start at the wrong point. It is becoming more and more the standard principle of historical research that, in attempting to reconstruct a portion of the past out of fragmentary evidence, one must begin at the point where the evidence is least subject to doubt or conflicting interpretation. Thus in the quest for the historical Baptist one does not begin with the Lucan nativity stories or speculations about John's relationship with Qumran, or even with the evidence of the Second and Fourth Gospels, in which John appears merely as a forerunner of Jesus. One begins with the Q tradition of John's preaching.

In the case of Jesus, there are six common points at which scholars have started, and at which we might begin.

(*a*) We could begin with the one saying of Jesus which for most people clearly has to do with politics: 'Pay to Caesar what is due to Caesar, and to God what is due to God' (Mark 12: 17 and par.). But what does this saying mean? It could be taken to mean that Christians live in two separate and independent worlds, to each of which they owe a duty and a loyalty, and that the sphere of politics belongs to Caesar and the sphere of religion to God. But this would be a serious mistake.[10]

(*b*) We could, following T. W. Manson,[11] begin with the theme of the fatherhood of God. But again this puts us into the thick of debate. Did Jesus address God as Father? Certainly, yes. But did he therefore describe himself as 'the Son'? Here we will find ourselves in the heart of Christological controversy, on which there will be little agreement. We cannot, of course, run away from such questions, and in the end they will be critical to our discussion of the theology of Jesus. But if we *start* here we will rapidly find ourselves in a cul-de-sac.

(*c*) We could begin with Matthew's Sermon on the Mount, which to the average person represents the most familiar and accessible

---

[10] To begin with such a division could easily lead to an interpretation of Jesus' teaching according to a theology of the two realms (as later made famous by Luther). But this would be totally alien to Jesus' understanding of the nation of Israel. A full-length treatment of the complexities of Mark 12: 17 is given in H. Loewe, *Render unto Caesar: Religion and Political Loyalty in Palestine* (Cambridge, 1940). A more limited suggestion is provided by J. D. M. Derrett, *Law in the New Testament* (London, 1970), 335.

[11] T. W. Manson, *The Teaching of Jesus* (Cambridge, 1945), 89 ff.

example of Jesus' teaching. But most scholars believe that this 'sermon' comes to us in a framework of the evangelist's theology of ethics. Thus, apart from any other considerations, this will lead us off on a wrong path, since whatever else Jesus' teaching may have been, it was not primarily ethics.[12]

(*d*) We could start with the parables of the Kingdom. But if a teacher spends an enormous amount of time telling people what the Kingdom of God is like, we can reasonably assume that the idea being presented is different from the popular one. But *how* different? Was Jesus saying to his contemporaries, 'You think that the Kingdom of God is all bound up with national politics, but I am going to tell you about a Kingdom of God that is purely religious and personal'? Again, this is the wrong way to approach the parables and the Kingdom of God in Jesus' teaching—although it is the way generations of Christians continue to use them.

(*e*) We could, as the vast majority of scholars since Johannes Weiss and Albert Schweitzer have done, begin with eschatology. But we saw in Chapter 7, that, far from being the key to the study of the Gospels, there are hardly two scholars who can agree on the meaning of the word 'eschatology'. The use of this as a platform on which to erect the teaching of Jesus has been one of the worst historical decisions of the century.

(*f*) Or, finally, we could, as so many modern works on New Testament Christology have done, start with a treatment of the titles by which Jesus came to be addressed or described. But we have seen that each of these titles is an area of maximum ambiguity. To use them as a foundation is to build on sand. We must look for another starting point which will enable us to reduce the range of ambiguity, or at least to come to terms with it.

9.2. THE BIRTH OF CHRISTIAN THEOLOGY

The quest for the historical Jesus has so far largely failed because it has been pursued by those who accept the humanity of Jesus as a dogma but do not grasp it as a historical fact. But we shall not find Jesus even indirectly relevant to our age unless we first find him directly relevant to his own. Those in too much of a hurry to progress

[12] Cf. Bruce Chilton and J. I. H. McDonald, *Jesus and the Ethics of the Kingdom* (Grand Rapids, 1987), 1 ff.

from the particular to the universal on this point would do better to listen to a profound hint dropped by C. F. D. Moule:

Jesus, in an extraordinary way, turned out to be occupying the position that, according to the Scriptures, had always been intended for Israel, and, through Israel, for all mankind . . . A widely shared and recognized experience had found in Christ that corporate sonship, that true Israel, indeed that Adam or renewed mankind, by belonging to which Christians found a right relation both to God and to one another as fellow-members of the People of God.[13]

The idea that Jesus' relationship to the human race is rooted in his relationship to Israel was earlier adumbrated in the work of T. W. Manson, C. H. Dodd, J. Munck, and J. Jeremias.[14] They suggested that the belief in the solidarity of Jesus with all humanity is historically credible only if it first suffered the scandal of particularity. The conviction that Jesus has taken away the sin of the world, enshrined as it is in scripture, hymn, and creed, is something which prima facie is so difficult that it is hardly surprising if millions of our contemporaries find it incredible. The hypothesis that Jesus, being a Jew, felt himself to be so implicated in the history and destiny of his people, so identified even with those from whose attitudes he profoundly dissented that he could not but suffer for their sins—this is at least historically manageable.[15]

---

[13] Moule, *Origin of Christology*, 129, 131.

[14] Manson, *The Teaching of Jesus*, 171–236; C. H. Dodd, *According to the Scriptures* (London, 1952); J. Munck, *Paul and the Salvation of Mankind* (Richmond, 1959); J. Jeremias, *Jesus' Promise to the Nations* (London, 1958); cf. also J. A. T. Robinson, *Jesus and His Coming* (London, 1957). Recent work into the historical Jesus continues to explore the relationship of Jesus and Judaism. See for instance J. H. Charlesworth, *Jesus Within Judaism* (New York, 1988); R. A. Horsley, *Jesus and the Spiral of Violence: Popular Resistance in Roman Palestine* (San Francisco, 1987), and *Sociology and the Jesus Movement* (New York, 1989); R. Leivestad, *Jesus in His Own Perspective* (Minneapolis, 1987); J. K. Riches, *Jesus and the Transformation of Judaism* (London, 1980); and N. T. Wright, *Jesus and the Victory of God* (Minneapolis, 1995); cf. also his ' "Constraints" and the Jesus of History', *SJT* 39 (1986), 189 ff. To these should be added the works of Borg, Meyer, and Sanders mentioned below. The study of J. D. Crossan, *The Historical Jesus: The Life of a Mediterranean Jewish Peasant* (San Francisco, 1991), labours under the view that later, Gnostic sources are to be preferred over the canonical Gospels for the life of Jesus; the result is a naïve and oversimplified Cynic teacher, devoid of any true theological understanding for his actions.

[15] In examining the titles in Ch. 8, we noted one element which, despite their ambiguity, is overwhelmingly clear: of the six titles most commonly used by the writers for Jesus (Messiah, King of Israel, Son of David, Son of God, Servant, Lord), the first five either express or are capable of expressing an identification with Israel. The first three are synonyms: each relates the holder of the title to Israel as a ruler in whom divine authority

And it is just such a hypothesis which points us in the direction of our own starting point for reconstructing the theology of Jesus. Recalling our warning that we should begin where the evidence is least subject to doubt, we turn to the one undoubted *fact* in the history of Jesus: *He was crucified*. Apart from those few on the lunatic fringe who have denied that Jesus actually existed,[16] nobody in our time has attempted to deny that Jesus died on a Roman cross.

But can we accept a fact without also asking *why*? One plausible reason for the writing of the Gospels, of course, was precisely to answer this question. Most modern scholars believe that underlying the Gospel of Mark, for instance, was the question of Roman Christians: 'If Jesus was the Son of God, why did he have to die?' And one of the answers provided is that the prime movers in bringing about the death of Jesus were the Jewish leaders, notwithstanding the clear fact that crucifixion was a Roman form of punishment and must have been executed on the order of the Roman governor. But here we run into a major hazard. Many writers, beginning with Reimarus[17] and extending to some eminent contemporary scholars,[18] have argued that any implication of certain religious and political leaders in the death of Jesus is the product of the fertile imagination of the early Church and of their struggle for survival against the threat of Roman persecution. The reasons for this are not far to seek. Modern writers continue to battle against centuries of anti-Semitism, with many claiming that the gospel story was invented to lay upon the Jews the charge

is vested; and it is this aspect of their meaning which is relevant to questions about the relation of Jesus to God. But we have also seen that it is characteristic of ancient ideas of kingship that from a different point of view the king *is* the nation; its national identity is summed up in his representative person. Nation and king are therefore to a large degree interchangeable.

[16] A recent defence of this view is G. A. Wells, *Did Jesus Exist?* (Buffalo, 1975), and *The Historical Evidence for Jesus* (Buffalo, 1988).

[17] On Reimarus see above, p. 243, n. 17.

[18] Cf. for instance H. Cohn, *The Trial and Death of Jesus* (New York, 1971); G. Vermes, *Jesus and the World of Judaism* (Philadelphia, 1984), 54 ff.; and E. Rivkin, *What Crucified Jesus?* (Nashville, 1984). As implied by the title, Rivkin argues that Jesus was killed by a political process rather than by 'the Jews'. J. H. Charlesworth, on the other hand, asks, 'Is it not axiomatic . . . that only people, not a political system, can condemn and kill?' (*Princeton Seminary Bulletin*, 9 (1988), 247). *Editor's note*: Caird, in answer to this question, would undoubtedly have replied that *both* are true: people work *through* political systems (*Principalities and Powers*, 22 ff.), but political systems cannot operate without people to administer them.

of deicide. But while no respectable historian will give any basis to anti-Semitism, it a mistaken policy on the part of modern apologists, Jewish or Gentile, to imagine that they could correct a centuries-old wrong by a ruthless attempt to rewrite the history of the first century. What we are here facing, of course, is the charge of bias: the assertion that the Gospels are thoroughly untrustworthy because those who wrote them were not objective. But in fairness it must be recognized that bias is not always all on one side: it can have various causes, even on the part of New Testament critics.

If we are to relieve the Gospel writers from the charge of bias, on the other hand, we cannot simply be content with placing blame for the Cross on the shoulders of certain first-century religious and political authorities unless we ask another equally significant question: 'What was the nature of the controversy between Jesus and the Jewish authorities which could have contributed to this denouement?' If the Cross is central to the story, the controversies which led up to it must be equally central. Here the points of disagreement between Jesus and the authorities would, if recoverable, constitute an entry into the material which might bring us close to the centre of Jesus' message. But the only accounts we have of these are the Gospels, and we are once again faced with the charge that they reflect not a situation in the life of Jesus but that between Church and society when the Gospels were written. This has been particularly said of Matthew's Gospel, not without some justification. Matthew was not writing simply to record, in an objective and unbiased fashion, the life of Jesus. He was writing and editing his sources to make them useful for a Church engaged in deep controversy with the Synagogue. We have seen that Matthew and the Church to which he was writing have strongly Jewish characteristics, while at the same time his Gospel is the most anti-Jewish of the four. But to make allowance for bitter controversy with the Synagogue is quite different from saying that Matthew has fabricated his material. In the long passage of woes to the Pharisees (Matt. 23: 13–36), Matthew has elaborated and accentuated the hostility of his source material, perhaps even directing against the Pharisees criticisms which, in the tradition which lay before him, were originally directed against a more general public. But if we accept the view that Matthew used Mark and Q, then by comparison with the other two Synoptic Gospels we may find that the controversies which Matthew edits and elaborates were already felt in the sources available to him. His bias, in other words, did not cause him to invent the controversies.

In Luke's Gospel there is a different hazard of bias, for Luke looks out upon a Gentile world. Dedicated to Theophilus, an educated Greek, Luke's two-volume work is apologetic. He is writing to demonstrate to the Graeco-Roman world that it has nothing to fear from Christianity, and that Roman officials, when they have investigated it, have always found it to be harmless. Thus Pilate three times proclaims Jesus to be innocent (23: 4, 14, 22), while in Acts one Roman official after another declares that the Christian movement constitutes no offence against Roman law (13: 7 ff.; 18: 12 ff.; 26: 31 ff.). Pre-eminent is Gallio, for whom Paul's controversy with the Synagogue constitutes no test to be brought before a Roman lawcourt (18: 12 ff.). Thus again we are faced with the question of bias: if Luke has an apologetic concern, can we trust his account of the controversies? And again we face the same answer. Luke used Mark and Q. If he had an axe to grind (and his axe is different from that of Matthew), the Q material provides evidence for a previous tradition of Jesus in controversy with the Jewish leaders. The hazard of bias therefore has to be moved back behind both evangelists (where there is evidence to support it) to the earliest possible point at which such evidence is lacking.

While there are therefore grounds for claiming that Christians who were engaged in controversy in the early Church used the tradition of Jesus for their own purposes, *they did not invent it*. And we are forced back to the view that the Gospels present us with sufficient evidence to reconstruct the situation which existed between Jesus and his contemporaries.

But there is one more hazard of bias, that of the modern interpreter. What if the New Testament theologian is also *a Christian*? Should the reconstruction of the controversies attempt to paint Jesus as the hero, with the Pharisees as the villains? The answer, of course, must be *emphatically, no*. The theologian/historian will attempt to understand both points of view, hoping to discover not the basis of a value judgement (although the Christian will in the end inexorably find that), but a clash of sincerely held opinions. This point, of course, has been somewhat disguised by that element in the Gospels which we owe primarily to Matthew—the designation of the Pharisees as 'hypocrites' (Matt. 23: 13; cf. Luke 12: 1). The popular assumption from this statement is that the Pharisees were insincere. The impression of the Pharisees provided by the Gospels and the later records of Judaism, on the other hand, is that they were deeply religious and deeply sincere.[19] They were convinced that what they were doing was the will of God.

On this point the evidence of Paul is of first-class value. Here speaks one who *was* a Pharisee. We are, of course, faced with the bias of the convert who looks back on the life he has deserted. But at least he knows *at first hand what it is to be a Pharisee*. Having set aside his Pharisaism, he still looks back on it with pride. If his opponents boast, he claims, 'I can outboast them' (Gal. 1: 14 ff.). 'You know my life in Judaism, how in my zeal for the ancestral traditions, I outstripped all my contemporaries' (v. 14). Paul the Christian has a vivid enough memory of Paul the Pharisee to recognize that in his Pharisaic days he had a deeply felt passion for the Law, and he recognizes in other Pharisees the same zeal for the ancestral traditions of Judaism.

The importance of this evidence is that, having seen through the eyes of Paul a profound piety and sincerity among the Pharisees, we may be prepared to come back to the Gospels and find, notwithstanding the provocative term 'hypocrite', that Jesus recognizes in his opponents a depth of passion and sincerity which he himself feels.

To this it may be added that other Pharisees besides Paul either became Christians or were sympathetic to Jesus and/or the Christian movement (cf. Luke 23: 51 (Mark 15: 43); 13: 31; 7: 36 ff; 11: 37; 14: 1; John 19: 38; 7: 50, 19: 39).[20] The Gospel tradition, in other words, does not preserve a simple, straightforward debate.

Having dealt with the hazards of bias, we now return to our main question: *why* was Jesus crucified? And here we face an inexorable fact about the Gospels, namely that Jesus' teaching has within it a strong political element. It has, of course, been crusted over by centuries of piety which has distinguished between religious concerns and politics; and this is the format which all New Testament theologies have implicitly employed in their consideration of the teaching of Jesus. It is, after all, New Testament theology, not New Testament history.[21]

---

[19] The sincerity of the Pharisees is well documented, from somewhat different directions, by E. P. Sanders, *Jesus and Judaism*, esp. 276 f., and M. Borg, *Conflict, Holiness and Politics in the Teaching of Jesus* (New York, 1984), *passim*.

[20] These texts will not, of course, be judged by scholars to be of equal weight; and since all of them come from the Gospels there will inevitably be those who dismiss the evidence out of hand. This is yet another example of how bias will control one's conclusions.

[21] *Editor's note:* Following on Caird's work, M. Borg has attempted to undermine the traditional division between religion and politics in two works (*Conflict, Holiness and Politics*, and *Jesus: A New Vision* (San Francisco, 1987)). See the pertinent remarks of

But this distinction breaks down very quickly. If Jesus had no interest in politics, why go to Jerusalem at all? Why not be content to train his disciples in the calm of the Galilean hills? Why this headlong clash with authority? And at the last, when he is aware that treachery is afoot, why not simply slip away quietly, under cover of darkness, to a place where his enemies could not get at him?

Such questions require an answer. One answer of course is that he exposed himself to certain danger because he believed he was fulfilling the scriptures. But apart from attributing to Jesus a one-dimensional understanding of this world and his role in it, such an answer does not account for much information in the Gospels which relates to Jesus' concern for the Jewish nation. If he found himself at the end embroiled in a political crisis which resulted in his execution on the order of a Roman governor, it was not because he avoided politics. *It was because for him politics and theology were inseparable.*

This assertion however puts us on more dangerous ground than we have touched thus far. Since Reimarus, a succession of writers have claimed that Jesus was deeply involved in Near-Eastern politics, and all, nearly without exception, have argued that Jesus was not merely involved in politics; he was deeply involved with the 'National Liberation Front'.[22] It was for this that he was crucified. That the evidence points to the contrary—that Jesus repudiated the 'National Liberation Front'[23]—has not much mattered. It can only be viewed as fortunate that the adherents of this view are few in number. But it is also part of the illogicality of modern Gospel criticism that, while most scholars have remained unconvinced, they have gone on to argue that, since Jesus was not a member of the National Liberation Front, *therefore he was not interested in politics.* Herein lies one of the most colossal 'undistributed middle terms' which any logician has ever laid bare.[24]

Much of the modern difficulty in attempting to incorporate the

Tom Wright in S. Neill and T. Wright, *The Interpretation of the New Testament* (New York, 1989), 388 ff.

[22] The term 'National Liberation Front' is here used as a shorthand term for a number of different groups (cf. Borg, *Jesus: A New Vision*, 90).

[23] The most famous exposition of the view that Jesus was a revolutionary remains that of S. G. F. Brandon, *Jesus and the Zealots* (Manchester, 1967). A sedulous, painstaking rebuttal of Brandon is found in the various essays in E. Bammel and C. F. D. Moule (eds.), *Jesus and the Politics of His Day* (Cambridge, 1984).

[24] It would be tantamount to saying, 'Mr Ian Paisley is not a member of the Irish Republican Army; therefore he is not interested in politics.'

teaching of Jesus into a New Testament theology thus results from the conventional division between religion and politics, a division which allows modern interpreters to continue thinking of the Torah as merely the Jewish religion. But Torah, then as now, was to the Jew *both* the religious charter and the corpus of civil and criminal law of the Jewish nation. Scholars still argue over how to translate the term *grammateus*;[25] it has been variously rendered in English 'scribe', 'teacher', 'teacher of the Law', 'doctor of the Law', and sometimes, simply, 'lawyer'. In retrospect it would have been better to settle for 'lawyer' in every instance. The scribes were the experts of the Law, not simply in the sense of university professors of jurisprudence, but in the sense of its *practitioners*.

It was impossible for a first-century Jew to draw the kind of distinction between religion and politics which is built into the American way of life. Moreover, to the question 'What is Israel?' Christian theologians have tended to respond as if Israel were the Old Testament *Church*. But Israel was, and continues to be, a *nation*; and those embroiled in controversy over the nature of Israel would of necessity be discussing its *nationhood*.

In the end Jesus came before the Sanhedrin, which modern pietists continue to see as the Jewish Church Assembly. But the Sanhedrin was more like the British High Court of Parliament or the American Supreme Court; it was the highest tribunal of the land. And while the Jewish people were not politically independent, the Roman Emperor allowed to his provinces the highest measure of local government.[26] Pontius Pilate was the representative of the Roman Emperor, much as the Governor General represented the Crown in a British dominion during the first half of the twentieth century, with a local parliament carrying on day-to-day affairs.

There continue to be strenuous debates about the 'trial' of Jesus, with the Gospel records sometimes characterized as dubious fiction in so far as they do not conform to the regulations in the Mishnah for the conduct of trials before the Sanhedrin.[27] The Sanhedrin however could call before it anybody it wanted to examine. Clearly it was not

---

[25] *Grammateus* occurs approximately 60 times in the Synoptics (often as a synonym for *nomikos*), 4 times in Acts, and once in Paul's letters. Cf. Jeremias' discussion in *TDNT* i. 740 ff.

[26] Cf. A. E. Harvey, *Jesus and the Constraints of History* (Philadelphia, 1982), 25 f., who argues convincingly that the Jews had considerable judicial authority under Pilate.

[27] See in particular Cohn, *The Trial and Death of Jesus*.

a trial but an inquiry into the nature of Jesus' claims in order to decide whether to present evidence to the local governor.[28]

A prima facie case therefore exists for claiming that Jesus was crucified for political reasons, not simply because of any concern for individual souls in the hereafter. He addressed an equally great question: What does it mean for the nation of Israel to be the holy people of God in the world as it is? Ultimately of course the individual and the national will not be unrelated. To claim that Jesus was embroiled in the politics of first-century Judaism hardly sends into limbo his many sayings which reflect his concern for the individual, and any approach to the teaching of Jesus which is unable to integrate such a concern is to be resoundingly rejected. But it is also true that the nineteenth-century picture of Jesus as the Saviour of individual souls only, that his exclusive concern was the relationship of individuals to their Maker, leaves out of account too much Gospel material, with too many crucial questions left unanswered.

Ultimately the decision to include Jesus in a New Testament theology will depend upon what we mean by 'theology'. Will it be static formulations about God and the timeless truths of eternity? Or will it be a dynamic intimately bound up with the politics, history, and daily affairs of the nation into which Jesus was born? Only in the latter case will 'the theology of Jesus' be an appropriate term. Only then will we guarantee that the particulars of history are not too quickly swallowed up by its universals. And only then will our final chapter have a place in an overall treatment of the theology of the New Testament.[29]

9.3 THE GATHERING STORM

It is the consensus of all four Gospels, confirmed in the preaching tradition recorded in the speeches of Acts, that the beginning of the gospel was the baptism proclaimed by John and the fact that Jesus

---

[28] Borg, *Jesus: A New Vision*, 180, claims something similar to this, although following E. Rivkin he seems to lapse into the very distinction between religion and politics which elsewhere he vigorously denies by distinguishing 'the political Sanhedrin' from 'the religious council'.

[29] This is the thrust of much of Borg's work on Jesus, although he falls short of describing authentic material in the Gospels as Jesus' 'theology'. His emphasis is rather on the socio-religious milieu of Jesus' historical message; hence the connection is between politics and 'religion', or politics and 'holiness'. While his reticence to advance into the more embattled terrain of 'theology' is perhaps understandable, it leads Borg

went to be baptized.[30] It was John who announced the imminent arrival of a crisis, which he called 'the wrath to come'.

John has sometimes been portrayed as a prophet of gloom, who took a ghoulish delight in the coming destruction of the ungodly; but this is to do less than justice to his imagery. The object of winnowing is not to collect enough chaff to have a glorious bonfire; it is to gather the wheat into the granary; the bonfire is purely incidental. In other words, John's crisis was one which would determine who among the Jews belonged to the true Israel. ' "Do not say," he warned them, " 'I am racially descended from Abraham'; for God can raise up children to Abraham from the stones of the desert" ' (Matt. 3: 9; Luke 3: 8). Descent from Abraham will not guarantee membership in the new Israel, nor will lack of it be a disqualification. In the coming crisis race will not count, only conduct. John accordingly summoned the Jews to a national movement of repentance, and his baptism was the proleptic symbol of admission to the Israel of the new age.

And Jesus went to be baptized. Why? We have already seen some of the universal and soteriological implications of this act. To this it needs to be added that Jesus apparently recognized the national character of John's summons to repentance and accepted his own involvement in the national life of his people. But this is to say that from the outset of his ministry Jesus was concerned with questions of national policy: What does it mean to be the chosen nation of God? How can Israel preserve its character as the holy nation in a world overrun and controlled by pagans? What must Israel do if, at God's winnowing, she is to prove wheat, and not chaff?

This impression receives further confirmation from the fact that in the middle of his ministry Jesus is said to have sent his disciples out on a missionary tour (Matt. 10: 1–15; Mark 6: 7–13; Luke 9: 1–16). The instructions given to them have survived in several forms, drawn from at least three strands of tradition; and in details they differ significantly. But in one essential respect they agree: the mission was to be conducted with the utmost urgency. The missionaries were to travel light and travel fast. They were to greet nobody on the road; not because Jesus set a premium on bad manners, but because the endless

into difficulty on certain questions. A case in point is his treatment of Jesus and the Son of Man, which is disappointingly brief.

[30] Matt. 3: 6 ff.; Mark 1: 5 ff.; Luke 3: 7 ff.; John 1: 25 ff.; Acts 1: 22; 10: 37; 13: 24.

civilities of oriental etiquette would consume more time than they could afford. They were to eat whatever was put before them, without pausing to enquire, as a good Pharisee would, whether their host had conformed with all the Levitical food laws, all of which Peter had observed from his youth (cf. Acts 10: 14). They were not to waste time in any place that was slow to give them a hearing. Why the desperate hurry? Albert Schweitzer (above, Ch. 7) chose this question as the key to his understanding of Jesus' ministry. His answer has long since been found inadequate, but the question remains: Why the hurry? The most probable answer is that Jesus was working against time to prevent the end of Israel's world; the haste of the mission was directly connected with the many sayings which predict the fall of Jerusalem and the destruction of the Temple. For Jesus, Israel was at the cross-roads; it must choose between two conceptions of its national destiny, and the time for choice was terrifyingly short. This explains why, in his instructions to his disciples, he speaks of 'towns where they receive you' and 'towns where they do not receive you'. He seems to have expected not individual but mass response. 'It shall be more tolerable for Sodom and Gomorrah in the judgement than for that town' (Luke 10: 12 = Matt. 10: 15). The disciples were not evangelistic preachers sent out to save individual souls for some unearthly paradise. They were couriers proclaiming a national emergency and conducting a referendum on a question of national survival.

The criticisms Jesus is recorded to have made against his contemporaries is further evidence of this. According to Mark (8: 11 ff.) Jesus said: 'An evil and adulterous generation asks for a sign, and no sign shall be given them.' Matthew (12: 38 ff.) and Luke (11: 29 ff.) add 'except the sign of Jonah', and each supplies his own explanation of the enigmatic phrase. We may take Mark's word for it that Jesus met the demand for irrefragable proof of his credentials with a flat negative, to which 'except the sign of Jonah' does not constitute a serious qualification. Jonah was sent to Nineveh with a message of extreme urgency: 'Within forty days Nineveh shall be destroyed' (Jonah 3: 4); and the Ninevites did not wait to examine his credentials. To those who were spiritually alive, the urgent warning of Jesus should have needed no more authentication than Jonah had; and, because they failed to recognize the word of the God they claimed to serve, they were stamped as an irreligious and disloyal generation. To this saying both Matthew and Luke have added the twin sayings about the Queen of Sheba and the men of Nineveh (Matt. 12: 41–2; Luke 11: 31–2). On this passage Kümmel has commented:

The Judgment which will then be held will extend over the whole of mankind. Consequently it presupposes the general resurrection of the dead . . . Since Jesus speaks here of the rising up of 'this generation' also, it is clearly expected that at least many of Jesus' contemporaries will die before the rising up and the judgment comes. This confirms the fact established by Mark 9: 1 that Jesus expected the coming of the eschaton to be at hand but not yet very near.[31]

Thus are theological silk purses made out of linguistic sows' ears. Matthew and Luke agree in using *egeirō* in the one instance and *anistēmi* in the other, and these two verbs are used regularly and interchangeably of the final resurrection. But both verbs are used in a variety of other senses; both can mean simply 'to appear'. One is actually almost a technical term for a witness appearing in court to give evidence (Mark 14: 57). It is in this last sense, and this sense alone, that the verbs are used in the passage under consideration. *No reference to the general resurrection or to the Last Judgement is intended.* At the Last Judgement all alike will be on trial. But in the present context the Ninevites and the Queen of Sheba will appear as witnesses for the prosecution at the trial of 'this generation'. We have already noted that the use of courtroom imagery in descriptions of the administration of divine justice in the daily life of men, women, and nations is frequent in both testaments. Job's confidence that after his death his *go'el*, his defence counsel, will stand up in court to vindicate his good name against all charges implies no belief in an afterlife for him. In the Fourth Gospel, John the Baptist is summoned as a witness in God's lawsuit with the world without having to be raised from the dead to give his evidence.[32] Above all, there is the court scene in Daniel. 'Thrones were set in place, and the Ancient in Years took His seat . . . The court sat, and the books were opened' (Dan. 7: 9–10, REB). Even if it be granted that the author of Revelation borrowed and adapted this imagery for his own picture of the Last Judgement (Rev. 20: 11–15), no such idea was in the mind of the author of Daniel.

Nor does the idea of a Last Judgement underlie the important *logion* preserved in Luke 11: 49–51 (= Matt. 23: 34 f.), where the whole nation at the time of Jesus, in the preaching of John and Jesus, has been given an opportunity to break with the past, and, if it refuses this chance, must answer at the bar of history for the accumulated guilt of

---

[31] W. G. Kümmel *Promise and Fulfilment* (London, 1957), 44.
[32] Cf. A. E. Harvey, *Jesus on Trial* (London, 1976), 18 ff.

former generations. This generation is in imminent danger of being the last generation in Israel's history.

The same may be said of Jesus' pronouncements on the scattered towns of Galilee (Luke 10: 12, 14). Again, the interpretation of these verses has been dictated by the obvious fact that the only assize in which the people of Sodom, Phoenicia, and Galilee could appear together in the dock is the Last Judgement. It is, of course, true that nothing is said here about imminence. Nevertheless this interpretation must be judged implausible. In any passage of the New Testament which unquestionably deals with the Last Judgement, this is the occasion on which *individual* destinies are decided: 'They were judged, each on the record of his deeds' (Rev. 20: 13). But here we have judgement on towns. Moreover, there has been a principle of law which has operated often in human history that nobody shall be put on trial twice for the same offence, and we have no reason to think that the New Testament writers believed that the God of the New Testament had departed from this rule. God's judgement on Sodom belongs to the past. 'Remember Sodom and Gomorrah and the neighbouring towns . . . in eternal fire they paid the penalty, a warning for all' (Jude 7, REB; cf. 2 Pet. 2: 6). 'So too in the days of Lot, they ate and drank, they bought and sold; they planted and built; but the day that Lot left Sodom, fire and sulphur rained from the sky and made an end of them all. It will be like that on the day when the Son of Man is revealed' (Luke 17: 28–30, REB). The suggestion that there is a future judgement awaiting the cities of the Plain or the cities of Phoenicia, which have already been destroyed in the past, is nothing more than a trick of syntax. Greek has no future-perfect tense, and the simple future must do service for both. 'It *will have been* more bearable for Sodom', i.e. the past judgement on Sodom will turn out to have been more bearable than the coming judgement on the towns of Galilee. What this comparison meant on the lips of Jesus would have been obvious to anyone who knew the Hebrew scriptures. 'The punishment of my people is worse than the penalty of Sodom, which was overthrown in a moment and no hands were wrung' (Lam. 4: 6). The author of Lamentations envies the people of Sodom because their doom was swift, unheralded, merciful, and complete—unlike the long-drawn-out agonies of Jerusalem under Babylonian siege, in which 'those who died by the sword were more fortunate than those who died of hunger' (Lam. 4: 9).

It is, of course, proper to respond that Jesus may have used scriptural terms and images to express ideas different from those of the context in which he found them. There is certainly an emphasis in his recorded teaching on a God who, at the Last Judgement, would inflict prolonged suffering on unbelievers in comparison with which the quick doom of Sodom would seem preferable (Matt. 5: 29 f.; Luke 16: 23 f.; Matt. 25: 41 ff.; etc.). What is beyond doubt, however, is that Luke at least understood Jesus' predictions of judgement otherwise, and classified them with the ancient Hebrew prophecies which they closely resembled. In a series of scorching passages peculiar to his Gospel he portrays Jesus warning Jerusalem of the imminence of a divine retribution, to be executed by Roman armies, in which all the horrors of 586 BC would be re-enacted (19: 41–4; 21: 20–4; 23: 27–31), with particularly gruesome consequences for pregnant women and the mothers of small children. This was the fate worse than that of Sodom which lay in store for the cities of Galilee if they rejected the proclamation of the Kingdom, because, like Jerusalem, they had failed to recognize the day when God was visiting His people or to know what made for their peace. There is therefore good reason to think that Luke's interpretation of Jesus was right on this point.

To any fair-minded observer, furthermore, the reasons for Jerusalem's impending fate in Jesus' mind must at least partially be rooted in the city's long and dubious pedigree. In answer to a threat from Herod, Jesus is said to retort: 'I must be on my way tomorrow, and the next day; for it cannot be that a prophet should meet his death outside Jerusalem' (Luke 13: 33). Jesus is safe in Herod's territory. As T. W. Manson once put it, 'Herod must not be greedy: for Jerusalem has first claim on the blood of God's messengers.'[33] Here, as in the previous passage and in the parable of the wicked tenants,[34] Jerusalem is treated as heir to a long national tradition. In Luke's Gospel this saying of savage irony is followed by another of deep pathos, in which God[35] is the Speaker:

[33] T. W. Manson, *The Sayings of Jesus* (London, 1949), 277.

[34] The parable (with or without a Christological gloss) continues to be viewed by many as authentic. Cf. in particular C. H. Dodd, *The Parables of the Kingdom* (London, 1941), 70 ff.; J. A. T. Robinson, *Twelve More New Testament Studies* (London, 1984), 12 ff.; J. D. Crossan, 'The Parable of the Wicked Husbandmen', *JBL* 90 (1971), 451 ff.; J. Jeremias, *The Parables of Jesus* (New York, 1963), 70 ff.; and K. Snodgrass, *The Parable of the Wicked Tenants* (Tübingen, 1983).

[35] This, of course, is not the traditional viewpoint, which regards Jesus as the speaker—referring possibly to previous visits to Jerusalem. But see G. B. Caird, *The Gospel of St Luke* (London, 1968), 173 f.

Jerusalem, Jerusalem, the city that kills prophets and stones the messengers sent to her! How often have I wanted to gather your children as a hen gathers her brood under her wings, and you would not let me. Look how your temple is left deserted! I tell you, you shall not see me until the time comes when you say, 'Blessed is he who comes in the name of the Lord!' (Luke 13: 34, Matt. 23: 37).

Shortly before the destruction of Jerusalem by the Babylonians in 586 BC, Ezekiel had a vision in which he saw the glory of the Lord abandon the Holy of Holies, leaving Temple and city deserted by the divine presence and exposed to enemy attack. Jesus has seen Jerusalem similarly deserted and exposed because it has not been prepared to welcome the one who came in the name of the Lord. Not long afterwards Luke shows us Jesus weeping over Jerusalem, because it did not recognize the day in which God was visiting it (19: 44).

We have seen how Jesus' predictions of the end of the city are commonly taken in this sense. It continues to be said that for Jesus the destruction of Jerusalem and the *eschaton* are one and the same event, or follow one another in such close proximity that they can barely be distinguished. But we have also seen that there is a strong case for saying that the Day of the Son of Man in the teaching of Jesus remained firmly in the sphere of national eschatology. Here, as in the book of Daniel, the coming of the Son of Man on the clouds of heaven was never conceived as a primitive form of space travel; it was a symbol for a mighty reversal of fortunes within history and at the national level.

What, then, was the connection between this eschatological crisis and the other national crisis which, as we have seen, bulked so large in the teaching of Jesus? Manson is again worth citing, only now to illustrate how careful scholars can sometimes misinterpret their own evidence. For Manson the Day of the Son of Man could never be an event in Israel's national history. 'For the Fall of Jerusalem as a fulfilment of the prophecy there is simply nothing to be said. The ruthless suppression by a great military empire of an insane rebellion in an outlying part of its territory has as much—and as little—to do with the coming of the Kingdom of God in power as the suppression of the Indian Mutiny.'[36] But the connection between Jerusalem and the Kingdom of God cannot be so easily discarded. There was in fact all the difference in the world between the Jewish revolt against the Roman rule and the Indian revolt against British rule. Jesus believed

[36] T. W. Manson, *Teaching of Jesus*, 281.

that Israel was called by God to be the agent of His purpose, and that he himself had been sent to bring about that reformation without which Israel could not fulfil its national destiny. If the nation, so far from accepting that calling, rejected God's messenger and persecuted those who responded to his preaching, how could the assertion of God's sovereignty fail to include an open demonstration that Jesus was right and the nation was wrong? How could it fail to include the vindication of the persecuted and the cause they had lived and died for? 'Shall not God vindicate His elect, He who listens patiently while they cry to Him day and night? I tell you, He will vindicate them speedily. Nevertheless, when the Son of Man comes, will he find faith on the earth?' (Luke 18: 7–9).

To such passages may be added others: the picture of Jerusalem surrounded by avenging armies (Luke 21: 20–4), the cleansing of the Temple (Mark 11: 15–19), the prediction that not one stone will be left on another (Mark 13: 1–2); and the words to the weeping women (Luke 23: 27–31) that if the Romans do this when the tree is green (when the victim is innocent of political offence), what will they do when the tree is dry (when all Israel is tinder, ready to be ignited by the first spark)? Certainly not all these passages are generally agreed to be genuine sayings of Jesus, but they make a cumulative impression to which we may properly apply the more conservative of Bultmann's principles: the certainty with which the Christian community puts this preaching into the mouth of Jesus is hard to understand if he did not really preach it.

We have also seen how in more than one strand of the Gospel tradition the coming of the Son of Man and the fall of Jerusalem are inextricably interwoven, and that at least Luke and Mark understood the coming of the Son of Man as an answer to the disciples' question about the date of the fall of Jerusalem. Is it indeed credible that Jesus, the heir to the linguistic and theological riches of the prophets, and himself a greater theologian and master of imagery than them all, should ever have turned their symbols into flat and literal prose? Can we really be satisfied with such a solution?

9.4. THE KINGDOM OF GOD

In Chapter 4 we saw that the three-tense structure of salvation is applied by the New Testament writers to the Kingdom of God. But when we turn to Jesus himself, while there is little doubt that the

proclamation of the Kingdom was central to his message,[37] we still find
no hint of a consensus concerning what the phrase could have meant
for him.[38] Much of the problem continues to rest on a misunderstanding. The normal procedure has been to go back to the Old Testament,
or more particularly to the references of contemporary Judaism, to
discuss what this term meant or could have meant in this or that
context, and then to use such evidence to set the limits on what the
expression could have meant in the teaching of Jesus. But if the Synoptic Gospels are right to insist that Jesus spent much of his time explaining what *he* meant by the Kingdom, would it not follow that he did
not mean what everybody else meant by it? Those who have insisted
otherwise tend to exhibit what Ronald Knox has called the 'token
word' fallacy.[39] Words become 'tokens' when they become a form of
coinage with a uniform and invariable rate of exchange. Knox correctly
attacked this schoolboy method of translation (a method which,
through the astonishing advocacy of J. B. Lightfoot, became the basis
of the old Revised Version). The alternative principle, on which the
whole of modern linguistic science is founded, is simply stated: Words
have multiple meanings, and images are certainly not less multivocal
than are other forms of language. Thus, in the study of the phrase
'the Kingdom of God' or 'the Son of Man' (below), it will be unwise
to decide prematurely which *one* of its possible senses can be ascribed
to Jesus.

We have seen that in the Hebrew scriptures God is eternally King,
Creator of heaven and earth, and Lord of history. In a more limited sense
he is King over Israel, in so far as, within the Covenant bond, Israel

[37] The centrality of the Kingdom in Jesus' teaching is denied, however, by Borg, *Jesus:
A New Vision*, 203 n. 20. Following Burton L. Mack (*Myth of Innocence: Mark and
Christian Origins* (Philadelphia, 1988)), Borg claims that 'a century of scholarship has
been bewitched by Mark's advance summary of Jesus' message (Mark 1: 15), treating
it as if it were accurate historical recollection rather than the Marcan redaction it clearly
is'. What is clear to one scholar of course may be signally unclear to another, and it is
always possible that modern writers may be bewitched by other modern writers.

[38] Among the many works on the Kingdom which might be cited in addition to those
below are B. D. Chilton's *God in Strength* (Freistadt, 1979), and his 'Regnum Dei Deus
Est', *SJT* 31 (1978), 261 ff.; G. Lundstrom, *The Kingdom of God in the Teaching of Jesus*
(London, 1963); N. Perrin, *Jesus and the Language of the Kingdom* (Philadelphia, 1976);
R. Schnackenburg, *God's Rule and Kingdom* (New York, 1963); and A. N. Wilder,
Eschatology and Ethics in the Teaching of Jesus (1950) and *Early Christian Rhetoric* (Cam-
bridge, 1978).

[39] R. Knox, *On Englishing the Bible* (London, 1949), 11.

acknowledges His royal authority. In a third sense His reign belongs to the eschatological future. These three are legitimate contexts in which to understand Jesus' sayings. But how often have we been told that it is only in the third sense that God's rule can be understood?

We have also seen the attempt of Dalman[40] and those who have followed him to distinguish between the Kingdom as a sovereignty rather than a 'realm'. That it should not be both is hardly obvious. In English 'kingdom' does service for both, with few kings exercising kingship without also having a realm over which to exercise it. We shall find ourselves in jeopardy if, when we hear Jesus speak of entering the Kingdom, there is no realm into which his followers can enter.

Obviously the understanding of the Kingdom of God in Jesus' teaching depends on the presuppositions with which one begins.[41] Those who follow Dodd's interpretation will put most of the stress on the presence of the Kingdom. And here it cannot be denied that Dodd spoke more sense on the subject than most. The presence of the Kingdom in the ministry of Jesus is one of the few clear data from which other aspects of his teaching may be construed.[42] But Dodd initially went too far. Like his opponents, he began with a definition of the Kingdom which allowed for no other interpretation. It had no future element, and Dodd was subsequently attacked as a Platonist.[43] His futurist opponents, on the other hand, started with a definition of the Kingdom as a state of affairs in which God's will is fully and finally realized, all wrongs are righted, and there is justice, light, and peace. And if one defines the Kingdom in those terms, it will be idiotic to suggest that it arrived in the ministry of Jesus. Both approaches were too exclusive, and the subsequent debate proved meaningless.

And yet: *The fact that such questions can be asked is an indication that*

---

[40] G. Dalman, *The Words of Jesus* (Edinburgh, 1902), 91 ff. Cf. above, p. 32.

[41] Cf. e.g. R. Scroggs, 'The New Testament and Ethics: How Do We Get from There to Here?' in C. H. Talbert (ed.), *Perspectives on the New Testament* (Macon, Ga., 1985), 84 ff.; B. D. Chilton (ed.), *The Kingdom of God in the Teaching of Jesus* (Philadelphia, 1984), *passim*; and B. D. Chilton and J. I. H. McDonald, *Jesus and the Ethics of the Kingdom* (Grand Rapids, 1987), *passim*.

[42] Cf. above, p. 32 f., and L. D. Hurst, 'The Ethics of Jesus', in Joel B. Green and Scot McKnight (eds.), *Dictionary of Jesus and the Gospels* (Downers Grove, Ill., 1992), 211 ff. There the presence of the Kingdom in Jesus' teaching is spelt out under eight headings.

[43] Cf. R. N. Flew, *Jesus and His Church*, 44 n. 1. But see also the persuasively succinct defence of Dodd's position in W. D. Davies, *Paul and Rabbinic Judaism* (London, 1955), 320.

the Kingdom in Jesus' teaching is all of these, and more besides. Only the context will tell which aspect might be uppermost at any one time. Any classification of the Kingdom as 'an eschatological concept' hardly severs its connection with history and politics, nor does it diminish the unique role which Israel was expected to play in the realization of God's world-wide sovereignty.

For Jesus, entering the Kingdom was synonymous with the life of discipleship—of submitting to the demands of the God who is King. His teaching is dominated by the central burning conviction that God's rule is now actively present in the affairs of individuals, kings, and nations. Ultimately, of course, such a view of the Kingdom turns upon the notion of divine sovereignty. For centuries the Jews had been preoccupied with questions about their national destiny as the chosen people, particularly with their undeserved suffering at the hands of pagan empires. But when God established His Kingdom of justice and peace, there would be a great reversal of fortunes, with Israel coming out on top. God would entrust to it His own royal authority, and it would reign over the other nations, to the great advantage of all. Jesus never questions the close link between the reign of God and Israel's election; but he insists on making God's sovereignty the primary consideration. First let Israel discover what it means for God to reign over Israel; then they will know what part Israel is to play in the plan of God.

9.5. THE SON OF MAN

Any appreciation of Jesus' original message is bound to address at some point the pressing questions[44] which surround the important designation 'the Son of Man'.[45] But like 'the Kingdom of God', the phrase

---

[44] Cf., in addition to the literature cited below, M. Black, 'The Son of Man Problem in Recent Research and Debate', *BJRL* 45 (1962–3), 305 ff.; F. H. Borsch, *The Son of Man in Myth and History* (Philadelphia, 1969); C. C. Caragounis, *The Son of Man* (Tübingen, 1986); O. Cullmann, *The Christology of the New Testament* (London, 1963) 137 ff.; J. D. G. Dunn, *Christology in the Making* (London, 1980), 65 ff.; F. Hahn *The Titles of Jesus in Christology* (London, 1969), 15 ff.; A. J. B. Higgins, *Jesus and the Son of Man* (London, 1964); J. Jeremias, *New Testament Theology*, i. 257 ff.; R. Maddox, 'The Function of the Son of Man According to the Synoptic Gospels', *NTS* 15 (1968–9), 45 ff.; I. H. Marshall, *Jesus the Saviour* (1990), 73 ff.; H. E. Tödt, *The Son of Man in the Synoptic Tradition* (Philadelphia, 1965); and D. R. N. Hare, *The Son of Man Tradition* (Philadelphia, 1990).

[45] In its anarthrous form the Hebrew is *ben adam* or *ben enosh*; the anarthrous Aramaic form is *bar enash* or *bar enasha*.

'the Son of Man' (*ho huios tou anthrōpou*) is ambiguous, raising more questions than it answers. While we cannot hope to treat every question, we can attempt to clear away some of the major misconceptions, erecting at least a substructure in their place. We begin with seven observations:

1. In the Gospels 'the Son of Man' occurs approximately eighty times, and is attributed exclusively to Jesus. Elsewhere in the New Testament it occurs only on the lips of the dying Stephen (Acts 7: 56). In Heb. 2: 6 and Rev. 1: 13 the phrase 'Son of Man' occurs without the definite article.

The Stephen reference is insignificant, in so far as Luke is drawing a parallel between the death of the first martyr and the death of Jesus; one can easily see why he has put it there. Hebrews 2: 6–8, on the other hand, is an extensive quotation from Psalm 8, while Revelation 1: 13 is clearly a reference to Daniel 7.[46] From these facts can be drawn two preliminary conclusions:

(*a*) 'Son of Man' was not an expression in general use in the early Church. Those who would attempt to claim that its usage in the Gospels is the product of later Church theology[47] have little foundation on which to base their case.

(*b*) The two writers (the author of Hebrews and John the Seer) who link the phrase to Psalm 8 and Daniel 7 were closer to their sources than are we. Thus it will be reckless to assert, without argument, that they did not know what they were talking about.

2. The Son of Man passages in the Gospels are normally divided into three categories: ministry, Passion, and apocalyptic sayings. Examples of each may be provided:

(*a*) *Ministry sayings*. Some sayings are set in the present ministry of Jesus. The Son of Man 'has nowhere to lay his head' (Matt. 8: 20; Luke 9: 58), 'came to seek and to save that which was lost' (Luke 19: 10), has 'authority on earth to forgive sins' (Mark 2: 10; Matt. 9: 6;

---

[46] Cf. G. B. Caird, *The Revelation of St John the Divine* (London, 1985²), 19, where it is said that a number of phrases from Dan. 7 'set the echoes of memory and association ringing'.

[47] As argued, e.g., by P. Vielhauer, 'Gottesreich und Menschensohn in der Verkündigung Jesu', in W. Schneemelcher (ed.), *Festschrift für Günter Dehn* (Neukirchen-Vluyn, 1957), 51 ff., and 'Jesus und der Menschensohn', *ZTK* 60 (1963), 133 ff.; E. Käsemann, 'The Problem of the Historical Jesus', in *Essays on New Testament Themes* (London, 1964), 43 f.; and H. Conzelmann, 'Jesus Christus', *RGG*³ (1959), iii. 619 ff.

Luke 5: 24), 'Lord of the sabbath' (Mark 2: 28), and 'comes eating and drinking' (Matt. 11: 19; Luke 7: 34).

(*b*) *Passion sayings.* Some sayings clearly predict the sufferings of the Son of Man. The most famous are the three from Mark's Gospel: 8: 31 (cf. Luke 9: 22); 9: 31 (Matt. 17: 22, Luke 9: 44); and 10: 33f. (Matt. 20: 18; Luke 18: 31; see below). Here the betrayal, death, and resurrection of the Son of Man are predicted with varying degrees of vividness. Elsewhere the Son of Man will give his life as a ransom for many (Mark 10: 45) and will be betrayed by one of his followers (Mark 14: 21 = Matt. 26: 24 = Luke 22: 22; Luke 22: 48; Mark 14: 41 = Matt. 26: 45).

(*c*) *'Apocalyptic' sayings.* Some sayings are 'apocalyptic', pointing either to a coming of the Son of Man or to a Day of the Son of Man. 'Whoever is ashamed of me and my words in this adulterous and sinful generation, the Son of Man will be ashamed of him when he comes in the glory of his Father with the holy angels' (Mark 8: 38; Matt. 16: 27; Luke 9: 26). 'Then they will see the Son of Man coming on the clouds with great power and glory' (Mark 13: 26 = Matt. 24: 30 = Luke 21: 27). '"I am", said Jesus. "And you will see the Son of Man seated at the right hand of the Power and coming on the clouds of heaven"' (Mark 14: 62 = Matt. 26: 64 = Luke 22: 69).[48]

Considerable debate continues to surround which of the Son of Man sayings may be seen as authentic. Many have accepted that some of the ministry sayings are genuine, but only if the Son of Man is understood as a paraphrase for the first person singular (below). Others claim that only the 'apocalyptic' sayings are genuine.[49]

Still less agreement surrounds the Passion sayings, with attention often drawn to two odd facts: they are confined to Mark and L, and they do not occur in Q and M. At first blush these could be seen as facts of some significance. Since the sayings are not preserved in Q, we may be dealing with Marcan theology rather than authentic material. But against this is the fact that Q and M have no Passion narrative, and it is therefore hardly surprising that they do not include predictions of the Passion (as opposed to Mark and Luke's special

---

[48] Cf. also the following: From Q, Matt. 24: 27; Luke 17: 24; Matt. 24: 37–9; Luke 17: 26 f.; and Matt. 24: 44; Luke 12: 40. From M, Matt. 24: 30; 25: 31; 13: 41; 19: 28; 10: 23; and 16: 28. From L, Luke 12: 8; 10: 32; 17: 22; 17: 24 f.; 18: 8; 21: 36.

[49] This view, normally associated with Rudolf Bultmann, almost always carries with it the corollary that these sayings refer to a figure other than Jesus himself.

source, which have Passion narratives and are interested in the process which led up to them).

3. Some predictions are more graphic than others. Note the three from Mark:

> And he began to teach them that the Son of Man had to undergo great sufferings, and to be rejected by the elders, chief priests, and doctors of the Law; to be put to death, and to rise again after three days (8: 31).

> For he was teaching his disciples, saying to them, 'The Son of Man is now to be given up into the hands of men, and they will kill him; and when he is killed, after three days he will rise again' (9: 31).

> 'Behold, we are going to Jerusalem, and the Son of Man will be given up to the chief priests and scribes; they will condemn him to death and hand him over to the Gentiles; and they will mock him, and spit on him, flog and kill him; and after three days he will rise' (10: 33).

Such variations make it prudent to admit the possibility that some passages have been elaborated in the light of the event. The last, for instance, may follow too closely the arrest, trial, and death of Jesus as recorded in the Gospels. The second, however, is bald in its simplicity (Luke's version, 'For the Son of Man shall be delivered into the hands of men' (9: 44), is even balder). And Jeremias, to name just one writer, has argued that Jesus predicted the death and resurrection of the Son of Man, but in the simple form, adding that part of our difficulty is that the basic prediction has been elaborated in the light of the event.[50]

4. In some apocalyptic sayings Jesus appears to distinguish himself from the *coming* Son of Man. Compare Luke 12: 84 f.: 'I tell you this: everyone who acknowledges me before men the Son of Man will acknowledge before the angels of God; but he who disowns me before men will be disowned before the angels of God.'[51]

This feature of the sayings tradition is important, and will have to be addressed eventually. But it will be unwise to address it before other evidence has been considered.

5. The Gospel tradition contains places where the Son of Man is clearly secondary. Two examples—one simple, one complex—illustrate the point.

---

[50] J. Jeremias, *New Testament Theology*, i. *The Proclamation of Jesus* (New York, 1971), 277–86. M. D. Hooker, *The Son of Man in Mark* (Montreal, 1967), 103 ff., argues similarly.

[51] For a helpful discussion of the authenticity of this saying, cf. I. H. Marshall, *Jesus the Saviour* (London, 1990), 88 ff.

(*a*) According to Matthew 16: 13, Jesus asks, 'Who do people say that the Son of Man is?' Mark's version is even simpler: 'Who do people say that I am?' (8: 27). Here it is obvious that Matthew has editorially inserted the 'Son of Man' expression into a context where it did not originally stand.

(*b*) According to Luke 12: 9–10, 'Whoever disowns me before others will be disowned before the angels of God. Anyone who speaks a word against the Son of Man will be forgiven; but for him who slanders the Holy Spirit there will be no forgiveness' (REB; cp. Matt. 12: 31f.). But in the previous chapter (11: 20) Luke understands Jesus to have claimed that the exorcisms were performed by the power of the Spirit, and that by casting out demons through the Spirit of God the Kingdom of God had come upon his hearers; thus we must ask in what way blasphemy against the Son of Man can be forgivable, while blasphemy against the Holy Spirit is unforgivable. The two would appear to be synonymous in so far as Jesus claims that the Spirit is at work in him.

The problem is clarified if we turn to Mark's version of the saying (3: 28 f.): 'All sins shall be forgiven to the sons of men, but he who blasphemes against the Holy Spirit will never be forgiven, but is guilty of an eternal sin.' Here the contrast is between sins in general and those committed against the Holy Spirit, and clearly Luke and Mark preserve variants of the same Aramaic saying. 'The son of man' (or 'a son of man') stood in the original, with two surviving translations giving a different nuance. There can be little doubt that Mark's version is closer to the original, with the Lucan 'the Son of Man' a titular phrase which was not part of the intention of Jesus. 'Son of man', meaning 'human being', has been developed into a title. Now it could be argued that this is what 'the Son of Man' *regularly* meant—'human being'[52]— and that the impression that Jesus used it as a Messianic title is 'Church theology'. But this is a large conclusion to base on one mis-translation.

6. The expression 'Son of Man' occurs occasionally in the Hebrew

---

[52] Suggested originally by H. Lietzmann, *Der Menschensohn* (Freiburg, 1896). A recent modification of this view is that of B. Lindars, *Jesus and the Son of Man* (London, 1983), and M. Casey, *Son of Man* (London, 1979). Lindars argues that the Son of Man in Jesus' usage refers to a class of people in a particular situation. Casey denies any influence of Dan. 7 upon Jesus, adding that only twelve Son of Man sayings are authentic, and in each Jesus merely refers to himself in a very general way.

scriptures, exemplifying what grammarians call 'the *ben* of classification'. Here the Hebrew noun *ben* (Aramaic *bar*) is used simply for classification purposes. Thus 'the sons of the prophets' (2 Kings 2: 3, 5, 7, 15) are members of the prophetic trade guild, 'sons of Belial' (Judg. 19: 22; 1 Sam. 2: 12) are scoundrels, 'sons of Aaron' are priests (Num. 10: 18), etc. The '*ben* of classification' tells us nothing about parentage, but everything about classes. Just so 'Son of Man', in its oldest contexts, is simply a human being. The clearest example is Psalm 8: 4: 'What is man, that you remember him, or the son of man, that you care for him?' The parallelism requires that 'son of man' is a paraphrase for the human race, *adam*.

Occasionally 'son of man' in the Hebrew scriptures is used not merely to denote a member of *homo sapiens*, but has a value judgement built in: it is the human race in all its creatureliness and insignificance. One finds an element of this in the psalmist's question, 'What is man?', answered by the claim that God has intended the human race to be the crown of creation, exercising His delegated authority over the world. But it is true especially of Ezekiel, where it is used over eighty times, mostly with the same sense: 'You, little man ... prophesy to this people.'

Thus it may be said that, in its origins at least, 'Son of Man' has more to do with grammar than with theology.

7. Old Testament and Jewish literature provides a variety of possible backgrounds for the use of the expression in the Gospels. These may be delineated as follows:

(*a*) *Psalm 8*. As we have seen, 'Son of Man' in Psalm 8 is a paraphrase for the human race, raised to a position of glory and honour, exercising an authority over creation exemplified in its domination of the beasts (v. 7).

(*b*) *Psalm 80*. The great 'vine' psalm ('You brought a vine out of Egypt', v. 8) uses 'son of man' and 'the son of your right hand' (v. 17), with 'son of man' meaning Israel, in only a slightly extended sense from its basic meaning of the human race. The psalmist could equally well have described Israel as 'the man of God's right hand', 'the man whom he has chosen', and 'the son of man', with all three phrases familiar to users of the psalms as an ideogram for the nation.

(*c*) *The Similitudes of Enoch*. Considerable discussion continues to focus on the central section (chs. 37–71) of the pseudepigraphic Book of Enoch, in so far as it also uses the expression.[53] There the Son of Man appears for the first time in 46: 1–2.

Before we discuss this text, several things must be said about the present state of the work. The only complete manuscript of 1 Enoch which has survived is an Ethiopic translation from the tenth century AD. The section comprising chapters 37–71, the 'Similitudes' or 'Parables', were thought for some time to have been part of the original prophecy; there is now no certainty that this was the case. Most recent opinion even questions whether the Similitudes are pre-Christian, largely because the fragments of 1 Enoch found in the Qumran caves include every part of the Book of Enoch *except* the Similitudes. If this is true, they could hardly have constituted any influence upon the New Testament.[54]

And yet, even if the Similitudes could be shown to be pre-Christian, it is clear that their author is simply adapting Daniel, not producing an independent myth. As with the author of 4 Ezra (below), the Similitudes are adapting the symbolism of Daniel for special purposes. So 46: 5: 'He shall depose the kings from their thrones and kingdoms.' Why? They do not acknowledge 'the source of their kingship'. This passage clearly depicts Nebuchadnezzar. The one point on which the Similitudes go beyond Daniel is in making the Son of Man more of an individual and less of a corporate figure (on Daniel's corporateness see below). But we must also reckon with the explicit statement of the last chapter: '*You* are the Son of Man, who is born in righteousness and upon whom righteousness has dwelt; the righteousness of the Ancient of Days will not forsake you' (71: 14, my emphasis). Here the Son of Man is Enoch; and he is clearly a heavenly Son of Man, not because he has been in heaven from all eternity, but because he has been taken away to heaven and kept there, awaiting a special purpose.

We may now appreciate that in chapter 46 the author is not departing from Daniel. The Enoch of Genesis 5: 18–24 is a symbol of the righteous person who in past days pleased God, and may therefore be used to fill out the picture of ideal Israel.

---

[53] See e.g. Dunn, *Christology*, 75 ff.

[54] This is recognized by most writers on the Son of Man question (so e.g. Hooker, *Son of Man*, 48). The arguments of E. Isaac, 'Ethiopian Apocalypse of Enoch', in J. H. Charlesworth (ed.), *The Old Testament Pseudepigrapha* (New York, 1983), i. 6 f., against the late dating of J. T. Milik cannot be said to be representative, and hardly eliminate the problem of the absence of the Similitudes in any text of Enoch prior to the Ethiopic translation.

(*d*) *4 Ezra*. The apocalyptic prophecy of 4 Ezra (2 Esdras) provides a vision of the Son of Man coming out of the sea (13: 1–3), and then coming with the clouds of heaven to receive a Kingdom, after which he is identified with 'my son the Messiah' (7: 28). Again there are doubts about dating. Most commentators date 4 Ezra *circa* AD 100, and as it stands it is heavily interpolated with Christian additions.[55] The first two chapters are a Christian introduction which were not part of the apocalypse, and it is difficult in the rest of the work to know when one is dealing with Christian interpolations of a Jewish work. Certainly serious doubt must exist about a work to be dated seventy years after Jesus.

On the whole it is clear that the Similitudes, 4 Ezra, and the Gospels go back to a common source, Daniel, with no direct link between them. But 4 Ezra has this in common with the materials we have thus far discussed: it is concerned with the destiny of the nation of Israel, and in particular with the problems raised for the nation brought about by the destruction of Jerusalem in AD 70.

(*e*) *Daniel 7*. The most decisive occurrence of the 'Son of Man' expression in the Jewish scriptures occurs in the vision of Daniel 7. There we have seen that the writer describes night visions in which four successive monsters rise from the sea, each symbolizing a world empire. Then, says the prophet,

in my night vision I looked, and saw one like a Son of Man, coming with the clouds of heaven. He came to the Ancient of Days and was brought into His presence. To him was given authority, glory and power; every people, nation and men of every tongue worshipped him. His dominion is everlasting and will not pass away, and his Kingdom will never be destroyed.

Several points here need to be addressed:

(i) In Daniel 7 the Son of Man is a symbol, with the symbolism clarified in v. 27; the Son of Man represents the saints of the Most High, Israel.

(ii) The fact that the four bestial figures represent four kings is important to any understanding of the symbolism. The symbol may represent either the kingdom or the king who is its figurehead. Because the author varies between the two, it is clear that it hardly matters to

---

[55] Cf. B. M. Metzger, 'The Fourth Book of Ezra', in Charlesworth, ibid. 520, who dates 4 Ezra 'about AD 100', adding that 'near the middle or in the second half of the third century four chapters were added, two at the beginning and two at the end, by one or more unknown Christian writers'.

him; he is talking about the same political entities, whether using the abstract 'kingdom' or the concrete 'king'. The human figure belongs to the same series as the beasts—it is a fifth symbol, and the fact that it is human rather than bestial is critical to its symbolism.

(iii) When the figure like a Son of Man comes on the clouds of heaven to the Ancient of Days, this is an enthronement scene. It has, of course, been correctly said that this is not a coming from heaven to earth, but of earth to heaven—there is no *Parousia* here. But such a statement takes the imagery too literally, failing to recognize that *the entire scene is symbolic*.[56] The journey on the clouds of heaven brings the human figure, the Son of Man, to the Ancient of Days, where he is enthroned (given authority). The symbol which represents Israel comes on the clouds which are in turn a symbol used to reinforce visually the authority and kingly power which the Son of Man is to receive.

But even the expression 'kingly power' will not advance our investigation unless we are prepared to see it in context. The power given to the Son of Man is the power *which has been taken away from the previous symbolic figures—the four beasts. It is in fact world empire.* What the author means by this can be seen if we go back to Nebuchadnezzar's dream (4: 10 ff.), where Nebuchadnezzar eats grass like an ox, after which we are told the significance of the dream. *Three times* this is said to have happened in order that Nebuchadnezzar may know that *the Most High controls world sovereignty and gives it to whomever He will* (4: 17, 25, 32). The characteristics of Nebuchadnezzar (e.g. nails like eagle's talons) in his grass-eating phase are strikingly like the first beast of the night visions, which represents Babylon. Nebuchadnezzar is the first holder of world empire in the sense intended by Daniel, and imperial power passes from him to the second beast/empire, then to the third beast/empire, then to the fourth beast/empire, and finally to the Son of Man. Clearly the prophet is discussing world power, not some highly spiritualized ideal.

(iv) The central image of Daniel is the throne, symbolizing judgement: 'I saw the thrones set up, and the Ancient of Days took his seat' (7: 9). We have seen how too much of the interpretation of biblical imagery has been based on the assumption that whenever we come

---

[56] 'The important point is not whether in Daniel the scene is laid in heaven or earth: the locus of an apocalyptic vision, like that of a dream, is, literally, neither here nor there. What is indisputable is that it is a scene of vindication and that the Son of Man comes *to* the Ancient of Days' (Robinson, *Jesus and His Coming*, 45 n. 2).

across the idea of judgement it is the *Last* Judgement. The judgement envisaged by Daniel is as much in the midst of history as in the earlier Old Testament writings. The case before the heavenly court is an appeal from the plaintiff Israel for redress against the tyrannical treatment it has received at the hands of successive world empires. The only 'end' to which the author looks is the one to which we are referred in the last chapter: 'When the shattering of the power of the holy people comes to an end, all this will be completed' (Dan. 12: 7). When judgement is given in favour of the saints of the Most High, the last of the pagan kings is stripped of his imperial power, and world sovereignty passes, by legal confiscation, to the nation he has tried to exterminate. Thus are we to understand that the divine court of appeal keeps close watch over the corruptions of imperial power, and that in the end the age of the Son of Man is to be imperial power *with a difference*: while in the past it has been bestial, in the future *it will be humane*. Herein lies the true significance of the Danielic Son of Man: in the judgement process whereby power passes to the Son of Man lies the fulfilment of the vision of human destiny in the eighth psalm, whereby the human race, humbled for a season, is to inherit glory and honour, with even the beasts subject to human authority. Thus Daniel 7 preserves the earliest known biblical midrash of Psalm 8.[57]

(v) The Son of Man expression *does not require that we fix to it one particular meaning.* As with so many other expressions used by or for Jesus, discussion has tended to centre on questions such as: Was it a title? Did it carry Messianic connotations? Was it an oblique self-designation? Did it refer to the human race? Arguments against authenticity have in turn rested almost automatically on the assumption that 'the Son of Man' in Jewish tradition must have been a title for a heavenly Messiah, and since there is good reason to suppose that Jesus did not explicitly refer to himself as Messiah, a fortiori he did not claim to be 'the Son of Man'. But this argument falls to the ground if the 'heavenly Son of Man' never existed, or if the Son of Man did not have 'Messianic' connotations in Jesus' day. The ambiguous dating of 1 Enoch 37–71 and 4 Ezra only accentuates the precariousness of assigning traditional Jewish 'Messianic' connotations to Jesus' use of 'the Son of Man'.

As with the Kingdom of God, we need to assume a greater flexibility of meaning and range of possible applications for 'the Son of Man'.

---

[57] Here the backward progression would be Dan. 7 → Ps. 8: 6 → Gen. 1: 26.

Why could not sayings which refer in one place to Jesus' ministry and in another to his Passion *both* be authentic? Is language always constant? Again, 'the token word' mentality in dealing with other phrases Jesus is said to have used will land us in deep trouble. What did he mean for instance by 'the birds of the air'? Will *that* be given a fixed value? In the parable of the Sower they are the Devil (Mark 4: 4, 15), while in the parable of the Mustard Seed (Mark 4: 31–2) they roost in the branches of the great bush, which in turn represents the Kingdom of God. Jesus could well have used 'the Son of Man' in connection with his own ministry in some contexts, while in others he looked forward to 'a Day of the Son of Man', meaning that 'Day' when the throne of judgement will be established and God will vindicate His people—'the saints of the Most High'.

A recognition of this complexity has unfortunately been impeded by G. Vermes, for whom the Aramaic phrase *bar nash[a]* in the Gospels is always a self-reference, meaning simply 'I', 'this son of man', or what in pidgin English would be 'this child'.[58] But again, granted that 'the Son of man' could be a way of talking about oneself, must it follow that this is what it *always* means? The eighth psalm and the Book of Daniel were parts of the scriptures of those who spoke Aramaic; Aramaic speakers must therefore have had a way of talking about Daniel 7.[59] What was possible to say in Daniel must certainly have been possible to say in the contemporary language of Jesus.[60]

There is in fact no tangible evidence to prevent us from concluding what on other grounds any competent linguist would have already concluded: Jesus used the 'Son of Man' expression in a variety of ways, and may have adopted it precisely *because* of its value in conveying the multivalent ambiguity inherent in the concept of 'the one and the

---

[58] G. Vermes, 'The Use of *bar nāsā/bar nās* in Jewish Aramaic', in M. Black, *An Aramaic Approach to the Gospels and Acts* (Oxford, 1967³), 310 ff.

[59] And even this overlooks the fact that Dan. 7 was written in Aramaic!

[60] It is of course well known that the Aramaic of Dan. 7: 13 does not have the definite article, whereas the Gospels refer to *ho huios tou anthrōpou* ('*the* Son of Man'). But to this observation should be brought the equally weighty point of C. F. D. Moule (*Origin of Christology*, 11 n. 1, and 13 ff.) that there would have been in the time of Jesus 'a straightforward Aramaic demonstrative phrase' which referred to *that* Son of Man, i.e. the figure recorded by Daniel. According to Moule, 'I have told this story dozens of times now, and the fact that I am still in a small minority makes me wonder what is wrong with it. But I can, so far, not find the flaw.' Cf. also Jeremias, *New Testament Theology*, 260 ff.

many'.[61] In this case the expression would come close to Isaiah's Servant. The Son of Man is a 'job description' for the New Israel, with Jesus inviting any and all applicants to join with him in fulfilling God's full intention, first for Israel, and then for all the nations of the earth.

Such a supposition would support an old argument of T. W. Manson[62] which, while much discussed, continues to be much dismissed.[63] 'The Son of Man has nowhere to lay his head' (Matt. 8: 20; Luke 9: 58) does not mean that Jesus is alone in that condition, but that those of the Kingdom, those who have enlisted in the Israel of the new age, share with Jesus the same homelessness. The Son of Man is an *open-ended* term which includes all who are prepared to respond to the preaching of the gospel of the Kingdom, who share with Jesus the demands the Kingdom is making on the Israel of the new age. Thus the first prediction of Jesus' Passion (Mark 8: 31) includes a summons to the disciples to join Jesus and take up their cross with him, to count their life lost for the sake of the gospel. It would also explain why in Luke 9: 59–62 and Mark 10: 39 Jesus suggests that others would share his vocation. Theirs will be the sufferings of the Son of Man, whatever may lie beyond. Manson admits this concept to be consonant with the idea that Jesus recognized early in his ministry that others might not, or probably would not, rise to the calling. Nevertheless 'the Son of Man' would remain for Jesus to the end potentially inclusive.

In Chapter 7, Gospel traditions concerning the Day of the Son of Man were found to be intimately linked with the fall of Jerusalem, which could also be seen as the day spoken of by Daniel when God vindicates His people against the bestial oppressors of the past. For Jesus 'the Son of Man' would then be the new Israel, which, rejected by the contemporary Jewish generation, was shortly to be vindicated.

---

[61] *Contra* e.g. D. Guthrie, *New Testament Theology*, 709, who rejects a variation of meaning because it 'implies that the Son of Man title was used ambiguously, sometimes in a collective sense, and sometimes in an individual sense. It would have been confusing for Jesus' contemporaries'.

[62] Cf. T. W. Manson, *The Teaching of Jesus* (Cambridge, 1935), 227 f. The corporate interpretation in Jesus' teaching has been adopted for instance by C. H. Dodd, *The Founder of Christianity* (New York, 1970), 116 f.; Moule, *Origin of Christology*, 14; and Hooker, *Son of Man*, 181 f. L. Hartman and A. A. Di Lella, *The Book of Daniel* (Garden City, NY, 1978), 85 ff. and E. W. Heaton, *Daniel* (London, 1956), 182 ff., argue for the corporate dimensions of the phrase 'Son of Man' in Dan. 7 itself.

[63] It is rejected by virtually all German and American scholars, not to mention many conservative evangelicals of all continents, for whom it ostensibly subverts the uniqueness of Jesus and subtracts from his divinity.

But such a reconstruction requires two significant differences between the teaching of Jesus and Daniel: (1) For Jesus the rejectors of the Son of Man are not the Gentile nations but the Jewish nation itself; the vindication of the Son of Man therefore takes the form not of God's judgement on the Gentile world but on the Israel which has rejected Jesus' proclamation of the gospel. (2) Unlike Daniel's Son of Man, who is to be served by all (Dan. 7: 14), Jesus' Son of Man is to serve all (Mark 10: 44 f.). The Greek verbs (*douloō*, Dan. LXX; *diakoneō*, Mark) are different, but there is no reason to suppose that the Aramaic underlying both accounts was not the same.[64] But this will in turn pose another question: to what extent did Jesus think of himself as bringing into existence the Israel of the new age? Manson's suggestion that the Son of Man is a term covering not only Jesus but the disciples as well (in so far as they were prepared with him to take upon themselves the yoke of the Kingdom) will become more attractive in proportion to other evidence which can be found in the Gospels that Jesus thought in such terms.

But is there other evidence? Here the work of R. N. Flew, while written several decades ago,[65] remains remarkably relevant. Flew set out to answer a very different question from ours: Did Jesus intend to found a Church? He dismissed the possibility that Jesus intended to found what we might understand by a church—an ecclesiastical structure—largely because he was intelligent enough to note that behind the word 'church' stood the Greek *ekklēsia*, which had a specific meaning in Judaism. Throughout the Greek Old Testament *ekklēsia* is used to translate the Hebrew *kahal*, 'the congregation', and particularly the congregation of Israel. For Flew the very word *ekklēsia* has national connotations.

But clearly there is one problem with this argument: the word *ekklēsia* does not occur in Mark, Luke, and John. It is found only in Matthew, and there only twice. And both passages for many scholars are suspect.[66] The first is the famous 'Petrine' passage (Matt. 16: 18), while the other concerns the errant member of the community who is eventually to be brought before the *ekklēsia* (18: 15–17)—an idea

---

[64] The Aramaic verb is *pelach* (Dan. 7: 14), roughly synonymous with the Hebrew *abad*.

[65] Published in 1938, Flew's work remains required reading for any serious appreciation of Jesus' teaching on the subject.

[66] It may go without saying that most German interpreters reject both texts as inauthentic. Among English-speaking writers 16: 18 is accepted as genuine by B. Meyer, *The Aims of Jesus* (London, 1979) 193 ff., and in a modified sense by Sanders, *Jesus*, 146 f.

which apparently envisages the Church structure of Matthew's day.

What is seldom asked of course is this: In the first half of the first century what might the term *ekklēsia* have meant? Could Matthew 18: 15–17 be understood as spoken by Jesus to his disciples during his earthly ministry? And in fact both sayings may be regarded as authentic if the term *ekklēsia* is given a genuinely Jewish meaning.[67] An *ekklēsia* was the town meeting of a Jewish community in any of the towns of Palestine. In the immediate background to the New Testament the term was never used simply of the whole congregation of Israel but of a congregation of Israel *anywhere it may gather*. In Ecclesiasticus 39: 10, which speaks of those prominent 'in the assembly' (*ekklēsia*), the assembly is the Synagogue which meets for worship; but it is also the town meeting that transacts local business. It is a lawcourt, the community gathering for all purposes; in effect it is *Israel*. Thus if Jesus used the word *ekklēsia* (or the Aramaic word underlying it), what he meant by it would have been peculiarly Israelite.

Still more arguments require airing. While it is speculative to claim that Jesus used a word which occurs in only two places in one of the four Gospels, other evidence can be found that Jesus intended to found a new community, an *ekklēsia*:

1. We have seen that (a) the common testimony of the four Gospels is that the beginning of the gospel was John the Baptist, and that it was he who prepared for the coming of Jesus, and that (b) John's preaching was a summons to admission to the Israel of the new age, with Jesus obeying the summons by being baptized in the Jordan. Thus if Jesus recognized in John his predecessor who had paved the way for him, it may be well to interpret Jesus' mission in the light of what preceded it. Both John and Jesus were looking to the new Israel.

2. Out of a large number of disciples, Jesus chose twelve. Why *twelve*? We have seen that the figure is prima facie significant in as much as the early Church had little interest in the members of the group. Most simply disappeared from view. While we have in the New Testament four lists of the Twelve (Mark 3: 13–19; Matt. 10: 1–4; Luke 6: 12–16; Acts 1: 13), they do not agree; even the identity of the Twelve is in doubt. It was not *who* they were that matters, but their *twelveness*. This is supported by Paul, whose description of the resurrection appearances records that Jesus appeared to 'the Twelve' (1 Cor. 15: 5). This, of course, is not precisely accurate; one was dead.

[67] Cf. R. N. Flew, *Jesus and His Church* (London, 1938), 48 ff.

But they were 'the Twelve', even before they elected a successor to Judas. The obvious explanation of this phenomenon is that the number is symbolic of the twelve tribes of Israel. This is hardly conjectural, for one saying, recorded by Matthew (19: 28) and Luke (22: 29 f.), makes the very link: 'You are those who have accompanied me through my trials, and as my Father has covenanted to me a Kingdom, so I covenant with you, that you shall sit with me in my Kingdom, judging the twelve tribes of Israel.' This saying is almost certainly genuine.[68] For Jesus the Twelve are a symbolic group representing Israel. See also Luke 12: 32: 'Fear not, little flock, it is your Father's good pleasure to give you the Kingdom.' The term 'flock' (Greek *poimnion*, Heb. *tson*) has a long history as a designation for Israel,[69] and therefore an expression of compassion on the people because 'they were like sheep without a shepherd' involves more than saying that they looked like a parish without a parson. A flock without a shepherd is a nation without a leader.

3. The false witnesses at Jesus' hearing before the Sanhedrin accuse him of saying, 'I will destroy this temple, and after three days I will build it again' (Mark 14: 58). According to Mark they were false witnesses—but how 'false'? Had Jesus said nothing of the kind, or had they got it wrong? According to the Fourth Gospel, Jesus said something very much like this ('Destroy this temple, and in three days I will raise it up', 2: 19). That Jesus predicted the destruction of the Temple, saying something about its replacement with a new Temple, is now beyond doubt.[70] The predictions include Mark 13: 32 and the story of Stephen's death (Stephen is accused of repeating what Jesus has said, Acts 6: 14). The tradition is thus deeply embedded in the records. But if Jesus looks to the building of a new Temple, with or without hands, his expectation must be part of a new age for Israel.

4. We saw in Chapter 6 that three accounts of the Last Supper have survived—those of Mark, Luke, and 1 Corinthians—and that

---

[68] That Jesus made a link between the 12 tribes and the disciples is argued strongly by Sanders, *Jesus*, 104, 115, 118, 156, 229 f., and 233.

[69] Cf. Jer. 13: 17; Isa. 40: 11; Ezek. 34: 31; Mic. 7: 14; Zech. 10: 3; Pss. 79: 13; 95: 7; 100: 3. For God as Shepherd, cf. Pss. 23; 28: 9; 68: 8 f.; 74: 1; etc.; Jer. 23: 2; Ezek. 34: 11 f.; Isa. 40: 10 f.; 49: 9; Mic. 4: 6f.

[70] Cf. Sanders, *Jesus*, 99 ff., against Vielhauer, who claims that it is a creation of the early Church. Sanders (p. 61 ff.) sees Jesus' action in the Temple as 'symbolic of its destruction' (75); but see B. D. Chilton, 'Jesus and the Repentance of E. P. Sanders', *TB* 39 (1988), 16 f. n. 36.

they agree that on the night of his arrest Jesus celebrated a meal with his disciples, in the course of which he said either, 'This is my blood of the covenant' (Mark), or 'This is the new covenant in my blood' (Paul). Luke does not preserve those words, but he does have, 'As my Father covenanted to me the Kingdom, so I covenant with you' (Luke 22: 29–30). Thus Luke omits the noun, but retains the verb.

The point of this is simple. We have three witnesses who attest that in the upper room Jesus did actions and spoke words about 'a covenant'. *But a covenant is a covenant with the nation.* Paul, of course, uses the expression '*new* covenant' (1 Cor. 15: 25); but whether Jesus said '*new* covenant', or whether Paul is interpreting it, we have reason to suppose that the saying goes back to Jeremiah's prediction (31: 31 ff.) that in the latter days God will make a new covenant with the new house of Israel. Later Christian tradition, embodied in Hebrews (8: 8; 9: 15; 12: 24) and 2 Corinthians (3: 6), speaks of a new covenant in contrast with the old. But if Jesus contracted with his disciples a new covenant, this can only mean that he saw in them the new Israel.

5. The idea of the Church as the new Israel occurs not only in words attributed to Jesus but in Paul. Paul mentions the 'Israel of God' in Galatians 6: 16, and elsewhere applies scriptural quotations concerning Israel to the Church. For him the Spirit has been given to the *ekklēsia* (cf. Rom. 8; Gal. 3: 14; 4: 6) as God's eschatological gift to Israel.[71] Paul also spent much of his life trying to prove to his fellow Christians that Gentiles are equal with Jews in the Church of Christ (Gal. 3: 28). In Christ there is neither circumcision nor uncircumcision, male nor female, slave nor free. Yet the great advocate of Gentile equality has no doubt that it is an Israelite body to which the Gentiles are being admitted (Rom. 11: 16–24). Now if the champion of Gentile equality can never quite get away from the idea that the Church is Israel, may we not be allowed to conjecture that this was how Jesus himself viewed it? Jesus' primary intention was not to found what we would call a Church, but to reconstitute the nation of Israel according to the promises of Daniel and the other Old Testament prophets.

[71] Ezek. 36: 27; 37: 14; 39: 29; Isa. 44: 3; Joel 2: 28–32; Zech. 12: 10; Test. Jud. 24: 2f.; see above, p. 205.

9.6. THE LAW

But if this was the nature of the true Israel, what becomes of the Law?[72] We have noted the impression which is so often given that Jesus intended to institute a new Torah, or at least that Matthew held this view of Jesus' teaching. But both impressions are false. The evidence that, for Matthew, Jesus is a new lawgiver is limited mainly to the arrangement of his teaching in five lengthy discourses, the first of which is given on a mountain, and the six antitheses of Matthew 5: 21–48.[73] But over against these must be set other passages, particularly Matthew 5: 17–20 (above, Chapter 6). While few will question that Matthew 5: 17–20 enshrines Matthew's view of law and ethics, the question which remains is whether, and to what extent, it represents Jesus' view. Much depends in particular on the 'jot' (*iota*) and 'tittle' (*keraia*) of v. 18, or 'the least of these commandments' of v. 19, all of which appear to indicate a legalism of a meticulous and literalistic kind.[74] But again this is in flat contradiction to the manner in which Jesus behaves throughout the rest of Matthew's Gospel. There he is attacked by the Pharisees precisely because he is *not* a legalist. Matthew 5: 17–20, of course, may be seen not as Jesus' teaching but as Matthew's.[75] But this is unlikely in so far as we find the same tension preserved in Luke. Luke contains three verses (16: 16–18), sand-

---

[72] In addition to the treatments of Borg, Banks, Derrett, Guelich, Gundry and Sanders (q.v.), cf. H. von Campenhausen, 'Jesus and the Law in the Gospel Tradition', in *The Formation of the Christian Bible* (Philadelphia, 1972), 1 ff.; J. Muddiman, 'The Fasting Controversy in Mark' D.Phil. thesis, Oxford, 1976; S. Westerholm, *Jesus and Scribal Authority* (Lund, 1978); S. Branscomb, *Jesus and the Law of Moses* (New York, 1930); and S. Zeitlin, 'The Halaka in the Gospels and Its Relation to the Jewish Law at the Time of Jesus', *HUCA* 1 (1924), 357 ff.

[73] Cf. e.g. the discussions of R. Mohrlang, *Matthew and Paul on Ethics* (Cambridge, 1984), 23; W. D. Davies, *The Setting of the Sermon on the Mount* (Cambridge, 1966), 83, 92 f., and 107 f.; and Guelich, *The Sermon on the Mount* (Waco, Tex. 1982) 136 ff., esp. 148: 'Matthew has neither a New Moses christology nor a "rabbinic" tendency to view Jesus as the Messianic interpreter of the Law anymore than did Paul (cf. Rom. 13: 8–10; Gal. 5: 14).'

[74] This much discussed passage has sometimes even been understood as an attack on Paul and his teaching (cf. T. W. Manson, *Sayings of Jesus*, 24). Others have attempted to see in 'the least of these commandments' a reference to Jesus' own commands in the Sermon (e.g. R. Banks, *Jesus and the Law in the Synoptic Tradition* (Cambridge, 1975), 223). This position, while easing the apparent legalism, has not won general assent (cf. Guelich, *Sermon*, 150 ff.).

[75] Cf. Banks, *Jesus and the Law*, 204 ff., and the authorities cited there.

wiched between two Lucan parables which are commonly attributed to the Q source, but which make an odd sequence. It does not take long, on the other hand, to see the link. All three concern the Law. The first affirms that the Law has passed away, the second that the Law can never pass away, while the third demands an obedience to the Law even more radical than that of the Pharisees. By every canon of synoptic criticism these Lucan verses provide justification for thinking that Matthew 5: 17–20 are not peculiarly Matthean. The only sense in which they can be seen as such is that Matthew may have isolated them in his source and stitched them together in his own interesting juxtaposition. But there is no longer any reason to doubt that Matthew could here be representing the viewpoint of Jesus.[76]

In Matthew *and* Luke we are here facing a mystery, a distinctly paradoxical quality of Jesus' teaching. Part of the explanation has to be rooted in the Jewish love of juxtaposing opposites, part in the complexity of the Jewish Law, and part in the uniqueness of Jesus' teaching.[77] We have seen that the Law was not simply the Jewish religion; it was also the civil and criminal code, with the Pharisees its lawyers. In this case Matthew 5: 20, Luke 16: 17, and Matthew 23: 2 f. are similar to Romans 13: 1–4: the civil powers are ordained by God, therefore accept their authority.

But if Jesus was not a new lawgiver, what might he have been doing? The simplest explanation is that he was drawing a number of precise distinctions, and the best way to appreciate the pattern is to begin with the sabbath.

While a subject of continuing debate, the breaking of the sabbath by Jesus and his disciples continues to be seen as one of the major causes of friction between Jesus and the Pharisees.[78] In justice to the Pharisees, it is important to realize what the sabbath meant to them. The sabbath was the sign of the covenant with Israel (Exod. 31: 12–17). On this one point the Diaspora Jew was duty-bound to make a public profession of faith by abstaining from work one day in seven. The sabbath was therefore the chief, almost the sole, safeguard against the lapse of Jews into the beliefs and practices of their pagan neighbours, and to take away this safeguard meant the end of Judaism. The

---

[76] Cf. R. Banks, 'Matthew's Understanding of the Law: Authenticity and Interpretation in Matthew 5: 17–20', *JBL* 93 (1974), 226 ff.

[77] Cf. Guelich, *Sermon on the Mount*.

[78] Cf. Borg, *Conflict, Holiness and Politics*, 145 ff. This is denied by Sanders, *Jesus and Judaism*, 264 ff.

Pharisees believed they were fighting for the very existence of Israel.[79]

Thus it is the more surprising that the Gospels represent Jesus as not only breaking the sabbath, but breaking it deliberately. This could be seen as a violation of Pharisaic and Mishnaic religion. But here we need to understand the Pharisaic point of view as precisely as possible, at least so far as it is preserved. For many of the Pharisees all 613 commandments must be lived out in daily life, and in contrast to the conservative and backward-looking Sadducees, they were progressive in so far as they recognized that one needs to know what the Law *means*. What, for instance, is 'work'?

The Mishnah defines work as thirty-nine different activities.[80] This in turn gave rise to many debates, some important, some trivial. One of the most important concerned whether the doctor may work on the sabbath. And on this point most of the Pharisees were not as hard-hearted as they are often depicted. Doctors were allowed to work on the sabbath where there was imminent danger of death. But in all other cases they must refrain. This latter ruling was accepted by the people with whom Jesus dealt, for we are told that they waited until sunset brought the sabbath to an end before bringing out the sick to him for healing (Mark 1: 32).

Jesus had no such scruples. There are four recorded instances in which he incurred the criticism of the authorities by healing on the sabbath,[81] and none of the four invalids could be said to have been in any real danger. One has a withered hand (Mark 3: 1–6), one suffers from dropsy (Luke 14: 1–6), and of the two paralytics one has had the affliction for eighteen years (Luke 13: 10–17), the other for thirty-eight (John 5: 2–18). In each case there was substance to the objection of the Pharisees that the cure could have waited another day. And yet in each case Jesus is said to have taken the initiative, deliberately choosing the sabbath as the right day for his acts of mercy.

It has been suggested that the intention of Jesus would not have been to break the sabbath, only to sweep aside the Pharisaic tradition

[79] Cf. Borg, *Conflict, Holiness and Politics*, 145 ff.

[80] *Shabbath* 7: 2.

[81] The historical genuineness of this conflict has been questioned by some recent studies on Jesus. Sanders (*Jesus and Judaism*, 264 ff.) denies that the Pharisees would have had any quarrel with Jesus' laying hands upon the sick on the Sabbath. For Borg, on the other hand, 'these violations of sabbath law ... *seem to be programmatic, flowing out of the alternative paradigm which Jesus taught: the sabbath was a day for works of compassion*' (*Conflict, Holiness and Politics*, 151, italics mine).

as to how the sabbath should be kept. But while at other times Jesus is said to have displayed contempt for the tradition of the elders (Mark 7: 1–13), this theory hardly explains the intense hatred which Jesus' behaviour apparently engendered in the religious authorities. The influential school of Hillel believed in a liberal interpretation of the Law, and the Sadducees rejected the tradition of the elders altogether. The authorities believed that Jesus was setting himself above the sabbath law itself, and that he was arrogating to himself the right to change the Law of Moses, just as on another occasion they believed him to be claiming the authority to forgive sins (Mark 2: 1–12). If they had been wrong there would be some evidence that Jesus corrected their misapprehension rather than allow it to build into a hatred which would issue in his death.

What possible justification then can we find for the idea that Jesus healed on the sabbath? The answer may be found in Luke's account of the paralytic woman. 'Was it not necessary that this woman, a daughter of Abraham whom Satan has bound for eighteen years, be loosed from this bond on the sabbath day?' (Luke 13: 16). While in Mark's Passion Predictions (8: 31; 9: 31; 10: 33 f.) the word *dei*, 'it is necessary', denotes a divine necessity laid down for Jesus in scripture, there was also a divine necessity for healing on the sabbath, the reason being that the sabbath was intended by God to be for Israel a foretaste or earnest of the Kingdom. Jesus, by healing the children of Abraham, had overthrown the kingdom of Satan and had ushered in the Kingdom of God (Luke 11: 20). The miracles of healing were the acts of the Messiah (Luke 7: 19–23). And if the sabbath was the day of the Kingdom, no better day could be imagined for him to perform his acts. Because the Kingdom was now present, the Son of Man was Lord of the sabbath.

This interpretation is supported by Mark 2: 23–8. The plucking of grain on the sabbath was an act which constituted two offences, reaping and threshing. Jesus' response is in turn shocking: 'Have you not read how David, when hungry, persuaded Ahimelech to part with the shewbread because he was "on the Lord's business"?' (1 Sam. 21: 1–6). The subsequent pronouncement that 'the sabbath was made for humankind, not humankind for the sabbath' indicates that which the Pharisees had missed, the humanitarian purpose of the sabbath in Deuteronomy. To interpret it in an antihumanitarian fashion is to misinterpret it. The claim made in Matthew 12: 5–7 (a passage peculiar to Matthew) makes the same point. If the Kingdom has arrived, all this activity is justified. The Pharisees, of course, do not accept that the Kingdom has arrived.

Nor can we be sure that the Jews of Jesus' day interpreted the sabbath as an earnest of the Kingdom. The Coronation Psalms (93, 97, 99, etc.), which begin with the phrase 'The Lord reigns', were probably sabbath psalms, but beyond this the evidence does not go. There can be little doubt, however, that this is the way Jesus interpreted it, and that the author of Hebrews is a faithful exponent of his teaching in representing the sabbath as a shadow of that rest that remains for the people of God when they enter the Kingdom (Heb. 3: 1 ff.). The disciples of Jesus live in a perpetual sabbath because they live in the Kingdom. They are the weary and heavy-laden who have found rest (Matt. 11: 28).

Such a concentration on 'the weightier matters of the Law' is also seen in Jesus' treatment of divorce (Mark 10: 11 f. = Matt. 5: 27 ff.; 19: 9 Luke 16: 18), and in the saying on mint and herb (Luke 11: 42 = Matt. 23: 23).[82] For Jesus the scrupulous observance of niggling rules only leads in the end to a neglect of the cardinal principles. It is a psychological inevitability that such concerns concentrate on what is *doable*—the visual, perceptible things—to the neglect of 'the weightier matters'.

To concentrate on outward acts is, of course, not in itself wrong. Its danger is that it may involve a preference of the good over the best. The clearest illustration of this is provided by the saying on oaths: 'Let your Yes be Yes and your No be No; anything more than this comes from the evil one' (Matt. 5: 37, corrected by comparison with Jas. 5: 12; Matthew's unintelligible version is presumably the product of mistranslation from the original Aramaic). If the assumption behind oath-taking is that one who is not on oath is free to tell a lie, then the whole practice is a Satanic lowering of the general standards of honesty.

One need not here enter into the debate concerning the extent to which the accusations against the Pharisees were justified. It is enough to say that, far from innovating, Jesus reminded his fellow Jews where the heart of their inherited religion lay; and no doubt many Pharisees appreciated what he was saying.[83] Matthew includes his

---

[82] On these two issues cf. Banks, *Jesus and the Law*, 146 ff., 178 ff., and Hurst, 'Ethics of Jesus', 219.

[83] This of course is the thrust of Sanders' work, although it may be said that in the process the differences have been severely underestimated.

accusations in his account not as a polemic against Jews, but as a warning against a similar scrupulosity within his own Christian community. In his day, as in many later periods of the Church's history, there was a tendency to turn the ethical demands of Jesus into a new legalism; and it was Matthew's concern to point out that the effect of this was to *reduce* their scope.

What Jesus appears to be doing, as reflected in the antitheses in Matthew and Luke (and throughout the rest of his teaching), was therefore not a rescinding of the Decalogue. It was a claim that a superficial interpretation and obedience to the Decalogue is not radical obedience to the purposes of God. Such radical obedience is the righteousness which exceeds that of the Scribes and Pharisees (Matt. 5: 20).

That such obedience needs to be coupled with actions is also seen in a number of recorded sayings, most notably that with which the Sermon on the Mount ends (Matt. 7: 24–7). These indicate that, as much as any Pharisee, Jesus required that principles of character should find their way into action. But at the same time for him actions are clearly not enough.

Jesus' teaching about the Law may now be summarized in five propositions: (1) There are lighter and weightier matters to the Law. (2) One needs to penetrate behind the Law's letter to its original divine intention. (3) One needs to penetrate behind action to character. (4) Those who love have fulfilled the Law. (5) It is possible to take this view of the Law because the Kingdom of God has arrived.

The last statement is the most radical, comprehensive, and potentially offensive. Here priority must to be given to Mark 10: 42–4 (Matt. 20: 25–7). 'You know that among the Gentiles the recognized rulers lord it over their subjects, and the great make their authority felt. It shall not be so with you; among you, whoever wants to be great must be your servant, and whoever wants to be first must be the slave of all' (REB). This text can be generalized as one of the major headings of the ethical teaching of Jesus. Among whom? *Among you who have entered the Kingdom.* The ethical teaching of Jesus is the way of the Kingdom. His teaching is not to be interpreted prescriptively as commandments to be obeyed as the Jews obeyed the Decalogue. Jesus' ethics are *descriptive*; they illustrate how men and women *will* behave in the Kingdom. 'If you enter the Kingdom, this is what you will be taking on—a higher standard of ethical observance than can ever be enforced by law.' Note especially the reference to the heart (Mark 7:

18–23; Matt. 15: 17–20). Whatever may be decided about the correctness of Mark's interpretation on this point,[84] what is clear is that the heart is the source of evil, and it must be changed, with behaviour following spontaneously.

And where for Jesus does the Law and his own example fit into this pattern? The tree is known by its fruit (Matt. 7: 17 ff. = Luke 6: 43 f.). Behaviour flows from the heart, and if the heart is changed, then with the Law of Moses and the example of Jesus as a guide, men and women can find their way to the practical application of their obedience to the law of love and to the radical demands of the God who is King.

Upon this premiss are predicated Jesus' most bitter recorded attacks on the Pharisees. Those who wish to be on firmer historical ground will here follow the Lucan version (11: 37–52), which has undergone less editing than Matthew's (23: 13–36). For Jesus the Pharisees concentrated on minutiae to the neglect of the weightier matters (Luke 11: 42).[85] They are like unmarked graves which men and women walk over without being aware of the contamination they incur (Luke 11: 44; par. Matt. 23: 27)[86]—a comment clearly showing Jesus at his most savagely ironic. The Pharisees attacked Jesus for not avoiding the company of contaminating people; Jesus turned the Pharisees on their

---

[84] There continues to be much debate over this question. For Sanders (*Jesus*, 266) the whole passage is impossible to consider as authentic. G. N. Stanton (*The Gospels and Jesus* (New York, 1989) 244) thinks it likely that Jesus originally said only 'there is nothing outside a man which can defile him', with no specific reference to food laws. Banks (*Jesus and the Law*, 144 ff.) likewise sees Mark as adapting Jesus' teaching to a Gentile setting—'clarifying the situation with respect to foods involved in idol-worship for his Gentile Christian readers'. C. E. B. Cranfield (*The Gospel According to St Mark*, (Cambridge, 1959), 244 f.), on the other hand, sees the entire saying, and Mark's interpretation of it, as authentic and correct: Jesus saw himself as 'the goal of the Law' (cf. Rom. 10: 4), which is 'no longer binding'.

[85] This has been denied particularly by Sanders. In his two major works on Paul and Jesus he has attempted with great sensitivity to allow the Rabbis to speak for themselves, with the result that to a large degree they are seen as very *un*legalistic. Yet it may be doubted whether this one rule is method enough by itself. Those who expound their own faith and practice are unlikely to dwell on abuses such as those of which the Pharisees are accused in the Gospels; yet the accusations may have been true, at least of those whom the cap fitted. Adverse criticism is not primary evidence or unbiased evidence, but it is evidence; and surely we are entitled to listen not only to what the Rabbis and others say about themselves, but also to what they incidentally disclose about themselves.

[86] On the priority of Luke's version over Matthew's, cf. Caird, *St Luke*, 158, and Borg, *Conflict, Holiness and Politics*, 113 ff.

heads by telling the crowds, 'Beware the leaven of the Pharisees' (Mark
11: 15). Leaven here is a symbol for silent, pervasive, spreading evil.
For Jesus the Pharisees were superficial environmentalists: concerned
with all kinds of outward pollution, they perpetuated a deeper, more
insidious and virulent form of contamination—that which comes from
those who claim to know everything about God but do not understand
Him in the slightest. They were those who take away the key of knowledge; they refuse to enter the Kingdom, and hinder those who are
entering (Luke 11: 52; Matt. 23: 13). In this context 'knowledge'
means more than knowing *about* God; it is knowing God, loving Him,
and responding with awe and fear in the presence of the holy and the
transcendent. The Pharisees refuse to use the 'key' themselves, and
hinder those who wish to do so.

A similar attack on the Pharisaic position is implicit in the parables
of crisis. But not all the parables of crisis are overtly directed against
Pharisees; in fact they are not overtly directed against *anyone*. A parable
is now being understood as a 'cap to be worn by the one it fits'; and
it so happened that the Pharisees fitted most of the caps. They were
those who could not discern the signs of the times (Matt. 16: 3); they
were the householder who did not stay awake and who let the house
be invaded by burglars (Matt. 24: 43);[87] they were the foolish brides-
maids (Matt. 25: 1–13); they were the guests who accepted an invitation to a wedding and then found reasons for not attending (Matt.
22: 1–4).

The same emphasis may be found from the 'reverse' angle, the
recorded criticisms of Jesus *by* the Pharisees. Here we get *their* point
of view, and the Gospels are remarkably frank in preserving their
complaints. This would indicate another certain bedrock fact: *Jesus
was a scandalous figure.* Such a recurring theme would hardly have been
preserved had it not been central to the preaching of Jesus about the
Kingdom. He profoundly shocked the authorities by what he did and
by what he said. Pronouncing forgiveness of sins (Mark 2: 1–12) and
keeping bad company (Mark 2: 13 ff.—a charge he accepted
and gloried in), he enjoyed likening his work to a doctor and the sick.
The attitude of the authorities is tantamount to insisting that doctors
visit only the well lest they catch a cold. Self-regarding and apprehen-
sive, they feared that the holiness of Israel will be contaminated by
what it touches. To Jesus the holiness of God can look after itself; it

---

[87] But see the application to the disciples in Mark 14: 38 ff. (cf. 13: 36 f.).

is an outgoing power reaching all who need help. It is incapable of being contaminated, except by selfishness.

Clearly Jesus and many of the religious authorities in his day had different views of the sinner. For some the sinner will suffer the judgement of God, and is to be repudiated. For Jesus on the other hand the sinner is the sick. The theology of Jesus entails a comprehensive concern for the holiness of Israel. His opponents were concerned with a small remnant; the rest could go to ruin. His mission was to seek and save that which was lost (Luke 19: 10), restoring the despised to their place in the national life. While in the past it has of course been claimed that there is a disagreement between Jesus and his opponents on this critical point,[88] it has almost always been treated as a matter of religious rectitude. For Jesus however the redemption of the lost *must be built into the very structures of the national life*. It must be part of what it means for Israel to be the holy people of God.

But if Jesus and his opponents were not able to agree on this central point, it was also because they had pivotally different conceptions of God. To them God was a lawgiver who approves of and rewards those who keep His Law. To Jesus He was the heavenly Father who loves even His erring children and whose sovereign grace is a dynamic, redemptive force let loose into the world to restore and redeem. Those who took the 'harder' view of God were few, because in order to please such a deity one would have to be a professional; obeying 613 commandments would be a full-time job. The leaders 'load them with intolerable burdens, and will not lift a finger to ease the load' (Luke 11: 46). For Jesus the Law is the gift of a gracious God, and to interpret it as an intolerable burden is to misunderstand the God from whom it comes. If ordinary men and women break down under the strain of obedience to the Law, then there must be something seriously wrong with that reading of the will of God.

9.7. THE NATIONS

The question of Jesus' approach to the Gentiles is yet another acute problem for the historical theologian. Now according to our one indubitably pro-Gentile writer, the Church in its early years was devoid of

---

[88] On the problem of Jesus, the Pharisees, and 'the sinners', in addition to the discussions of Davies, Meyer, Sanders, and Borg, cf. Chilton, 'Jesus and the Repentance of Sanders', pp. 1 ff.

all concern for the preaching of the gospel to the Gentiles. The Christians were assiduous in their attendance at Temple and Synagogue, and in all outward respects remained good Jews; and the Pharisees, led by Gamaliel, were content to have it so. When later, through Peter's experience with Cornelius, the Church faced for the first time the prospect of having Gentiles among their number, they received the invitation, not indeed with reluctance, but with unfeigned astonishment. 'So then to the Gentiles also God has granted repentance leading to life!' (Acts 11: 18). Now this might be allowed to pass without remark, were it not for the fact that in the Gospels we find Jesus so often saying and doing things which imply the universality of the gospel. The picture of the symbolic figure whom Daniel had seen coming on the clouds of heaven, and to whom 'was given dominion and glory and sovereignty, that all peoples, nations, and languages should serve him' (Dan. 7: 14), is adopted by Jesus, but as we have seen with the last part inverted. And when he rode into Jerusalem,[89] he is said to have reminded the spectators of another prophet's vision:

> Rejoice greatly, daughter of Zion!
> Shout aloud, daughter of Jerusalem!
> See, your king comes to you;
> Triumphant and victorious is he,
> Humble and riding on an ass,
> On a colt, the foal of an ass . . .
> And he shall command peace to the nations.
> His dominion shall be from sea to sea,
> From the River to the ends of the earth.
> (Zech. 9: 9–10; Matt. 21: 5 ff. = Luke 19: 38)

In the Gospels Jesus repeatedly compares Gentiles favourably with his fellow Jews—the Queen of Sheba, the people of Nineveh, Naaman the Syrian, the widow of Zarephath, the people of Tyre and Sidon, even those of Sodom and Gomorrah (Mark 6: 11; Luke 4: 25 ff.; 10: 12 ff.; 11: 29 ff.; Matt. 10: 15; 11: 23 f.).[90]

---

[89] There is no valid reason to question the historicity of this event simply because of its later interpretation in the light of Zechariah. As Sanders (*Jesus*, 235) suggests, it is a 'prophetic and symbolic action' which 'speaks for itself'. He goes on: 'Jesus saw himself as one who was a servant of all . . . not their glorious leader in a triumphal march through parted waters.'

[90] *Contra* e.g. G. Vermes, *The Gospel of Jesus the Jew* (Newcastle upon Tyne, 1981), 45, who equates the 'dogs' of Mark 7: 27 and Matt. 15: 27 (on this episode cf. below, p. 395) with the 'swine' of Matt. 7: 6. But the latter most certainly refers to those Pharisaic and Sadducean authorities, who in a way far worse than the Roman armies,

There is, of course, the notorious problem of the Syro-Phoenician woman,[91] to whom, in response to her request for healing, Jesus is said to have remarked. 'It is not fair to take the children's bread and throw it to dogs' (Mark 7: 27; Matt. 15: 27). Much has been built on this one passage in depicting Jesus' attitude to Gentiles, as if on it hinges everything else. But apart from the obvious danger of building an entire reconstruction on one reported incident, one must be especially aware of the problem incurred by the loss of *tone* in any reported saying of Jesus. Anyone today who attempts to read the Bible in public knows what a change in meaning can be effected by changing the inflexions of the voice.[92] Jesus' words, which in cold print seem so austere, were almost certainly spoken with a smile and a tone of voice which invited the woman's witty reply. Jesus must have been aware of the prejudice against Gentiles which existed among many of his contemporaries, and in view of the use of irony found elsewhere in his teaching,[93] it would be surprising not to find a vestige of it in this, one of the most crucial points of concern among the 'pure' Jews of his day.[94]

are 'trampling upon' the people of the land. For a brief but useful treatment of Sadducean abuse of the Jewish people, cf. J. H. Charlesworth, 'Caiaphas, Pilate, and Jesus' Trial', *Explorations* 7 (1993), 3 f.; and D. Flusser, '. . . To Bury Caiaphas, Not to Praise Him', *Jerusalem Perspective* 4 (July/Oct., 1991), 24, cited in Charlesworth. Charlesworth, quoting Flusser, claims that it is possible that one of these abuses 'was the "persecution of Jesus and his first disciples"' (4).

[91] For an analysis of this enormously difficult passage and its possible implications for Jesus' theology, cf. S. G. Wilson, *Gentiles and the Gentile Mission in Luke–Acts* (Cambridge, 1973), 9 ff., who on the whole follows Munck's reconstruction (cf. esp. p. 12).

[92] On voice inflexion, cf. Caird, *Language and Imagery of the Bible*, 53 f.

[93] For examples of irony in Jesus' teaching see Mark 7: 9 ('You have a fine way of setting aside the commandment of God in order to maintain your tradition'); Matt. 6: 5 ('They have their reward'); Luke 7: 24 ('What did you go out into the wilderness to behold? A reed shaken by the wind?'); and Matt. 16: 18 ('You are Peter, and upon this rock I will build my Church'). On the subject in general cf. C. H. Dodd, *The Founder of Christianity* (New York, 1970), 40 f., and E. Trueblood, *The Humor of Christ* (San Francisco, 1964), ch. 3. According to Trueblood, 'the dividing line which separates humor and sarcasm is sometimes a narrow one and is easily crossed' (p. 64).

[94] This is hardly to claim that all Jews except Jesus hated or condemned Gentiles to perdition, a point made forcibly by Sanders, *Jesus*, 213 ff., 218 ff. See also his scathing denunciation of Jeremias in 'Jesus and the Kingdom: The Restoration of Israel and the New People of God', in Sanders (ed.), *Jesus, the Gospels, and the Church*, 228 ff. According to Sanders, Jeremias, by depicting first-century Jews as predominantly anti-Gentile, 'simply created a fiction and handed it down to those who admire his learning and piety' (p. 230).

We have seen the hypothesis of Munck and Jeremias that Jesus believed that his ministry should be restricted to recalling Israel to its role as a beacon or magnet to the nations, with the actual missionary work left to his followers.[95] It is interesting that this view of the mission of Jesus is preserved even in the Fourth Gospel. 'The hour is coming when neither on this mountain nor in Jerusalem will you worship the Father. You worship what you do not know; we worship what we know, for salvation comes from the Jews' (John 4: 21–2). In God's new order all earthly worship will be transcended and all the earth's peoples will be one; but, until that time arrives, it remains true that 'salvation is of the Jews'.

It is understandable, then, that after Jesus left them, the Jerusalem church might have felt their immediate task to be to pick up where he left off, the winning of Israel to an acceptance of its role as God's missionary nation. 'Repent therefore and return to God, so that your sins may be blotted out, that God may grant you a period of recovery, and that He may send the Messiah appointed for you, Jesus, who must remain in heaven until the time for the universal restoration (*apokatastasis*) of which God spoke through His holy prophets in days of old' (Acts 3: 19–21). The winning of the Gentiles, they believed, belonged to that universal restoration which would begin just as soon as Israel had accepted the demand and invitation of the gospel.

Two other pieces of evidence support this interpretation.

1. *The Cleansing of the Temple (Mark 11: 15–19 = Matt. 21: 12–17 = Luke 19: 45–8)*. This episode occurs in Mark, Matthew, and Luke, and we have therefore no reason to assume that the latter two had any independent source. The usual interpretation of Jesus' double quotation (from Isa. 56: 7 and Jer. 7: 11), 'My house shall be called a house of prayer for all nations, but you have made it a den of robbers (*lēstai*)', is that the Temple authorities, whose sole reason for existence was to bring worshippers into vital contact with the living God, were wilfully frustrating that purpose by allowing the profiteers to grow rich at the expense of the pilgrims.[96] But there is no reason to suspect that the issue was dishonesty. The Temple tax was to be paid in holy rather than ordinary currency, and the moneychangers performed a necessary function. The real objection is rooted in the term *lēstēs*, normally translated 'thief'. The ordinary word for 'thief', however, was *kleptēs*.

---

[95] See above, pp. 52, 352.
[96] Cf. Borg, *Jesus: A New Vision*, 174 ff.

A *lēstēs* was a 'bandit', a different class of person. *Lēstēs* was the pejorative term used by the respectable for those we wrongly call the 'Zealots'. Jesus was crucified between two *lēstai* (Mark 15: 27 and par.), and the term used by Josephus for the Jewish insurrectionists was *lēstai* or *to lēstrikon*.[97] The Temple authorities were turning the Temple into a banditry hideout. Here we do well to look to Jer. 7: 10–14, a partial source of the quotation:

> Will you then come and stand before me in this house, which bears my name, and say, 'We are safe'; safe, you think, to indulge in all these abominations? Do you regard this house which bears my Name as a bandit's cave? . . . Go to my shrine at Shiloh, which once I made a dwelling for my name, and see what I did to it because of the wickedness of my people Israel . . . Therefore what I did to Shiloh I will do to this house which bears my name, the house in which you put your trust, the place I gave to you and your forefathers; I shall fling you away out of my presence, as I did with all your kinsfolk, all Ephraim's offspring (REB).

The same Temple ideology existed in Jesus' day. The inhabitants of Jerusalem thought they were safe, but in fact they were practitioners of Jewish nationalism trading on the supposed presence of their God. It is easier to understand Jesus' words if they are translated 'My house shall be called a house of prayer for all nations, but you have turned it into a nationalists' hideout'. Neglecting their missionary task, and so forfeiting their calling, they filled the court of the Gentiles with a market, with the Gentiles prevented from having a place to sacrifice and worship. Therefore, rather than being the centre of a world religion, the Temple had degenerated into a source of nationalism and division.[98]

2. *The Lamp Placed under a Bushel Basket (Matt. 5: 14–16 = Mark 4: 21 = Luke 8: 16; 11: 33).* 'When a lamp is lit, it is not put under a bushel basket, but on the lamp-stand, where it gives light to all in the house.' Again, this text is usually interpreted in pietistic, individualistic, and purely religious terms. But it was clearly intended to be a

---

[97] On the meaning of *lēstēs*, cf. Borg, *Conflict, Holiness and Politics*, 174, and G. W. Buchanan, 'Mark 11: 15–19: Brigands in the Temple', *HUCA* 30 (1950), 169 ff. Buchanan, sadly, takes Jesus' words literally: revolutionaries were occupying the Temple precincts. But Jesus was speaking figuratively ('you have made it *like* a den of *lēstai*'), comparing the *consequences* of the actions of the Temple authorities with those of the *lēstai*; each, by their approach to the Gentiles, had achieved the same result, exclusion from the redemptive purposes of God.

[98] So also Chilton, 'Jesus and the Repentence of Sanders', 16 f. n. 36.

parable concerning Israel, the nation called to be a light to the Gentiles. Jesus accuses his Israel of putting its light under a bushel. And if we ask why anyone would do that, the answer is clear. Those who live in a draughty Palestinian house take the risk of having a lamp blown out. But if it is under a bushel, it cannot be extinguished. Of course the lamp does no good; but it is *safe*. Israel, so concerned to protect its sanctity, its lamp, has forgotten what the lamp is *for*. The normal understanding any Israelite would put on the comment may be best appreciated by referring to Isaiah 42: 6 f.: 'I have given you as a covenant to the people, a light to the Gentiles, to open the eyes that are blind, to bring the captives out of the dungeon, out of the dungeons where they lie in darkness.' Again Jesus is not concerned so much with individual response as with the enormous *political* question: what does it mean for Israel to be the holy people of God? To what destiny is Israel called? And what are the choices for the nation at this momentous juncture in its history, when it must choose between life and death, once and for all?

9.8. SONSHIP

Another certain fact about Jesus is his use of the word 'father', attested by the Aramaic word *abba* in the records. The prayer in Gethsemane (Mark 14: 36) ('*Abba*, Father . . .') is on all hands recognized as an authentic word of Jesus, for two good reasons: (1) In normal Jewish usage the form *abba* was not used in prayers: the Jewish usage was the more formal *abinu*, 'Our Father'. (2) The word *abba* occurs twice in the Pauline Epistles: Galatians 4: 6 ('God has sent into our hearts the Spirit of His son crying, "*Abba*, Father"') and Romans 8: 17 ('the Spirit of adoption which leads us to say, "*Abba*, Father"'). The presence of an Aramaic word in a Greek epistle is a clear indication that it was deeply embedded in the early Christian tradition, and that Mark's use of it in the story of Gethsemane is authentic in representing Jesus on this point.

At the height of nineteenth-century liberal Protestantism, the teaching of Jesus was fondly described as 'the fatherhood of God and the brotherhood of man'.[99] Such a summary suggested that when Jesus

---

[99] For the Fatherhood of God in Jesus' teaching cf. T. W. Manson, *Teaching of Jesus*, 89 ff.; H. F. D. Sparks' discussion in D. E. Nineham (ed.), *Studies in the Gospels: Essays in Honour of R. H. Lightfoot* (Oxford, 1955), 241 ff.; C. H. Dodd, *The Epistle to the*

talked about the divine fatherhood he talked about a universal fatherhood. But that was doubly false. Nowhere in the Gospels does Jesus talk about the fatherhood of God in a universal sense. At times he speaks of God as 'your Father', i.e. the father of those who worship, recognize, and put themselves under His authority as His children. In other places He is the God of all people, whether they know it or not. But both affirmations differ from a belief in a universal fatherhood.

Second, even the reference to God as *your* father is not central to the tradition. While present in all strands, it occurs mainly in Matthew.[100] It is from Matthew that we get the impression that Jesus constantly talks about God as 'your heavenly Father'. When we turn from Matthew to the other Gospels, we find something very different. We have noted that there are in Mark only four passages in which Jesus refers to God as Father. Mark 8: 38 ('the Son of Man coming in the glory of his Father'); 11: 25 ('If you do not forgive others their sins, your Father in heaven will not forgive you your sins'); 13: 32 ('Of that day no one knows, no angel, not the Son, but only the Father'); and 14: 36 ('*Abba*, Father, remove this cup from me'). Thus only four instances in Mark designate God as Father, and all are different: 'his Father, your Father, the Father, and Father'. *In only one is God 'your Father'*. In the first He is Father of the Son of Man, in the third He is Father in a reciprocal relationship with the Son, and in the fourth He is addressed as Father in prayer. Thus if we were to draw a general impression from Mark alone, we should say that Jesus spoke of God as Father with great reticence, and that when he did, in the majority of cases God is *his* father, particularly in correlation with his sense of being 'son'.

Returning to Matthew, there are three passages in Mark where Jesus refers to God without using the word 'father', but where Matthew has inserted it (Mark 3: 35 = Matt. 12: 50; Mark 10: 40 = Matt. 20: 23; Mark 14: 25 = Matt. 26: 29). These three are enough to show that some instances of the word 'father' in Matthew are clearly editorial.

When we come to Q we discover a very similar phenomenon: a number of passages in the Matthean version contain the word *patēr*,

Romans, 130 f.; and R. Hamerton-Kelly, *God the Father: Theology and Patriarchy in the Teaching of Jesus* (Philadelphia, 1979).

[100] Matthew has 31 occurrences of 'Father' as opposed to only 4 in Mark (see below). For a useful chart, cf. J. D. G. Dunn, *The Evidence for Jesus*, 44.

whereas the Lucan does not.[101] We shall therefore suspect that the Lucan version is original and that Matthew is doing with Q what he has done with Mark. But before a firm conclusion on this question may be drawn there are several Q passages in which Matthew and Luke agree on the use of 'father' (Luke 6: 36; Matt. 5: 48; Luke 10: 21 f., Matt. 11: 25 ff.; Luke 11: 13; Matt. 7: 11). Now this is justification for saying that, although Matthew is fond of inserting the expression 'your heavenly Father' into his sources, there are places where it stood in Q. Matthew is therefore simply dispersing the designation from a limited number of occurrences in his sources.

Coming finally to the L material, we find the following: Luke 2: 49; 11: 2—here, in the Lord's prayer, Luke begins with *patēr*, but we can safely see behind it *abba* (Matthew, conversely, has, 'Our Father in heaven'); 22: 29; 23: 34, 23: 46; and 24: 49 ('*My* father'). The L evidence is therefore more overwhelming than the Marcan. Every single instance is either 'my Father' or the vocative 'Father', addressed to God in prayer.

From these statistics three conclusions may be drawn. (1) Matthew introduces the idea of divine fatherhood into contexts where it did not originally stand. (2) Matthew is partial to the expression 'heavenly Father', which he did not invent. (3) In sources other than Matthew the references to God as Father are few. On the whole they express Jesus' consciousness of his filial relationship to God rather than any doctrine of universal fatherhood.

Nor it is possible to argue[102] that the idea of Jesus as 'the Son' is Church theology retroactively injected into the record. The evidence points in fact in the opposite direction. Where we can detect editorial work (as in the case of Matthew), it *broadens* the divine fatherhood to include the disciples. *The further back we go, the more we discover the intense conviction of Jesus that God is his Father and he is His son.* This is supported by the word *abba*, an address used at times by children to their father, indicating an intimacy and directness not contained in

---

[101] Matt. 5: 45; Luke 6: 35; Matt. 6: 26; Luke 12: 24; Matt. 7: 21; Luke 6: 46; Matt. 10: 29; Luke 12: 6; Matt. 10: 32 f.; Luke 12: 8 f.

[102] Cf. e.g. R. Bultmann, *The Theology of the New Testament* (New York, 1951) i. 28, 32, for whom Jesus was the Son of God because the Aramaic-speaking Church saw him as the fulfilment of a Messianic interpretation of Ps. 2: 7, not because he actually thought of himself in any special way as the Son of God.

the more formal *abinu*.[103] Certainly other Jews believed in the fatherhood of God, but this was a credal affirmation, with God seen as the Father of the nation, and in a more particular sense as the Father of the Messiah. This background underlies somewhat the terms *patēr* and *huios* in the teaching of Jesus. Yet it would be wrong to regard 'son' as though it were simply a synonym for 'Messiah'. The synoptic passages speak of an intimacy of filial relationship which goes beyond traditional Jewish concepts of Messiahship. For Jesus the fatherhood of God has become a profoundly personal religious experience, long before it became a doctrine to be communicated to others.

What may be said of the experience? It may well have begun at the baptism (or at least in any demonstrable form—Luke traces it back further, 'I must be about my Father's business', 2: 49). Here, as with the later episode of the transfiguration (Mark and par.), the voice addresses Jesus as 'my Son'. We should next look at three crucial passages which provide an indication of what that sonship might have meant to Jesus.

1. The first, the Gethsemane prayer (Mark 14: 36), preserves the words, '*Abba*, Father, all things are possible with you; remove this cup from me . . . nevertheless, not what I will, but what you will.' This saying conveys two remarkable elements of the divine fatherhood. (*a*) 'All things are possible'—complete trust in the providential ordering of God. (*b*) 'Remove this cup from me, nevertheless, not what I will but what you will'—complete obedience. To the Jew the first connotation of the fatherhood of God is the right to obedience. It is important to emphasize these two aspects of the prayer in Gethsemane lest we be overawed by Chalcedonian definitions and trinitarian formulations which will inexorably lead us into metaphysics. Such speculation may lie in the background, but we are here dealing with the human Jesus in his attitude of total trust and obedience to the God whom he terms 'Father'.

2. The second passage, the so-called 'Great Thanksgiving' (Matt. 11: 25–7 = Luke 10: 21–2),[104] introduces another element, mutual

---

[103] On *abba*, see J. Jeremias, *The Prayers of Jesus* (London, 1967); Dunn, *Evidence for Jesus*, 47 ff.; G. Vermes, *Jesus the Jew* (London, 1973), 210 ff.; J. Barr, '"Abba" Isn't "Daddy"', *JTS* NS 39 (1988), 28 ff.; and B. Witherington, *The Christology of Jesus* (Minneapolis, 1990), 216 ff.

[104] While this passage is considered by many to be inauthentic, others have no difficulty seeing it as genuine. Cf. M. Hengel, *The Son of God*, 69; J. A. T. Robinson, *The*

understanding between Father and Son. He who speaks is pre-eminently the Son, the one who knows God as Father in a way others do not. 'No one knows the Father save the Son, and he to whom the Son wills to reveal Him.' Included here is a fourth element, mediation. As 'Son' Jesus enables others to share the experience of divine fatherhood.

3. The third passage travels outside the synoptic tradition to the Fourth Gospel. 'My Father is working up to now, and I am working' (John 5: 17). For this writer God's work of grace and mercy goes on seven days a week; he who is His earthly agent works as God works, all the time. The Jews then seek to kill Jesus because he calls God his Father, thus making himself equal with God (v. 18). John however goes on to say that this is precisely what Jesus was *not* doing. 'The Son cannot do anything on his own authority—of himself—except what he sees the Father doing'. In the 'parable of the apprenticed Son', John may have glossed over an original parable about sonship by making it Christological. 'The Father loves the Son and shows him His whole trade.' For John, Jesus is comparing himself to an apprenticed son who from day to day is in communication with his Father in his Father's workshop, wholly dependent on the One to whom he is apprenticed. Such dependence is more vigorously expressed in John's Gospel than in any of the other three. It is an experiential knowledge which the Son enters into from day to day as the Father shows him new 'tricks of the trade'. The Great Thanksgiving in Matthew and Luke is the only synoptic parallel to such a motif, but it may be enough to suggest that Jesus thought in this way, and that the Fourth Gospel does not here represent a later theological development.

These three passages, along with the baptism, allow us to see, however dimly, that to Jesus 'sonship' was not what it is often taken to mean—a claim to be the second person of the Trinity. Far from being a Docetic Christ, he is a *man*—certainly one for whom sonship carries with it supreme authority—but only because as Son his life is characterized by complete trust in, obedience to, and under-standing of the God he knows as Father. And it is part of his sonship

Human Face of God (Philadelphia, 1973), 186 f; Meyer, *Aims of Jesus*, 152, quoting Dalman ('he who stands in so uniquely close a relation to God is God's "only possible" and "absolutely reliable" revealer'); and Dunn, *Christology*, 199 f. For a useful summary of the complexities surrounding the passage, cf. Hugh Anderson, *Jesus and Christian Origins* (New York, 1964), 156 ff.

that he is commissioned to communicate that understanding of God to others ('he to whom the Son wills to reveal Him').

This communication of sonship which stands at the heart of Jesus' theology is pre-eminently contained in the Lord's Prayer. 'Teach us to pray' (Luke 11: 1). Here we may be misled by the more familiar Matthean version, which begins 'Our Father'. Luke's version (11: 2) gives the address as simply *patēr*, and since in all other prayers of Jesus recorded in the Gospels Jesus' own address is in the same form, we are entitled to conclude that Jesus taught his disciples to address God in the same style of intimacy which he was accustomed to use himself. This is part at least of the process by which he is revealing that Father whom he as Son knows. One can then expound the various parts of the prayer as the unpacking of the concept of the divine fatherhood.

T. W. Manson's comment on the prayer concludes by saying, 'And the significant thing is not so much its contents as the fact that it is a *prayer*.'[105] It is certainly worth noting that in a great proportion of the sayings in which Jesus refers to God as Father, the context is prayer.

There is no suggestion here that the idea of God as Father would have been strange or foreign to the disciples before he spoke about it. What Jesus communicates is a new *style* of sonship, *a style of what it means to know God as Father, which comes directly out of his own experience.* 'You shall be sons of the Most High' (Luke 6: 35). To be sons and daughters of the Most High is to be like God, to live a life of imitation of the Father. 'He forgives, thus you must forgive; you must take after your Father.' And in the Gospels this is the beginning of what will later be called Christology. But originally the likeness to God is worked out in moral terms.

The fatherhood of God was not so much a concept which Jesus taught as something he lived and shared with his disciples, pre-eminently by introducing them into his own prayer. The twin ideas of the fatherhood of God and the sonship of Jesus may lead the reader of the New Testament close to the heart of the Gospels. But they also leave major theological questions suspended in mid-air. How does one *become* a child of God? What part in the process is played by the Cross? If Jesus was sinless, was his sonship different *in kind* from that of others? To these questions there is little answer in the synoptic tradition. One becomes a child of God by being like God. But how

---

[105] T. W. Manson, *Teaching of Jesus*, 115 (italics his).

does one set about that? The only answer is the invitation to enter the Kingdom, to become a disciple of Jesus, to deny oneself, to take up one's cross and follow him. And to follow him is to enter the Kingdom, the life of imitation of the Father.

And yet the synoptic writers also had little doubt that the centre of their preaching was the Cross. This brings us to an inescapable fact about the teaching of Jesus. No one who participated in the writing of the New Testament imagined that the teaching of Jesus was in itself a complete entity apart from the life on which that teaching was a commentary. The answers to the above questions are contained in their dramatic account of the life and death of Jesus rather than in any direct appeal to his teaching. And yet with that caveat we may see that the teaching and the teacher are one and the same. What Jesus says about the fatherhood of God agrees with what we have observed about the Kingdom of God. The Jesus of the Gospels summons men and women to enter the Kingdom which in him has arrived; they are to submit themselves in radical obedience to his—and its—demands. But for Jesus, the King who asserts His kingly authority is also the divine Father, and the two pictures of God stand together in his teaching, inevitably qualifying one another, until finally they converge into a single, coherent image of the beloved son who is also the King's most obedient servant.

9.9. DEATH

A final topic which many New Testament theologians and historians continue to avoid is Jesus' understanding of his own death. But here, despite the obvious critical hazards involved, we will offer two ideas, one focusing on his vocation as Servant, the other on the sacrificial aspects of his death.

Despite the arguments of some, we have seen that the Servant concept can be supported from the Gospels. An allusion to the Isaianic Servant Songs implicit in the choice of the term *euangelion* for Jesus' message is difficult to deny. The voice at the baptism, furthermore, implies the belief that Jesus saw this event as his anointing as Messiah (cf. also Acts 10: 38), and that at this time the concept of Messiah was fused in his mind with that of the Lord's Servant (Isa. 42: 1). It is also worth noting that Jesus is said to have introduced the theme of service into his reply to the first Satanic assault on his sonship (Matt. 4: 10; Luke 4: 8). There can be little doubt that he would have been familiar enough with the prophecies of Isaiah to understand, even at this early point, that his baptism was also an initiation into his death. Two sayings link the ideas of baptism and death: (1) Just as water baptism had inaugurated his earthly servanthood, so the baptism of death was to be the inauguration of a servanthood which would not be subject to the limitations of this world. 'I have a baptism to be baptized with, and how I am restricted until it is accomplished!' (Luke 12: 50).[106] What was anticipated in the prophetic symbolism of the Jordan had to be acted out in the grim realism of Golgotha. (2) Jesus not only speaks of his death as his own baptism, but as something others might share: 'With my baptism you shall be baptized' (Mark 10: 38 f.). It should therefore come as no surprise that a later writer such as Paul could see baptism as a putting on of Jesus crucified, a symbolic union with him in death (Rom. 6: 3).

The second approach is to go back to ancient Hebrew notions of sacrifice. From the inception of the Mosaic covenant one of the dominating questions had been how sinful human beings could enter the presence of a holy God. The answer offered was sacrifice, even though it was an answer about which there was constant uneasiness, and the prophets were particularly outspoken on the subject. Amos (5: 21–7), Isaiah (1: 10–15), and Hosea (6: 6) all denounced the use of outward forms of religion with no corresponding inner loyalty, and Micah summed up their teaching in a great utterance (6: 6–8). Jeremiah likewise protested that the distinctive thing about the demands of the Lord was not sacrifice but obedience (7: 21–3).

Prophetic criticism in time produced profound effects on the interpretation of sacrifice. Early in Israel's history sacrifice had been a happy event, a time when men and women 'rejoiced before the Lord'. It was an act of communion, a meal shared by the worshippers with their God (1 Sam. 1: 4–18; 9: 11–24).[107] But as progressively more emphasis was placed on the holiness of God, Israel became increasingly conscious of the notion of sin, a gulf opened up between God and His creatures, communion disappeared from worship, and only the High Priest once a year was allowed to enter the Holy of

---

[106] Here Jesus almost certainly echoes the teaching of John the Baptist, incidentally demonstrating the gulf which lay between him and his predecessor. John had prophesied the coming of one who would baptize with the fire of divine judgement: it had never occurred to him that the Coming One would be the first to undergo that baptism.

[107] Cf. W. T. McCree, 'The Covenantal Meal in the Old Testament', *JBL* 45 (1926), 120 ff.

Holies. After the exile of 586–539 BC, greater prominence was given to the sacrifices of atonement, but the Priestly Code legislated only for unintentional sin; for sins committed 'with a high hand' it continued to know of no atonement.

Sacrifice was also regarded as a gift; but we now know that some recognized that it was at best a symbol of another gift, that of perfect obedience; and this other gift was beyond the competence of Israel to offer. The covenant had also been inaugurated with sacrifice (Exod. 29: 12), but it had failed in its purpose of producing perfect obedience, and a new covenant was needed. Thus in several respects the institution of sacrifice day by day bore mute testimony to the incompleteness of the religion of Israel. Even the Day of Atonement, which was intended to cover the national sin, only reinforced the sense of separation of the average Israelite from God. Only Passover maintained a vital connection with the life of the people, reminding them that God had redeemed them from slavery in Egypt.

According to two passages preserved only by Matthew, Jesus reiterated the prophetic criticism of sacrifice (Matt. 9: 13 and 12: 7, both quoting Hos. 6: 6). While these alone are not conclusive, two other passages in the synoptic tradition give grounds for thinking that he interpreted his own death in the prophetic sacrificial sense. 'The Son of Man came not to be served, but to serve, and to give his life a ransom for many' (Mark 10: 45). While the authenticity of this passage continues to be hotly debated, there are reasons for seeing in this one verse four echoes of the vicarious sacrifice of the Lord's Servant, whose life is made 'an offering for sin', so that he could 'justify the many' and bear 'the sin of many' (Isa. 53: 10–12). The word 'ransom' (*lutron*) is of particular importance. One might be ransomed or redeemed by animal sacrifice (Lev. 25: 25–55; Exod. 13: 12–13). But in Israel there were some conditions from which redemption was humanly impossible:

> They that trust in their wealth,
> and boast themselves in the multitude of their riches;
> None of them can by any means redeem his brother,
> Nor give to God a ransom for him . . .
> That he should live always,
> And that he should not see corruption.

> (Ps. 49: 6–9)

A special kind of ransom was required when a life had been forfeited. Was Jesus familiar enough with ancient Hebrew notions of sin and sacrifice to know that he was dealing with those whose lives were forfeited through sin? 'What shall it profit one to gain the whole world and forfeit one's very life? Or what shall one give as a ransom for one's life?' (Mark 8: 36–7). It is certainly conceivable that what sinful people could not do for themselves Jesus believed he was doing by giving his life 'a ransom for many'.

We have also seen that in the many volumes written on the identity of the Servant in Isaiah 53 it has been seldom recognized that the prophet himself probably did not know the identity of the person he was depicting. In this sense it was a 'situation vacant' title, an unfulfilled 'job description', which Jesus himself—and perhaps any who might be willing to join with him—was determined to fill. Too much discussion has centred on such questions as whether the Servant in Isaiah was a 'willing' sacrifice, or to what extent that sacrifice was 'vicarious', and too little on the originality of Jesus. Certainly the Targum of Isaiah 53 was known by Jesus,[108] and if so it may well have been seen by him as a 'situation vacant', in which case he would have taken it up and given it a new significance out of his own penetrative insight into the meaning of Hebrew notions of sacrifice (cf. Heb. 9: 28–10: 5, undoubtedly the most percipient interpretation of Jesus on this point among the New Testament writings).

The suggestion of a sacrificial significance to Jesus' death is made the more persuasive by the words he is recorded as speaking over the cup at the Last Supper, either in the form provided by Paul or by Mark ('This cup is the new covenant in my blood,' 1 Cor. 11: 25; 'This is my blood of the covenant, which is shed for many' Mark 14: 25). Behind this saying lies both the description of the sealing of the covenant with the blood of sacrifice (Exod. 24: 3–8) and the vision of the New Covenant—'I will forgive their iniquities, and I will remember their sins no more' (Jer. 31: 34). In making such allusions Jesus would not be giving a sacrificial significance to the Last Supper itself, only to his death. The Last Supper was a prophetic act. As Jeremiah smashed the earthen pot to demonstrate the imminent destruction of Jerusalem (Jer. 19), so Jesus broke the bread in token of the breaking of his body, handing round the bread and cup in token of the benefits of his death. It would be as sensible to think that Jeremiah's pot

---

[108] See above, p. 312, 315, n. 65.

became the city of Jerusalem as to imagine that the significance of the Last Supper for Jesus lay in the elements of bread and wine. The significance resided in the *acts*, which represented Jesus' coming act of sacrifice on behalf of all who would accept it.

It would be difficult to find in any of these passages an explicit idea that Jesus' coming death was a vicarious sacrifice for the sins of the whole world, as found in later hymn and creed. Such a claim looks at first like a quantum leap ahead of the evidence. Yet the seeds for such a belief are there if one is disposed to draw out the implications of Isaiah 53 and of Jesus' concern for the role of Israel in God's plan for the Gentile nations. And there is indeed no evidence to suggest that one who found this plan outlined in the scriptures could not have made just such a leap, long before it was made by a later writer such as Paul. The traditional difficulty of Christian theology, of course, has been that it made Jesus' death of universal significance too fast and too easily, at the expense of his Jewishness. But as a Jew he would also have seen his death as intimately bound up with the people into whom he had been born, and to whom he had been called—first as a prophet, and later as the fulfilment of everything to which the far-reaching hopes, visions, and dreams of the prophets had pointed.

'How dull you are . . . How slow to believe all that the prophets said! Was not the Messiah bound to suffer in this way before entering upon his glory?' Then, starting from Moses and all the prophets, he explained to them in the whole of scripture the things that referred to himself (Luke 24: 25–7, REB).

To those who believe Luke's testimony, no further explanation is necessary. To those who do not, no further explanation is possible.

10.

Summary and Conclusions: Jesus and the Apostolic Conference

Chapters 2–8 attempted to allow the New Testament writers to speak for themselves, to engage in an imaginary conversation, with the experiment in dialogue leading ultimately to the theology of Jesus. The chair of the conference will now 'take the sense of the meeting', summarizing the distinctive features of the discussion, with the additional step of asking at certain points how these different themes may relate to the teaching of Jesus.

1. Chapter 1 discussed the various approaches to writing a New Testament theology. After a survey of the pitfalls and advantages of the dogmatic, the chronological, the kerygmatic, and the author-by-author approaches, the conference table model was adduced from Paul's description of the Jerusalem Conference in Galatians 2: 1–10. This model was seen to have the unique advantage of interrogating witnesses. Through the life-blood of imagination the modern scholar is allowed to reanimate figures from the past, enabling them to speak, both to one another and to the modern time-traveller.

2. Chapter 2 explored the plan of salvation as it is developed by the New Testament writers. It was foretold in the Old Testament scriptures that God would one day actively come upon the stage of human history through His chosen people, Israel. Of the New Testament writers, Luke develops the theme of the divine visit most explicitly. Beginning his two-volume story with a group of devout Jews, whose eyes of faith are turned to the future of the nation of Israel, he climaxes his story with Paul telling the Ephesian elders, 'I never shrank from declaring to you the whole purpose of God.' In Ephesians the idea of God's purpose is seen as a divine mystery which now 'in the last days' is being unfolded. Elsewhere it is a plan which works through a chosen group, Israel, which through a faithful remnant is progressively narrowed through various rejections, until at last it is reduced to one,

Jesus the promised Messiah. All except him have failed, but by his resurrection God's promise will be fulfilled to all nations (Rom. 5–11). Jesus is the head of a new people, and thus the inclusive movement has started, but with a new direction. Israel had been separated from the world and drawn towards Jerusalem, but the real separation was to be found on Calvary. God had purposed that the city should be a starting point for a movement outwards, with the representatives of the twelve tribes, the apostles, sent out with a gospel. The direction is changed by the descent of God into the common world.

It was also seen that C. H. Dodd discovered a pattern of exegesis among the New Testament writers, by which certain important Old Testament contexts enhanced the themes of Israel's suffering, the new Israel, the righteous sufferer, and the Exodus. Dodd suggested that Jesus, out of his distinctive understanding of the Jewish scriptures, bequeathed to his followers a principle of selection and interpretation of his ministry which was later explored by Paul, John, and others in a way which was diverse yet compatible with the original intention. And when Jesus is depicted by John the Seer as breaking the seals of the scroll of the destiny of the human race, it is only to follow to a logical conclusion the mastery of his own destiny which Jesus had learned from reading the scriptures during his earthly life.

3. Chapter 3 developed the need of salvation as it is spelt out by the New Testament writers. The moral bankruptcy of a fallen cosmos is expressed in terms of universal judgement, metaphors for sin (guilt, stain, enmity, bondage), the primal sin of Adam, the principalities and powers, Satan, the Antichrist, and the unforgivable sin. In each case it was seen that the universal nemesis of God's purposes is the corruption of that which is good. The sinful life is the life turned in upon itself, whether by the open roads of self-indulgence and self-assertion, or by the more secret paths of self-esteem and self-protection.

To a considerable degree Jesus saw human sin as embodied in the perverted sincerity and self-regard of Jerusalem's religious leaders, an idea later amplified by Paul in his idea of the principalities and powers. For Jesus *and* Paul the highest evil is the Adamic elevation of the secondary and derivative to a position of primacy. Later New Testament depictions of the Antichrist and the unpardonable sin may ultimately revert to Jesus, for whom 'the abomination which stands where it ought not' and the blasphemy against the Holy Spirit are the supreme examples of the rejection of the grace of God. For Jesus the whole duty of the human race consists in a love for God which so identifies itself with His purposes of grace that it works itself out in the service of His children. From this it follows that human sin consists in the diversion of love from its proper object, so that it becomes self-love. Evil deeds and evil thoughts are not themselves humanity's disease; they are only the symptoms of a more deep-seated malady which the victim cannot cure. To expect people to amend their ways is like asking a corrupt tree to produce good fruit. Nor can we expect them to expel the demons from their own hearts without inviting a more grievous invasion: only the Spirit of God can so fill the human house so that there is no room for squatters (Matt. 7: 18; Luke 11: 24–6). Here St Paul was the greatest exponent of the mind of Jesus. Out of his experience of emancipation he looked back into the life of bondage, and saw sin so dominating it that even the Law, itself holy, and just, and good, could be distorted into a weapon of seduction (Rom. 7).

4. Chapter 4 explored the three-tiered tense structure of New Testament language about salvation. Christians have been saved once and for all, they are being saved, and they look to a salvation yet to come. All attempts to give priority to one tense over another results in a distortion of the complete picture. This was seen with particular emphasis in the case of the Kingdom of God. The New Testament writers preserve a tension which may go back to Jesus himself, for whom the Kingdom has come in the proclamation of the gospel, is in process of coming as it encroaches upon the kingdom of Satan, and is yet to come in powerful future manifestations, climaxing with the final thunder-clap of history.

5. Chapter 5 understood the accomplished fact of salvation as it is developed by the themes of the one and the many, revelation, and atonement. The identification of a king with his people, the opening of eyes blinded to the truth, and the elimination of the sin-barrier which separates God from His creatures are explored by the writers through the use of rich and varied images. In particular the metaphors of salvation were seen to correspond to the sin-metaphors noted in Chapter 3 (guilt : justification; taint : sacrifice; enmity : reconciliation; bondage : emancipation).

If, of all these images, the terminology of sacrifice is most foreign to the modern mind, it is for a good reason: the institution of sacrifice forms no part of modern life or worship. For Jesus, however, sacrifice was a vital concept: it established communion between human beings and God, made atonement for sin, offered to God the gift of perfect obedience, inaugurated the new covenant, and was the new Passover, which delivered the human race from a worse bondage than that of Egypt—the tyranny of sin. He saw his sacrifice as giving new meaning to the gropings of the ancient Israelite religion, which tried to satisfy the requirements of God by offering 'a lamb without blemish and without spot' (Exod. 12: 5). Thus the New Testament writers are only drawing out what is implicit in Jesus' own thinking: 'This man, after he had offered one sacrifice for sins forever, sat down at the right hand of God' (Heb. 10: 12). 'Through him we . . . have access by one Spirit to the Father' (Eph. 2: 18).

6. Chapter 6 understood the present aspects of salvation in terms of new life, worship, grace, imitation of Christ, life in Christ, life in the Spirit, and life in the Church. Christians have been born anew to a life of pulsating spontaneity and freedom, a fresh plane of experience which allows them access to the presence of God in worship, freedom from the trammels of the Law, and the power to imitate in their own lives a sense of the presence of God and a self-subordinating love of others which characterized Jesus' own life. The experience is further defined as inclusion in the new humanity which is at the same time membership in the corporate body of Christ, a new state which makes possible the presence and gifts of God's Spirit and the fellowship and benefits of the communal life of the Church.

To the question, 'Did Jesus intend to found a Church?' there may be two possible answers: If by 'church' we mean an ecclesiastical structure, the answer must be, 'no'. But if we mean a community of individuals in whom Jesus is present, who put one another before themselves, and through whom God's redemptive power can reach out into the world, neutralizing evil and incorporating all, Jew and Gentile alike, into a community which is willing to put itself under His absolute sovereignty, the answer can only be a resounding 'Yes'.

7. Chapter 7 explored the eschatology of the New Testament writers under the heading 'the Hope of Salvation'. The ground of that hope was seen to be the resurrection of Jesus, an event in which Christians will one day share. Discussion then moved to the definition and subsequent application of the exalted term 'eschatology'. Two widely divergent qualifications of the term were seen to dominate modern discussion—'cosmic' and 'individual'. For the New Testament writers the 'end' was found frequently to be a very different 'end' from the *eschaton*.

In the case of Paul certain comments in his Thessalonian letters, Romans, and 1 Corinthians were seen to preserve the classic tension of 'already and not yet'. Mark, Luke, Matthew, and the other writers likewise contain, in the midst of much complexity and with varying degrees of emphasis, the eschatological paradox in which the ultimate 'End' is always intruding upon the temporal present, so as to make its demands crucially felt in the experiences and crises of everyday human occupations.

The New Testament writers' understanding of the individual's fate after death (the future of the body, one's whereabouts between death and resurrection, and eternal judgement) were also seen in many cases incapable of reduction to a single, coherent frame of reference which would be satisfactory to modern logic.

Finally, the New Testament writers' concern with the future of the cosmos was examined by looking at several images. The maturing purpose of God, initially treated in Chapter 2, will ultimately embrace all creation in its variegated diversity. In God's purposes even the principalities and powers will be saved, but only when a fractured and warring universe is finally brought into unity in the cosmic Christ. The City to come is a vibrant, functioning society, large enough to include all.

How much of this may go back to Jesus himself will remain a subject of debate. But what is clear is that the starting point of New Testament teaching about the last things was the salvation of the nation Israel. From there the writers moved out to larger concepts, paradoxically bringing into sharper yet more universal focus what had been forged in the midst of a heated political crisis.

8. Chapter 8 discussed the Bringer of Salvation, the one who accomplishes the results outlined in Chapter 5. Here it was seen that, whatever staggering affirmations they may have later made, the New Testament writers never ceased to think of Jesus as a human being. To begin with exalted and static formulations concerning his divinity will in the end lead to distortion.

The idea of development was likewise seen to be ill-conceived if logical and chronological development are naïvely equated. To claim that the New Testament writers progressed in their understanding of Jesus' nature and cosmic role is hardly to say that this progression can be charted on a time-graph.

Jesus' qualifications as the bringer of salvation were understood primarily in terms of his relations with the human race. In his normal human experiences (birth, growth, fatigue, death) and in his fulfilment of the soaring aspirations of Psalm 8, Jesus' humanity was seen to be a full humanity. But full humanity does not guarantee perfect human-ity. A perfect human being would be one who is fully and constantly in communion with the Creator, and here in a number of interesting ways the New Testament writers discuss Jesus' constant communion with his Father. Finally it was seen that, while a perfect human being might well aspire to full and perfect humanity, this does not necessarily indicate an identification with the human race in its abject need. The New Testament writers make an additional claim: Jesus stood with the human race in all its sinfulness. Thus they preserve a paradox by saying that Jesus is sinfully human without thereby being personally sinful.

The qualifications of Jesus to bring about salvation were further-more delineated by recourse to the so-called 'titles' used by the New Testament writers. Prophet, Messiah, Servant, Son of God, and Priest were seen not as 'ontological' entities in themselves, but as extensions of the functions of Chapter 5. Jesus is God's supreme agent because he acts on behalf of God and because God is present in him. This distinction is often lost on modern treatments of New Testament theology, for whom the titles of Jesus are treated as self-explanatory and derive from his eternal person and attributes. A filling out of the picture is Paul's claim in Philippians 2: 5–11 (cf. 2 Cor. 8: 9) that Jesus personally pre-existed, one of his more striking contributions to the apostolic conference table.

9. Chapter 9 suggested, from Jesus' recorded teaching, that the historical Jesus is recoverable and able to be seen as the starting point and goal of New Testament theology. Information in the Gospels which relates to Jesus' claims concerning Israel and its role in this world may properly be included under the heading 'theology', but only if that exalted term does not dislocate Jesus' message from the setting of the first-century political crisis in which he found himself embroiled. All of the things Christians normally associate with the term 'theol-ogy'—God, Creation, sin, salvation, grace *v.* law, the Kingdom of God, the last things, Jesus' person and work—were for him not abstract speculation, but were shaped and guided by his understanding of the calling and destiny of the nation of Israel. Thus in describing his political debates with his contemporaries we shall at the same time be describing his 'theology'.

Our findings may now give rise to the following six observations.

1. What we call 'the gospel of Jesus' was not in the first case a new

religion, but a political challenge to the nation of Israel, asking it to believe that God's power is always breathtakingly fresh, always ready to break in upon their history, always an outgoing and transforming power reaching into the lives of all who need help. But in order to receive the inbreaking power they must also accept a radically new understanding of what it meant for them to be the chosen people. They had been chosen not for privilege but for responsibility, not for authority and glory but for service and suffering; that through them God's power might reach out into the world, overthrowing the forces of evil. Instead of hating their national enemies and praying for their downfall they were to love them and pray for their well-being. Instead of avoiding their desecrating contact they were to make friends with them. And, in perhaps the most difficult piece of advice of all, they were to be content with the good government of Rome. Paying taxes to Caesar was not incompatible with giving to God a full and unconditional obedience (cf. Rom. 13: 1–7).

2. If Jesus considered his message to be a matter of extreme urgency, it was because for him Israel stood at a cross-roads. The road he advocated could be called 'gospel' in so far as he was confident that it was God's way of dealing with the problem of evil, and that, though it might lead God's people through suffering, in the end it would lead on to ultimate vindication and the triumph of the divine purpose. The other road was the road of Jewish nationalism, that path along which they had hoped to meet the Son of David, the Messiah of their traditional hopes. This was the road which was supposed to lead back to the political and economic glories of the reign of David. Jesus could see that in fact it would lead only to conflict with Rome and, in the end, to total, irretrievable disaster. Only an immediate and dramatic change of heart could save it from the frenzy of its futile Messianic dreams. When he rode into Jerusalem on a donkey, he was not offering to be the Messiah of the nationalists' fantasy; he was making his last appeal to a nation on the verge of suicide to accept him as the Messiah of God's Kingdom, the realm of self-negating sacrifice.

3. Jesus' invitation to enter the Kingdom was an appeal to the nation to put itself under God's sovereignty once and for all. Those who enter the Kingdom fulfil the Law of Moses in a way far deeper than the Pharisees, who through superficial observance of outward regulations erect a spiritual quarantine around themselves, therefore failing to penetrate to the Law's deeper intention of love and mercy.

4. Jesus moved constantly from national to individual concerns, and

vice versa. This is true in all four accounts of his teaching, but especially of Luke's, in which Jesus expresses great concern for the individual. And if the other New Testament interpreters show a stronger interest in the individual than in the Jewish national hope, the change of emphasis is also readily explained by Luke; it was the love which Jesus had for men, women, and children, and the conviction of Jesus that this love was not his alone but the love of the Father who had sent him. But this is not the same thing as saying that Jesus abandoned the hope of a national salvation for a religion of merely individual piety. The Jesus of Luke's Gospel justifies his actions on behalf of individuals on the ground that this man or that woman was a son or daughter of Abraham. Moreover all the Gospel writers believed that Jesus was the King of Israel, and a king, as John Milton said, 'is a body politick'. To acknowledge one as sovereign is to accept all that he or she stands for as a national way of life. Jesus intends his teaching and his example to be nationally implemented, embedded in the ethos and in the institutions of the national life. To be sure, he does not issue a manifesto; there is no detailed programme of political legislation. But neither did the prophets, and no serious student of the Old Testament would argue for that reason that the prophets did not expect their teaching about social justice to be implemented nationally, or even that to a large extent this actually happened.

This of course is dependent upon Luke's picture of Jesus. The question is thus bound to be asked in the name of *Redaktionsgeschichte* how much we should attribute to Luke, and how much to Jesus. But behind this legitimate question may lie the latent, less legitimate and even sinister assumption that to interpret is to *misinterpret*. It is a matter of professional prudence on the part of interpreters of literary texts to allow for the possibility that an interpreter may occasionally be right. And it is certainly conceivable that Luke, in interpreting his sources, has shown that he actually understood both the teaching of Jesus and the eschatological language in which it came to him.

5. If, as seen in Chapter 5, nation and king are sometimes interchangeable, so that the functions of the one may be fulfilled by the other, it will follow that texts applicable to the one may be transferred to the other. Thus in Daniel 7 and Isaiah 53, to name two, functions applied to the nation are transferred to its royal figurehead. The theme of the one and the many appears not only in Paul, John, and Hebrews, but in the synoptic tradition. But if it is feasible that the early Church advanced its thinking via the fruitful possibilities of ambiguity, there

is no a priori reason why Jesus could not have done the same. The case of those who argue for a discontinuity between the teaching of Jesus and that of the early Church continues to rest largely on the improbable premiss that the Christological 'titles' had one single, clearly defined sense, so that if they meant one thing they could not mean another. But Jesus certainly could have used the 'Son of Man' expression as a periphrastic self-reference *precisely because* of the ambiguity inherent in Daniel 7.

And if the imagery of suffering–vindication–authority in Daniel's Son of Man admirably covers the material (stated or implied) in all the Son of Man sayings[1] and Isaianic Servant allusions, it would appear that Jesus has fused the Servant and Son of Man models so as to create an extraordinary new twist: unlike Daniel's Son of Man, who *is to be served*, the Son of Man *is to serve*. Those acquainted either with the originality of Jesus' mind or with the fluidity inherent in the Hebrew concept of king and subjects will have no trouble placing the historical Jesus into his Jewish soil on this point.

It is not, however, so easy to disengage ourselves from our academic heritage. Because we have been so long accustomed to the notion that if Jesus had anything to say about his own person it must have been couched in the form of a dogmatic claim to a status of well-defined authority, it is difficult to adjust to any another view of him. Yet the fact that a great deal of Jesus' teaching comes in the form of a question should serve as a suitable warning. It has been said of the episode of Caesarea Philippi that the question is more significant than the answers: Jesus not only understands that he poses a problem to his contemporaries; *he considers it right that he should*! It may however equally be said that the episode exemplifies Jesus' most characteristic method of instruction in that it poses a question. Even the pronouncements of the so-called 'Pronouncement Stories' notoriously leave questions still to be asked (e.g. 'Pay to Caesar what is Caesar's, and to God what is God's'). In particular Mark 12: 35 ff. ('How can the scribes say that the Christ is the son of David? . . . David himself calls him Lord; so how is he his son?') depict Jesus as engaging in precisely this kind of exploration of ambiguity. Here it is important that, as so frequently occurs elsewhere, the teaching of Jesus is couched in the form of a question.

6. New Testament opinion has too long accepted the notion,

---

[1] A point made by C. Rowland, *Christian Origins*, 185 f.

recently articulated anew[2] by G. Vermes, that there is a 'simple Jewish person of the Gospels' who has been lost to us and will not again come into his own until he has been disencumbered of all the adventitious trappings of the Church's Christ. Like so many others, Professor Vermes lays the blame for the 'long exile' of the Jewish Jesus at the door of that villain Paul, who constitutes 'a fatal misrepresentation of Jesus, a betrayal of his ideals, and their replacement by alien concepts and aspirations'.[3] But the fact that Paul was not only a Jew but a Pharisee has led others to conclude that his evidence about the beginnings of Christianity cannot be so cavalierly brushed aside. S. Sandmel is surely right in arguing that Paul conceived the debate between himself and the Synagogue to be a debate within Judaism.[4] This leads on to a tantalizing question: What if scholars were to lay aside their hostility to Paul and engage as historians in a sympathetic quest for Paul the Jew? Might they not, to their own surprise, find themselves better able to paint a fuller and truer portrait of that other Jew to whom Paul gave his heart's allegiance, and of whose teaching he was the great expositor?

Thus we come to the end of our journey. For Jesus, Israel had been called to be the saved and saving nation, the agent through whom God intended to assert His sovereignty over the rest of the world; the time had arrived when God was summoning the nation once and for all to take its place in His economy as the Son of Man. If the nation would not listen, it must pay the price; but at least Jesus, and anyone else who would share it with him, must fulfil the national destiny. The light to the Gentiles, the Son of Man coming on the clouds of heaven, the son who clings to his Father for his very life, the king who ransoms the people for whom he must stand as surety, and the servant who dies for the many, fill out his picture of Israel as God intended it to be. So deeply does he love his nation, so fully is he identified with its life, so bitterly does he regret what he sees coming upon it, that only

---

[2] The idea is at least as old as E. Renan, who produced the famous epigram, 'Paul substituted a religion about Jesus for the religion of Jesus'. For a helpful discussion of Renan's comment, see S. Sandmel, *The Genius of Paul* (1970[3]), 211 ff.

[3] G. Vermes, *The Gospel of Jesus the Jew* (1981), 9.

[4] S. Sandmel, *The Genius of Paul*. Cf. esp. p. 218: 'It was Paul the Jew criticizing his inherited Judaism.' Unfortunately Sandmel adds to this legitimate comment the corollary that Paul has totally distorted that inheritance. For a helpful treatment of the surprising amount of common ground between Paul and the Judaism of his time, cf. G. P. Carras, 'Paul, Josephus, and Judaism: The Shared Judaism of Paul and Josephus', D.Phil. thesis, Oxford, 1989.

death can silence his reiterated and disturbing appeal. He goes to his death at the hands of a Roman judge on a charge of which he was innocent and of which his accusers, as the event proved, were guilty. And so, not only in theological truth but in historic fact, the one bore the sins of the many, confident that in him the entire Jewish nation was being nailed to the Cross, only to come to life again in a better resurrection, and that the Day of the Son of Man which would see the end of the old Israel would also see the vindication of the new.

And if the theology of the New Testament began with ways in which Jesus thought and spoke about himself and his people, it was precisely because, as the agent appointed by God to be the fulfilment of Israel's destiny, he later came to be recognized, first as the fulfiller of the destiny of the human race, and then, in consequence, as the bearer of a more-than-human authority and the embodiment of a more-than-human wisdom.

II.

Epilogue: Dialogue, Meaning, and Authority

We began this book with an idea of dialogue. And dialogue, however often it has been attempted in the Church, has seldom been effectively achieved, for one painfully clear reason: dialogue means honest listening, and theologians of whatever age have been all too content to score shabby victories by demolishing a mere caricature of another's position. Real and important differences are thus obscured by a welter of sheer and often unscrupulous fiction.

In place of real dialogue there continues to be the constant temptation to take the easier road of exercising tight control, whether political, ecclesiastical, or academic, over the human mind, extracting from it a rigid agreement. Usually this is done openly, through dictations oral and written, or more subtly, through the control of key appointments in political, academic, or ecclesiastical circles. The motives for this, of course, are not difficult to see; rigid confessionalism, in whatever form, often seems to be the only alternative to total chaos.

Human beings have always longed for a guarantee, for extraneous signs of what is true and false. Jesus was asked for a sign, for some demonstrative proof of his credentials. Not only did he refuse; he stigmatized his interrogators as a wicked and adulterous (disloyal) generation. If they knew God and loved Him as they claimed, they would recognize the word of God when they heard it. Christianity is, and always has been, a dangerous religion, and the greatest mistake is to try to make it safe. The only proper safeguards against rampant subjectivism are free academic debate, ruthless self-criticism in the examination of our own presuppositions, and, not least, a renewed confidence in the ability of God to watch over His Word.

This is supported if we take the time to discover the strong strain of discontinuity which exists throughout the Bible. Saul was anointed king and then deposed. David succeeded him and was given a promise that his dynasty would never fail; yet a little more than four centuries later the Davidic line was dethroned. There were prophets who belonged to professional guilds, and others, like Elisha, who were anointed by a predecessor. But the great prophets were not among them. Amos hotly denied standing in any succession or belonging to any trade union. 'I was no prophet or prophet's son . . . the Lord took me from following the flock.' John the Baptist warned his contemporaries that physical descent from Abraham would be no advantage in the coming crisis of divine judgement, since God can create children of Abraham from the desert stones; and Paul echoed his teaching when he said that the true children of Abraham are not those who can trace their lineage from him in unbroken descent, but those who share his faith. Jesus predicted that God's vineyard will be taken from its present tenants and given to others. Asked by the apostles to rebuke an unlicensed evangelist, he rebuked instead the apostles, and through them all who have supposed that there could be no authority without authorization, and have tried to confine the grace of God within official channels. And finally the Epistle to the Hebrews pointed out that Jesus, the great High Priest, could not have been a priest at all if he had had to rely on historical succession, since he came from Judah and a priest must be descended from Levi; on the contrary, Jesus stands in the order of Melchizedek, who is notorious for having no genealogy.

The question all this raises is not whether God makes occasional exceptions in favour of oddballs or nonconformists, but whether there is not ample evidence in the Bible and history that God regularly honours human faith and grants His presence in ways not allowed for by ecclesiastical or academic theorizing; that He regularly breaks in upon the *status quo* of human complacence, saying, 'Behold, I do a new thing!'; and that He regularly speaks His words of judgement, consolation, guidance, or demand through those who have no authorization other than His own.

On the other side of the scale must be weighed the equally important and historic belief that there is a finality to the New Testament revelation which requires that in Jesus God has spoken His last word. Certainly the early Church believed itself to be so led by the Spirit of God that it could respond to the prompting of that Spirit wherever He was at work. But in its revolt against legalism it never abandoned its belief in historic transmission. Historic transmission of some sort is inescapable in Christianity, since its faith is rooted in historic facts, with which we can have contact only because they are handed down to us across the centuries. Paul could insist that his apostleship and his gospel came to him direct from Christ and not from any human

source or through human mediation; but he could also speak of handing on what he himself had received. It will not do to say that the
whole apostolic tradition is contained in scripture, so that we need no
mediating tradition to put us in contact with the sources of the Christian faith; for we should never have read the Bible if it had not come
to us through the living experience of a community continuous with
the Church of past generations.

The tension between authority transmitted historically and authority
received directly is as old as religion itself. This was especially appreciated by John Cardinal Newman, who, just before he changed his
allegiance from the Church of England to the Church of Rome, wrote
a massive work in which he argued that any idea which is a living
force in human life and thought must of necessity be subject to development, and tried to define the limits within which a developing idea
could be said to have retained its identity.

The problem will always be with us, as will be the two extreme ways
of solving it. On the one hand there will always be those for whom
development is everything, with the original intention of the writer of
a religious text ultimately reduced to irrelevance in the search for
truth. Each new meaning given to ancient texts throughout the ages
is as valid, or even more valid, as that of the original.

But if God speaks through the writers of Scripture, He speaks not
only through their lips but through their minds. He does not indulge
in double-talk, allowing Isaiah or Paul to mean one thing by what
they say, while He Himself means another. If there is anything that
distinguishes Christianity from all other religions and philosophies it
is this: Christianity in the first instance is neither a set of doctrines
nor a way of life, but a gospel; *and a gospel means news about historical
events, attested by reliable witnesses, and having at its centre a historical
person.* Whenever Christians have attempted to give to the scriptures
a sense other than the plain sense intended by those who wrote them,
Christianity has been in danger of running out into the sands of Gnosticism. And the danger is at its greatest when dogma or philosophical
presuppositions are allowed to take control of exegesis.

One example may be given. In recent years theologians have been
much tempted to welcome the attempts made by literary critics and
structuralists to persuade us that a text, once launched into the world,
attains an existence of its own and can accumulate new meanings
which are quite independent of the original intention of the author.
Every verse of Scripture may thus yield some sense acceptable to the

reader. For many this is the hope of the future. But against all such Gadarene precipitations into the Dark Ages it must be asserted that such critics, whether they are studying a literary masterpiece or a book of the Bible, ought to be aware that perhaps they are in touch with a creative mind considerably more profound and percipient than their own. What right have they to assume that the glimpses of meaning which have occurred to them were hidden from the author? How often do we read commentaries on the Revelation, in which learned writers have argued that, although John was a simpleton who believed in the most naïve fashion that the world would end the day after tomorrow, nevertheless his work can be rescued from inanity if by the alchemy of modern sophistication we transmute his belief in temporal imminence into ultimacy of value, existential encounter, certainty of the triumph of God's purposes, the impact of the transcendent on the temporal, and so on. It never seems to occur to such writers that all of this and more may have been limpidly clear to John himself and a part of his intention in using what they are pleased to call his 'eschatological language and imagery'. Only in so far as we are able to suppress our temptations to intellectual and spiritual superiority are we likely to be able to listen accurately to what John has to say.

Language is in essence a medium of communication. If the hearer takes words in a sense not intended by the speaker, that is not an enlargement of meaning but a breakdown of communication. This claim applies to all uses of language, but it is especially apposite where a claim of revelation is involved. Certainly anyone, when reading a text of Scripture, may have a bright idea which is independent of the author's intention, but which comes upon the reader with all the force and persuasiveness of revealed truth. But when that happens it is the reader's idea, not the meaning of what he or she was reading; and any authority which we may attach to the text is irrelevant to the question of the truth or validity of the reader's idea.

At least a partial reason for the rise of the structuralist approach in biblical studies is that the modern Church has been living through a long period of scepticism about the historicity of its biblical records. But this scepticism has not been the inevitable result of objective historical research. For whenever secular historians have set their minds to the biblical evidence, they have commonly come to far more conservative conclusions than the theologians. Sceptical results have often been accepted in a naïvely uncritical fashion because they were congenial to the dogmatic presuppositions of the day or of the researcher. If, for example, you believe that true faith can never find support in anything other than the experience of the presence of God, you will be predisposed to welcome the idea that historical research cannot intrude upon that utter faith. If, on the other hand, you are committed to the Incarnation, you will find that any method of handling scripture which blunts the tools of the quest for the historical Jesus is doing a disservice to the gospel which the Church has always claimed to be preaching.

The other extreme solution is to deny the existence of development altogether. Here the Bible is read for its original intention, and then, once that intention is allegedly found, a wall of intolerance is erected around the interpretation. In this case the infallibility of Scripture becomes a cypher for the infallibility of the interpreter. Doctrinal 'tests' become normative in deciding whether or not individuals are in conformity with the discerned pattern. This may be called 'the Nehemiah solution'. Faced with the problem of how to define the Israel of his day against its enemies in the land, Nehemiah answered by surrounding Jerusalem on all sides with walls. This was not the approach of the first apostolic conference. For Paul and the others who met in Jerusalem the walls were down. It was in the crucible of dialogue that the living Spirit of God among His people was to be discerned.

One problem which the Church historically has had to bear is that far too often its leaders have held a destructively narrow view of the principalities and powers of this age. St Paul and Lord Acton would agree to the extent that power corrupts, and there is hardly any reason to suppose that corruption is limited to the 'secular' powers. Paul recounts how at one point he saw the Law as the means by which he was brought to God; but the Law had been a veil over his heart, whereby Satan, the God of this world, had blinded the minds of the unbelieving to keep them from seeing the light of the gospel of the glory of Christ. There is no human authority which is so high or so holy that it cannot become an instrument of Satan. This is true even of scripture. As soon as scripture is used for the purpose of coercion or regimentation, this principle comes into effect, and history is littered with and disfigured by its record.

What Paul expressed in highly theological language is illustrated in simpler terms in the gospel story. Jesus dealt leniently and sympathetically with the outcasts and untouchables, reserving his severest strictures for the ecclesiastical authorities. This judgement is amply borne out in the history of the Church. The astonishing theory that Christian ministers, officials, and teachers are less liable than others to sin and error has no basis in the New Testament. Certainly the Church is furnished by God with the gifts and graces necessary for its tasks; but there is no evidence whatever that permananent immunity from the corruption of power is one of those gifts.

This is something Christianity has had a hard time learning. Of course it has always had a need for formal appointments, and those who are given such appointments deserve respect. Appointments convey authority. But it is vital to distinguish in what sense appointment is the source of authority and in what sense it is no more than a recognition of it. A university may appoint people to professorial chairs, thereby declaring to the world its confidence that they are authorities on the subject they are professing. In virtue of their appointment they may be given authority to act, where they did not have it before, e.g. in directing a department and influencing or even deciding junior appointments in it. But their appointment will not of itself add one grain or scruple to the expertise which was their qualification for the chair, still less can it in any way make up for the lack of such qualification. It may indeed add to the public recognition of that expertise, thus rendering it more effective in producing persuasion or conviction in others; it may provide fresh opportunities for increasing the expertise; but it will not of itself convey it. The same argument not only applies to the New Testament writers, it is applied by these writers themselves. A successor to Judas must be found among those who have the qualifications; appointment can be no substitute for eyewitness, nor can an eyewitness have a successor. Paul insists that his qualification for his apostolic task comes from no human source and is mediated by no human appointment. No doubt the apostles needed successors for the carrying out of their apostolic tasks, and no doubt with their appointments God gave to those successors the grace to enable them. But for the preservation of apostolic meaning Paul's only successor is the one who understands Paul.

THE WRITINGS OF
GEORGE BRADFORD CAIRD

1950   *The Truth of the Gospel* (London, 1950).

1951   *The Shorter Oxford Bible* (with G. W. Briggs and N. Micklem) (London, 1951).

'Christ's Attitude to Institutions', *Exp.T.* 62 (1950–1), 259 ff.

The New Testament View of Life (Inaugural Lecture) (Montreal, 1951).

1952   'Recent Articles on Biblical Interpretation', *Int.* 6 (1952), 458 ff.

1953   'Introduction and Exegesis to I and II Samuel', in G. A. Buttrick, *et al.* (eds.), *The Interpreter's Bible* (Nashville, 1953), ii. 855 ff.

1955   *The Apostolic Age* (Essex and London, 1955).

1956   *Principalities and Powers* (Oxford, 1956).

'The Transfiguration', *Exp.T.* 67 (1955–6), 291 ff.

'Judgement and Salvation: An Exposition of John 12: 31–2', *CJT* 2 (1956), 231 ff.

1957   'Predestination: Romans 9–11', *Exp.T.* 68 (1956–7), 324 ff.

1958   'Christian Ethics and Nuclear Warfare', *Christus Victor* 102 (1958), 4 ff.

1959   'The Exegetical Method of the Epistle to the Hebrews', *CJT* 5 (1959), 44 ff.

'Everything to Everyone: The Theology of the Corinthian Epistles', *Int.* 13 (1959), 387 ff.

1961   'The Will of God in the Fourth Gospel', *Exp.T.* 72 (1960–1), 115 ff.

'Alexander Nairne's "The Epistle of Priesthood"', *Exp.T.* 72 (1960–1), 204 ff.

1961–2   'He Who for Men their Surety Stood', *Exp.T.* 73 (1961–2), 24 ff.

'The Kingship of Christ', *Exp.T.* 73 (1961–2), 248 ff.

1962   'Samuel', *Encyclopaedia Britannica* (Chicago, 1962; repr. 1972), xix. 984.

'On Deciphering the Book of Revelation' (four articles: 'I. Heaven and Earth'; 'II. Past and Future'; 'III. The First and the Last'; 'IV. Myth and Legend'); *Exp.T.* (1962–3), 13 ff.; 51 ff.; 82 ff.; 103 ff.

'The Chronology of the New Testament' *IDB* (Nashville, 1962), i. 599 ff.

'John, Letters of', *IDB* (Nashville, 1962), ii. 946 ff.

1963   'Paul the Apostle', in J. Hastings (ed.), *Dictionary of the Bible*, rev. edn. by F. C. Grant and H. H. Rowley (New York, 1963), 731 ff.

'Paul's Theology', in J. Hastings (ed.), *Dictionary of the Bible*, rev. edn. by F. C. Grant and H. H. Rowley (New York, 1963), 736 ff.

The Gospel of St Luke, paperback edn. (Harmondsworth, 1963), hardback edn. (London, 1968).

1964   'The Descent of Christ in Ephesians 4: 7–11', *Studia Evangelica*, 2, ed. F. L. Cross (Berlin, 1964), 535 ff.

The Unity We Seek: II, Making It Visible (London, 1964).

1965   'C. H. Dodd', *A Handbook of Christian Theologians*, ed. Martin E. Marty and Dean G. Peerman (Cleveland, 1965), 320 ff.

'The New Testament', in D. T. Jenkins (ed.), *The Scope of Theology* (Cleveland, 1965), 39–56.

'Expounding the Parables: I. The Defendant (Matthew 5: 25 f.; Luke 12: 58 f.)', *Exp.T.* 77 (1965–6), 36 ff.

Jesus and God (with D. E. Jenkins) (London, 1965).

Jesus and the Jewish Nation, Ethel M. Wood Lecture (London, 1965).

1966   *The Revelation of St John the Divine*, Black's New Testament Commentaries (London, 1966).

1967   *Our Dialogue With Rome: The Second Vatican Council and After*, the Congregational Lectures for 1966 (Oxford, 1967).

1968   'The Development of the Doctrine of Christ in the New Testament', in N. Pittinger (ed.), *Christ for Us Today* (London, 1968), 66 ff.

'Relations with Roman Catholics: A Congregationalist View', in B. Leeming (ed.), *Towards Christian Unity* (London, 1968).

'Towards a Lexicon of the Septuagint I', *JTS* 19 (1968), 453 ff.

1969   'Towards a Lexicon of the Septuagint II', *JTS* 20 (1969), 21 ff.

'Uncomfortable Words: II. Shake off the Dust from Your Feet (Mk. 6: 11)', *Exp.T.* 81 (1969–70), 40 ff.

'The Glory of God in the Fourth Gospel: An Exercise in Biblical Semantics', *NTS* 15 (1969), 265 ff.

The Open Heaven, by W. H. Cadman, ed. G. B. Caird (Oxford, 1969).

'Les Eschatologies du Nouveau Testament', *Revue d'histoire et de philosophie religieuses* (Paris, 1969), 217–27.

1970   'The Christological Basis of Christian Hope', in G. B. Caird
        (ed.), *The Christian Hope*, Theological Collections, 13 (London,
        1970), 19 ff.
        'The Bible and the Word of God', *Christian Confidence*, Theologi-
        cal Collections, 14 (London, 1970), 105 ff.

1971   *Christianity and Progress*, the twenty-sixth Shaftesbury Lecture,
        (London, 1971).

1972   'Paul and Women's Liberty', *BJRL* 54 (1972), 268 ff.
        'Saint Paul the Apostle', *Encyclopaedia Britannica*, 15th edn.
        (Chicago, 1972 and 1974), xiii. 1090 ff.

1973   'New Wine in Old Wine-Skins: I. Wisdom', *Exp.T.* 84 (1973),
        164 ff.

1974   'Charles Harold Dodd, 1884–1973', *The Proceedings of the British
        Academy*, 60 (1974), 497–510; offprint (1975), 3–16.

1976   'Eschatology and Politics: Some Misconceptions', in Johnston R.
        McKay and James F. Miller (eds.), *Biblical Studies: Essays in
        Honour of William Barclay* (London, 1976), 72 ff., 202 f.
        'Homoeophony in the Septuagint', in R. Hamerton-Kelly and R.
        Scroggs (eds.), *Jesus, Greeks and Christians: Essays in Honor of
        William David Davies* (Leiden, 1976), 74 ff.
        'The Study of the Gospels' (three articles: 'I. Source Criticism';
        'II. Form Criticism'; 'III. Redaction Criticism'), *Exp.T.* 87
        (1975–6), 99 ff.; 137 ff.; 168 ff.
        South Africa: Reflections on a Visit (with John Johansen-Berg)
        (London, 1976), 3 ff.
        'The New Testament Concept of Salvation', *Tantur Yearbook*
        (1976–7), Tantur, Jerusalem, 19–34.
        Paul's Letters from Prison, New Clarendon Bible (Oxford, 1976).

1978   Major review of E. P. Sanders, *Paul and Palestinian Judaism*
        (Philadelphia, 1977), in *JTS* NS 29 (1978), 540 ff.

1979   *The Word for Today* (Sackville, 1979).
        War and the Christian (Surrey, 1979).
        'Health', in *The Quality of Life*, Report of the British Association
        Study Group on Science and the Quality of Life, ed. Harford
        Thomas (London, 1979), 21 ff.
        'Biblical Classics: VIII. James Denney: The Death of Christ',
        Exp.T. 90 (1978–9), 196 ff.
        'Jesus Men Made Perfect', in Charles S. Duthie (ed.), *Resurrection
        and Immortality: Aspects of Twentieth Century Christian Belief*
        (London, 1979), 89 ff. repr. from *The London Quarterly and
        Holborn Review* (1966), 89 ff.

1980   *The Language and Imagery of the Bible* (Essex and London, 1980).

1982   'Ben Sira and the Dating of the Septuagint', *Studia Evangelica*,
        4, ed. E. A. Livingstone (Berlin, 1982), 95 ff.

        'Jesus and Israel: The Starting Point for New Testament
        Christology', *Christological Perspectives: Essays in Honor of Harvey
        K. McArthur*, ed. Robert F. Berkey and Sarah Edwards (New
        York, 1982), 58–68.

1983   'The One and the Many in Mark and John', in Horton Davies
        (ed.), *Studies of the Church in History: Essays Honoring Robert S.
        Paul on his Sixty-Fifth Birthday* (Allison Park, Pa. 1983), 39 ff.

1984   'Biblical Exegesis and the Ecumenical Movement', in John E.
        Booty (ed.), *The Divine Drama in History and Liturgy: Essays
        Presented to Horton Davies on His Retirement from Princeton Uni-
        versity* (Allison Park, Pa. 1984), 203 ff.

        'Son by Appointment', in William C. Weinrich (ed.), *The New
        Testament Age: Essays in Honor of Bo Reicke* (Macon, Ga. 1984),
        73 ff.

        Introduction to Paul S. Minear's *Matthew, the Teacher's Gospel*,
        British ed. (London, 1984).

1985   *The Revelation of St John the Divine*, 2nd ed. (London, 1985), with
        a new preface (written 5 Mar. 1984).

        'Perfection and Grace', in C. R. Young, R. A. Leaver, and J. H.
        Litton (eds.), *Duty and Delight: Routley Remembered*, memorial
        vol. for Eric Routley (Carol Stream, Ill. 1985), 21 ff.

1994   *New Testament Theology*, completed and ed. by L. D. Hurst
        (Oxford, 1994).

Book Reviews

Reviews published in over a dozen journals (most notably the *Journal of Theological Studies*) of over 100 books written in English, German, French, and
Italian.

SELECT BIBLIOGRAPHY

Not intended to be a comprehensive list, the following represents a sampling of the best work revelant to the subject of New Testament theology. Foreign works are listed in their English translation, if any.

ABBOTT, T. K., *A Critical and Exegetical Commentary on the Epistles to the Ephesians and Colossians* (Edinburgh: Clark, 1899).

ACHTEMEIER, P. J., *Mark* (Philadelphia: Fortress, 1975).

—— *Romans* (Atlanta: Knox, 1985).

—— *The Quest for Unity in the New Testament* (Philadelphia: Fortress, 1987).

ALLISON, D. C., *The End of the Ages Has Come* (Philadelphia, 1985).

ARNOLD, C. E., *Ephesians: Power and Magic* (Cambridge: CUP, 1989).

ASHTON, J. (ed.), *The Interpretation of John* (Philadelphia: Fortress, 1986).

—— *Understanding the Fourth Gospel* (Oxford, Clarendon, 1991).

ATTRIDGE, H. W., *The Epistle to the Hebrews* (Philadelphia: Fortress, 1989).

AULÉN, G., *Christus Victor: An Historical Study of the Three Main Types of the Idea of the Atonement* (New York: Macmillan, 1969).

AUNE, D. E., *The Cultic Setting of Realised Eschatology in Early Christianity* (Leiden: Brill, 1972).

—— *The New Testament in its Literary Environment* (Philadelphia: Westminster, 1987).

—— *Prophecy in Early Christianity and the Ancient Mediterranean World* (Grand Rapids: Eerdmans, 1983).

BAILLIE, D. M., *God Was in Christ* (London: Faber, 1955²).

BALCH, D. L., *Let Wives be Submissive: The Domestic Code in I Peter* (Chico, Calif.: Scholars, 1981).

BAMMEL, E. (ed.), *The Trial of Jesus* (London: SCM, 1970).

—— and MOULE, C. F. D. (eds.), *Jesus and the Politics of His Day* (Cambridge: CUP, 1984).

BANKS, R., *Jesus and the Law in the Synoptic Tradition* (Cambridge: CUP, 1975).

—— *Paul's Idea of Community* (Grand Rapids: Eerdmans, 1980).

—— (ed.), *Reconciliation and Hope: Essays on Atonement and Eschatology* (Exeter: Paternoster, 1974).

BARR, J. *Biblical Words for Time* (London: SCM, 1969²).

—— 'George Bradford Caird', *Proceedings of the British Academy*, 71 (1985), 493 ff.

—— *The Semantics of Biblical Language* (Oxford: OUP, 1961).

BARRETT, C. K., *A Commentary on the Epistle to the Romans* (New York: Harper, 1957).

—— *A Commentary on the First Epistle to the Corinthians* (London: Black, 1968).

—— *A Commentary on the Second Epistle to the Corinthians* (London: Black, 1973).

—— 'The Eschatology of the Epistle to the Hebrews', in D. Daube and W. D. Davies (eds.), *The Background of the New Testament and Its Eschatology* (Cambridge: CUP, 1956).

—— *Freedom and Obligation: A Study of the Epistle to the Galatians* (Philadelphia: Westminster, 1985).

—— *From First Adam to Last* (London: Black, 1962).

—— *The Gospel According to St John* (Philadelphia: Westminster, 1978).

—— *The Holy Spirit and the Gospel Tradition* (London: SPCK, 1947).

BARTH, M., *Ephesians*, 2 vols. (New York: Doubleday, 1974).

BARTSCH, H., *Kerygma and Myth* (London: SPCK, 1972).

BAUCKHAM, R. J., *Jude, 2 Peter* (Waco, Tex.: Word, 1983).

BEARE, F. W., *The First Epistle of Peter* (Oxford: Blackwell, 1958²).

—— *A Commentary on the Epistle to the Philippians* (New York: Harper, 1981).

—— *The Gospel According to Matthew* (Oxford: Blackwell, 1981).

BEASLEY-MURRAY, G. R., *Baptism in the New Testament* (Grand Rapids: Eerdmans, 1962).

—— *Jesus and the Future* (London: Macmillan, 1954).

—— *Jesus and the Kingdom of God* (Exeter, 1986).

BEKER, J. Christian, *Paul's Apocalyptic Gospel: The Coming Triumph of God* (Philadelphia: Fortress, 1982).

—— *Paul the Apostle: The Triumph of God in Life and Thought* (Philadelphia: Fortress, 1980).

BENOIT, P., *The Passion and Resurrection of Jesus Christ* (London: Darton, 1969).

BEST, E. *Following Jesus: Discipleship in the Gospel of Mark* (Sheffield: JSOT, 1981).

—— *One Body in Christ* (London: SPCK, 1965).

—— *1 Peter* (London: Oliphants, 1971).

—— *The Temptation and the Passion: The Markan Soteriology* (New York and Cambridge: CUP, 1965).

BETZ, H. D., *Galatians* (Philadelphia: Fortress, 1979).

BOERS, H., *What is New Testament Theology? The Rise of Criticism and the Problem of a Theology of the New Testament* (Philadelphia: Fortress, 1979).

BORG, M. J., 'An Orthodoxy Reconsidered: The "End-of-the-World Jesus"', in L. D. Hurst and N. T. Wright (eds.), *The Glory of Christ in the New Testament* (Oxford: Clarendon, 1987), 207–17.

—— *Conflict, Holiness and Politics in the Teaching of Jesus* (New York and Toronto: Mellen, 1984).

—— *Jesus: A New Vision* (San Francisco: Harper, 1987).

BORNKAMM, G., *Jesus of Nazareth* (New York: Harper, 1963).

—— BARTH, G., and HELD, H. J. (eds.), *Tradition and Interpretation in Matthew* (London: SCM, 1983²).

—— *Paul* (New York: Harper, 1975).

BORSCH, F. H., *The Son of Man in Myth and History* (London: SCM, 1967).

BOUSSET, W., *Kyrios Christos* (Nashville: Abingdon, 1970).

BRANDON, S. G. F., *Jesus and the Zealots* (Manchester: MUP, 1967).

BRAUN, F.-M., *Jean le Theologien; Les Grandes traditions d'Israël et l'accord des Écritures selon le Quatrième Evangile*, 3 vols. (Paris: Gabalda, 1959–72).

BROWN, C., *Jesus in European Protestant Thought* (Grand Rapids: Eerdmans, 1985).

BROWN, R. E., *The Birth of the Messiah: A Commentary on the Infancy Narratives in Matthew and Luke* (New York: Doubleday, 1977).

—— *The Community of the Beloved Disciple* (Ramsey, NJ: Paulist, 1979).

—— *The Gospel According to John*, 2 vols. (New York: Doubleday, 1966).

—— *The Virginal Conception and Bodily Resurrection of Jesus* (Paramus, NJ: 1973).

BRUCE, F. F., *A Commentary on the Acts of the Apostles* (Grand Rapids: Eerdmans, 1954).

—— *The Epistle to the Hebrews* (Grand Rapids: Eerdmans, 1964).

BRUNER, F. D., *A Theology of the Holy Spirit* (London: Hodder, 1970).

BUCHANAN, G. W., *Jesus the King and His Kingdom* (Macon, Ga.: Mercer, 1984).

BULTMANN, R., *The Gospel of John: A Commentary* (Philadelphia: Westminster, 1971).

—— *The History of the Synoptic Tradition* (London: Blackwell, 1972).

—— *Jesus and the Word* (London: Nicholson, 1935).

—— 'The New Testament and Mythology', in H. W. Bartsch (ed.), *Kerygma and Myth* (London: SPCK, 1972).

—— *Primitive Christianity in its Contemporary Setting* (London: Thames, 1956).

—— *The Theology of the New Testament*, 2 vols. (New York: Scribner's, 1951, 1955).

BURGE, G. M., *The Anointed Community: The Holy Spirit in the Johannine Tradition* (Grand Rapids: Eerdmans, 1987).

CADMAN, W. H., *The Open Heaven*, ed. G. B. Caird (Oxford: Blackwell, 1969).

CAMPENHAUSEN, H. VON, 'The Events of Easter and the Empty Tomb', *Tradition and Life in the Church* (London: Collins, 1968), 42–89.

CARAGOUNIS, C. C., *The Son of Man* (Tübingen: Mohr, 1986).

CARR, *Angels and Principalities* (Cambridge: CUP, 1981).

CARRAS, G. P., 'Paul, Josephus, and Judaism: The Shared Judaism of Paul and Josephus', D.Phil. thesis Oxford, 1989.

CASEY, M., *Son of Man* (London: SPCK, 1979).

CASSIDY, R. J., *Jesus, Politics and Society: A Study of Luke's Gospel* (New York: Orbis, 1978).

—— *Political Issues in Luke's Gospel* (New York: Orbis, 1983).

CATCHPOLE, D. R., *The Trial of Jesus* (Leiden: Brill, 1971).

CHARLESWORTH, J. H. (ed.), 'Caiaphas, Pilate, and Jesus' Trial', *Explorations*, 7 (1993), 3 f.

—— *Jesus Within Judaism* (New York: Doubleday, 1988).

—— (ed.), *The Old Testament Pseudepigrapha*, 2 vols. (New York: Doubleday, 1983–5).

—— 'A Prolegomenon to a New Study of the Jewish Background of the Hymns and Prayers of the New Testament', *JJS* 33 (1982), 265 ff.

CHILDS, B. S., *Biblical Theology of the Old and New Testaments* (Minneapolis: Fortress, 1993).

CHILTON, B. D., *A Galilean Rabbi and His Bible* (Wilmington, Del.: Glazier, 1984).

—— *God in Strength: Jesus' Announcement of the Kingdom* (Freistadt: Plöchl, 1979).

——(ed.), *The Kingdom of God in the Teaching of Jesus* (Philadelphia: Fortress, 1984).

—— and MCDONALD, J. I. H., *Jesus and the Ethics of the Kingdom* (Grand Rapids: Eerdmans, 1987)

COLLINGWOOD, R. G., *The Idea of History* (Oxford: Clarendon, 1949).

COLLINS, A. Y., *Crisis and Catharsis: The Power of the Apocalypse* (Philadelphia: Westminster, 1984).

CONZELMANN, H., *The Theology of St Luke* (London: Faber, 1960).

—— *An Outline of the Theology of the New Testament* (London: SCM, 1969).

CRANFIELD, C. E. B., *A Critical and Exegetical Commentary on the Epistle to the Romans*, 2 vols. (Edinburgh: Clark, 1975–9).

—— *The Gospel According to St Mark* (Cambridge: CUP, 1959).

CREED, J. M., *The Gospel According to St Luke* (London: Macmillan, 1930).

CROSSAN, J. D., *The Historical Jesus: The Life of a Mediterranean Jewish Peasant* (San Francisco: Harper, 1991).

CROWN, R. W., 'The Non-Literal Use of Eschatological Language in Jewish Apocalyptic and the New Testament', D.Phil. thesis, Oxford, 1986.

CULLMANN, O., *Baptism in the New Testament* (London: SCM, 1950).

—— *The Christology of the New Testament* (London: SCM, 1963).

—— *Early Christian Worship* (London: SCM, 1953).

—— *The Johannine Circle* (Philadelphia: Westminster, 1976).

CULPEPPER, R. A., *Anatomy of the Fourth Gospel* (Philadelphia: Fortress, 1983).

DAHL, N. *The Crucified Messiah and Other Essays* (Minneapolis, 1974).

—— *Jesus in the Memory of the Early Church* (Minneapolis, 1976).

—— *Jesus the Christ* (ed. D. Juel) (Minneapolis, 1991).

DALMAN, G., *The Words of Jesus* (Edinburgh: Clark, 1902).

DAVIES, W. D., *Jewish and Pauline Studies* (Philadelphia: Fortress, 1984).

—— *Paul and Rabbinic Judaism* (London: SPCK, 1955).

—— *The Setting of the Sermon on the Mount* (Cambridge: CUP, 1966).

—— and ALLISON, D. C., *A Critical and Exegetical Commentary on the Gospel of Matthew* (Edinburgh: Clark, 1988).

DEISSMANN, A. *Die neutestamentliche Formel 'In Christo Jesu'* (Marburg: Siebeck, 1892).

DENNEY, J., *The Christian Doctrine of Reconciliation* (London: Hodder, 1917).

—— *The Death of Christ* (London: Hodder, 1902).

DERRETT, J. D. M., *Jesus's Audience: The Social and Psychological Environment in Which He Worked* (New York: Seabury, 1973).

—— *Law in the New Testament* (London: Darton, 1970).

DIBELIUS, Martin, *From Tradition to Gospel* (New York: Scribner's, 1935).

—— and GREEVEN, H., *James* (Philadelphia: Fortress, 1976).

DILLISTONE, F. W., *The Christian Understanding of Atonement* (London: SCM, 1984).

DIX, G., *Jew and Greek: A Study in the Primitive Church* (Westminster: Dacre, 1953).

DODD, C. H., *According to the Scriptures: The Substructure of New Testament Theology* (London: Nisbet, 1952).

—— *The Apostolic Preaching and Its Developments* (London: Hodder, 1951[2]).

—— *The Bible and the Greeks* (London: Hodder, 1954[2]).

—— *The Epistle of Paul to the Romans* (New York: Harper, 1932).

—— *The Founder of Christianity* (New York: Macmillan, 1970).

—— *Gospel and Law: The Relation of Faith and Ethics in Early Christianity* (New York: Columbia University Press, 1951).

—— *Historical Tradition in the Fourth Gospel* (Cambridge: CUP, 1963).

—— *History and the Gospel* (London: Nisbet, 1938).

—— *The Interpretation of the Fourth Gospel* (Cambridge: CUP, 1953).

—— *The Johannine Epistles* (London: Hodder, 1963[2]).

—— *New Testament Studies* (Manchester: MUP, 1953).

—— *The Parables of the Kingdom* (London: Nisbet, 1941).

DUNN, J. D. G., *Christology in the Making* (London: SCM, 1980; 1990[2]).

—— *The Evidence for Jesus* (London: SCM, 1985).

—— *Jesus and the Spirit* (London: SCM, 1975).

—— *Jesus, Paul and the Law: Studies in Mark and Galatians* (Philadelphia: Westminster, 1990).

—— *The Partings of the Ways Between Christianity and Judaism and their Significance for the Character of Christianity* (London: SCM, 1991).

—— 'Pharisees, Sinners and Jesus', in J. Neusner *et al.* (eds.), *The Social World of Formative Christianity and Judaism* (Philadelphia: Fortress, 1988), 264 ff.

DUNN, J. D. G., *Romans 1–8* (Waco, Tex.: Word, 1988).

—— *Romans 9–16* (Waco, Tex.: Word, 1988).

—— *Unity and Diversity in the New Testament* (Philadelphia: Westminster, 1977).

—— and MACKEY, J. P., *New Testament Theology in Dialogue: Christology and Ministry* (London: SPCK, 1987).

EBELING, G., 'The Meaning of "Biblical Theology" ', *JTS* 6 (1955), 210 ff.

EDWARDS, R. A., *Matthew's Story of Jesus* (Philadelphia: Fortress, 1985).

ELLINGWORTH, P., *The Epistle to the Hebrews: A Commentary on the Greek Text* (Grand Rapids: Eerdmans, 1993).

ELLIOTT, J. H., *A Home for the Homeless: A Sociological Exegesis of 1 Peter, Its Situation and Strategy* (Philadelphia: Fortress, 1981).

ELLIS, E. E., *The Gospel of Luke* (London: Oliphants, 1966).

—— *Paul and His Recent Interpreters* (Grand Rapids: Eerdmans, 1961).

—— *Paul's Use of the Old Testament* (London: Oliver, 1957).

—— *Prophecy and Hermeneutic in Early Christianity* (Tübingen: Mohr, 1978).

EVANS, C. A., and HAGNER, D. A. (eds.), *Anti-Semitism and Early Christianity: Issues of Polemic and Faith* (Philadelphia: Fortress, 1993).

EVANS, C. F., *The Resurrection and the New Testament* (London: SCM, 1970).

FARRER, Austin, *The Revelation of St John the Divine* (Oxford: Clarendon, 1964).

FIORENZA, E. SCHÜSSLER, *The Book of Revelation: Justice and Judgment* (Philadelphia: Fortress, 1985).

—— *In Memory of Her* (New York: Crossroad, 1983).

FITZMYER, J., *Essays on the Semitic Background of the New Testament* (London: Chapman, 1971).

—— *The Gospel According to Luke*, 2 vols. (New York: Doubleday, 1981–6).

—— *Paul and His Theology: A Brief Sketch* (Englewood Cliffs, NJ: Prentice-Hall, 1989).

FLEW, R. N., *Jesus and His Church* (London: Epworth, 1938).

FOAKES-JACKSON, F., and LAKE, K., *The Beginnings of Christianity*, 5 vols., (London: Macmillan, 1920–33).

FORD, D., *The Abomination of Desolation in Biblical Eschatology* (Washington, DC: University Press of America, 1979).

FORTNA, R. T., *The Gospel of Signs: A Reconstruction of the Narrative Source Underlying the Fourth Gospel* (New York: CUP, 1970).

—— and GAVENTA, B. (eds.), *The Conversation Continues: Studies in Paul and John* (Nashville: Abingdon, 1990).

FRANCE, R. T., and WENHAM, D. (eds.), *Gospel Perspectives 2* (Sheffield: Sheffield Academic Press, 1983).

—— *Jesus and the Old Testament* (London: Tyndale, 1971).

FRASER, J., *Jesus and Paul: Paul as Interpreter of Jesus from Harnack to Kümmel* (Abingdon: Marcham Manor, 1982).

FULLER, R. H., *The Mission and Achievement of Jesus* (London: SCM, 1954).

—— *The Formation of the Resurrection Narratives* (New York: Macmillan, 1971).

—— *The Foundations of New Testament Christology* (London: Lutterworth, 1965).

FURNISH, V. P. *11 Corinthians* (Garden City: Doubleday, 1984).

—— *Theology and Ethics in Paul* (Nashville: Abingdon, 1985²).

GASQUE, W. W., *A History of the Criticism of the Acts of the Apostles* (Grand Rapids: Eerdmans, 1975).

—— and MARTIN, R. A. (eds.), *Apostolic History and the Gospel* (Exeter: Paternoster, 1970).

GASTON, L., *No Stone on Another: Studies in the Significance of the Fall of Jerusalem in the Synoptic Gospels* (Leiden: Brill, 1970).

GEDDERT, T. J., *Watchwords: Mark 13 in Markan Eschatology* (Sheffield: JSOT, 1989).

GIBSON, J. B., 'The Traditions of the Temptations of Jesus in Early Christianity'. D.Phil. thesis, Oxford, 1992.

GOPPELT, L., *Theology of the New Testament*, ed. J. Roloff, 2 vols. (Grand Rapids: Eerdmans, 1981–2).

GOULDER, M., *Incarnation and Myth: The Debate Continued* (Grand Rapids: Eerdmans, 1979).

—— *Paul and the Torah* (Vancouver: U. of British Columbia Press, 1987).

GREEN, J. B., *The Death of Jesus: Tradition and Interpretation in the Passion Narrative* (Tübingen: Mohr, 1988).

—— and MCKNIGHT, S., *Dictionary of Jesus and the Gospels* (Downers Grove, Ill.: Inter-Varsity, 1992).

GUELICH, R., *The Sermon on the Mount: A Foundation for Understanding* (Waco, Tex.: Word, 1982).

GUNDRY, R. H., *Matthew: A Commentary on His Literary and Theological Art* (Grand Rapids: Eerdmans, 1982).

—— *The Use of the Old Testament in St Matthew's Gospel* (Leiden: Brill, 1967).

GUNTON, C., *The Actuality of Atonement: A Study of Metaphor, Rationality and the Christian Tradition* (Edinburgh: Clark, 1988).

—— 'Christ the Sacrifice: Aspects of the Language and Imagery of the Bible', in L. D. Hurst and N. T. Wright (eds.), *The Glory of Christ in the New Testament* (Oxford: Clarendon, 1987), 229 ff.

GUTHRIE, D., *New Testament Introduction* (Downers Grove, Ill.: Inter-Varsity, 1990⁴).

—— *New Testament Theology* (Downers Grove, Ill.: Inter-Varsity, 1981).

GUTHRIE, G. H., 'The Structure of Hebrews: A Textlinguistic Analysis', Leiden: Brill, 1994.

HAGNER, D. A., *Hebrews* (San Francisco: Harper, 1983).

HAHN, F., *The Titles of Jesus in Christology* (London: Lutterworth, 1969).

HAMERTON-KELLY, R. G., *Pre-existence, Wisdom and the Son of Man* (Cambridge: CUP, 1973).

HANSON, A. T., *The Wrath of the Lamb* (London: SPCK, 1957).

HANSON, P. D., *The Dawn of Apocalyptic: The Historical and Sociological Roots of Jewish Apocalyptic Eschatology* (Philadelphia: Fortress, 1979²).

HARE, D. R. A., *The Son of Man Tradition* (Philadelphia: Fortress, 1990).

—— *The Theme of the Jewish Persecution of Christians in the Gospel According to St Matthew* (Cambridge: CUP, 1967).

HARVEY, A. E., 'Christ as Agent', in L. D. Hurst and N. T. Wright (eds.), *The Glory of Christ in the New Testament* (Oxford: Clarendon, 1987), 239 ff.

—— *Jesus and the Constraints of History* (Philadelphia: Westminster, 1982).

—— *Jesus on Trial: A Study in the Fourth Gospel* (London: SPCK, 1976).

HASEL, G., *New Testament Theology: Basic Issues in the Current Debate* (Grand Rapids: Eerdmans, 1978).

HAY, D., *Glory at the Right Hand: Psalm 110 in Early Christianity* (Nashville: Abingdon, 1973).

HAYS, R. B., *Echoes of Scripture in the Letters of Paul* (New Haven, Conn.: Yale, 1989).

—— *The Faith of Jesus: an Investigation of the Narrative Substructure of Galatians 3: 1–4, 11* (Chico, Calif.: Scholars, 1983).

HENGEL, MARTIN, *Acts and the History of Earliest Christianity* (Philadelphia: Fortress, 1980).

—— *The Atonement: The Origin of the Doctrine in the New Testament* (Philadelphia: Fortress, 1981).

—— *Between Jesus and Paul: Studies in the History of Earlier Christianity* (Philadelphia: Fortress, 1983).

—— *The Charismatic Leader and His Followers* (New York: Crossroad, 1981).

—— *Crucifixion* (Philadelphia: Fortress, 1977).

—— *The Johannine Question* (London: SCM, 1989).

—— *Judaism and Hellenism*, 2 vols. (Philadelphia: Fortress, 1974).

—— 'Literary, Theological and Historical Problems in the Gospel of Mark', in P. Stuhlmacher (ed.), *The Gospel and the Gospels* (Grand Rapids: Eerdmans, 1991), 209 ff.

—— *The Son of God* (London: SCM, 1975).

—— *Studies in the Gospel of Mark* (London: SCM, 1985).

—— *Was Jesus a Revolutionist?* (Philadelphia: Fortress, 1971).

—— *The Zealots: Investigations Into the Jewish Freedom Movement in the Period from Herod 1 Until 70 AD* (Edinburgh: Clark, 1989).

HÉRING, J., *The First Epistle of St Paul to the Corinthians* (London: Epworth, 1962).

HICK, JOHN (ed.), *The Myth of God Incarnate* (London: SCM, 1977).

HIERS, R. H., *Jesus and the Future* (Atlanta: Knox, 1981).

HIGGINS, A. J. B., *Jesus and the Son of Man* (London: Lutterworth, 1964).

—— *The Lord's Supper and the New Testament* (London: SCM, 1952).

HILL, D., *The Gospel of Matthew* (London: Oliphants, 1972).

HILL, D., *Greek Words and Hebrew Meanings* (London: CUP, 1967).

—— *New Testament Prophecy* (Atlanta: Knox, 1979).

HOLLADAY, C. H., *Theios Anēr in Hellenistic-Judaism: A Critique of the Use of this Category in New Testament Christology* (Missoula, Mont.: Scholars, 1977).

HOOKE, S. H., *The Resurrection of Christ as History and Experience* (London: Darton, 1967).

HOOKER, M. D., 'Christology and Methodology', *NTS* 17 (1970), 480 ff.

—— *From Adam to Christ: Essays on Paul* (Cambridge: CUP, 1990).

—— 'In His Own Image', in M. D. Hooker and C. J. A. Hickling (eds.), *What About the New Testament?* (London: SCM, 1975).

—— 'Interchange in Christ', *JTS* 22 (1971), 349 ff.

—— *Jesus and the Servant* (London: SPCK, 1959).

—— *The Message of Mark* (London: Epworth, 1983).

—— 'On Using the Wrong Tool', *Theology*, 75 (1982), 570 ff.

—— *Pauline Pieces* (London: Epworth, 1979).

—— *A Preface to Paul* (New York: OUP, 1980).

—— *The Son of Man in Mark: A Study of the Background of the Term 'Son of Man' and Its Use in St Mark's Gospel* (Montreal: McGill UP, 1967)

HORSLEY, R. A., *Jesus and the Spiral of Violence: Popular Resistance in Roman Palestine* (San Francisco: Harper, 1987).

—— *Sociology and the Jesus Movement* (New York: Crossroads, 1989).

HORTON, F., *The Melchizedek Tradition* (Cambridge: CUP, 1976).

HOSKYNS, E. C., and DAVEY, F. N., *The Fourth Gospel* (London: Faber, 1947[2]).

HURST, L. D., 'The Christology of Hebrews 1 and 2', in L. D. Hurst and N. T. Wright (eds.), *The Glory of Christ in the New Testament* (Oxford: Clarendon, 1987), 151 ff.

—— *The Epistle to the Hebrews: Its Background of Thought* (Cambridge: CUP, 1990).

—— 'The Ethics of Jesus', in J. Green and S. McKnight (eds.), *Dictionary of Jesus and the Gospels* (Downers Grove, Ill.: Inter-Varsity, 1992), 210 ff.

—— 'How "Platonic" are Heb. 8: 5 and 9: 23 f.', *JTS* NS 34 (1983), 156 ff.

—— 'Re-enter the Pre-Existent Christ in Phil. 2: 5–11?', *NTS* 32 (1986), 449 ff.

—— and Wright, N. T. (eds.), *The Glory of Christ in the New Testament* (Oxford: Clarendon, 1987).

HURTADO, L., *One God, One Lord* (Philadelphia: Fortress, 1988).

ISAACS, M., *Sacred Space: An Approach to the Theology of the Epistle to the Hebrews* (Cambridge: CUP, 1992).

JEREMIAS, J., *The Eucharistic Words of Jesus* (Oxford: Blackwell, 1955).

—— *The Parables of Jesus* (New York: Scribner's, 1963).

—— *Jesus' Promise to the Nations* (London: SCM, 1958).

—— *New Testament Theology: The Proclamation of Jesus* (New York: Scribner's, 1971).

——*The Prayers of Jesus* (London: SCM, 1967).

JERVELL, J., *Luke and the People of God* (Minneapolis: Augsburg, 1972).

JEWETT, R., *A Chronology of Paul's Life* (Philadelphia: Fortress, 1979).

——*A Letter to Pilgrims: A Commentary on the Epistles to the Hebrews* (New York: Pilgrim, 1981).

——*The Thessalonian Correspondence: Pauline Rhetoric and Millenarian Piety* (Philadelphia: Fortress, 1986).

JOHNSTON, G., *The Spirit Paraclete in the Gospel of John* (Cambridge: CUP, 1970).

JOHNSTON, L. T., *The Writings of the New Testament* (London: SCM, 1986).

JONGE, M. DE, *Christology in Context* (Philadelphia: Westminster, 1988).

——*Jesus: The Servant-Messiah* (New Haven, Conn.: Yale, 1991).

——*Jesus: Stranger from Heaven and Son of God* (Missoula, Mont.: Scholars, 1977).

JUEL, D. *Luke–Acts: The Promise of History* (Atlanta: Knox, 1984).

——*Messianic Exegesis: Christological Interpretation of the Old Testament in Early Christianity* (Philadelphia: Fortress, 1988).

KÄSEMANN, ERNST, *Commentary on Romans* (Grand Rapids: Eerdmans, 1980).

——*Essays on New Testament Themes* (London: Allenson, 1964).

——*Perspectives on Paul* (London: SCM, 1971).

——*The Testament of Jesus* (London: SCM, 1968).

——*The Wandering People of God* (Minneapolis: Augsburg, 1984).

KECK, L. E., *A Future for the Historical Jesus* (London: SCM, 1972).

——and MARTYN, J. L. (eds.), *Studies in Luke–Acts* (Nashville: Abingdon, 1966).

KEE, H. C., *Community of the New Age: Studies in Mark's Gospel* (London: SCM, 1977).

——*Jesus in History* (New York: Harcourt, 1977).

KEENER, K. S., *Paul, Women and Wives* (Peabody, Mass: Hendrikson, 1992).

KELLY, J. N. D., *A Commentary on the Epistles of Peter and Jude* (Grand Rapids: Baker, 1969).

KILPATRICK, G. D., *The Origins of the Gospel According to St Matthew* (Oxford: Clarendon, 1946).

KIM, S., *The Origin of Paul's Gospel* (Grand Rapids: Eerdmans, 1981).

——*'The Son of Man' as the Son of God* (Grand Rapids: Eerdmans, 1983).

KINGSBURY, J. D., *The Christology of Mark's Gospel* (Philadelphia: Fortress, 1983).

——*Matthew as Story* (Philadelphia: Fortress, 1986).

——*Matthew: Structure, Christology and Kingdom* (London: SPCK, 1976).

KIRK, K. E., *The Epistle to the Romans in the Revised Version* (Oxford: Clarendon, 1937).

KISTEMAKER, S., *The Psalm Citations in the Epistle to the Hebrews* (Amsterdam: Soest, 1961).

KLAUSNER, JOSEPH, *From Jesus to Paul* (Boston: Beacon, 1961).

KNOX, J., *Chapters in a Life of Paul* (New York: Abingdon, 1950).

——*The Humanity and Divinity of Christ* (Cambridge: CUP, 1967).

KNOX, W. L., *St Paul and the Church of the Gentiles* (Cambridge: CUP, 1961).

——*Some Hellenistic Elements in Primitive Christianity* (London: OUP, 1944).

KOESTER, HELMUT, *Introduction to the New Testament*, 2 vols. (Philadelphia: Fortress, 1972).

KRAELING, C. H., *John the Baptist* (New York: Scribner's, 1951).

KÜMMEL, W. G., *Introduction to the New Testament* (Nashville: Abingdon, 1966[14]).

——*The New Testament: The History of the Investigation of Its Problems* (London: SCM, 1972).

——*Promise and Fulfilment* (London: SCM, 1957).

——*The Theology of the New Testament* (London: SCM, 1974).

KUSCHEL, K.-J., *Born Before All Time? The Dispute Over Christ's Origin* (New York: Crossroad, 1992).

KYSAR, R., *The Fourth Evangelist and His Gospel: An Examination of Contemporary Scholarship* (Minneapolis: Augsburg, 1975).

——*John's Story of Jesus* (Philadelphia: Fortress, 1984).

LADD, G. E., *A Theology of the New Testament* (Grand Rapids: Eerdmans, 1974).

——*The Presence of the Future* (London: SPCK, 1974).

LAMBRECHT, J., *Once More Astonished: The Parables of Jesus* (New York: Crossroad, 1981).

LAMPE, G. W. H., and MACKINNON, D. M. (eds.), *The Resurrection* (London: Mowbrays, 1966).

LANE, W. L., *The Gospel According to Mark* (Grand Rapids: Eerdmans, 1974).

——*Hebrews 1–8* (Waco, Tex.: Word, 1991).

——*Hebrews 9–13* (Waco, Tex.: Word, 1991).

LAWS, S., *A Commentary on the Epistle of James* (San Francisco: Harper, 1980).

LEENHARDT, F. J., *The Epistle to the Romans* (London: Butterworth, 1961).

LEIVESTAD, R., *Jesus in His Own Perspective* (Minneapolis: Augsburg, 1987).

LEMCIO, E. E., *The Past of Jesus in the Gospels* (Cambridge: CUP, 1991).

LIGHTFOOT, J. B., *The Epistles to the Colossians and to Philemon* (London: Macmillan, 1890[9]).

—— *St Paul's Epistle to the Galatians* (London: Macmillan, 1876).

—— *St Paul's Epistle to the Philippians* (London: Macmillan, 1878[4]).

LIGHTFOOT, R. H., *The Gospel Message of St Mark* (Oxford: OUP, 1950).

LINCOLN, A. T., *Paradise Now and Not Yet: Studies in the Role of the Heavenly Dimension in Paul's Thought with Special Reference to His Eschatology* (Cambridge: CUP, 1981).

LINDARS, B., *Behind the Fourth Gospel* (London: SPCK, 1971).

—— *The Gospel of John* (London: Oliphants, 1972).

LINDARS, B., *Jesus Son of Man* (London: SPCK, 1983).
—— *New Testament Apologetic* (Philadelphia: SCM, 1961).
—— *The Theology of the Letter to the Hebrews* (Cambridge: CUP, 1991).
—— and SMALLEY, S. (eds.), *Christ and Spirit in the New Testament* (Cambridge: CUP, 1973).
LOHFINK, G., *Jesus and Community* (Philadelphia: Fortress, 1984).
LOHMEYER, E., *Kyrios Jesus: Eine Untersuchung zu Phil. 2: 5–11* (Heidelburg: C. Winter, 1961²).
LOHSE, E., *The History of the Suffering and Death of Jesus Christ* (Philadelphia: Fortress, 1967).
LONGENECKER, R. N., *Biblical Exegesis in the Apostolic Period* (Grand Rapids: Eerdmans, 1975).
—— *The Christology of Early Jewish Christianity* (London: SCM, 1970).
MACK, B. L., *A Myth of Innocence: Mark and Christian Origins* (Philadelphia: Fortress, 1988).
MCKNIGHT, S., *A Light Among the Gentiles* (Philadelphia: Fortress, 1991).
MADDOX, R., *The Purpose of Luke–Acts* (Edinburgh: Clark, 1982).
MALHERBE, A. J., *Paul and the Thessalonians* (Philadelphia: Fortress, 1987).
—— *Social Aspects of Early Christianity* (Philadelphia: Fortress, 1983).
—— and MEEKS, W. A. (eds.), *The Future of Christology* (Philadelphia: Fortress, 1993).
MALINA, BRUCE J., *The New Testament World: Insights from Cultural Anthropology* (Philadelphia: Fortress, 1981).
MANSON, T. W., *On Paul and John* (London: SCM, 1963).
—— *The Sayings of Jesus* (London: SCM, 1949).
—— *The Servant Messiah* (New York: CUP, 1953).
—— *The Teaching of Jesus: Studies in Form and Content* (Cambridge: CUP, 1945).
MARCUS, J., and SOARDS, M. L., *Apocalyptic and the New Testament* (Sheffield: JSOT, 1989).
MARSH, J., *The Gospel of St John* (Harmondsworth: Penguin, 1968).
MARSHALL, I. H., *The Gospel of Luke* (Exeter: Paternoster, 1978).
—— *Jesus the Saviour* (London: SPCK, 1990).
—— *Last Supper and Lord's Supper* (Exeter: Paternoster, 1980).
—— (ed.), *New Testament Interpretation: Essays on Principles and Methods* (Grand Rapids: Eerdmans, 1977).
—— *The Origins of New Testament Christology* (London: Paternoster, 1976).
MARTIN, R. P., *Carmen Christi* (Cambridge: CUP, 1967).
—— *Mark: Evangelist and Theologian* (Exeter: Paternoster, 1972).
—— *Philippians* (London: Oliphants, 1976).
MARTYN, J. L., *The Gospel of John in Christian History* (New York: Paulist, 1978).
—— *History and Theology in the Fourth Gospel* (New York: Harper, 1968).

MARXEN, W., *The Lord's Supper as a Christological Problem* (Philadelphia: Fortress, 1970).

—— *Mark the Evangelist* (Nashville: Abingdon, 1969).

MATERA, F. J., *Passion Narratives and Gospel Theologies* (New York: Paulist, 1986).

MEEKS, W. A., *The Prophet-King: Moses Traditions and the Johannine Christology* (Leiden: Brill, 1967).

—— *The First Urban Christians: The Social World of the Apostle Paul* (New Haven, Conn.: Yale, 1983).

MEIER, J. P., *The Vision of Matthew: Christ, Church, and Morality in the First Gospel* (Ramsey, NJ: Paulist, 1979).

—— *Matthew* (Wilmington: Glazier, 1983).

METZGER, B. M., 'The Punctuation of Rom. 9: 5', in B. Lindars and S. S. Smalley (eds.), *Christ and Spirit in the New Testament* (Cambridge: CUP, 1973).

MEYER, B., *The Aims of Jesus* (London: SCM, 1979).

—— 'Jesus Christ', in D. N. Freedman (ed.), *The Anchor Bible Dictionary*, 3 (New York: Doubleday, 1992), 773 ff.

MICHAELS, J. R., *Servant and Son: Jesus in Parable and Gospel* (Atlanta: Knox, 1981).

MICHEL, O., *Der Brief an die Hebräer* (Göttingen: Vandenhoeck, 1966[6]).

MINEAR, P. S., *The Commands of Christ* (Edinburgh: St Andrews, 1972).

—— *Images of the Church in the New Testament* (London: Lutterworth, 1961).

—— *I saw a New Earth* (Washington: Corpus, 1968).

—— *John: The Martyr's Gospel* (New York: Pilgrim, 1984).

—— *Matthew: The Teacher's Gospel* (New York: Pilgrim, 1982).

—— *New Testament Apocalyptic* (Nashville: Abingdon, 1981).

MOESSNER, D. P., *Lord of the Banquet: The Literary and Theological Significance of the Lukan Travel Narrative* (Philadelphia: Fortress, 1989).

MOFFATT, J., *A Critical and Exegetical Commentary on the Epistle to the Hebrews* (Edinburgh: Clark, 1924).

MOHRLANG, R. *Matthew and Paul on Ethics* (Cambridge: CUP, 1984).

MONTEFIORE, H. W., *The Epistle to the Hebrews* (London: Black, 1964).

MOORE, A. L., *The Parousia in the New Testament* (Leiden: Brill, 1966).

MORGAN, R., *The Nature of New Testament Theology* (London: SCM, 1973).

—— 'The Historical Jesus and the Theology the New Testament', in L. D. Hurst and N. T. Wright (eds.), *The Glory of Christ in the New Testament* (Oxford: Clarendon, 1987), 187 ff.

—— 'Theology, New Testament', in D. N. Freedman (ed.), *The Anchor Bible Dictionary*, 6 (New York: Doubleday, 1992).

MORRIS, L., *The Apostolic Preaching of the Cross* (London: Tyndale, 1955).

—— *Jesus is the Christ: Studies in the Theology of John* (Grand Rapids: Eerdmans, 1989).

MORRIS, L., *New Testament Theology* (Grand Rapids: Zondervan, 1986).

MORRISON, C. D., *Powers that Be: Earthly Rulers and Demonic Powers in Romans* (Naperville, Ill.: Allenson, 1960).

MOULE, C. F. D., *The Birth of the New Testament* (London: Black, 1972).

—— *Essays in New Testament Interpretation* (Cambridge: CUP, 1982).

—— *The Epistles to the Colossians and Philemon* (Cambridge: CUP, 1957).

—— *The Origin of Christology* (Cambridge: CUP, 1977).

—— *The Phenomenon of the New Testament* (London: SCM, 1967).

—— *The Sacrifice of Christ* (London: Hodder, 1956).

—— (ed.), *The Significance of the Message of the Resurrection for Faith in Jesus Christ* (London: SCM, 1968).

—— *Worship in the New Testament* (London: Lutterworth, 1961).

MUDDIMAN, J., 'The Fasting Controversy in Mark', D.Phil. thesis, Oxford, 1976.

MUNCK, J., *Paul and the Salvation of Mankind* (Richmond: Knox, 1959).

NAIRNE, A., *The Epistle of Priesthood* (Edinburgh: Clark, 1913).

NEILL, STEPHEN, *Jesus Through Many Eyes: Introduction to Theology of the New Testament* (Philadelphia: Fortress, 1976).

—— and WRIGHT, TOM, *The Interpretation of the New Testament 1861–1986* (New York: OUP, 1989).

NEUSNER, J. *Judaism in the Beginning of Christianity* (London: SPCK, 1984).

NYGREN, A., *Commentary on Romans* (London: SCM, 1952).

NYSTROM, D. P., 'Not Many Wise, Powerful, or Noble: The Sociology of Primitive Christianity', Ph.D. dissertation, University of California, Davis, 1992.

O'COLLINS, G., *Jesus Risen: An Historical, Fundamental, and Systematic Examination of Christ's Resurrection* (New York: Paulist, 1987).

PAINTER, J., *John: Witness and Theologian* (London: SPCK, 1975).

PATZIA, A. G., *Colossians, Philemon, Ephesians*, (San Francisco: Harper, 1984).

PERKINS, P., *Resurrection: New Testament Witness and Contemporary Reflection* (London: Chapman, 1984).

PERRIN, N., *Jesus and the Language of the Kingdom* (Philadelphia: Fortress, 1976).

—— *The Kingdom of God in the Teaching of Jesus* (London: SCM, 1963).

—— *Rediscovering the Teaching of Jesus* (London: SCM, 1967).

PETERSON, D., *Hebrews and Perfection: An Examination of the Concept of Perfection in the 'Epistle to the Hebrews'* (Cambridge: CUP, 1982).

PFEIFFER, R., *History of New Testament Times* (New York: Harper, 1949).

RÄISÄNEN, H., *Beyond New Testament Theology* (London: SCM, 1990).

—— *Paul and the Law* (Tübingen: Mohr, 1987²).

—— *The Torah and Christ* (Helsinki: Finnish Exegetical Society, 1986).

REICKE, Bo, *The Disobedient Spirits and Christian Baptism* (Copenhagen: Munksgaard, 1946).

—— *The Epistles of James, Peter and Jude* (New York: Doubleday, 1964).

REICKE, Bo., *The New Testament Era: The World of the Bible from 500 BC to 100 AD* (Philadelphia: Fortress, 1968).

REVENTLOW, H. G., 'Theology (Biblical), History of', in D. N. Freedman (ed.), *The Anchor Bible Dictionary*, 6 (New York: Doubleday, 1992).

RICHARDSON, A., *An Introduction to the Theology of the New Testament* (London: SCM, 1968).

RICHES, J. K., *Jesus and the Transformation of Judaism* (London: Darton, 1980).

RIDDERBOS, H. N., *Paul: An Outline of His Theology* (Grand Rapids: Eerdmans, 1975).

RIGAUX, B., *Dieu l'a ressuscité. Exégèse et théologie biblique* (Gembloux: Ducelot, 1973).

ROBINSON, H. W., *The Christian Doctrine of Man* (Edinburgh: Clark, 1926³).

ROBINSON, J. ARMITAGE, *The Epistle to the Ephesians* (London: Macmillan, 1922³).

ROBINSON, J. A. T., *The Body* (London: SCM, 1952).

—— *The Human Face of God* (Philadelphia: Westminster, 1973).

—— *In the End, God* (London: Clarke, 1950).

—— *Jesus and His Coming* (London: SCM, 1957).

—— *The Priority of John* (London: SCM, 1985).

—— *Redating the New Testament* (Philadelphia: Westminster, 1976).

—— *Twelve New Testament Studies* (London: SCM, 1962).

—— *Twelve More New Testament Studies* (London: SCM, 1984).

ROBINSON, J. M., *A New Quest of the Historical Jesus* (London: SCM, 1959).

—— *The Problem of History in Mark* (London: SCM, 1971⁴).

ROHDE, J., *Rediscovering the Teaching of the Evangelists* (Philadelphia: Westminster, 1968).

ROWLAND, C., *Christian Origins* (London: SPCK, 1985).

—— *The Open Heaven: The Study of Apocalyptic in Judaism and Early Christianity* (London: SPCK, 1982).

RUSSELL, D. S., *Apocalyptic: Ancient and Modern* (London: SCM, 1978).

SANDAY, W., and HEADLAM, A. C., *A Critical and Exegetical Commentary on the Epistle to the Romans* (Edinburgh: Clark, 1902).

SANDERS, E. P., *Jesus and Judaism* (Philadelphia: Fortress, 1984).

—— (ed.), *Jesus, the Gospels, and the Church* (Macon, Ga.: Mercer, 1987).

—— *Paul and Palestinian Judaism: A Comparison of Patterns of Religion* (Philadelphia: Fortress, 1977).

—— *Paul, the Law, and the Jewish People* (Philadelphia: Fortress, 1983).

—— *The Tendencies of the Synoptic Tradition* (Cambridge: CUP, 1969).

SCHLATTER, A., *Der Glaube im Neuen Testament* (Darmstadt: Wissenschaftliche Buchgesellschaft, 1963).

—— *Neutestamentliche Theologie* (Stuttgart: Verlag, 1922–3²).

SCHMIDT, J. E. C., 'Vermuthungen über den beyden Briefe', repr. in W. Trilling, *Untersuchungen zum zweiten Thessalonicherbrief* (Leipzig: St Benno, 1972), 159 ff.

SCHNACKENBURG, R., *The Gospel According to St John*, 3 vols. (London: Burns & Oates, 1968–76).

SCHOEPS, H. J., *Paul, The Theology of the Apostle in the Light of the History of Jewish Religion* (London: Lutterworth, 1961).

SCHWEITZER, A., *The Mysticism of Paul the Apostle* (London: Black, 1953²).

—— *Paul and His Interpreters* (London: Black, 1912).

—— *The Quest of the Historical Jesus* (London: Black, 1954³).

SCHWEIZER, E., *Church Order in the New Testament* (London: SCM, 1961).

—— *The Good News According to Mark* (London: SPCK, 1971).

—— *The Good News According to Matthew* (London: SPCK, 1976).

—— *The Lord's Supper According to the New Testament* (Philadelphia: Fortress, 1967).

—— *Luke: A Challenge to Present Theology* (London: SPCK, 1982).

—— *The Good News According to Luke* (London: SPCK, 1984).

—— *Theological Introduction to the New Testament* (Nashville: Abingdon, 1989).

SELWYN, E. G., *The First Epistle of Peter* (London: Macmillan, 1946).

SMALLEY, S. S., *John: Evangelist and Interpreter* (Exeter: Paternoster, 1984).

SMART, J. D., *The Past, Present and Future of Biblical Theology* (Philadelphia: Fortress, 1979).

SMITH, D. MOODY, *Johannine Christianity: Essays on its Setting, Sources and Theology* (Columbia, SC: University of South Carolina Press, 1984).

—— *John* (Philadelphia: Fortress, 1986).

SNYDER, J. I., 'The Promise of His Coming: The Eschatology of 2 Peter'. D. Theol. dissertation, Basel, 1986.

STACEY, W. D., *The Pauline View of Man* (London: Macmillan, 1956).

STANTON, G.N., *The Gospels and Jesus* (New York: OUP, 1989).

—— *A Gospel for a New People* (Edinburgh: Clark, 1992).

—— (ed.), *The Interpretation of Matthew* (Philadelphia: Fortress, 1983).

—— *Jesus of Nazareth in New Testament Preaching* (Cambridge: CUP, 1974).

—— 'Matthew as a Creative Interpreter of the Sayings of Jesus', in P. Stuhlmacher (ed.), *The Gospel and the Gospels* (Grand Rapids: Eerdmans, 1991), 257 ff.

STAUFFER, E., *New Testament Theology* (London: SCM, 1955).

STENDAHL, K., *The Bible and the Role of Women* (Philadelphia: Fortress, 1966).

—— *Paul Among the Jews and Gentiles, and Other Essays* (Philadelphia: Fortress, 1976).

—— *The School of St Matthew and Its Use of the Old Testament* (Philadelphia: Fortress, 1968).

STRECKER, G. (ed.), *Jesus Christus in Historie und Theologie* (Tübingen: Mohr, 1975).

—— *Das Problem der Theologie des Neuen Testaments* (Darmstadt: Wissenschaftliche Buchgesellschaft, 1975).

—— *The Sermon on the Mount* (Edinburgh: Clark, 1988).

STUHLMACHER, P., *Gottes Gerechtigkeit bei Paulus* (Göttingen: Vandenhoeck, 1965).

—— *Vom verstehen des Neuen Testaments* (Göttingen: Vandenhoeck, 1979).

—— *Reconciliation, Law, and Righteousness: Essays in Biblical Theology* (Philadelphia: Fortress, 1986).

SUGGS, M. J., *Wisdom, Christology and Law in Matthew's Gospel* (Cambridge, Mass.: Harvard University Press, 1970).

SWEET, J. P. M., *Revelation* (Philadelphia: Westminster, 1979).

TALBERT, C. H. (ed.), *Perspectives on Luke–Acts* (Danville, Va.: Association of Baptist Professors of Religion, 1978).

—— (ed.), *Perspectives on 1 Peter* (Macon, Ga.: Mercer, 1986).

—— *Reading Luke: A Literary and Theological Commentary on the Third Gospel* (New York: Crossroad, 1984).

TAYLOR, V., *The Atonement in New Testament Teaching* (London: Epworth, 1945).

—— *The Gospel According to St Mark* (London: Macmillan, 1966).

—— *Jesus and His Sacrifice* (London: Macmillan, 1937).

—— *The Passion Narrative of St Luke* (Cambridge: CUP, 1972).

TELFORD, W. R. (ed.), *The Interpretation of Mark* (London: SPCK, 1985).

THEISSEN, G., *The First Followers of Jesus* (London: SCM, 1978).

—— *Psychological Aspects of Pauline Theology* (Philadelphia: Fortress, 1987).

—— *The Shadow of the Galilean* (London: SCM, 1987).

—— *The Social Setting of Pauline Christianity: Essays on Corinth* (Philadelphia: Fortress, 1983).

THISELTON, A., *New Horizons in Hermeneutics: The Theory and Practice of Transforming Biblical Reading* (London: Harper Collins, 1992).

—— *The Two Horizons: New Testament Hermeneutics and Philosophical Description* (Grand Rapids: Eerdmans, 1980).

THOMPSON, M. M., *The Humanity of Jesus in the Fourth Gospel* (Philadelphia: Fortress, 1988).

TÖDT, H. E., *The Son of Man in the Synoptic Tradition* (London: SCM, 1965).

TOLBERT, M., *Sowing the Gospel: Mark's World in Literary-Historical Perspective* (Philadelphia: Fortress, 1989).

TRITES, A., *The New Testament Concept of Witness* (Cambridge: CUP, 1976).

TUCKETT, C. M. (ed.), *The Messianic Secret* (Philadelphia: Fortress, 1983).

VANDERLIP, D. G., *Christianity According to John* (Philadelphia: Westminster, 1975).

—— *John: The Gospel of Life* (Valley Forge, Pa.: Judson, 1979).

VAUX, R. DE, *Ancient Israel: Its Life and Institutions* (London: Darton, 1965).

VERMES, G., *Jesus the Jew: An Historian's Reading of the Gospels* (Philadelphia: Fortress, 1981).

—— *Jesus and the World of Judaism* (Philadelphia: Fortress, 1984).

VIA, D. O., *The Parables: Their Literary and Existential Dimension* (Philadelphia: Fortress, 1967).

VIELHAUER, P., 'On the Paulinism of Acts', in L. E. Keck and J. L. Martyn (eds.), *Studies in Luke–Acts* (Nashville: Abingdon, 1966).

WALKER, W. O., 'The Son of Man: Some Recent Developments', *CBQ* 45 (1983), 584 ff.

WALL, R. W., *Revelation* (Peabody, Mass.: Hendrikson, 1991).

—— and LEMCIO, E. E., *The New Testament as Canon* (Sheffield: Sheffield Academic Press, 1993).

WANAMAKER, C. A., 'Philippians 2: 6–11: Son of God or Adamic Christology?' *NTS* 33 (1987), 179 ff.

WATSON, F. W., *Paul, Judaism and the Gentiles: A Sociological Approach* (Cambridge: CUP, 1986).

WEDDERBURN, A. J. M., 'Adam and Christ: An Investigation into the Background of 1 Corinthians XV and Romans V. 12–21,' Ph.D. thesis, Cambridge, 1974.

—— *Baptism and Resurrection: Studies in Pauline Theology Against Its Graeco-Roman Background* (Tübingen: Mohr, 1987).

—— 'The Body of Christ and Related Concepts in 1 Corinthians', *SJT* 24 (1971), 74 ff.

—— *The Reason for Romans* (Edinburgh: Clark, 1988).

—— 'Some Observations on Paul's Use of the Phrases "in Christ" and "with Christ" ', *JSNT* 25 (1985), 83 ff.

WEISS, J., *The History of Primitive Christianity* (ET, New York, 1937), reprinted as *Earliest Christianity: A History of the Period AD 30–150* (Gloucester, Mass: Peter Smith, 1970).

—— *Jesus' Proclamation of the Kingdom of God* (Philadelphia: Fortress, 1971).

WELLS, G. A., *Did Jesus Exist?* (Buffalo: Prometheus, 1982).

WENHAM, D., *The Rediscovery of Jesus' Apocalyptic Discourse* (Sheffield: JSOT, 1984).

WESTCOTT, B. F., *The Epistle to the Hebrews* (London: Macmillan, 1892).

—— *The Gospel According to St John* (London: Macmillan, 1887).

—— *The Epistles of St John* (London: Macmillan, 1892[3], reprinted Appleford: Marcham Manor, 1966).

WESTERHOLM, S., *Israel's Laws and the Church's Faith: Paul and His Recent Interpreters* (Grand Rapids: Eerdmans, 1988).

WHITELEY, D. H. E., *The Theology of St Paul* (Philadelphia: Fortress, 1964).

WICKENHAUSER, A., *Pauline Mysticism: Christ in the Mystical Teaching of St Paul* (Edinburgh: Nelson, 1960).

WILCKENS, U. *Resurrection* (Edinburgh: St Andrews, 1977).

WILDER, A. N., *Eschatology and Ethics in the Teaching of Jesus* (New York: Harper, 1950[2]).

—— *Early Christian Rhetoric: The Language of the Gospel* (Cambridge: Harvard, 1978).

—— *Jesus' Parables and the War of Myths* (Philadelphia: Fortress, 1987).

WILLIAMS, R., *Resurrection: Interpreting the Easter Gospel* (Cleveland, Ohio: Pilgrim, 1982).

WILLIAMSON, R., *Philo and the Epistle to the Hebrews* (Leiden: Brill, 1970).

WILSON, S. G., *The Gentiles and the Gentile Mission in Luke–Acts* (New York: CUP, 1973).

WINDISCH, H., *The Spirit-Paraclete in the Fourth Gospel* (Philadelphia: Fortress, 1968).

WINK, W., *Naming the Powers* (Philadelphia: Fortress, 1984).

—— *Unmasking the Powers* (Philadelphia: Minneapolis, 1986).

—— *Engaging the Powers* (Philadelphia: Minneapolis, 1992).

WINTER, P., *On the Trial of Jesus* (Berlin: de Gruyter, 1961).

WITHERINGTON, B., *The Christology of Jesus* (Minneapolis: Fortress, 1990).

—— *Women in the Earliest Churches* (Cambridge: CUP, 1991).

WREDE, W., *The Messianic Secret* (London: Clarke, 1971).

WRIGHT, N. T., *The Climax of the Covenant: Christ and the Law in Pauline Theology* (Philadelphia: (Minneapolis: Fortress, 1995).

—— ' "Constraints" and the Jesus of History', *SJT* 39 (1986), 189 ff.

—— *Jesus and the Victory of God* (Philadelphia: Fortress, 1994).

—— 'Jesus, Quest for the Historical', in D. N. Freedman (ed.), *The Anchor Bible Dictionary*, 3 (New York: Doubleday, 1992), 795 ff.

—— 'The Messiah and the People of God: A Study in Pauline Theology with Particular Reference to the Epistle to the Romans', D.Phil. thesis, Oxford, 1980.

—— *The New Testament and the People of God* (Minneapolis: Fortress, 1992).

YODER, J., *The Politics of Jesus* (Grand Rapids: Eerdmans, 1972).

YOUNG, F., and FORD, D. F., *Meaning and Truth in 2 Corinthians* (London: SPCK, 1987).

ZIESLER, J. A., *The Meaning of Righteousness in Paul* (Cambridge: CUP, 1972).

—— *Pauline Christianity* (New York: OUP, 1983).

—— *Paul's Letter to the Romans* (London: SCM, 1989).

ZIMMERLI, W., and JEREMIAS, J., *The Servant of God* (London: SCM, 1957).

INDEX OF PASSAGES CITED

APOCRYPHA AND PSEUDEPIGRAPHA

JEWISH WRITERS

RABBINICAL LITERATURE

EARLY CHRISTIAN WRITINGS

GREEK AND LATIN AUTHORS

INDEX OF MODERN AUTHORS

INDEX OF SUBJECTS